T0053473

PIXAR

A MINIATURE ART COLLECTION

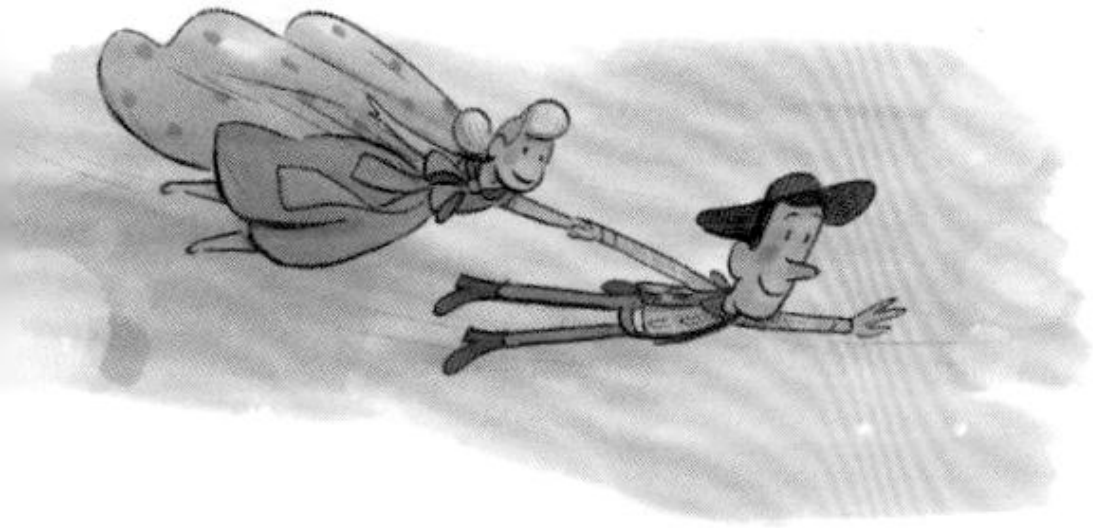

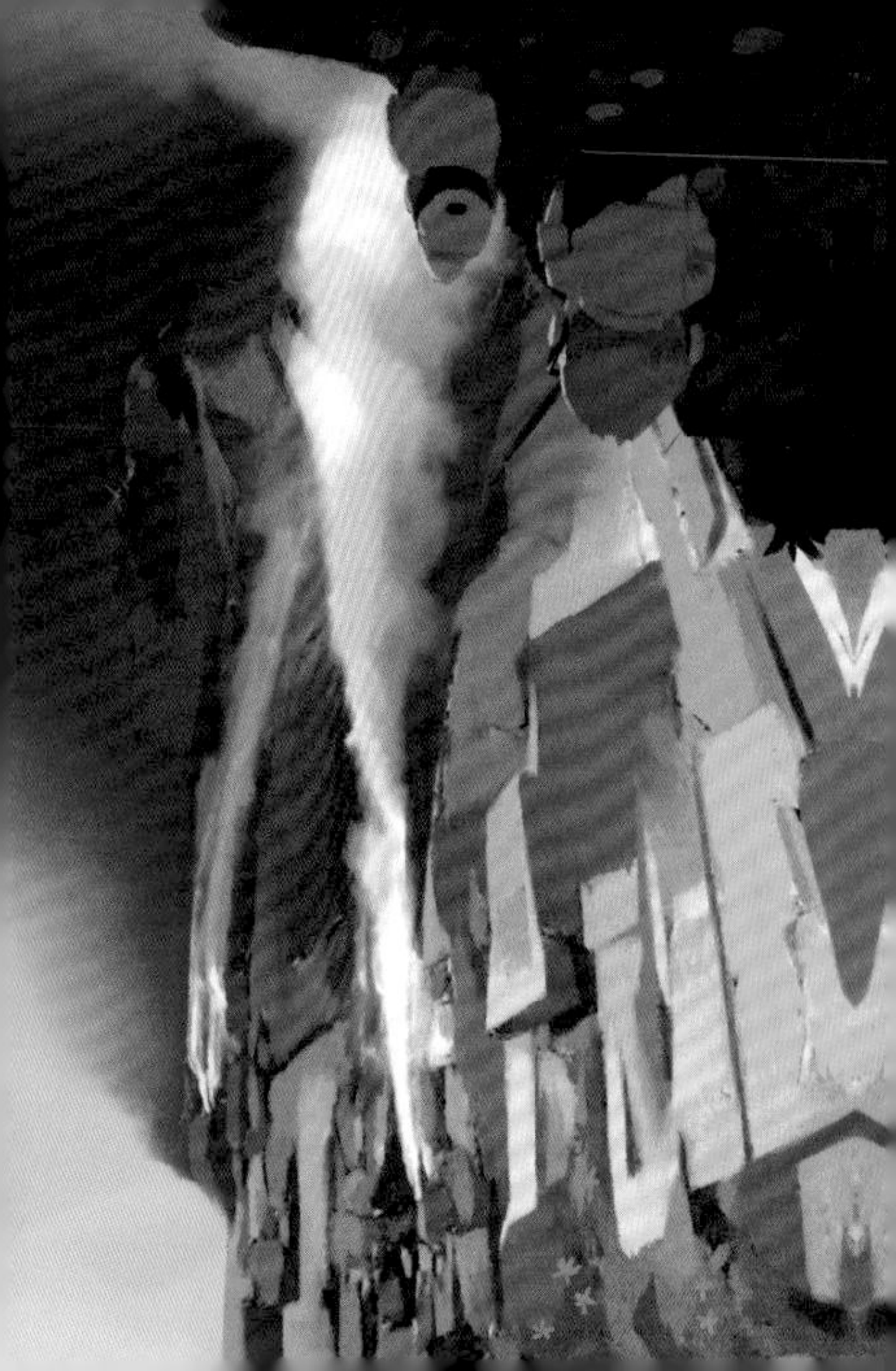

PIXAR

A MINIATURE ART COLLECTION

BY BROOKE VITALE

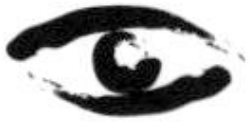

INSIGHT EDITIONS

SAN RAFAEL • LOS ANGELES • LONDON

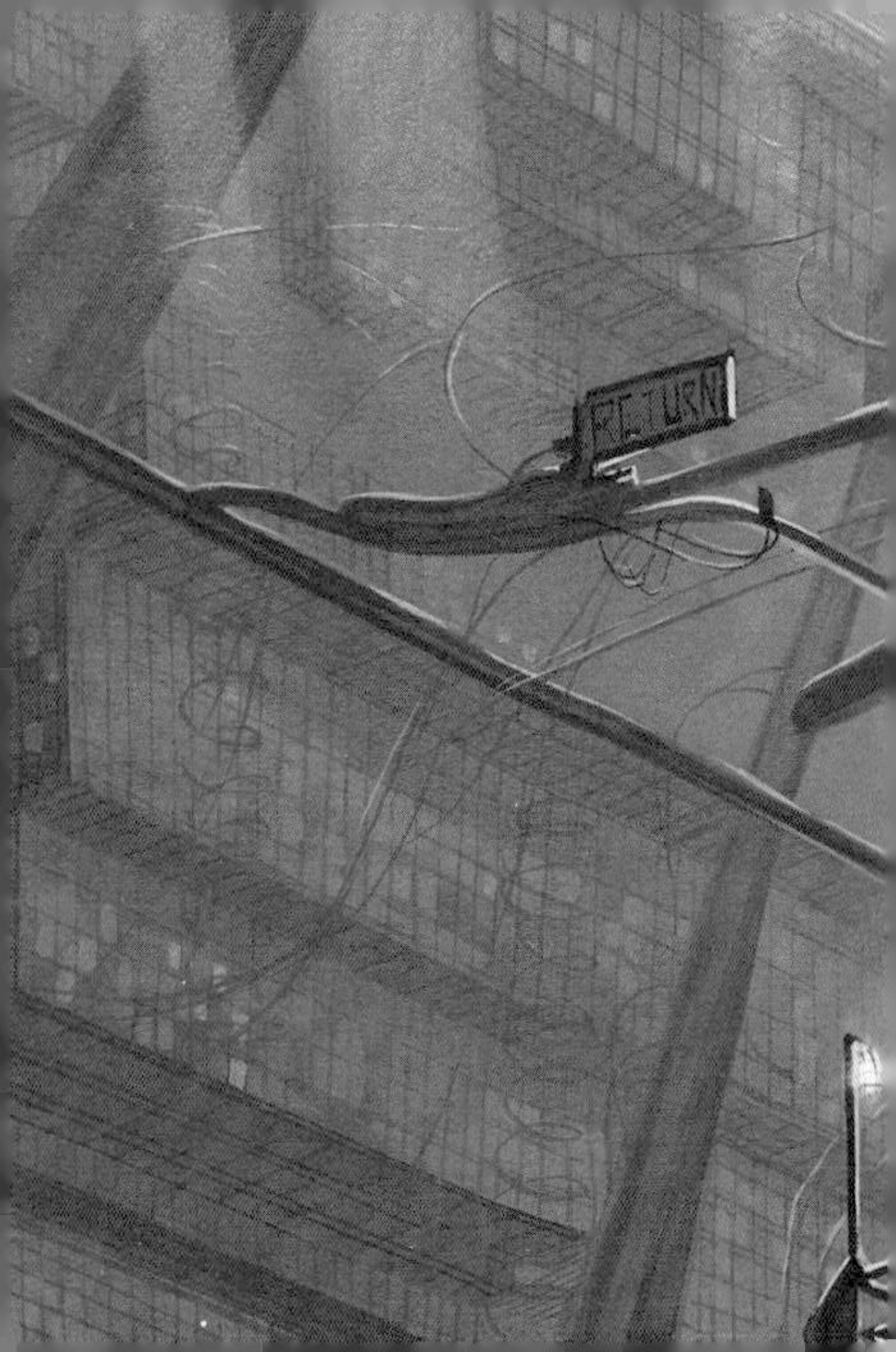
RETURN

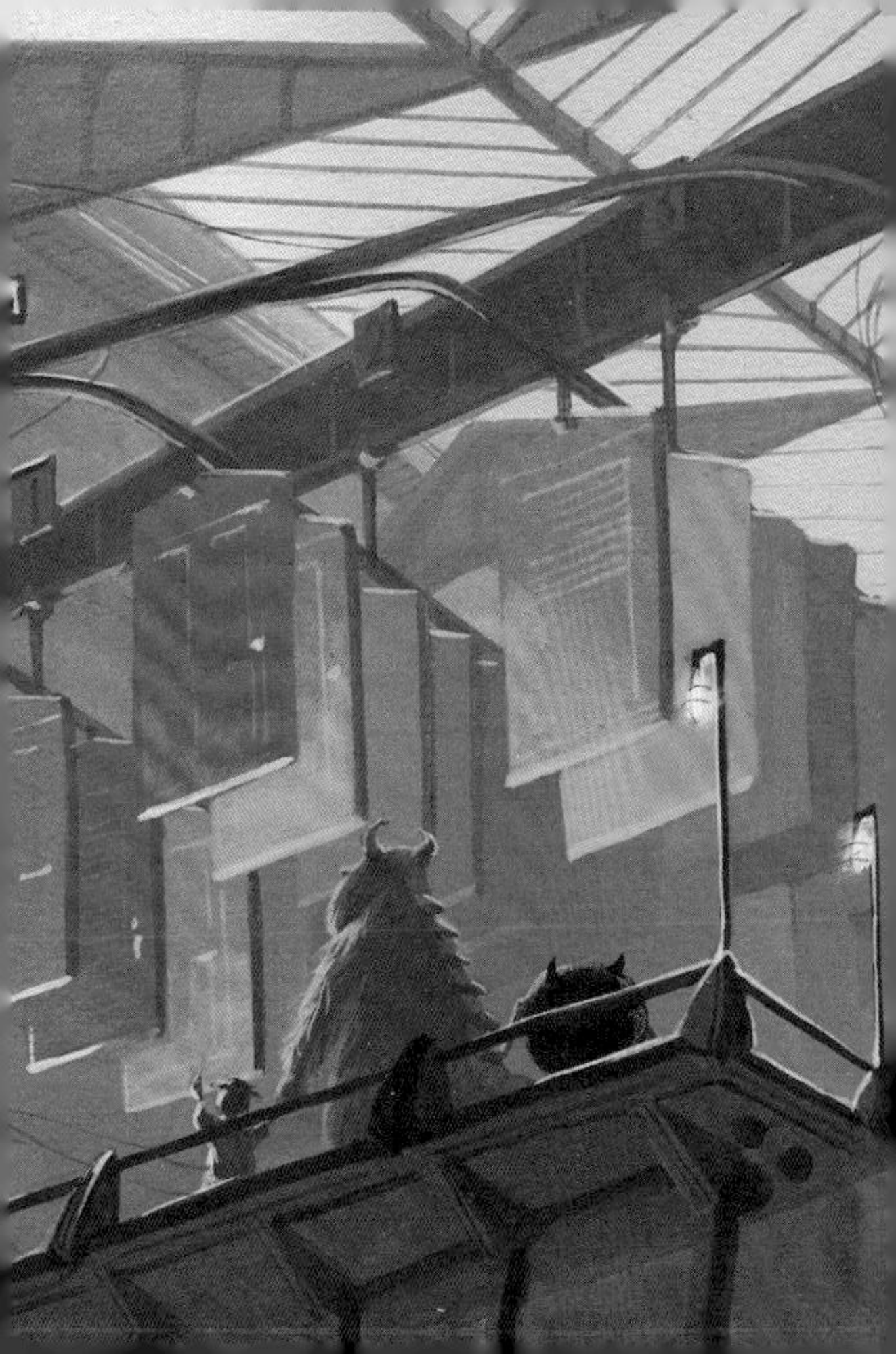

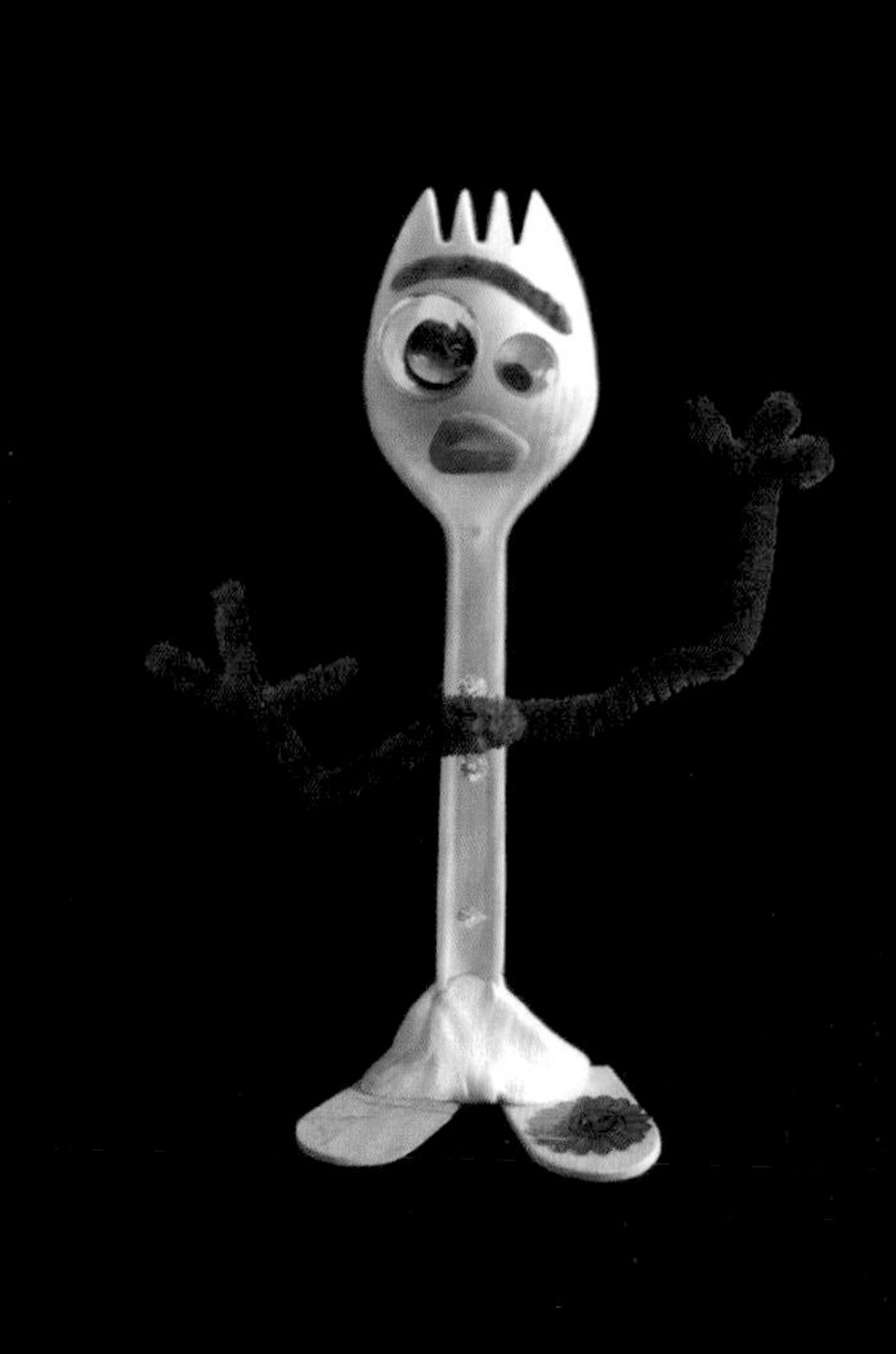

CONTENTS

INTRODUCTION 11

EARLY DAYS 16

1990s 39

2000s 69

2010s 151

2020s 273

CREDITS 290

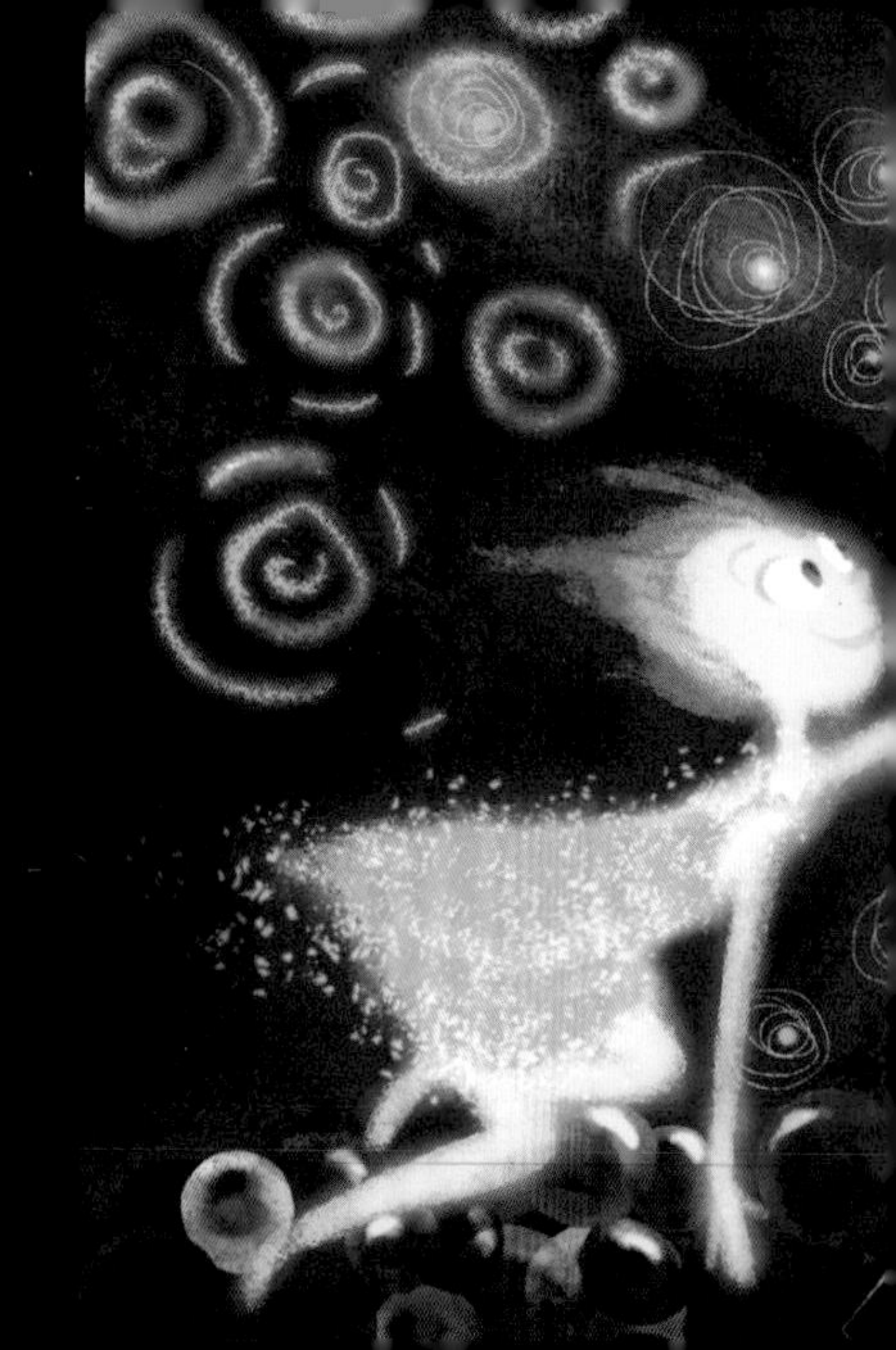

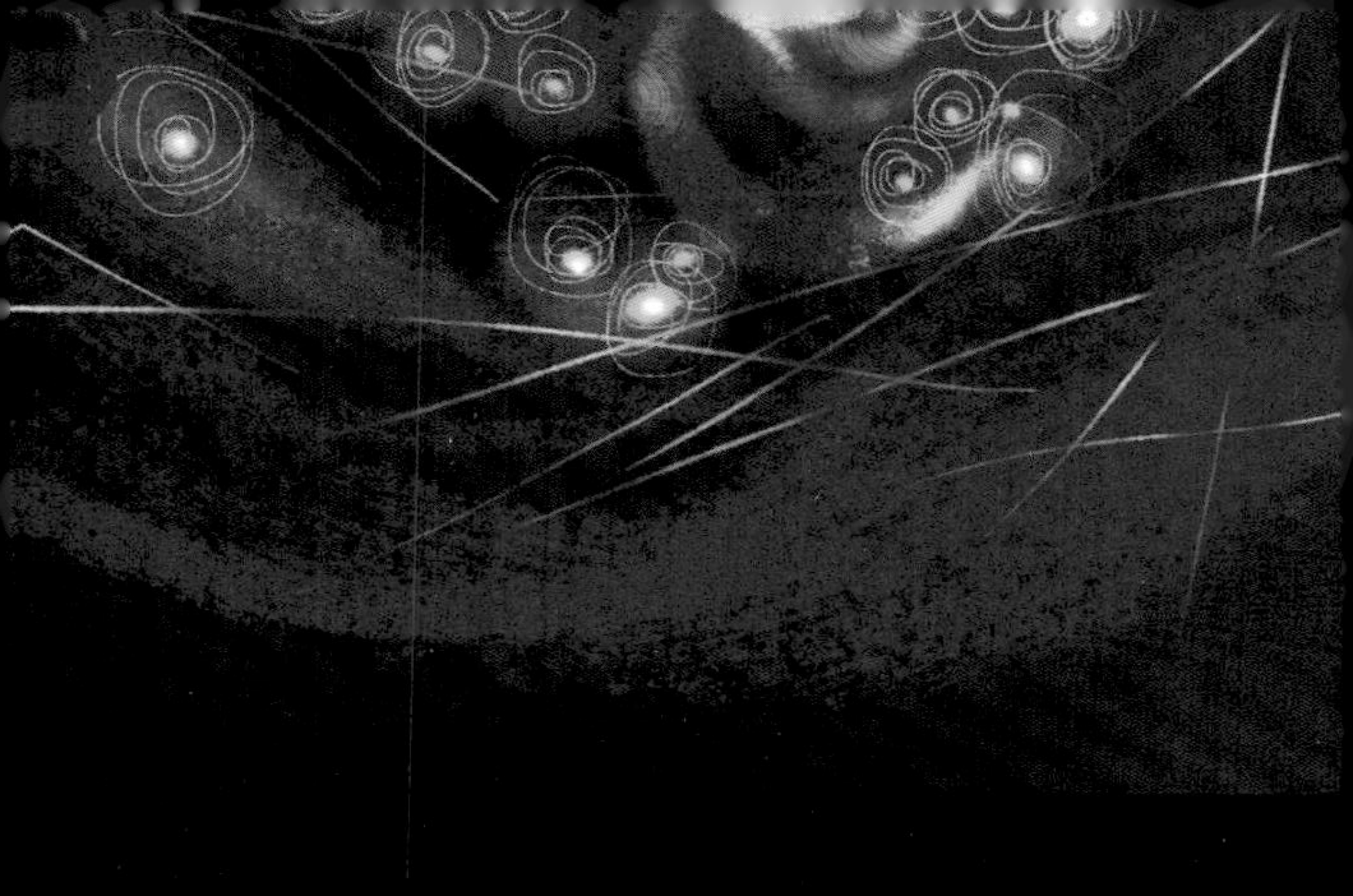

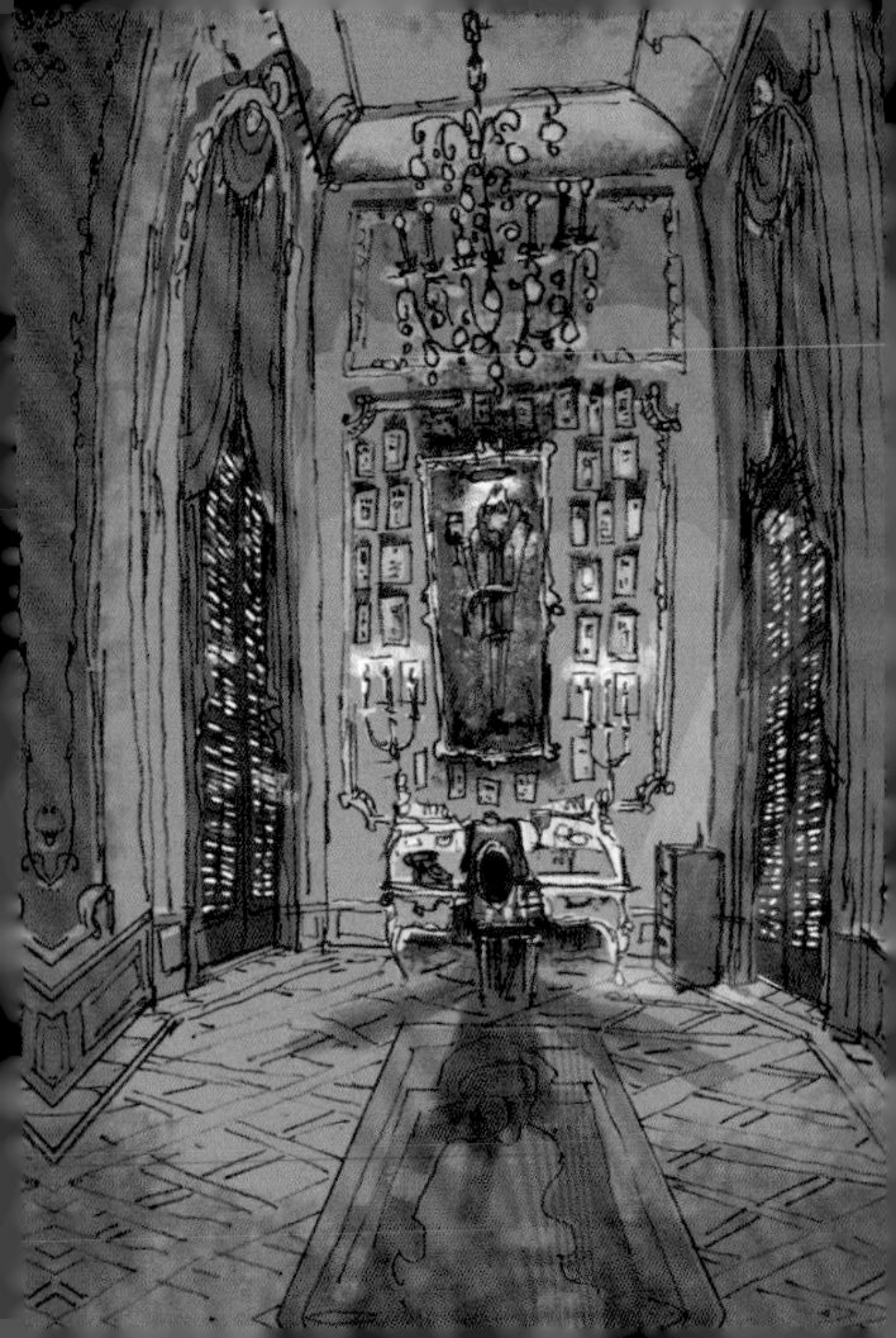

INTRODUCTION

Today, Pixar is known as one of the leading forces in computer animation and visual storytelling. The group that would eventually become Pixar began as a part of the Lucasfilm Computer Division. In 1979, computer scientist Ed Catmull joined the Computer Division there to head up a team focused on developing tools for advanced digital filmmaking. The company embraced this drive to create computer graphics, and

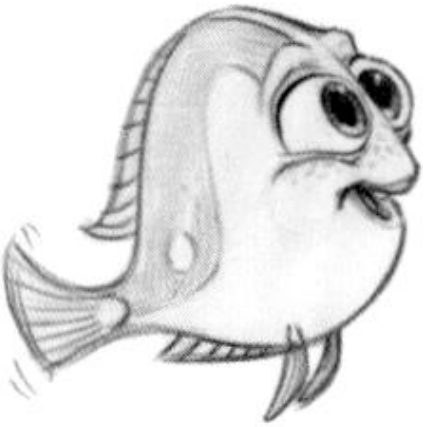

Catmull sought out like-minded artists, including former Disney animator John Lasseter. In 1986, Apple co-founder Steve Jobs purchased the computer graphics division from Lucasfilm. Under the direction of Catmull, Lasseter, and Jobs, the newly renamed Pixar focused on the hardware business, software business, and computer animation, setting their sights on creating the first entirely computer-animated feature film.

From the early days, to the release of *Toy Story*, to the next generation of animated films, Pixar has continually sought to reach new technological and artistic heights in the name of storytelling. In this miniature art book, fans will find a curated collection of art spanning the studio's extensive film library, from *Toy Story* to *Up*, to *Coco*, and beyond—a pocket-sized celebration of technology, artistry, and story.

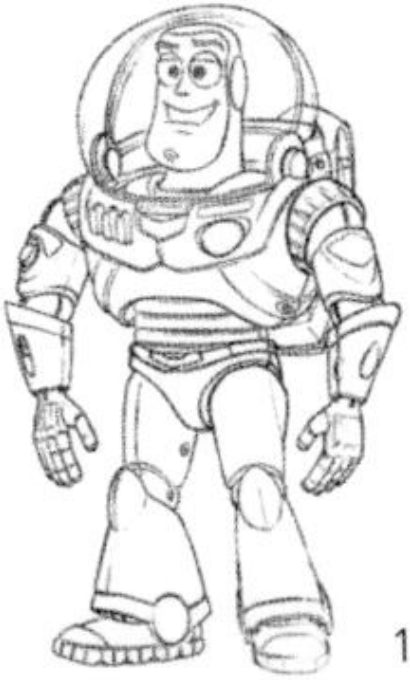

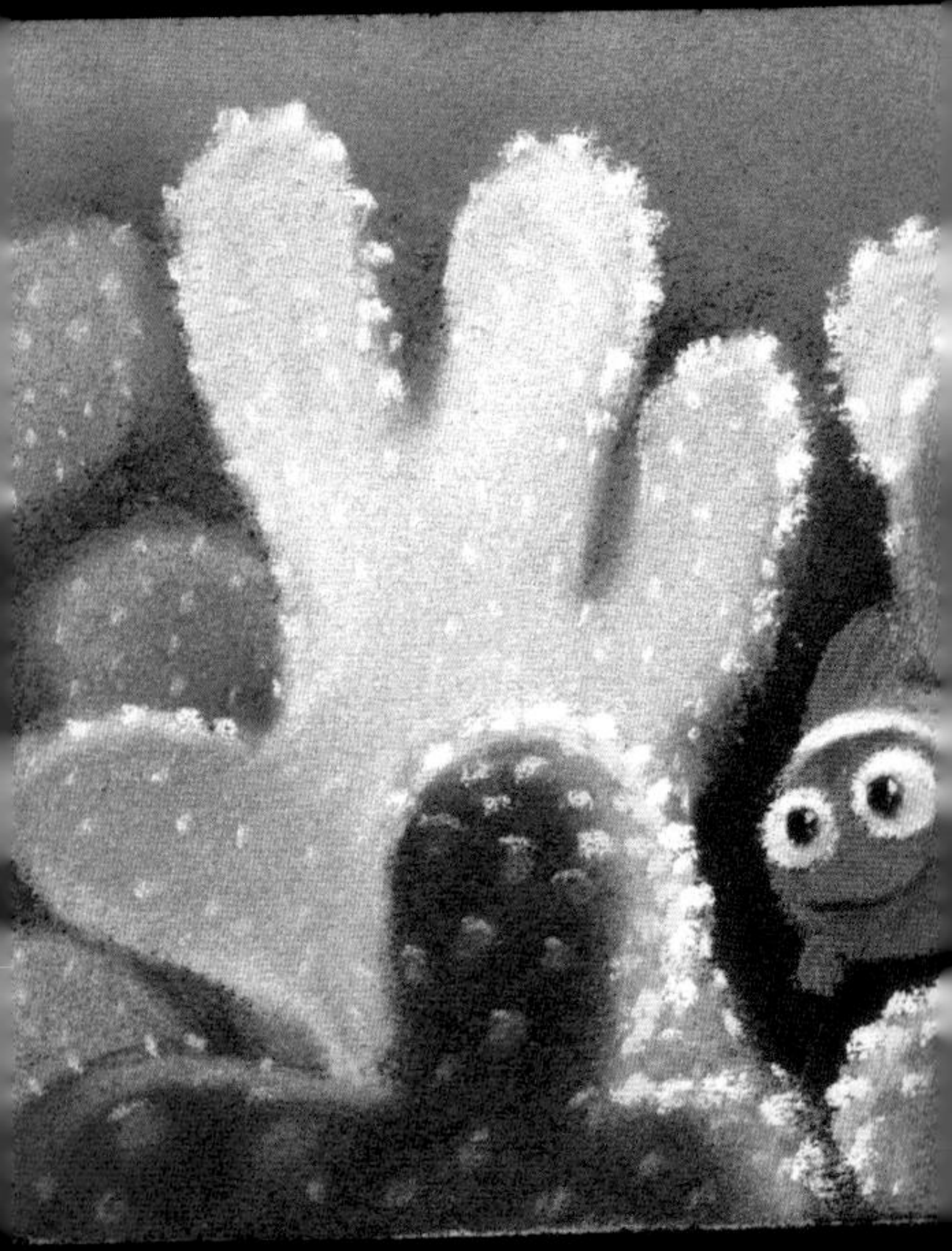

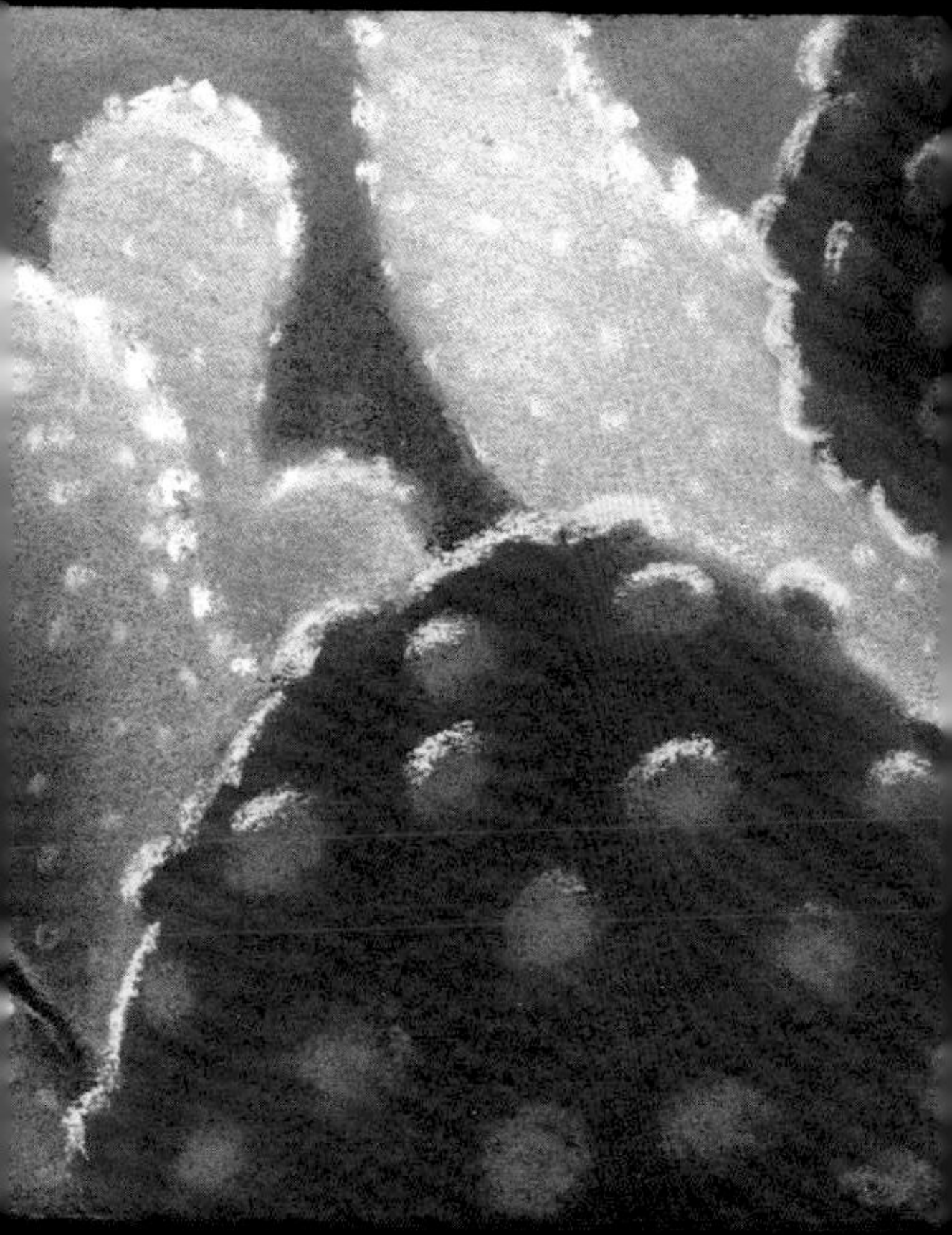

EARLY DAYS

From their earliest days, Pixar films offered a unique perspective that demonstrated the marriage of technology and artistic vision. While the Graphics Group was still under the ownership of Lucasfilm, they created the animated short *The Adventures of André & Wally B.*, which introduced the use of motion blur, complex backgrounds, and nongeometric shapes. Over the next five years, the studio continued to strive to innovate. By the end of the decade, the newly independent Pixar had earned two Academy Award nominations and one win for the short film *Tin Toy*, the first-ever CGI film to win an Oscar. Although lesser known than Pixar's feature films, it was these early films that helped to bring legitimacy to CGI films as an art form and laid the groundwork for many of the films we see today.

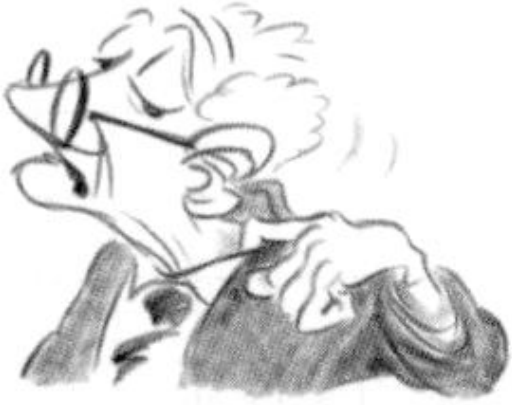

SHORT

THE ADVENTURES OF ANDRÉ & WALLY B.

1984

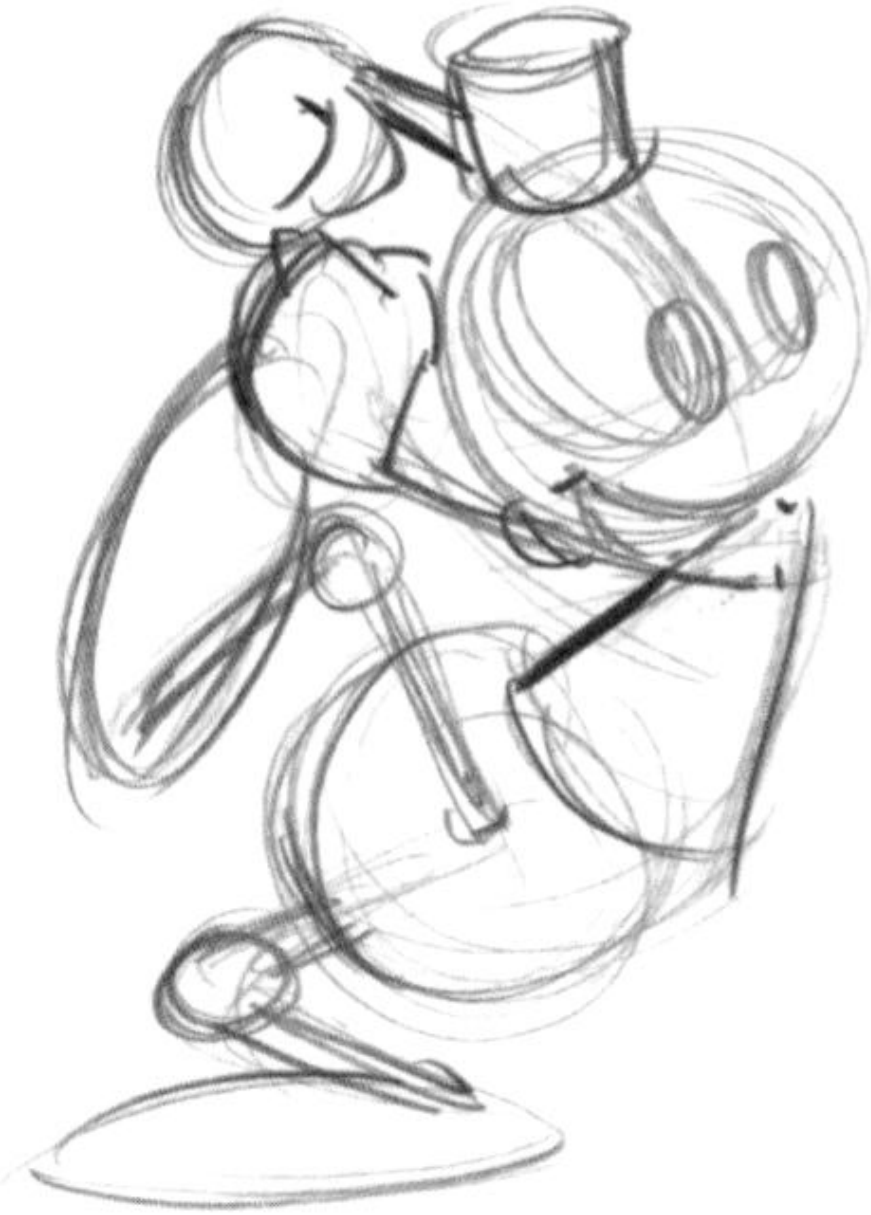

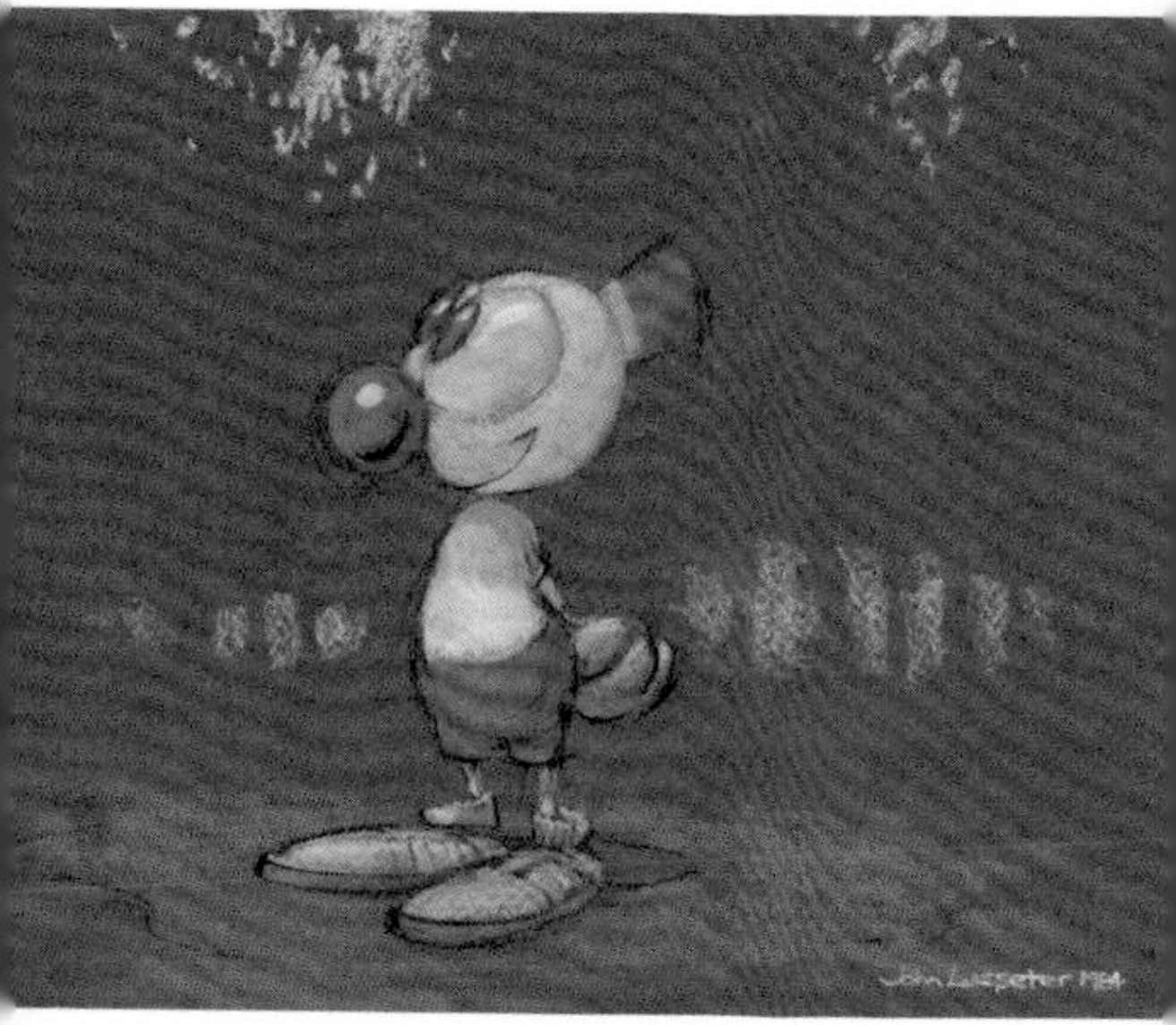
John Lasseter 1984

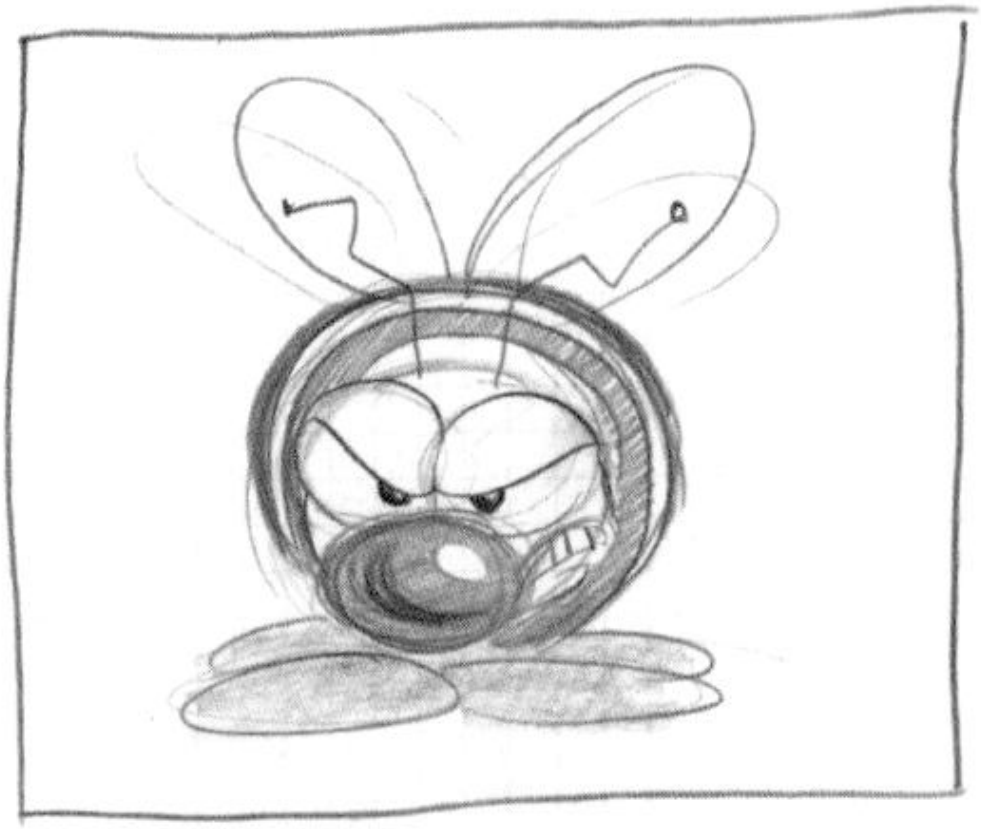

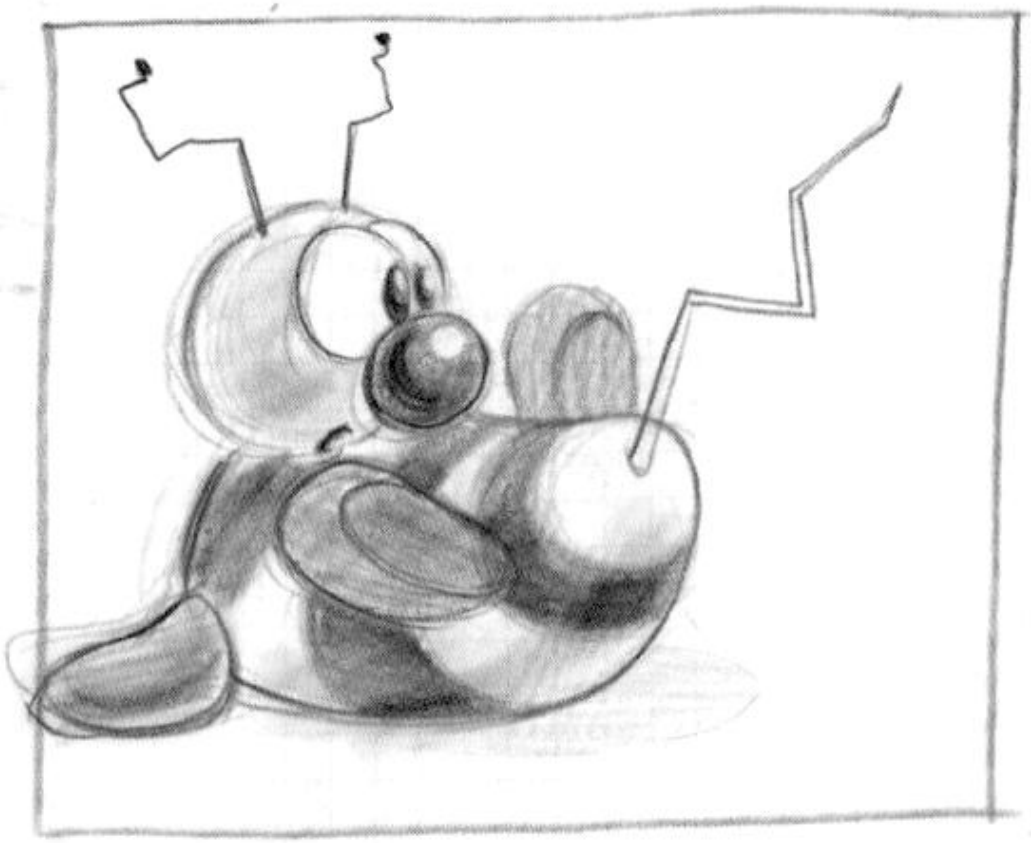

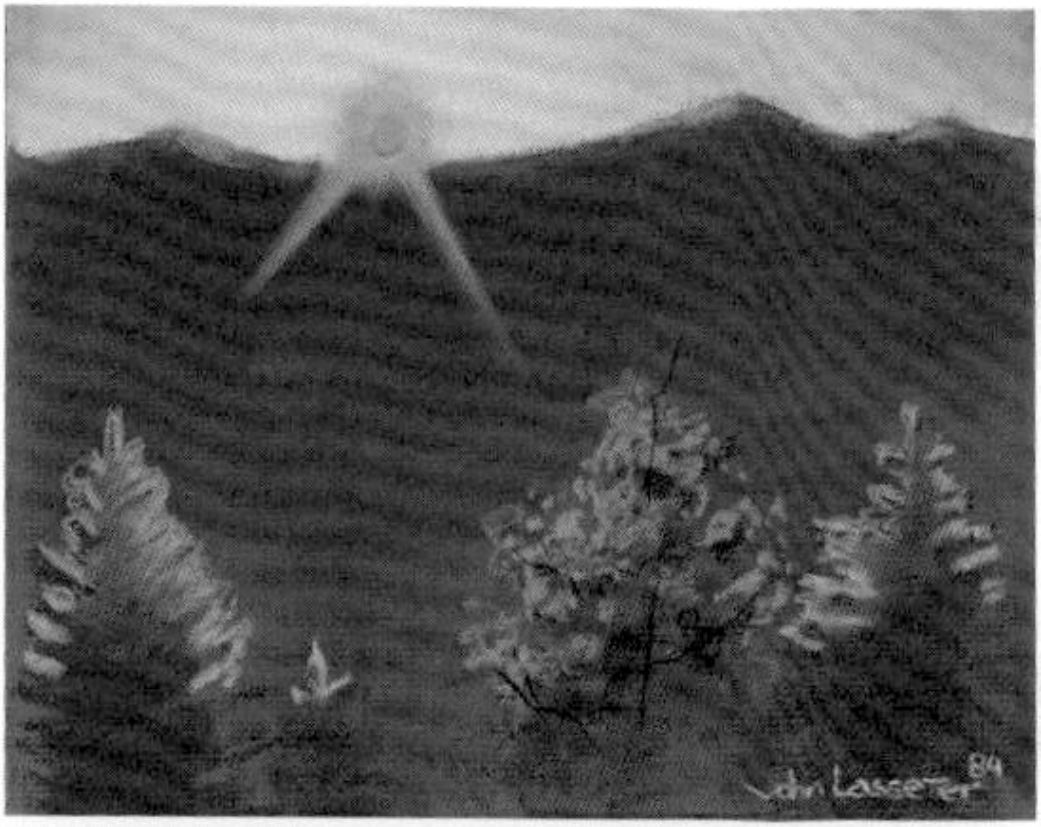
John Lasseter 84

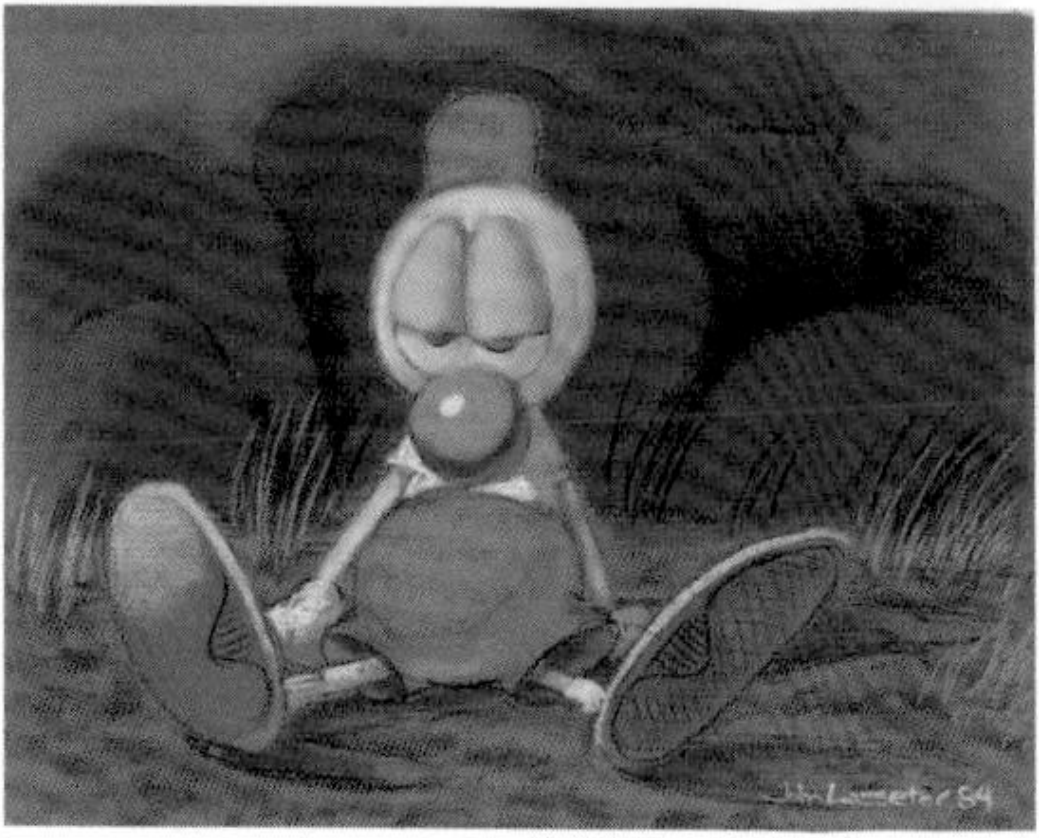
John Lasseter 84

SHORT

LUXO JR.

1986

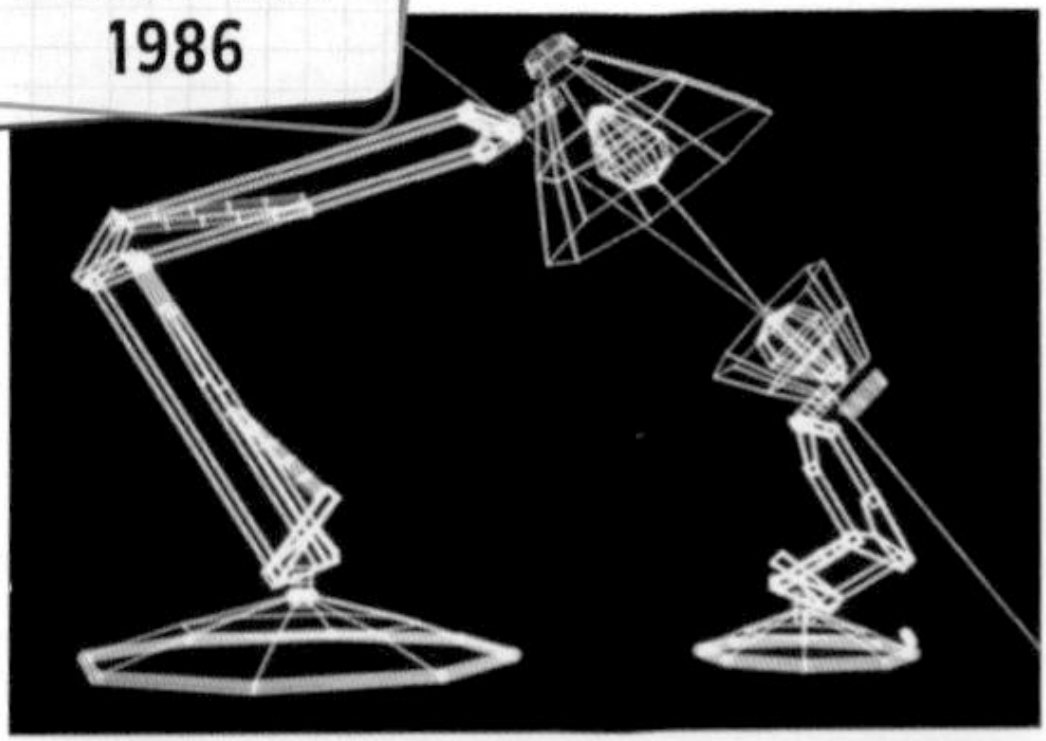

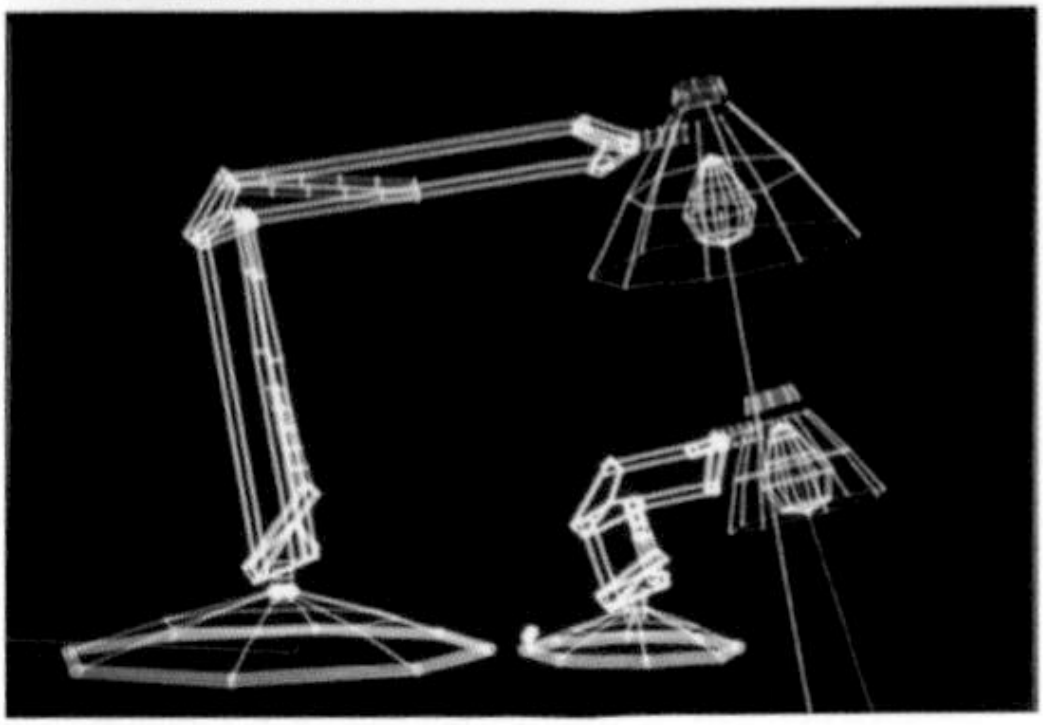

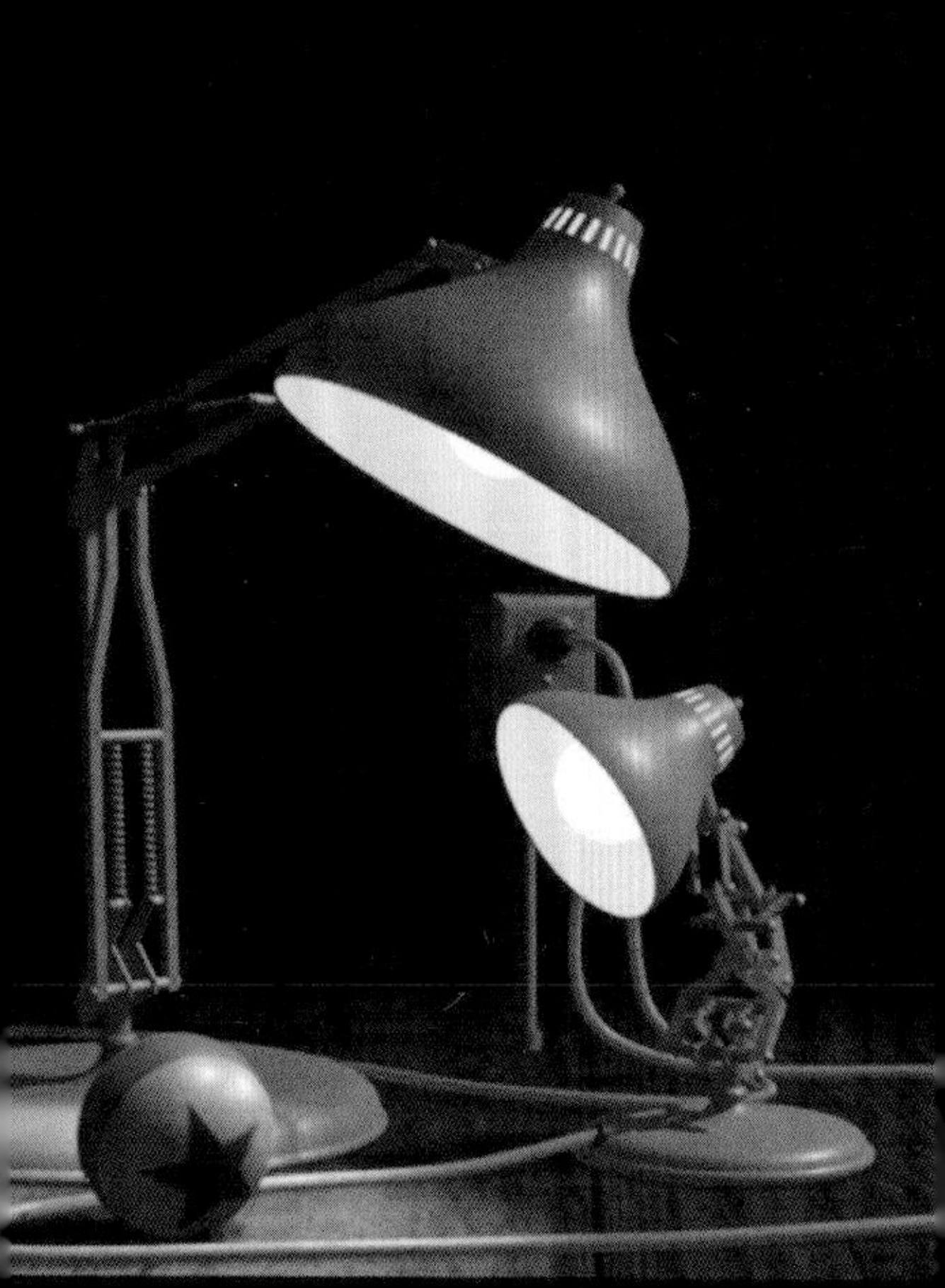

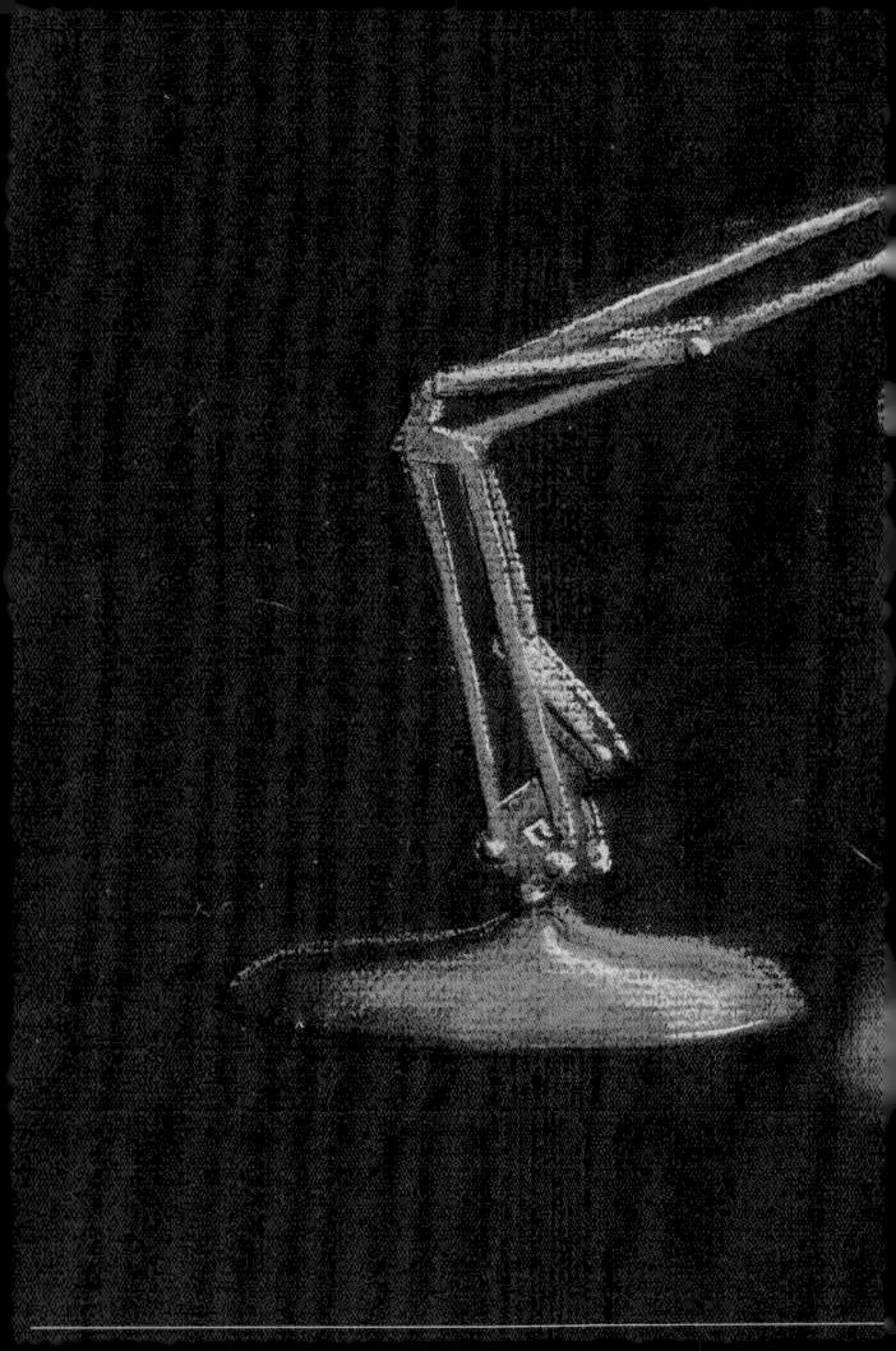

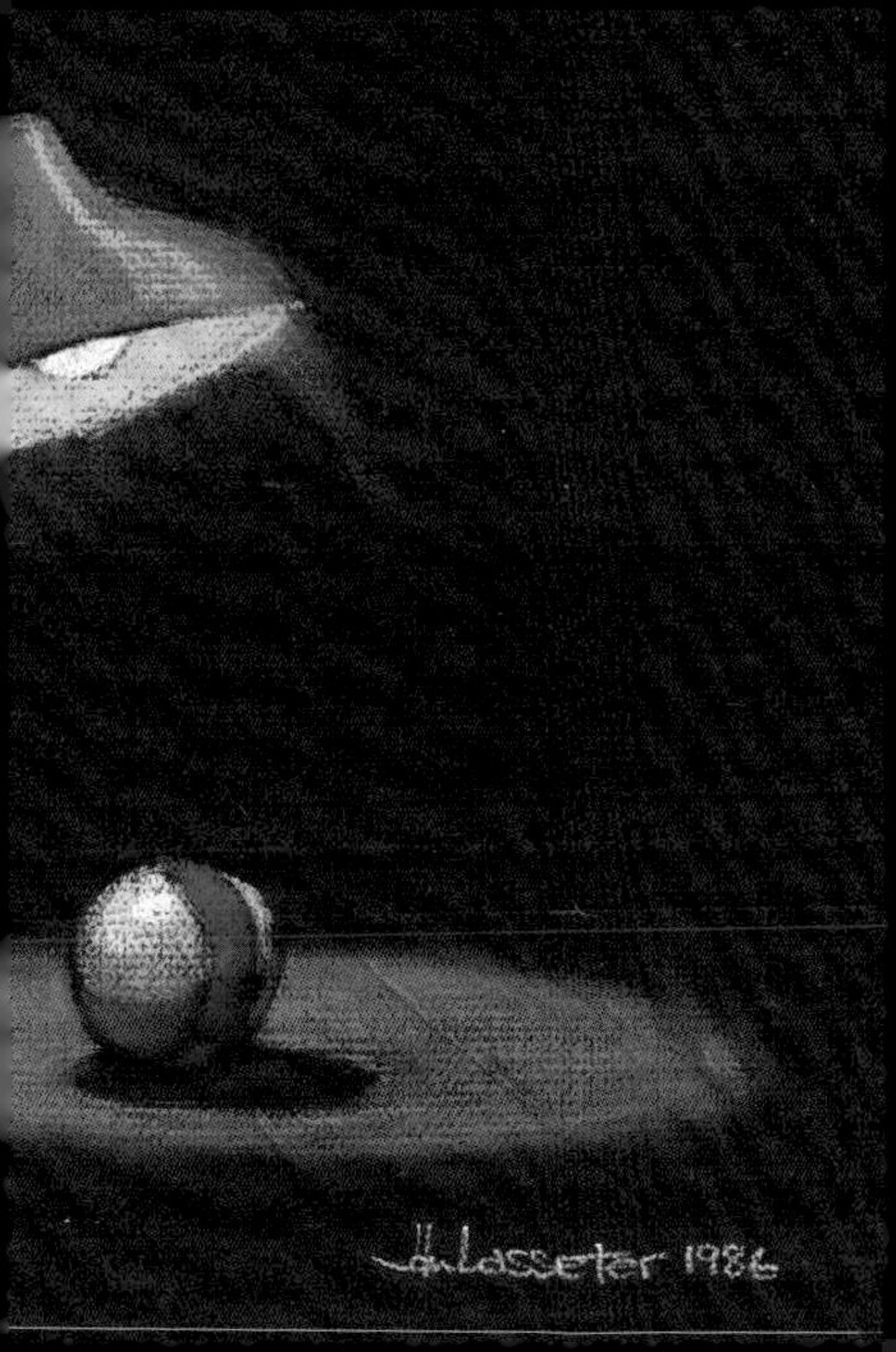
Lasseter 1986

SHORT

RED'S DREAM

1987

Company Confidential

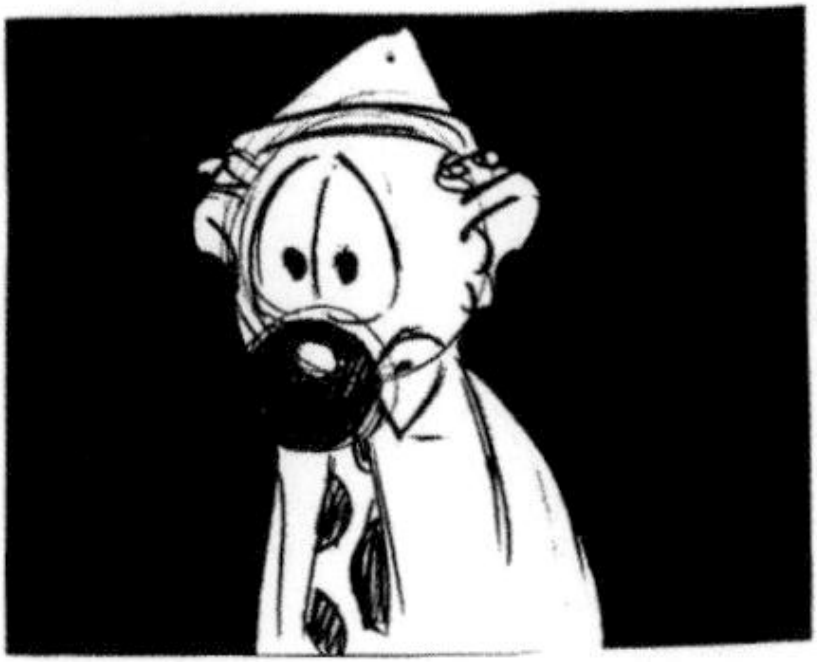

DESCRIPTION:	NOTES:	SEQUENCE:
THEN TO CAMERA		DS-
ELEMENTS / DATE:		Sheet: 2
	FRAME COUNT:	PAGE#: 46

Pixar 3-19-87

Company Confidential

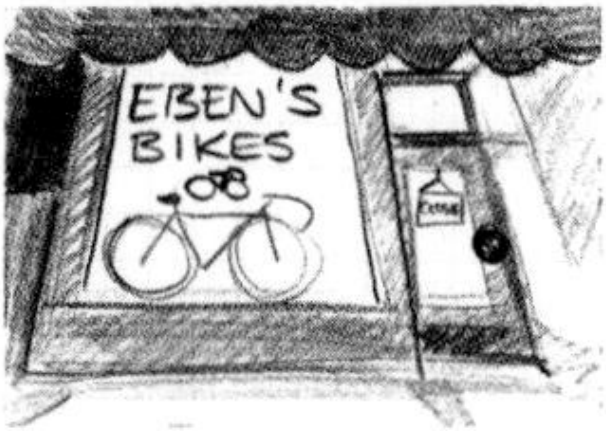

DESCRIPTION:	NOTES:	SEQUENCE/SHOT:
END ON EXTERIOR OF EBEN'S BIKES.	Use Last Shot of EB-1	SE-4
ELEMENTS / DATE:		Sheet:
bstore		
	FRAME COUNT:	PAGE#:
	5sec/120f	62

Page 3-19-97

Company Confidential

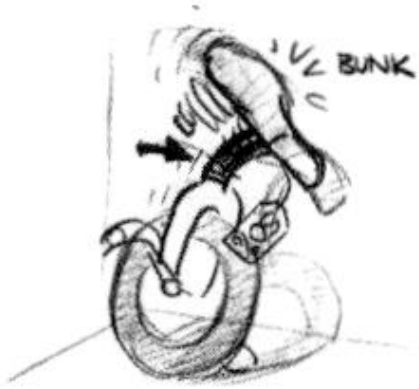

DESCRIPTION:	NOTES:	SEQUENCE/SHOT:
SLOWLY LEANS AGAINST WALL...		SE-3
ELEMENTS / DATE:		Sheet: 3
	FRAME COUNT:	PAGE#:
		60

Page 3-19-97

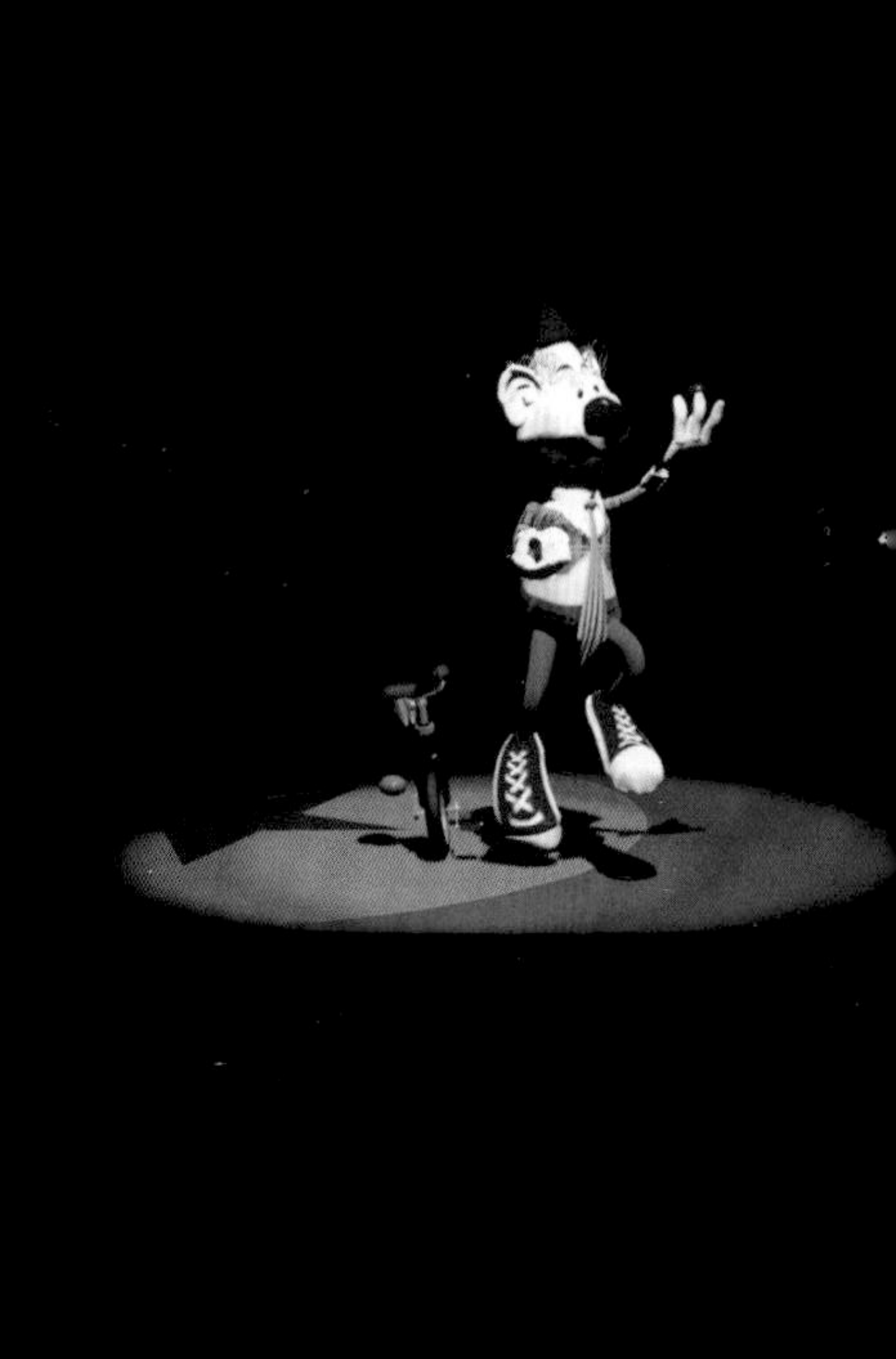

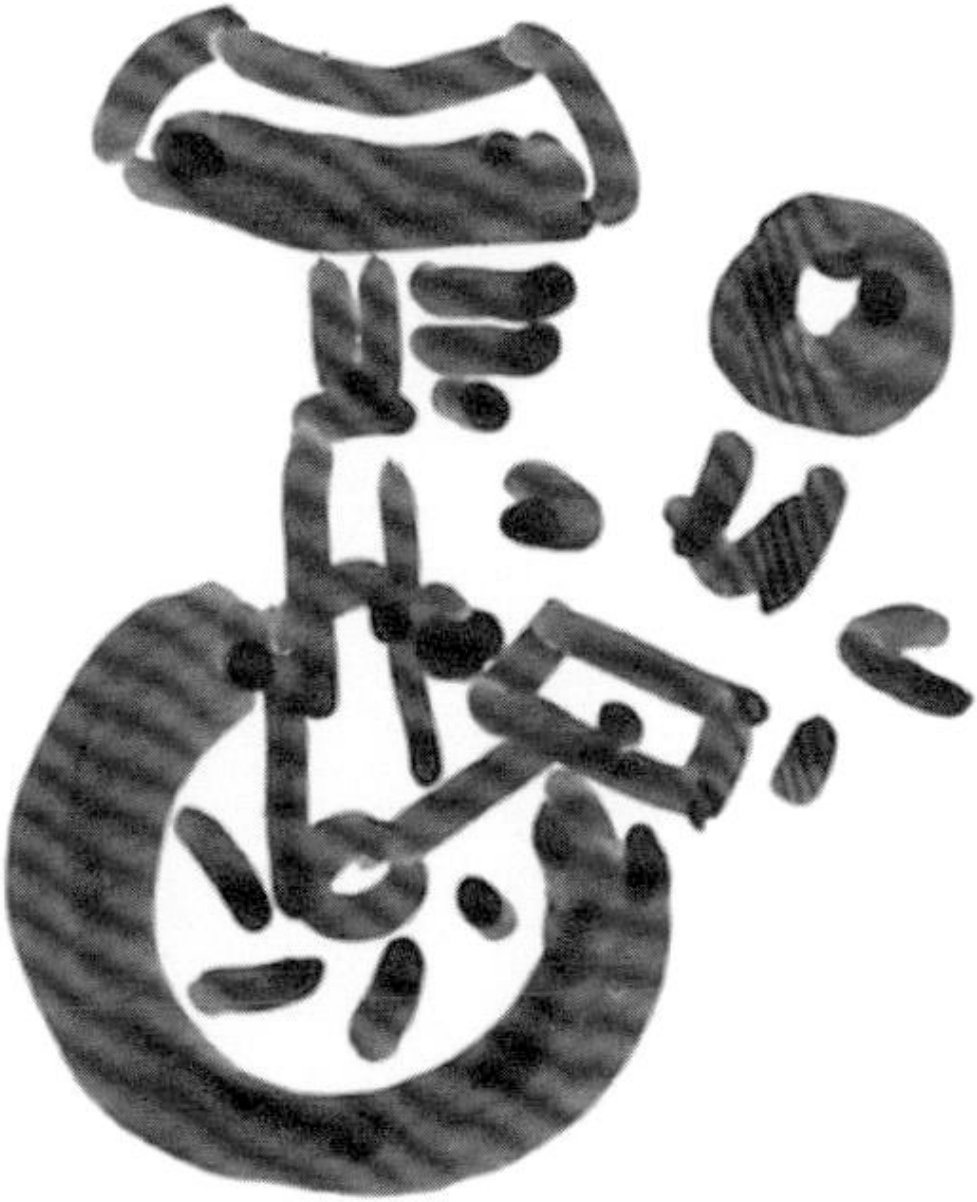

SHORT

TIN TOY

1988

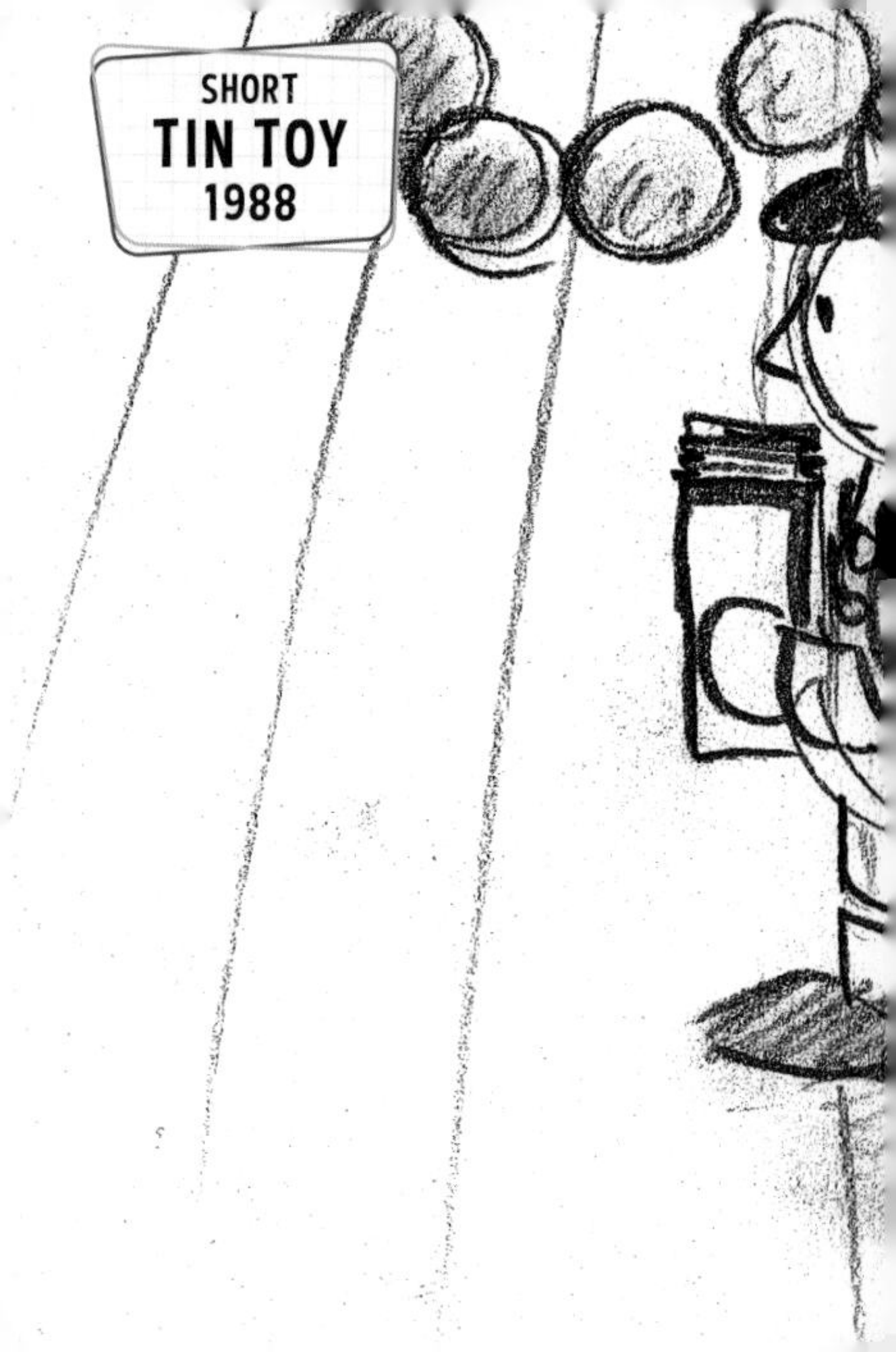

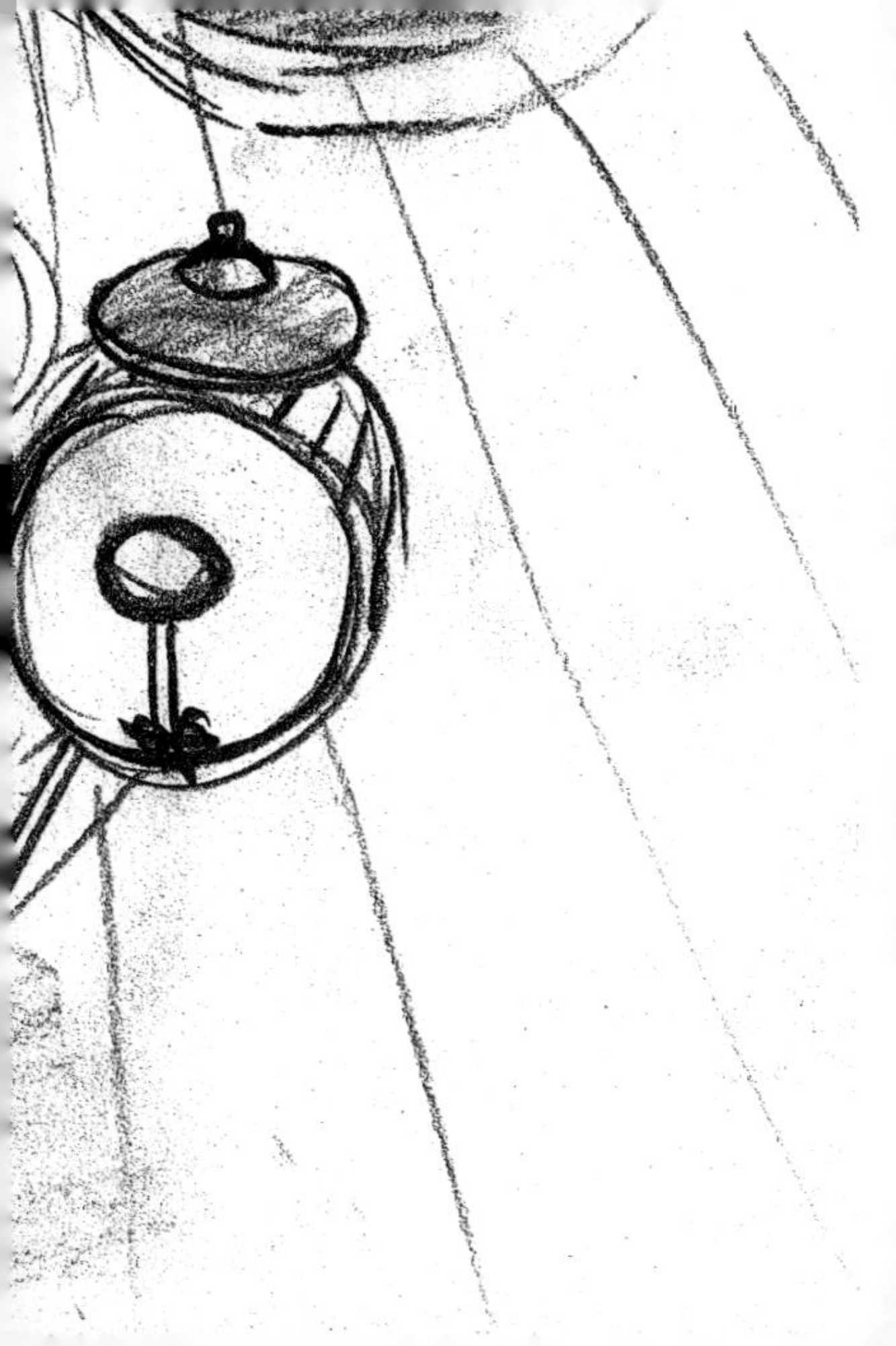

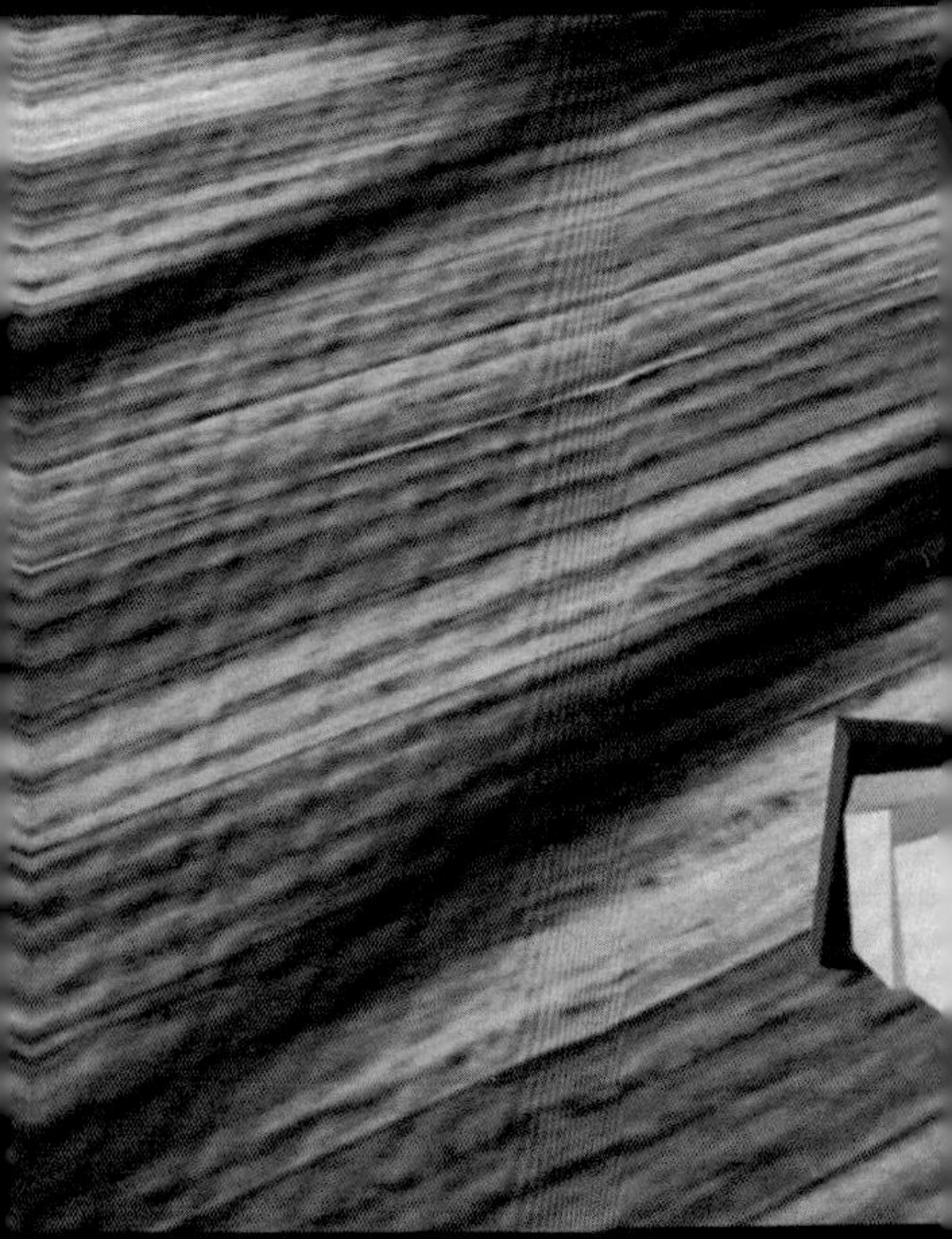

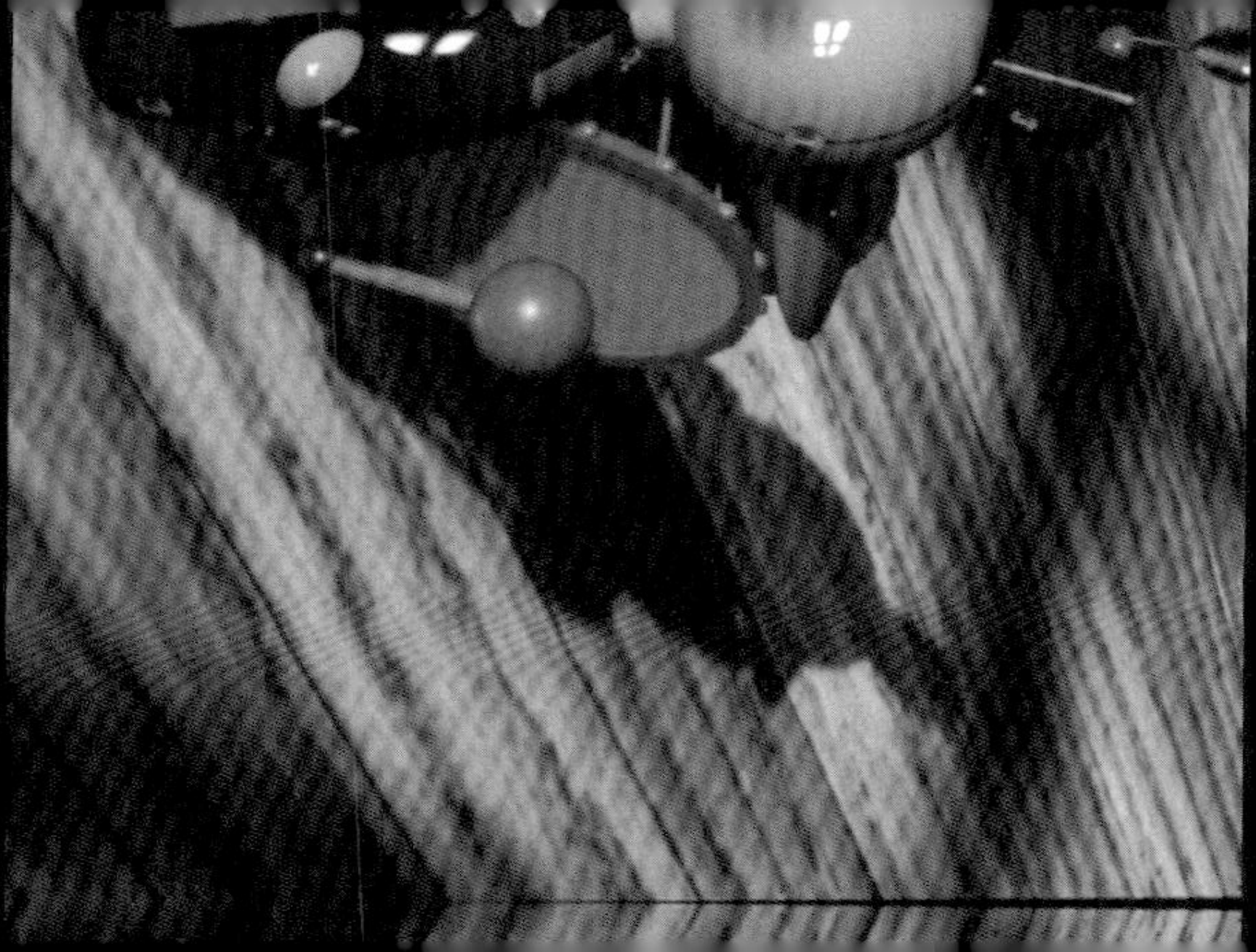

SHORT

KNICK KNACK

1989

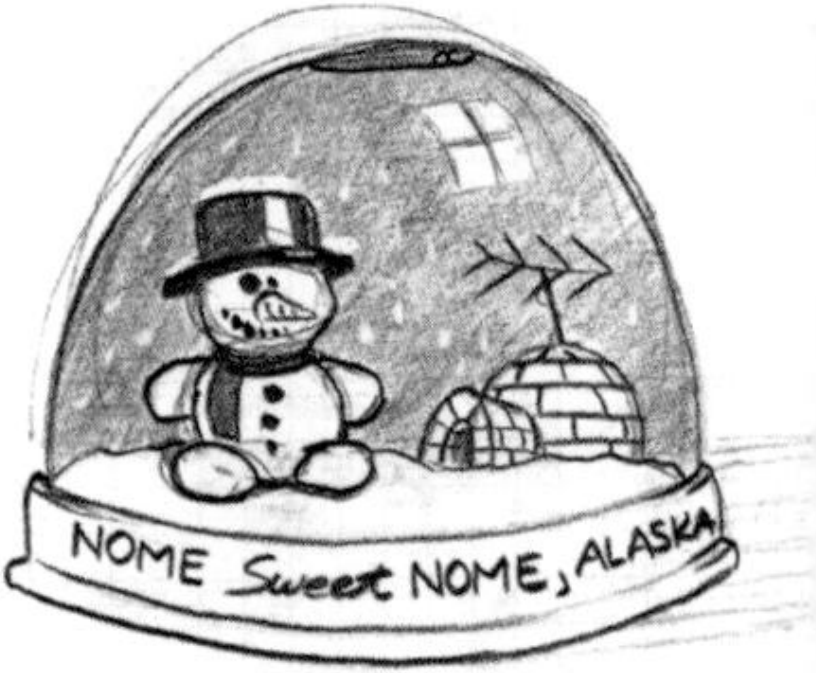

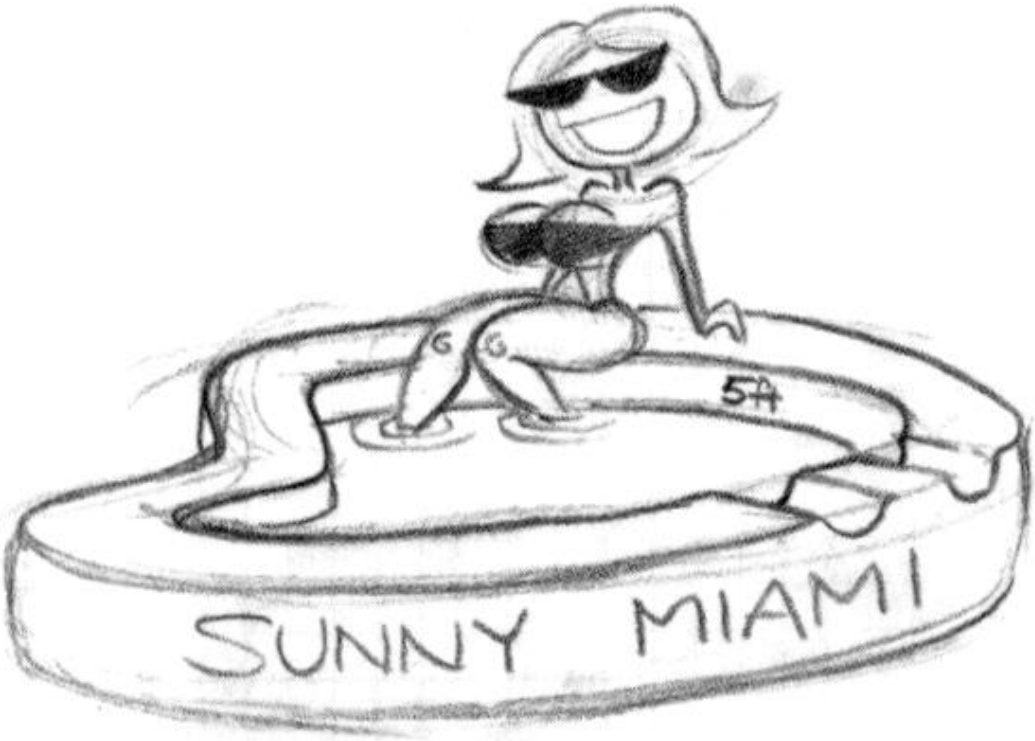

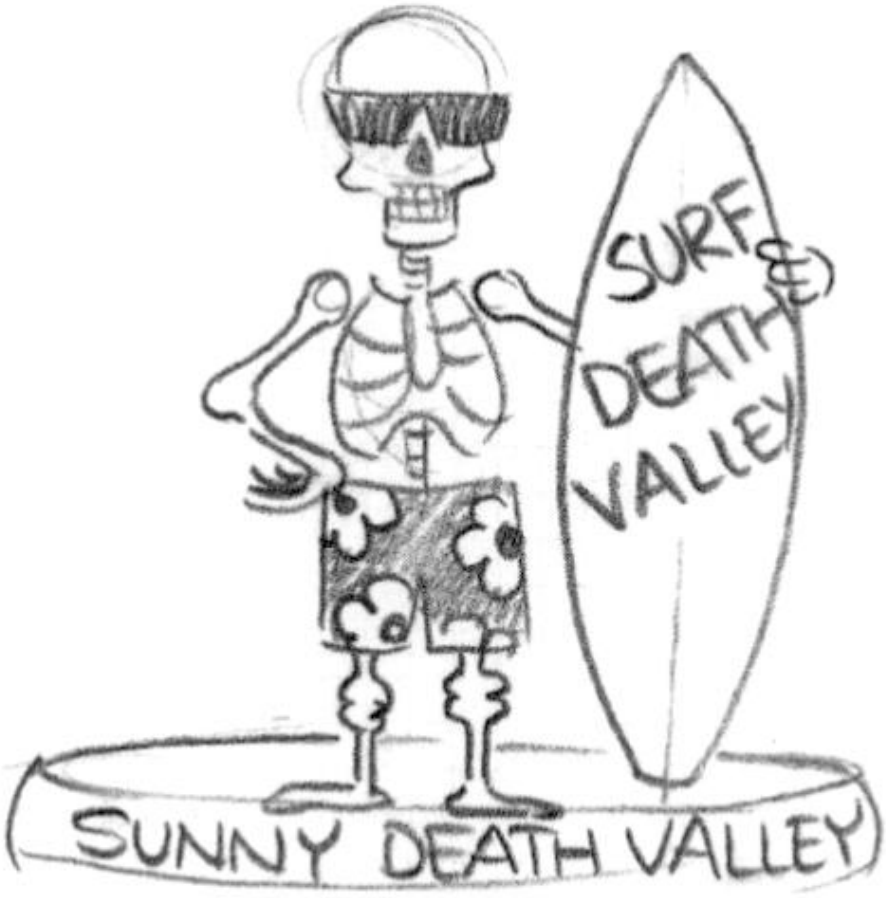
SURF
DEATH
VALLEY
SUNNY DEATH VALLEY

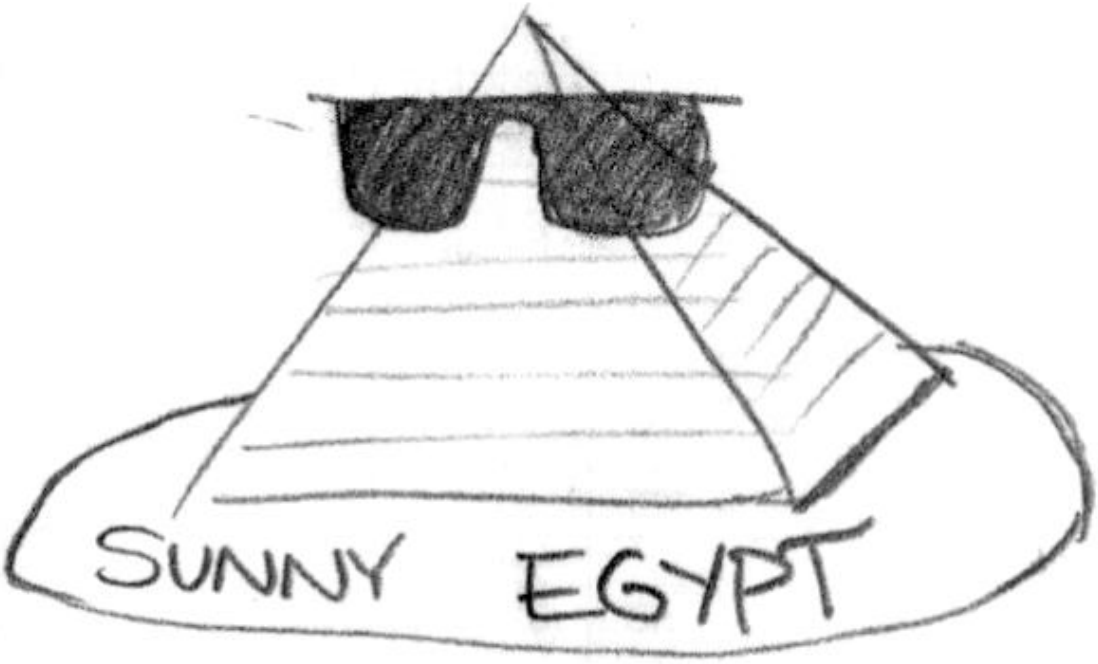
SUNNY EGYPT

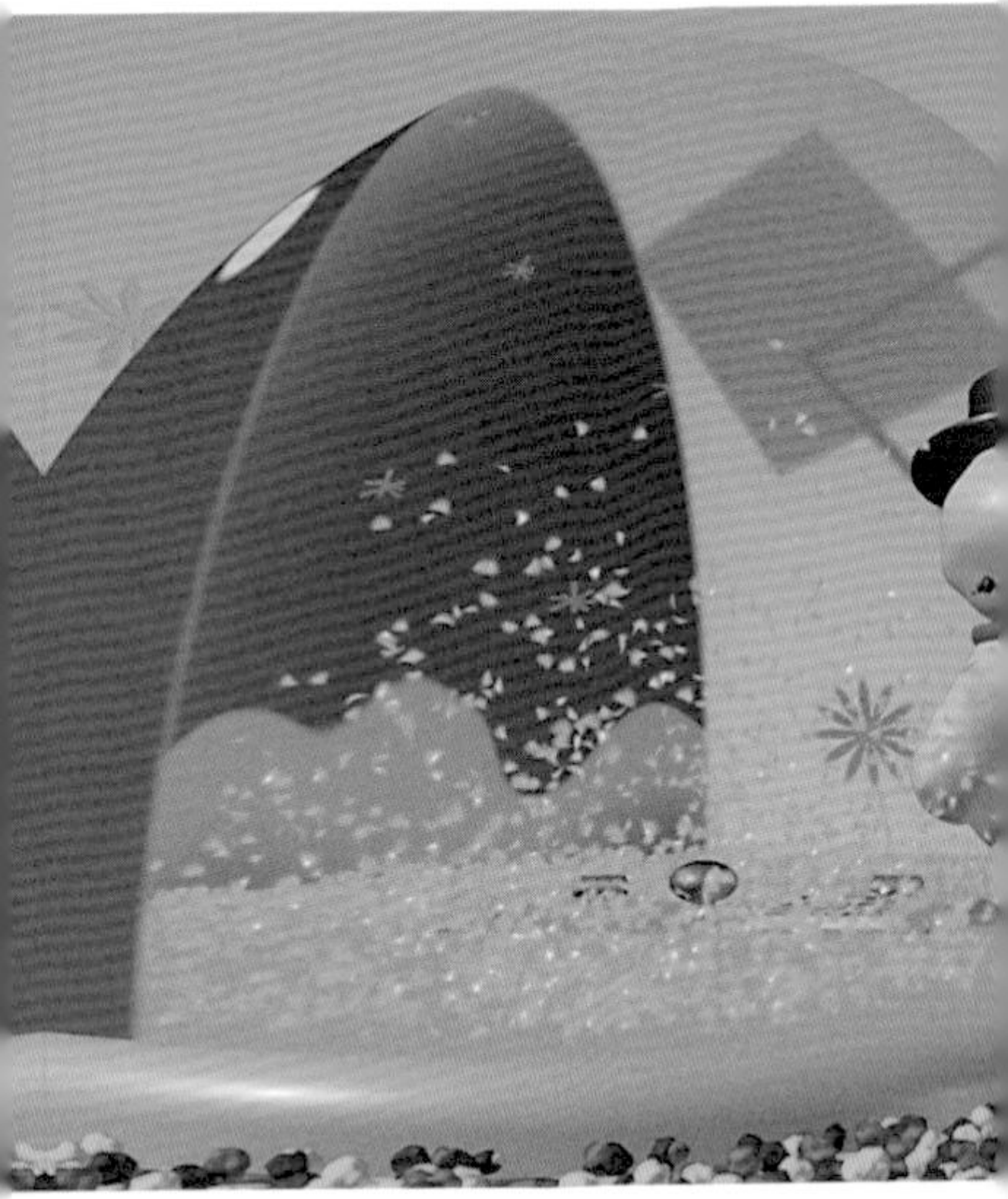

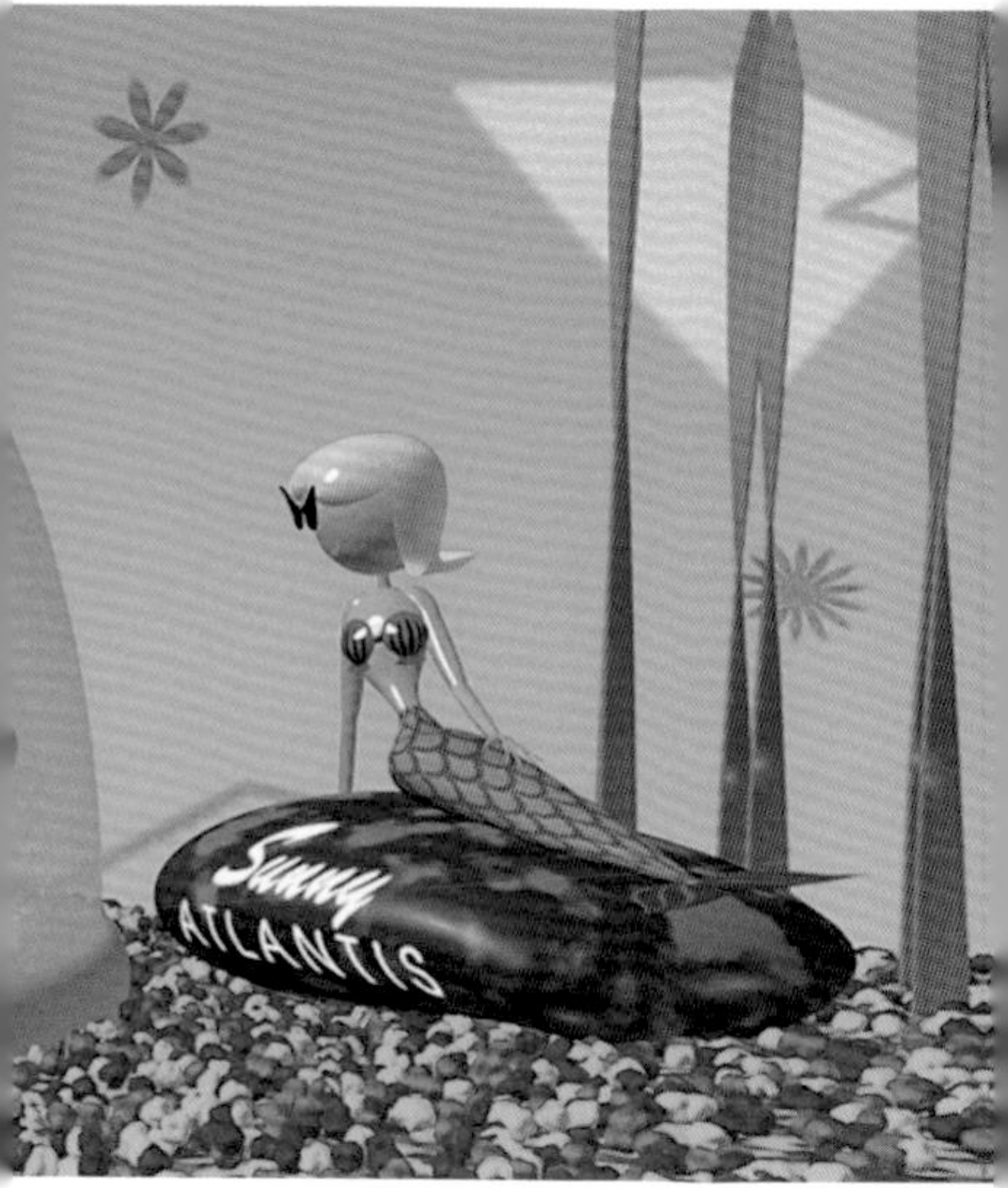
SUNNY
ATLANTIS

1990s

The 1990s saw the release of *Toy Story*, the first-ever fully computer-animated feature film, and a game changer for Pixar.

TOY STORY
1995

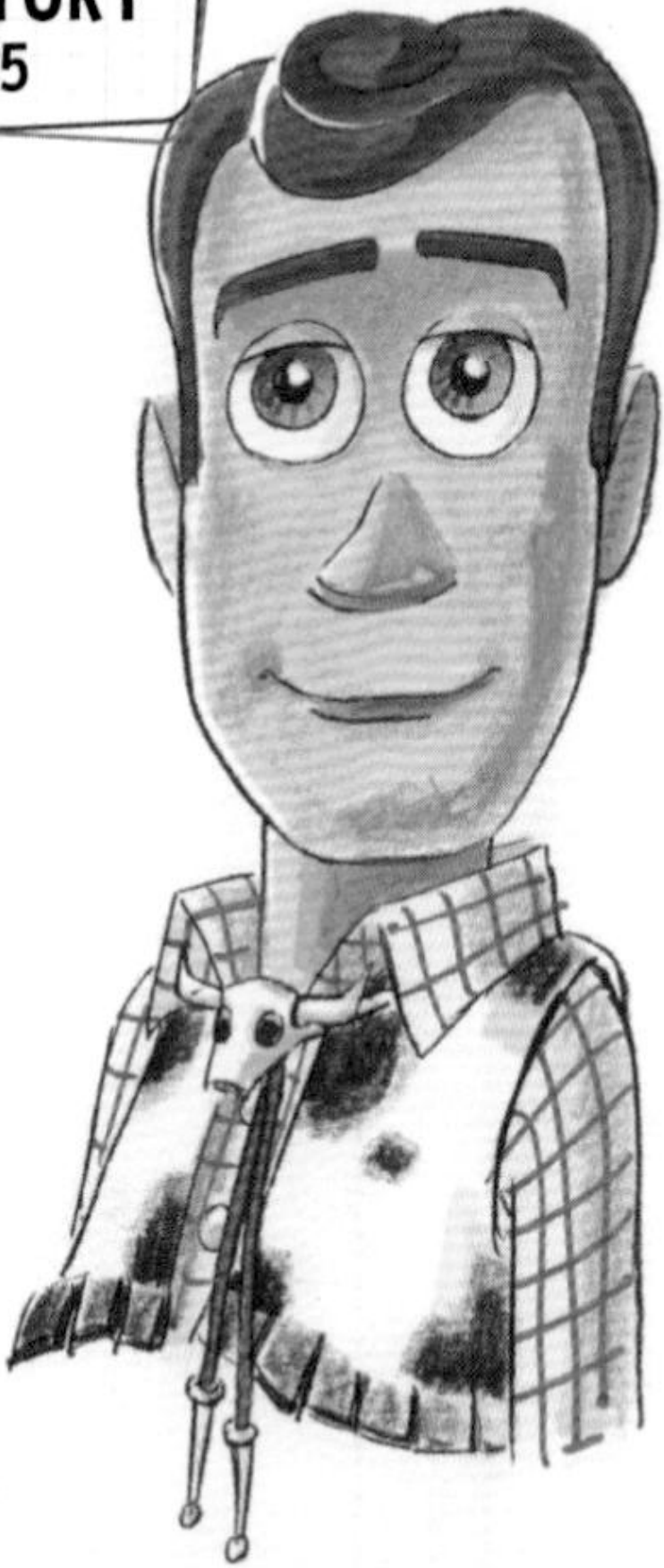

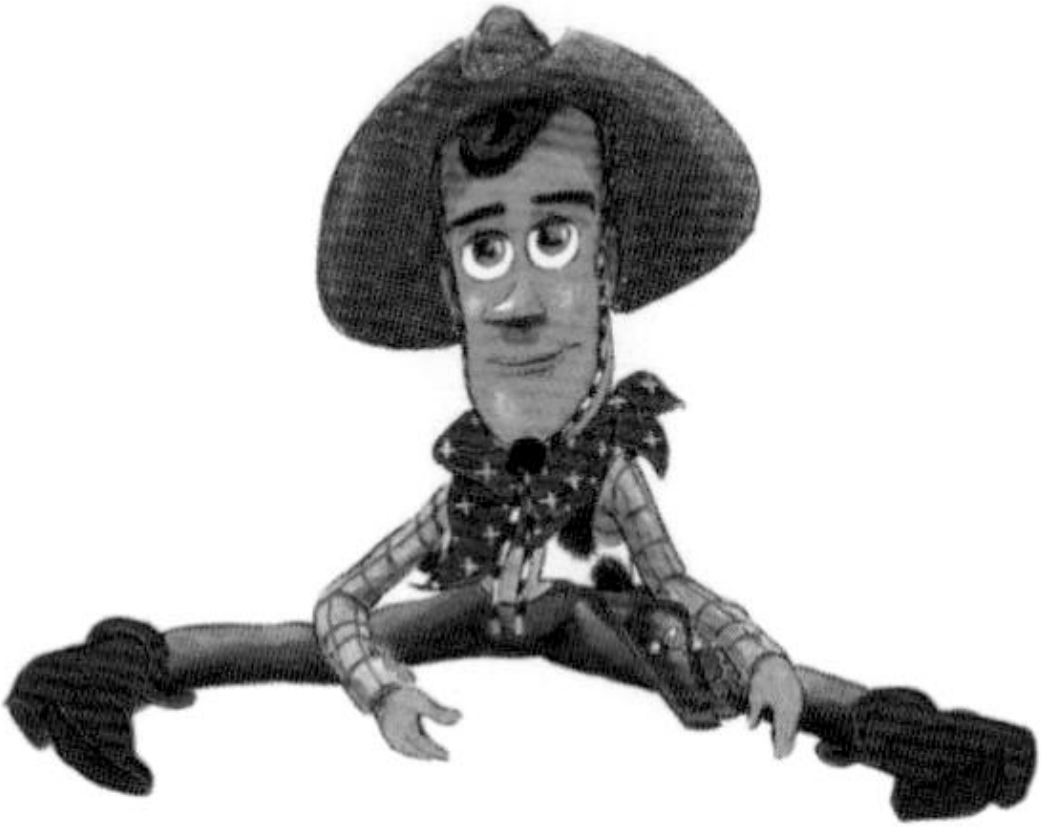

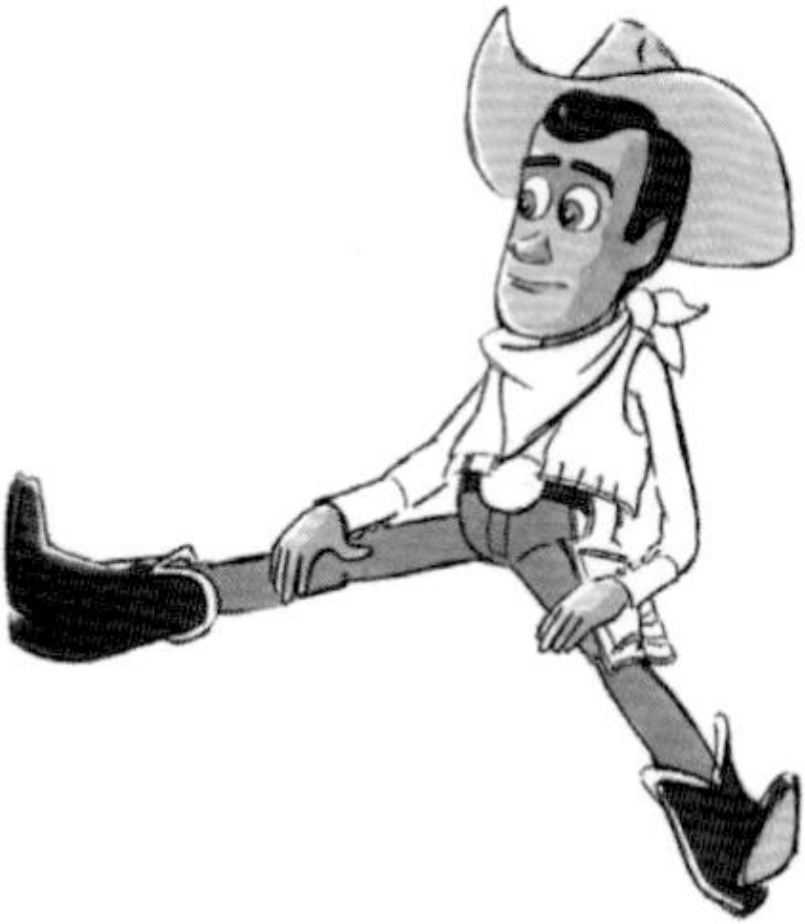

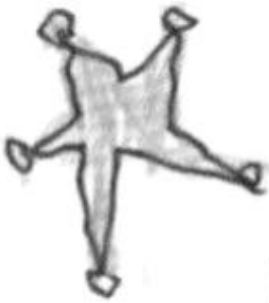

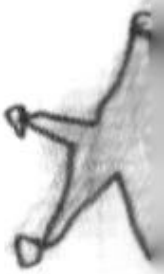

ANDYS
ROOM
KEEP OUT
except MOLLY

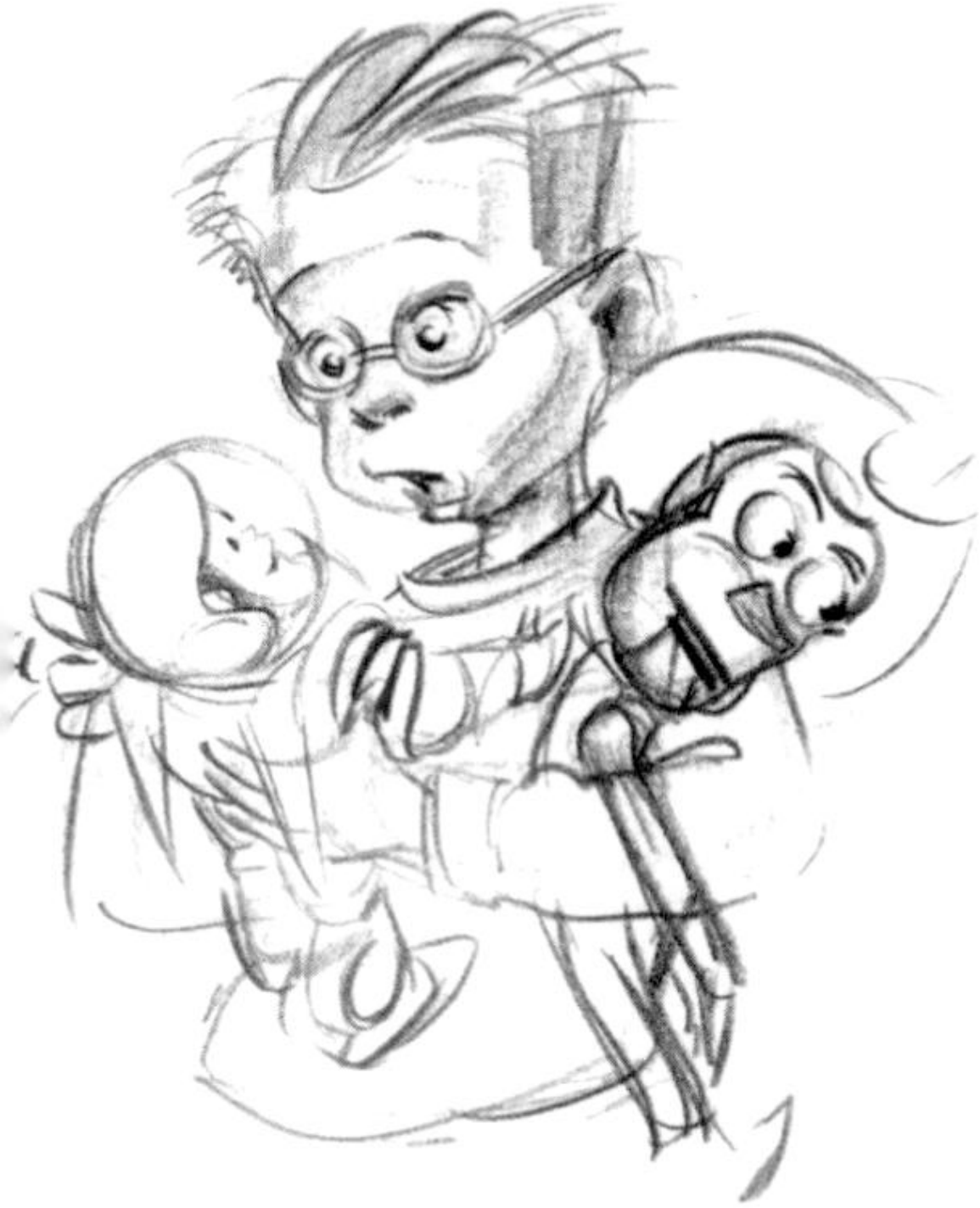

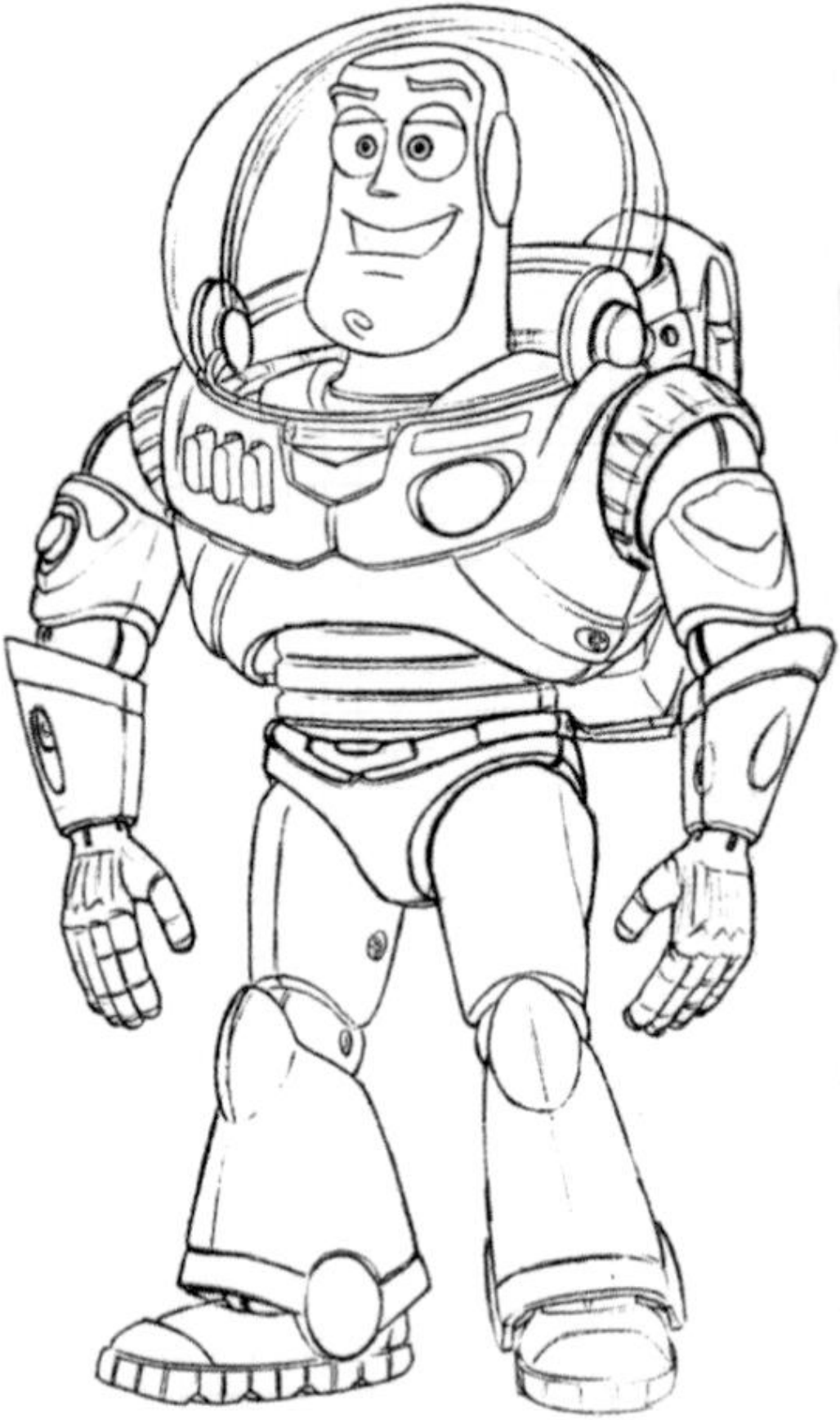

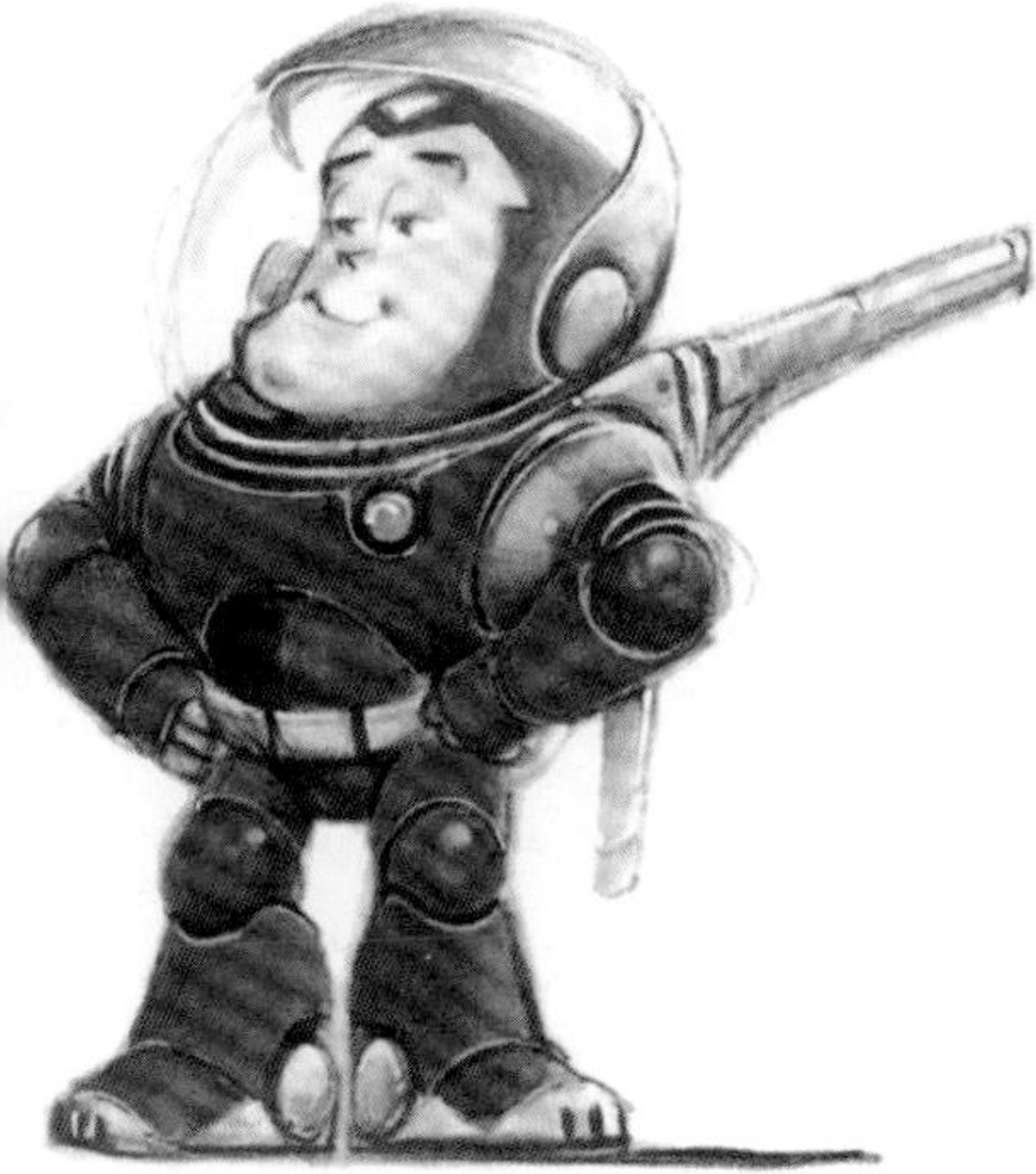

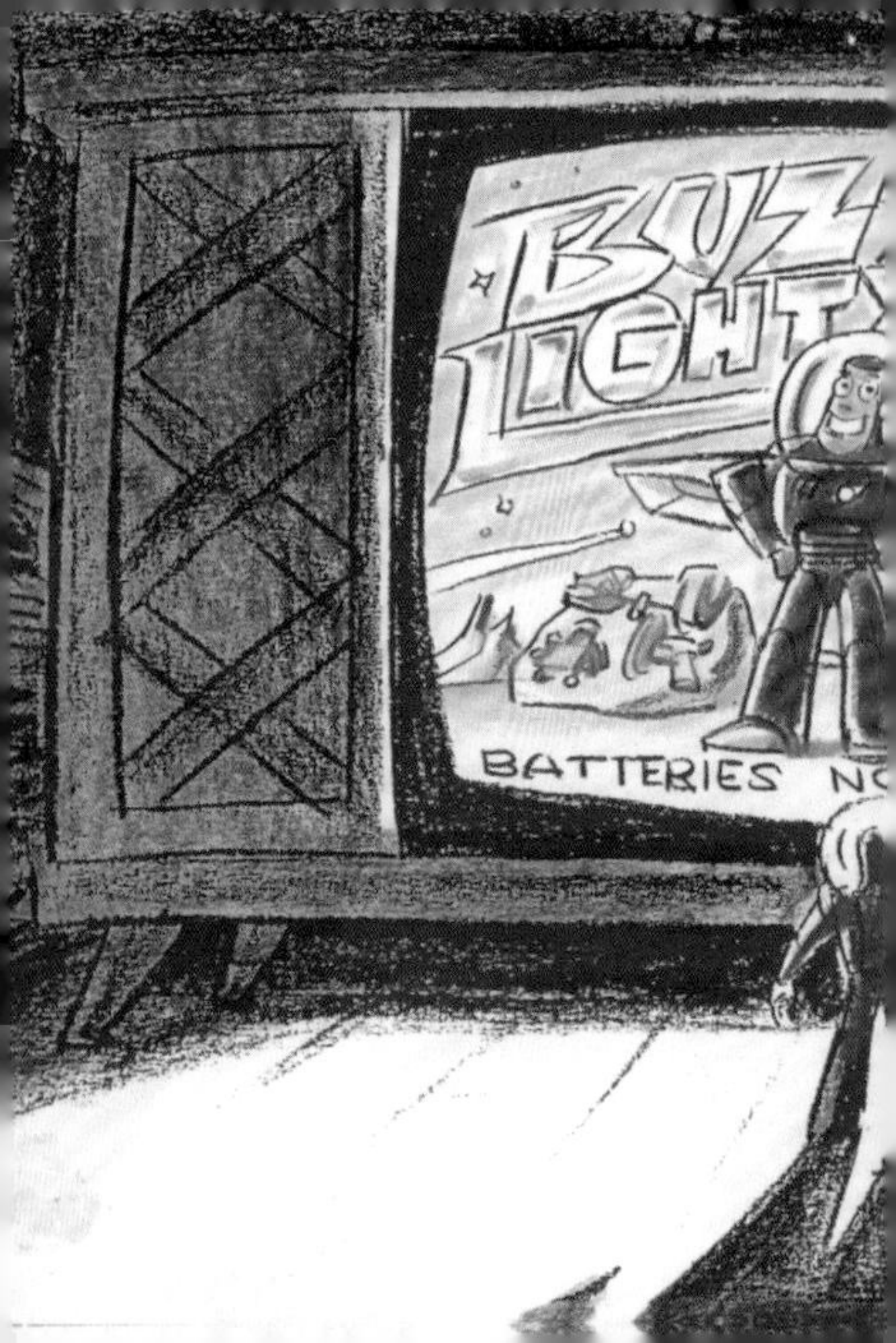
BUZZ
LIGHT
BATTERIES

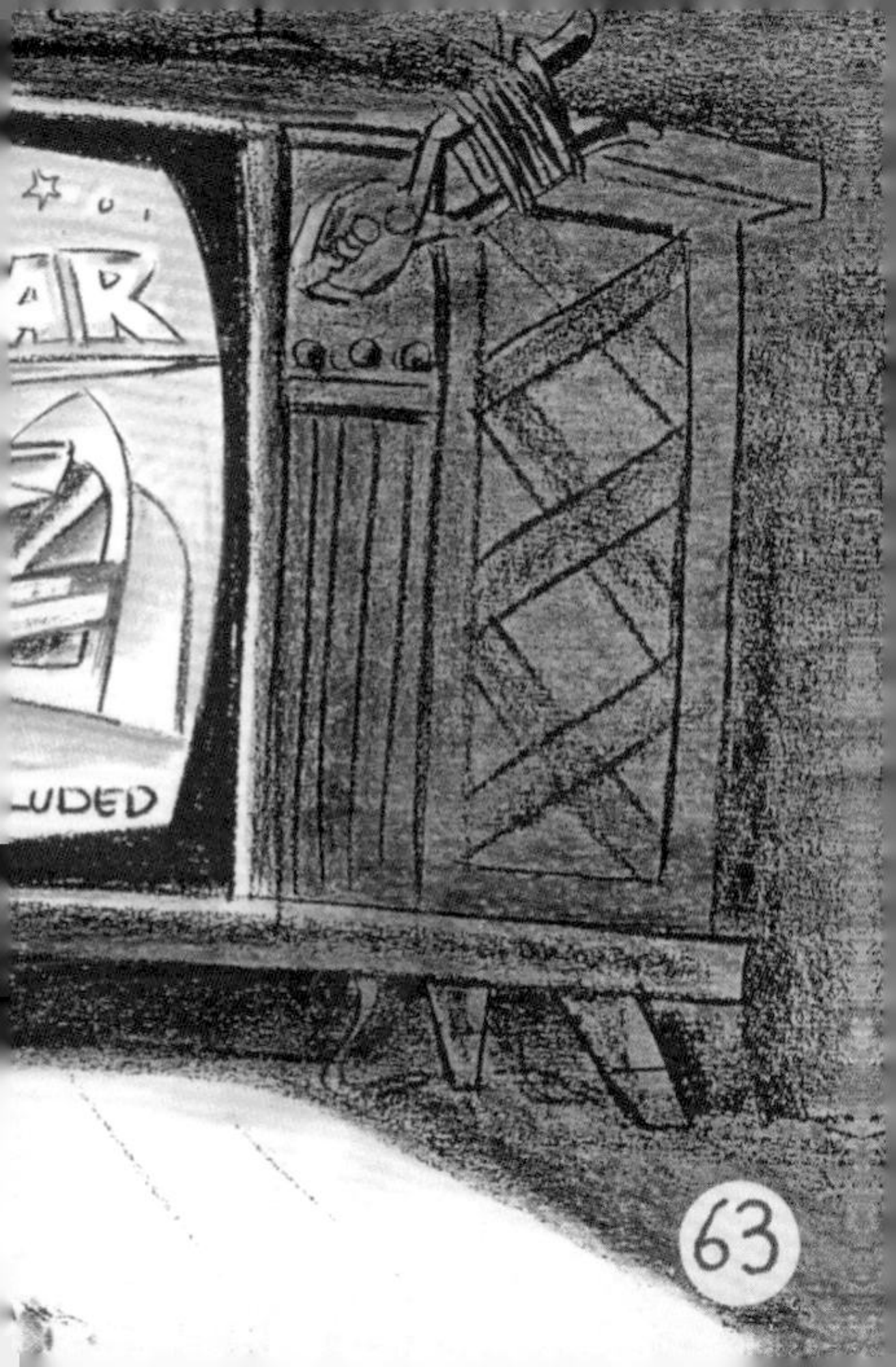
AR
UDED

SHORT

GERI'S GAME

1997

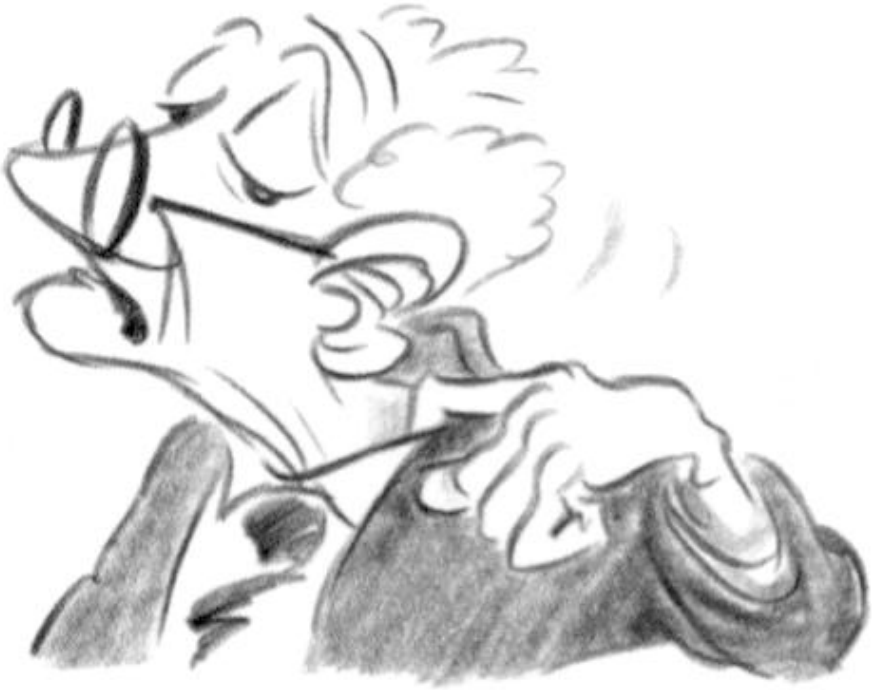

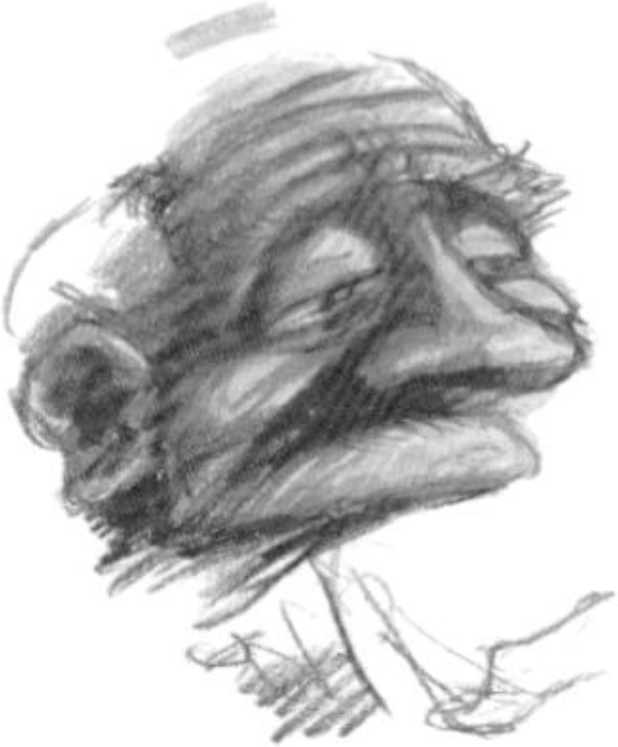

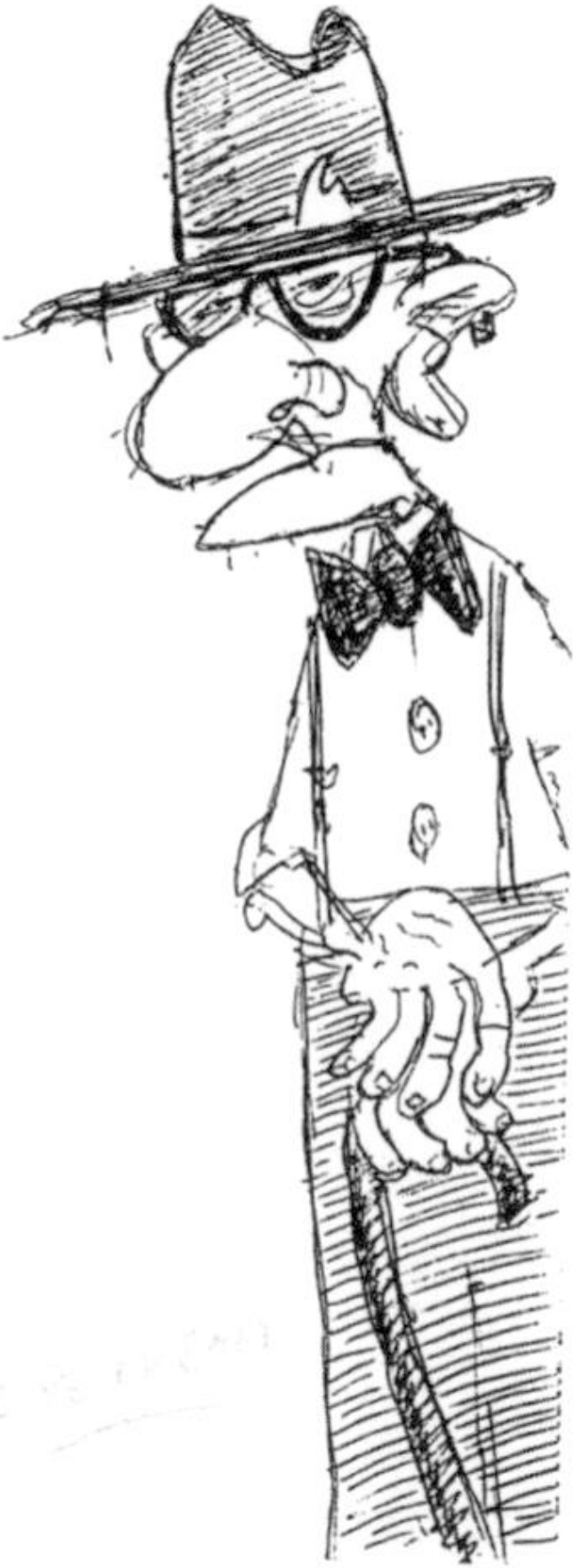

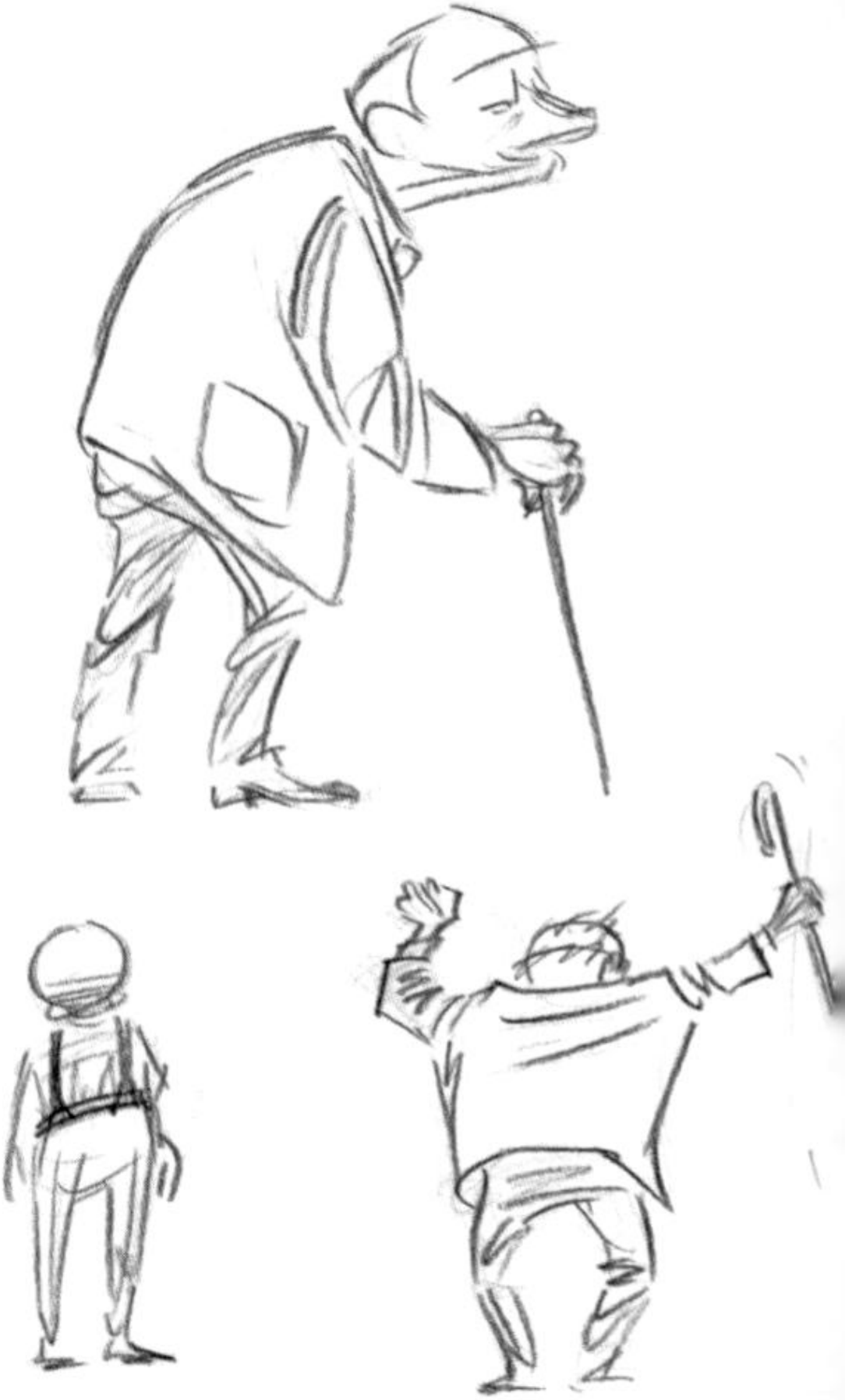

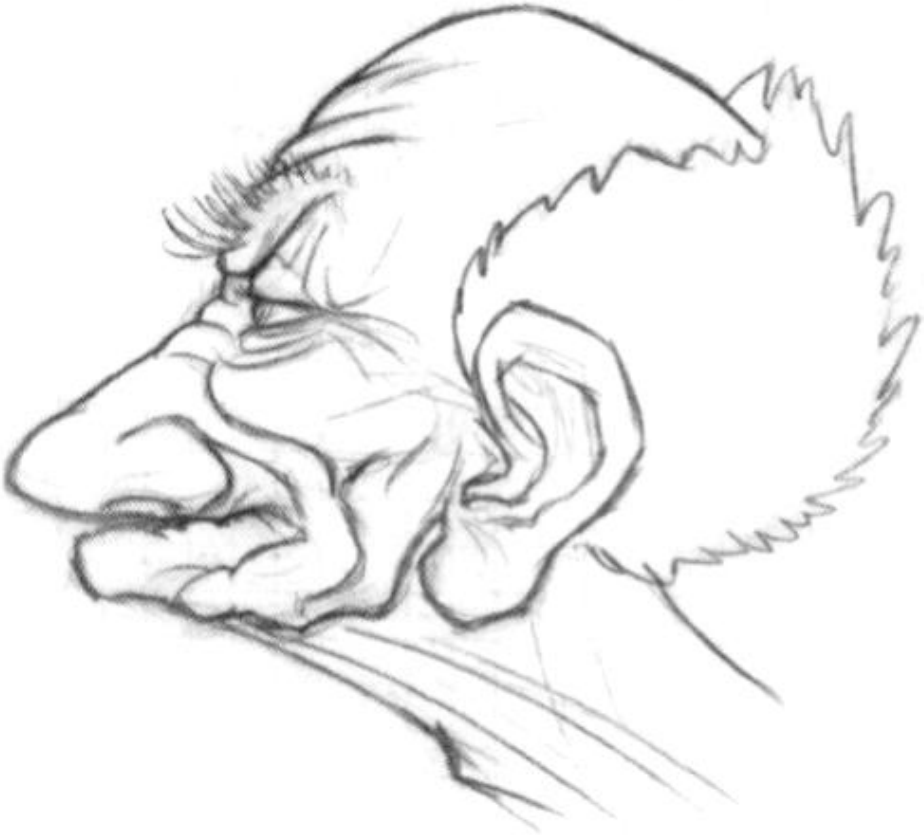

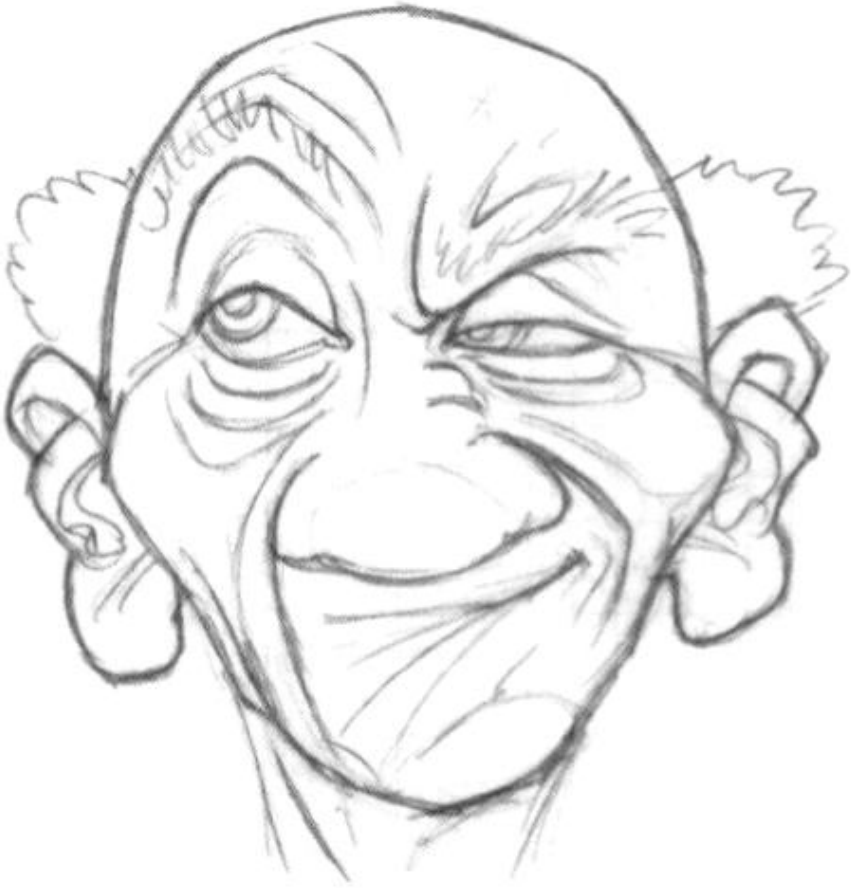

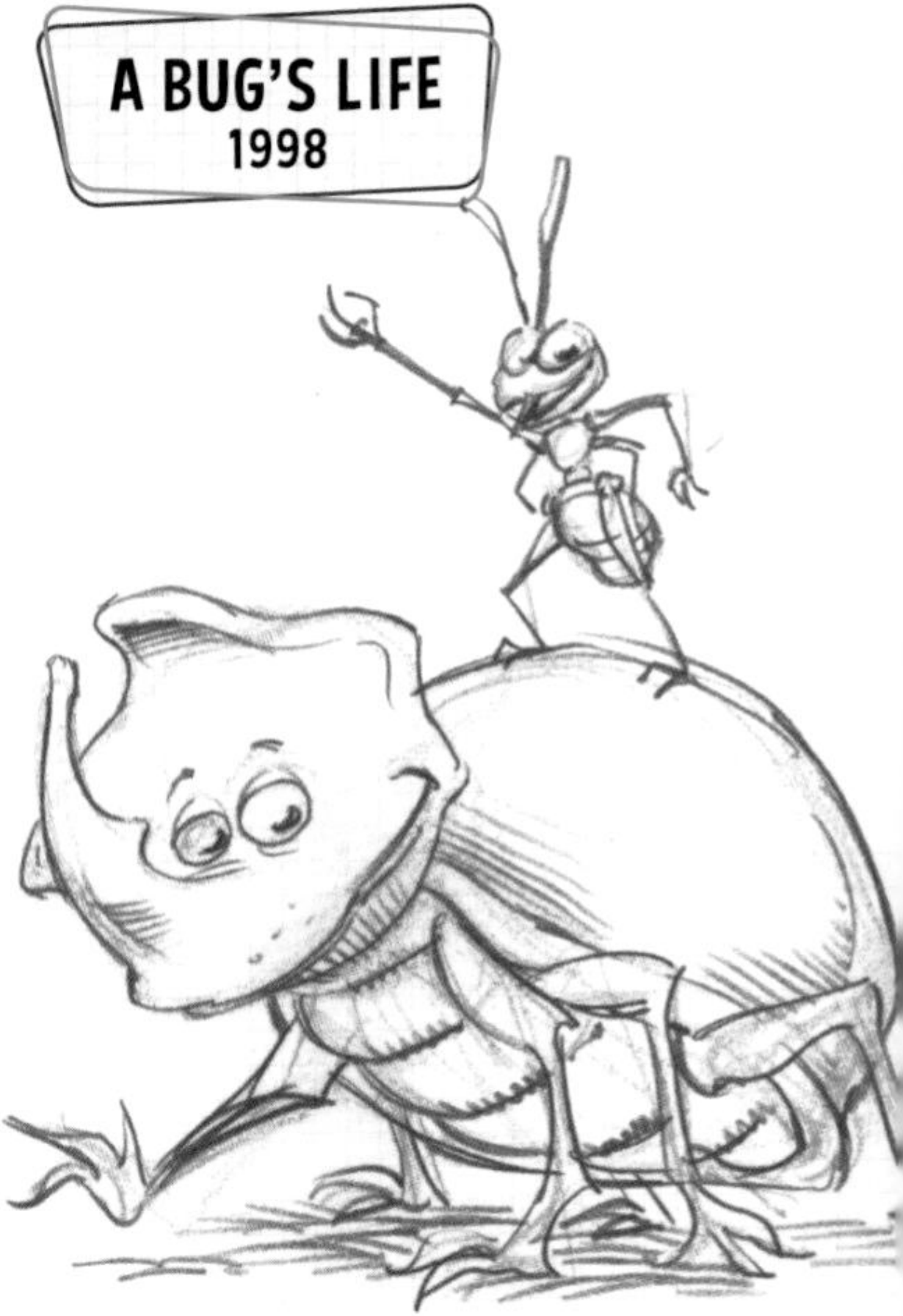
A BUG'S LIFE
1998

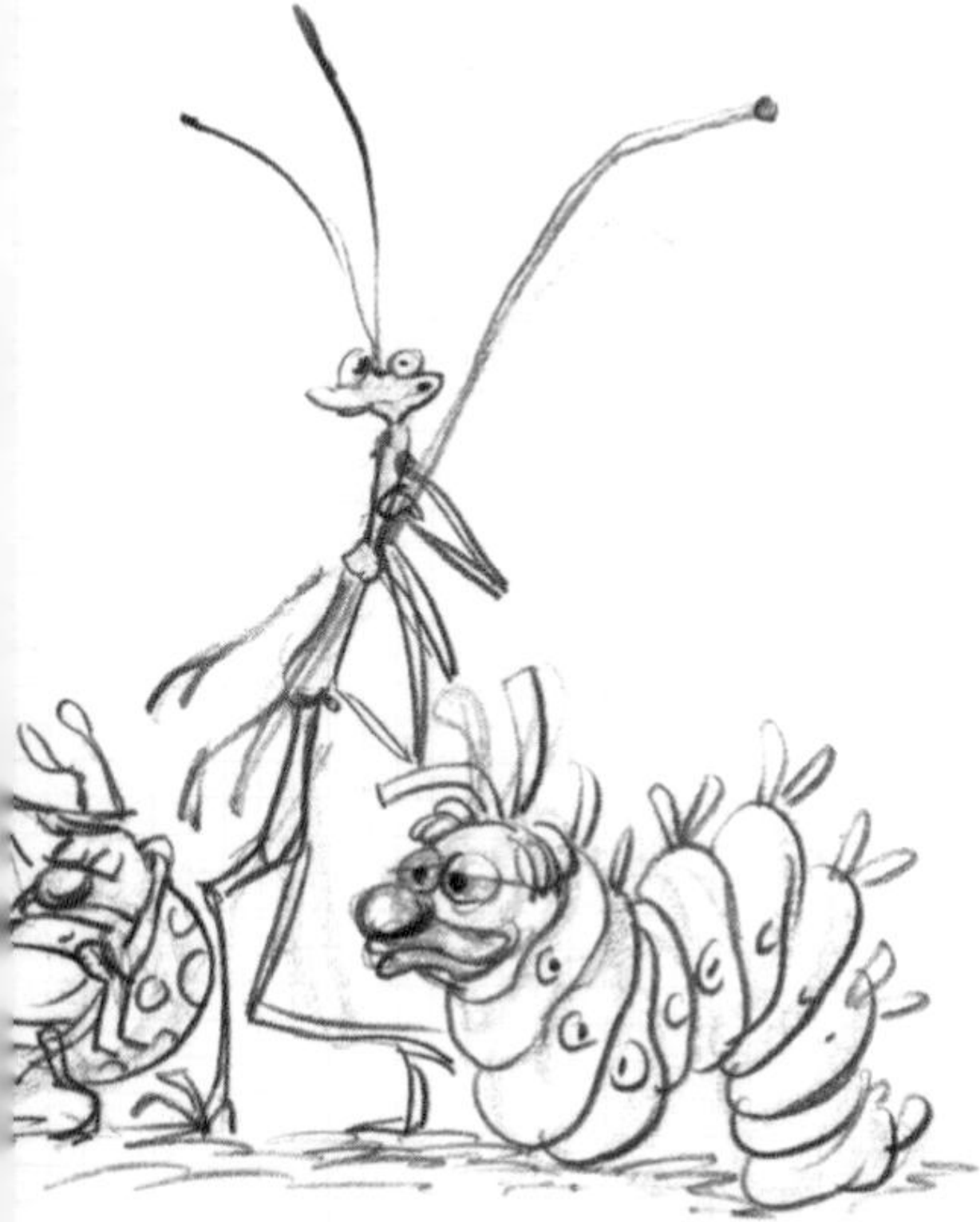

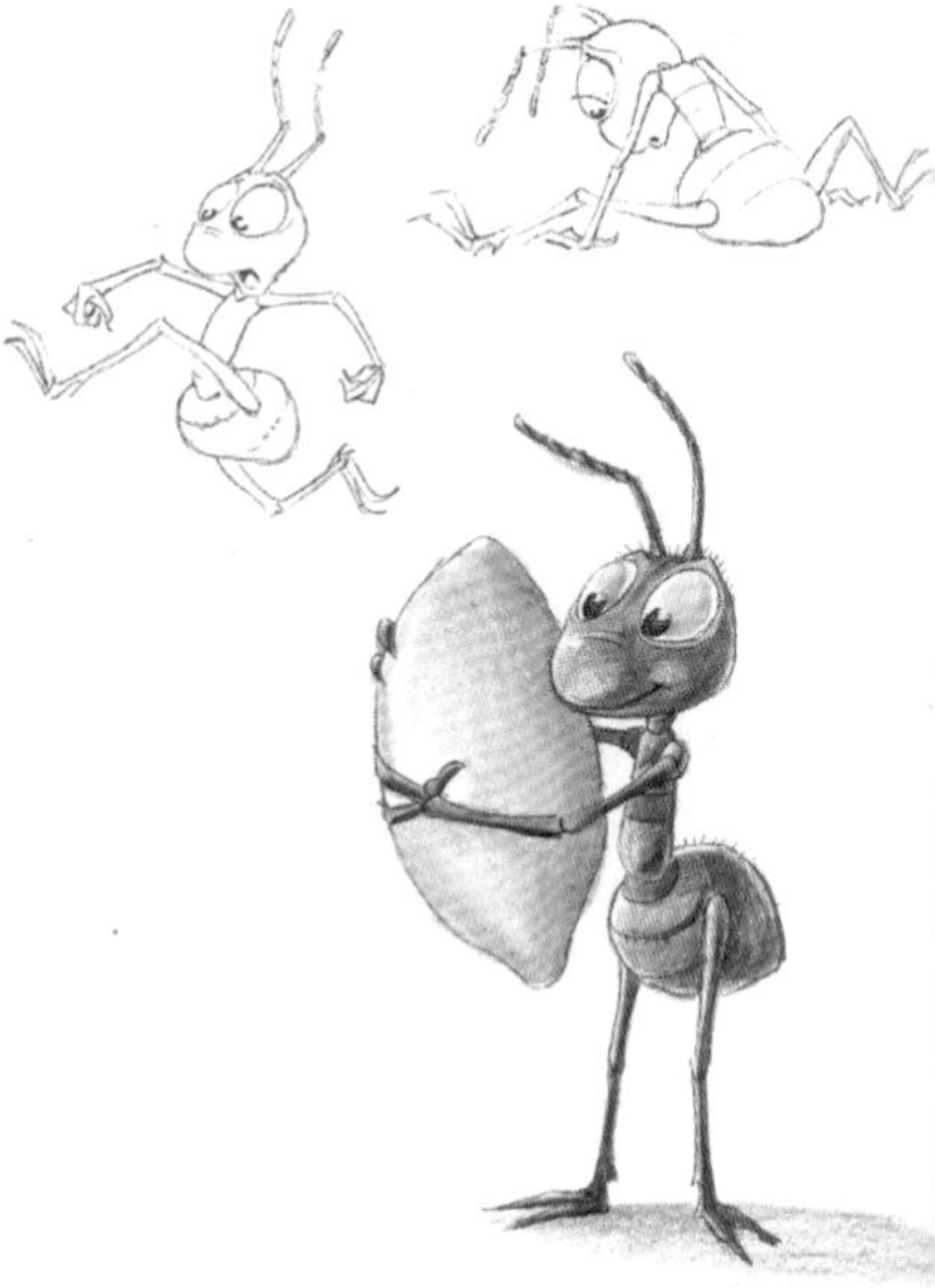

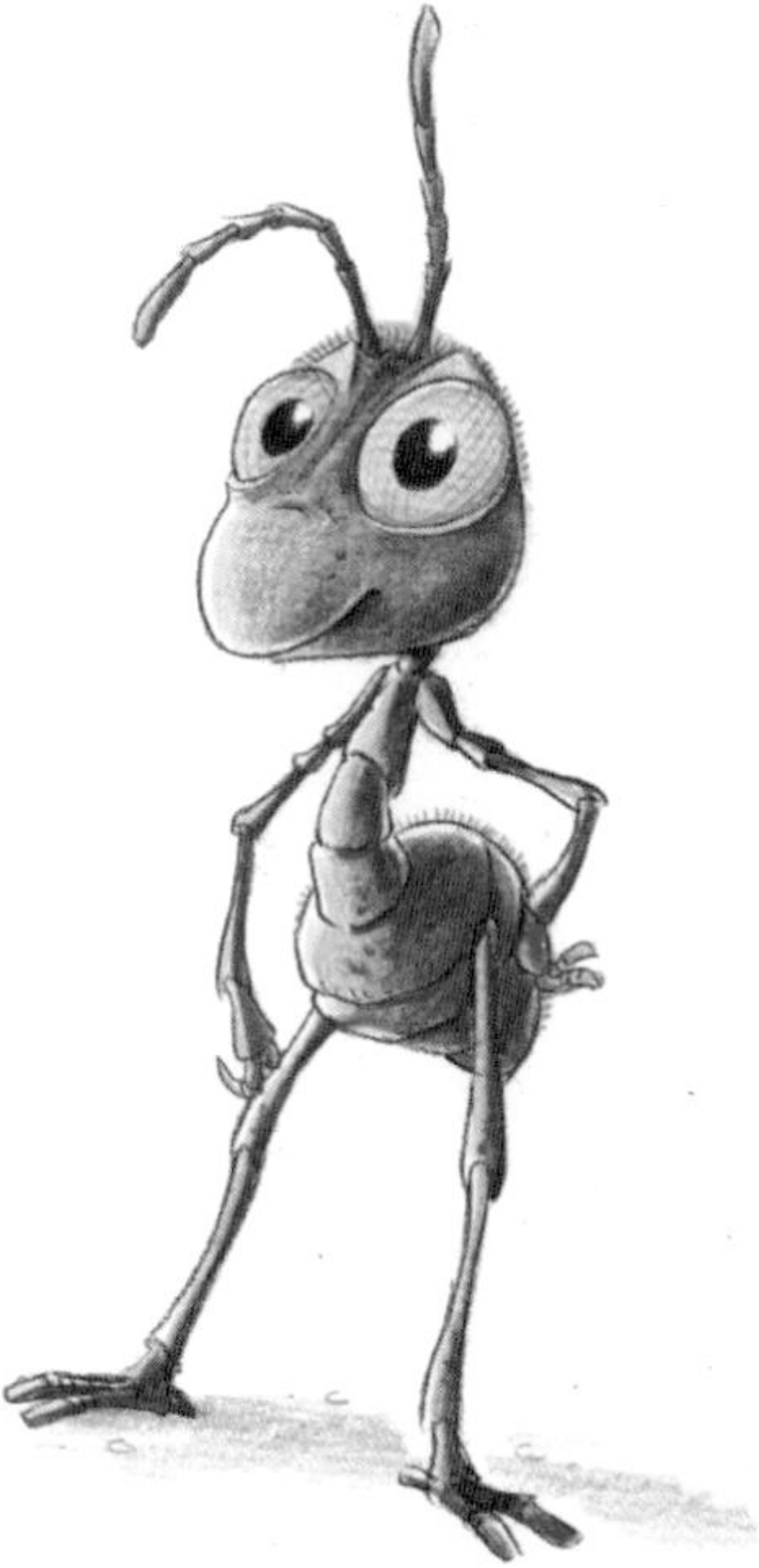

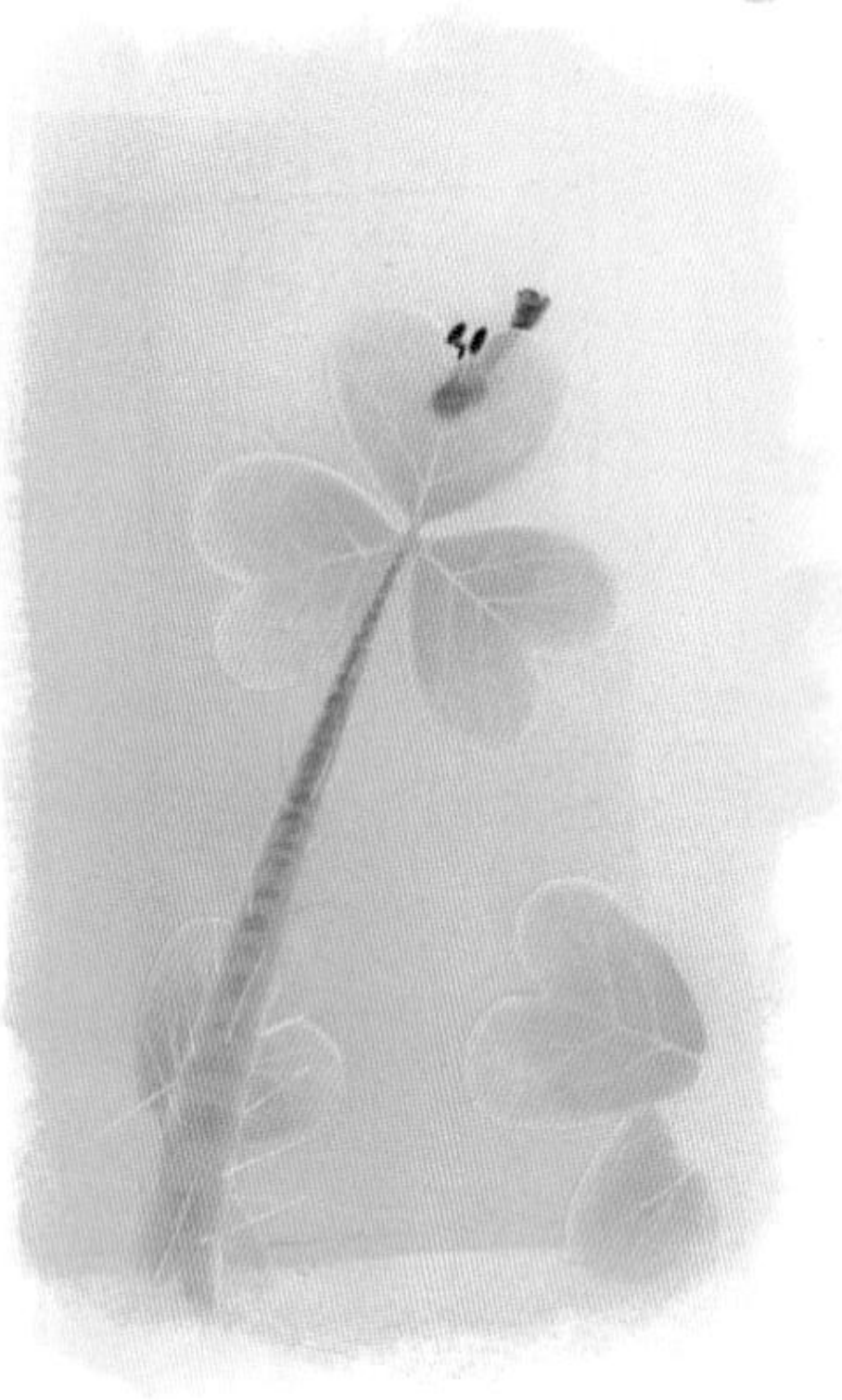

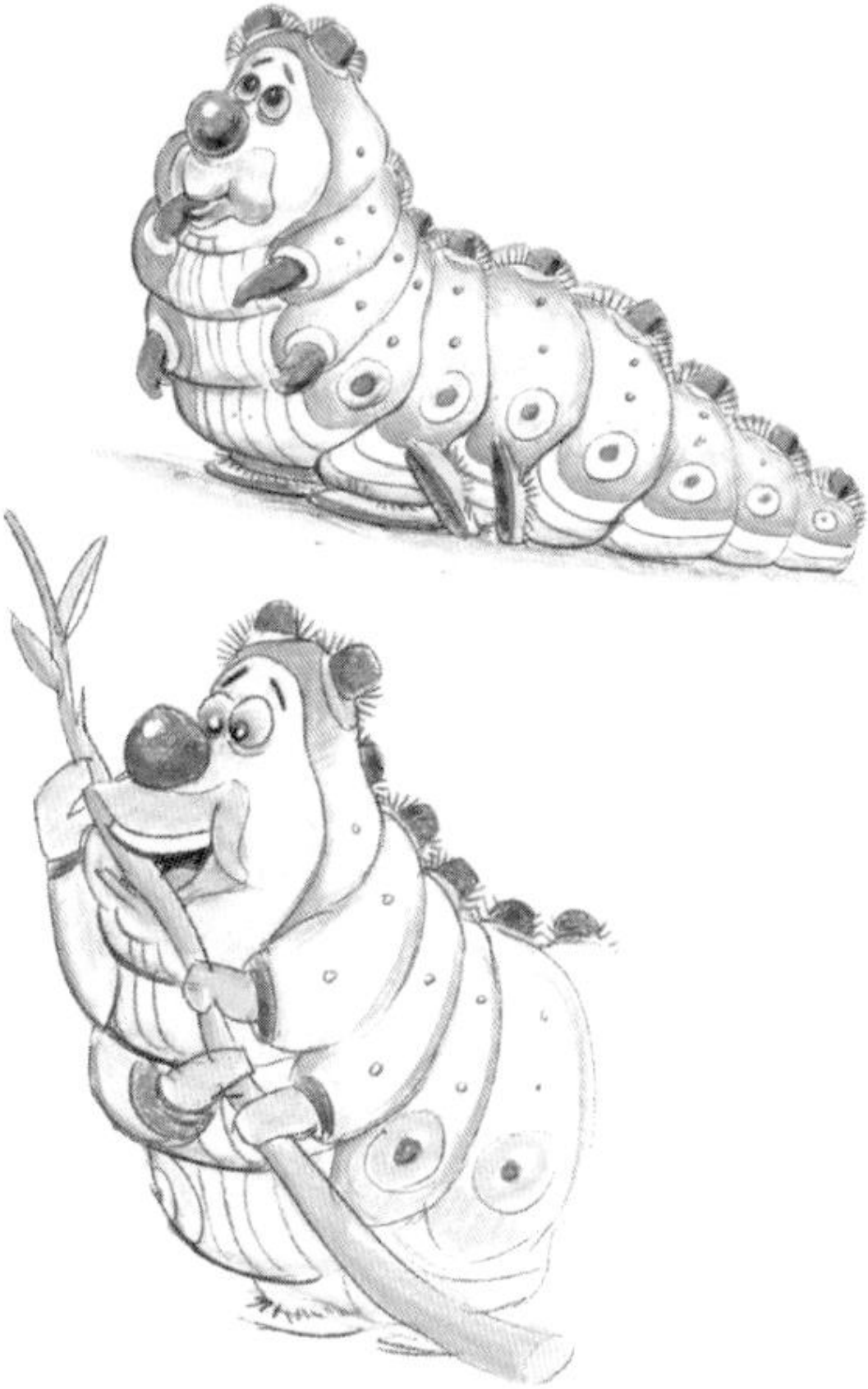

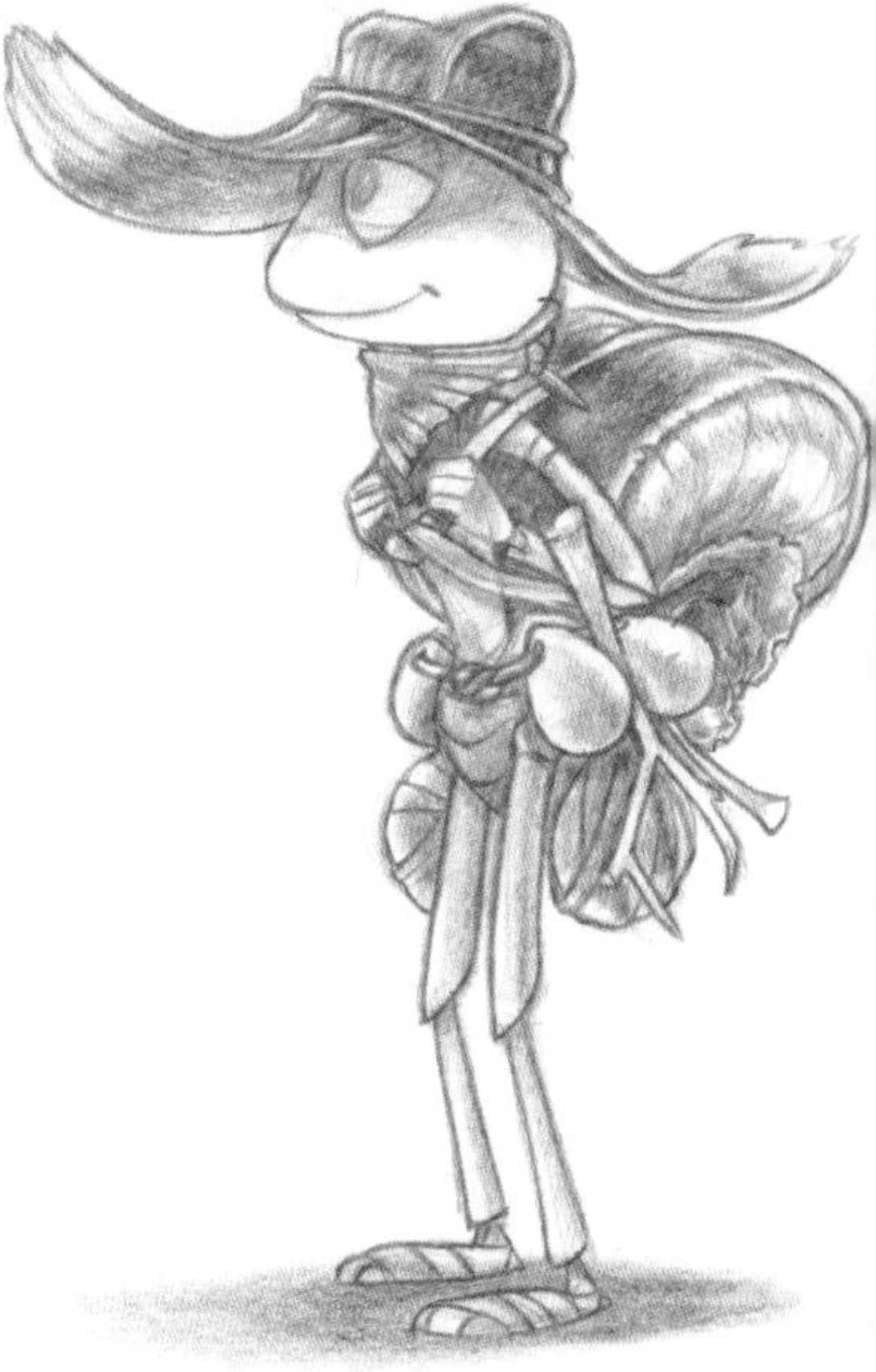

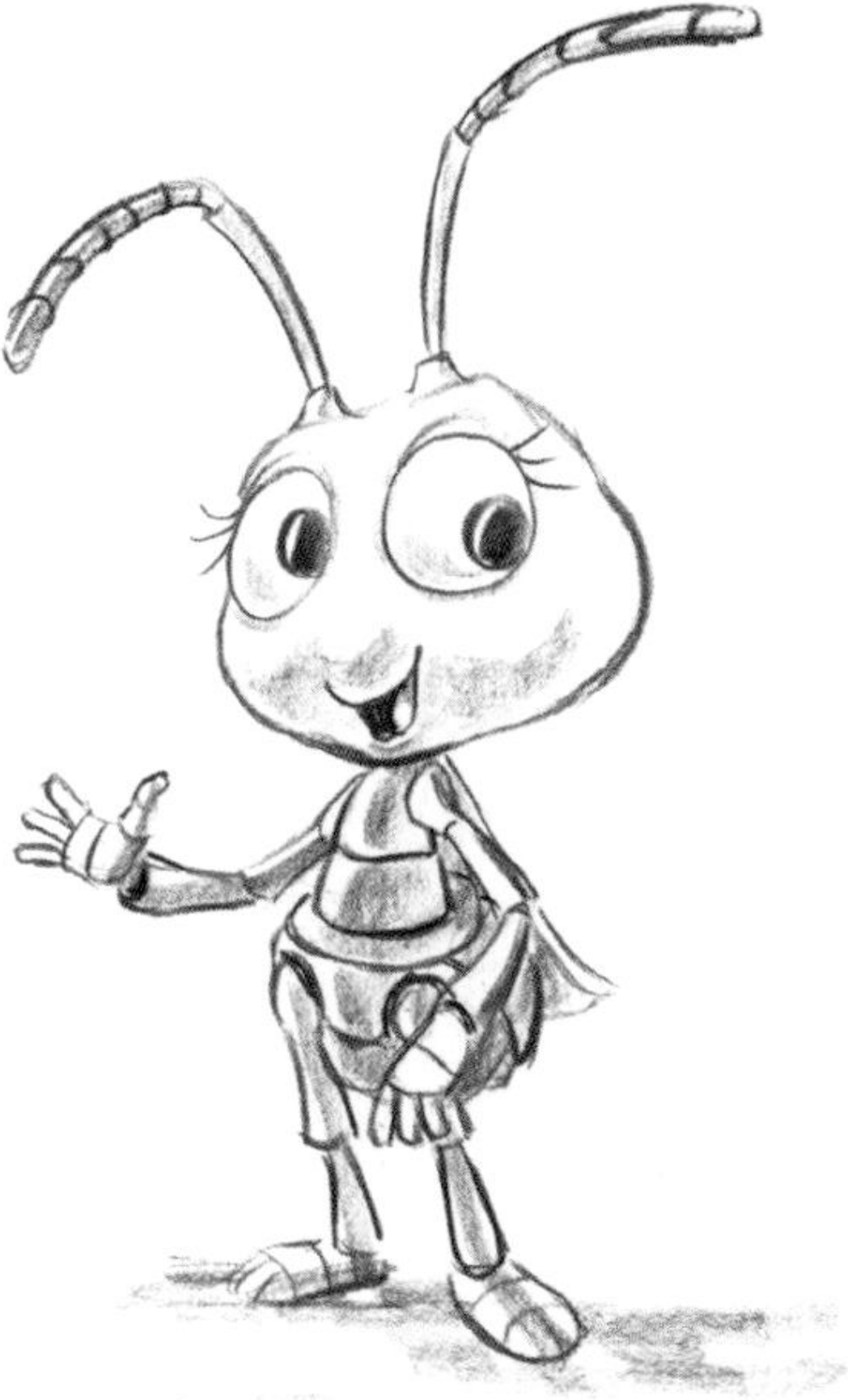

TOY STORY 2
1999

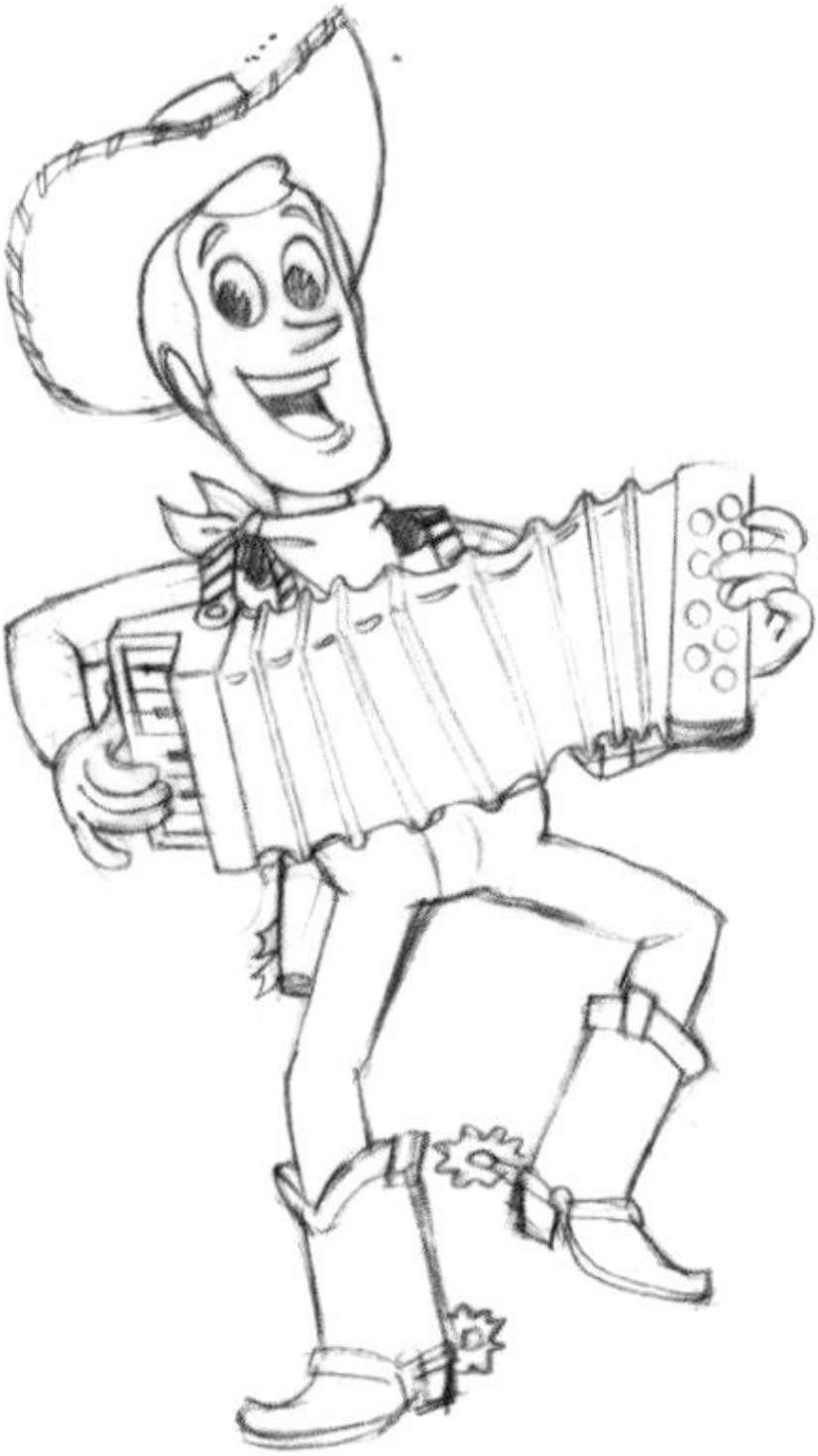

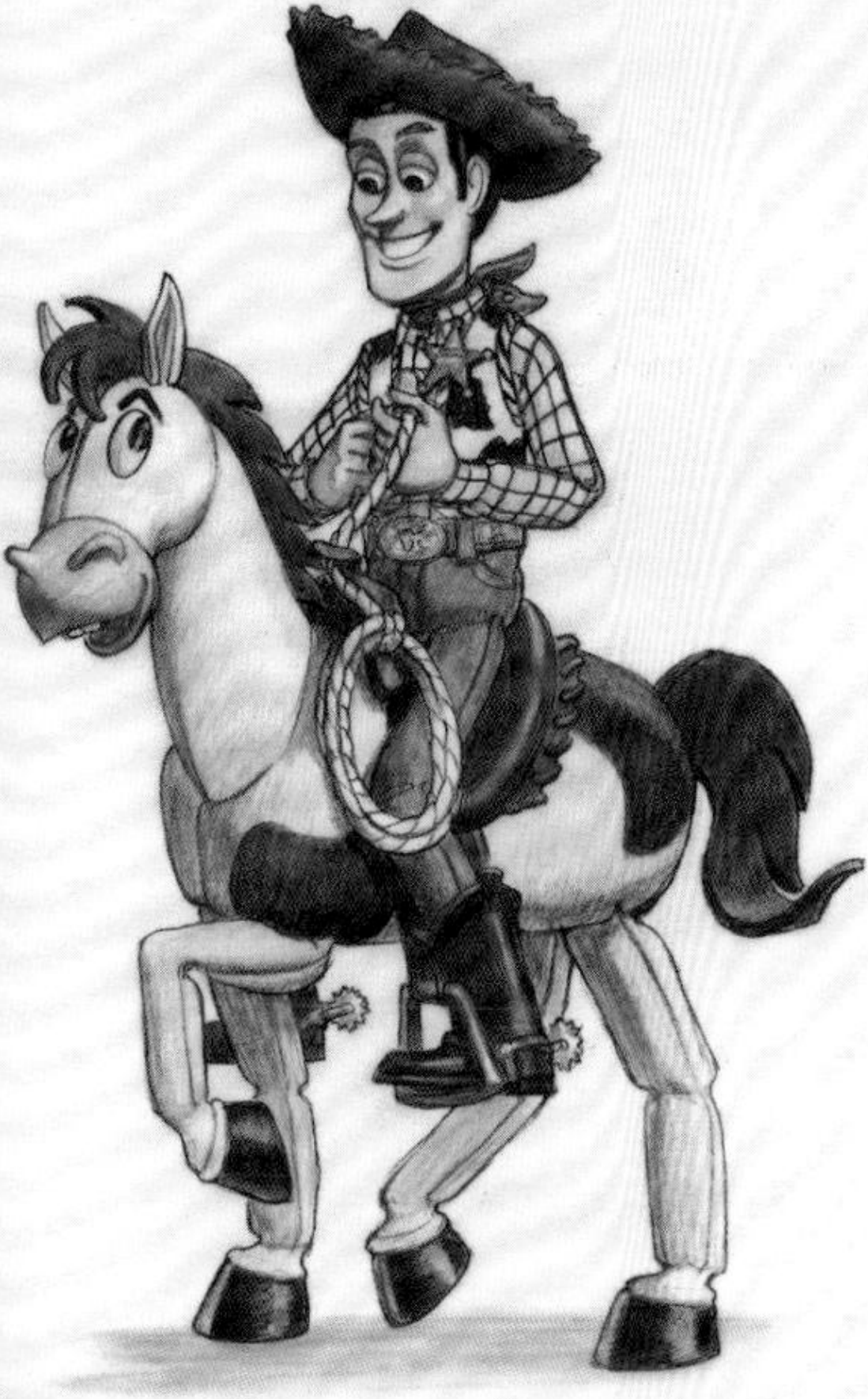

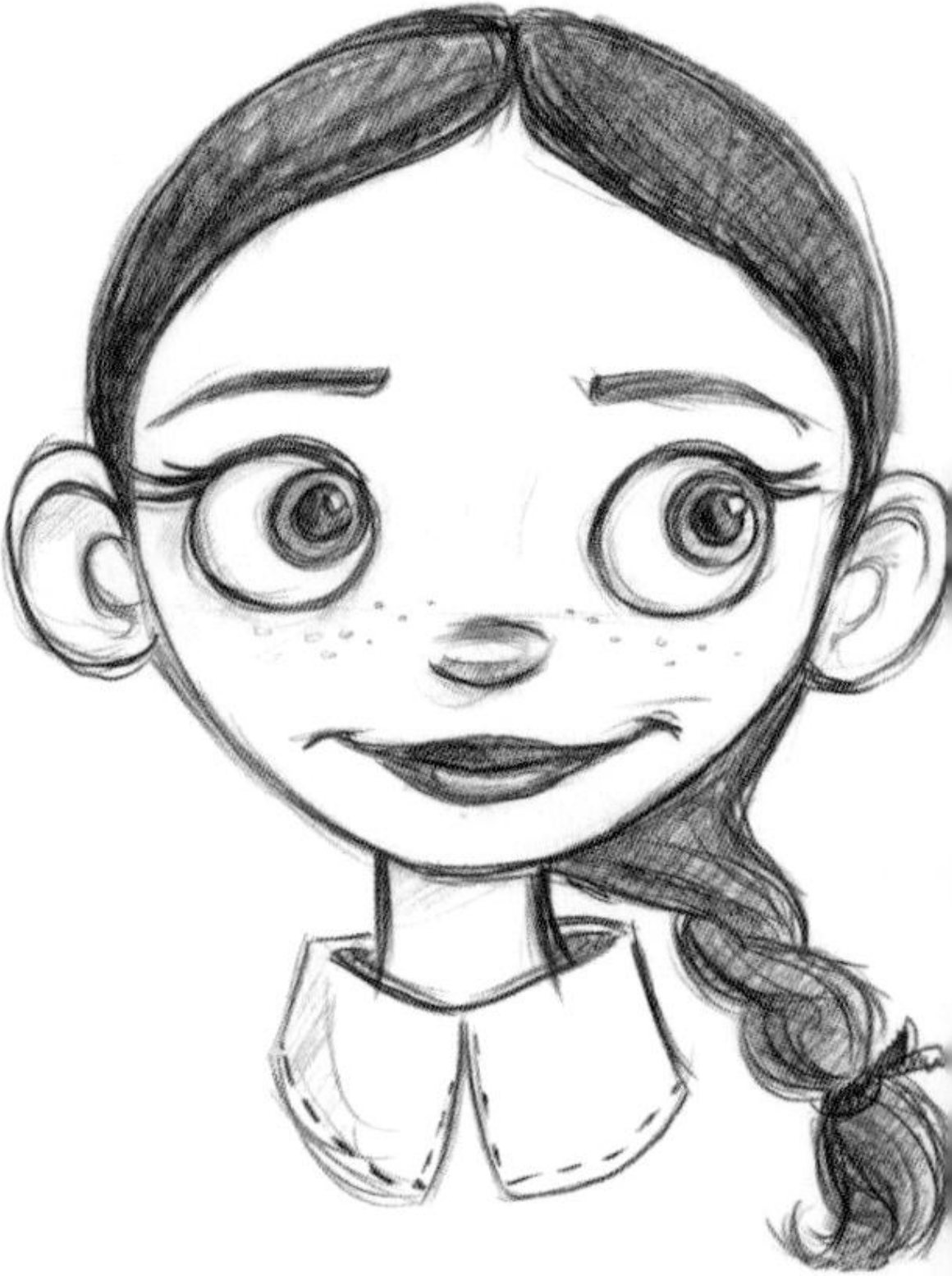

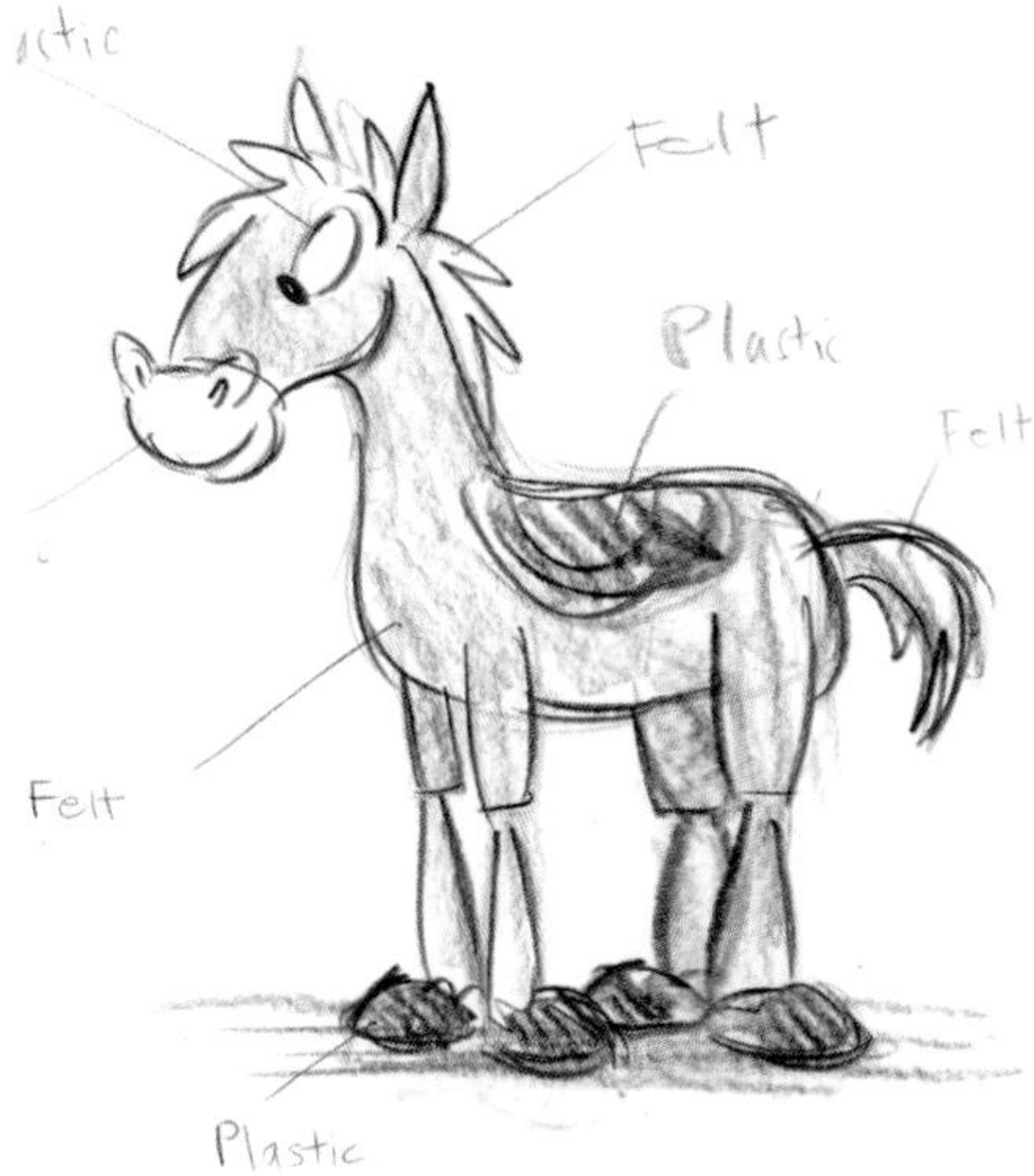
Felt
Plastic
Felt
Felt
Plastic

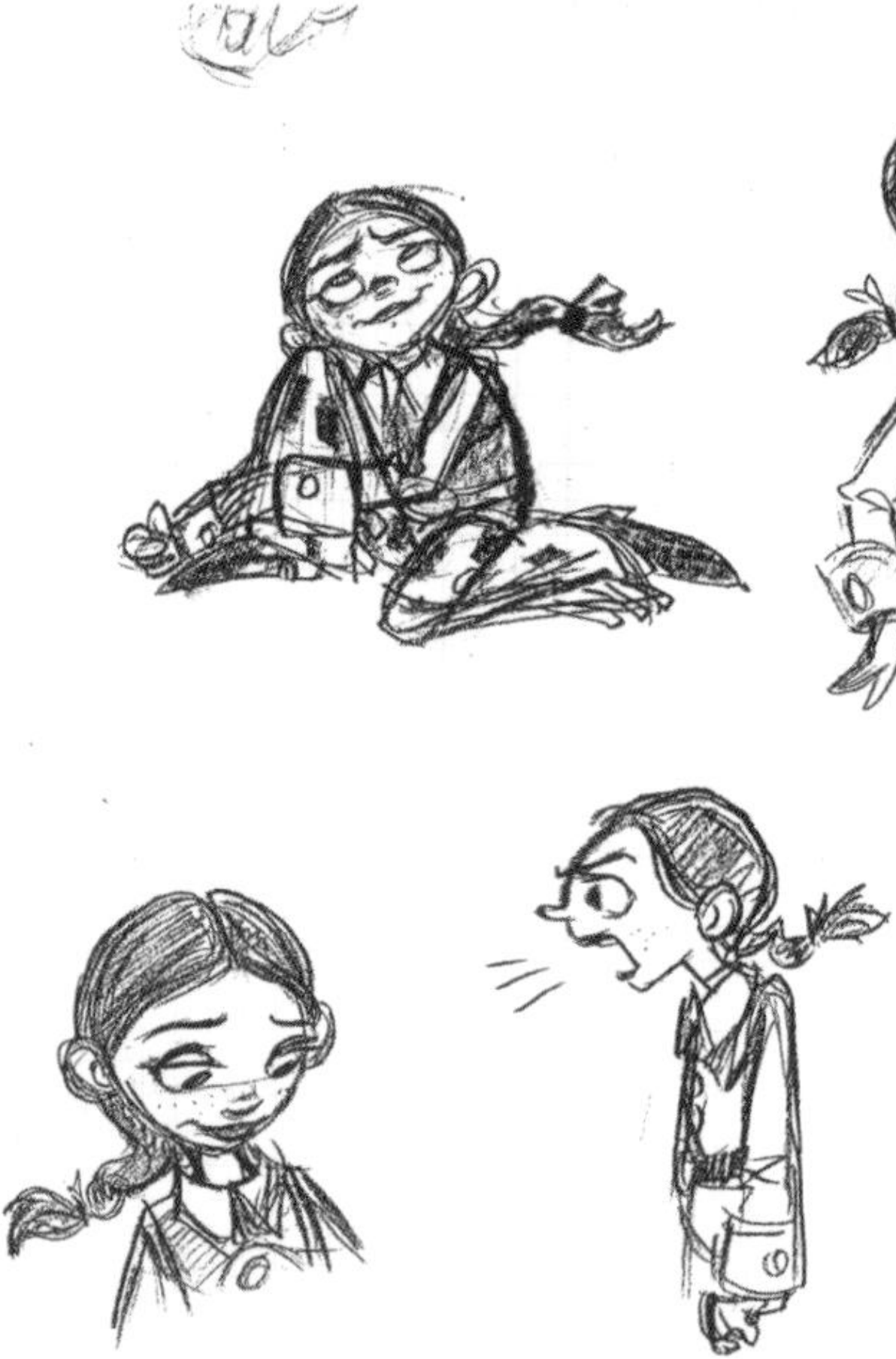

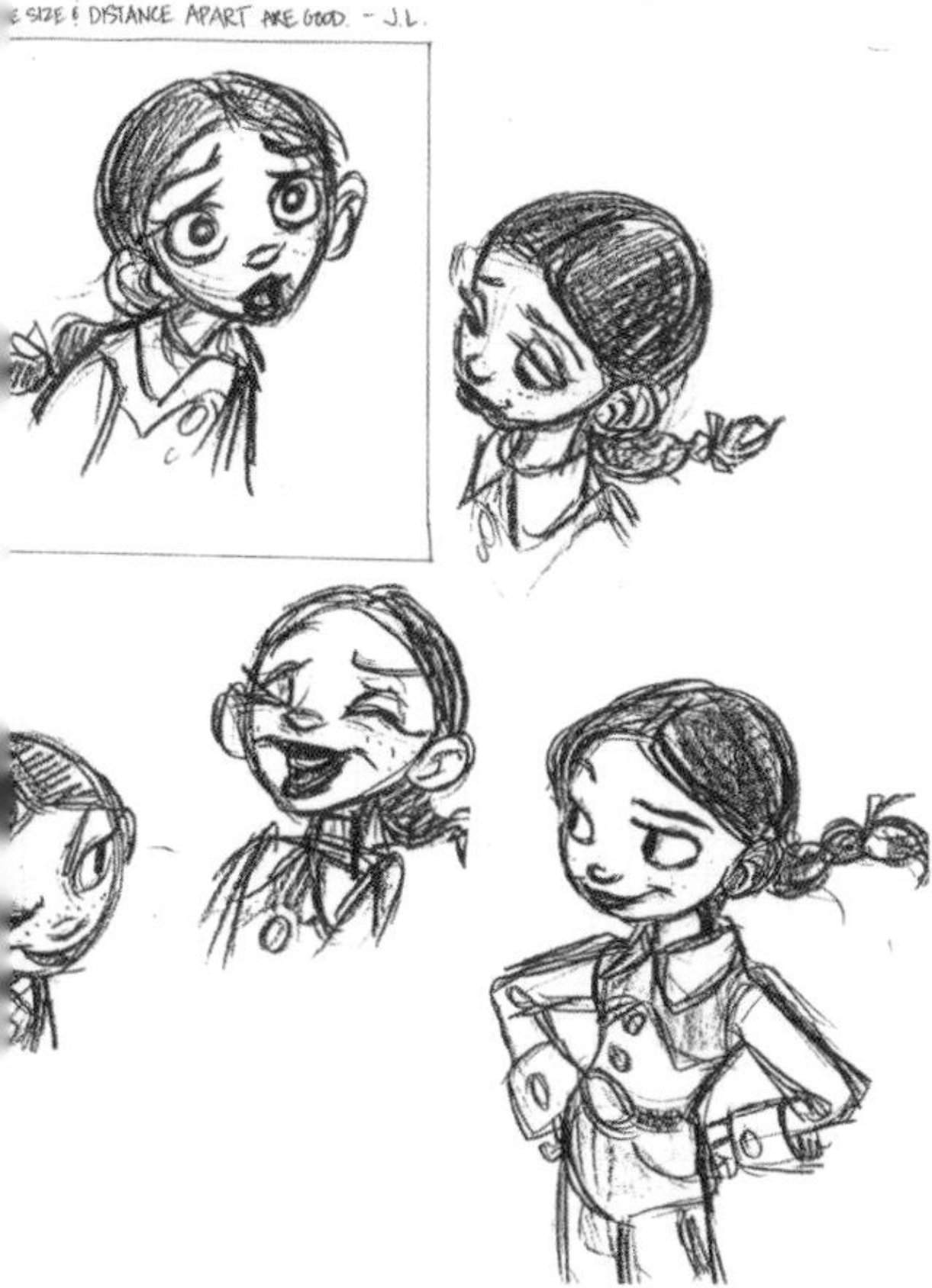
E SIZE & DISTANCE APART ARE GOOD. - J.L.

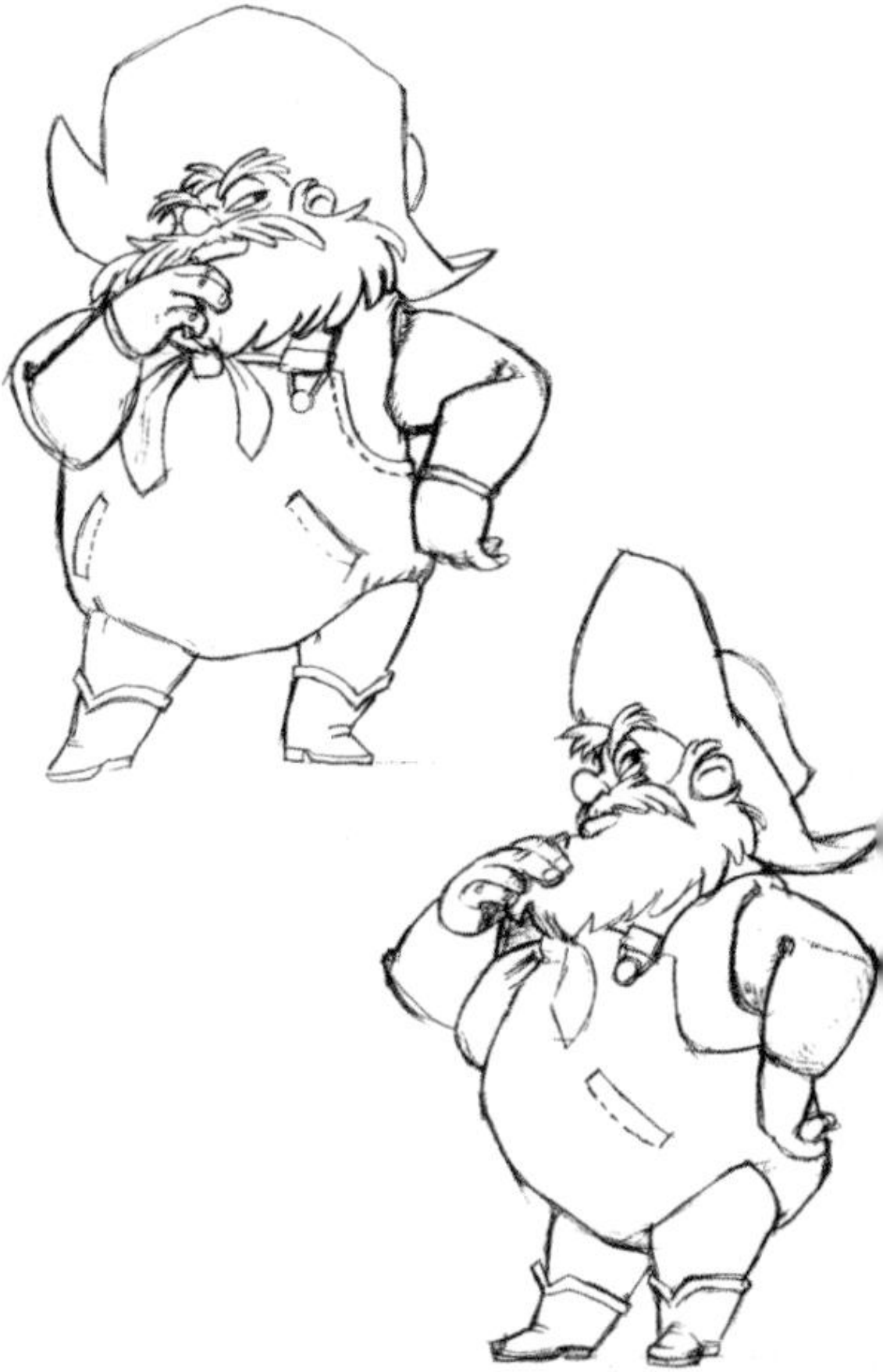

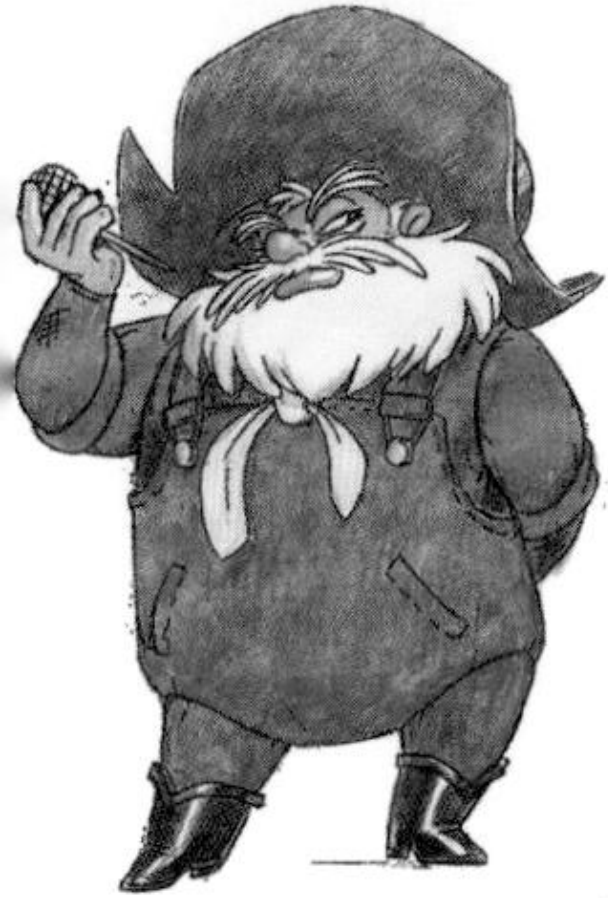

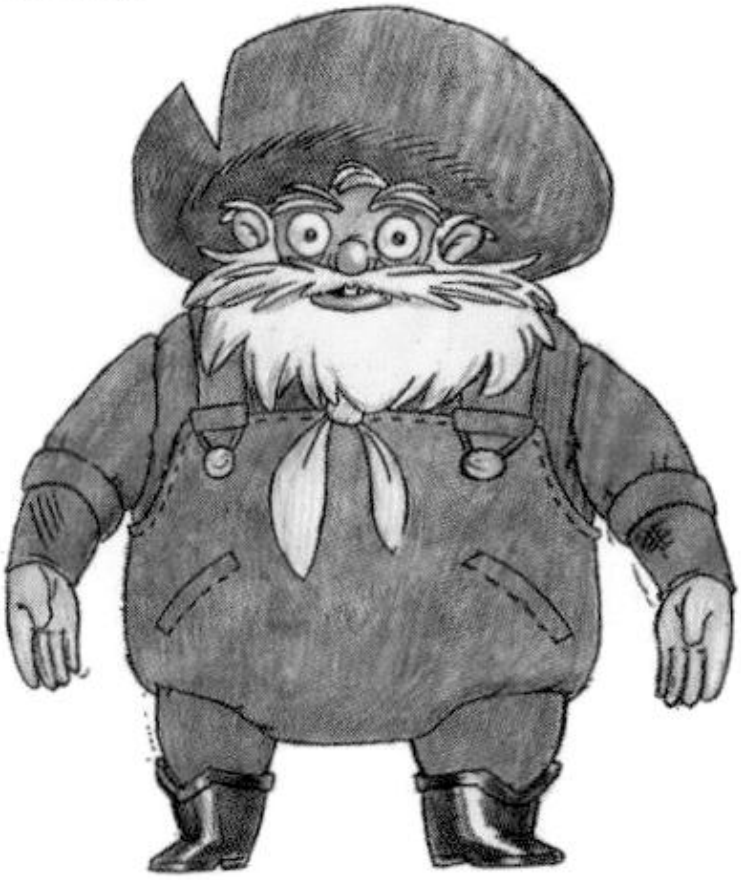

Ron dey Bennett

2000s

The 2000s was a time of continued innovation for Pixar. From developing methods that helped to make every hair on a monster's body properly lit to improving the realistic movement of fabric, the Pixar filmmakers brought their artistry to life with new techniques that are still used today by many across the film industry.

SHORT

FOR THE BIRDS

2000

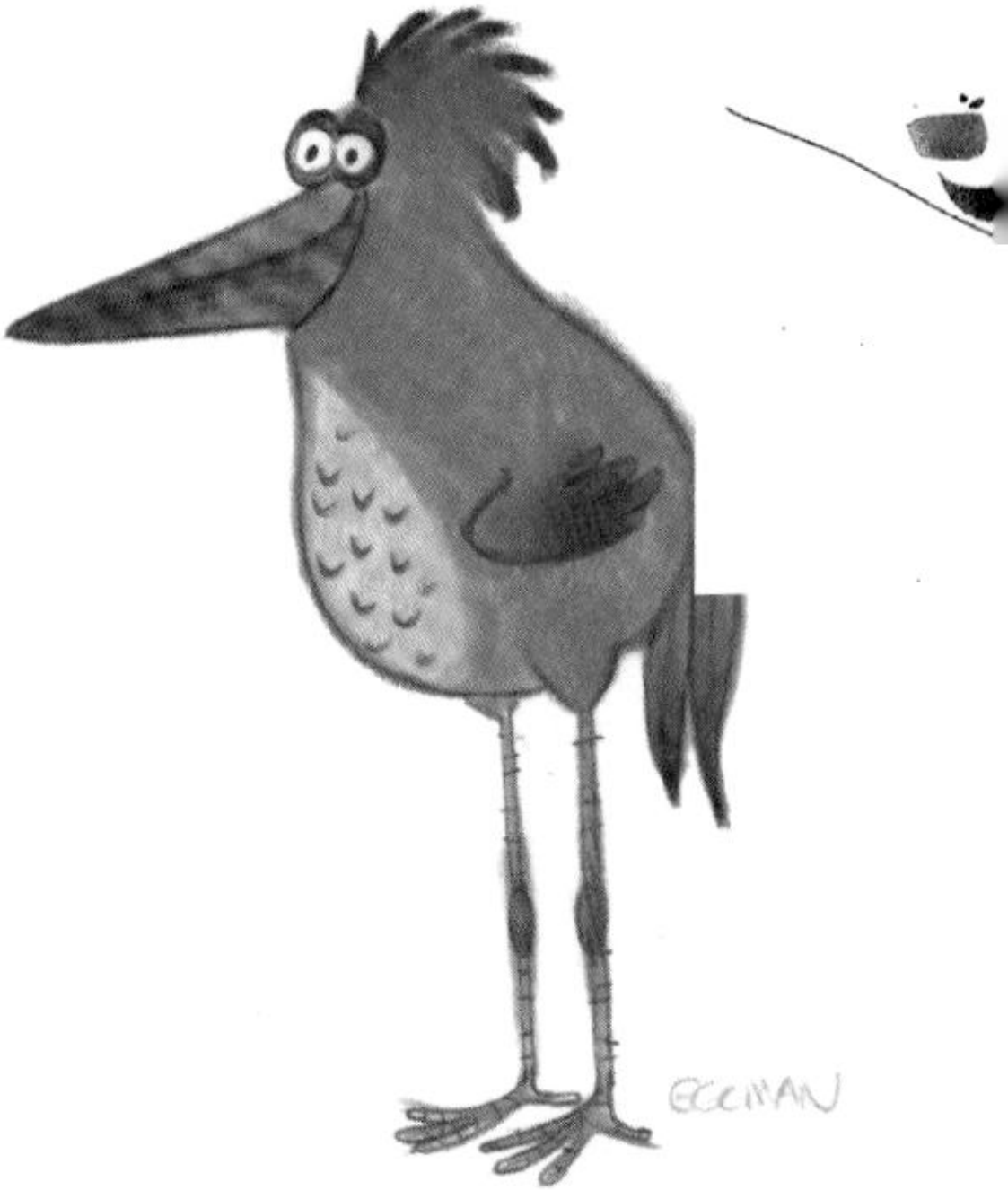

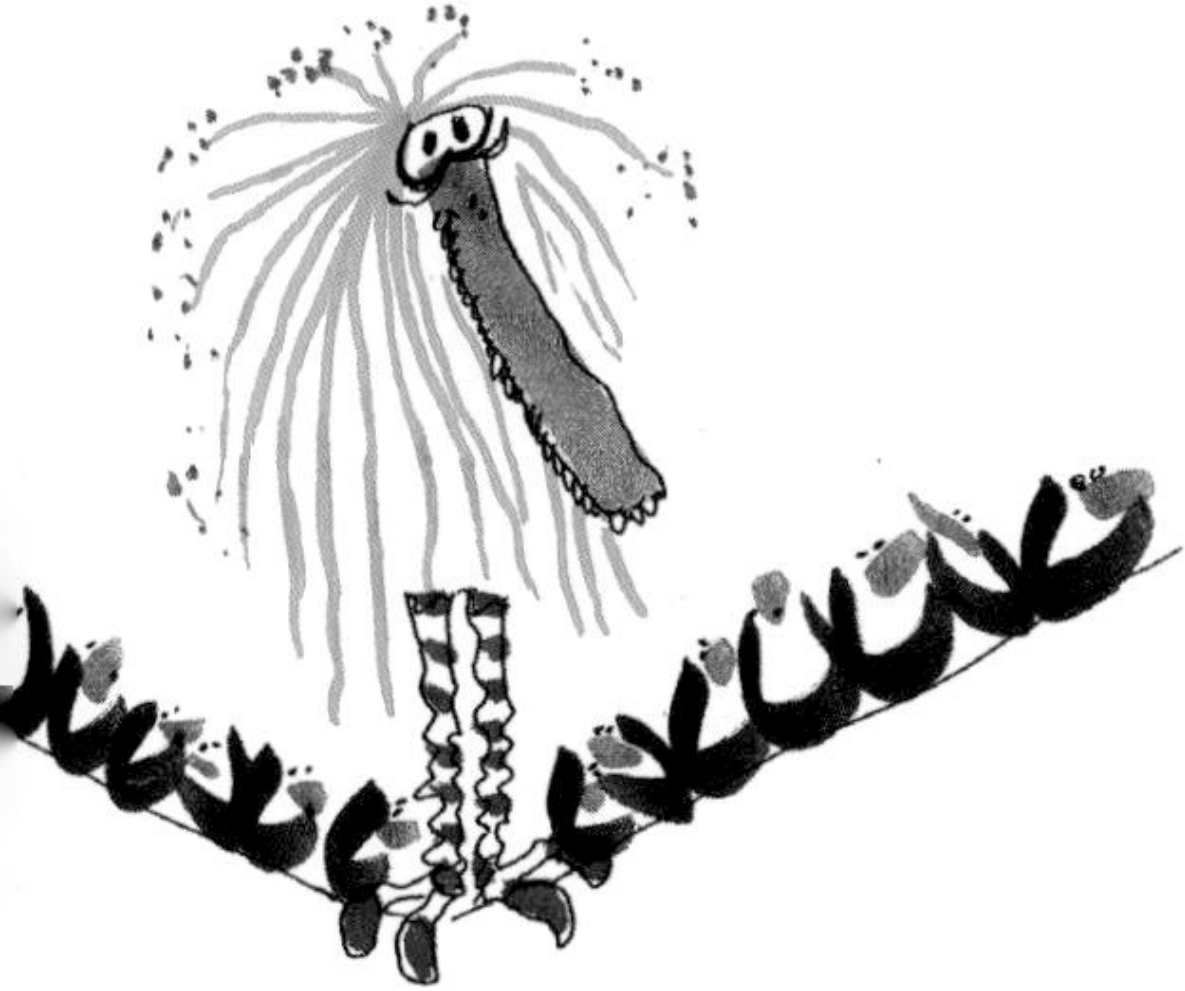

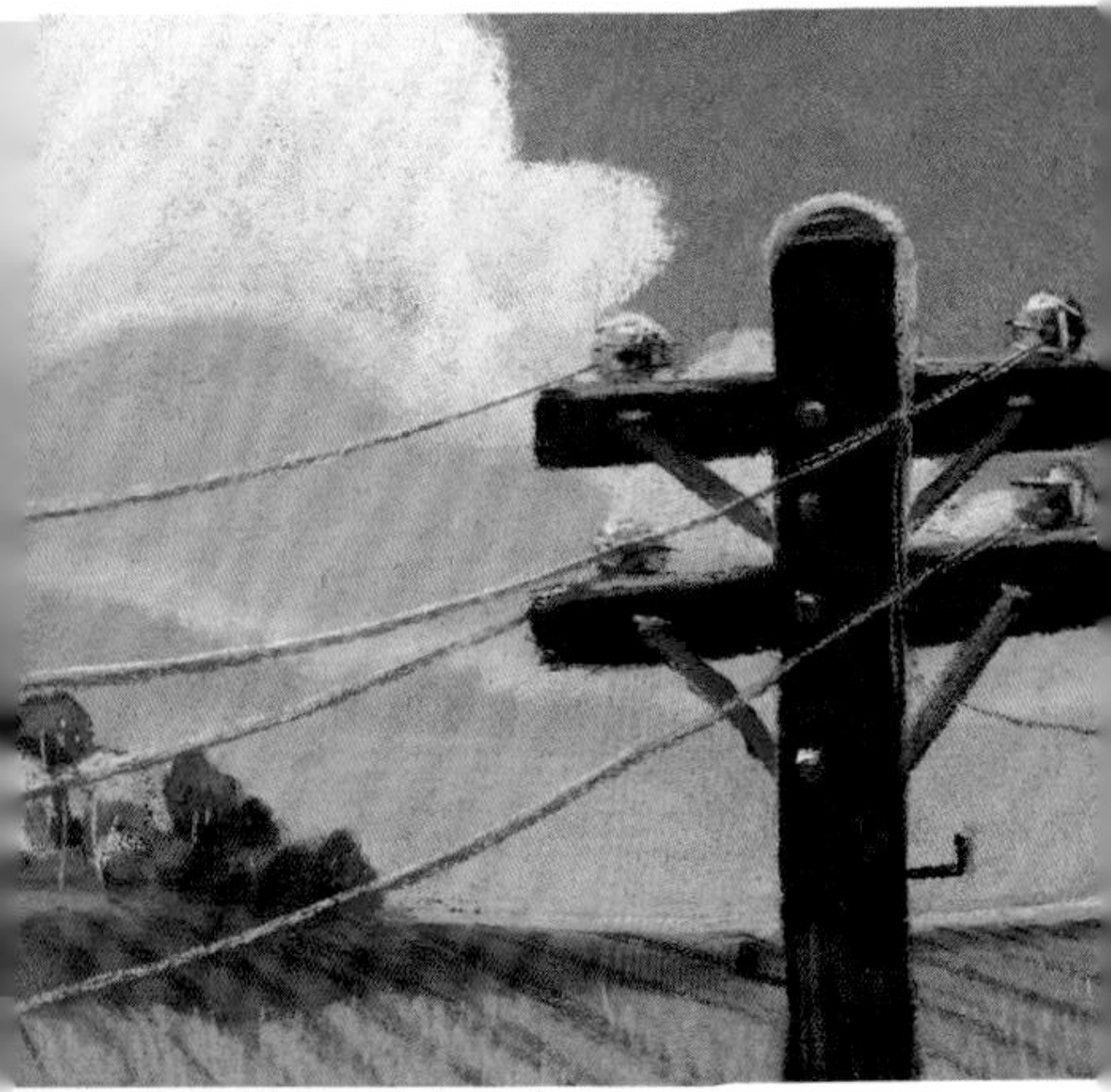

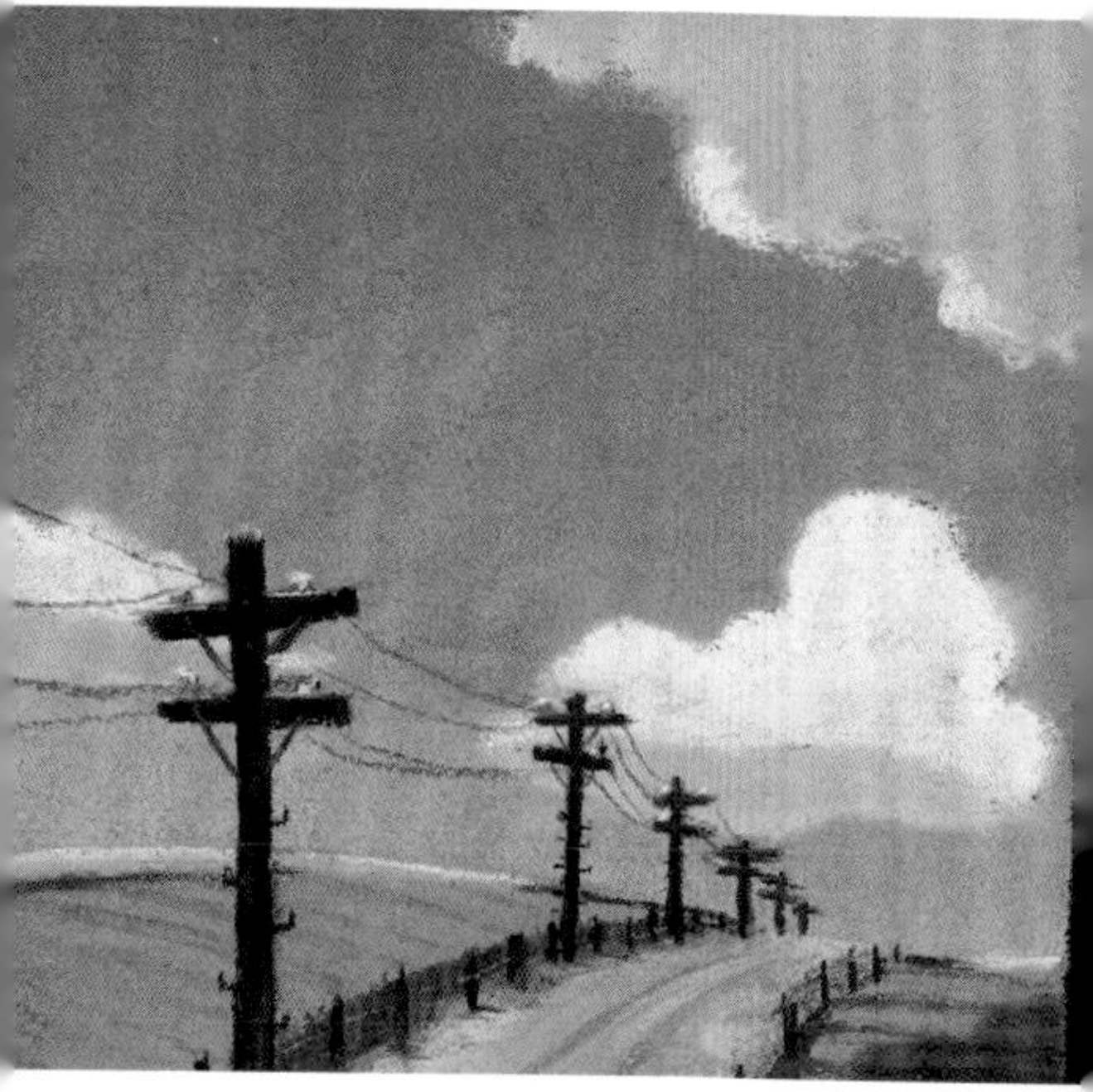

MONSTERS, INC.
2001

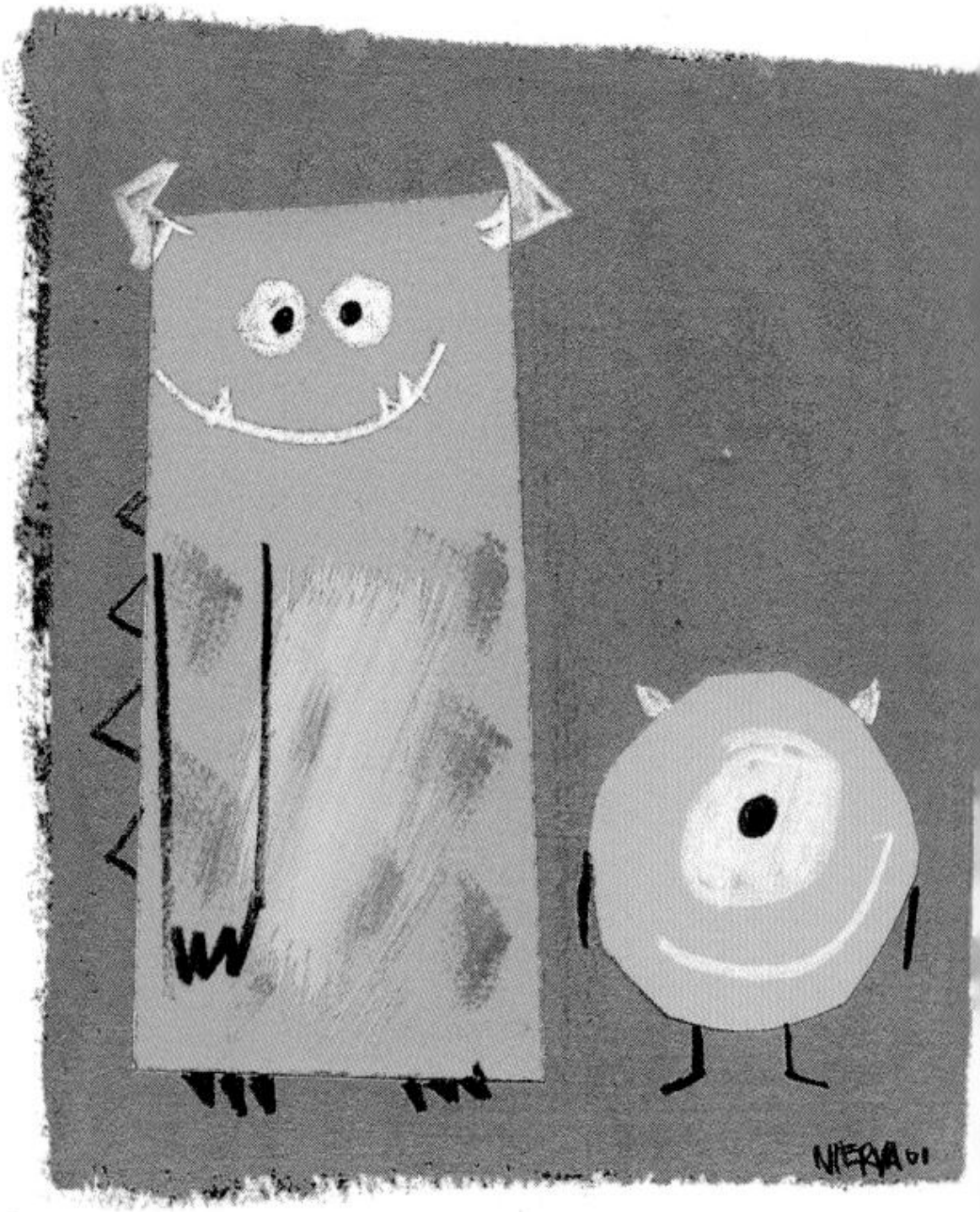

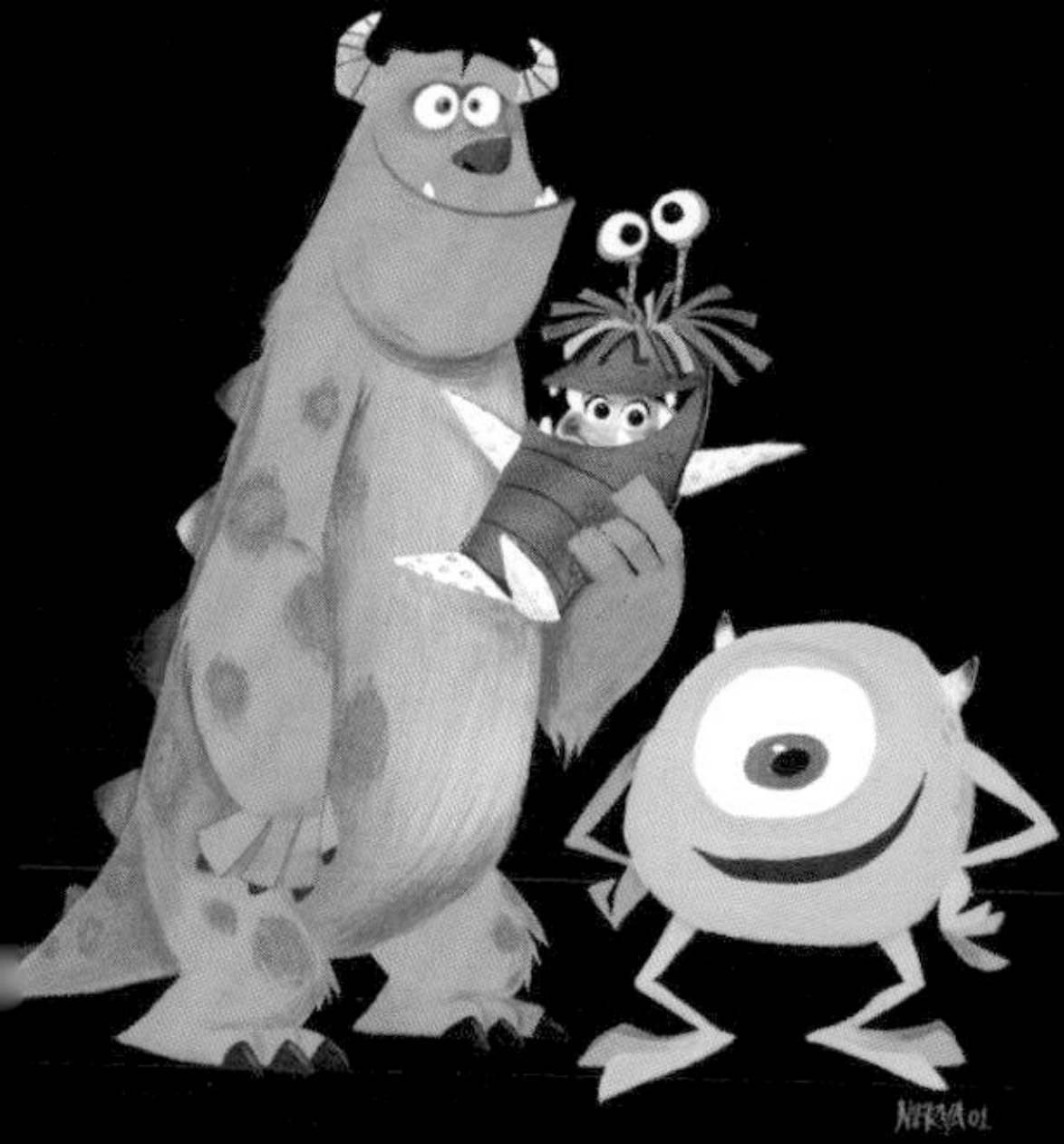
NERVA 01

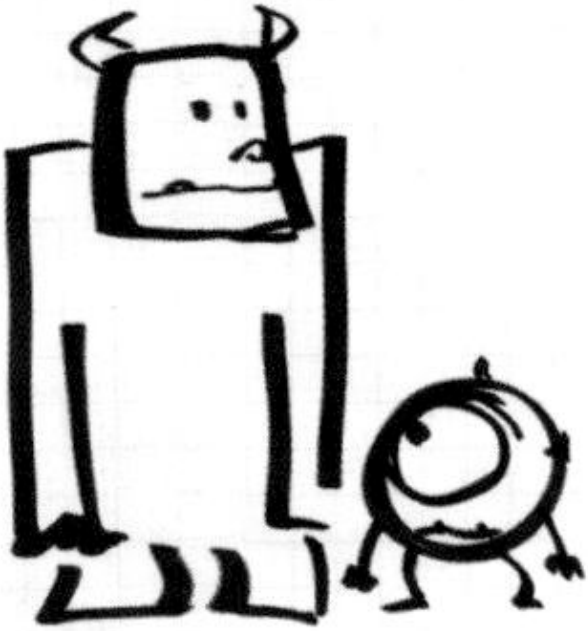

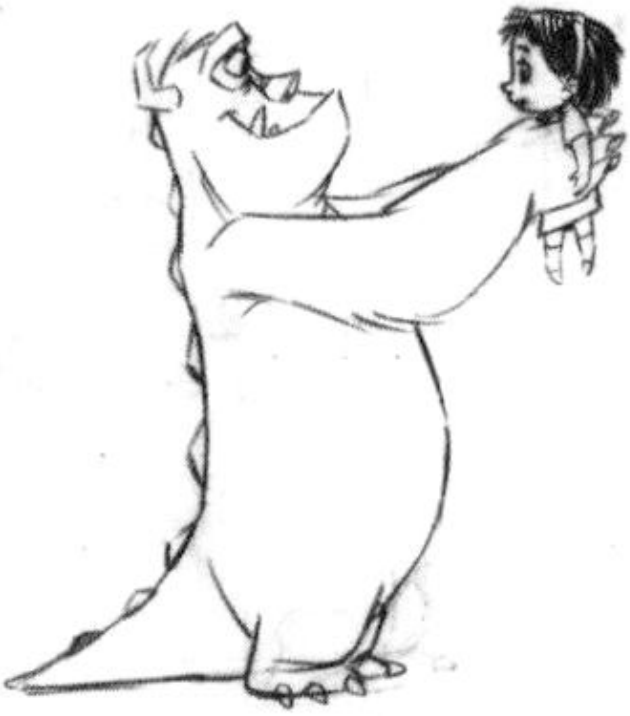

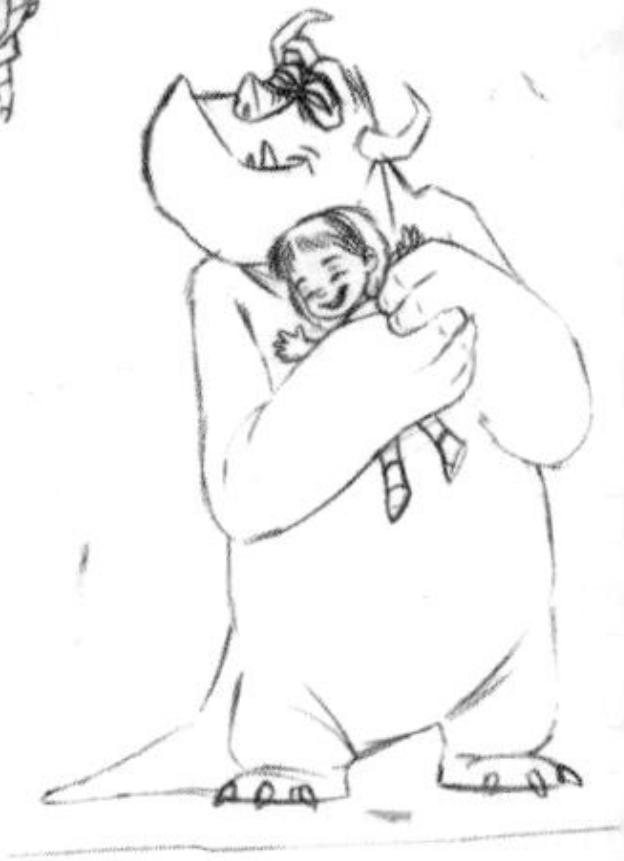

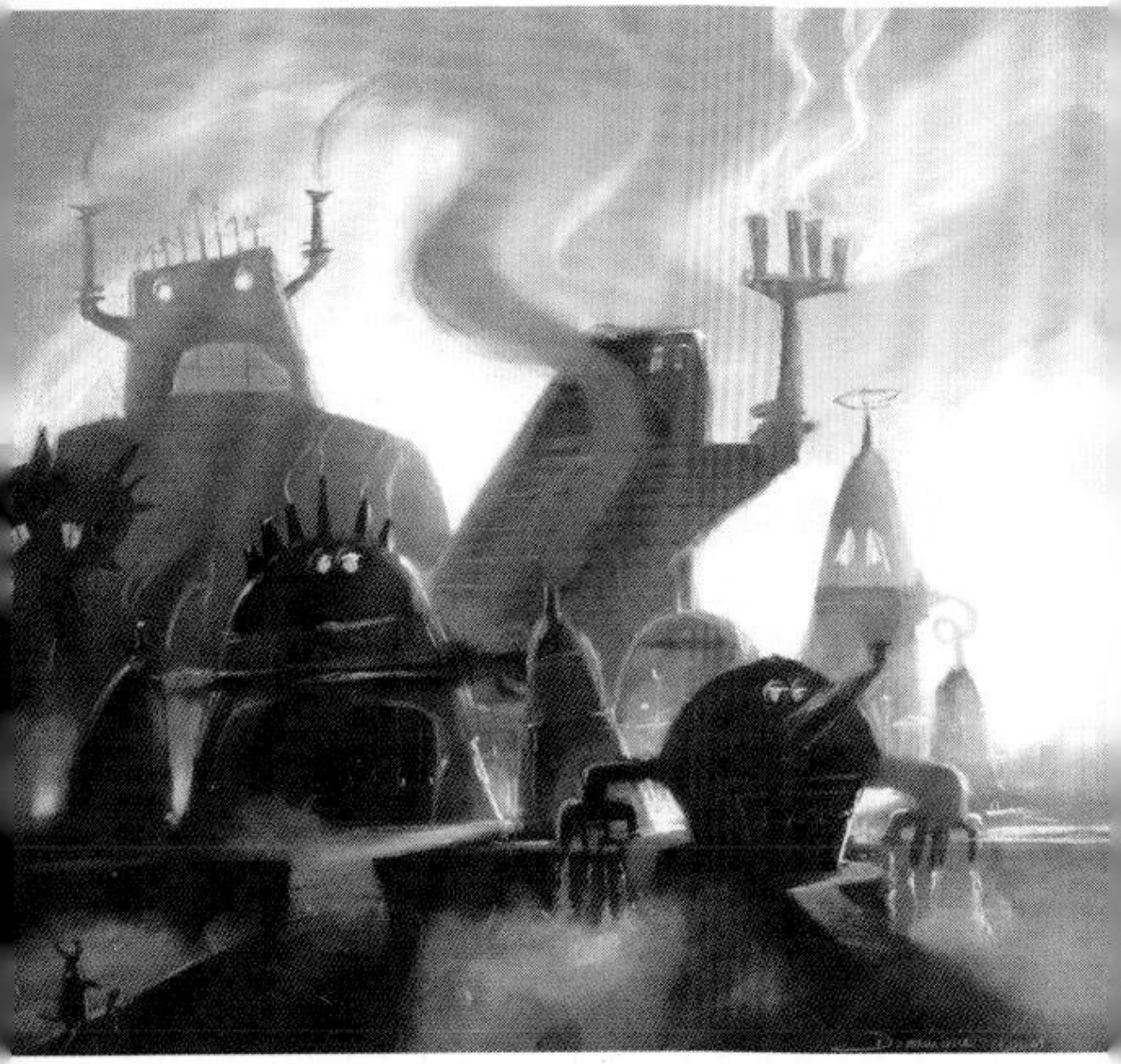

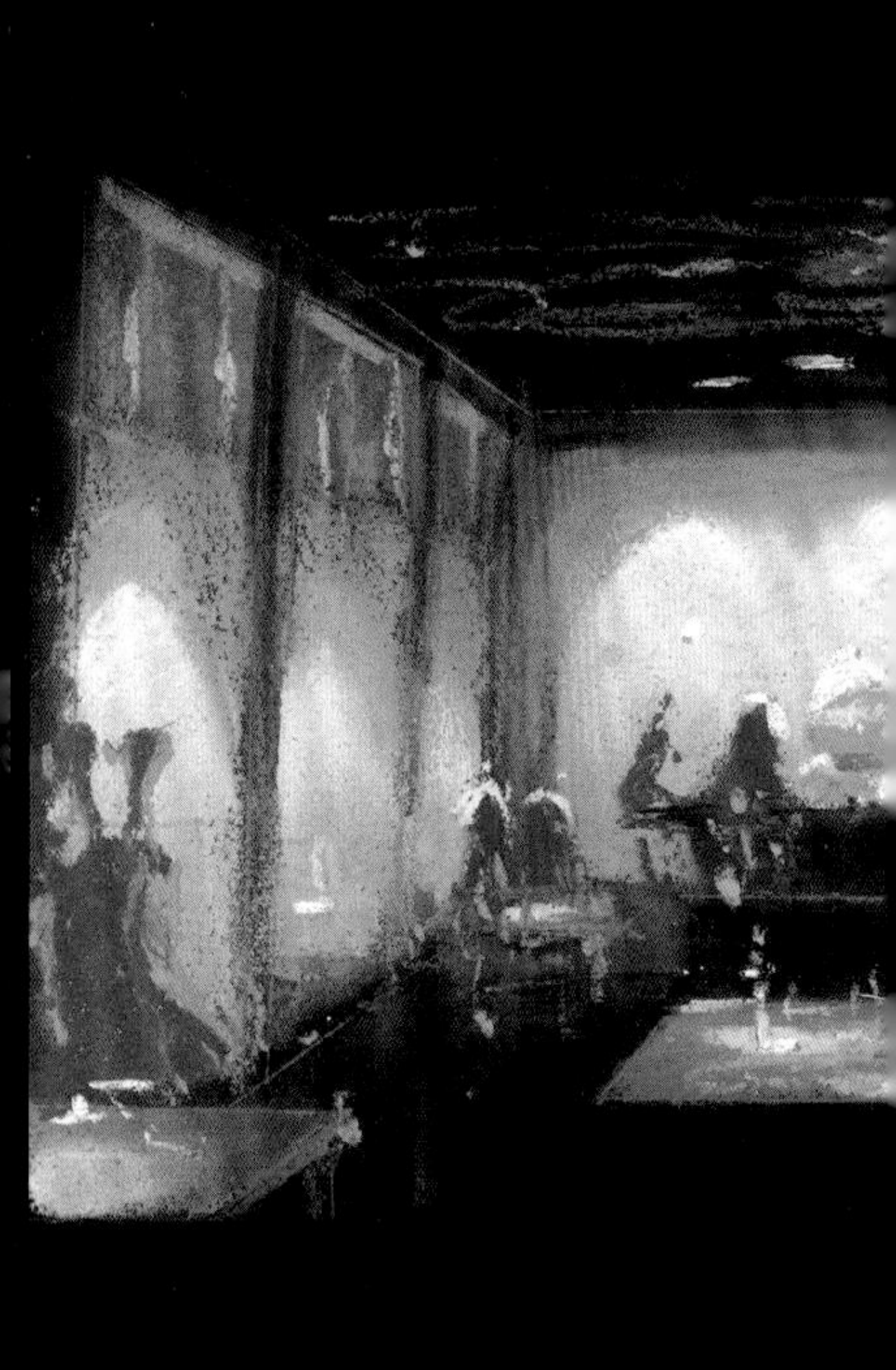

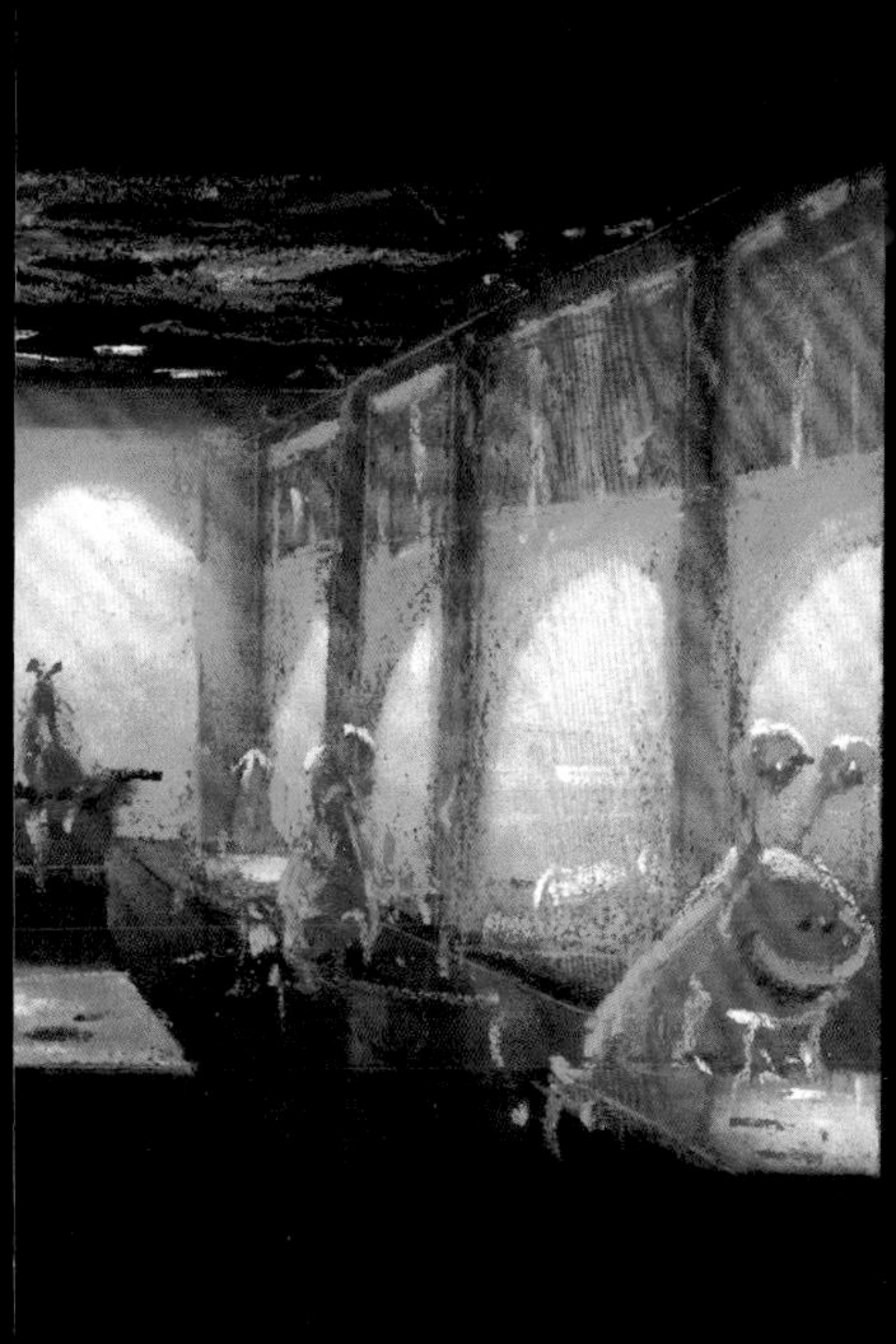

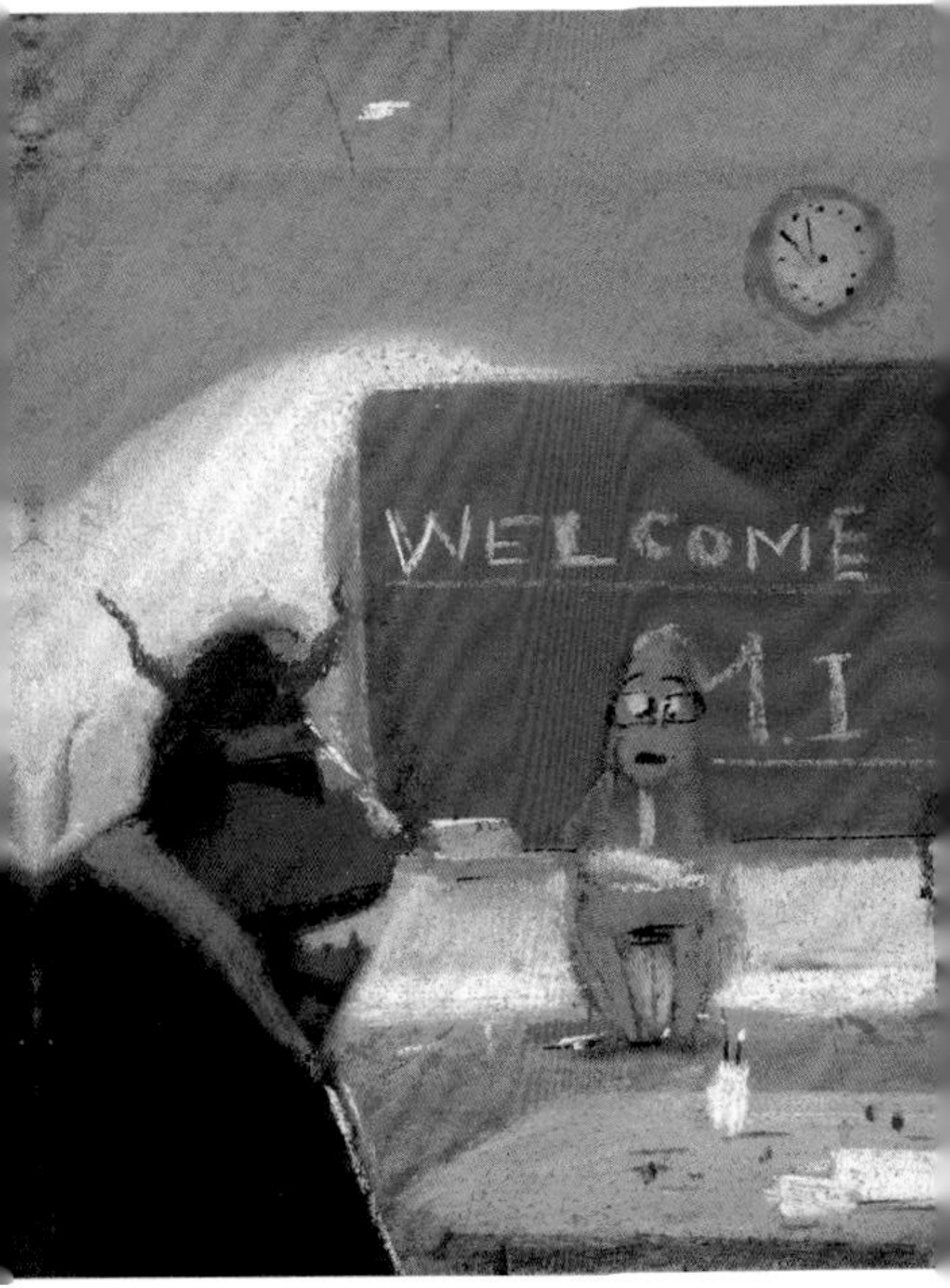
WELCOME
M.I

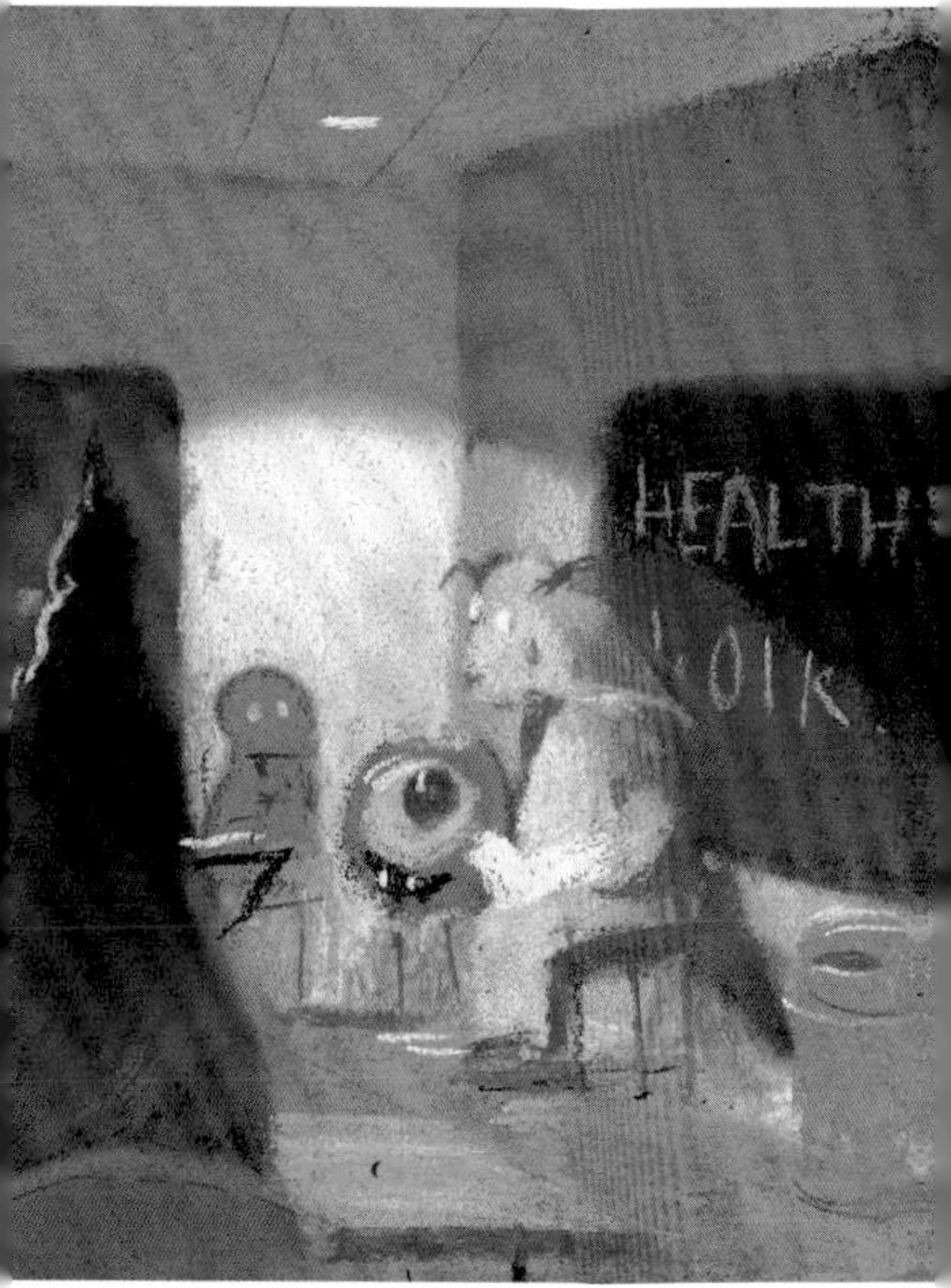
HEALTH
KOIK

FINDING NEMO
2003

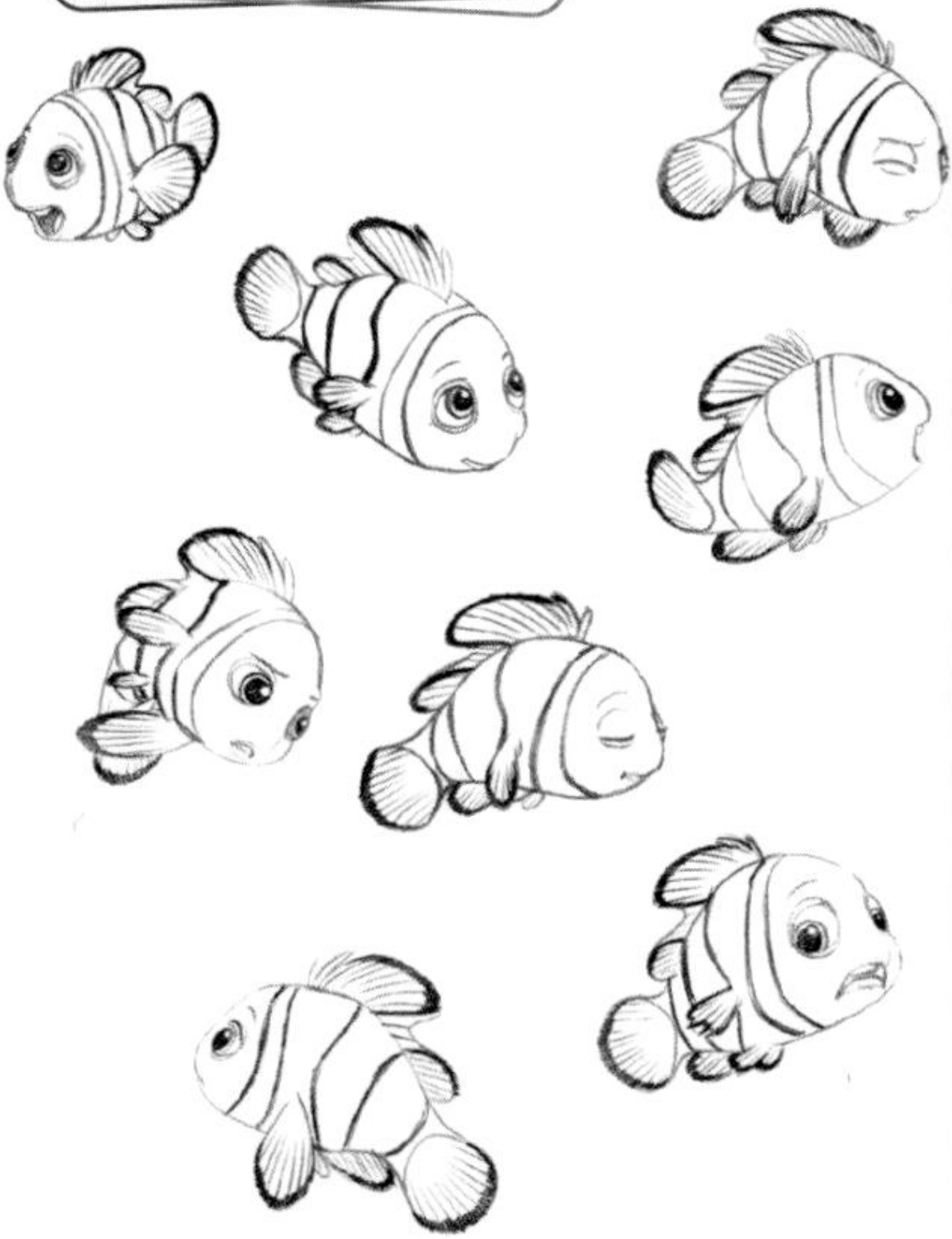

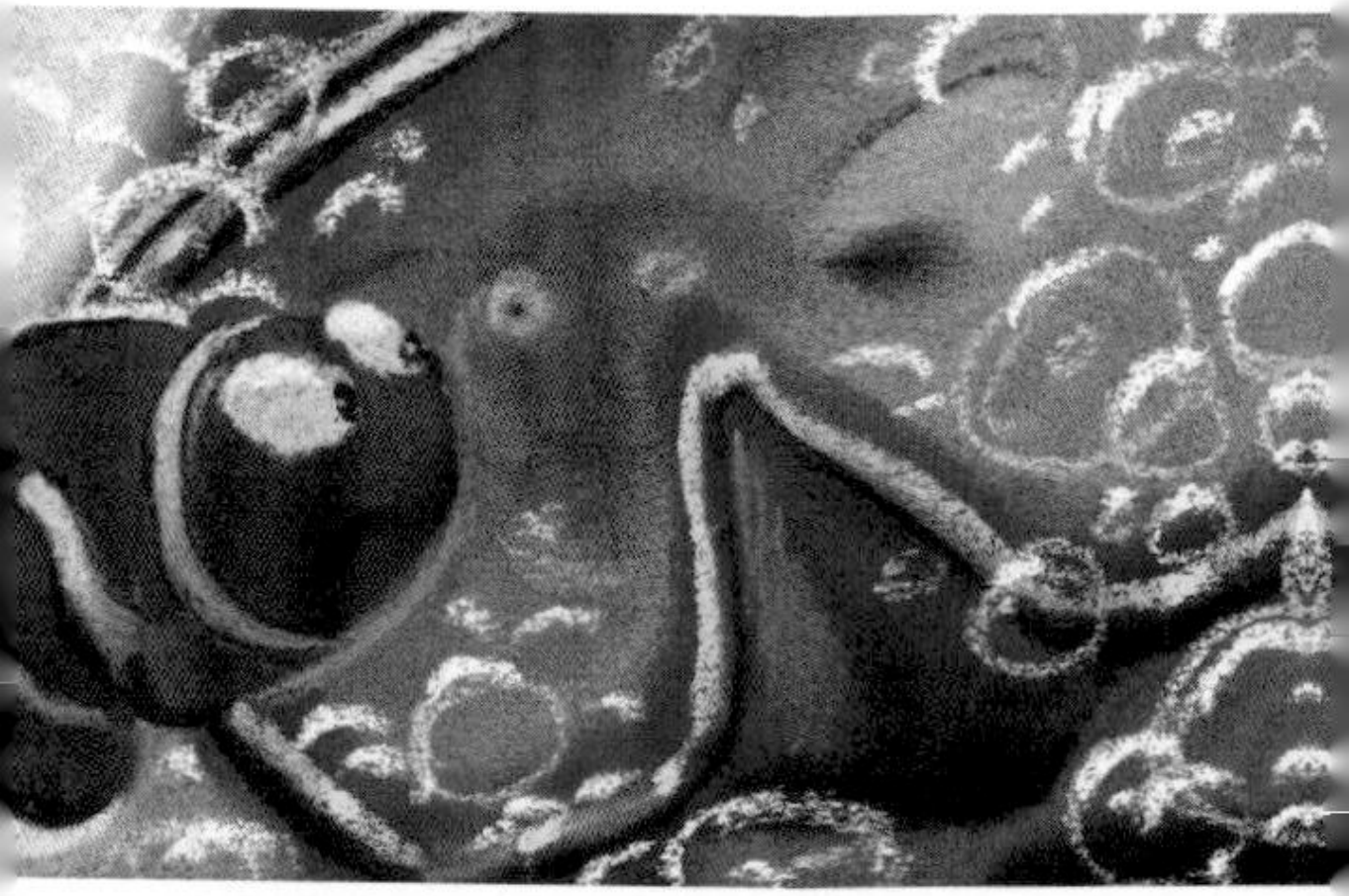

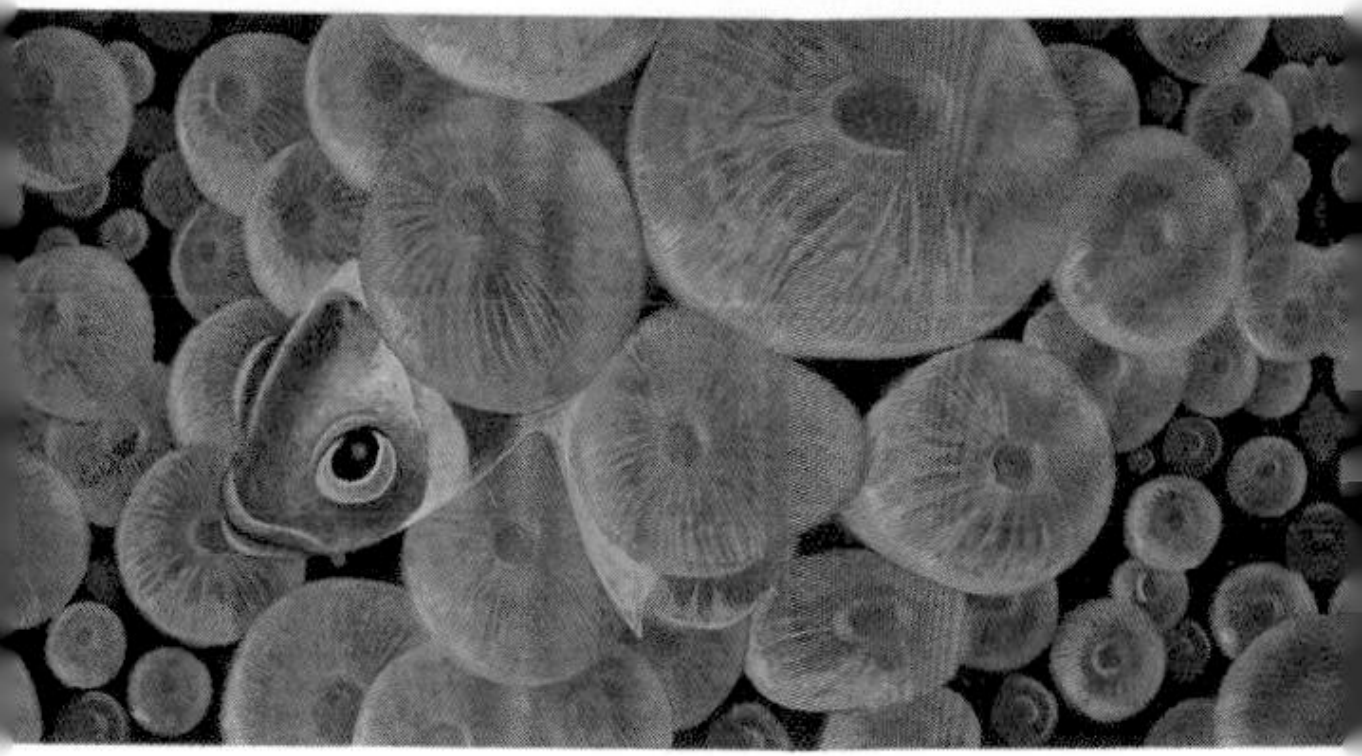

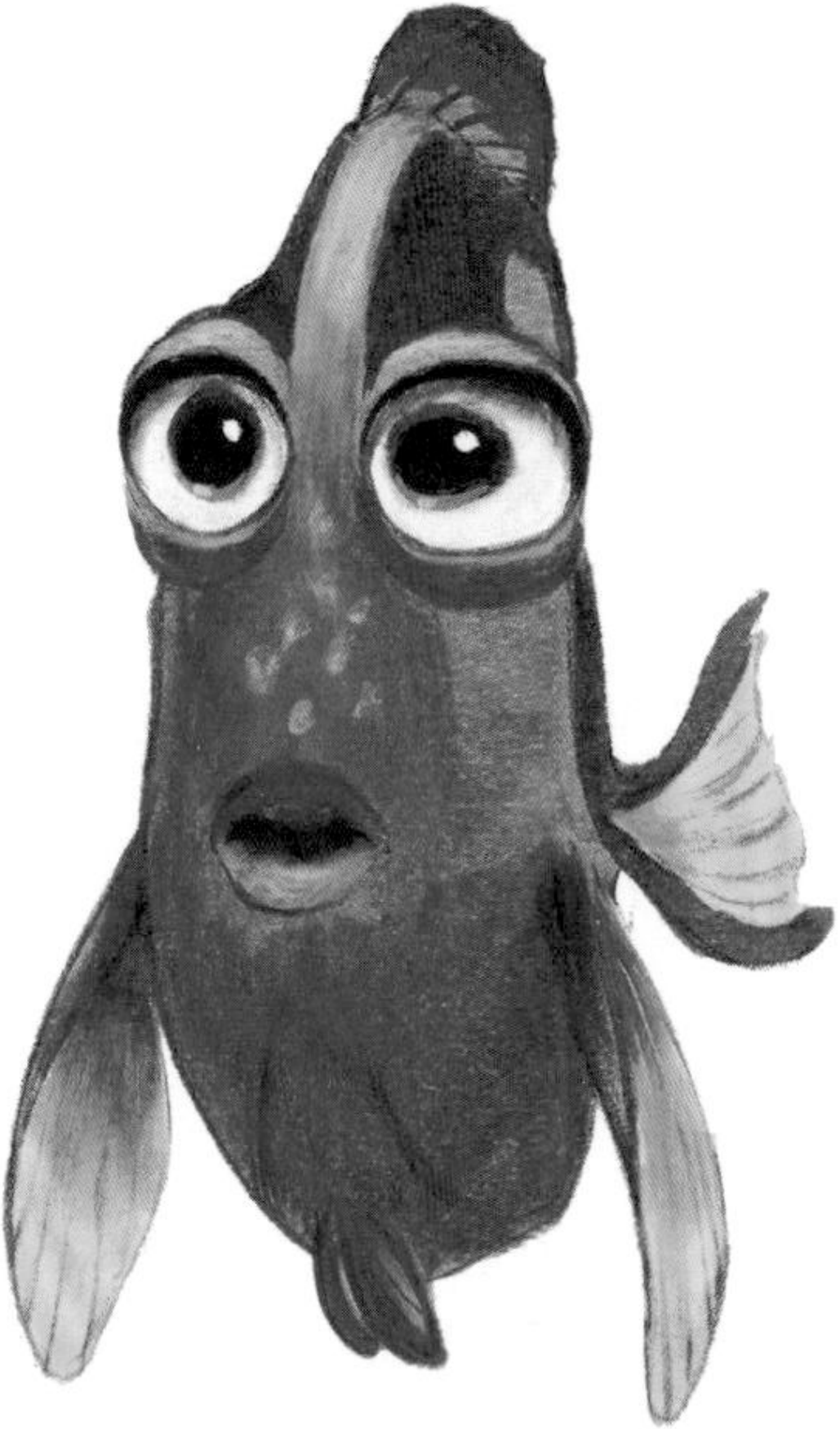

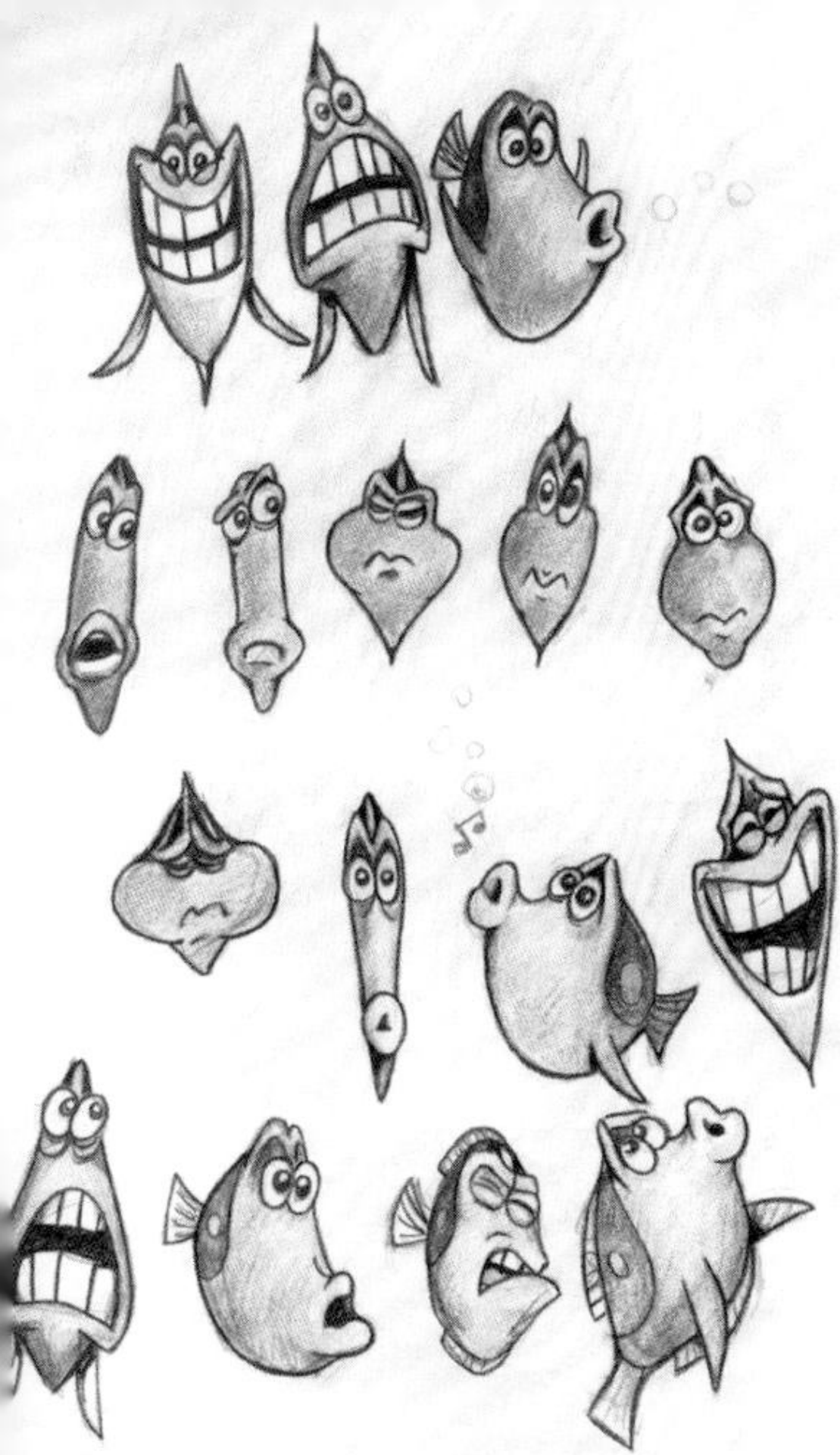

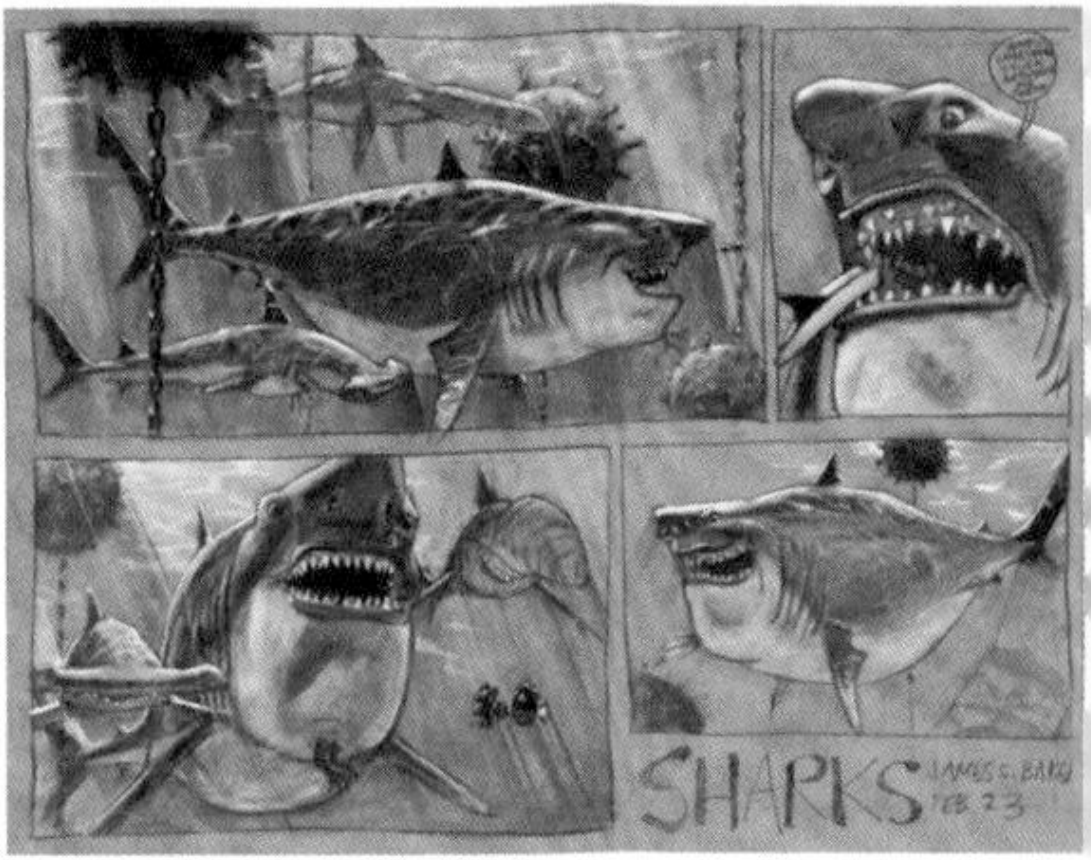
SHARKS

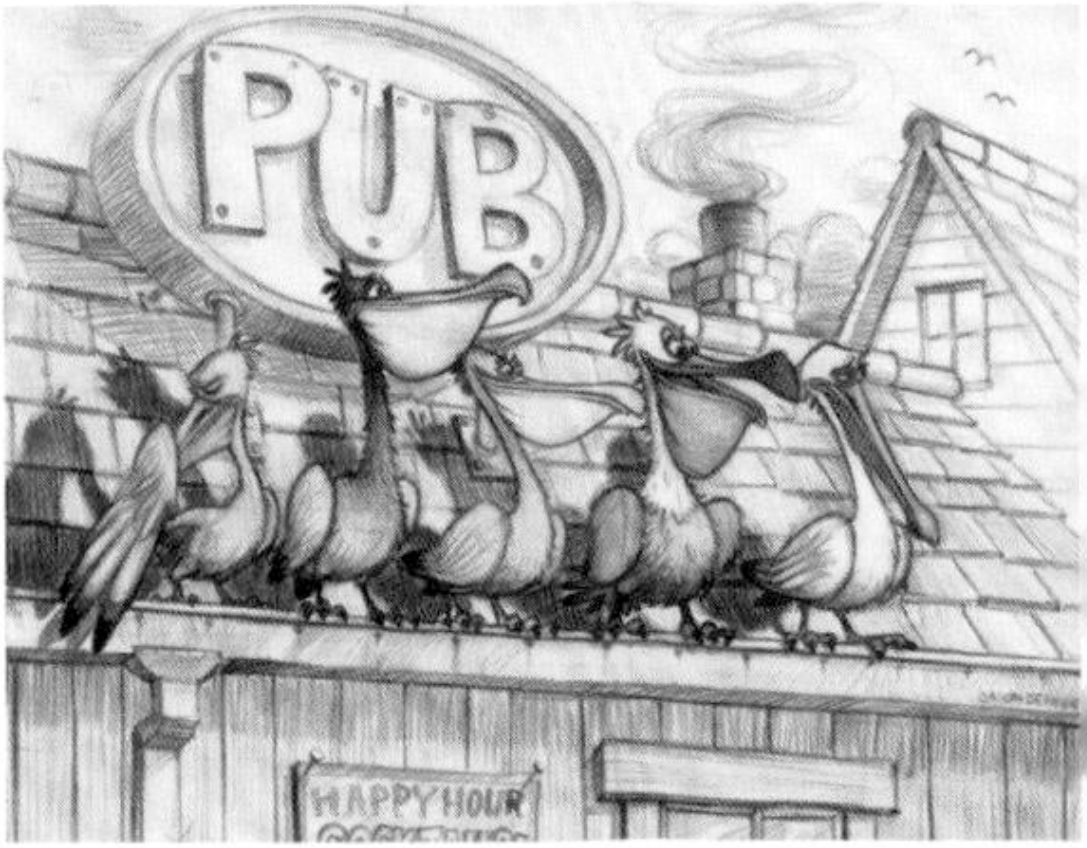
PUB
HAPPY HOUR

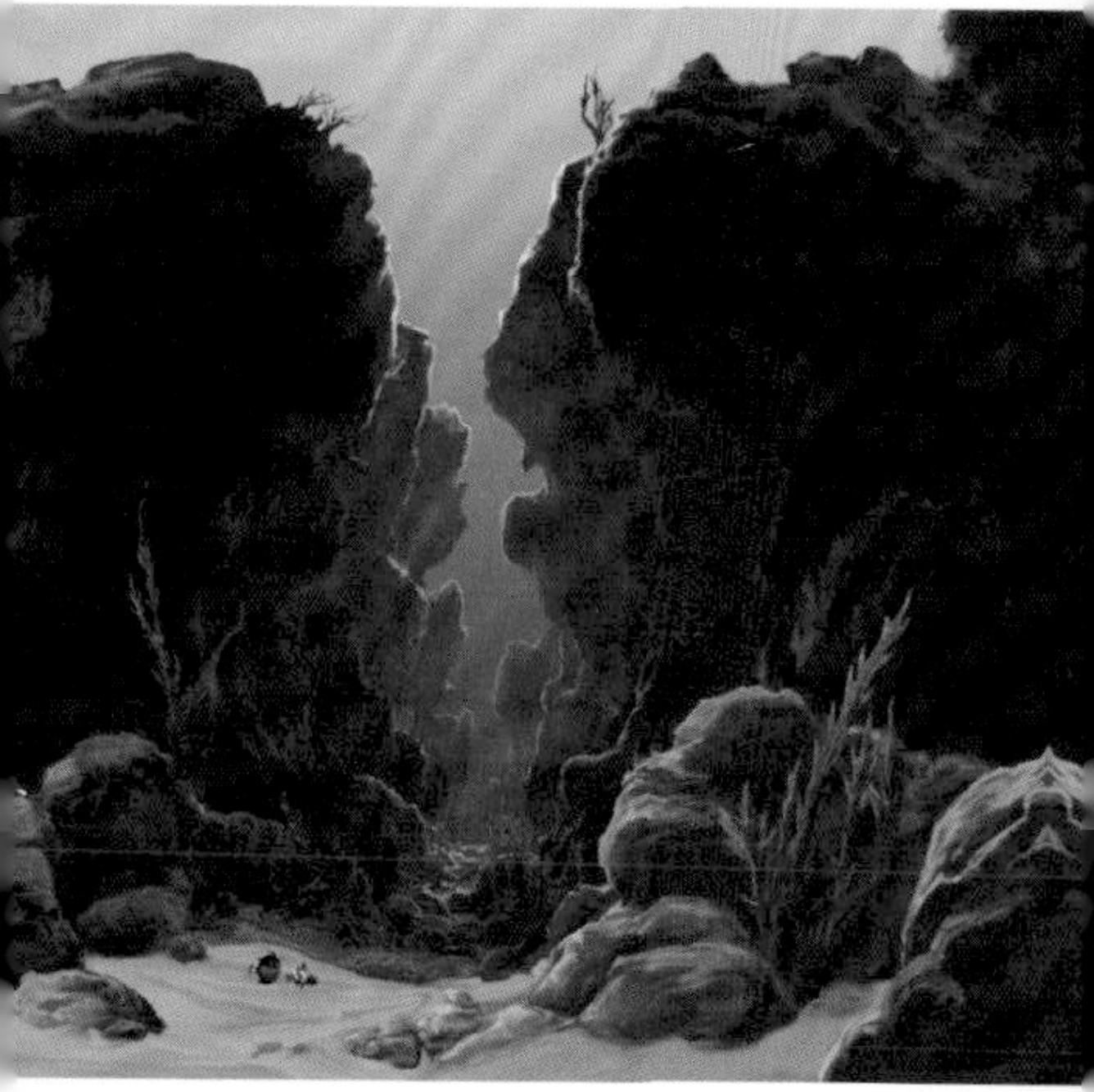

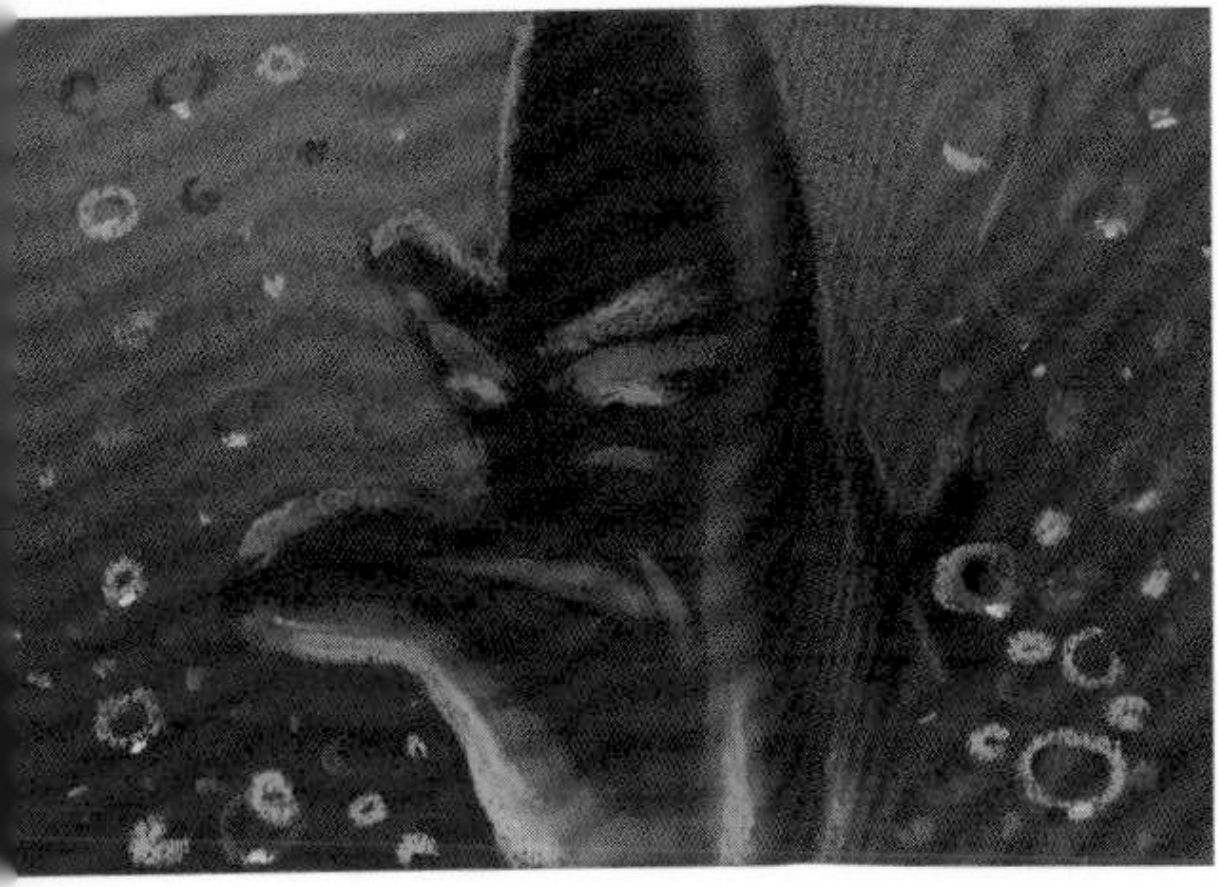

SHORT

BOUNDIN'

2003

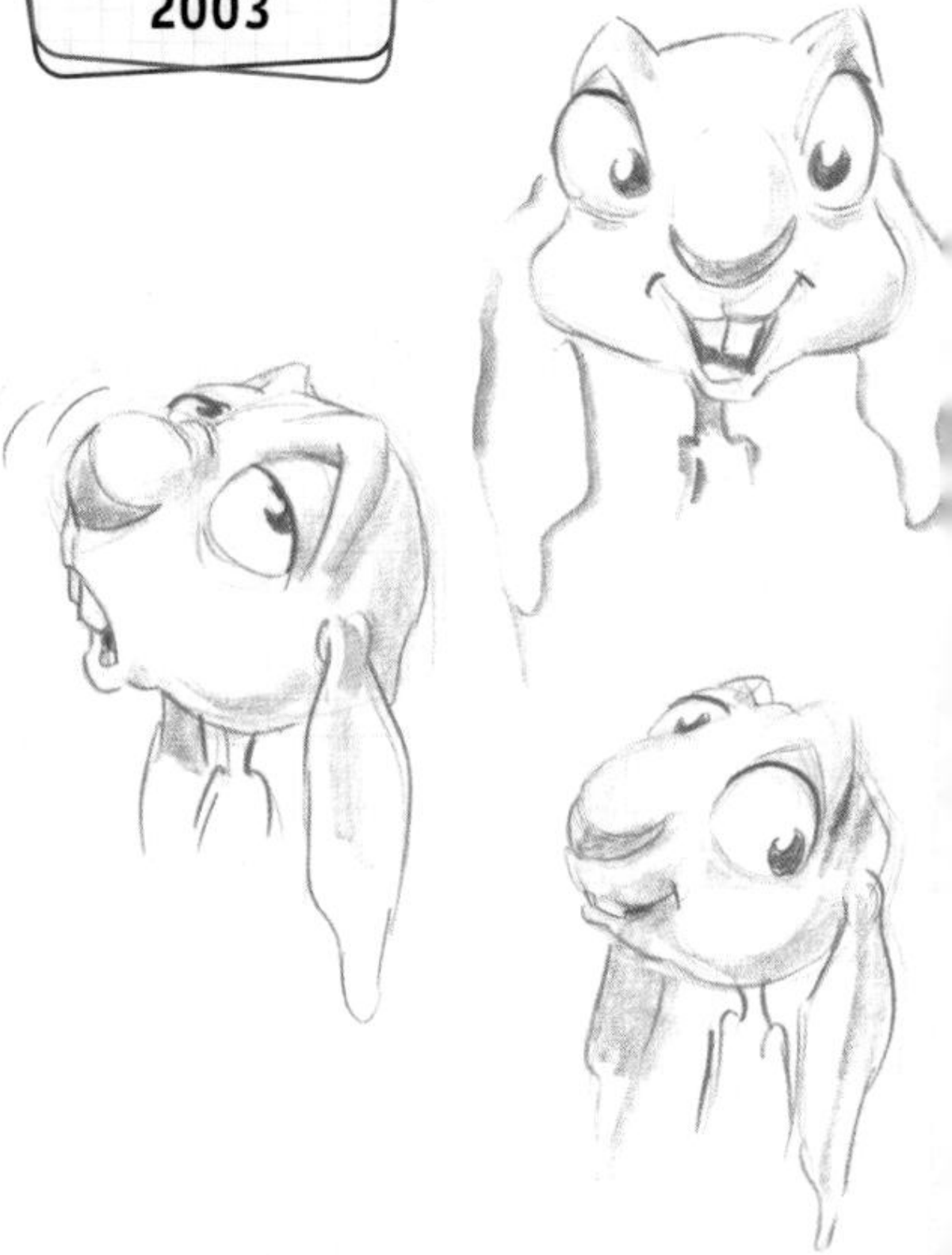

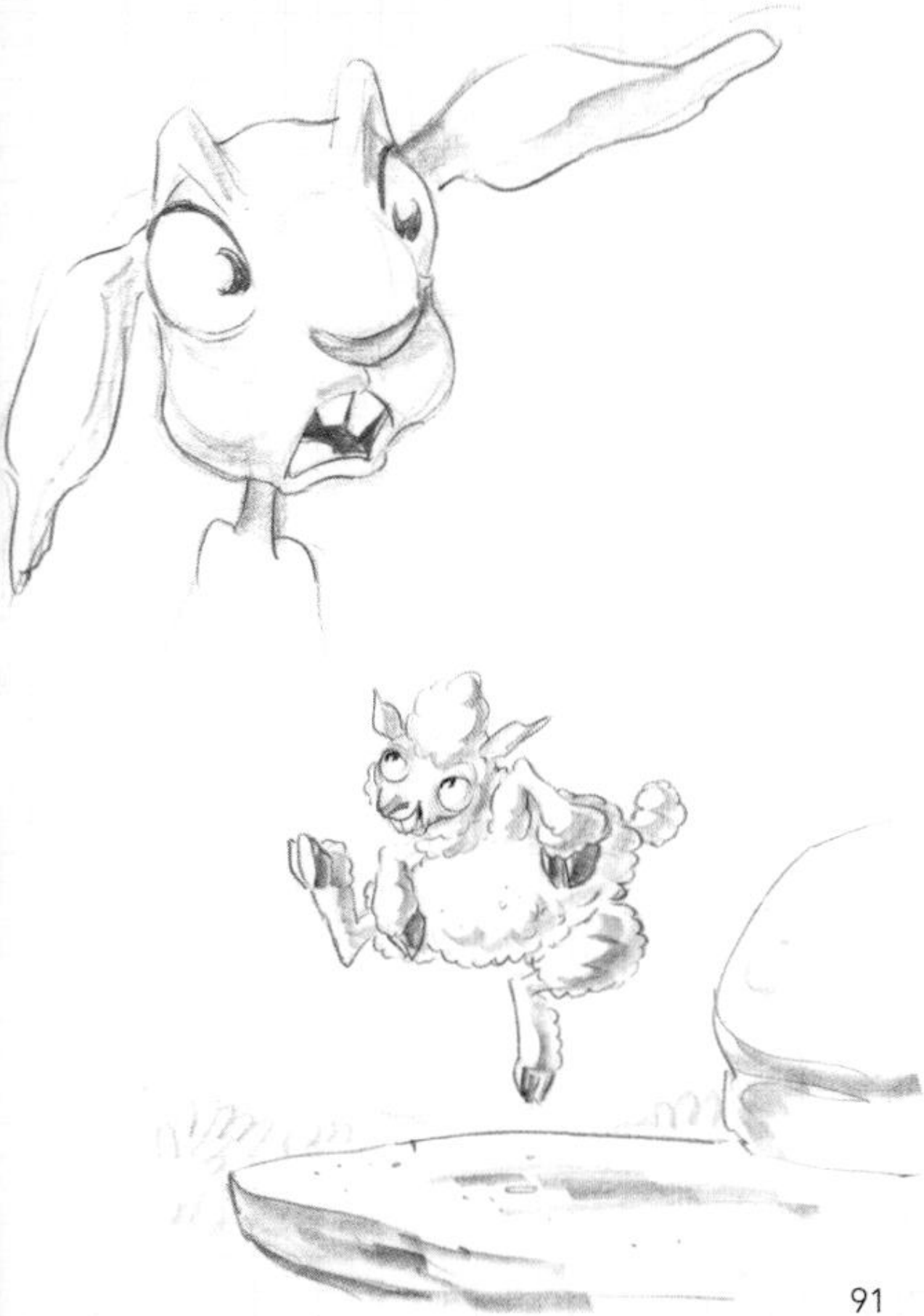

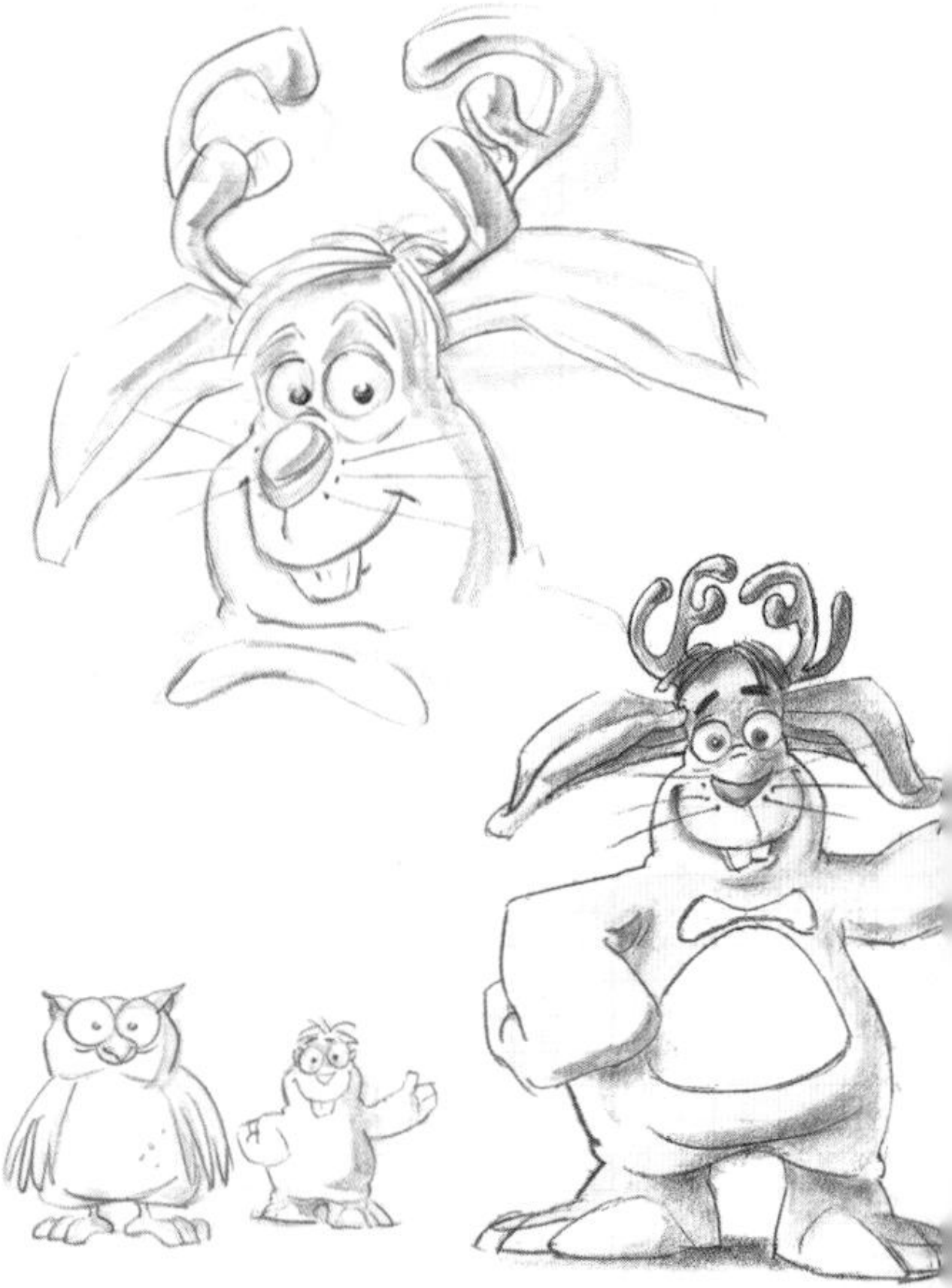

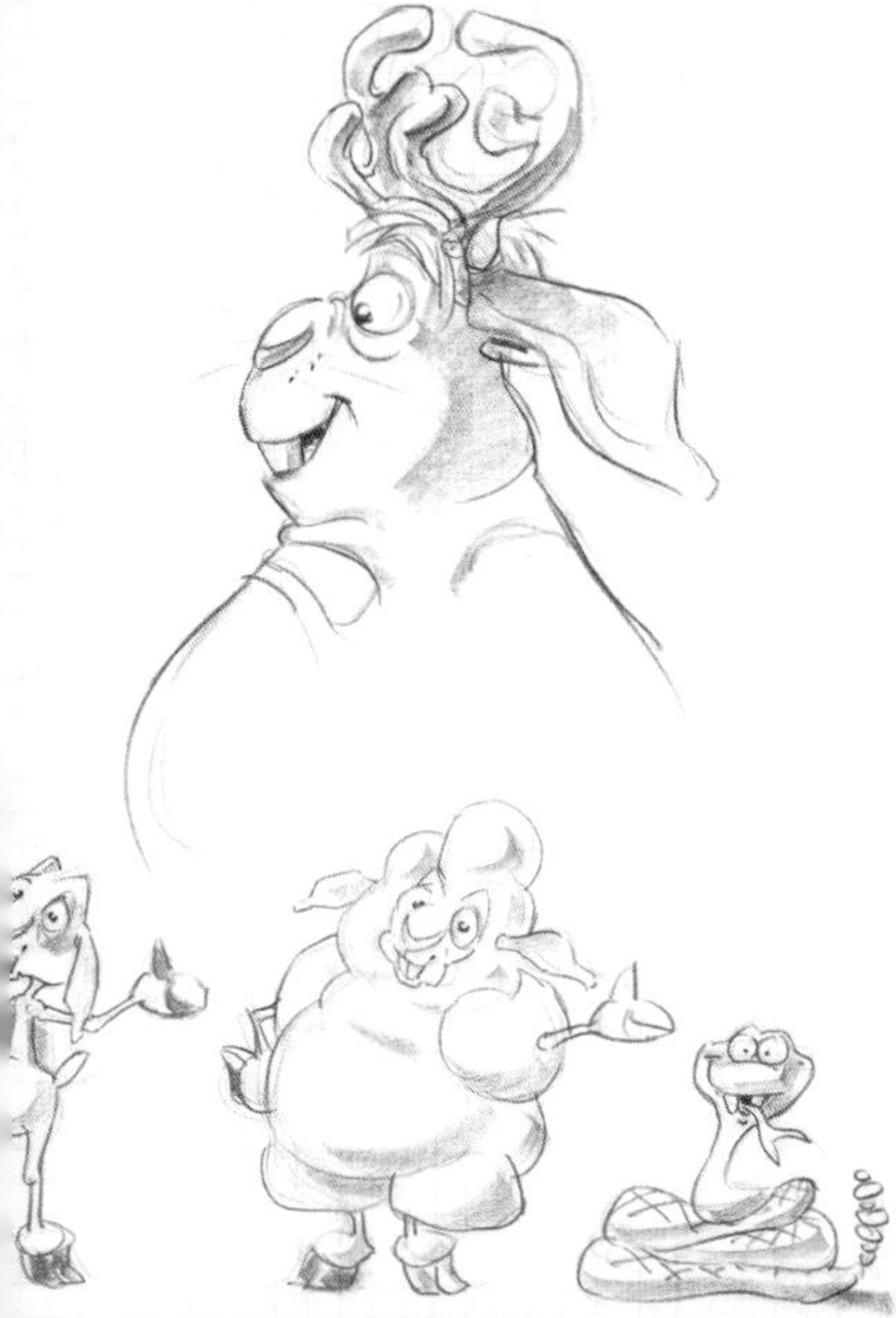

THE INCREDIBLES
2004

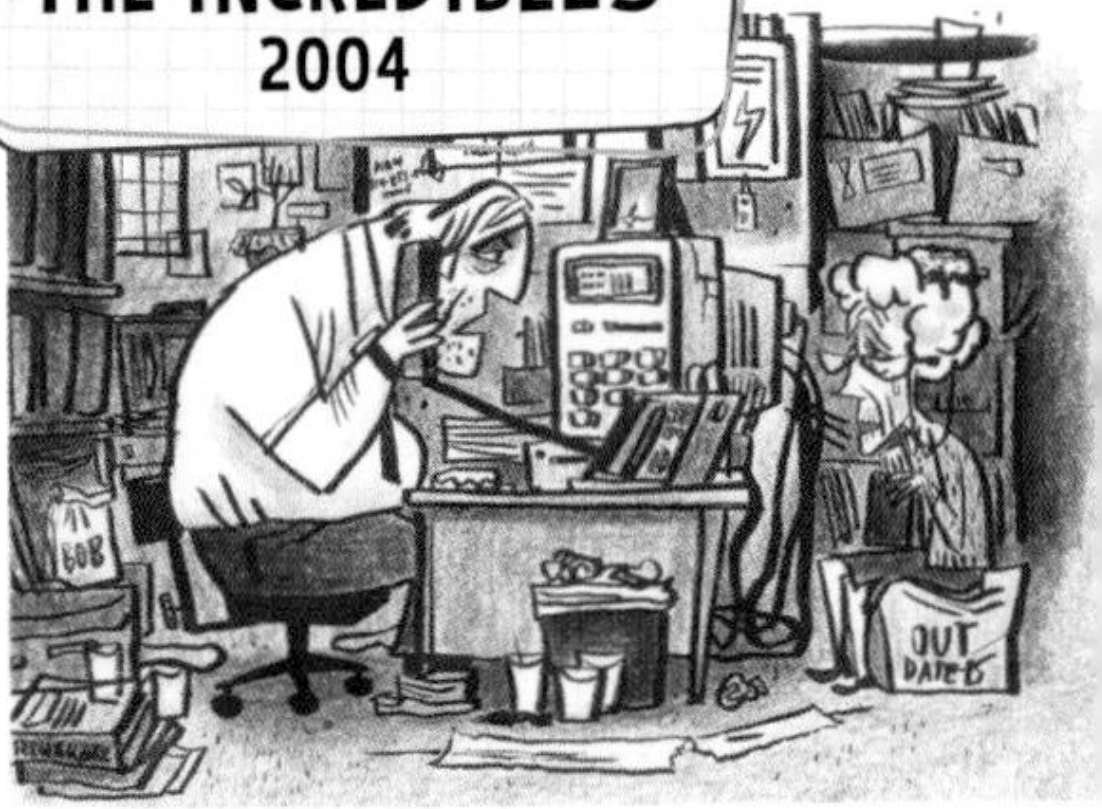

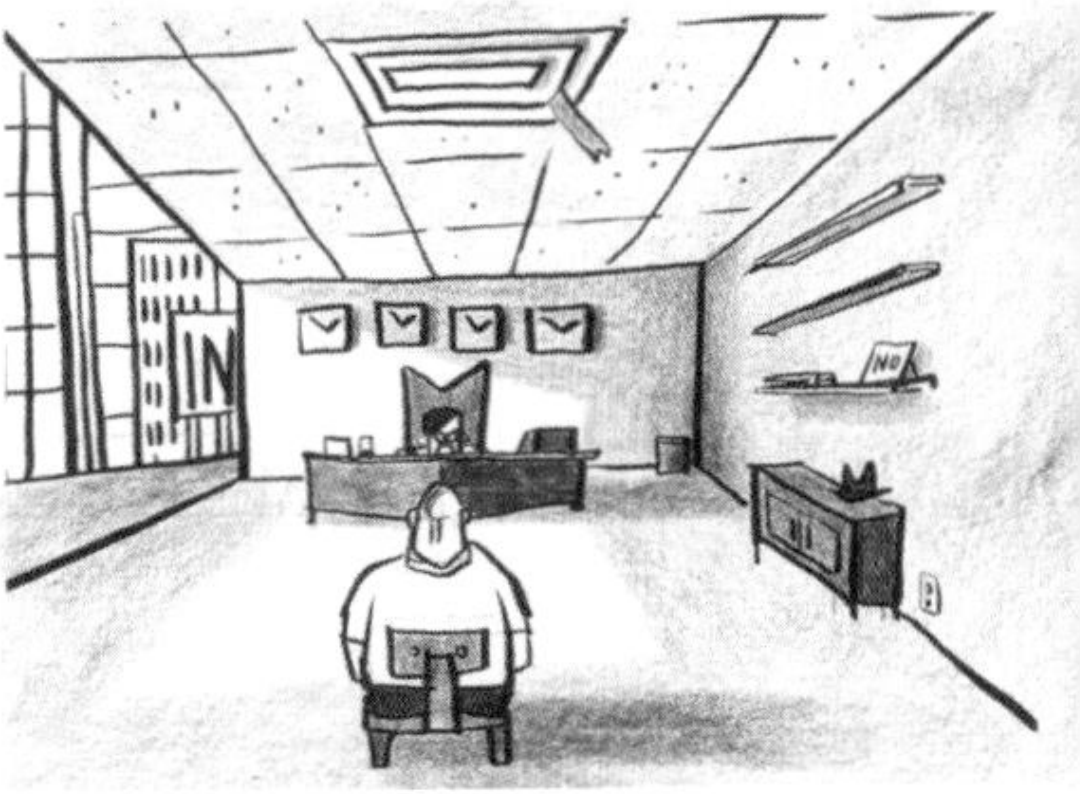

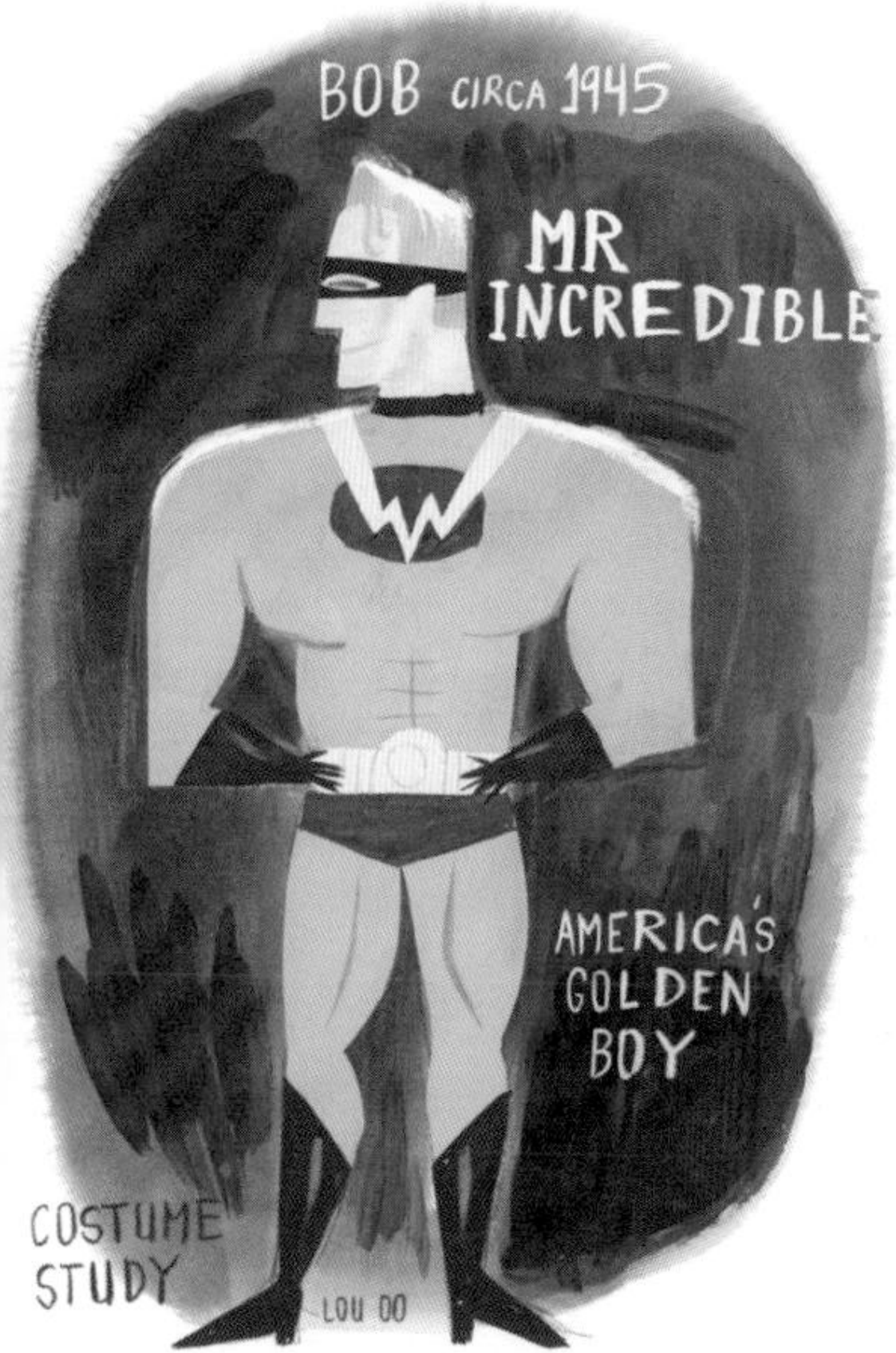
BOB CIRCA 1945
MR INCREDIBLE
AMERICA'S GOLDEN BOY
COSTUME STUDY
LOU DO

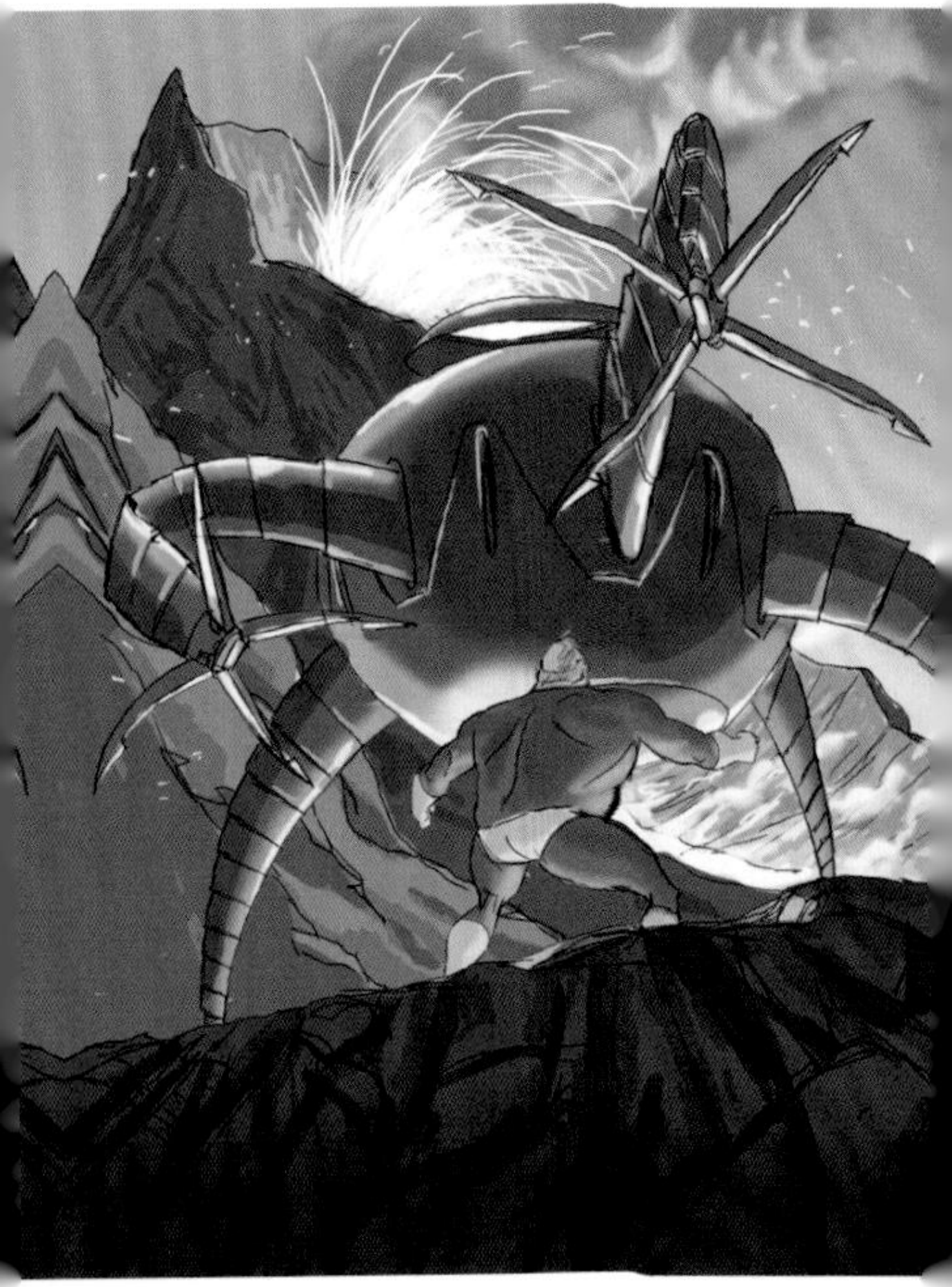

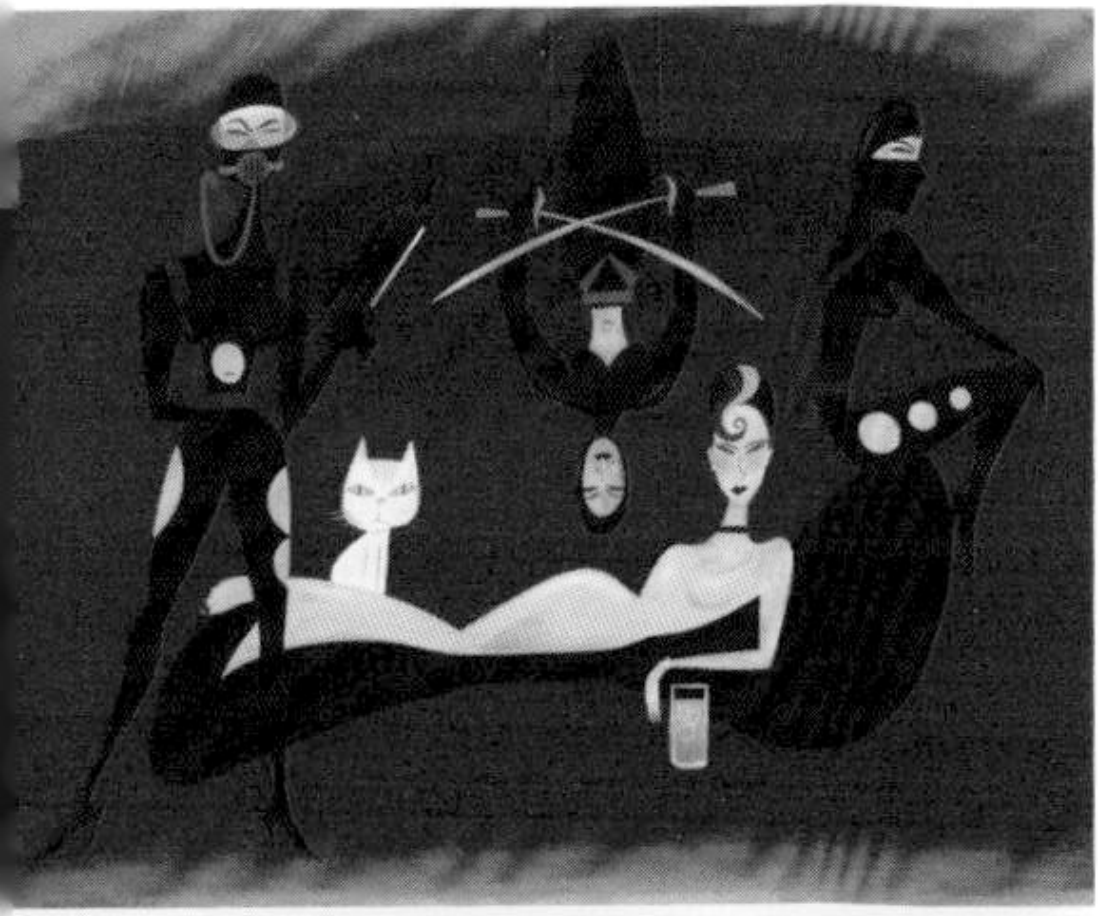

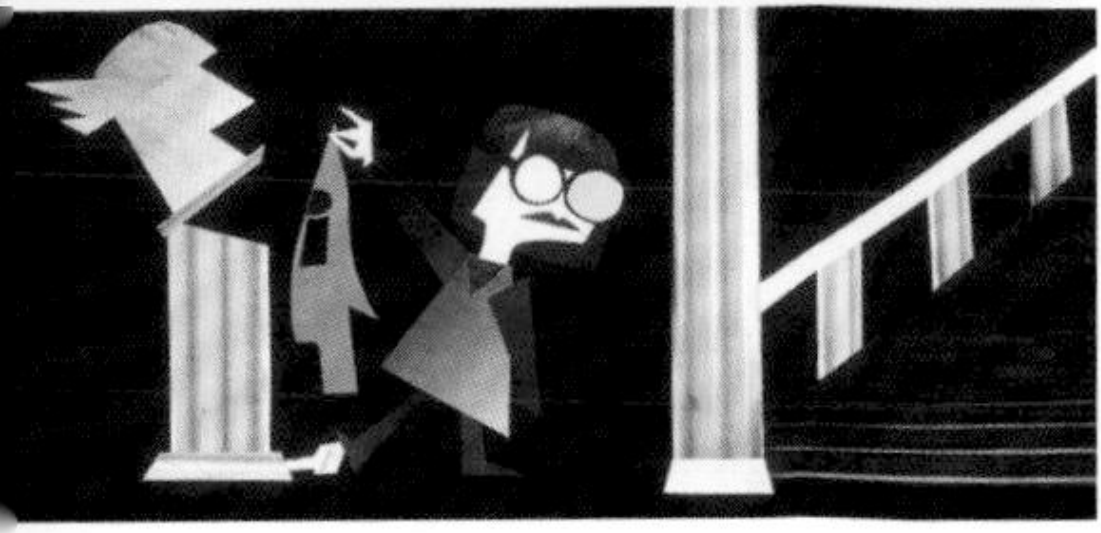

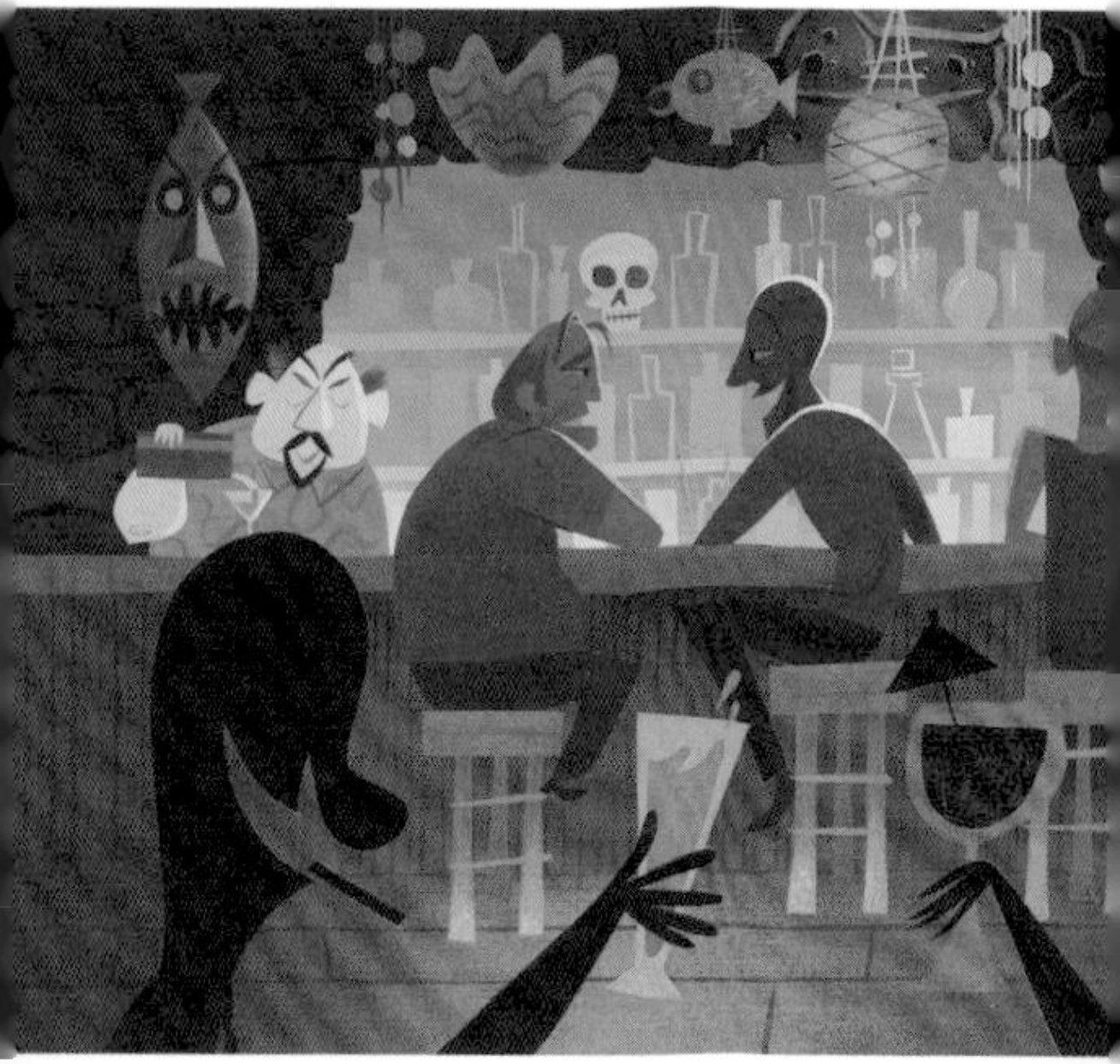

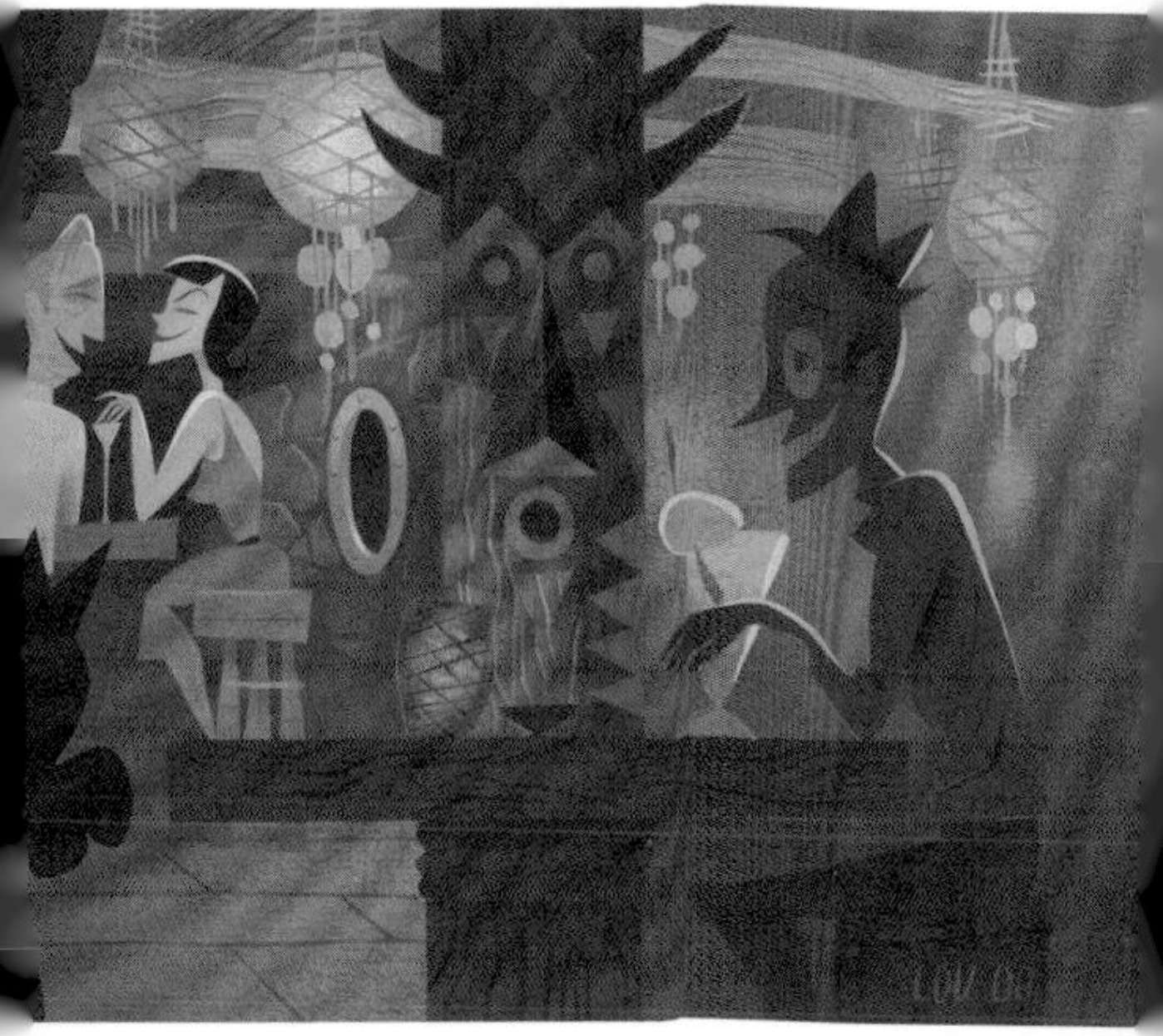

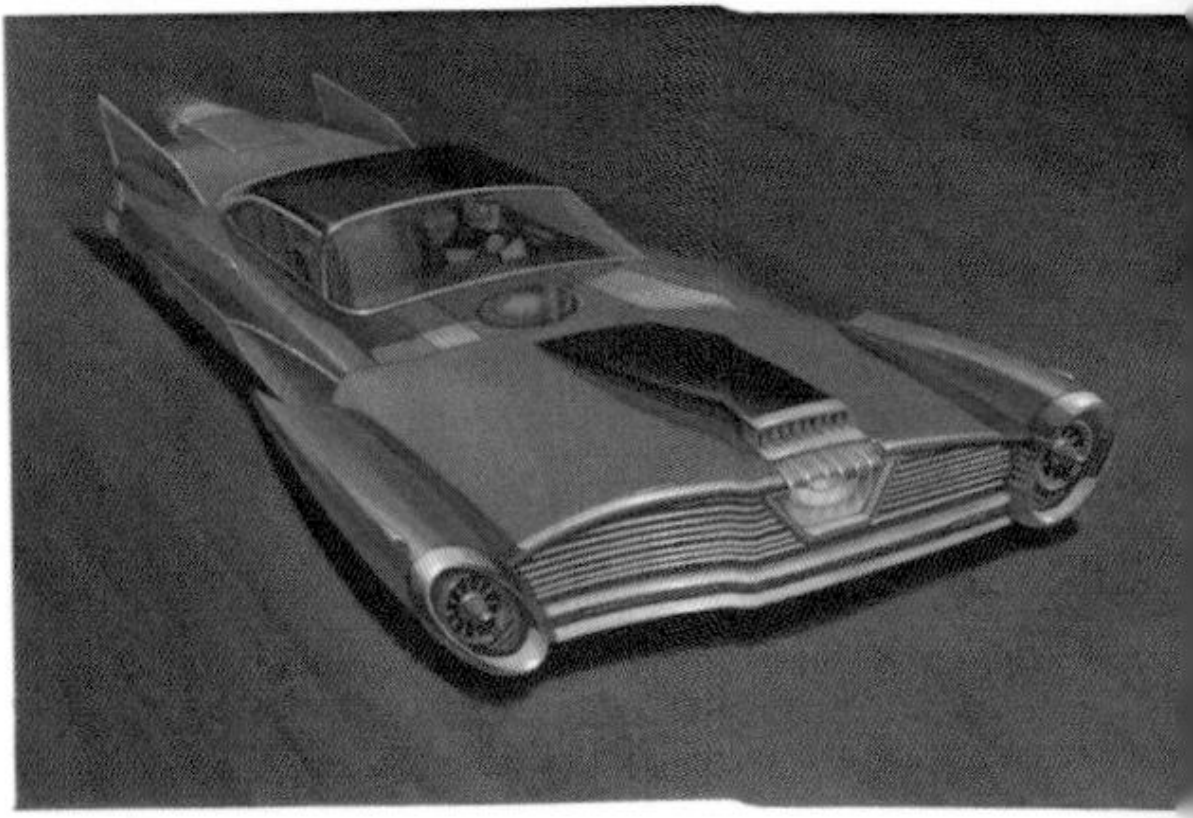

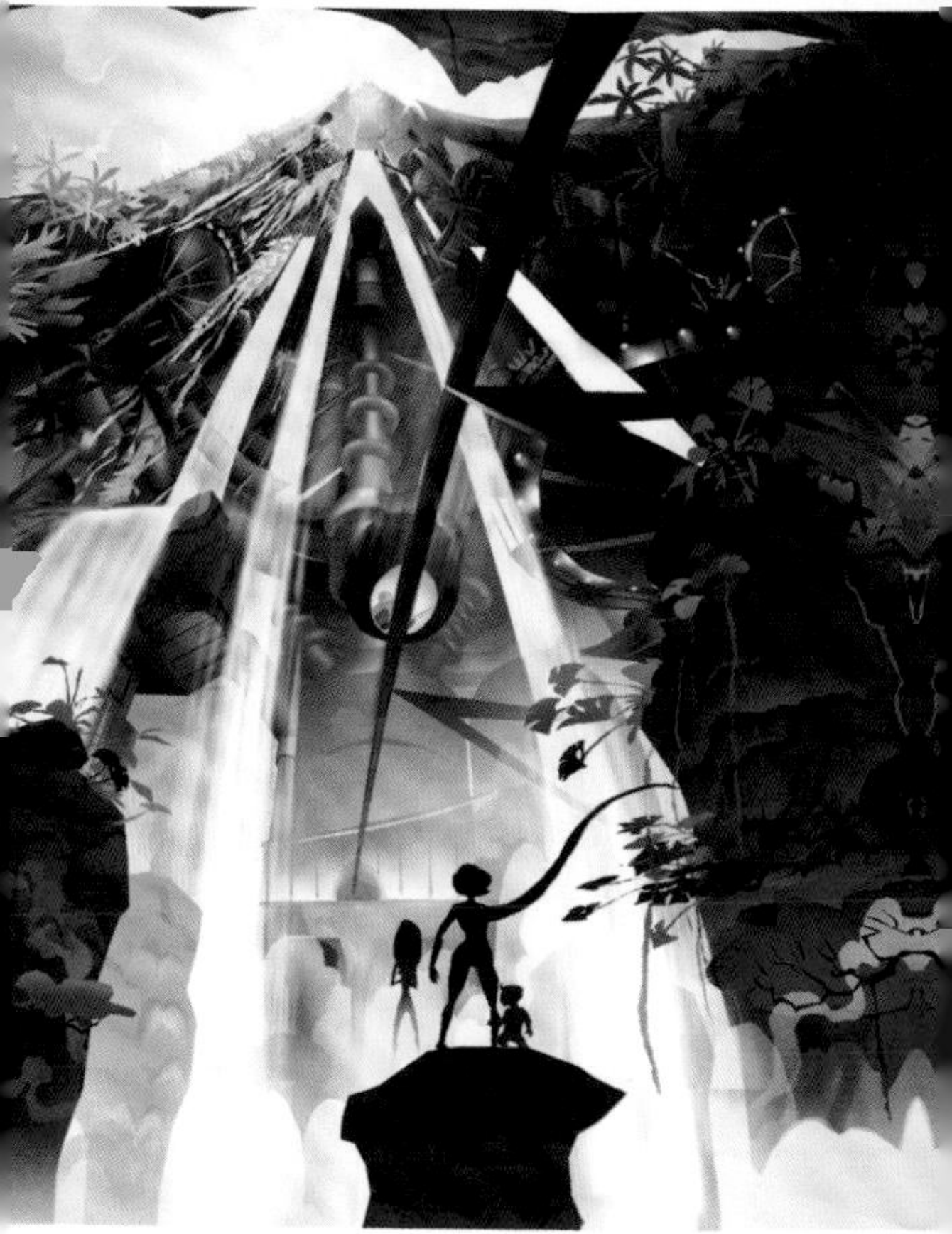

SHORT

ONE MAN BAND

2005

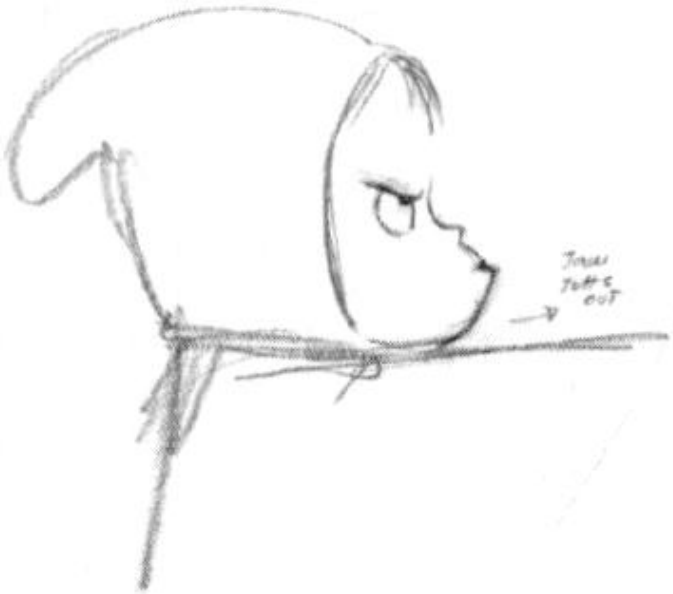

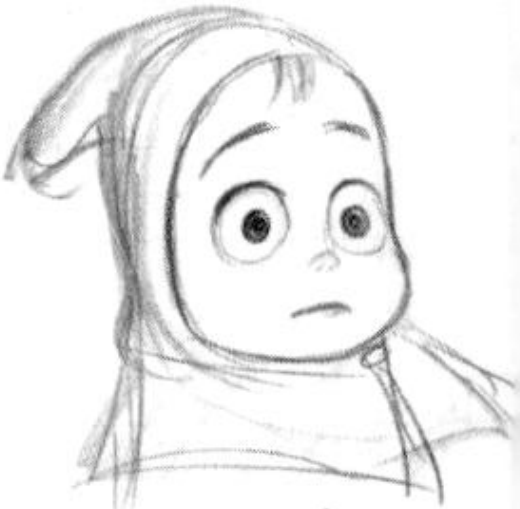

on my way to make a wish

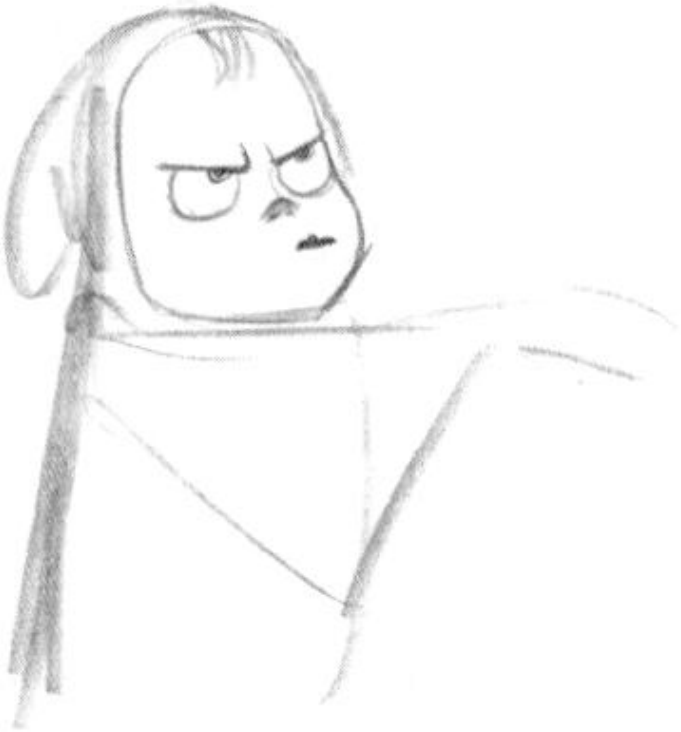

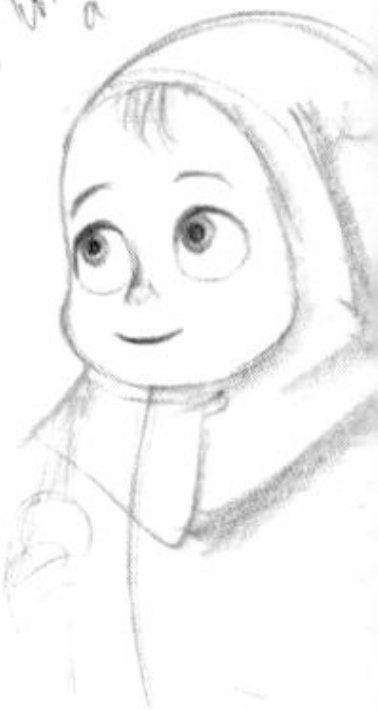

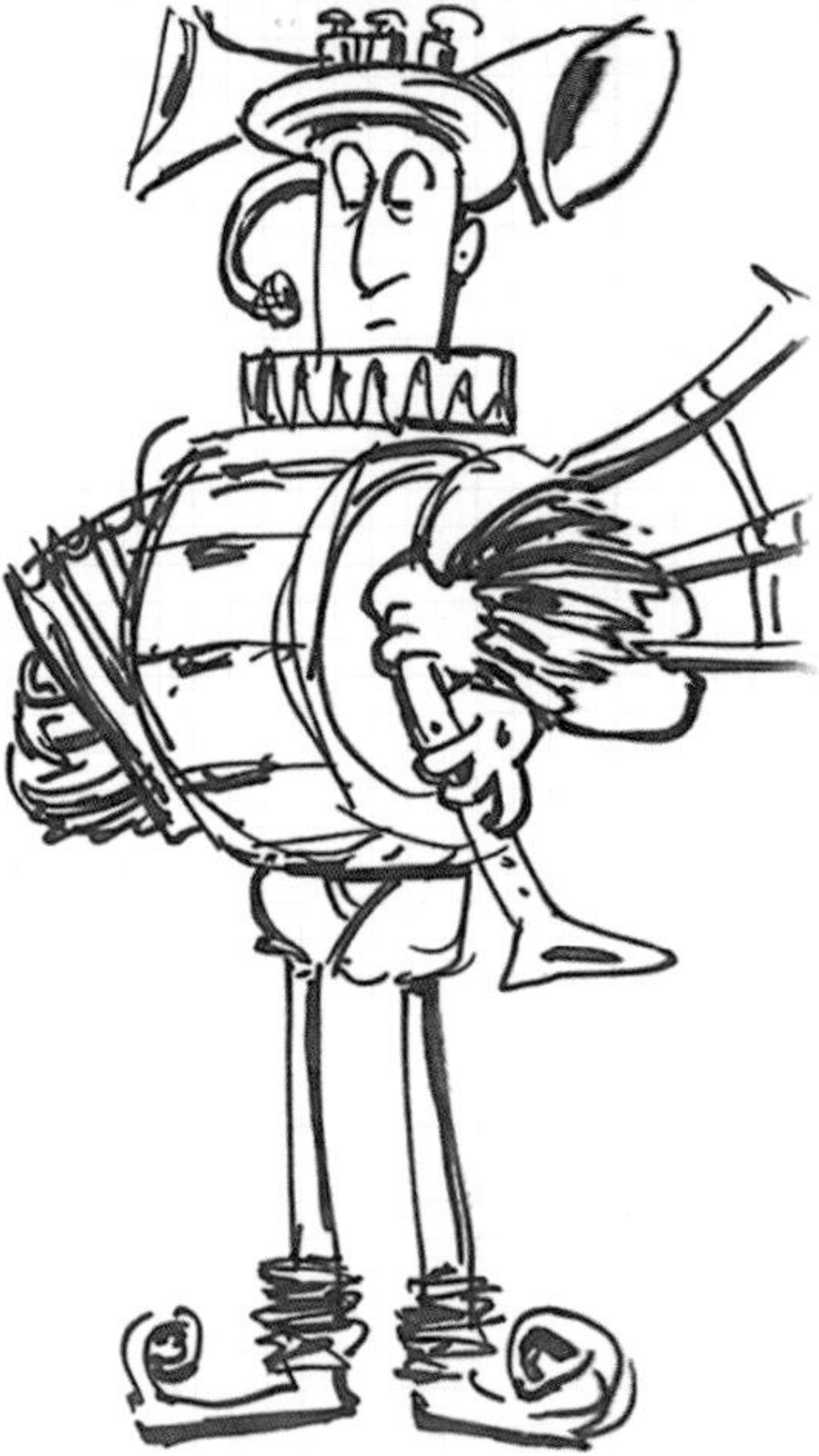

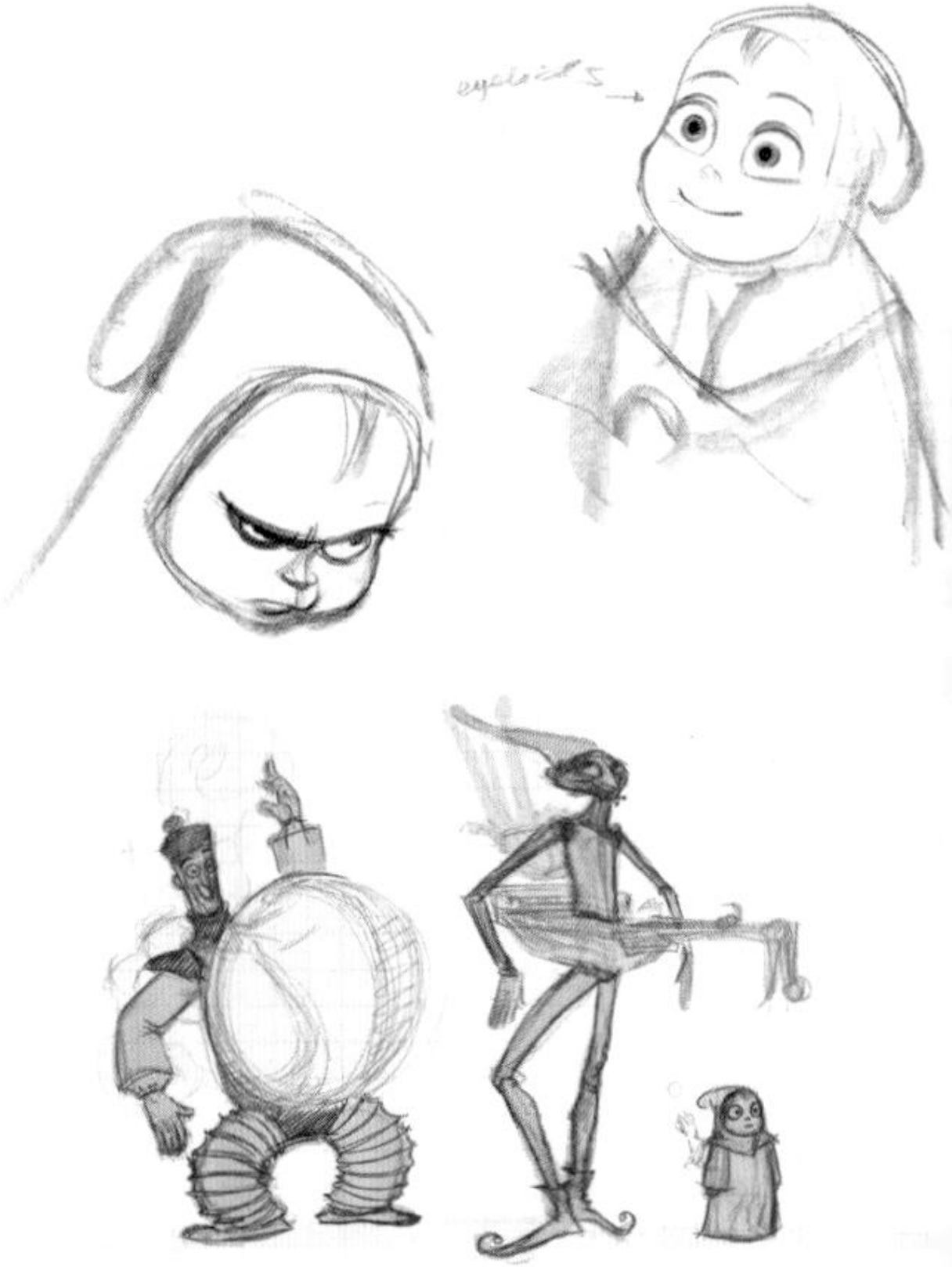

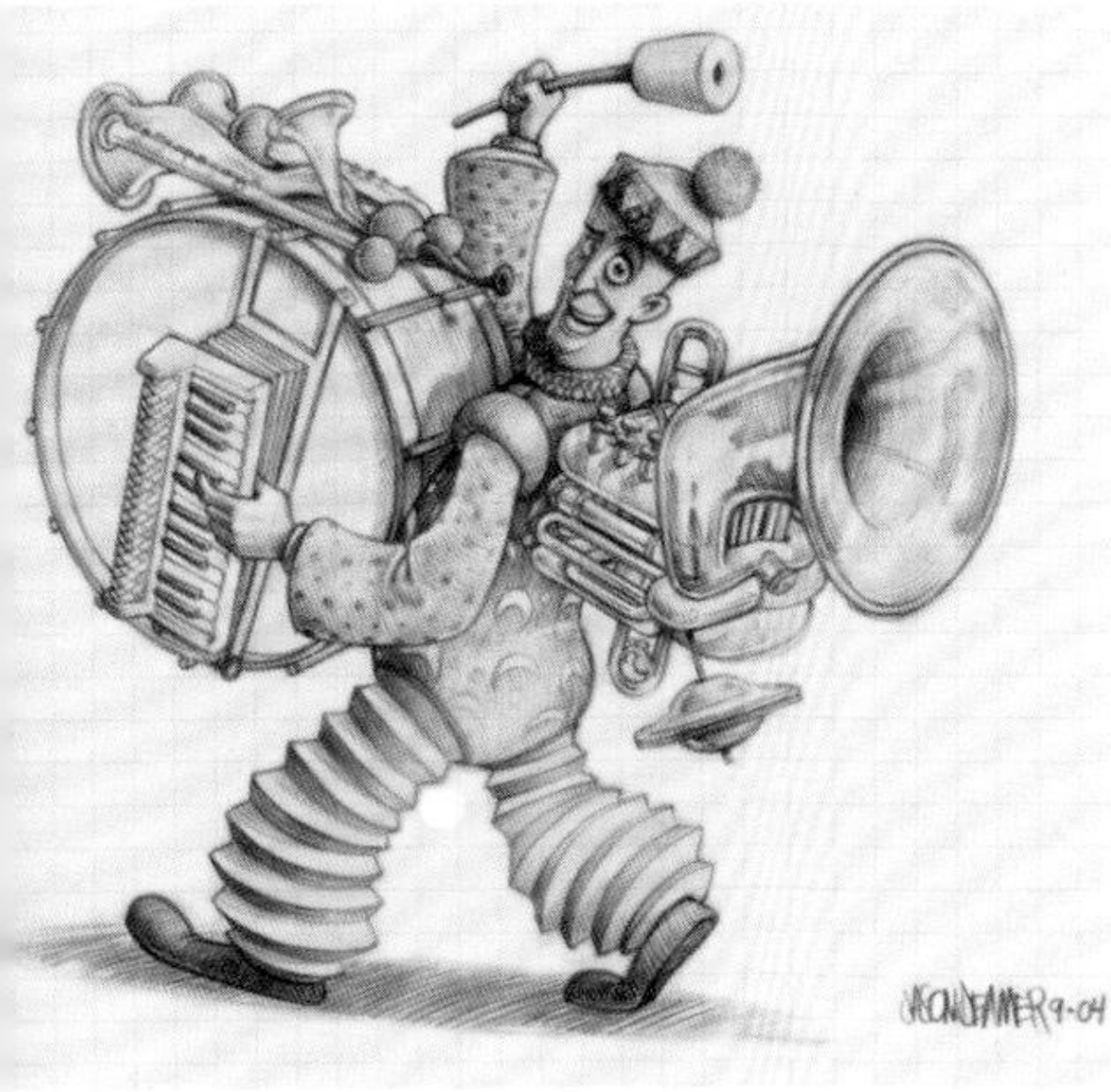

CARS
2006

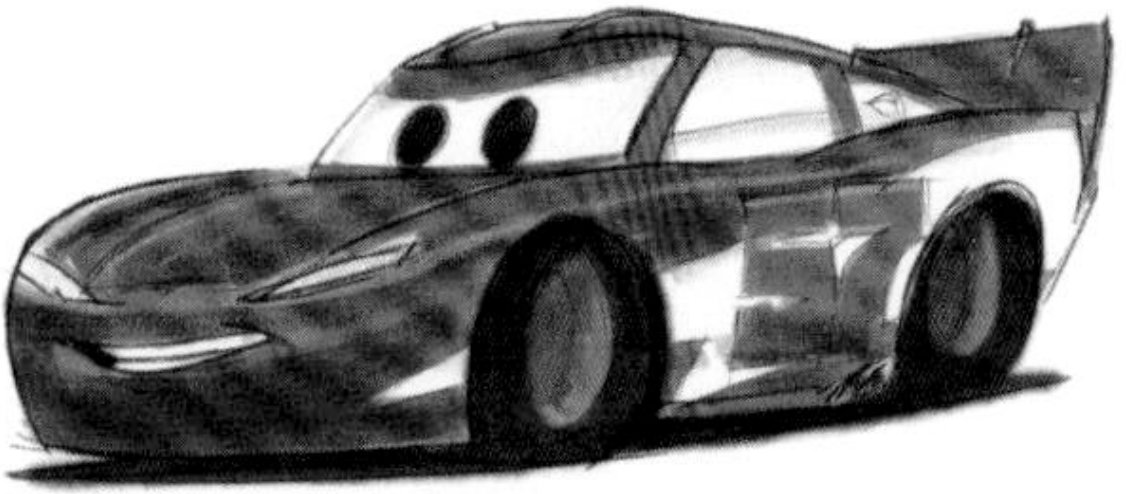

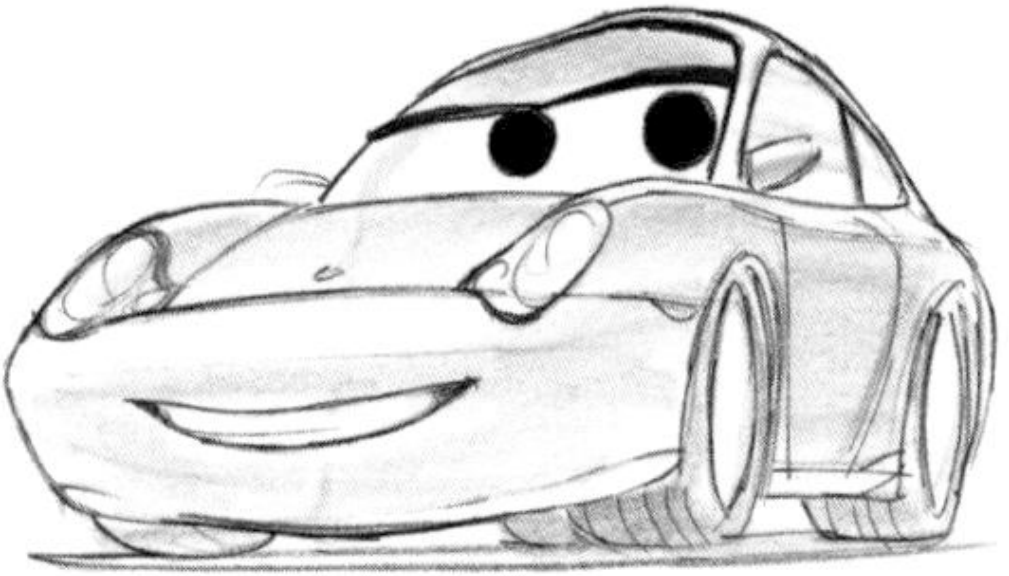

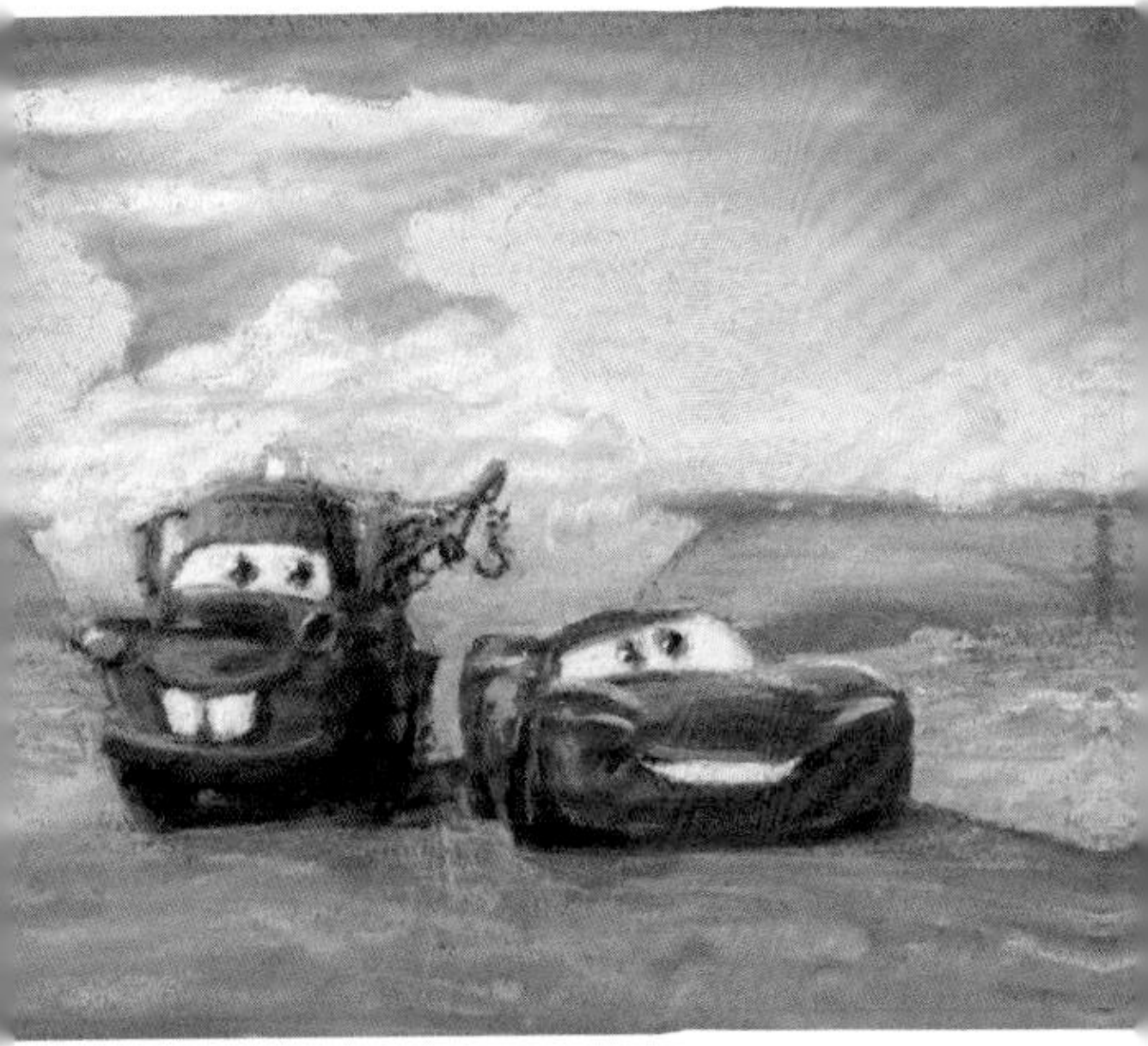

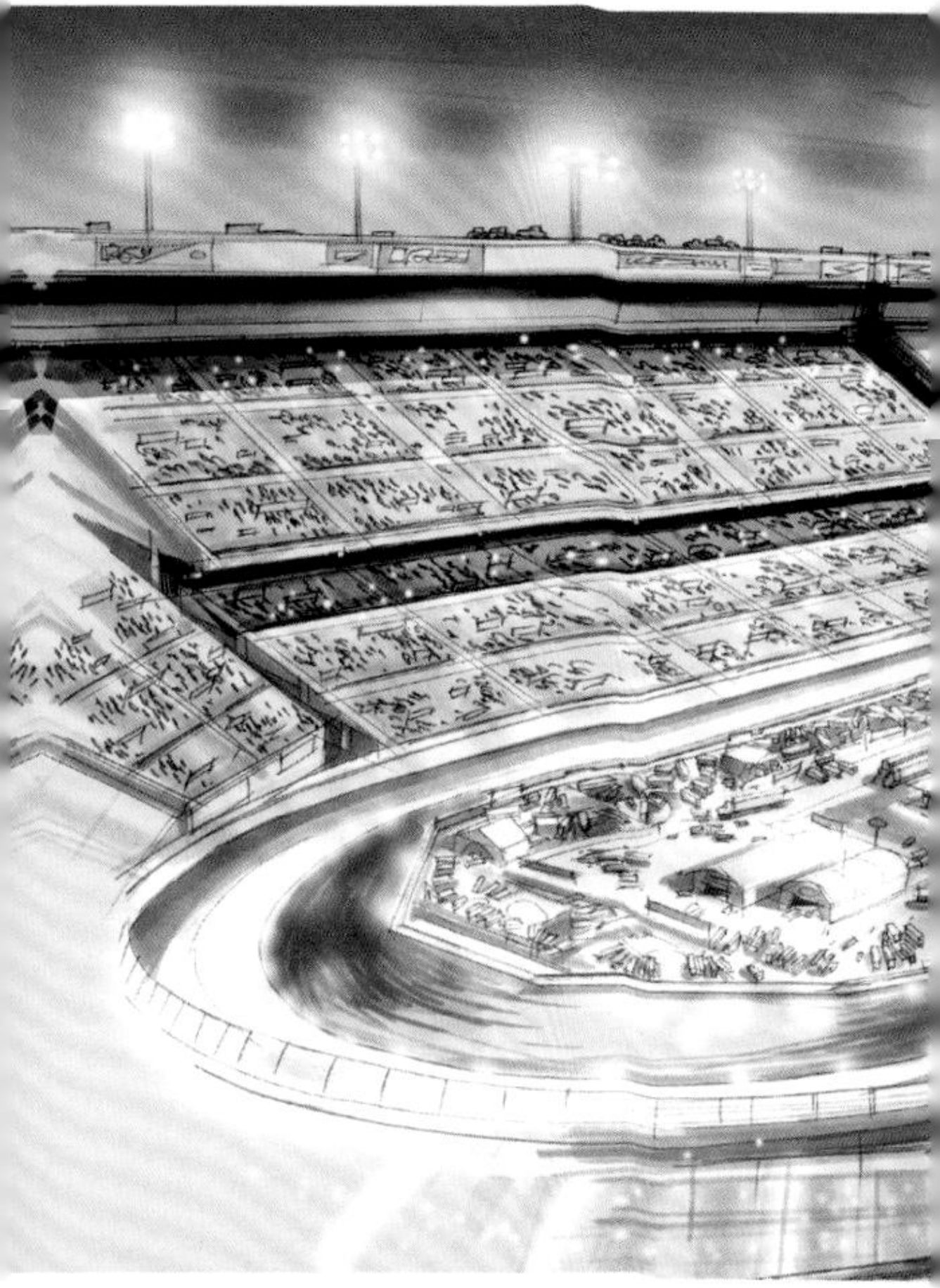

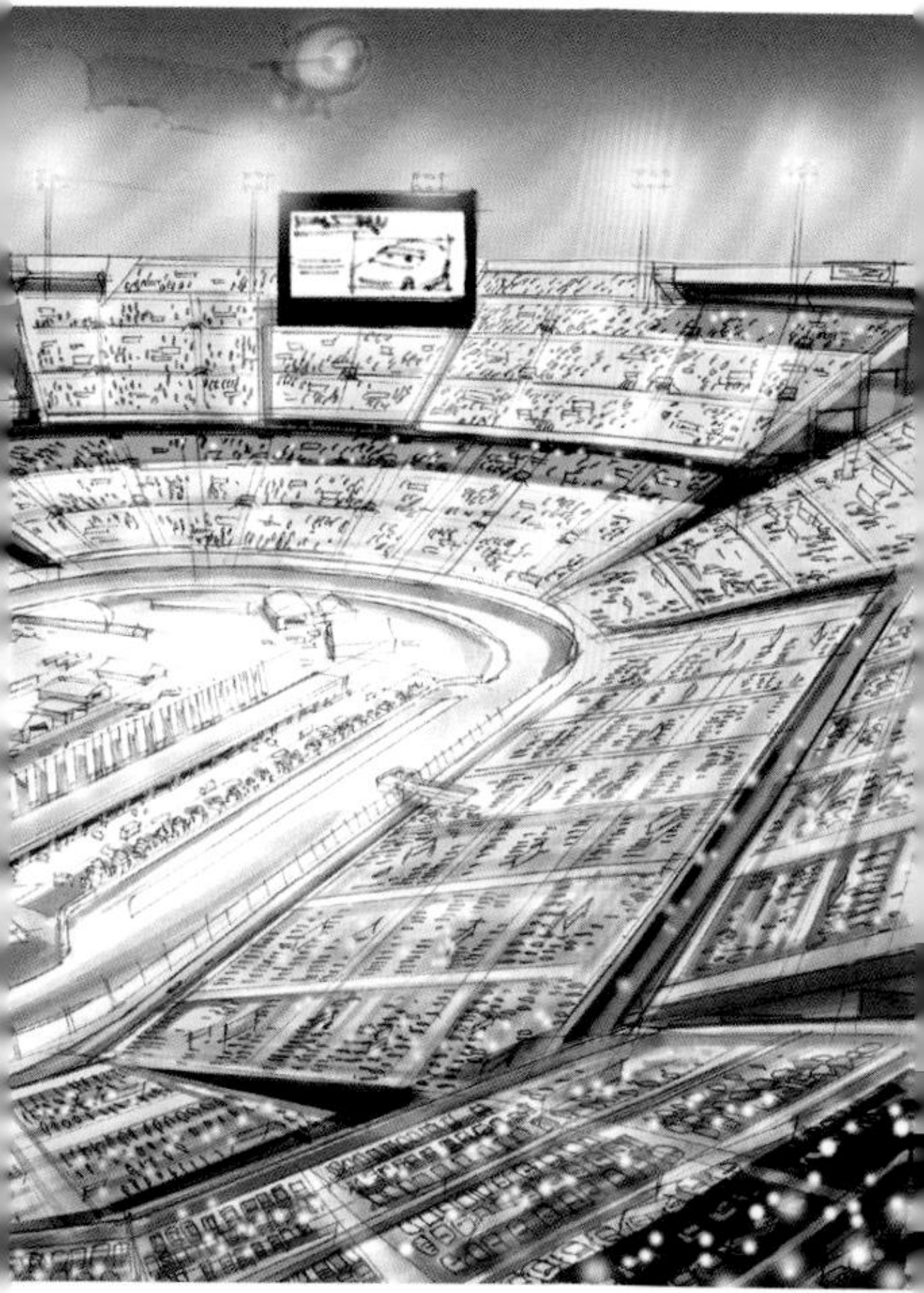

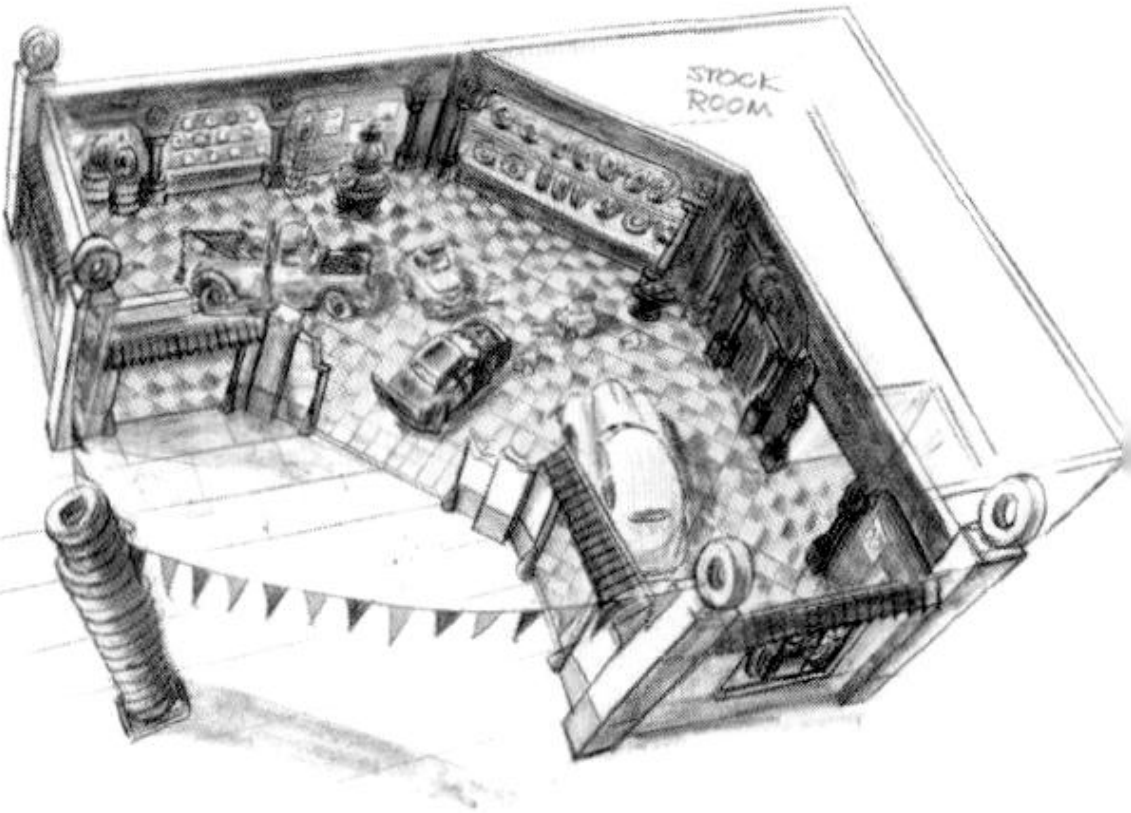
STOCK
ROOM

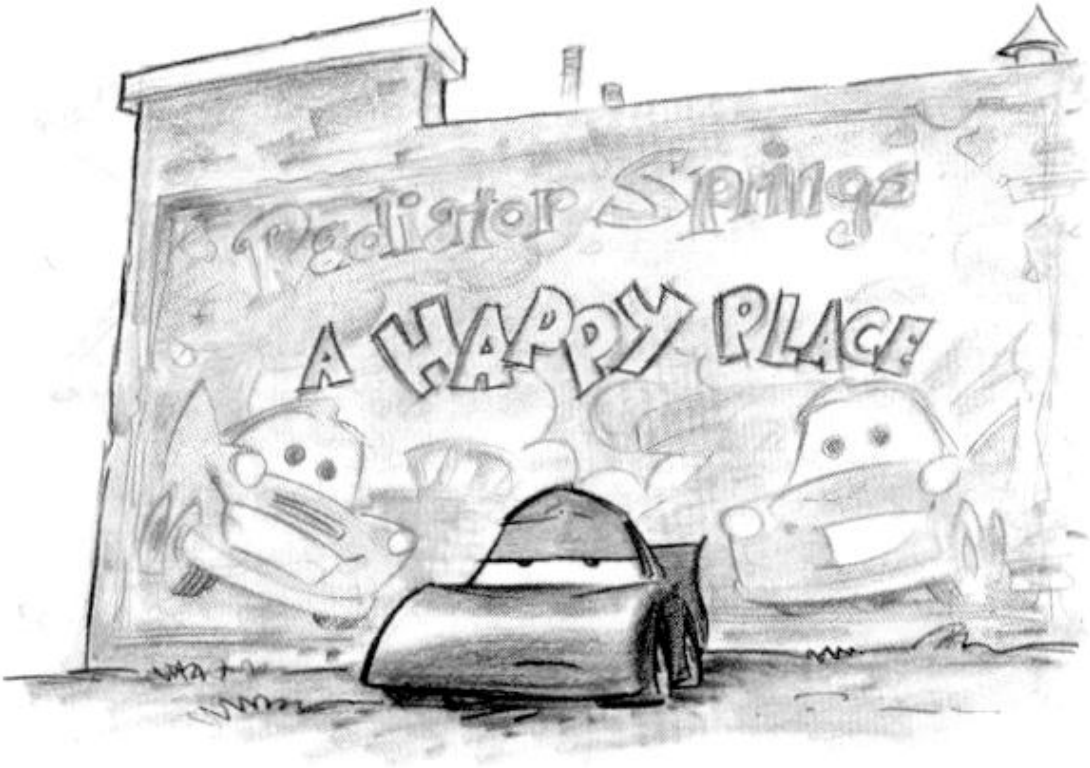
Radiator Springs
A HAPPY PLACE

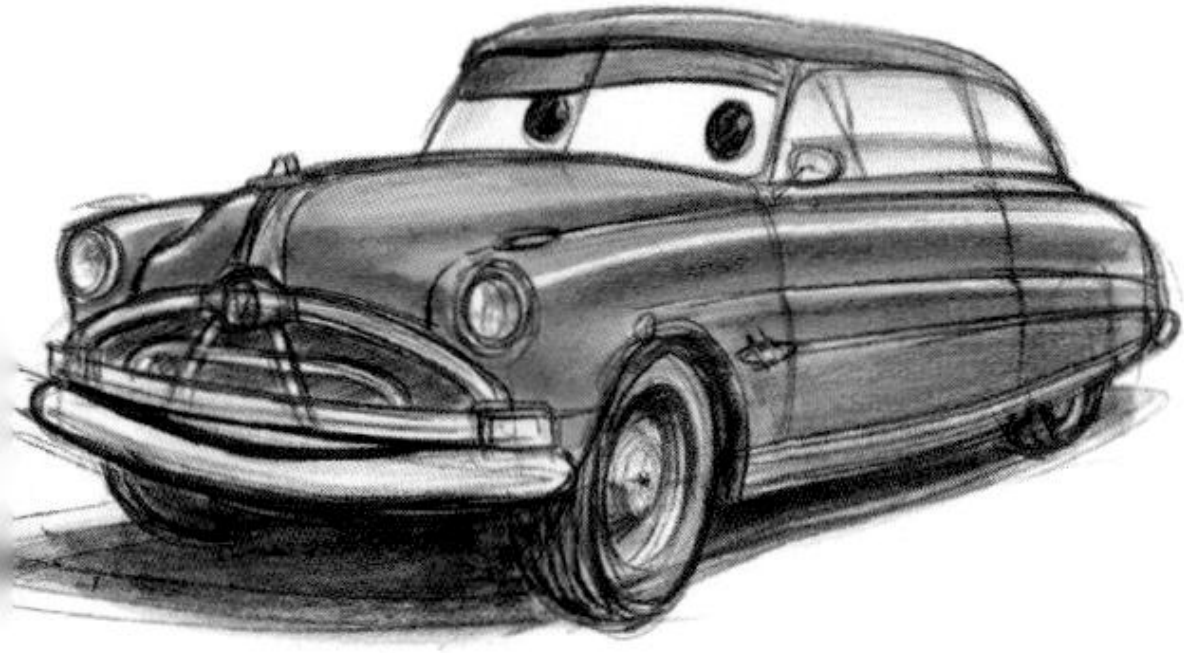

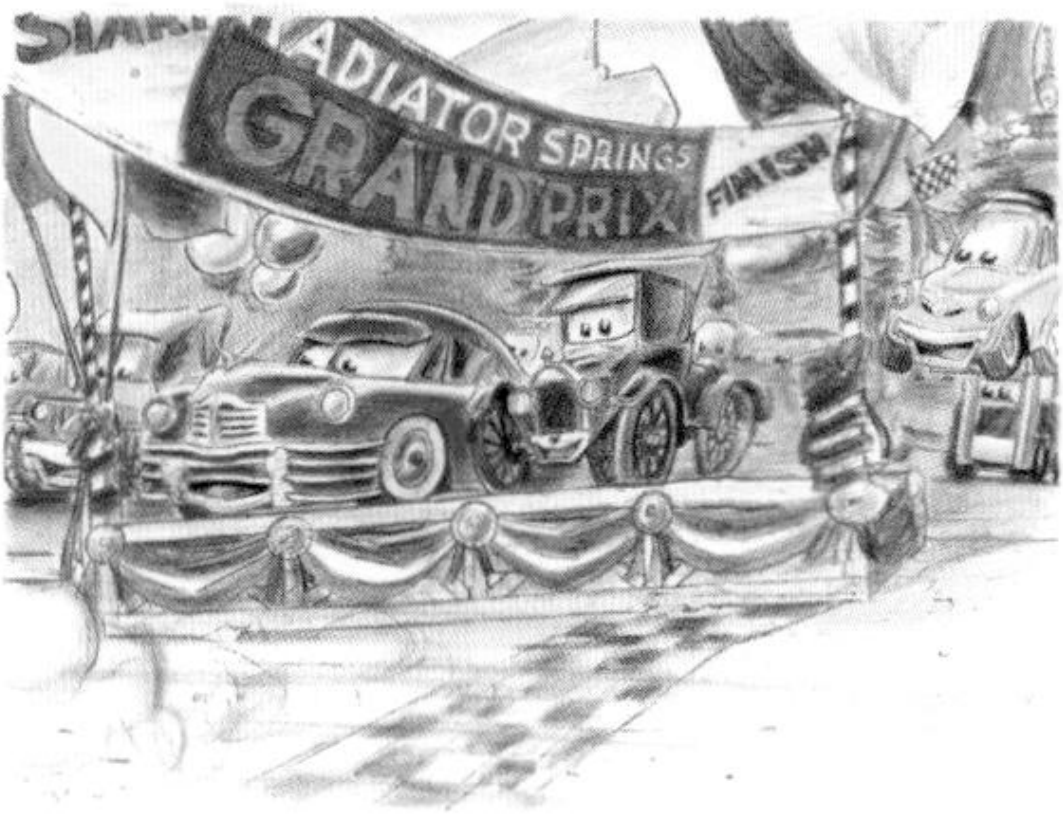
ADIATOR SPRINGS
GRAND PRIX
FINISH

SHORT
LIFTED
2006

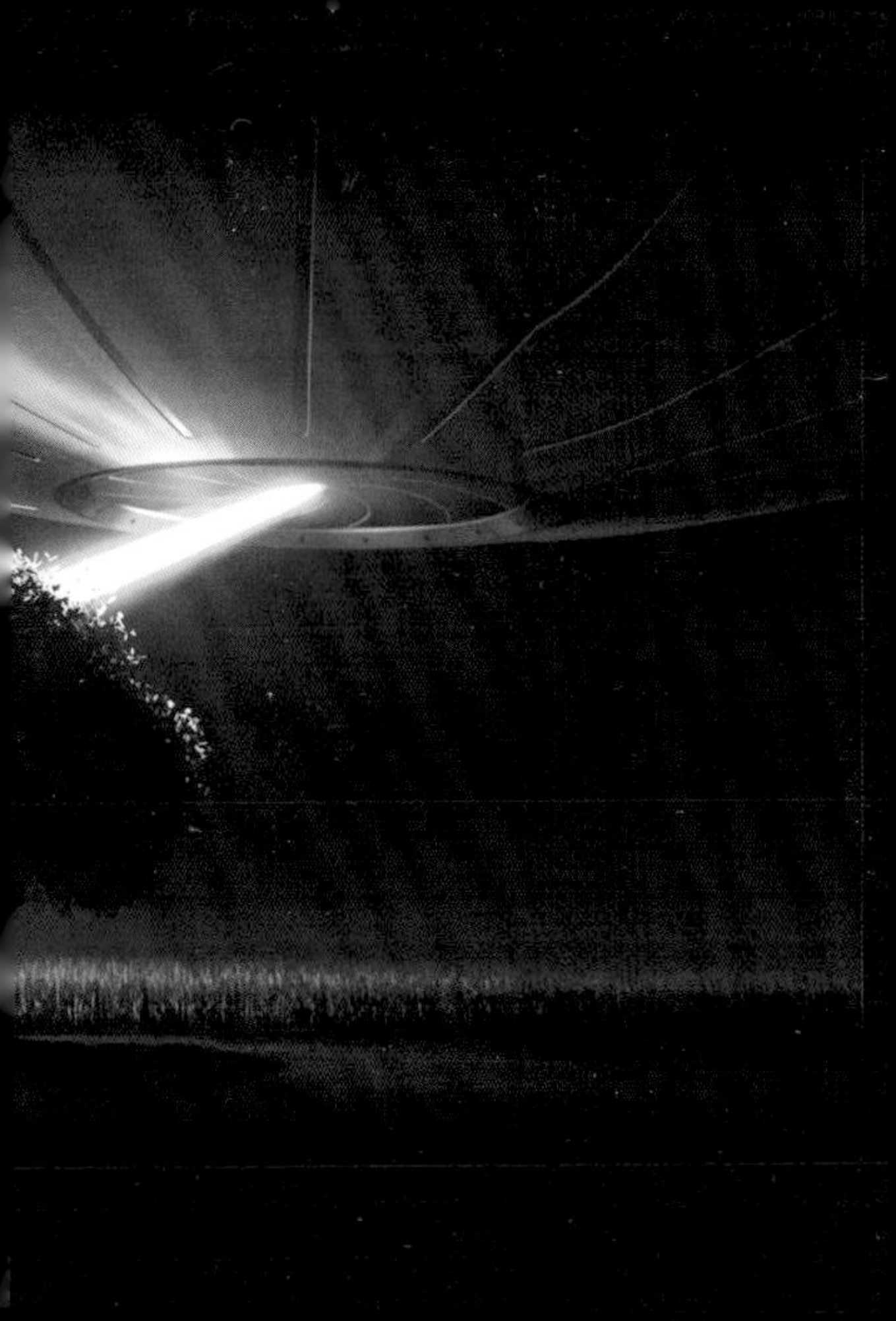

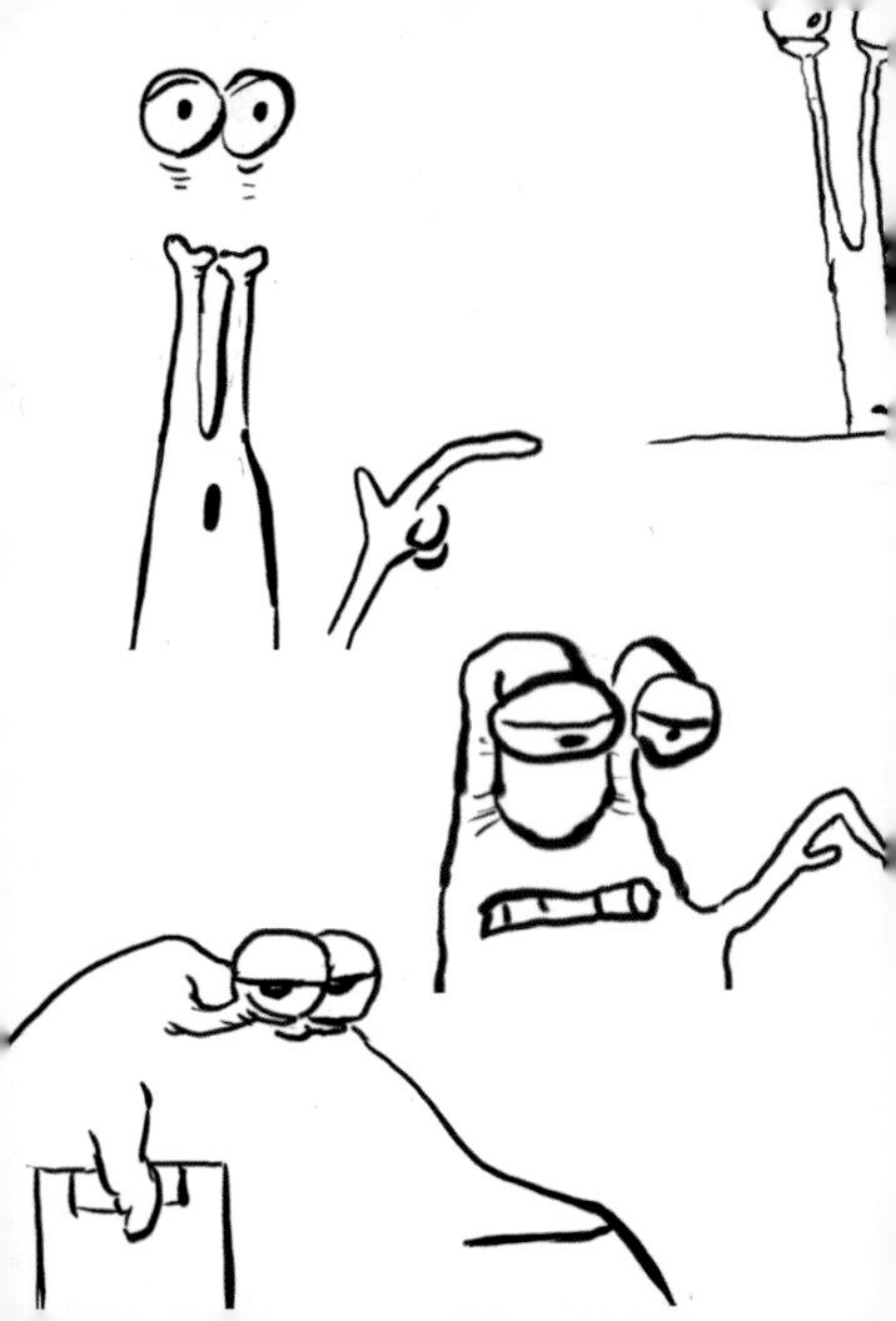

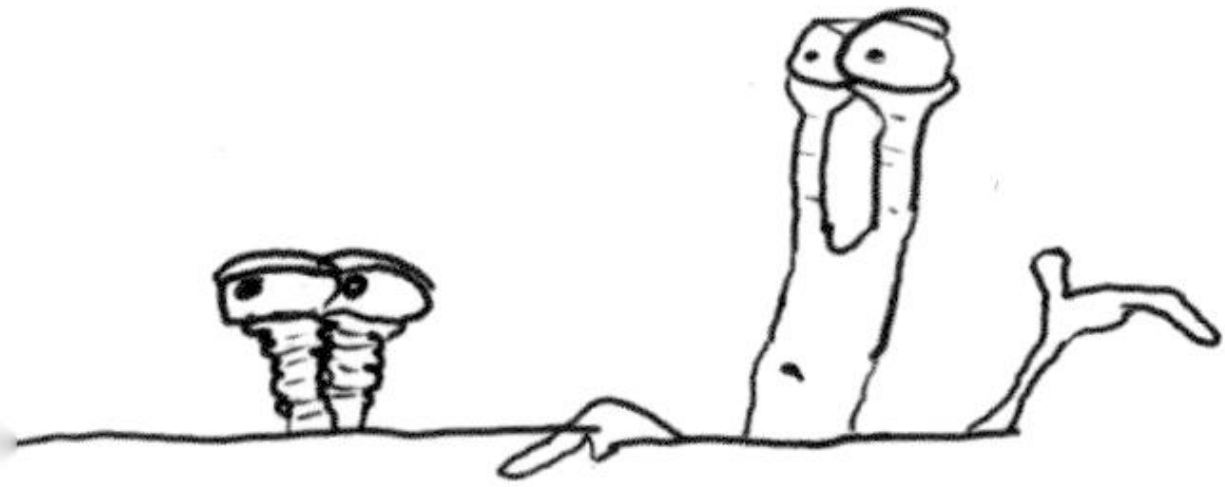

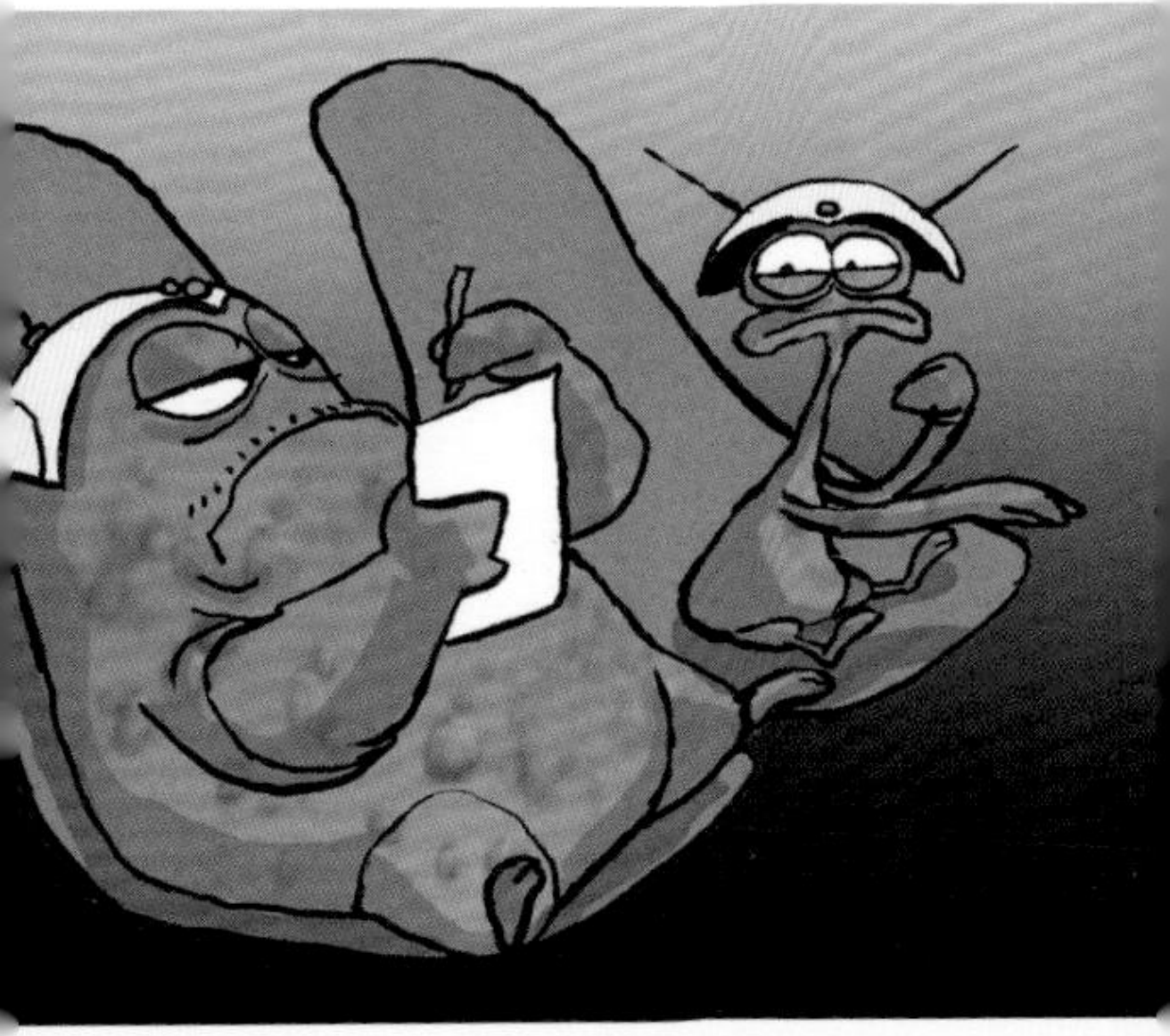

RATATOUILLE
2007

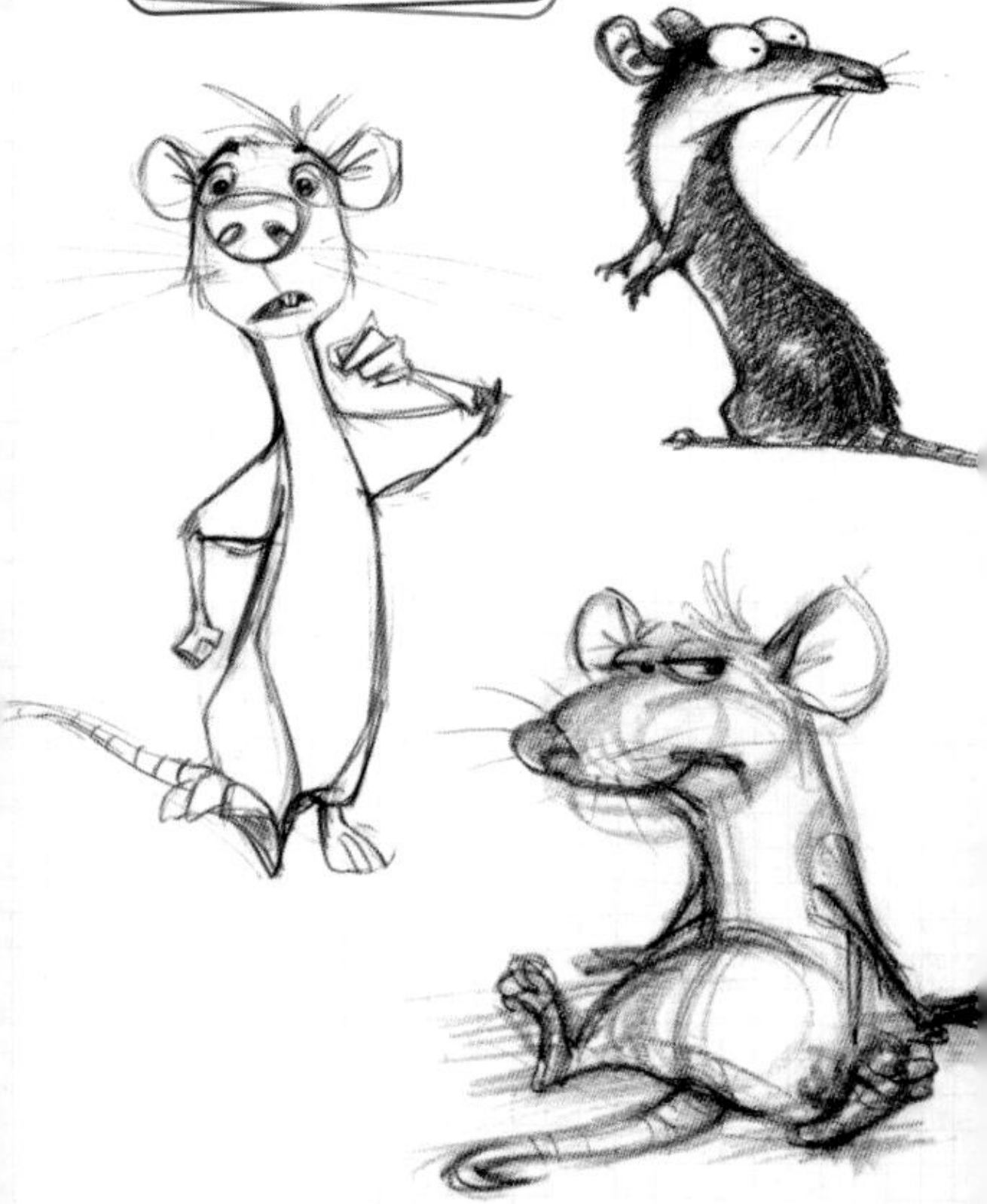

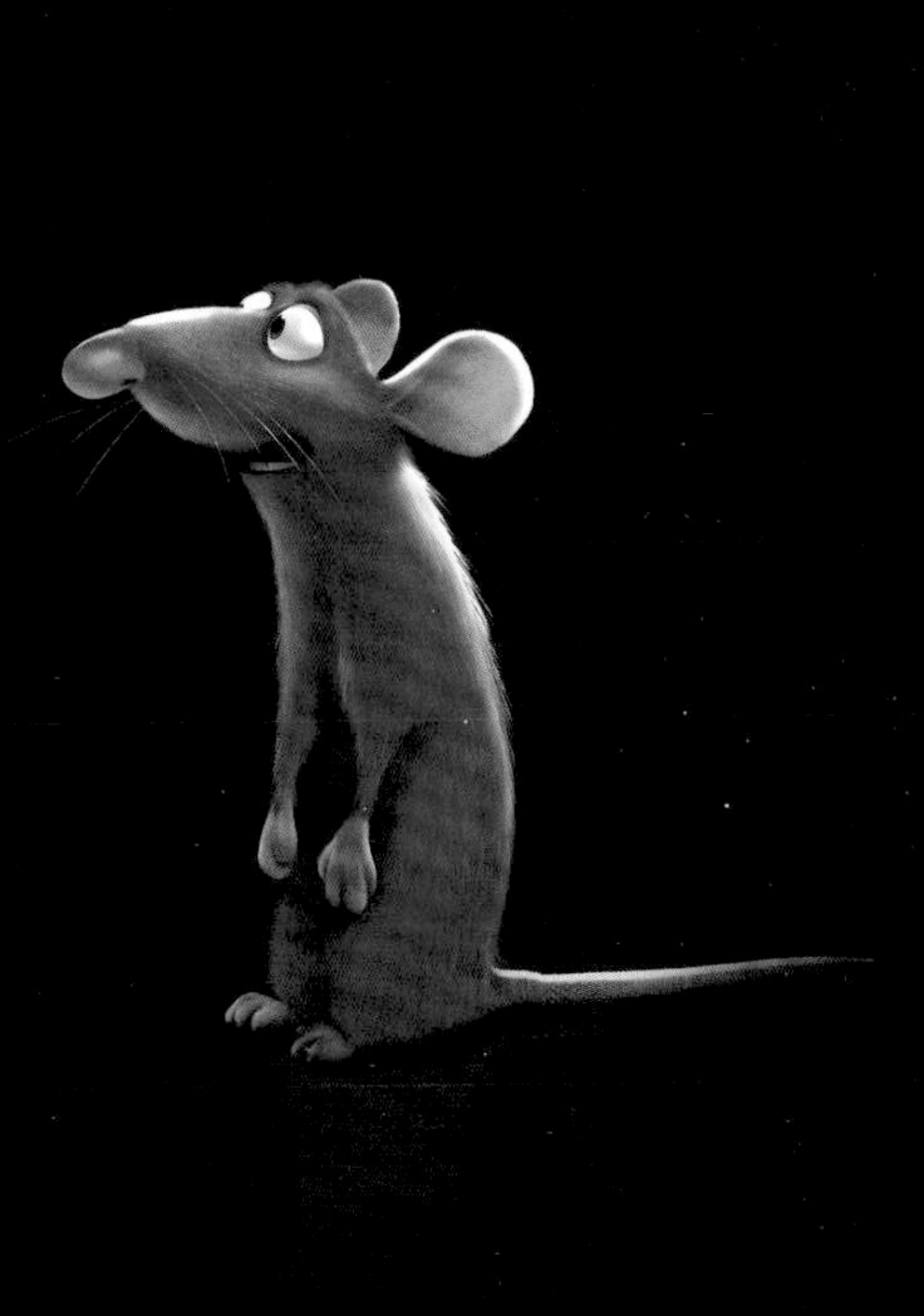

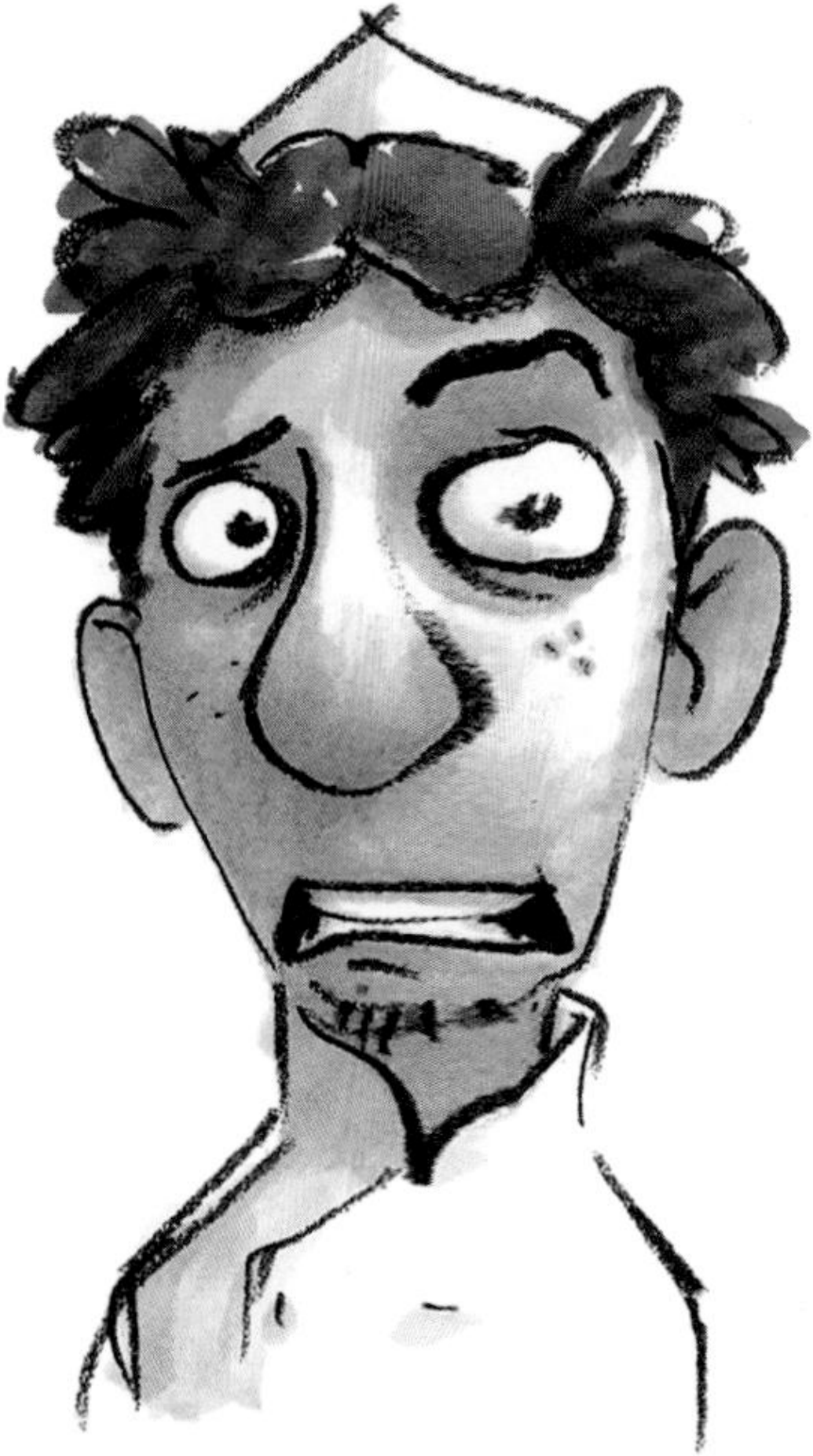

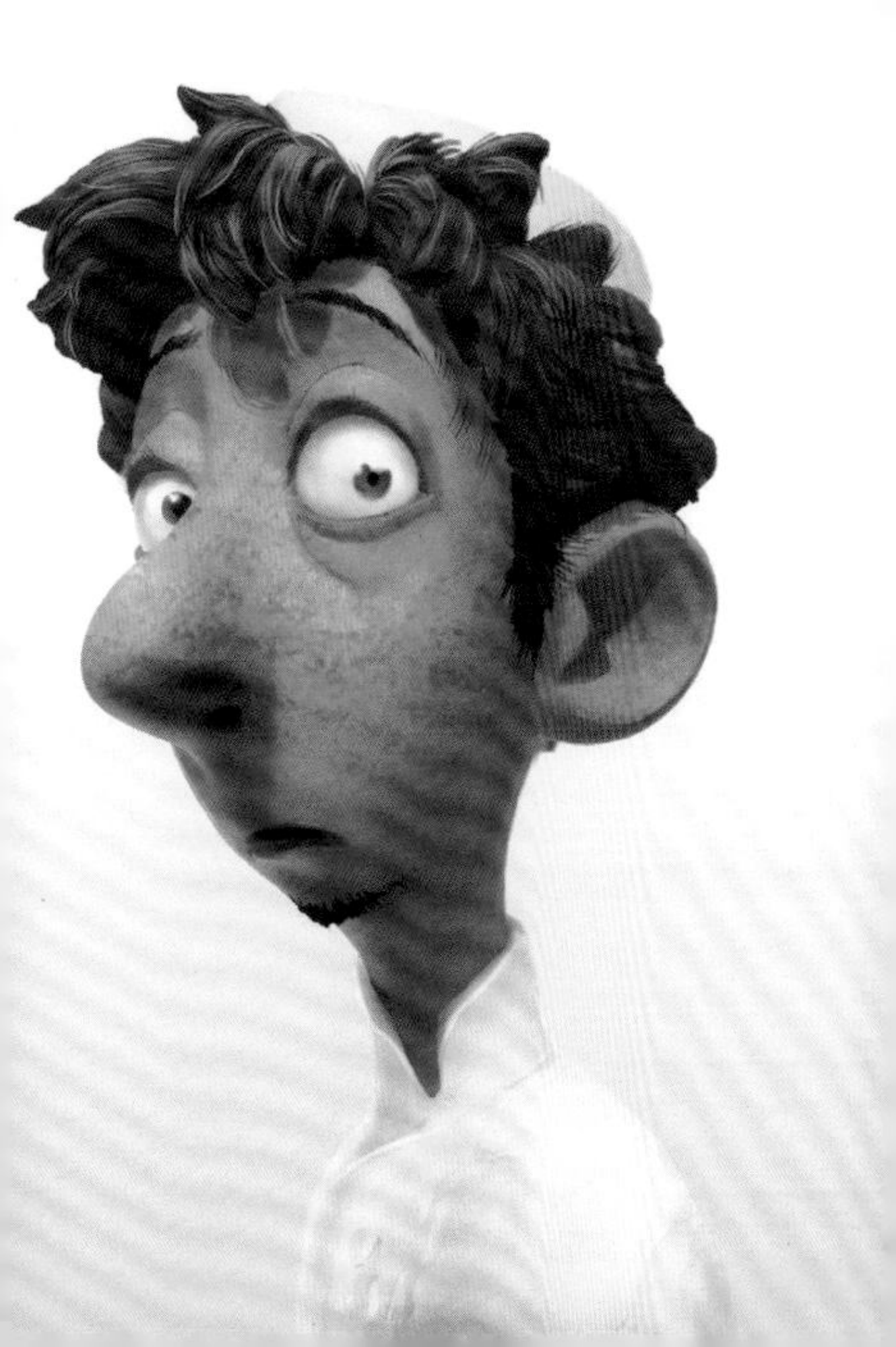

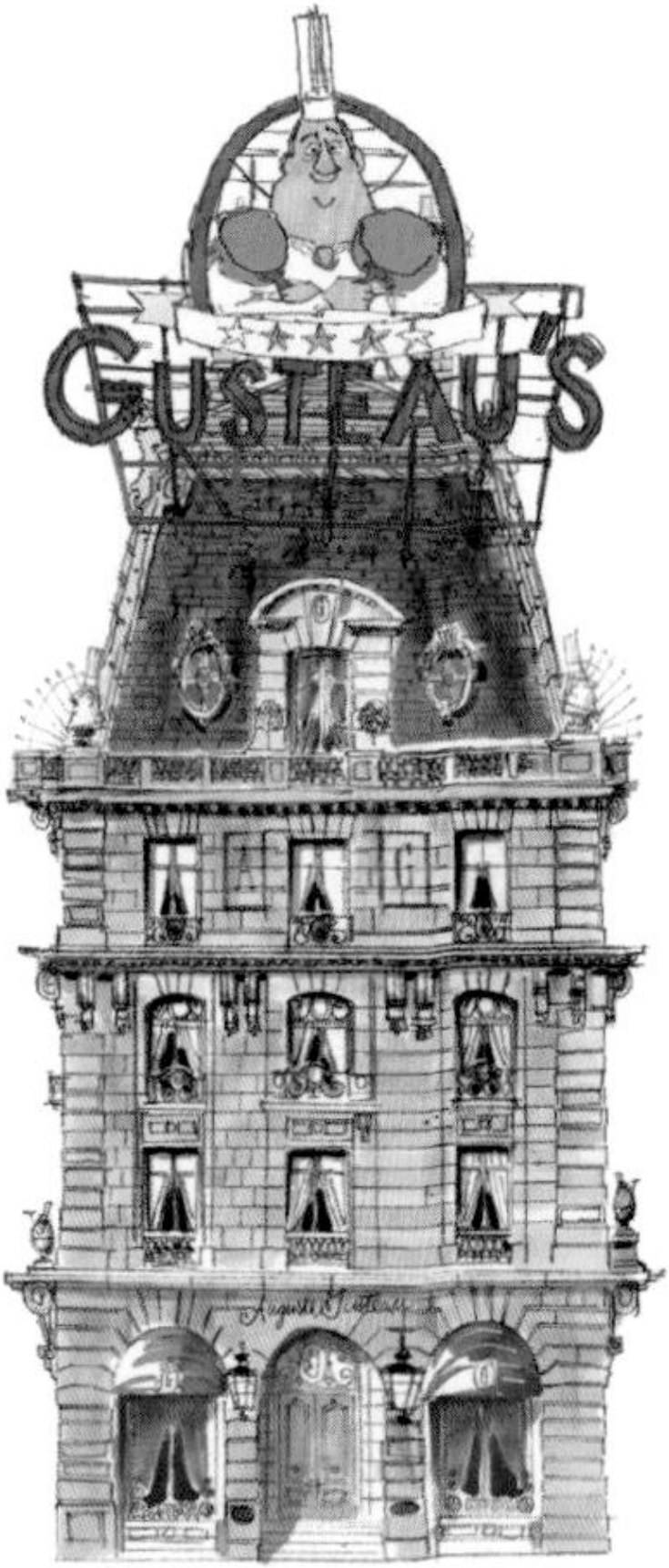
GUSTEAU'S

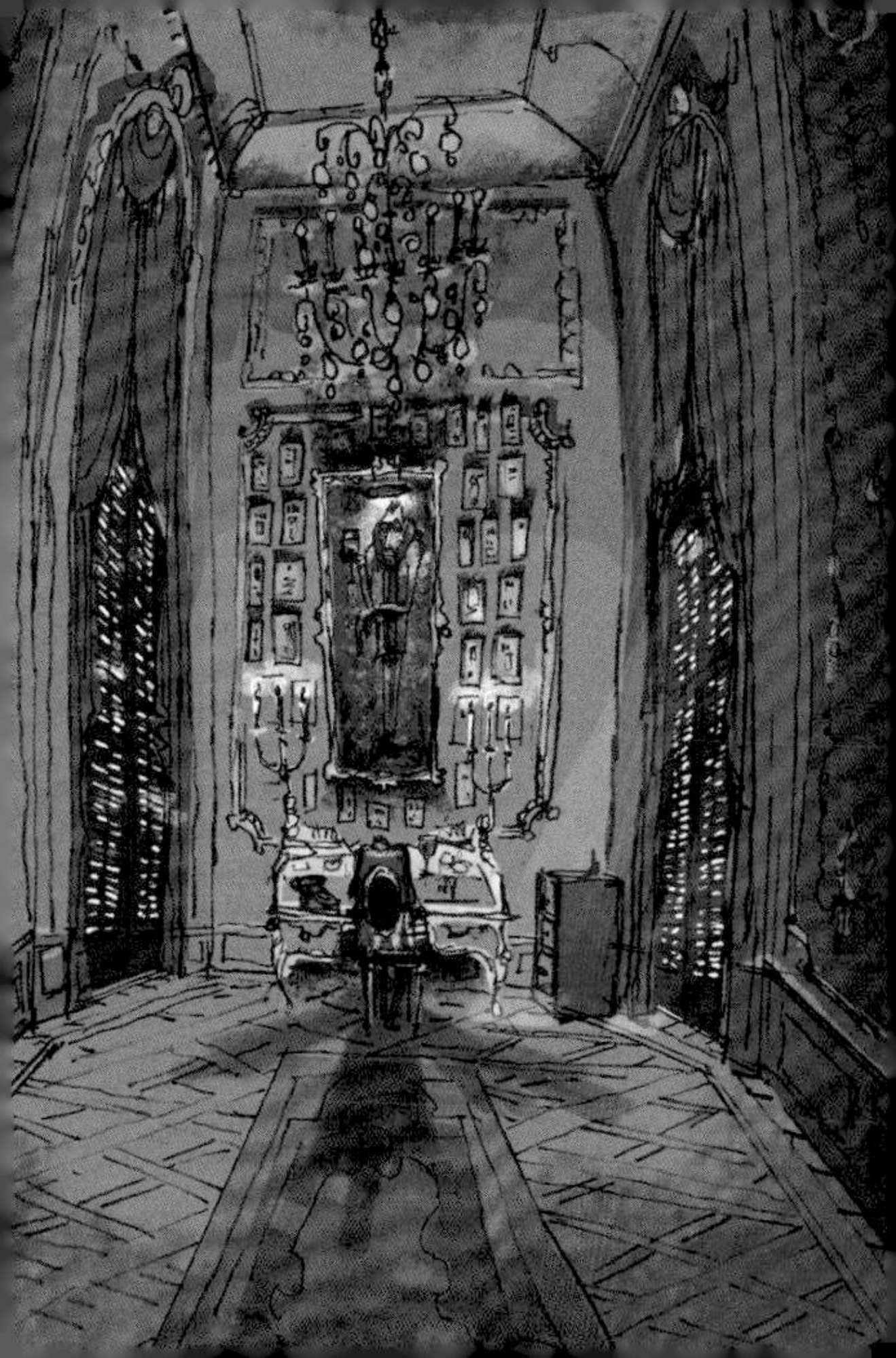

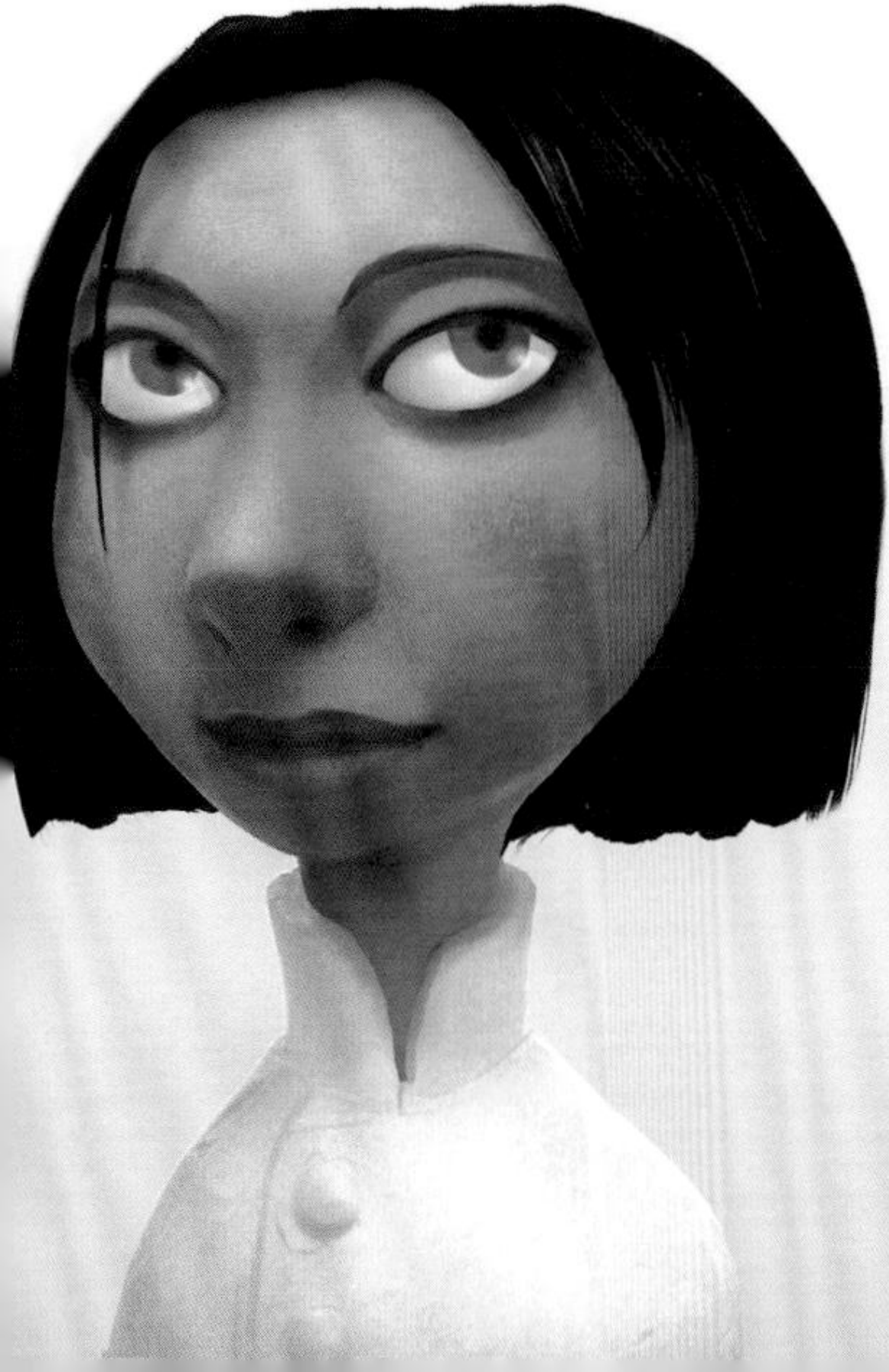

SHORT

PRESTO

2008

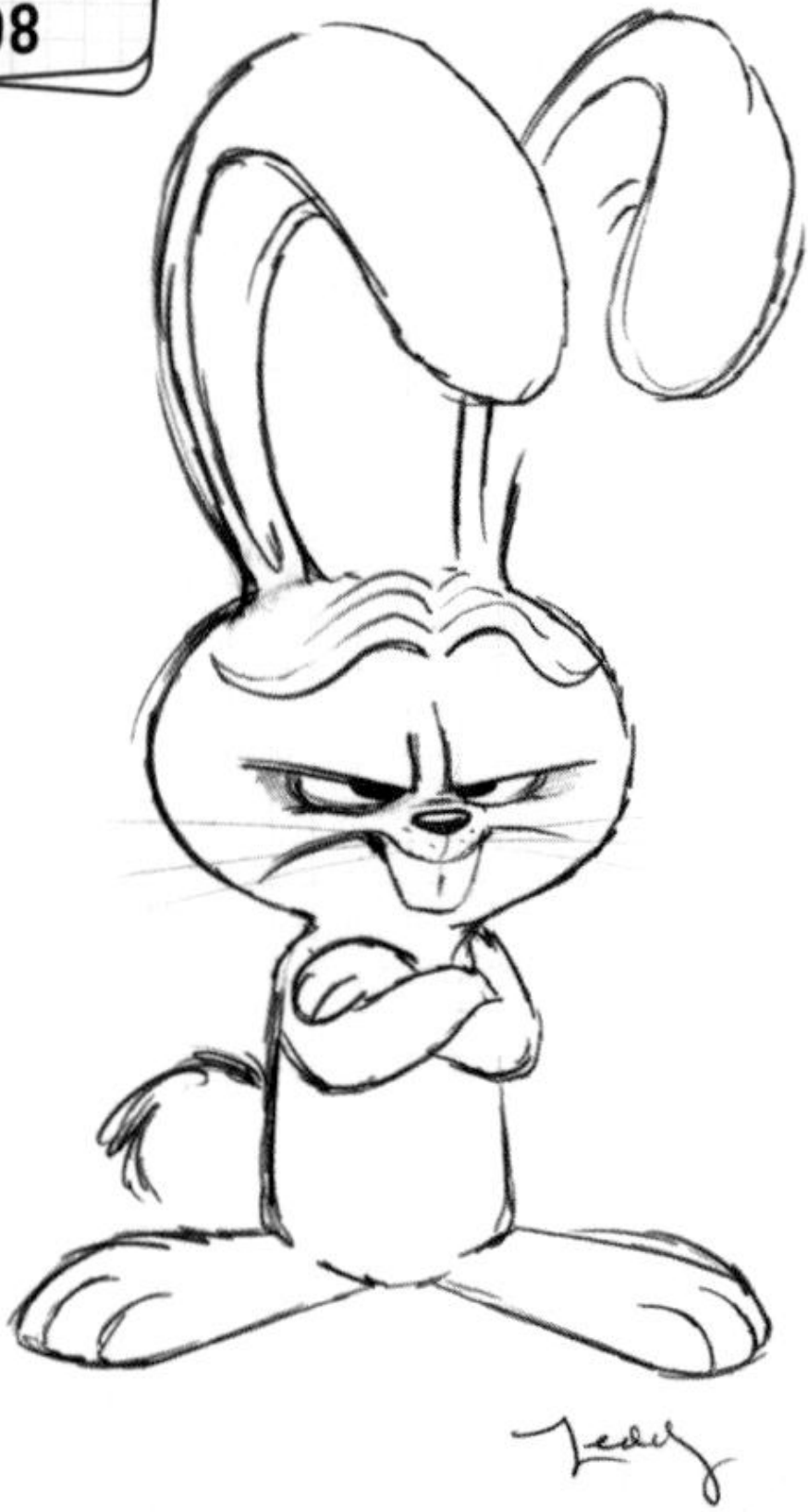

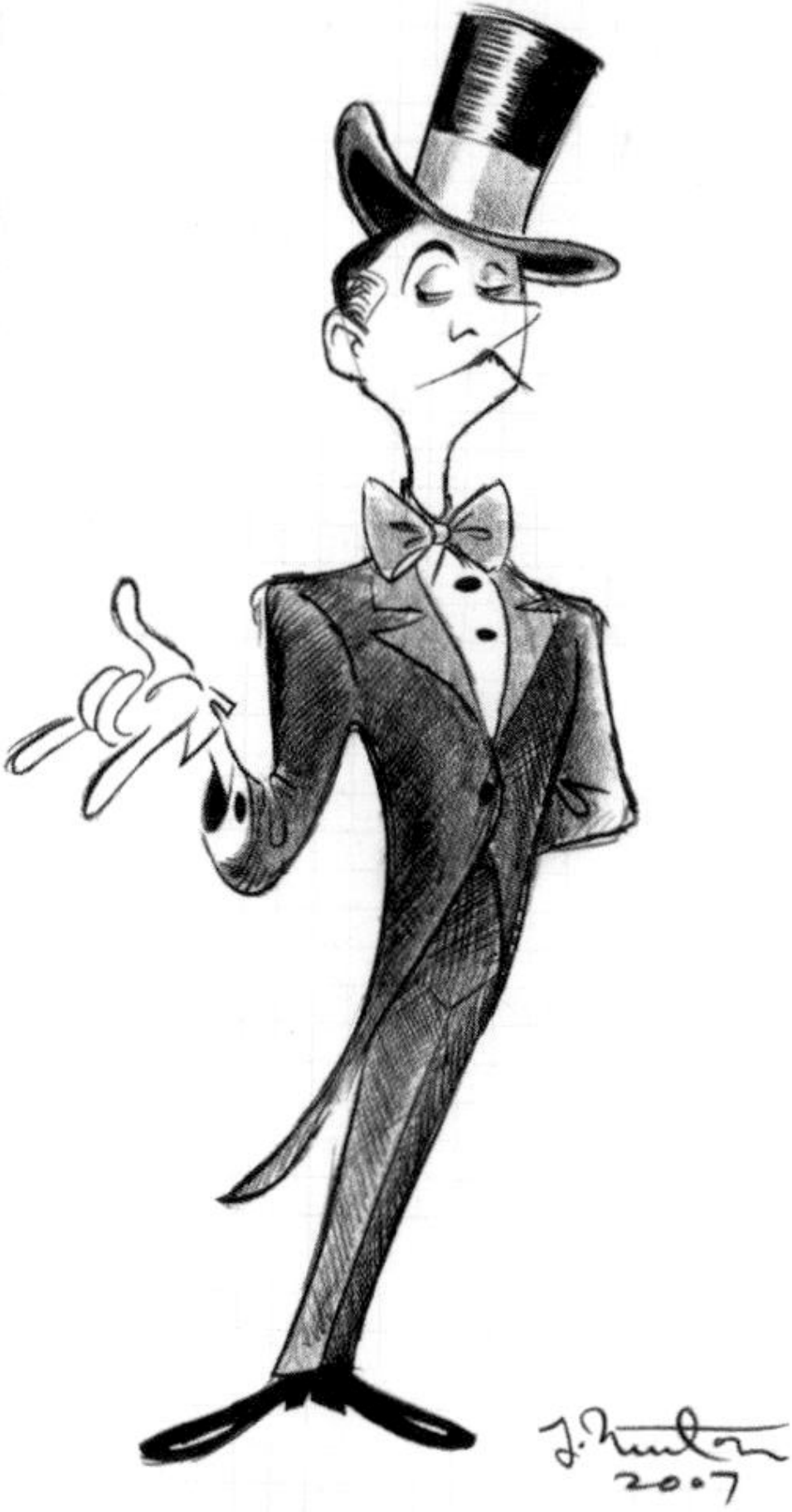
2007

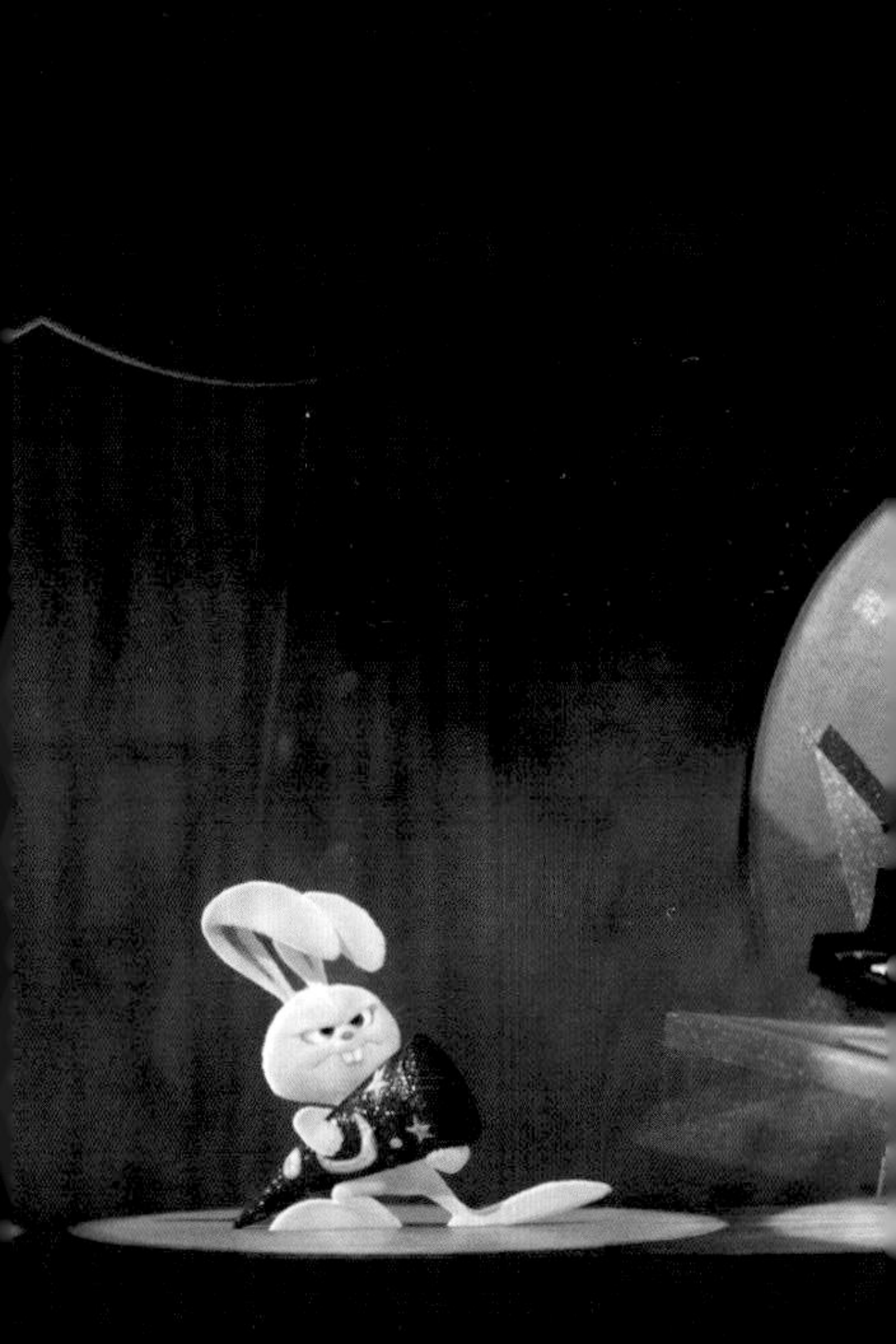

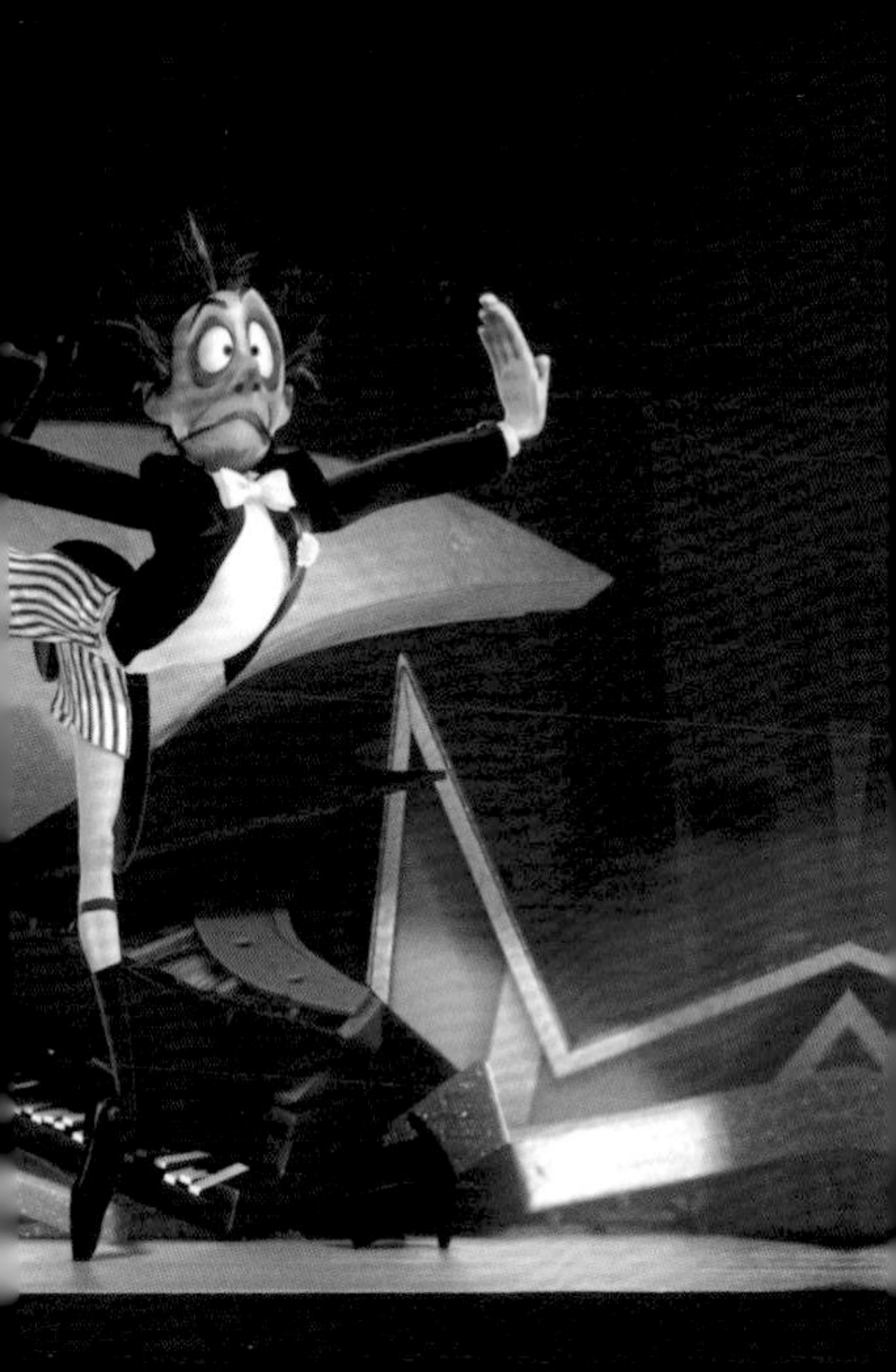

WALL-E
2008

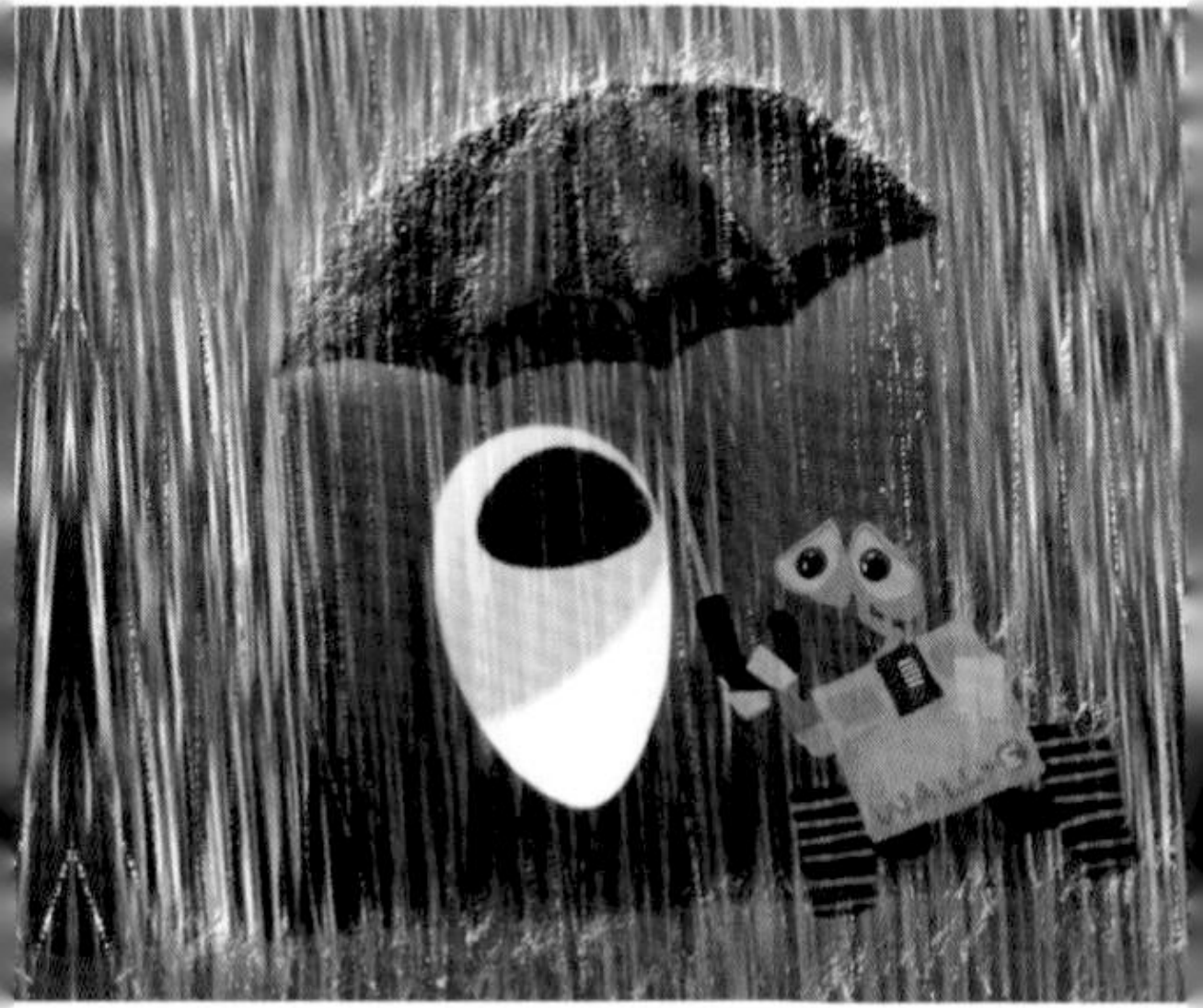

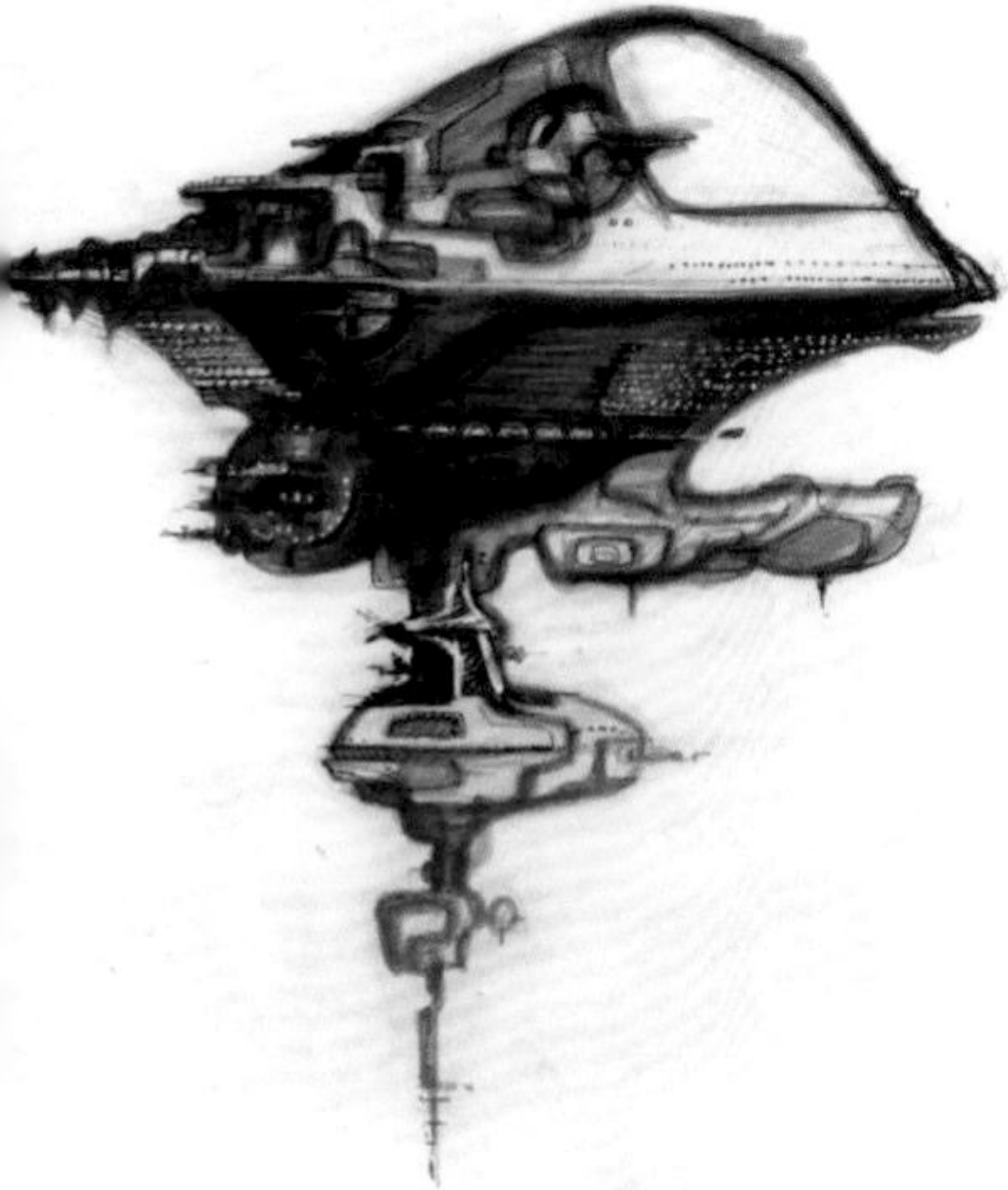

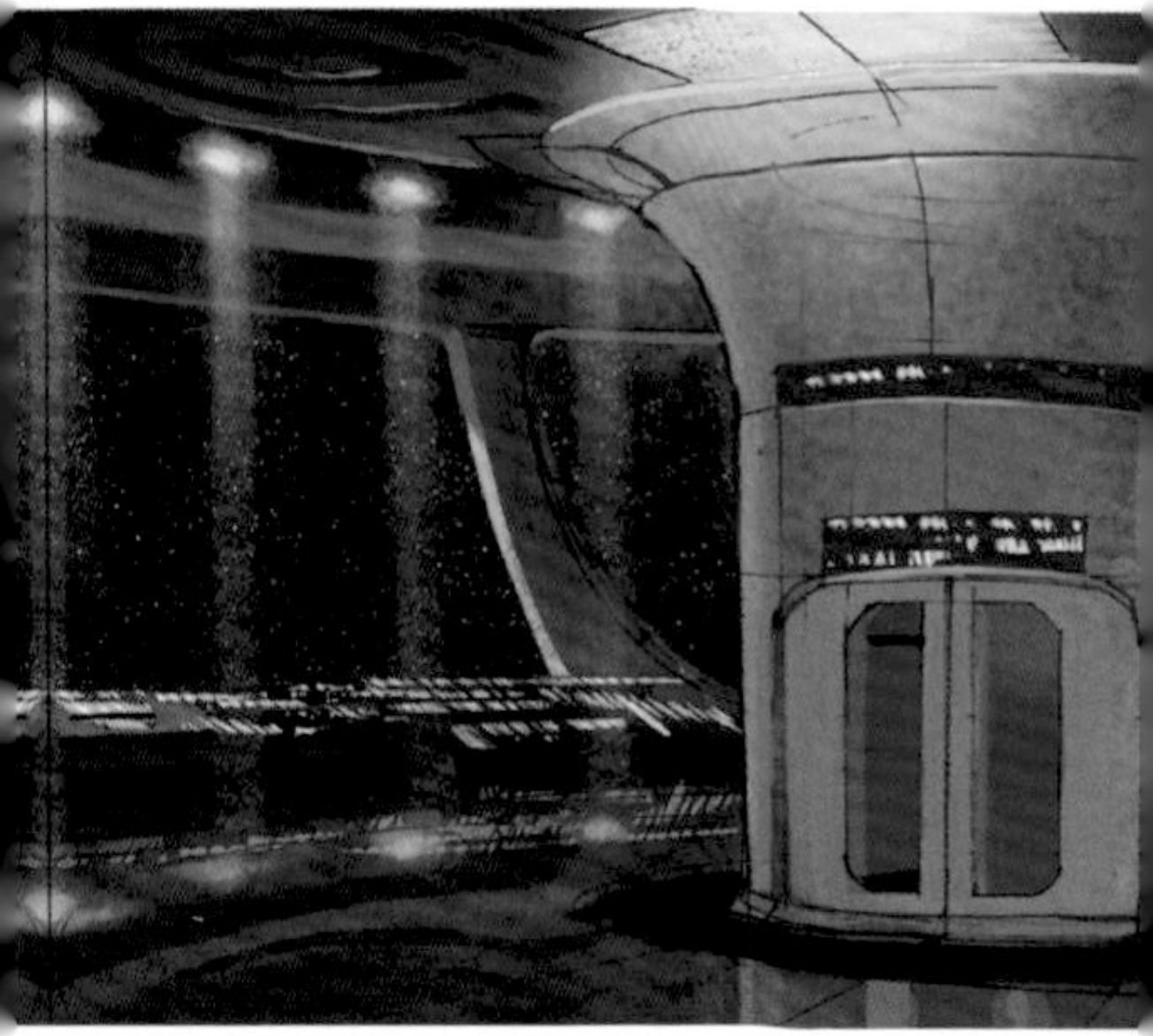

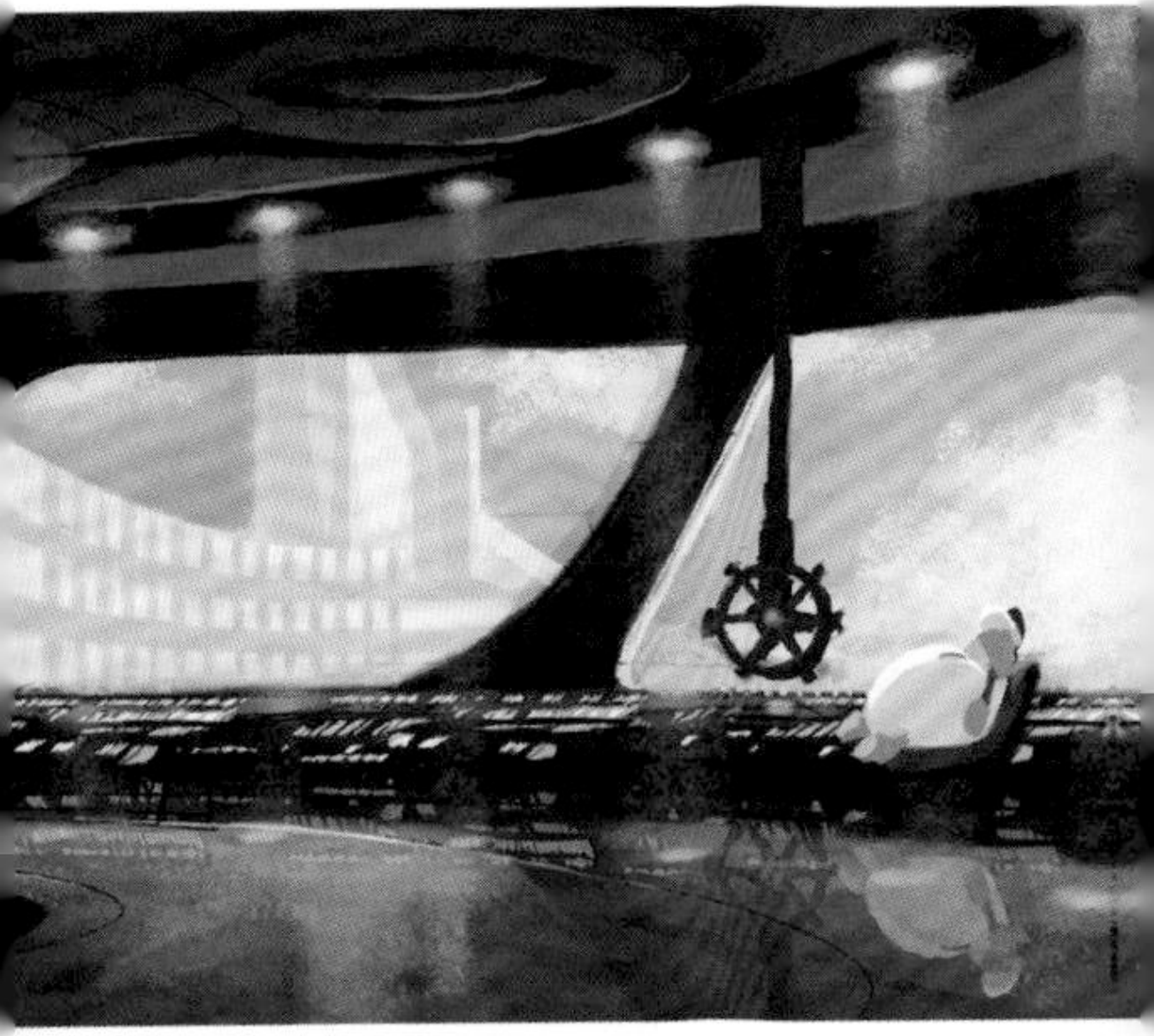

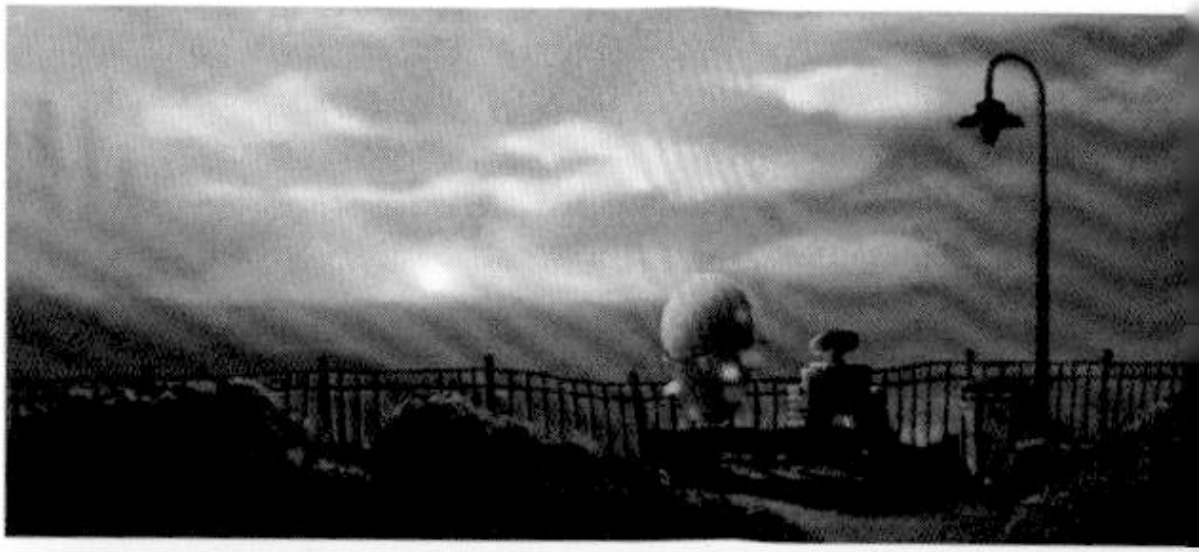

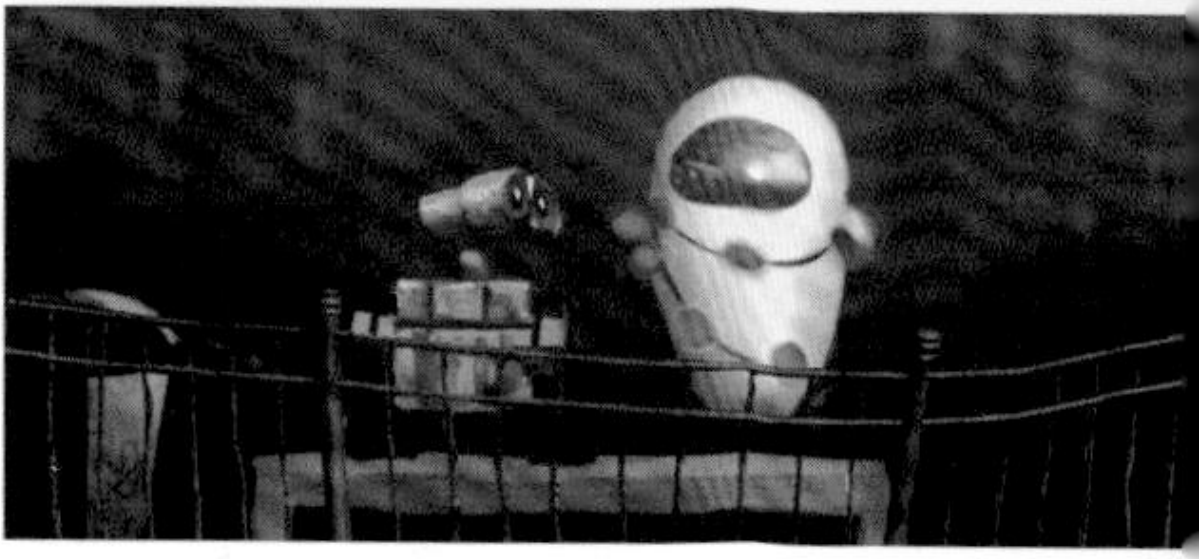

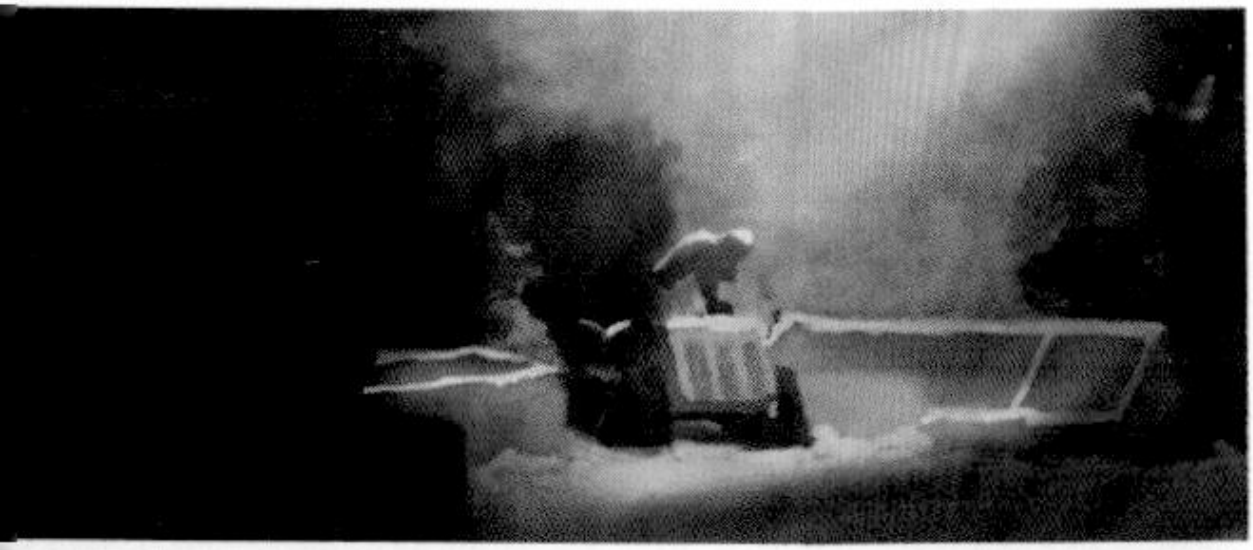

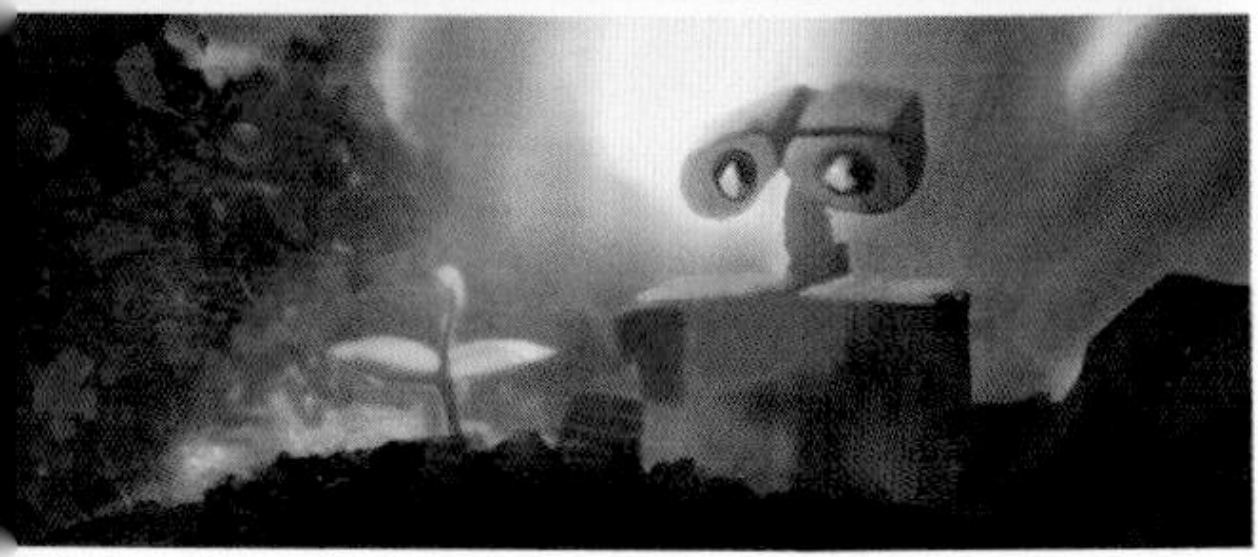

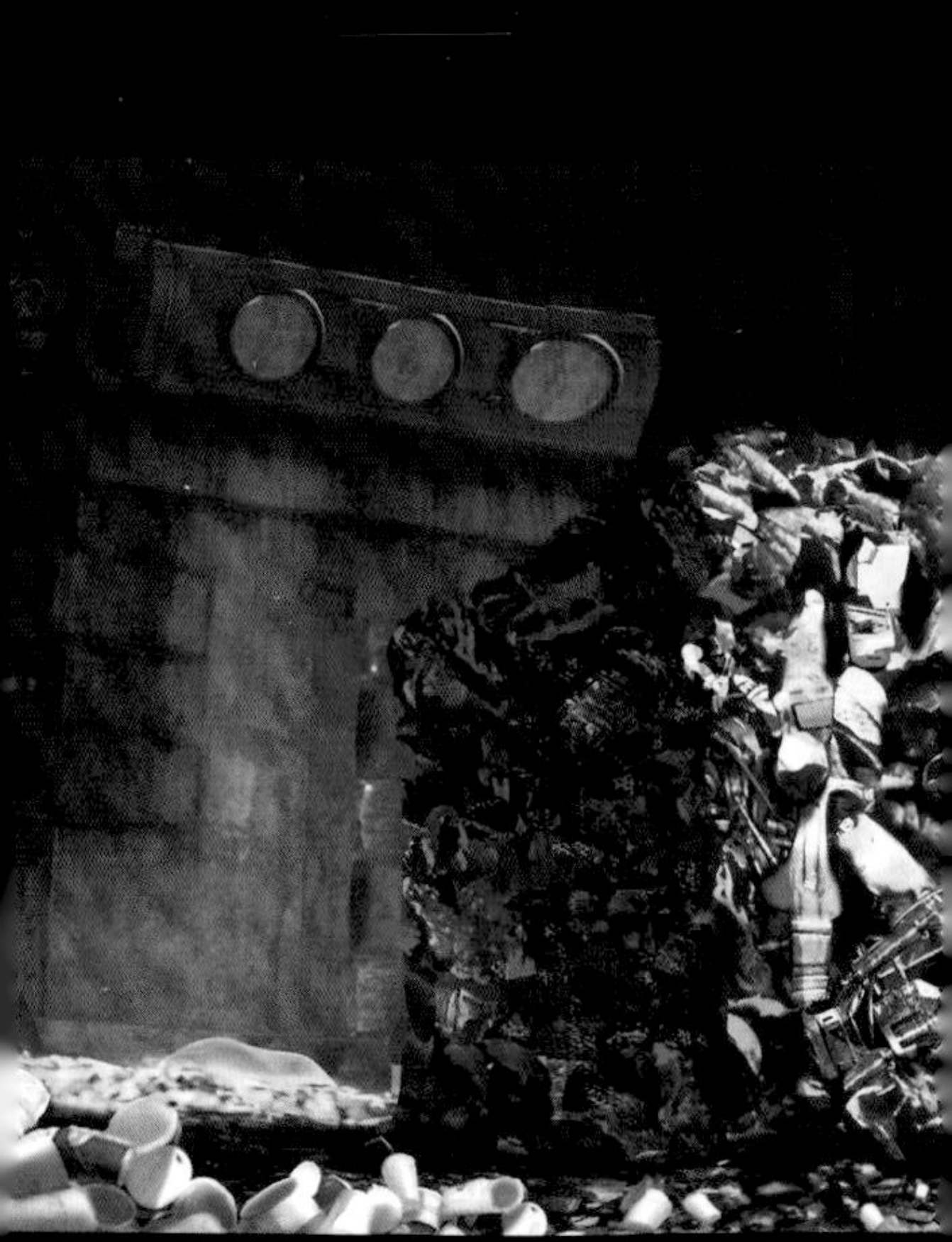

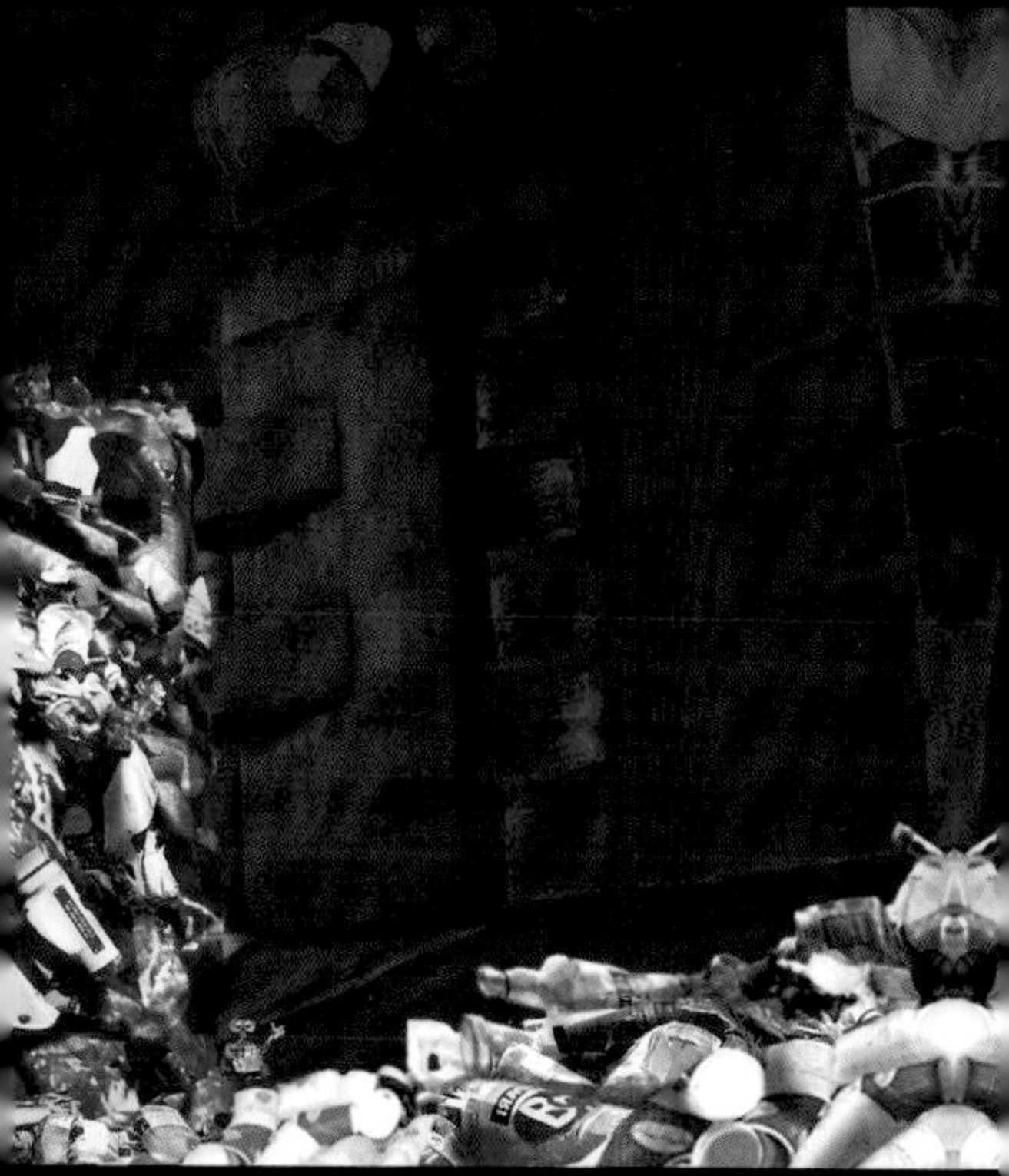

SHORT

PARTLY CLOUDY

2009

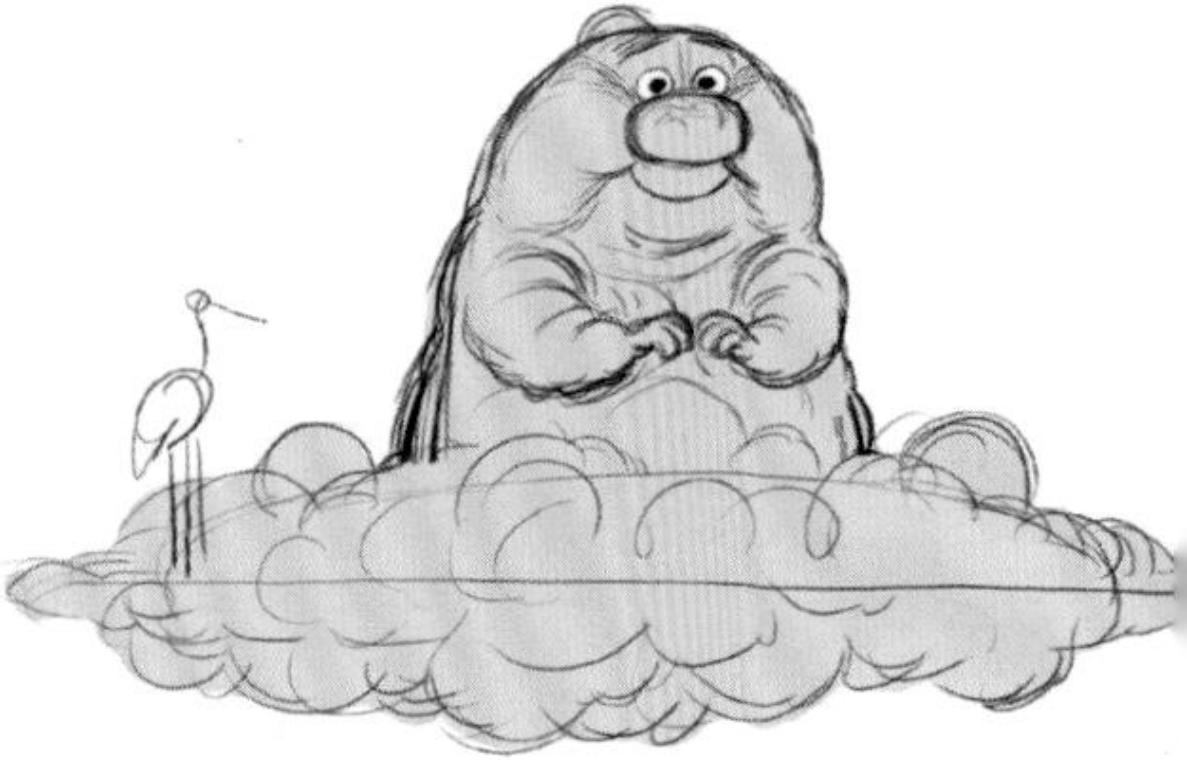

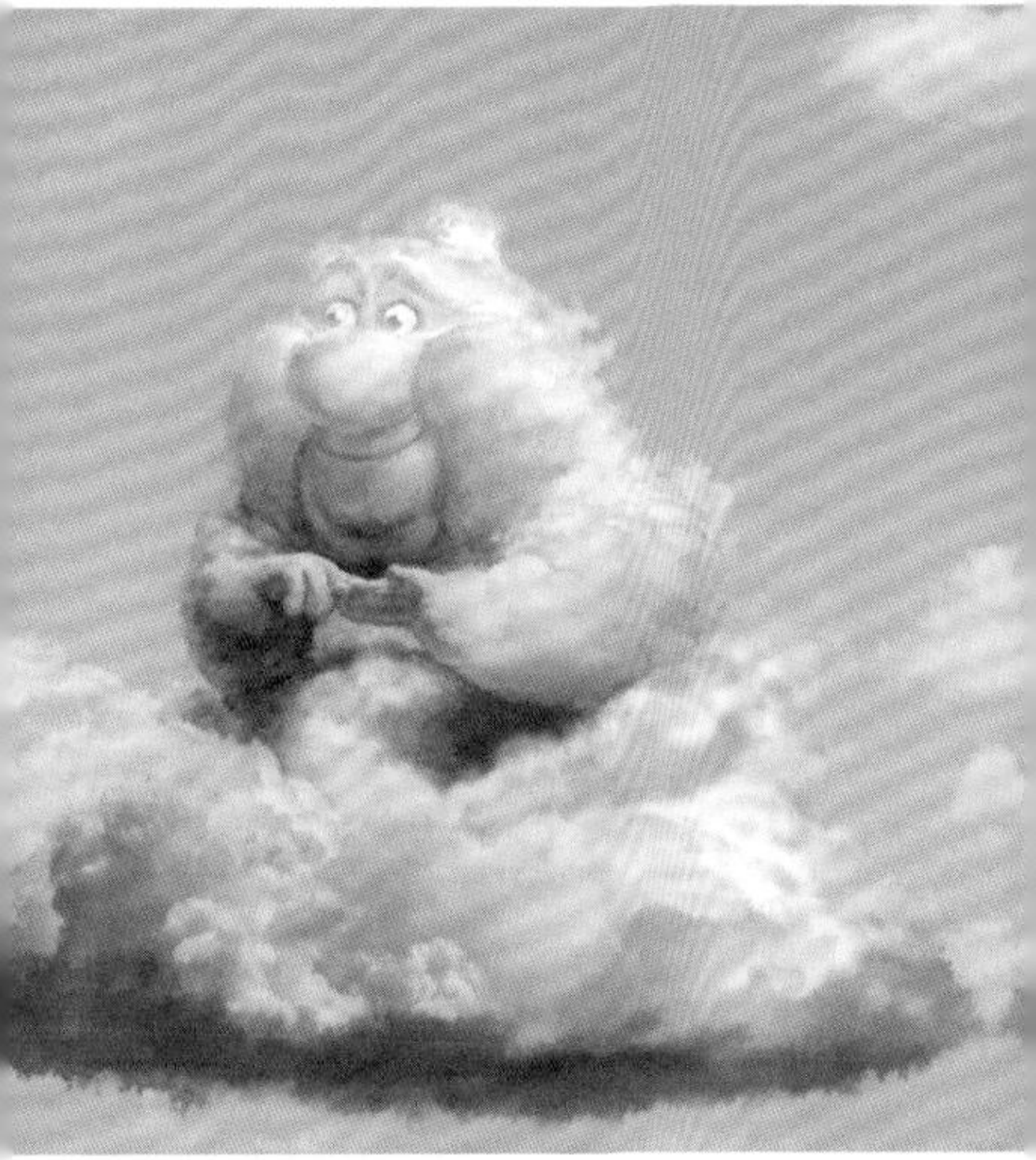

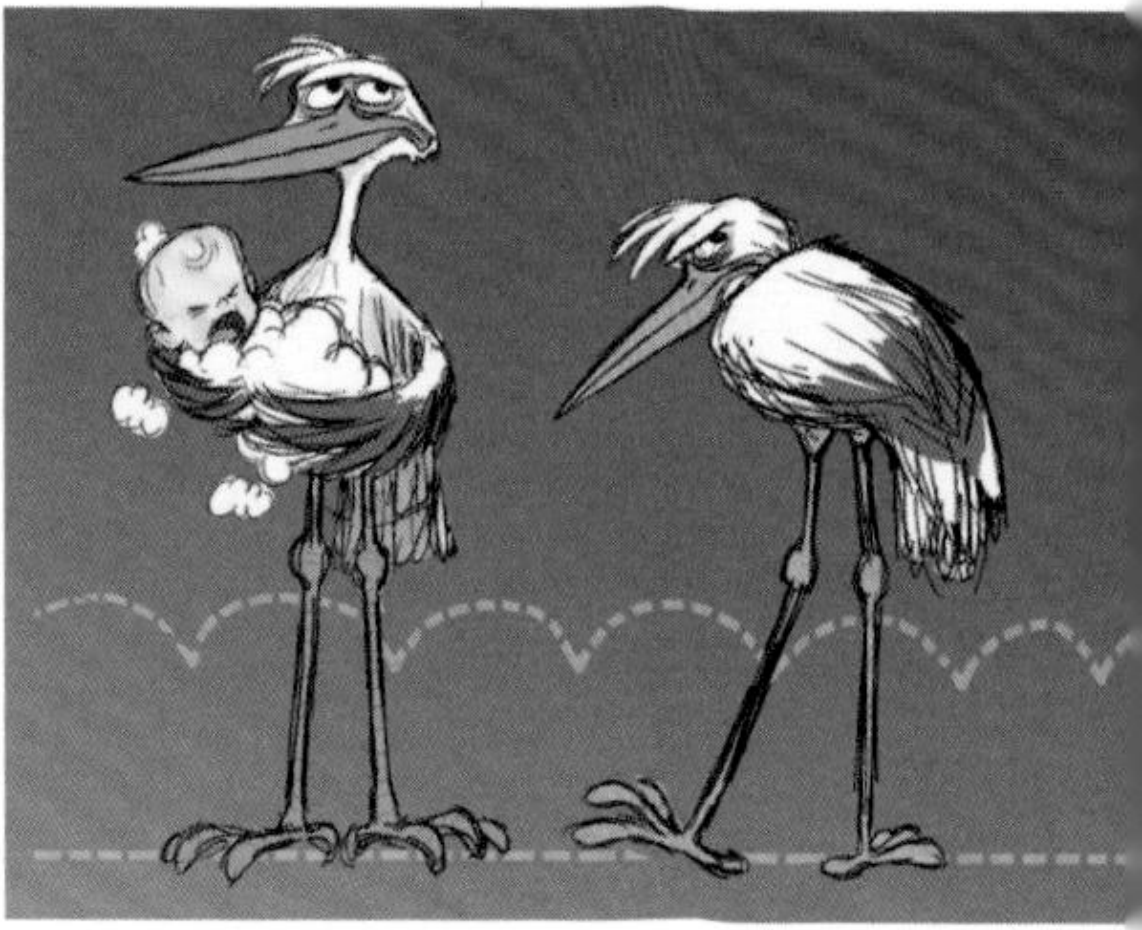

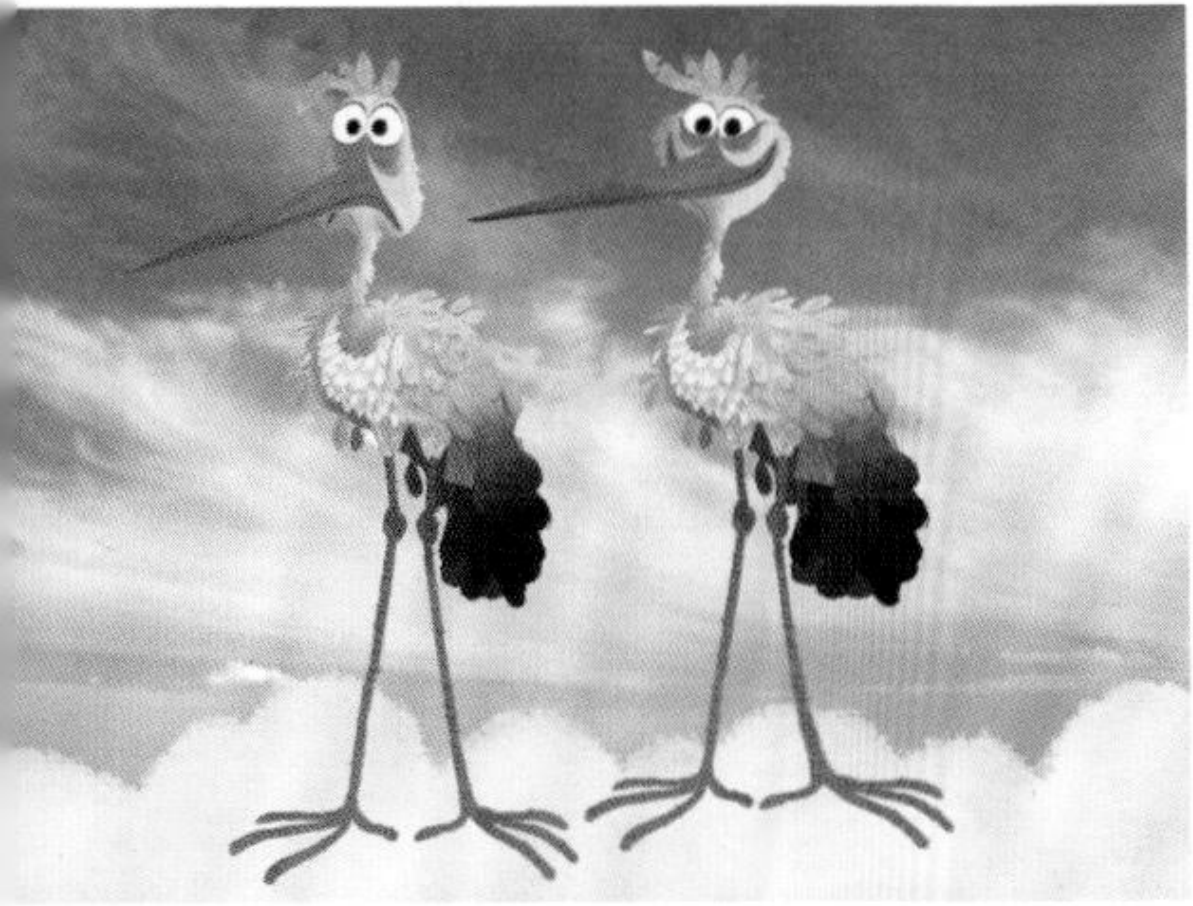

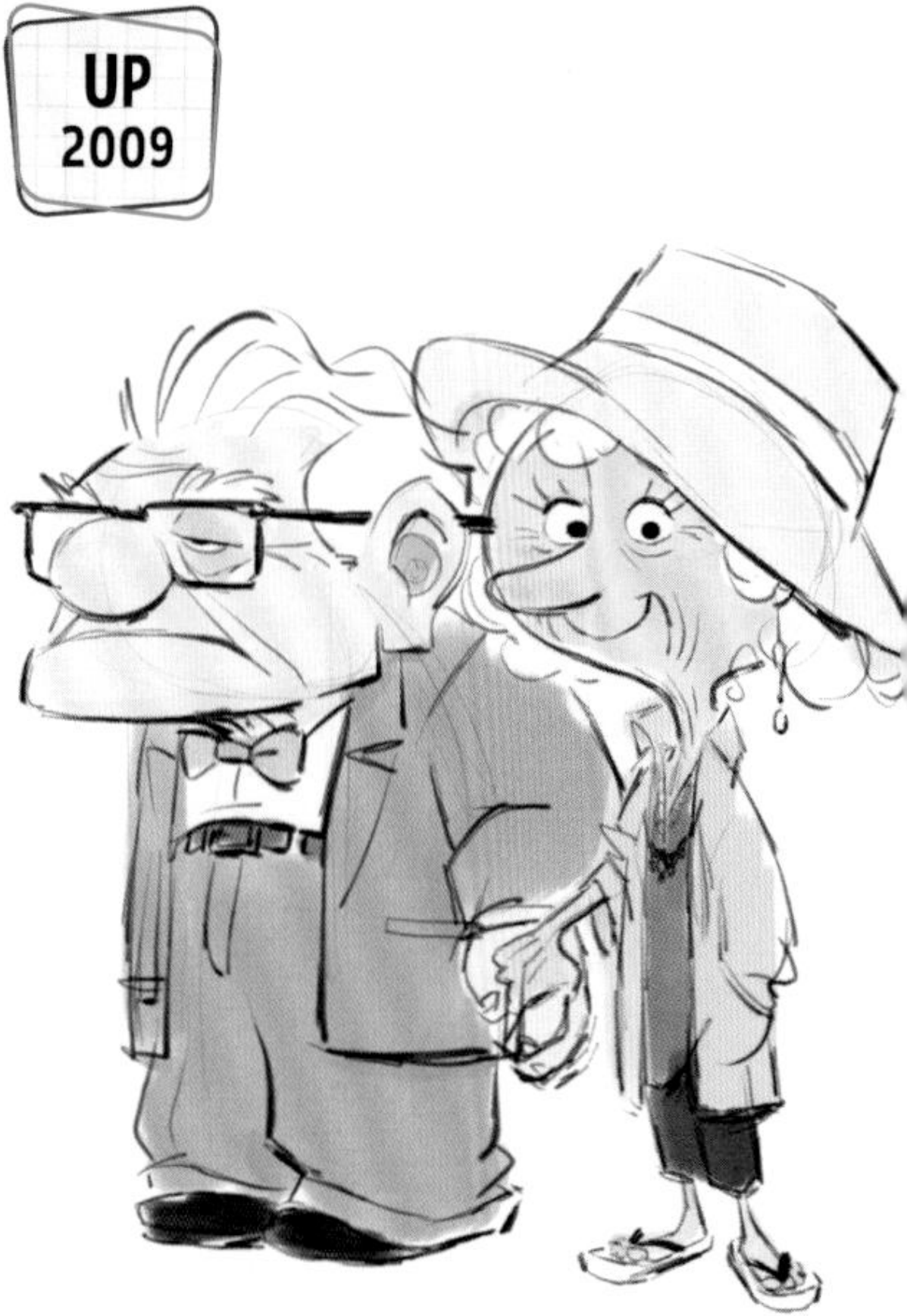
UP
2009

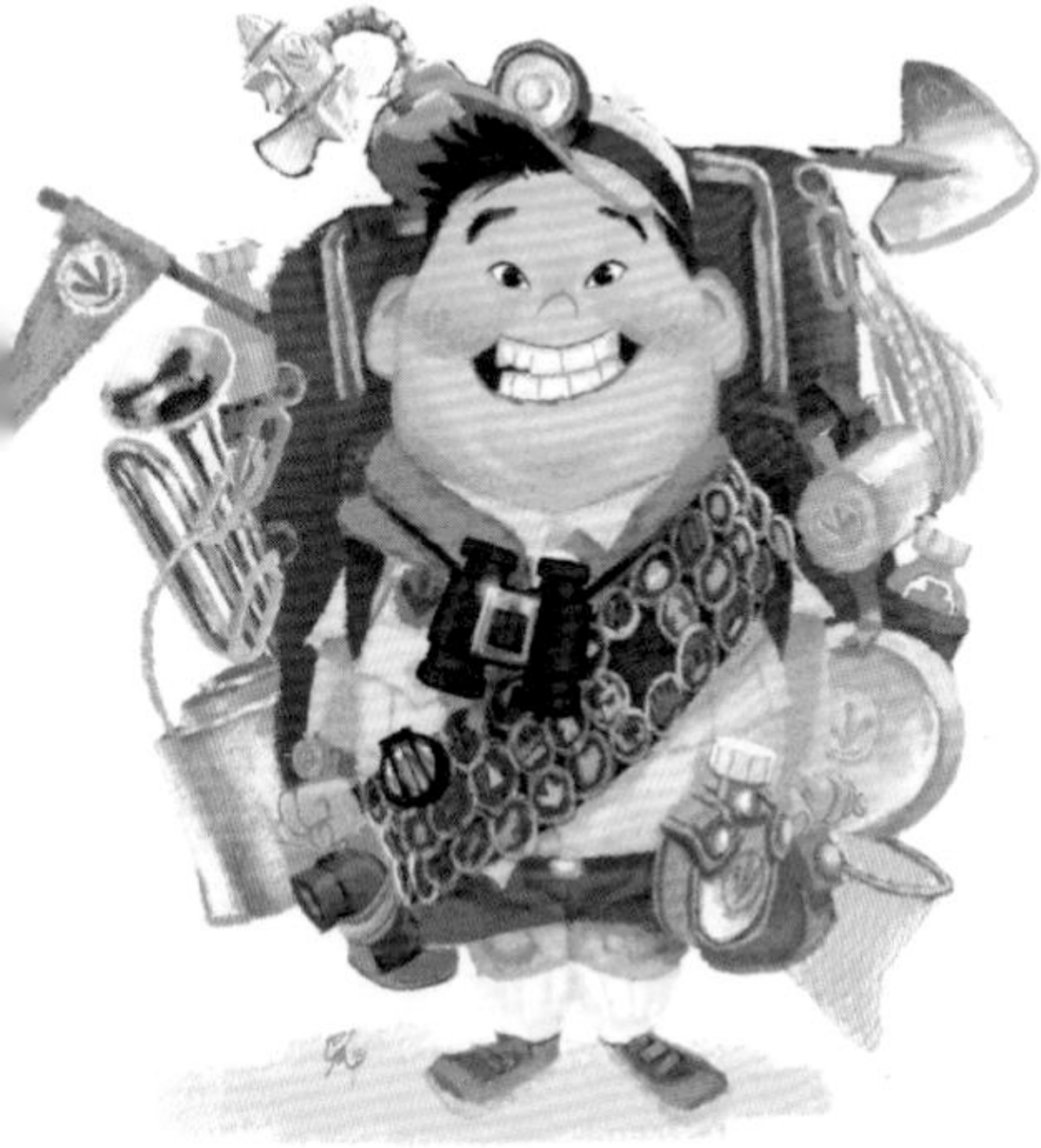

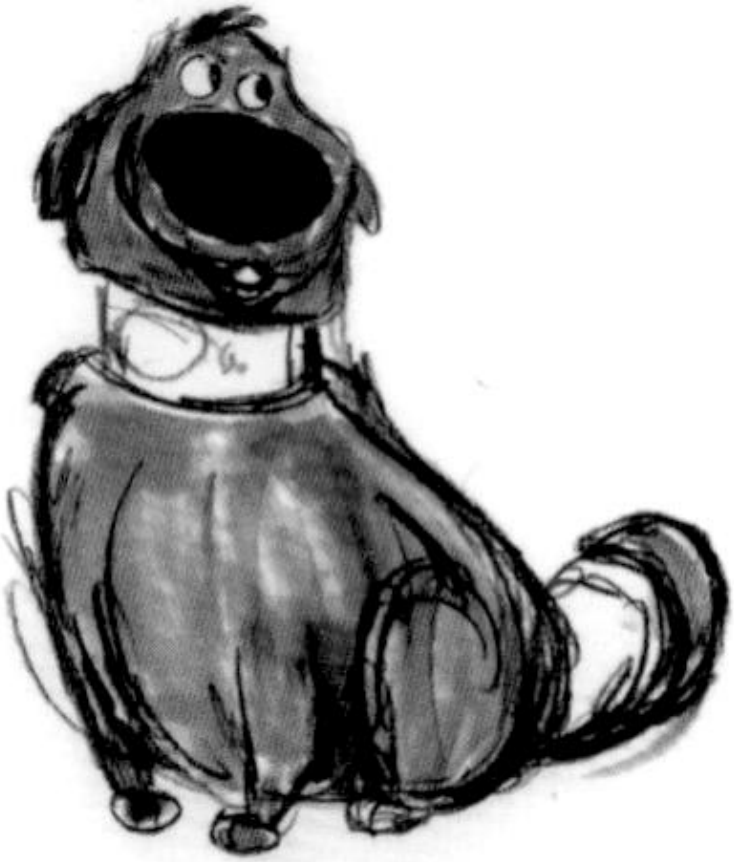

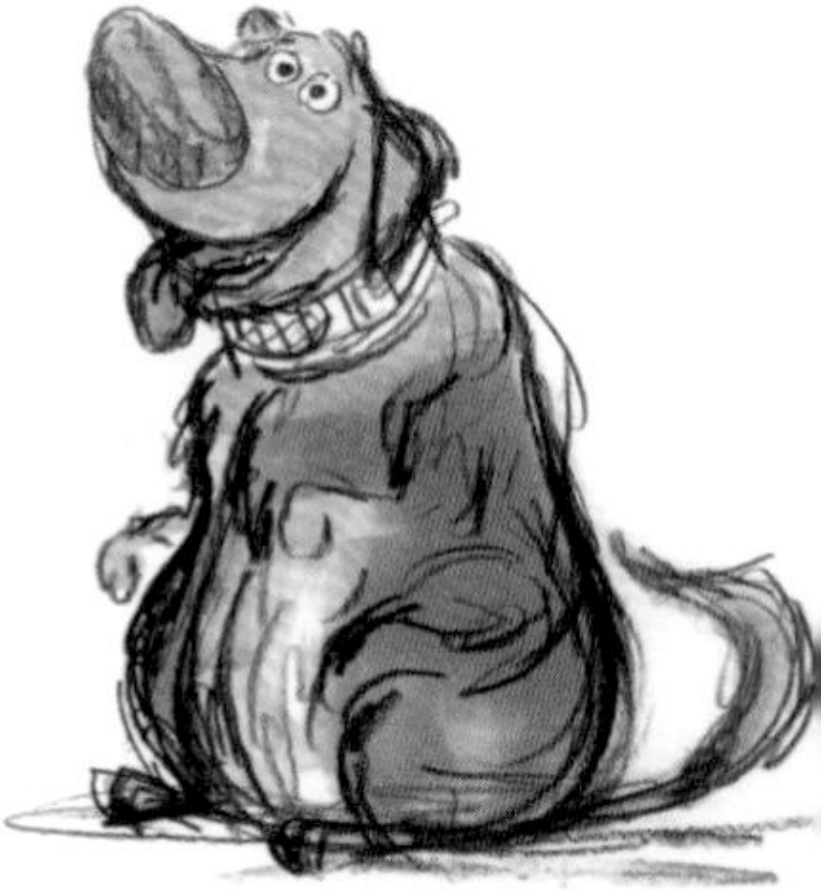

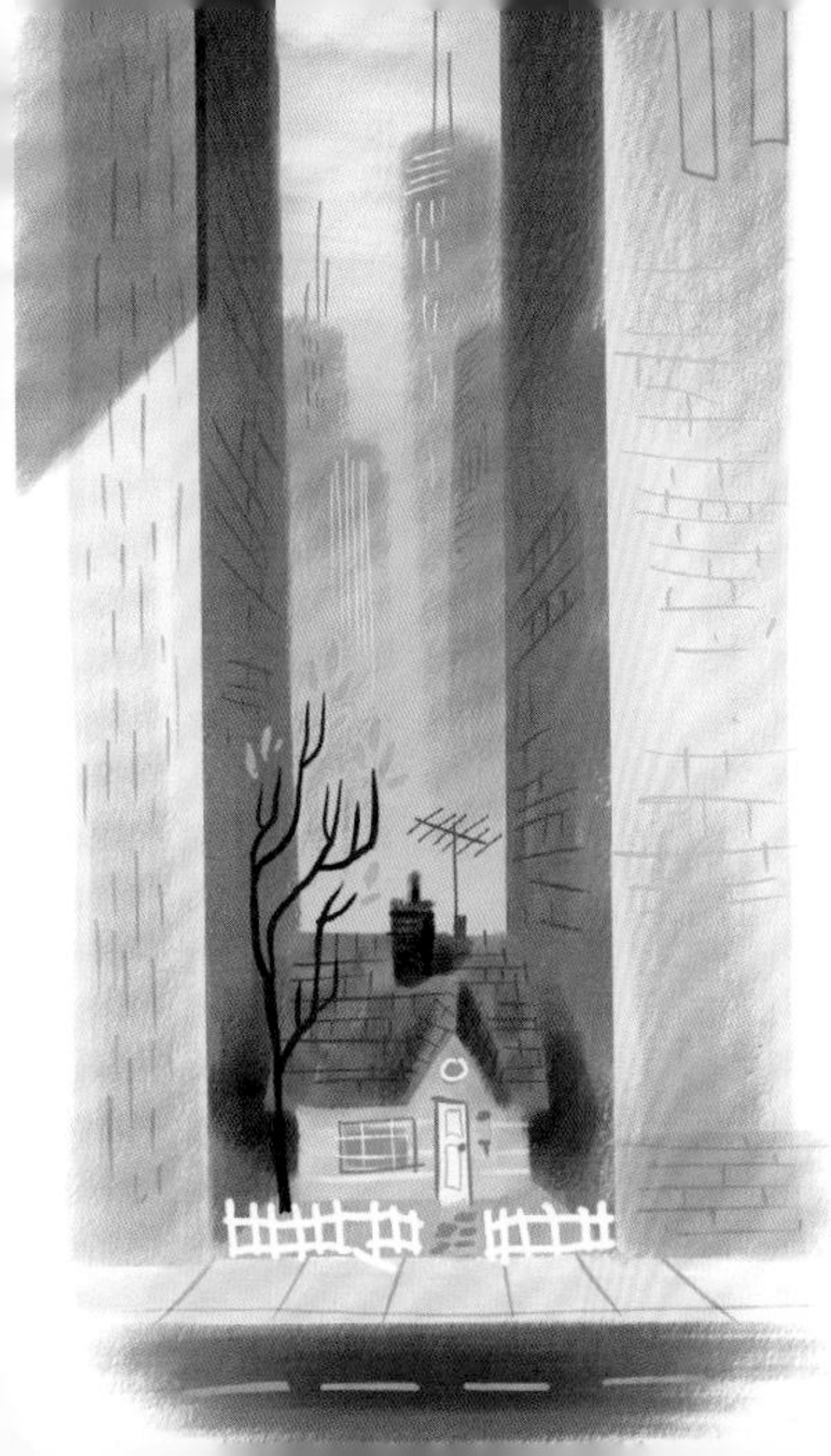

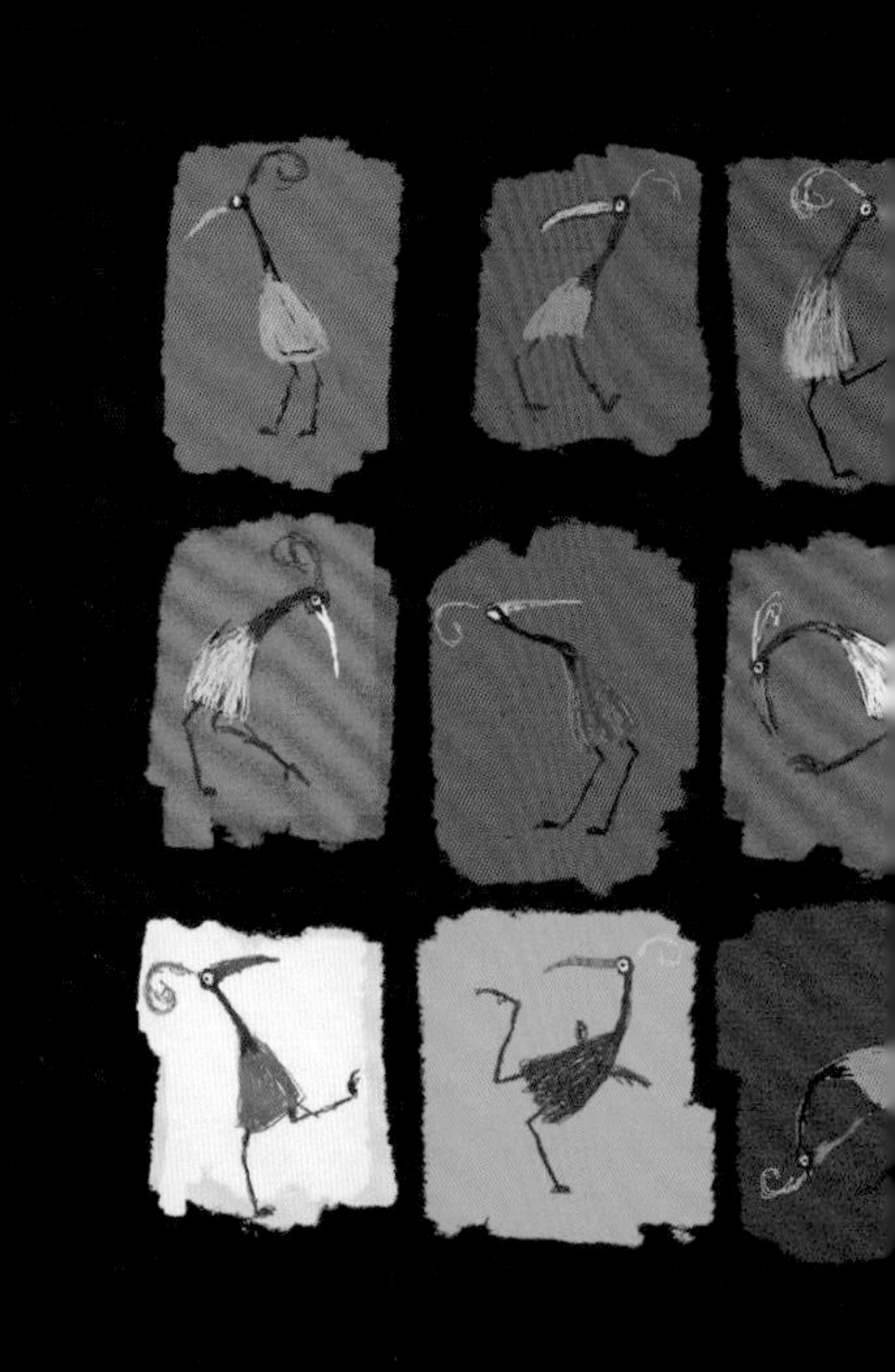

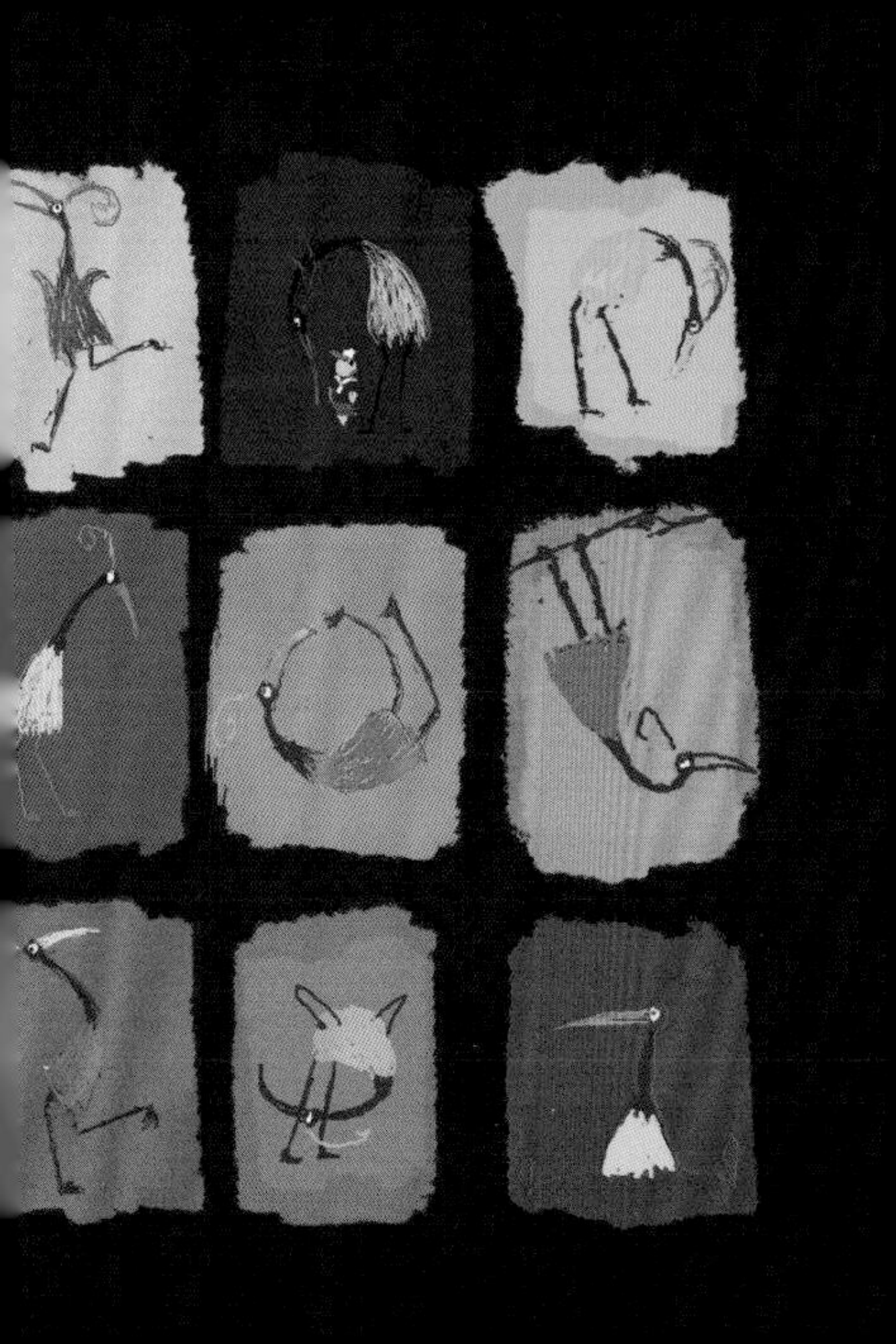

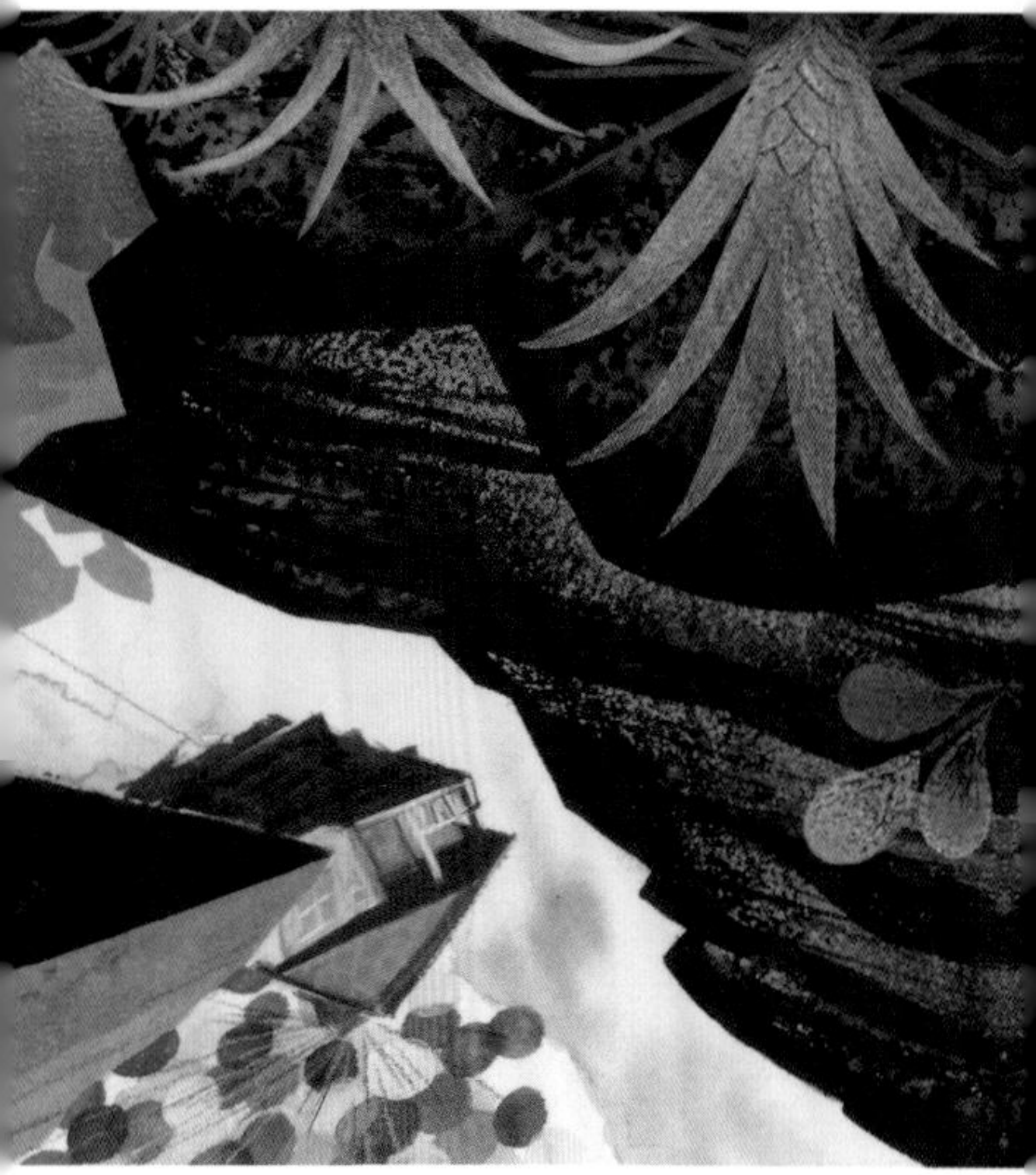

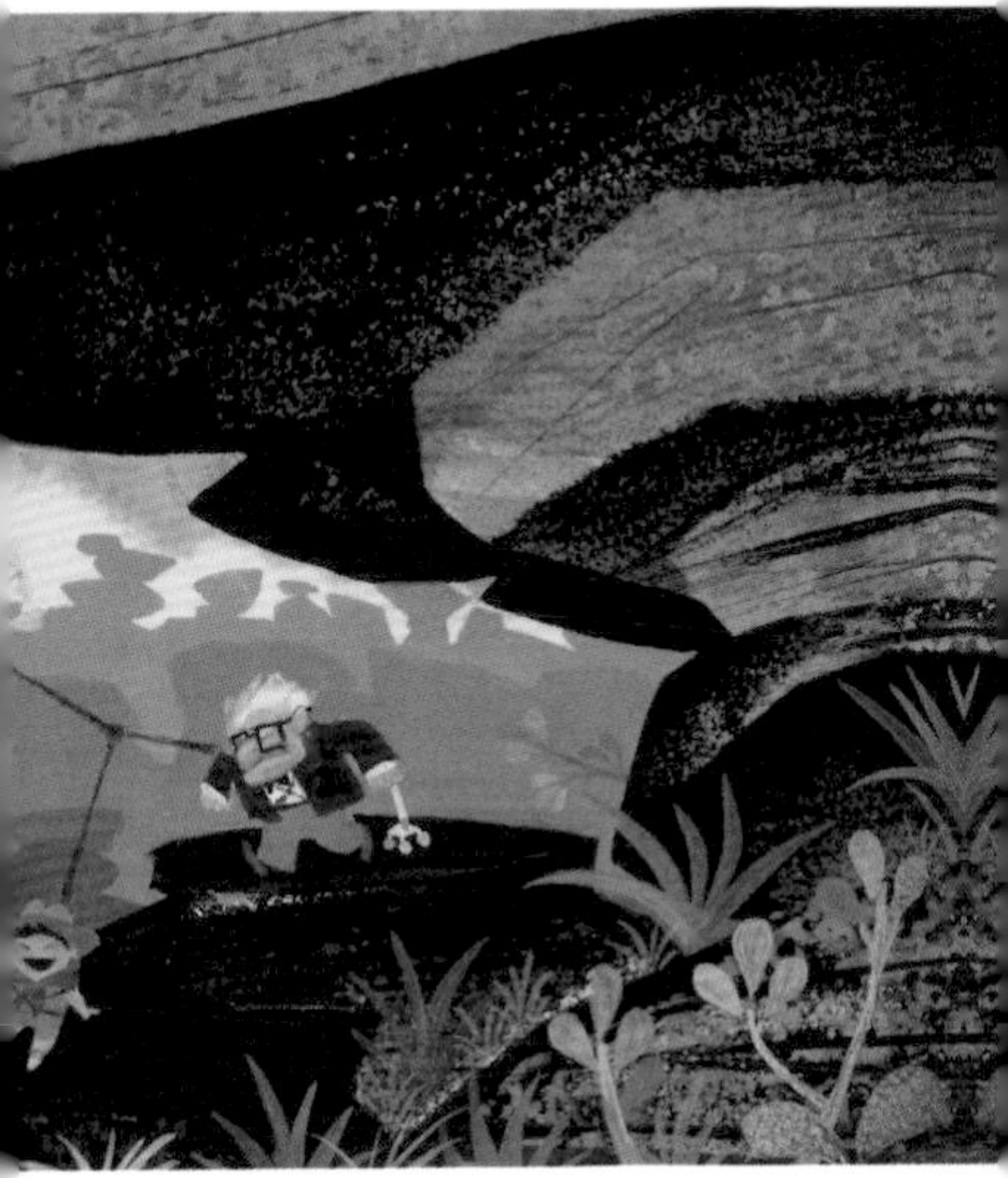

2010s

Pixar continued to deliver entertaining animated stories to a global audience. The 2010s took moviegoers on dazzling and far-reaching journeys, from the Highlands of Scotland to the realm of dinosaurs; from the Land of the Dead to our very own minds. The results have been an enthralling and wide-ranging collection of animated films.

SHORT

DAY & NIGHT

2010

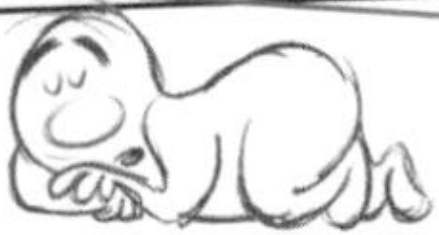

sleep

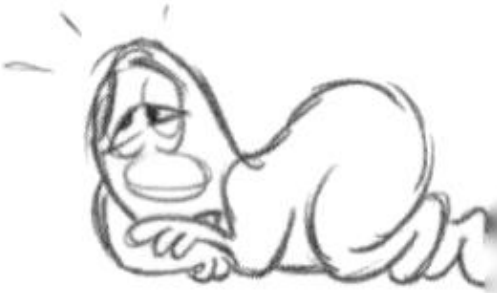

Rooster crows

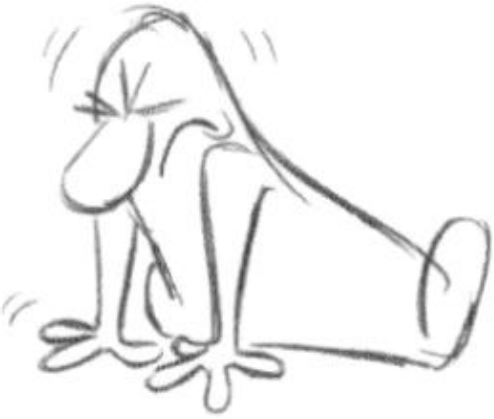

get up

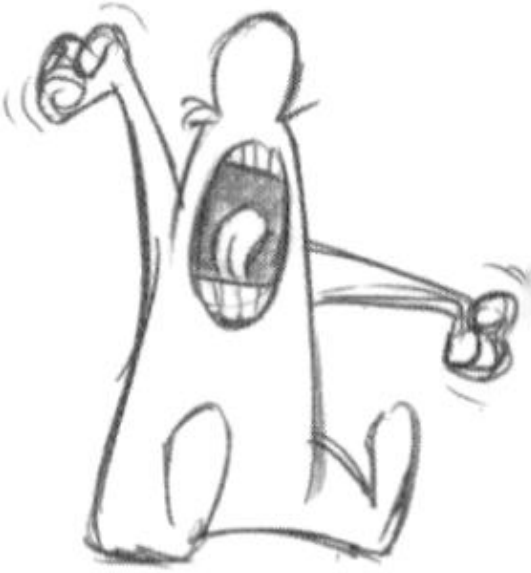

yawn.

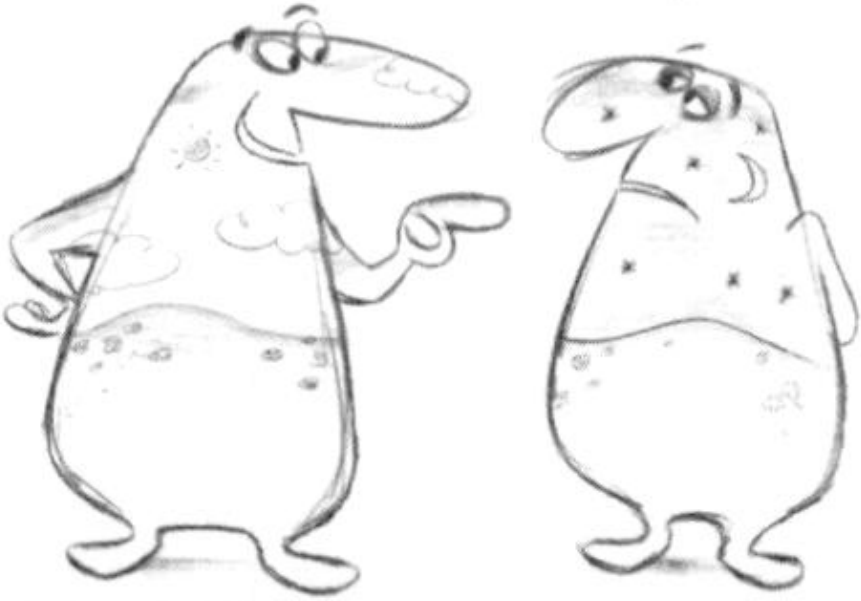

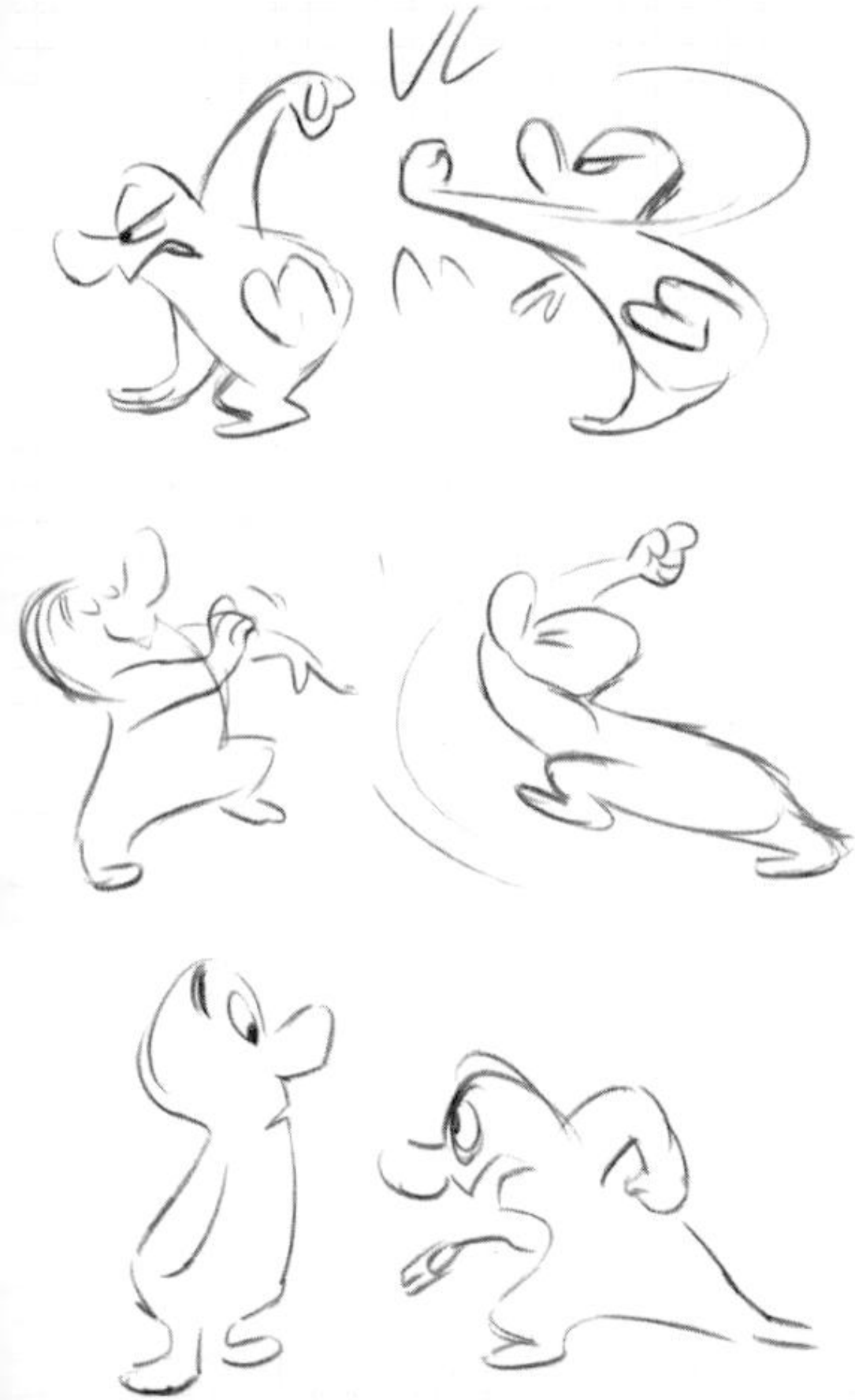

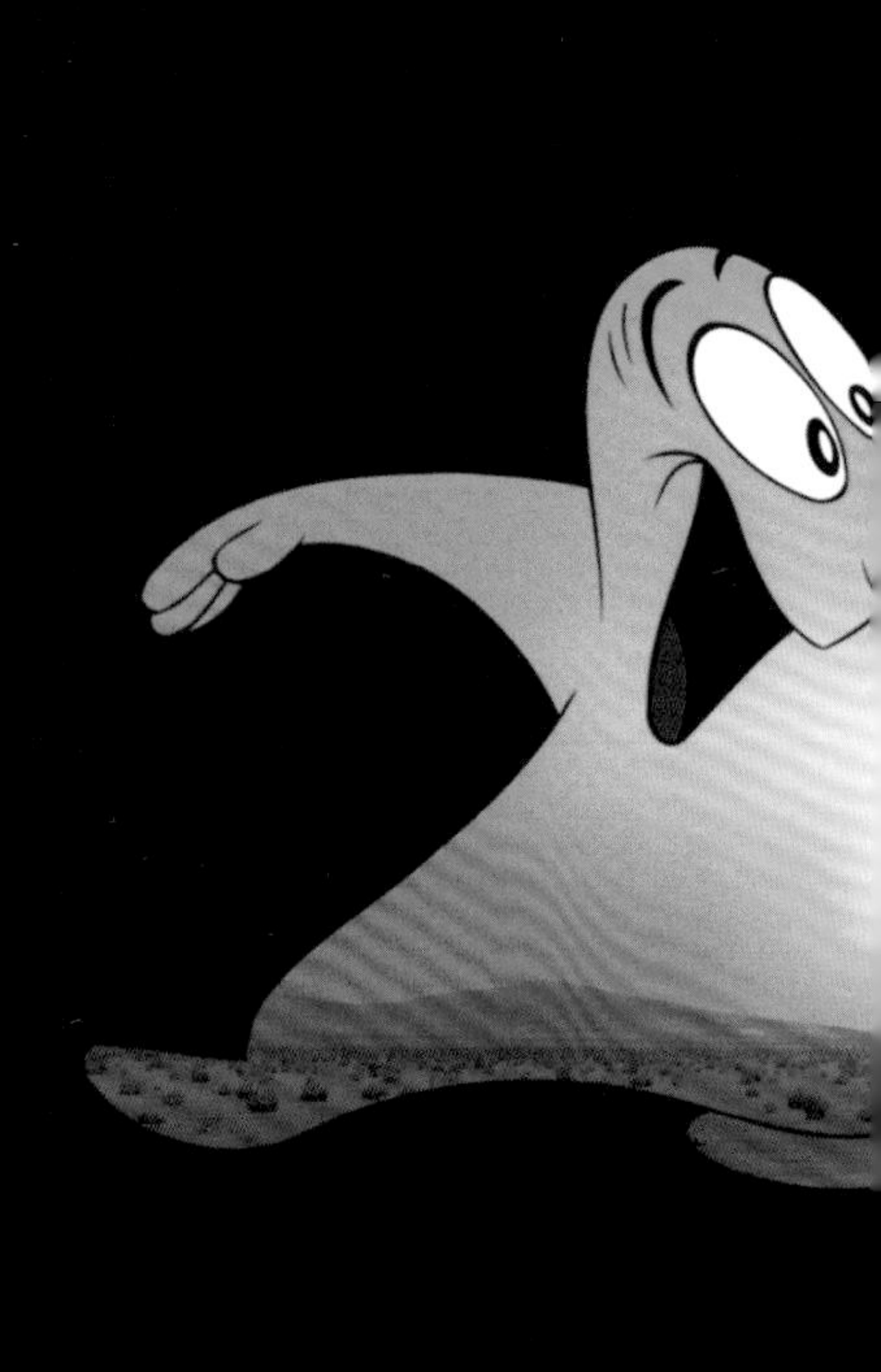

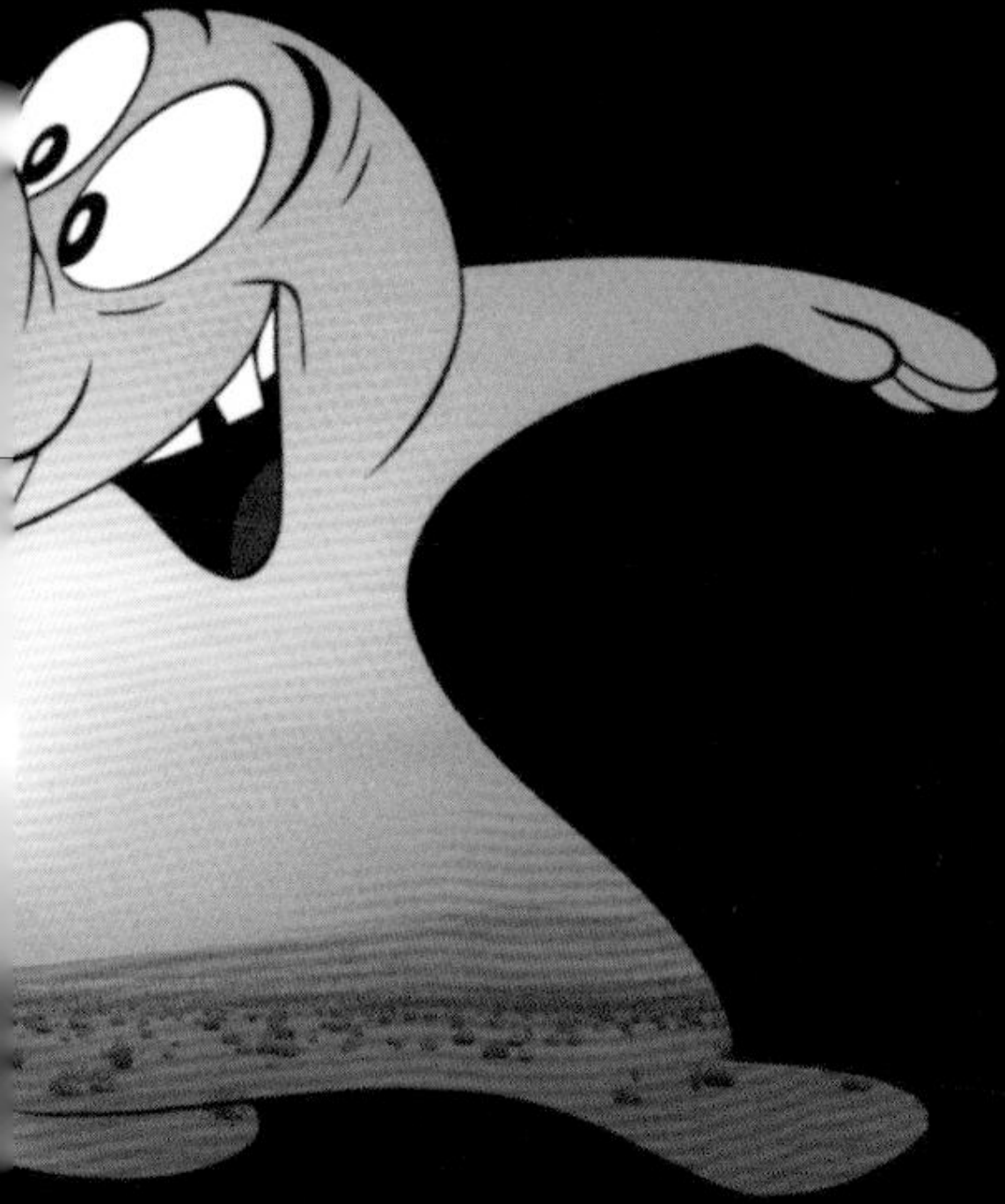

TOY STORY 3
2010

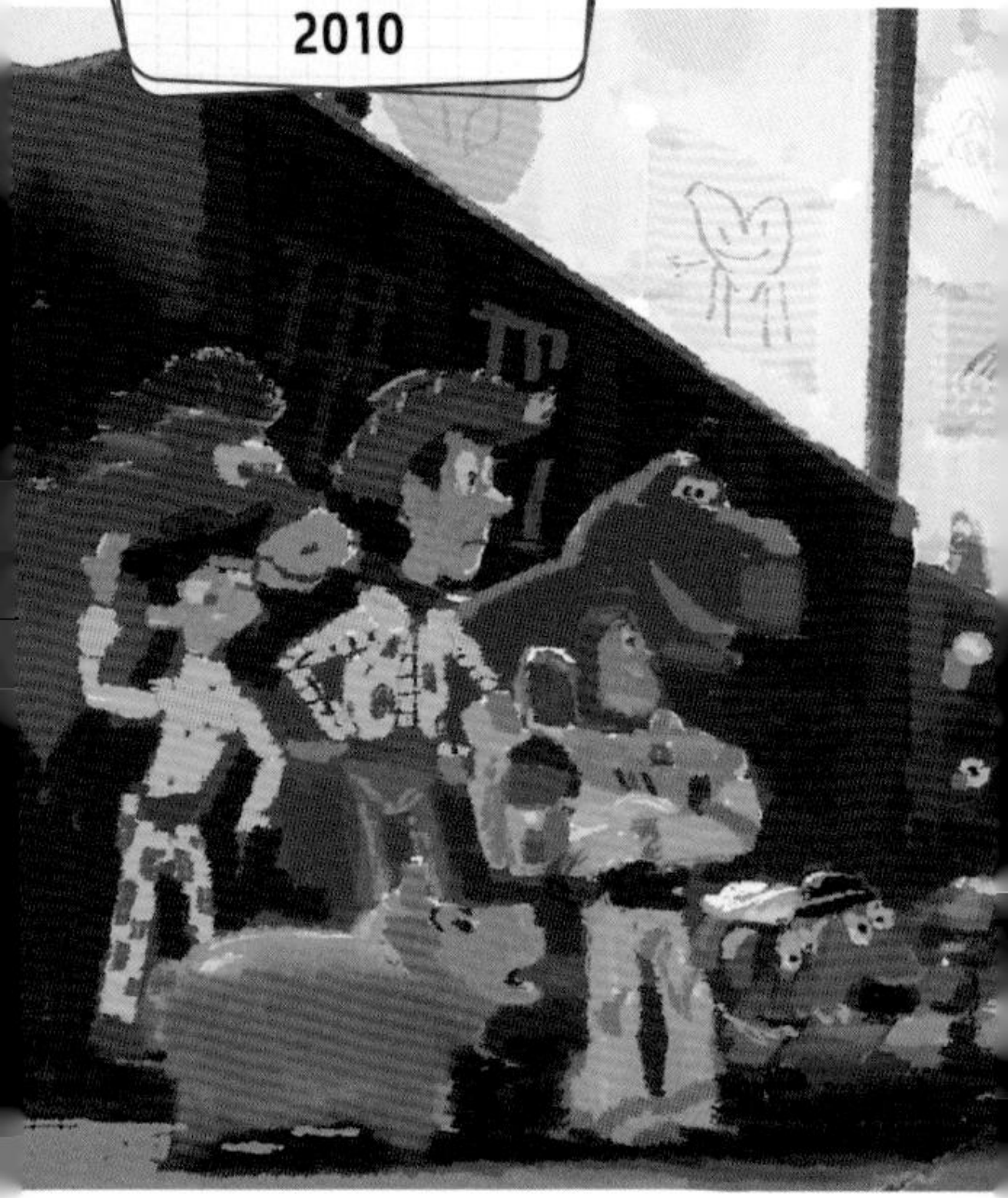

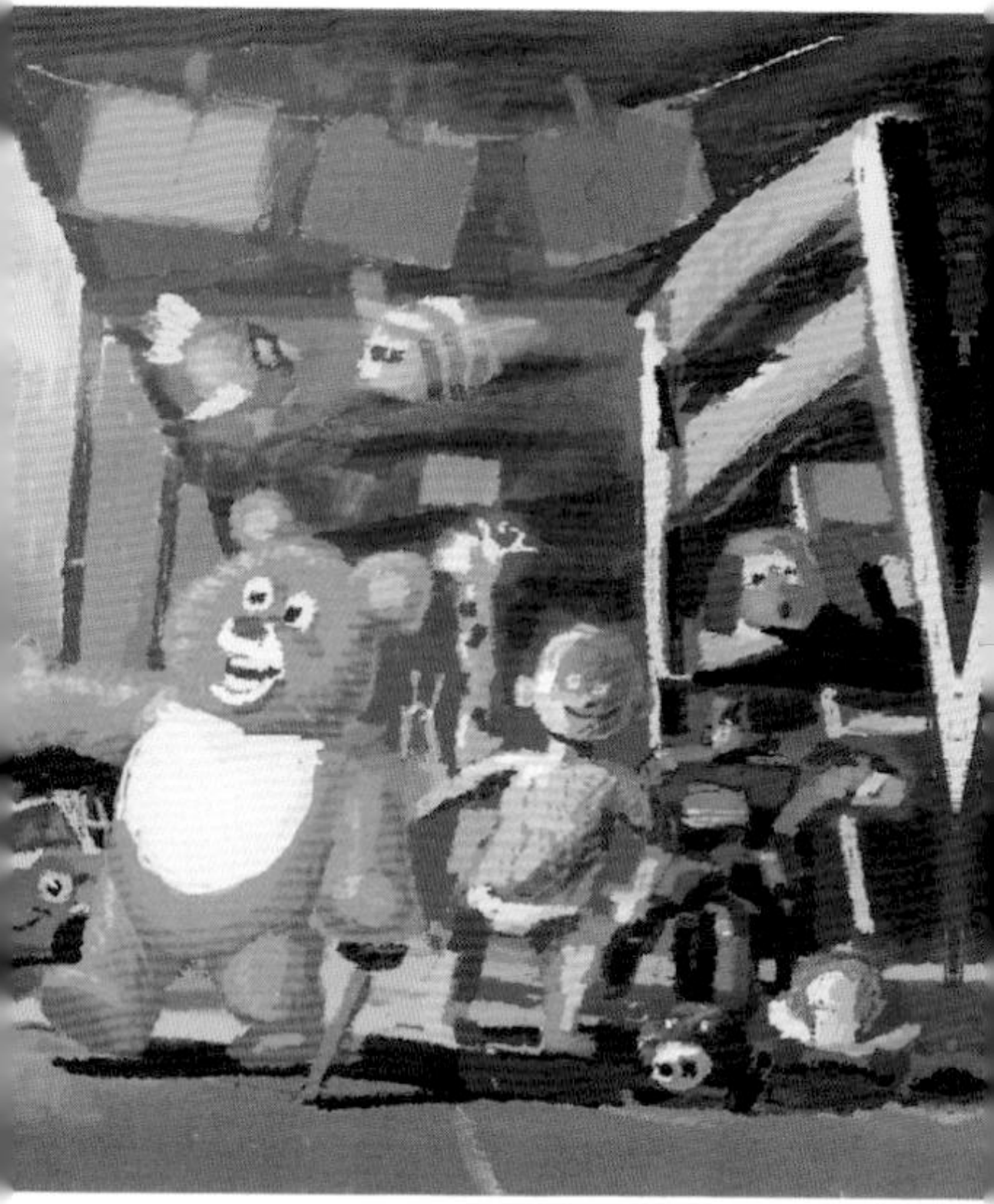

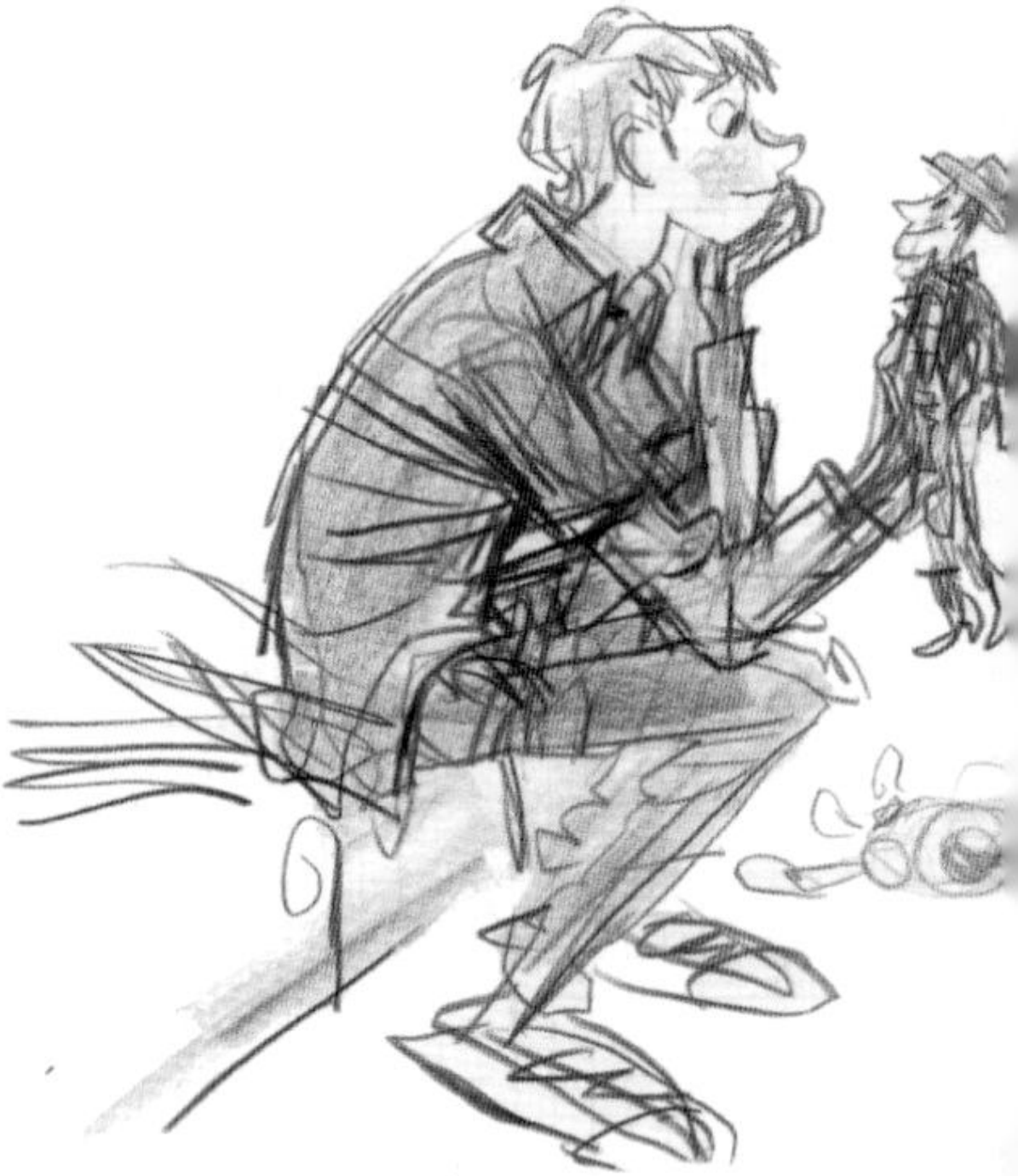

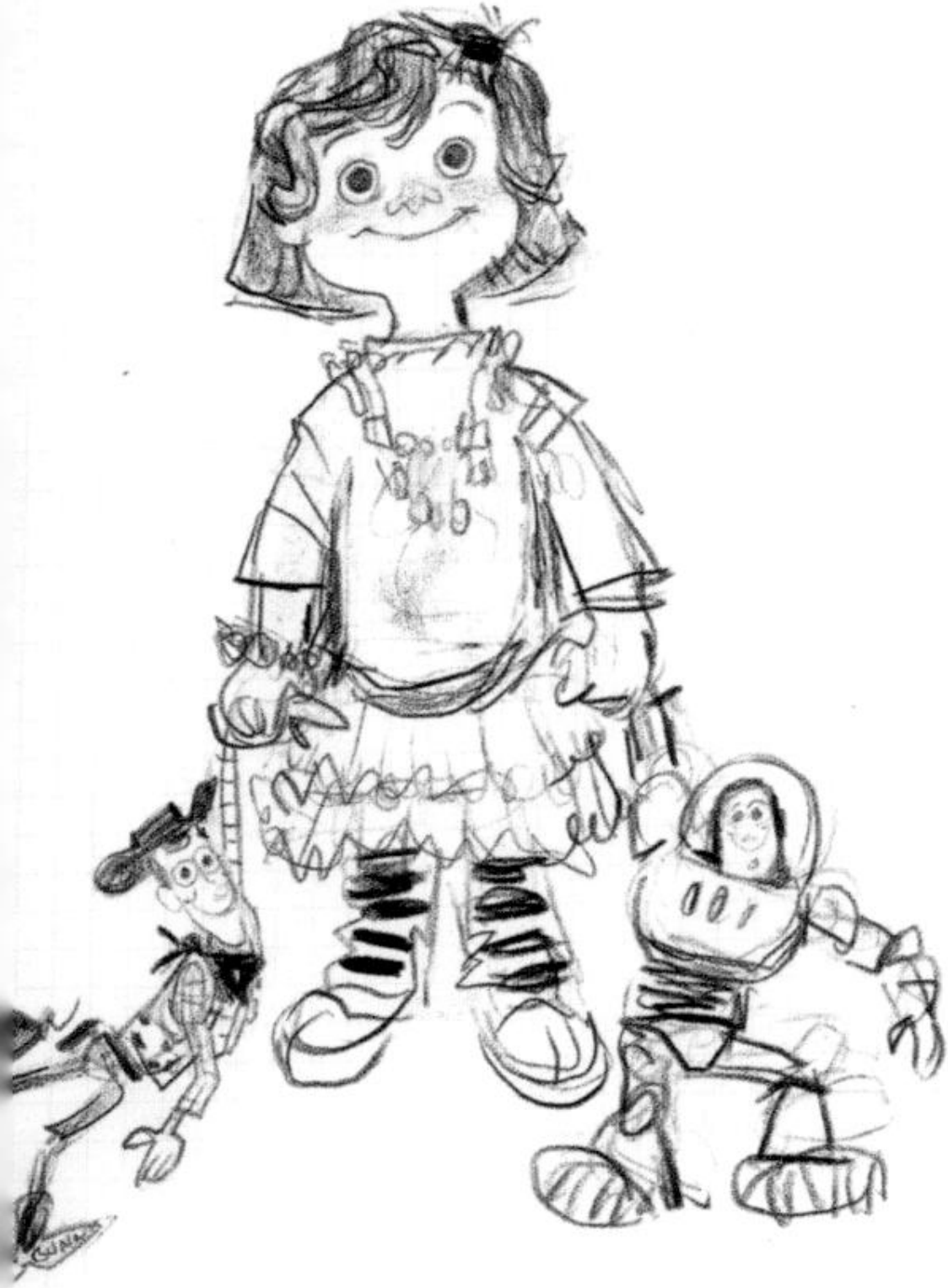

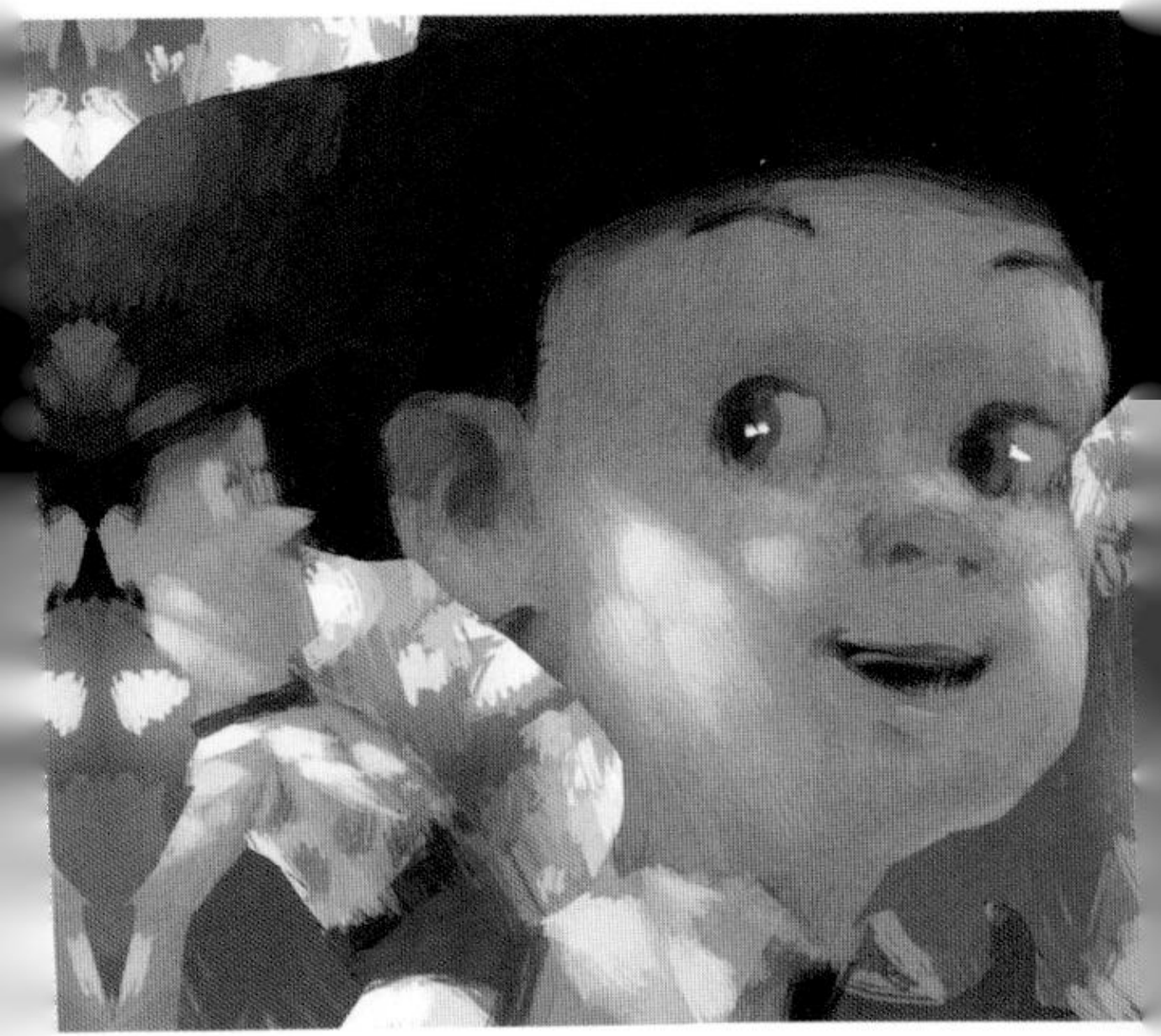

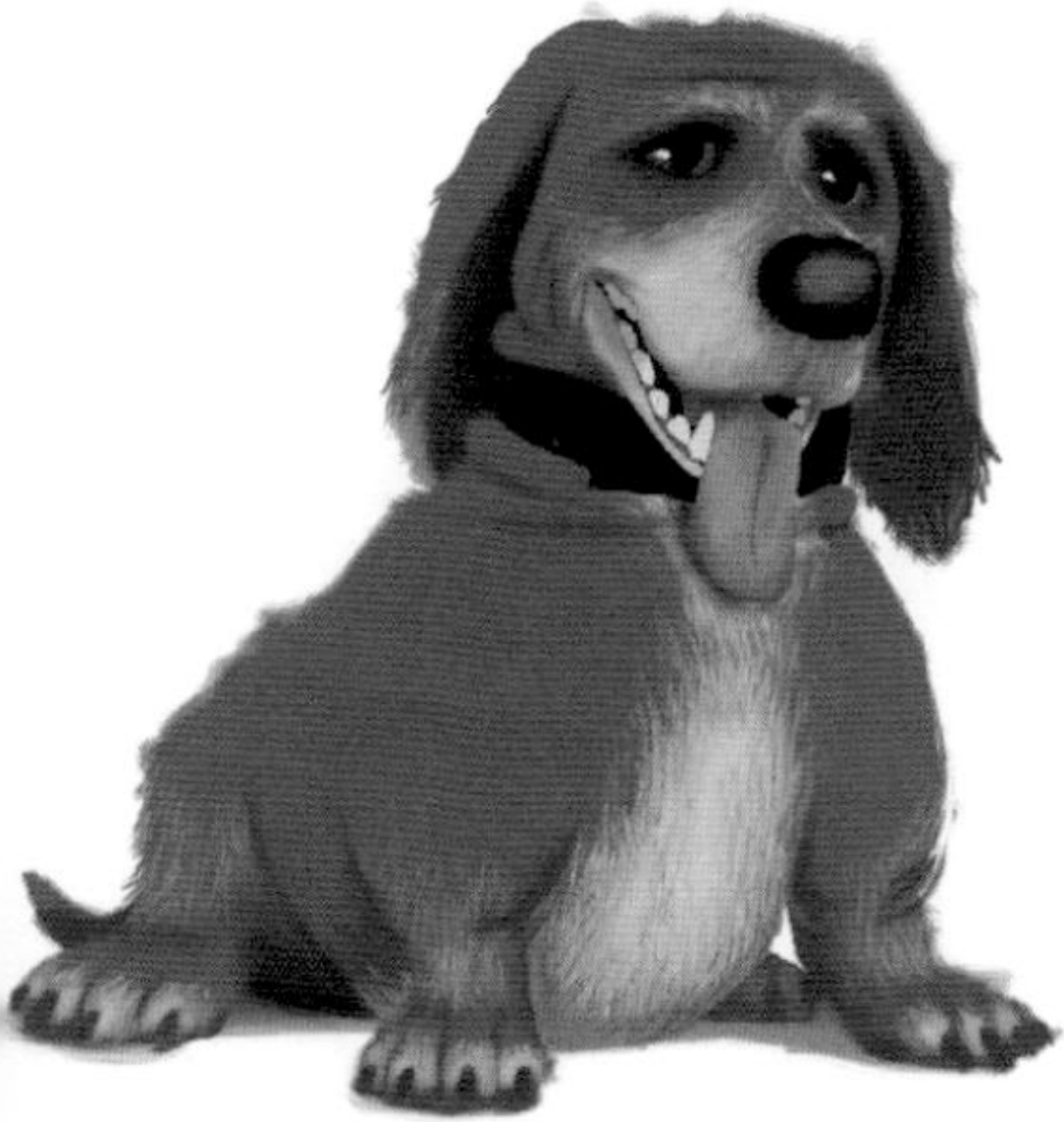

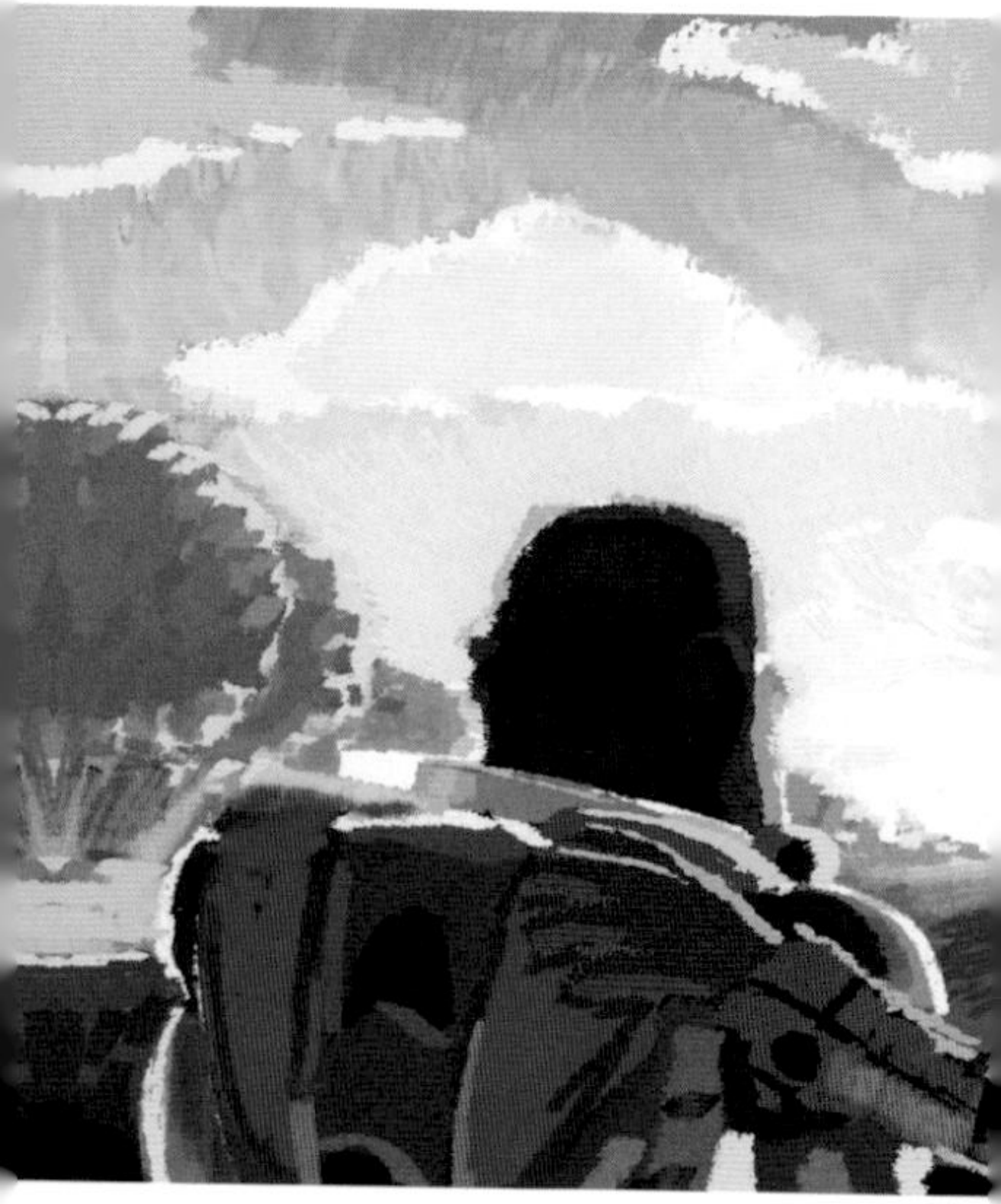

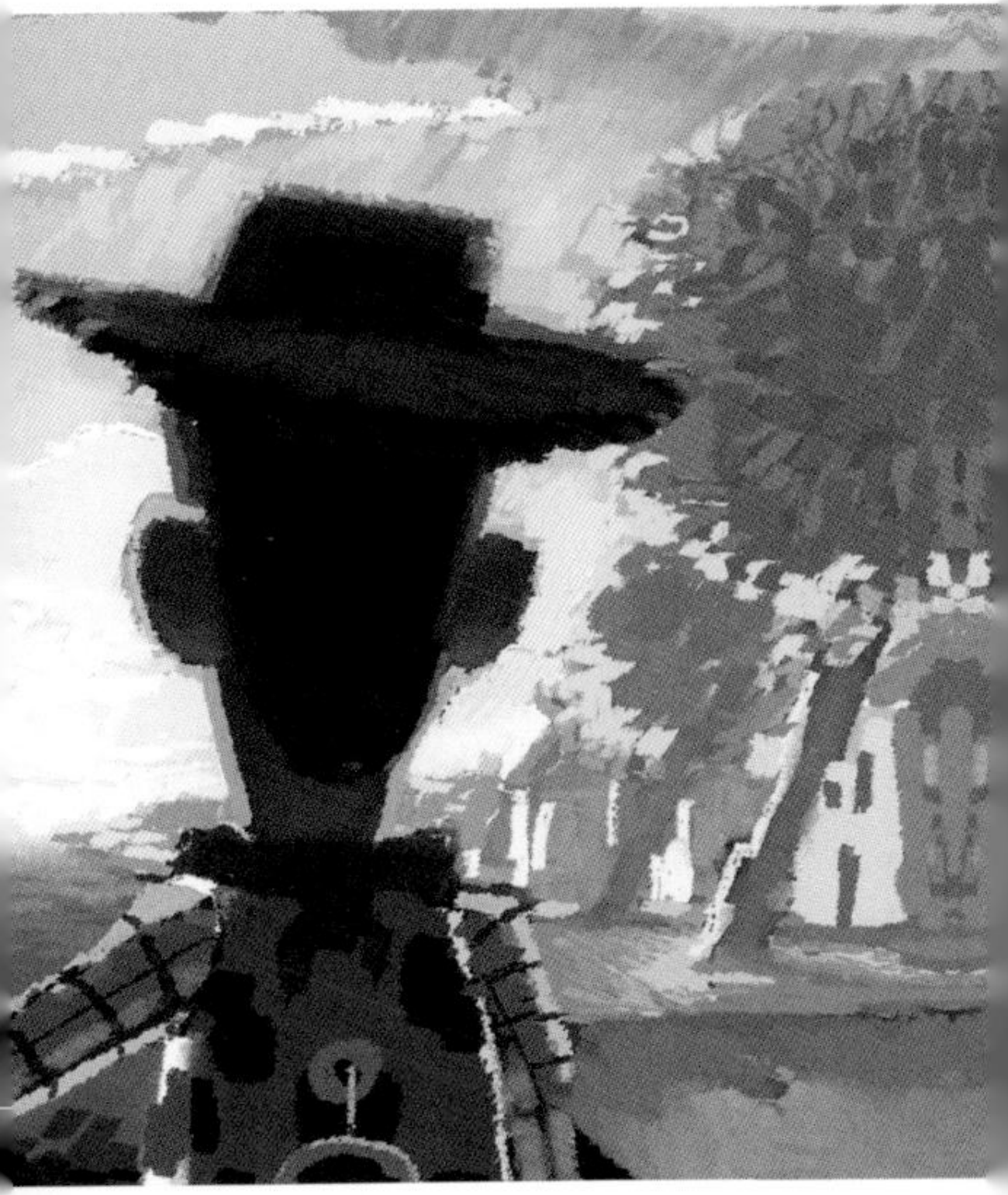

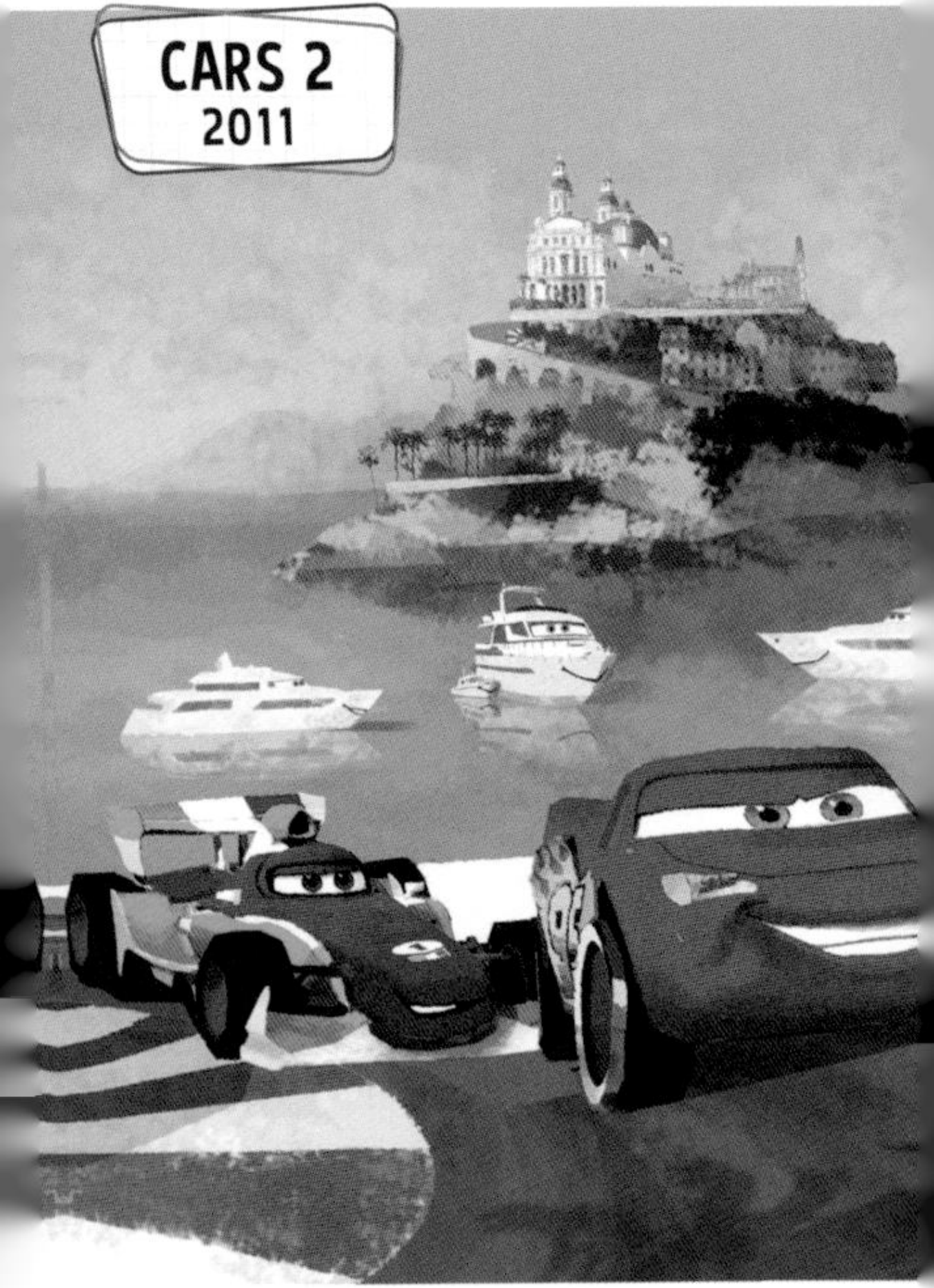
CARS 2
2011

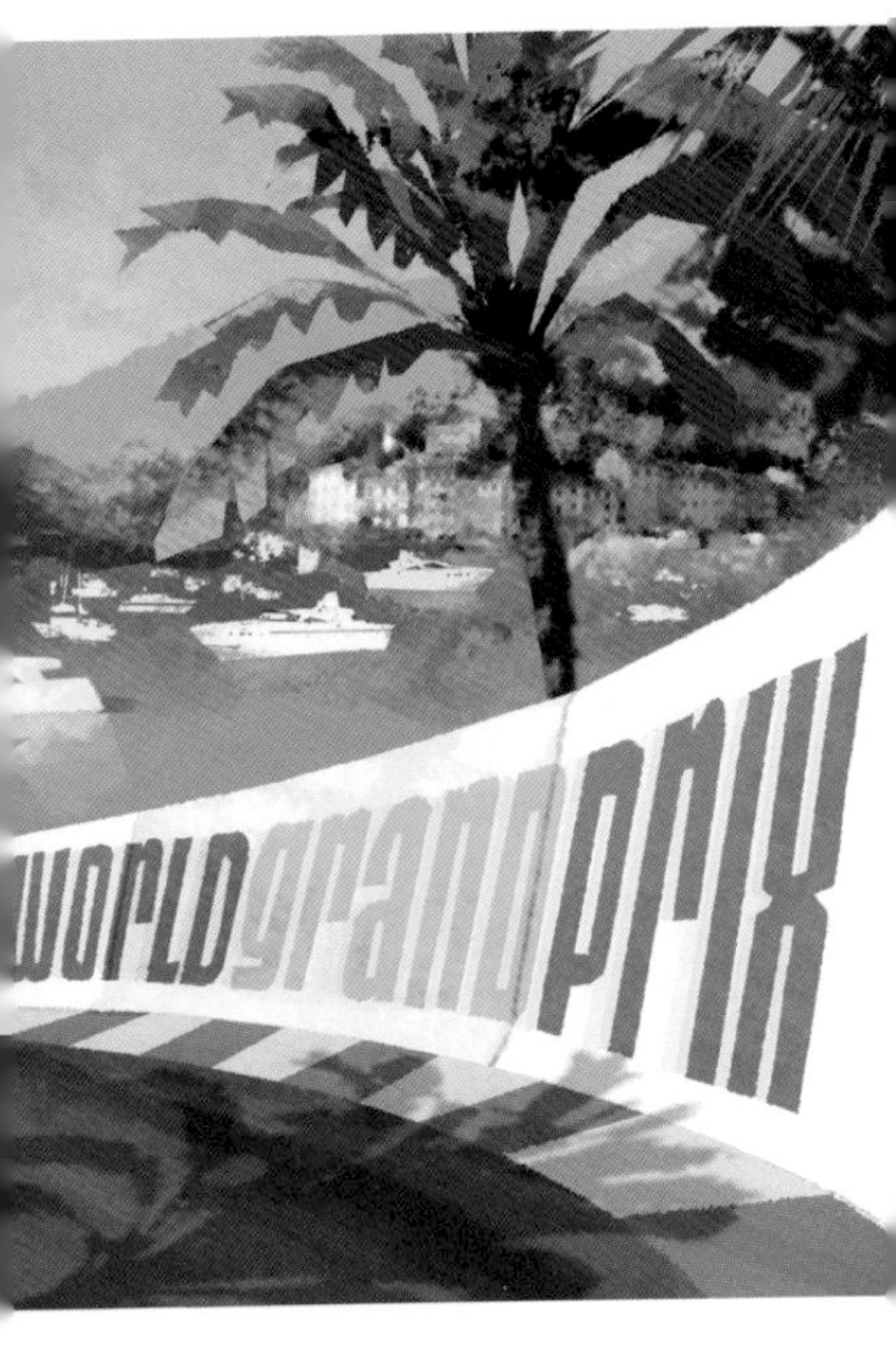
WORLD GRAND PRIX

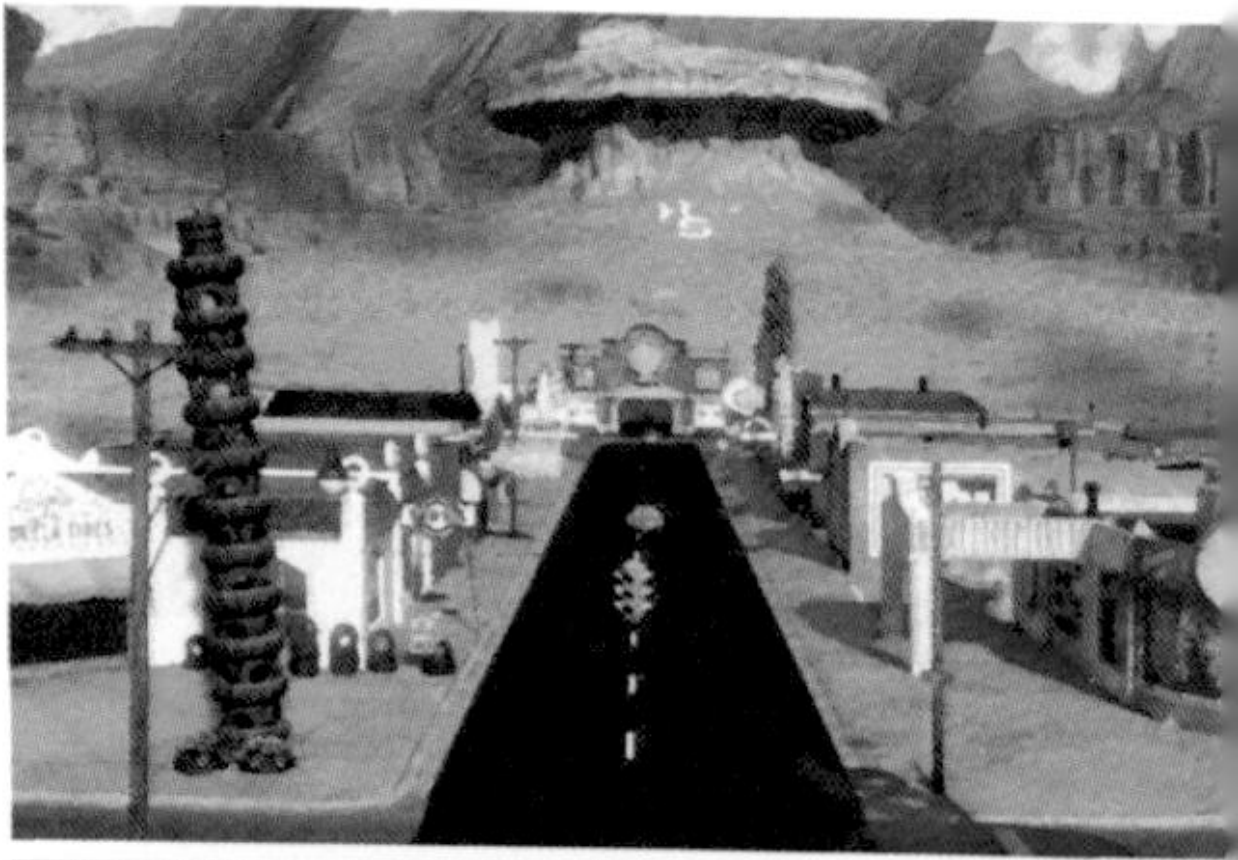

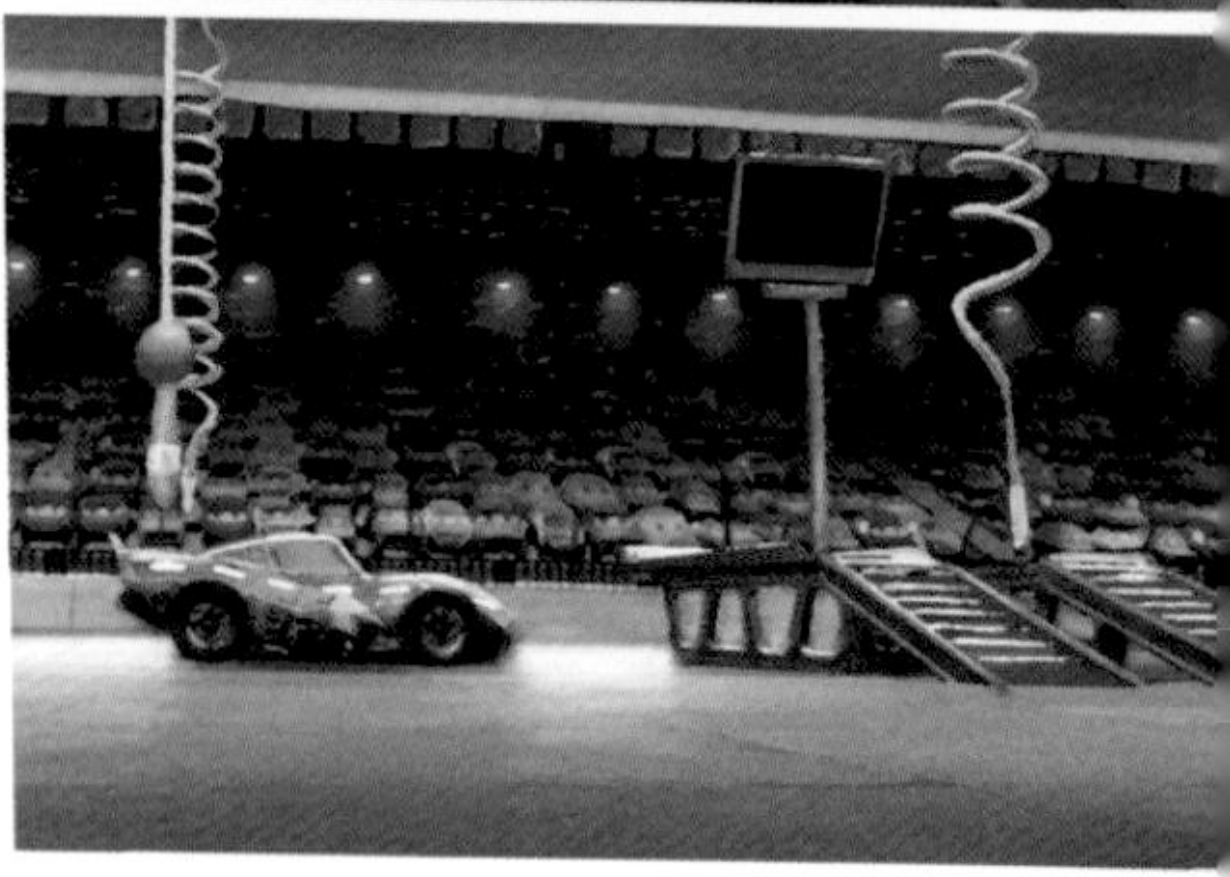

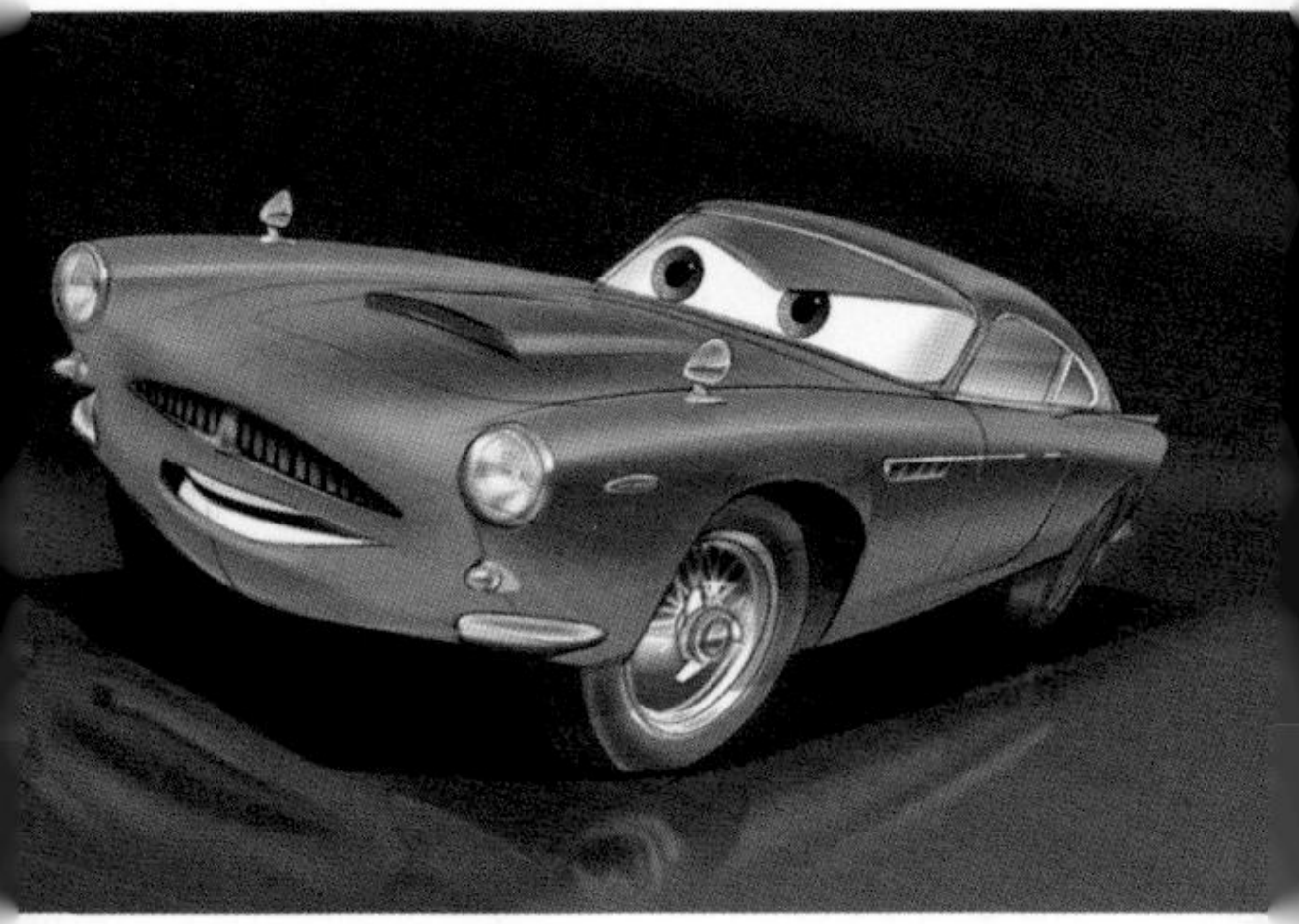

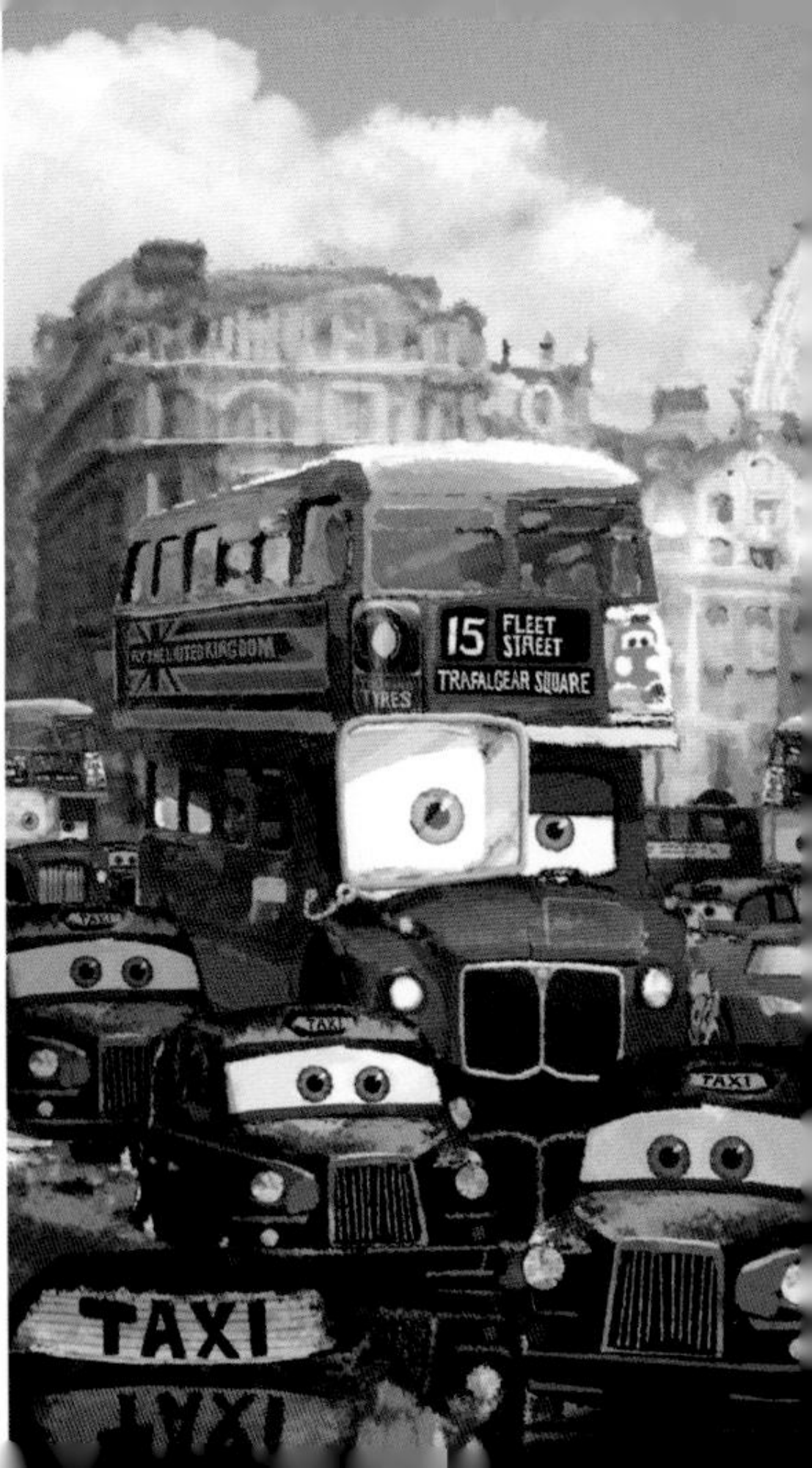
15 FLEET STREET
TRAFALGEAR SQUARE
TYRES
TAXI
TAXI
TAXI
TAXI

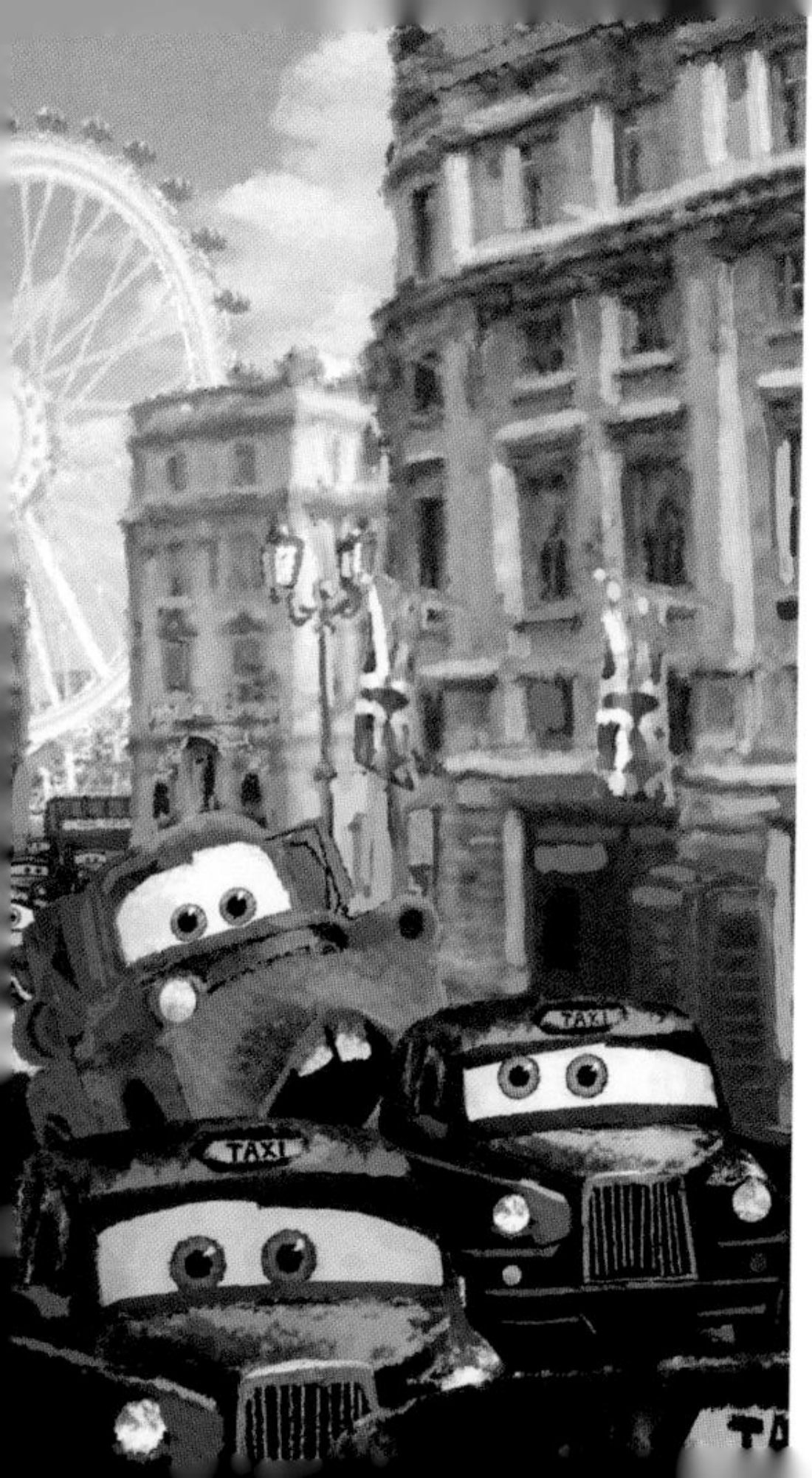
TAXI
TAXI

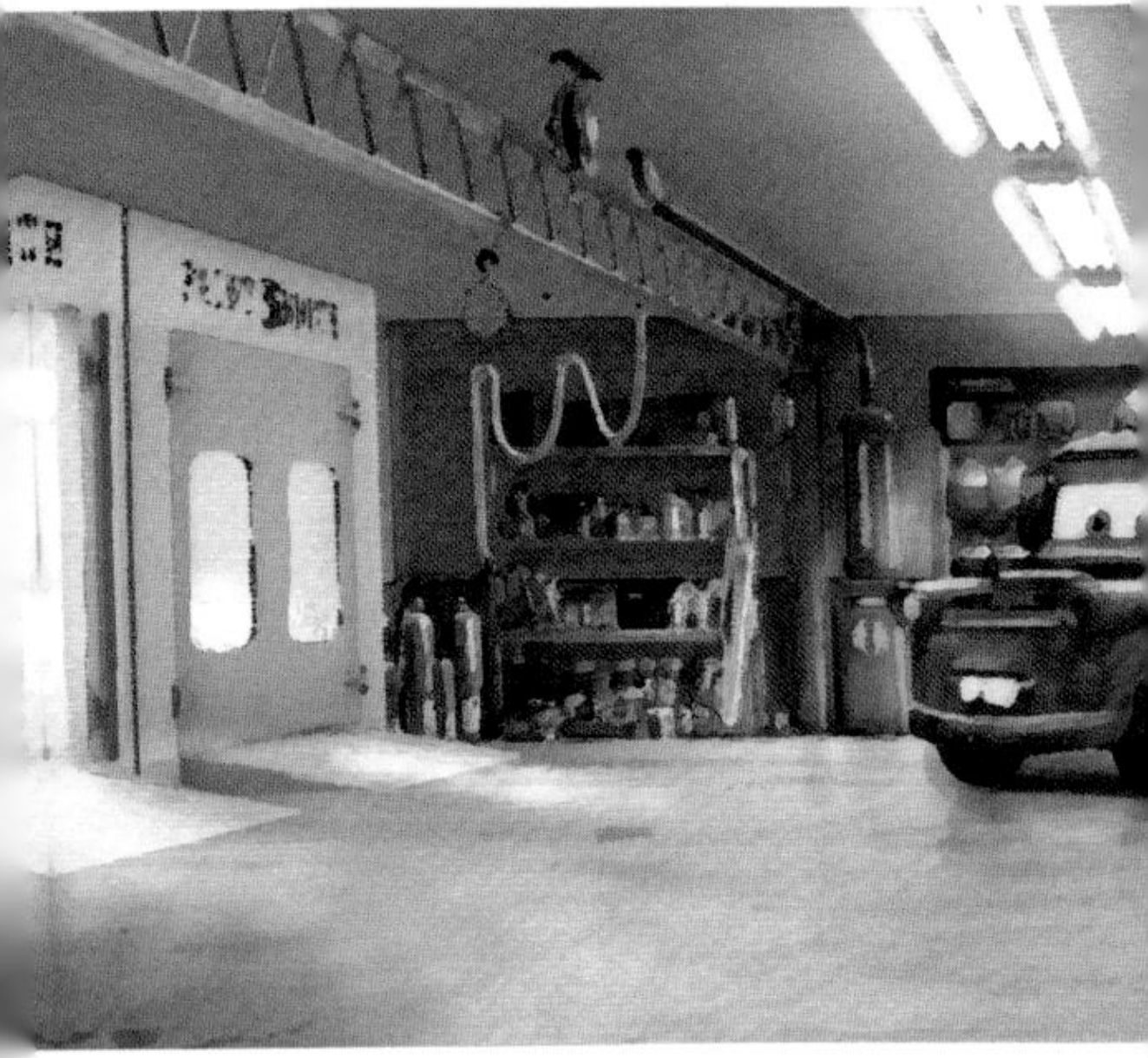

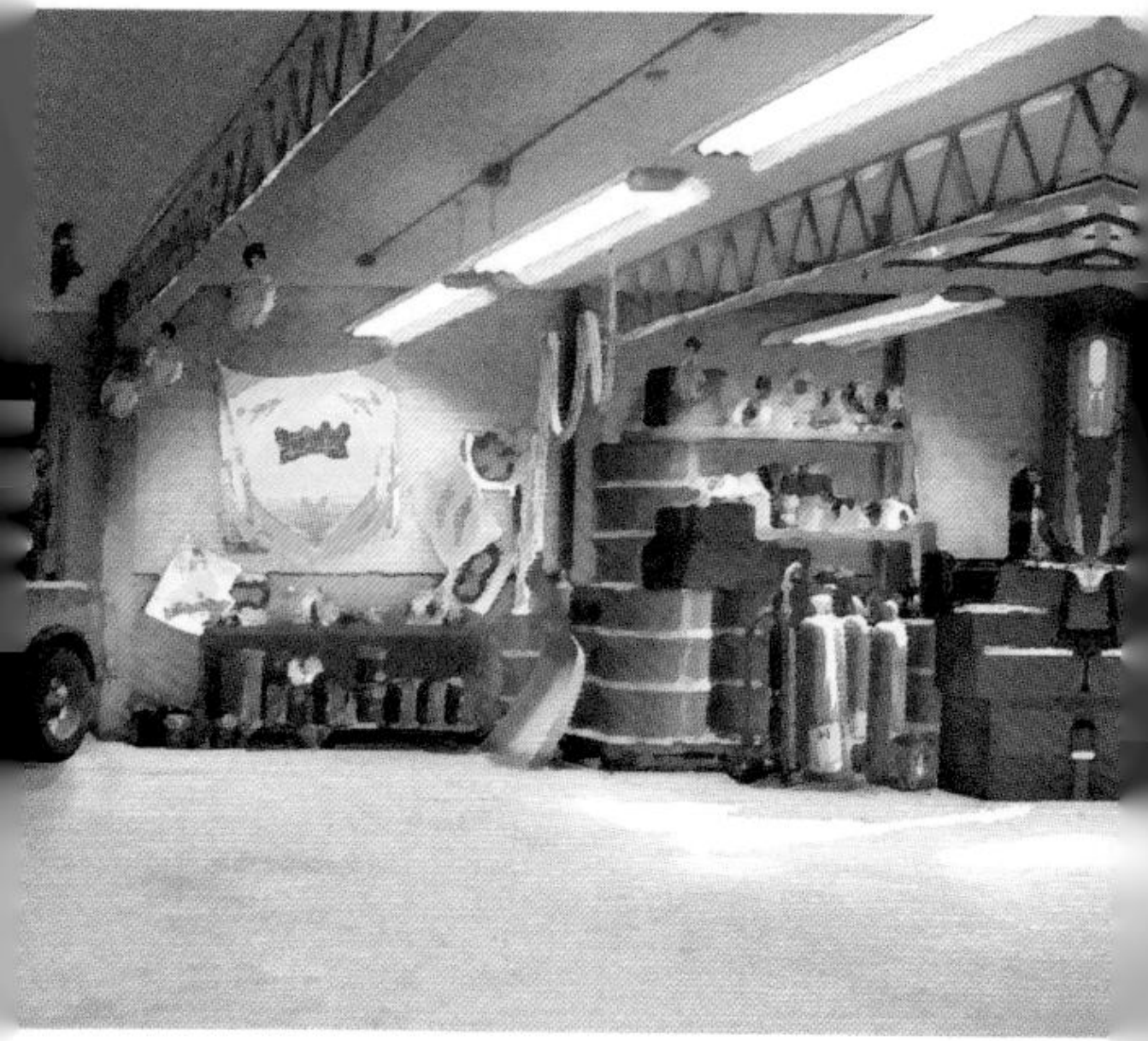

SHORT

LA LUNA

2011

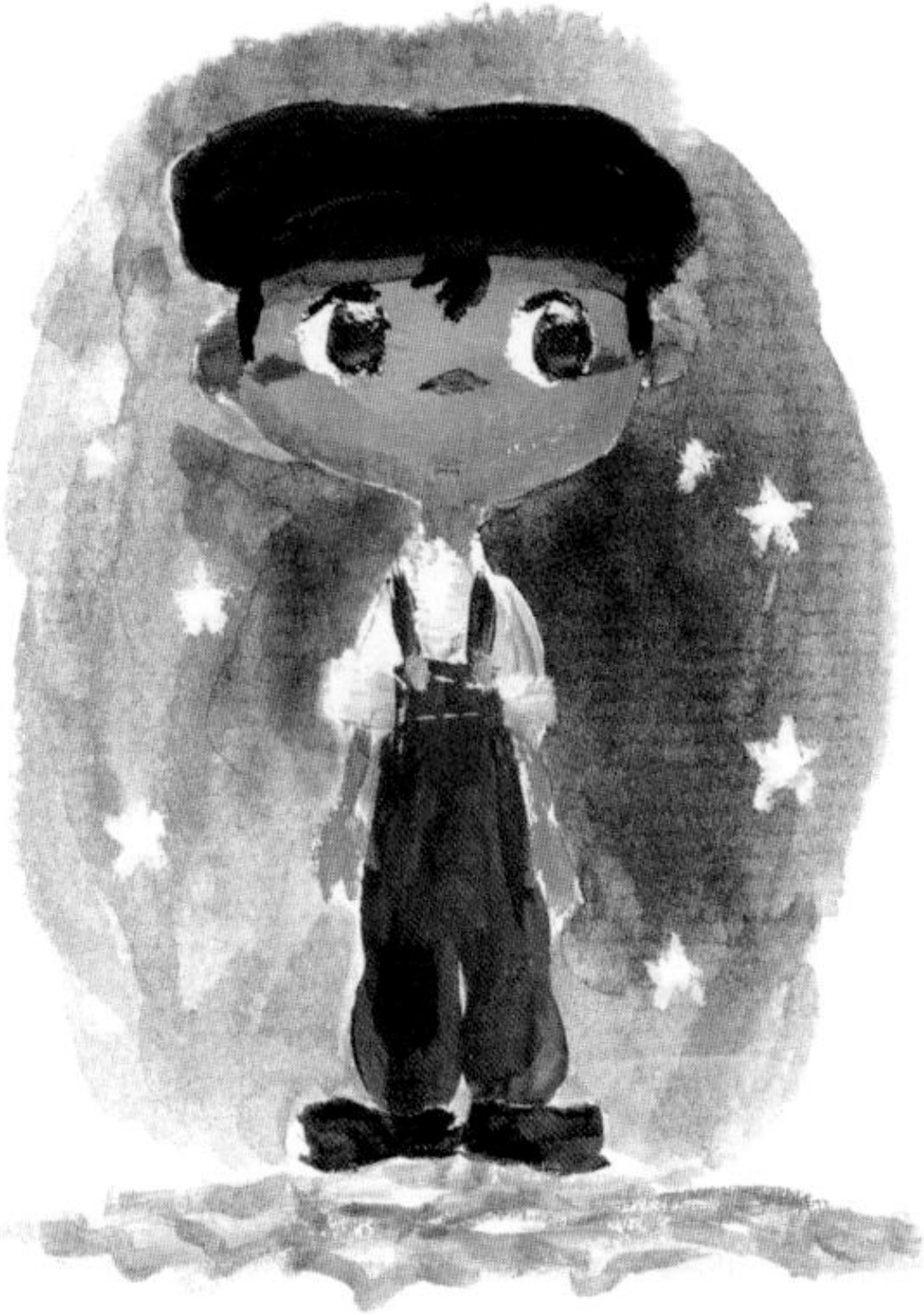

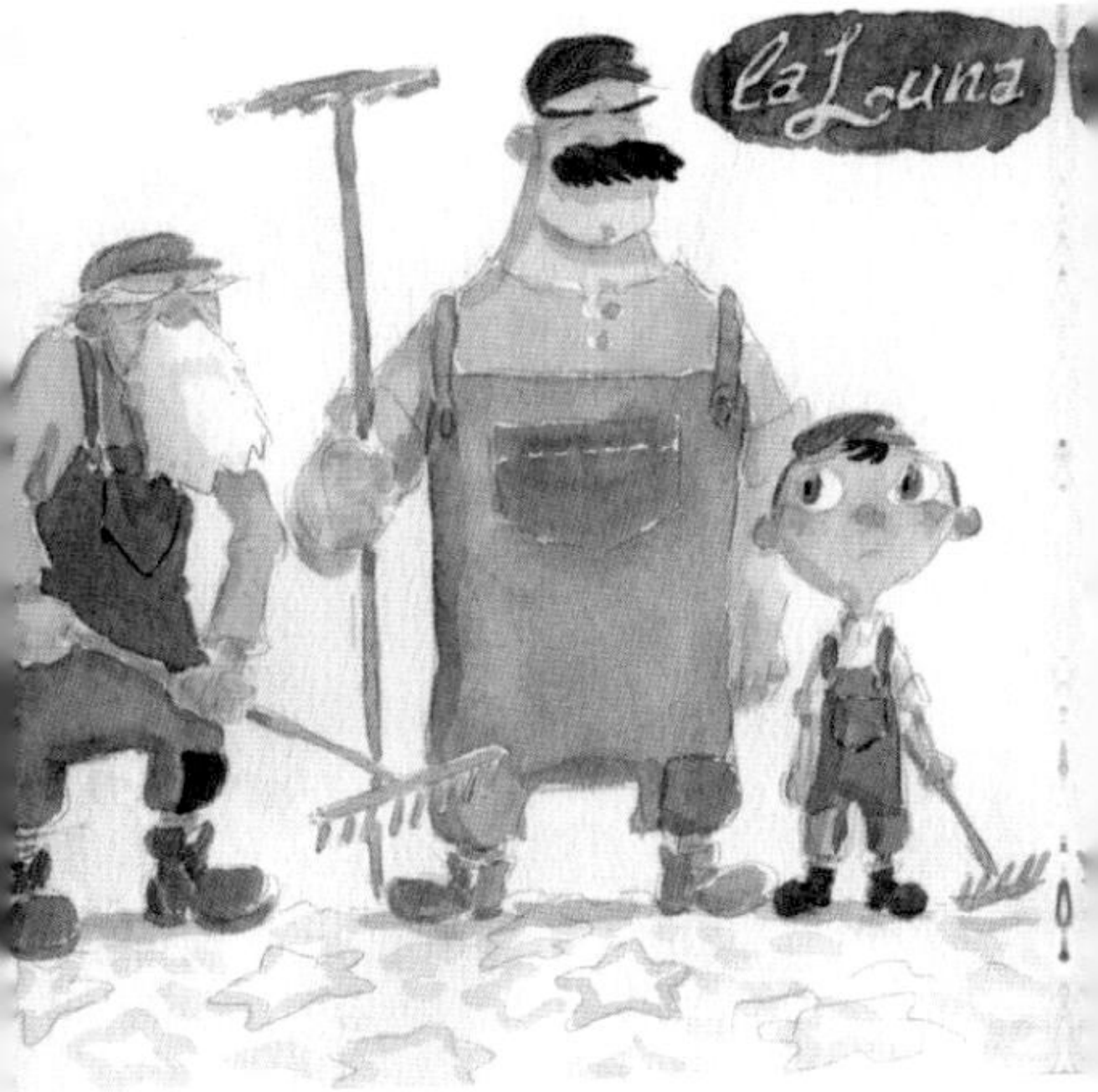
la Luna

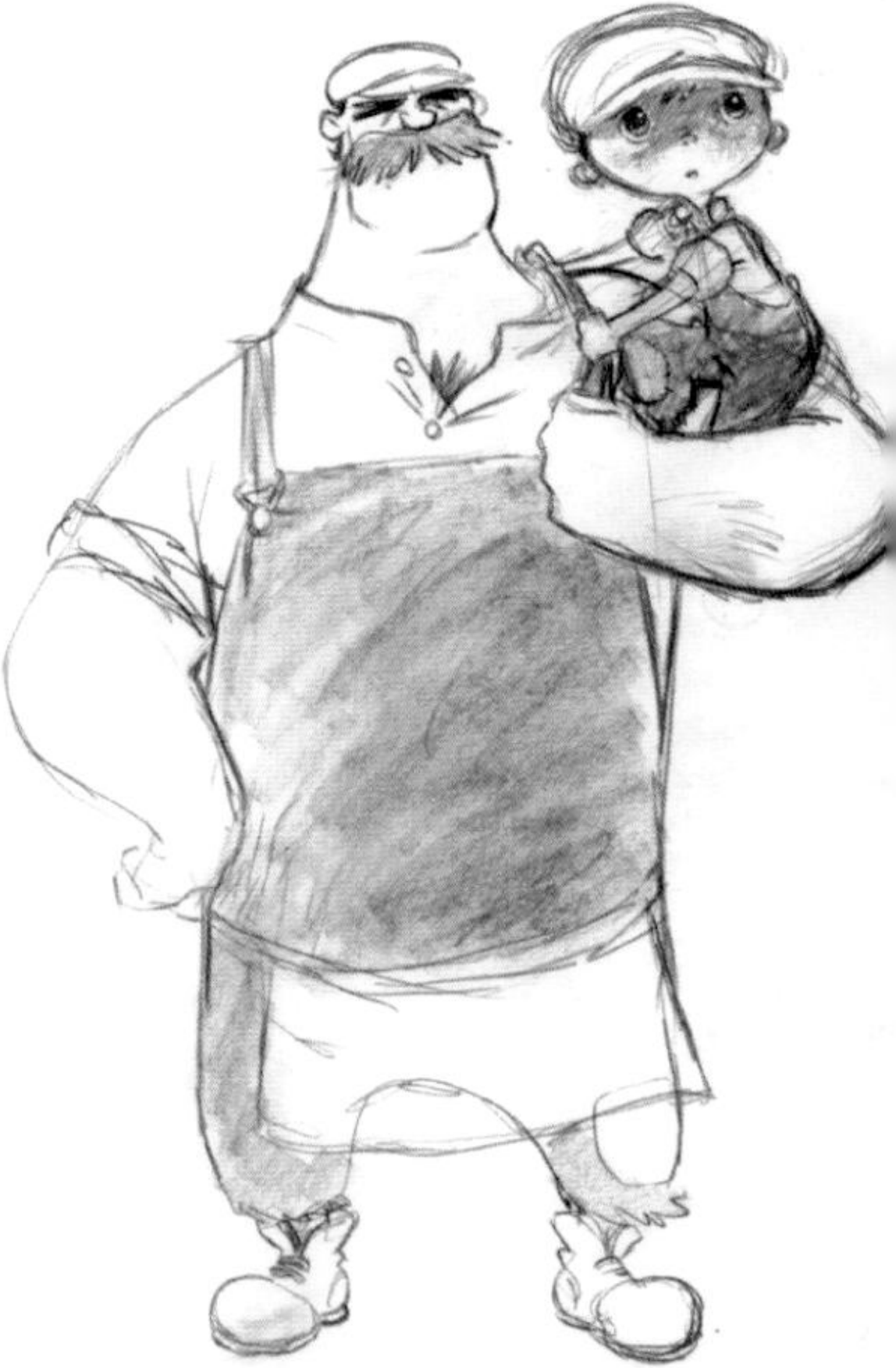

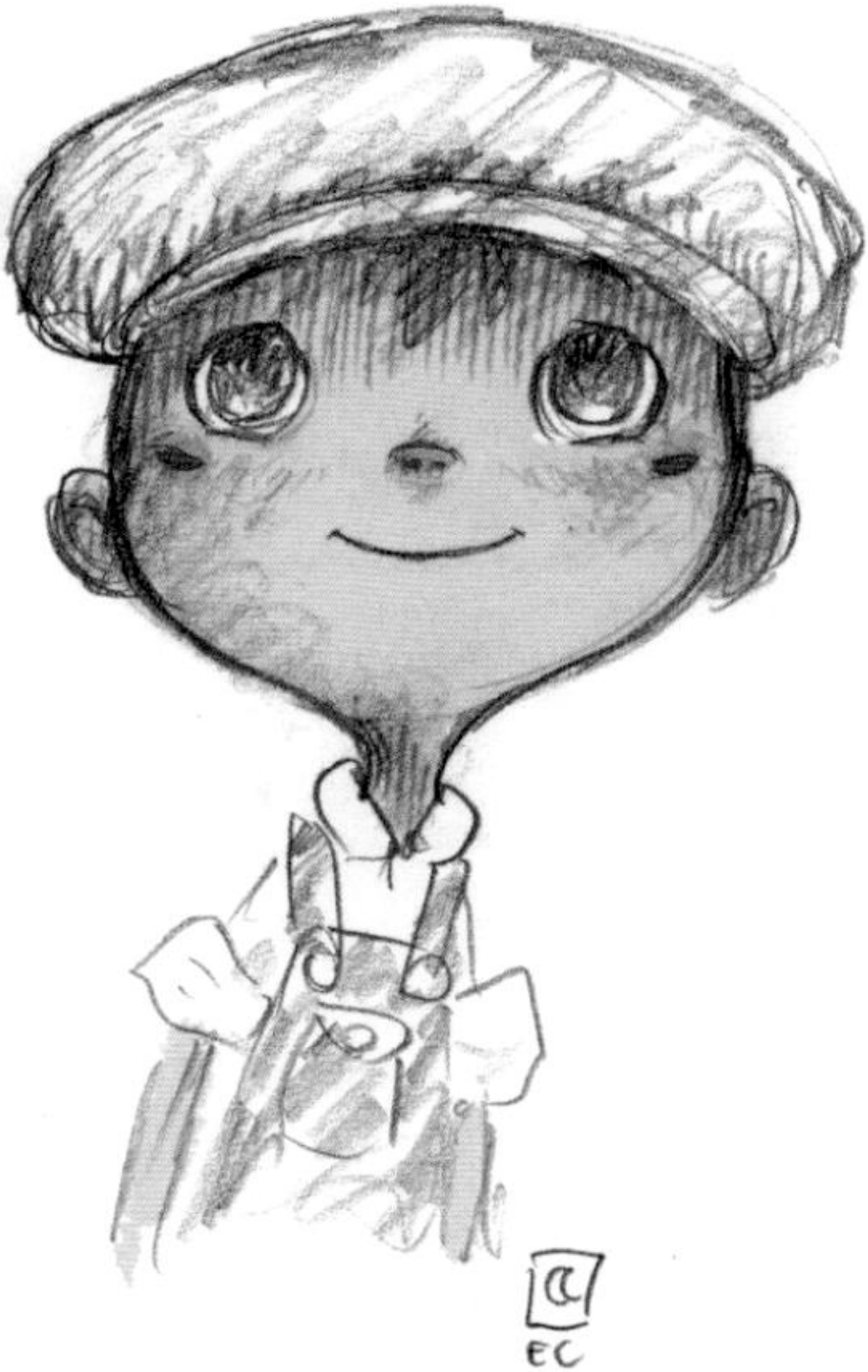
EC

BRAVE
2012

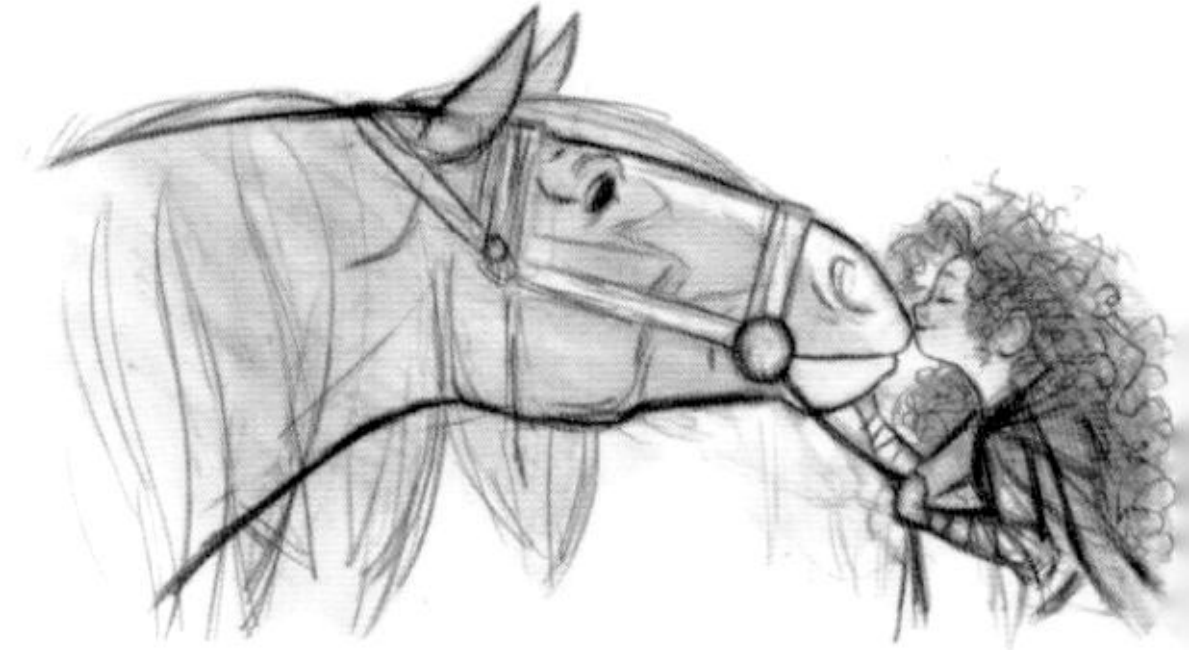

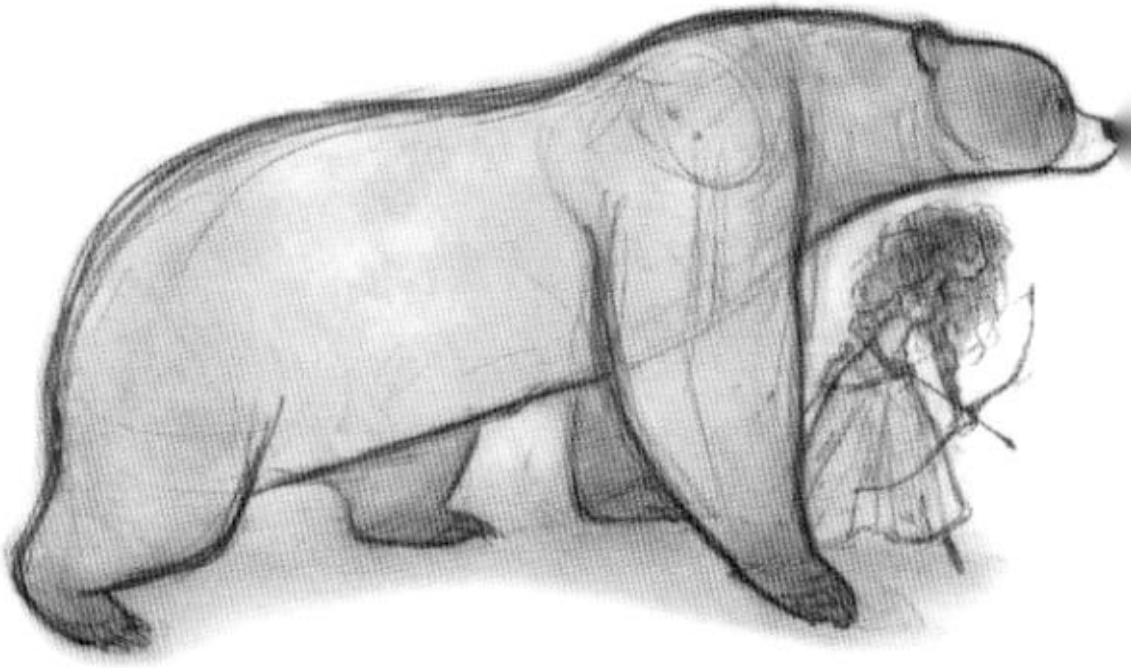

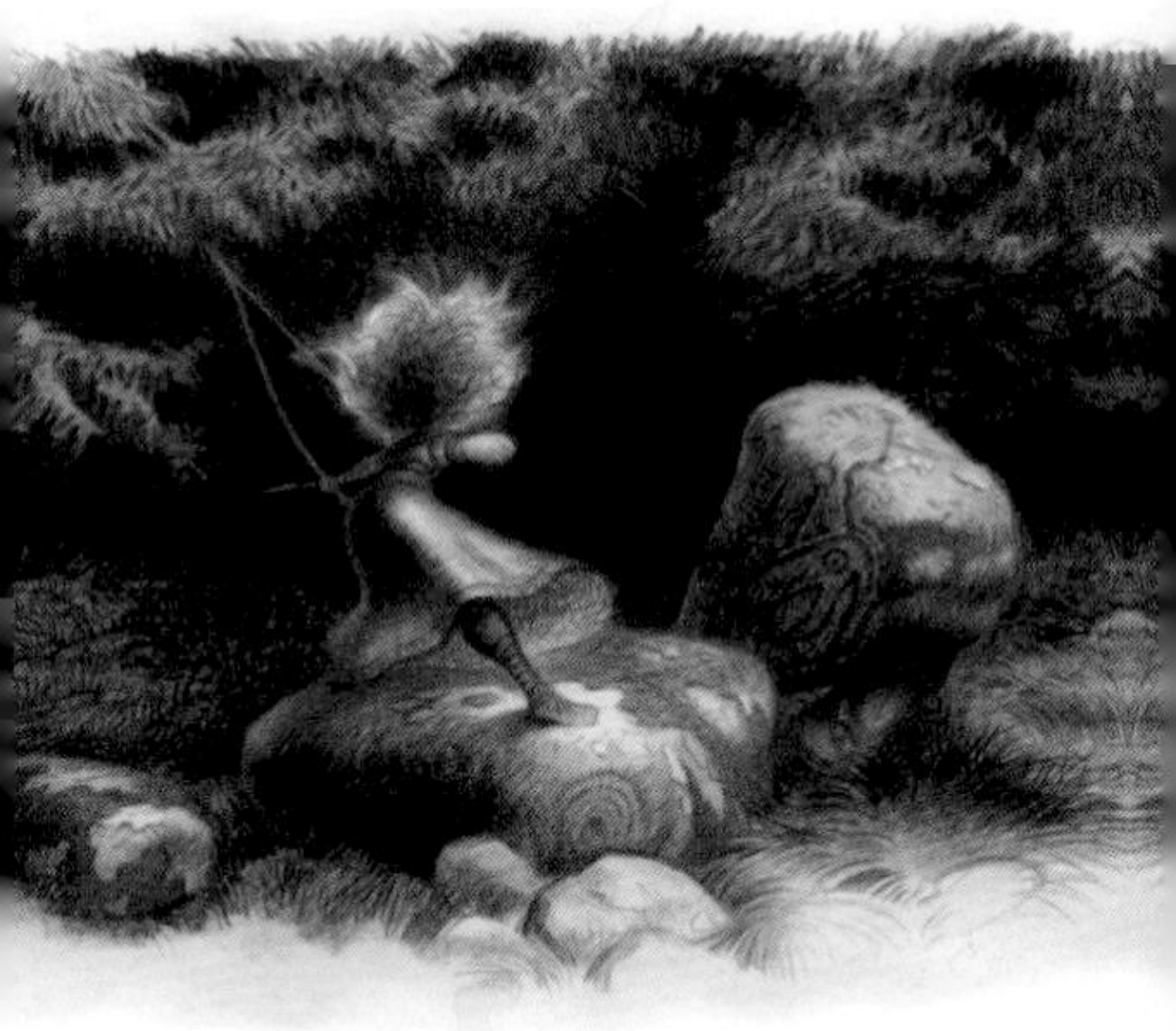

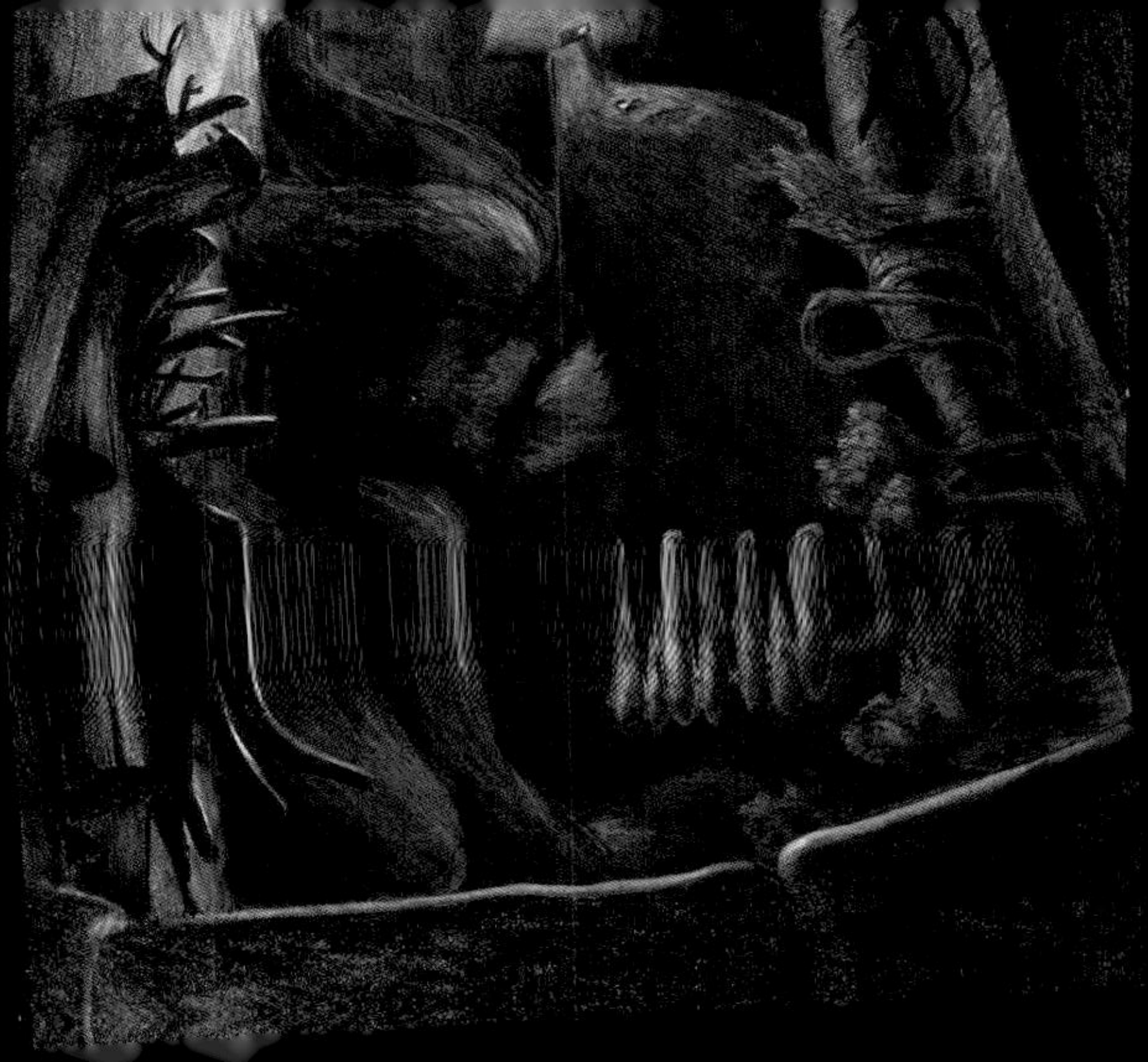

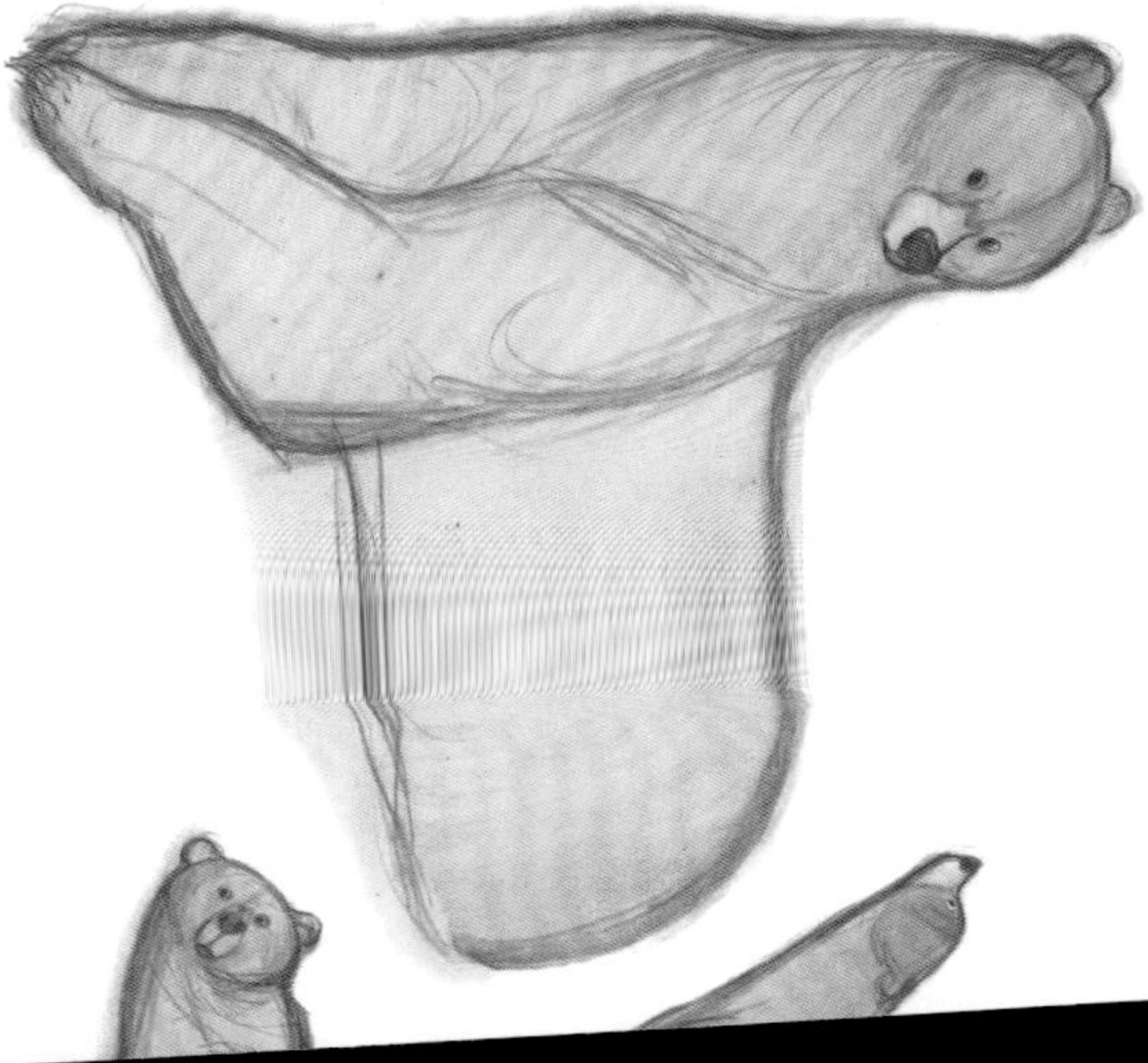

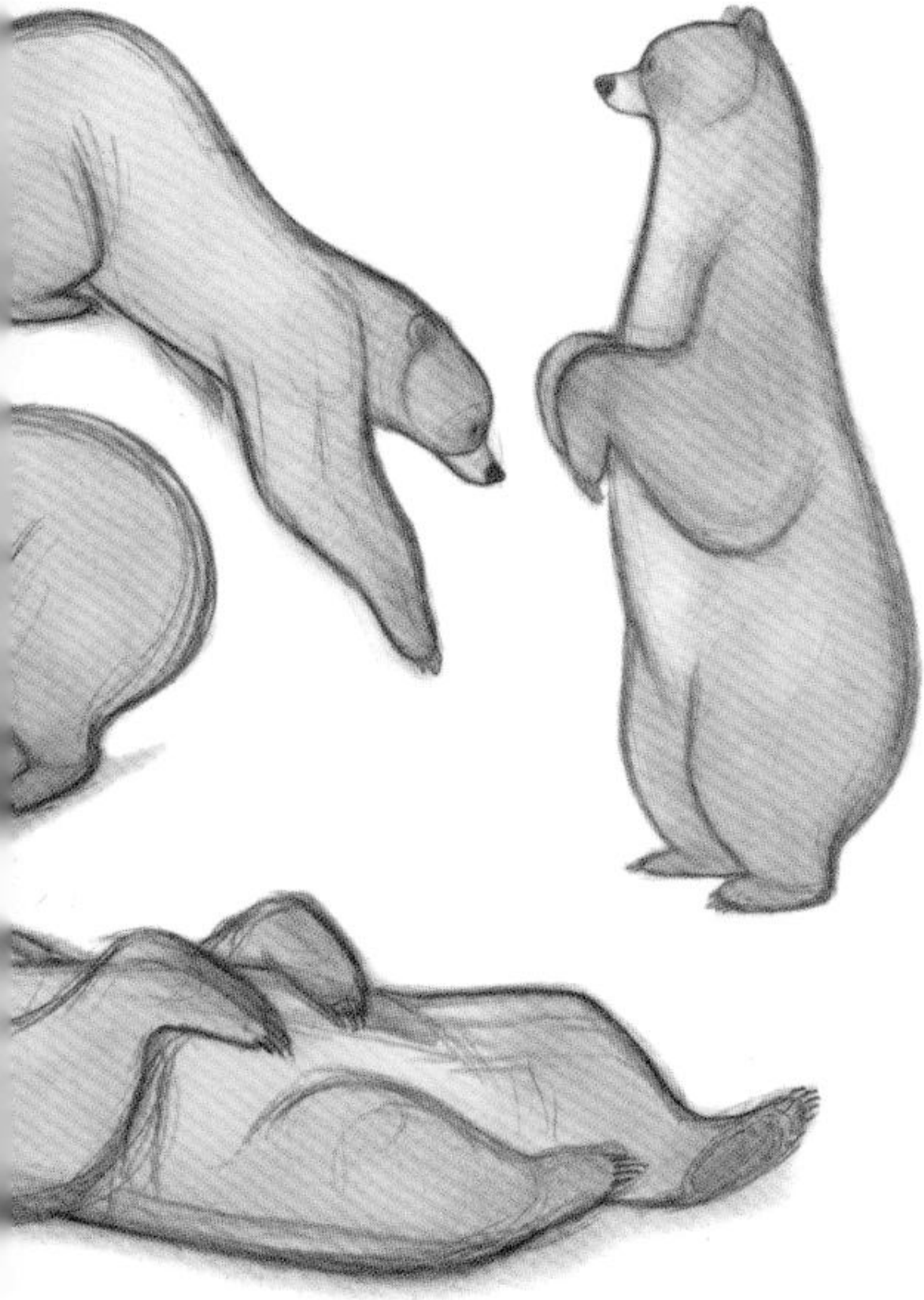

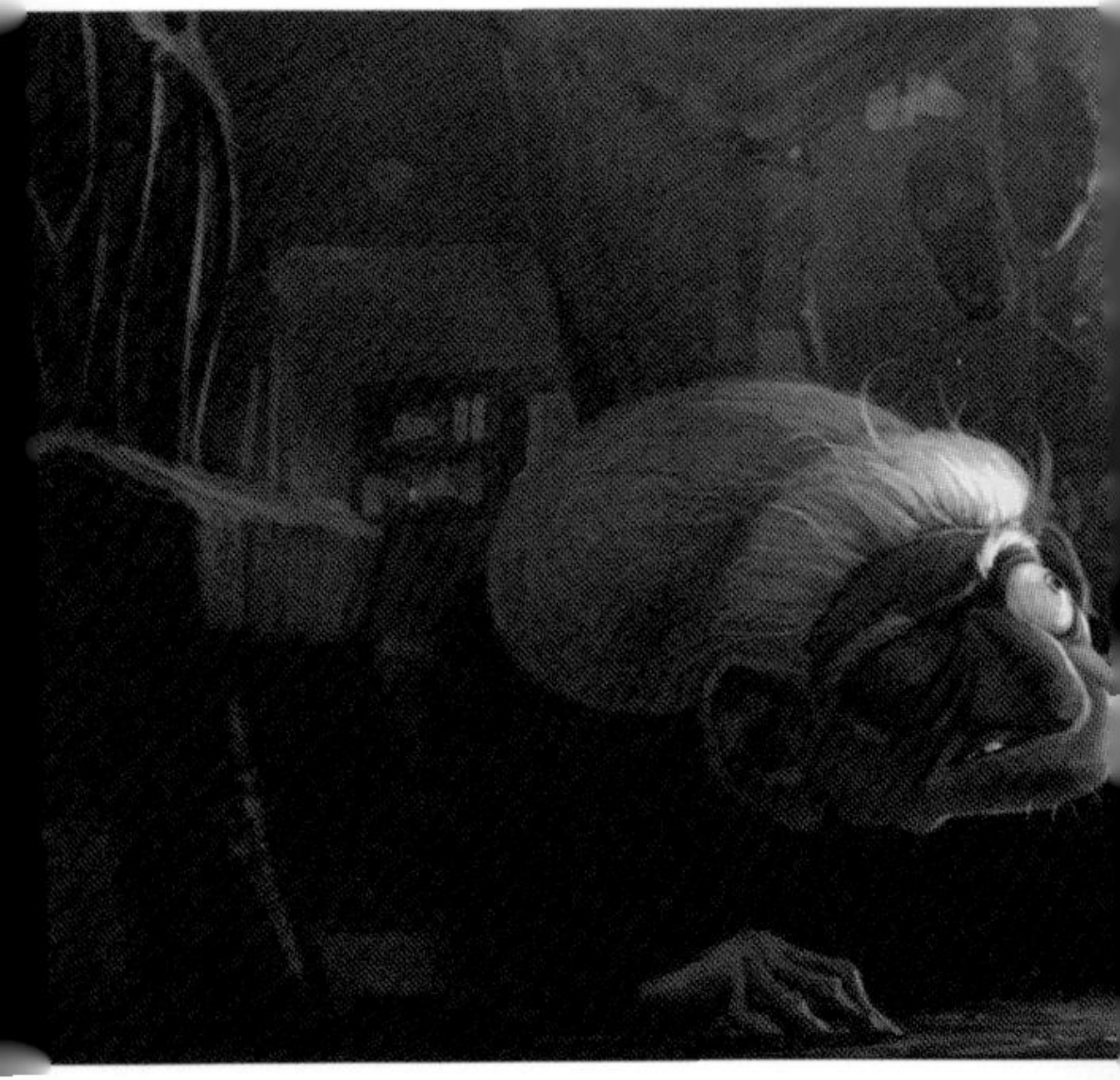

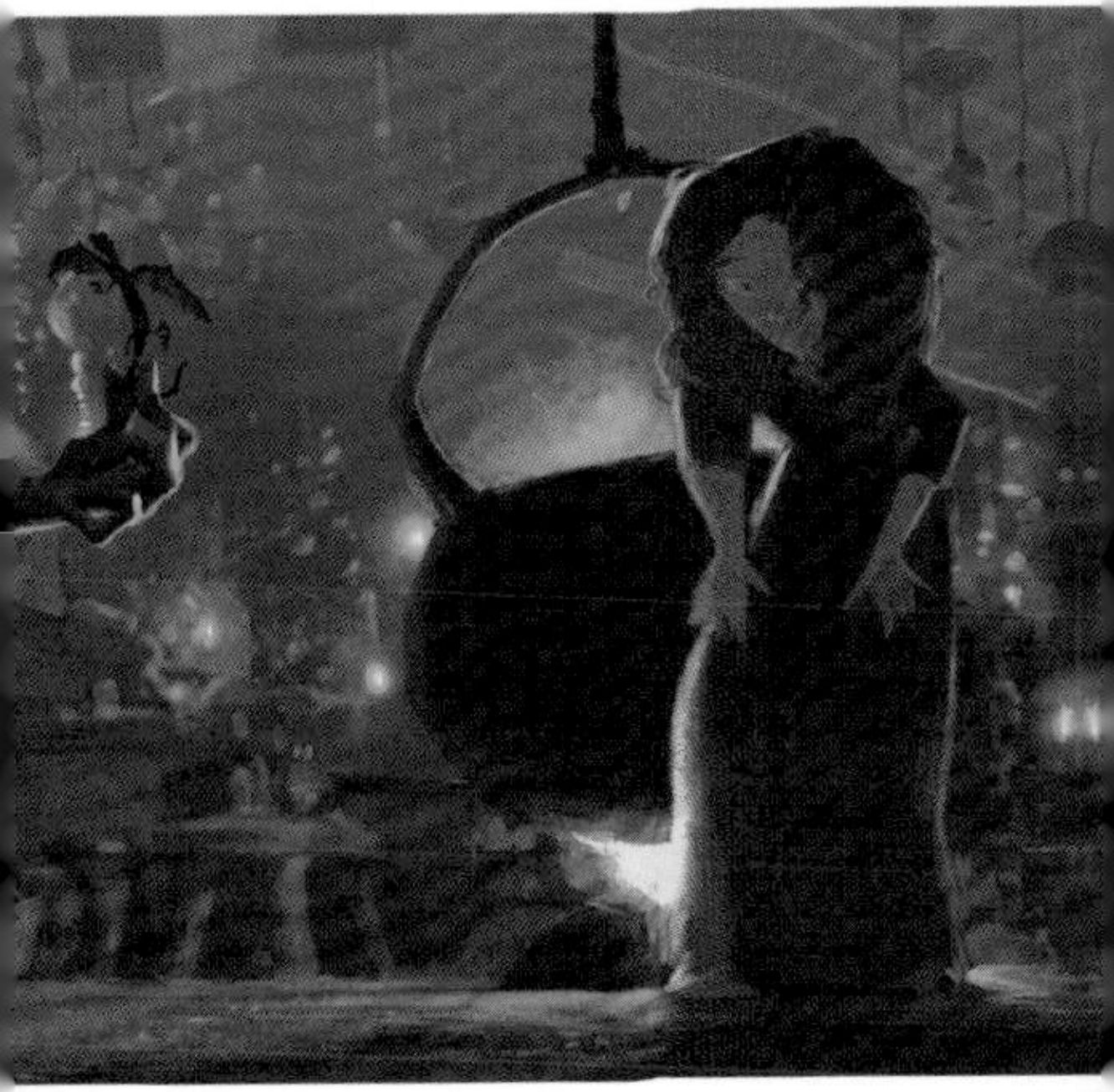

SHORT

THE BLUE UMBRELLA

2013

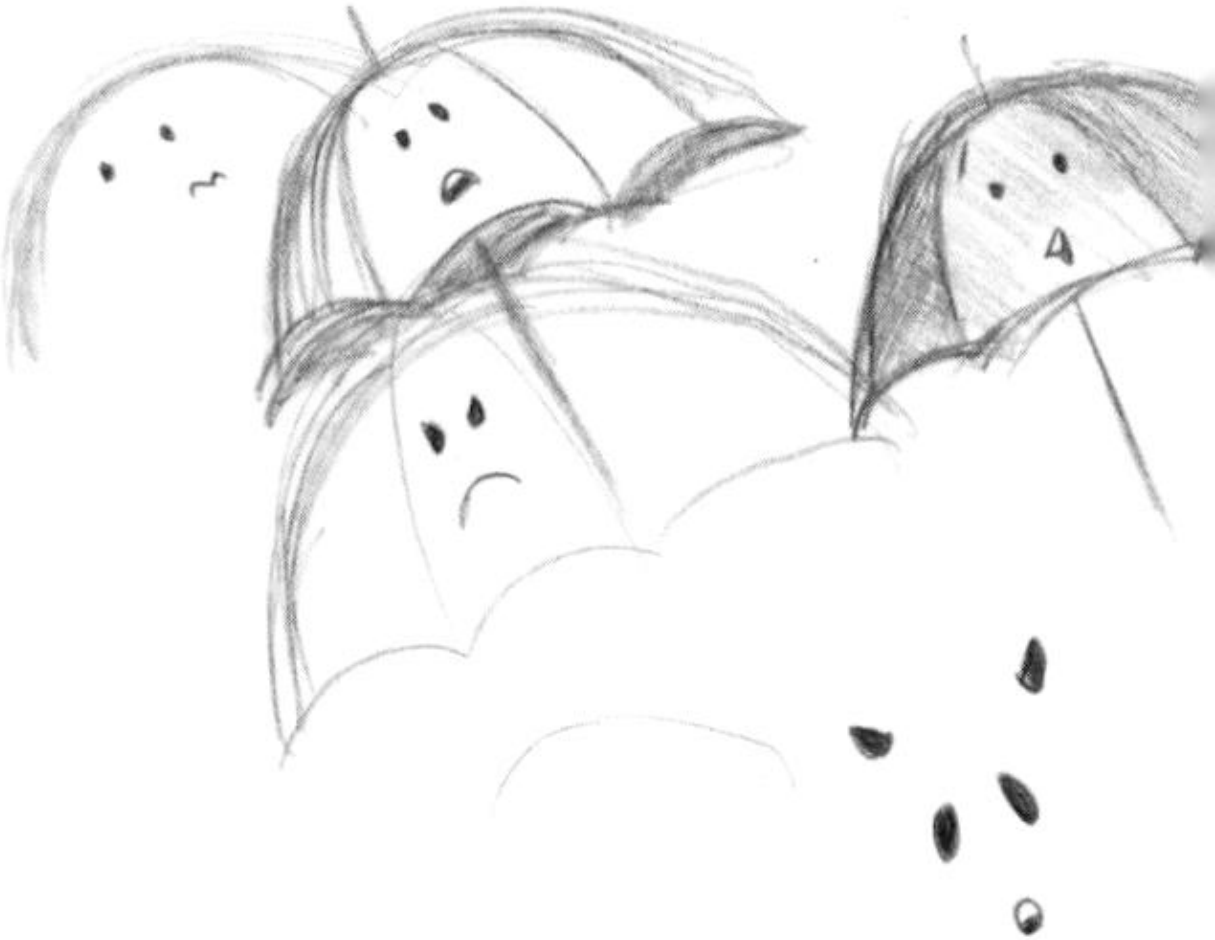

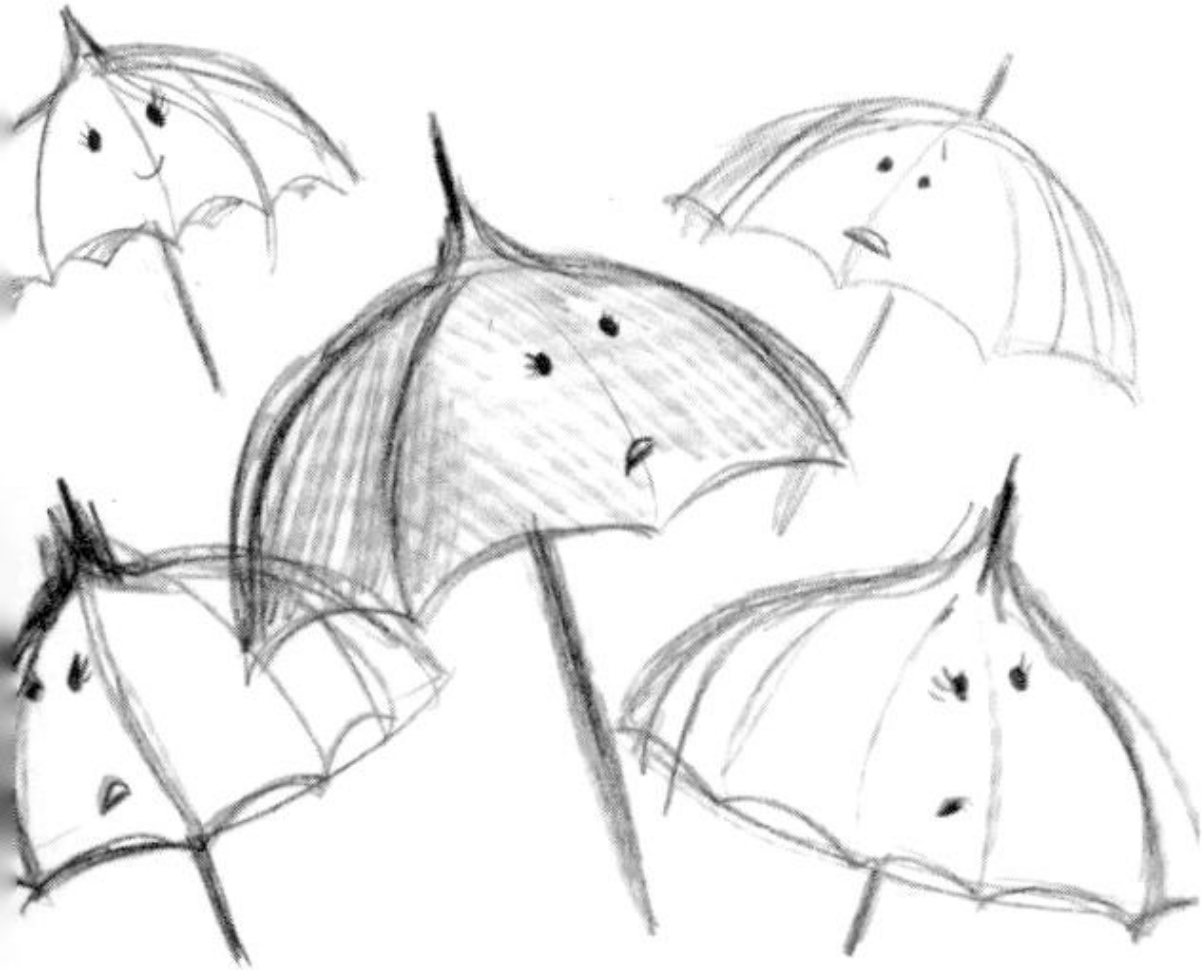

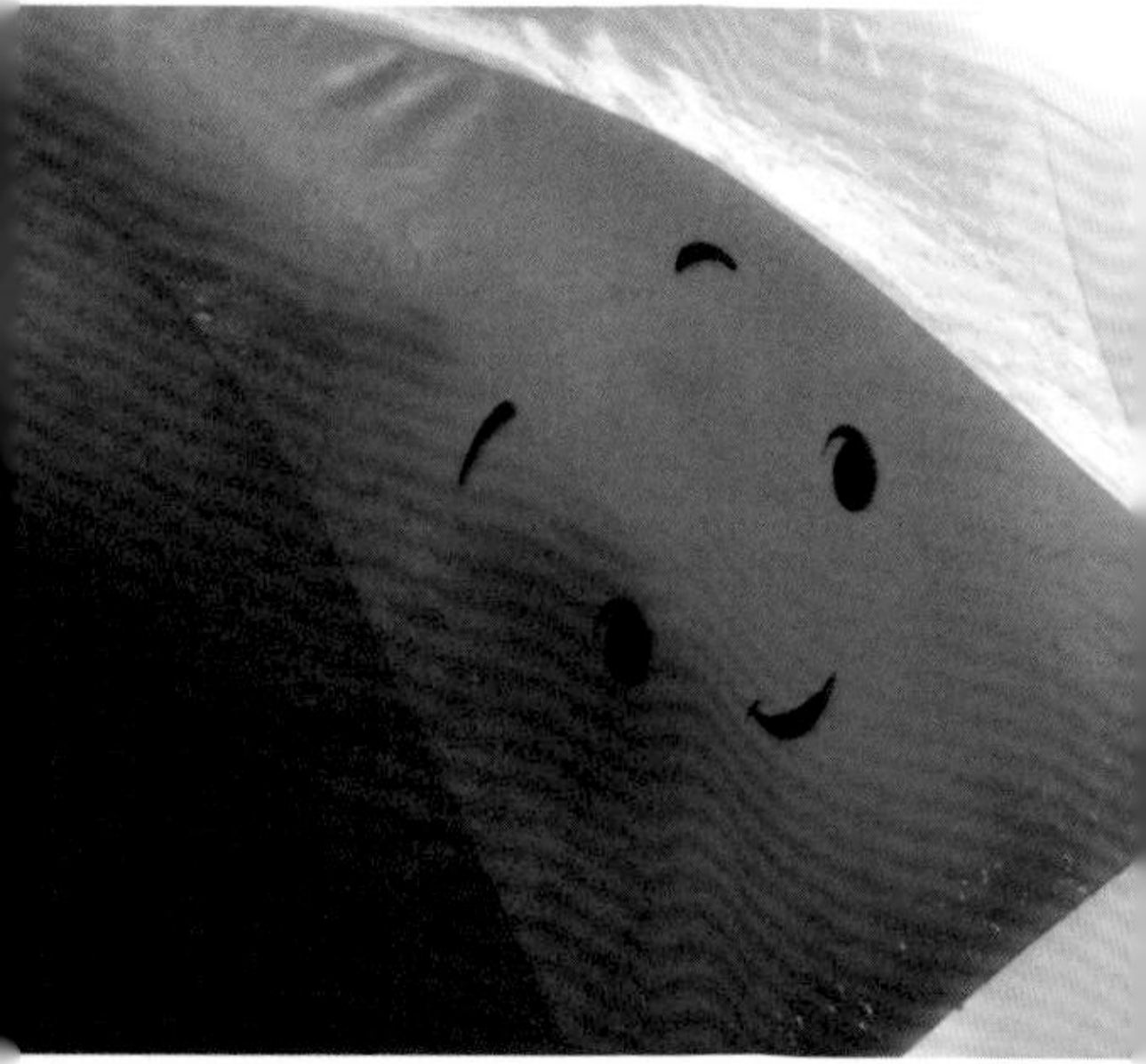

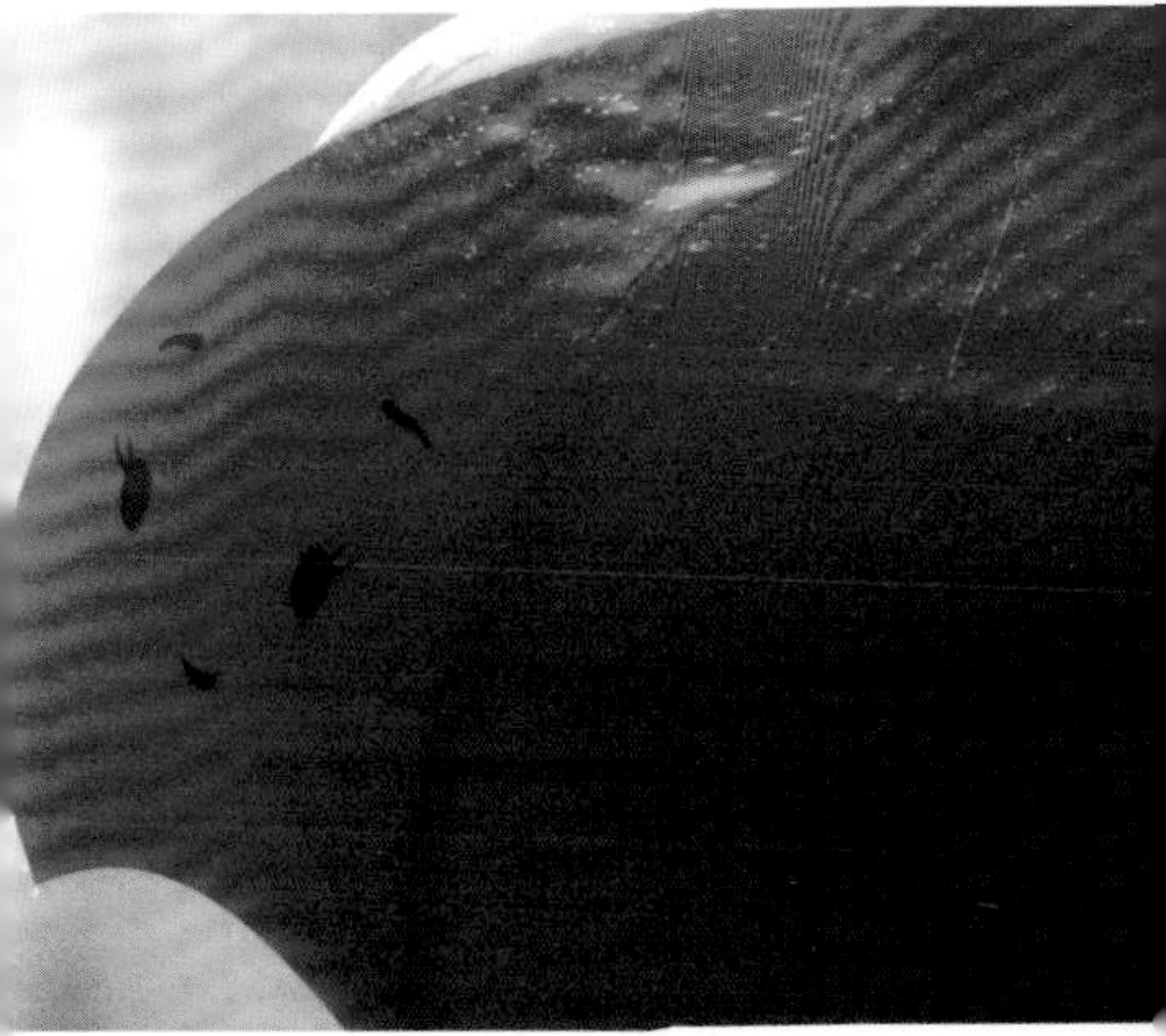

MONSTERS UNIVERSITY
2013

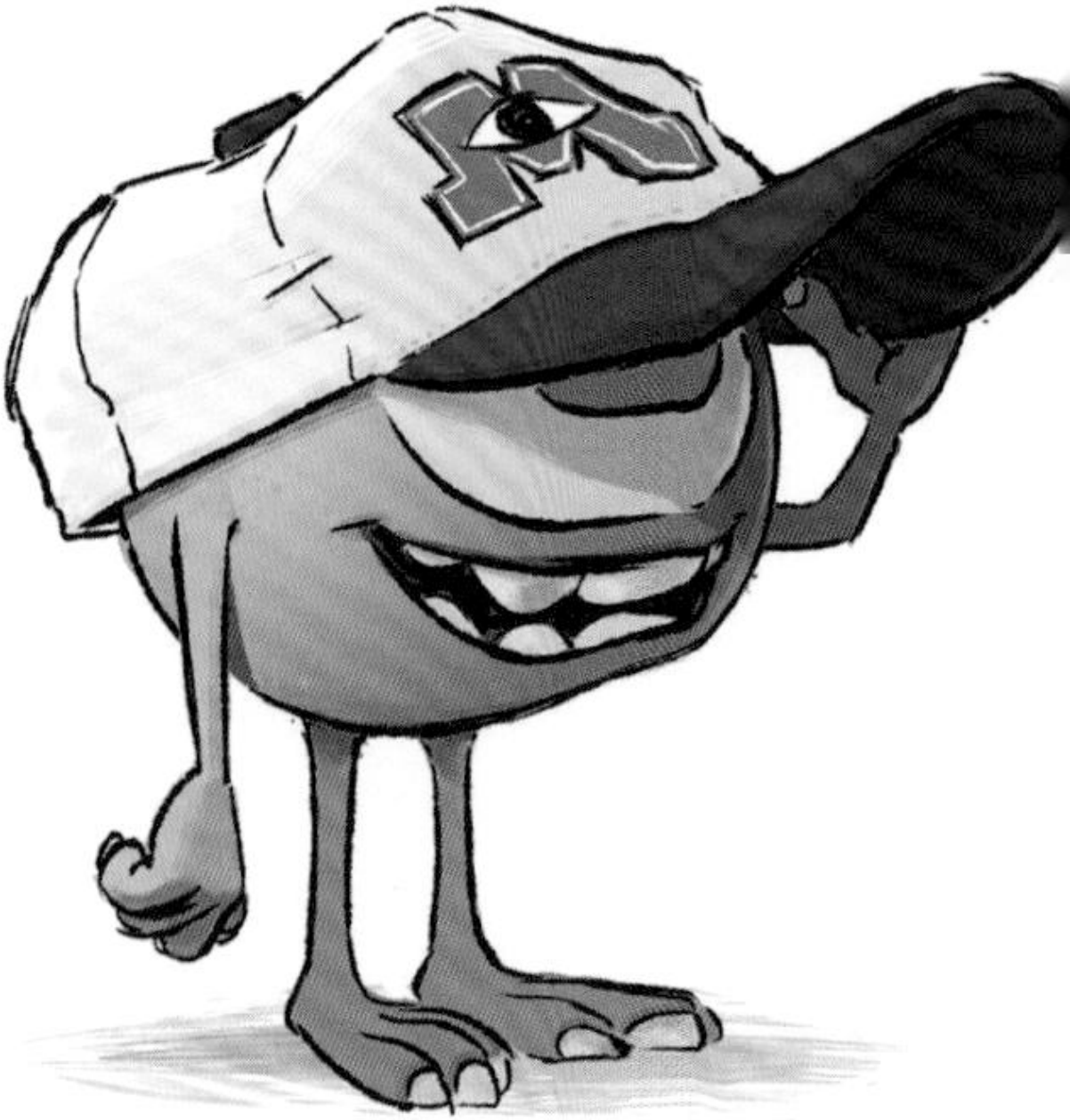

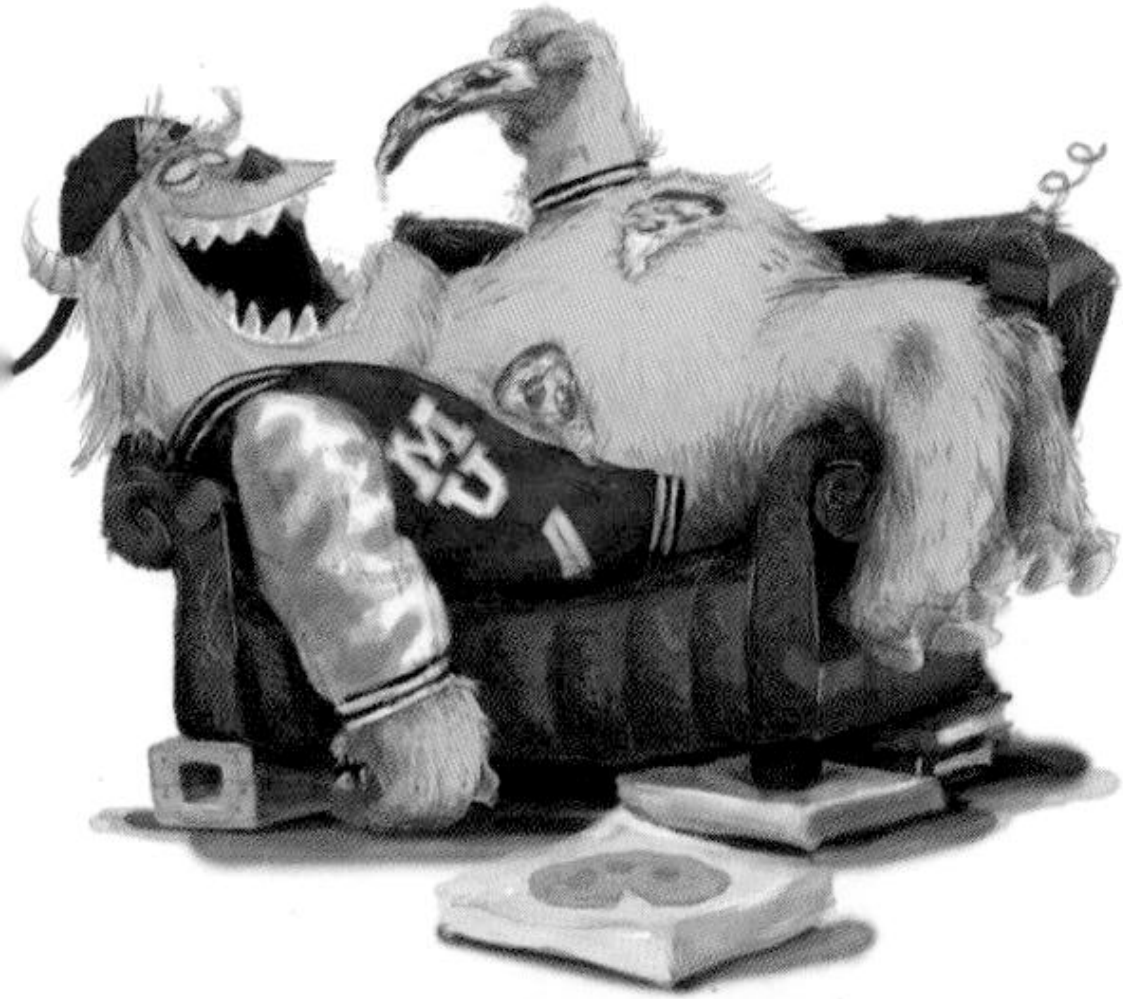

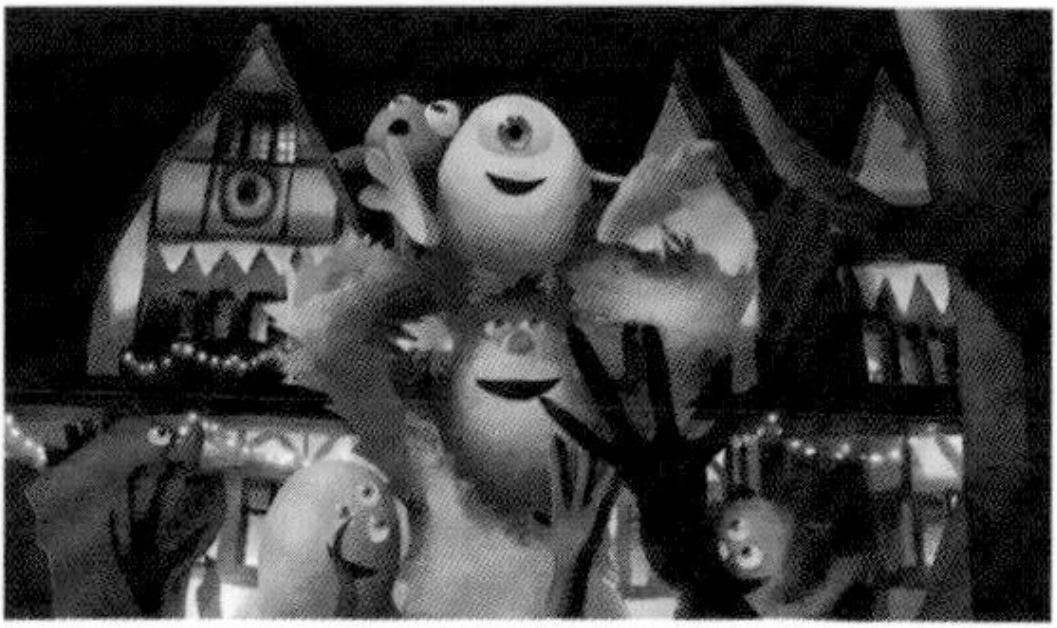

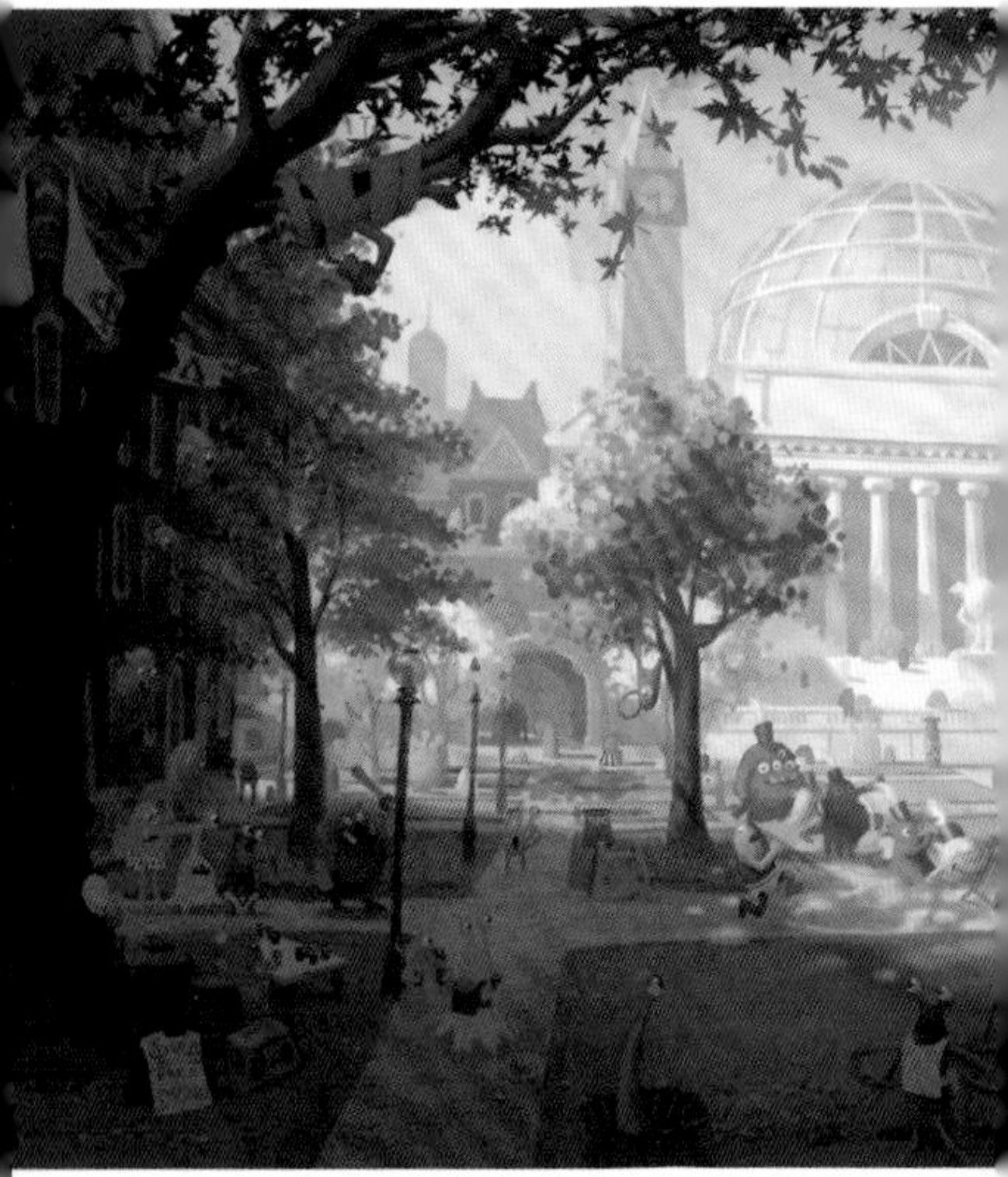

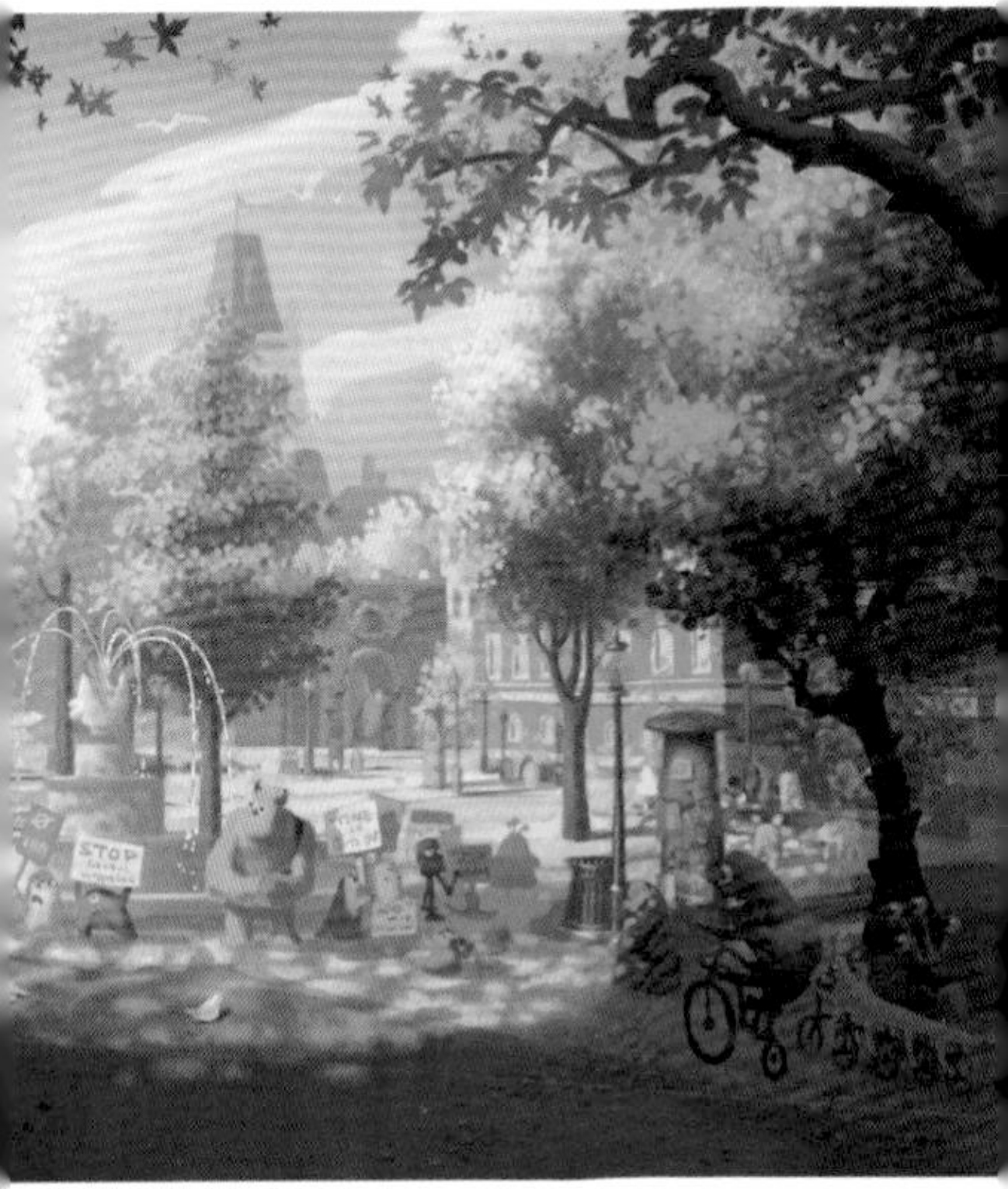
STOP

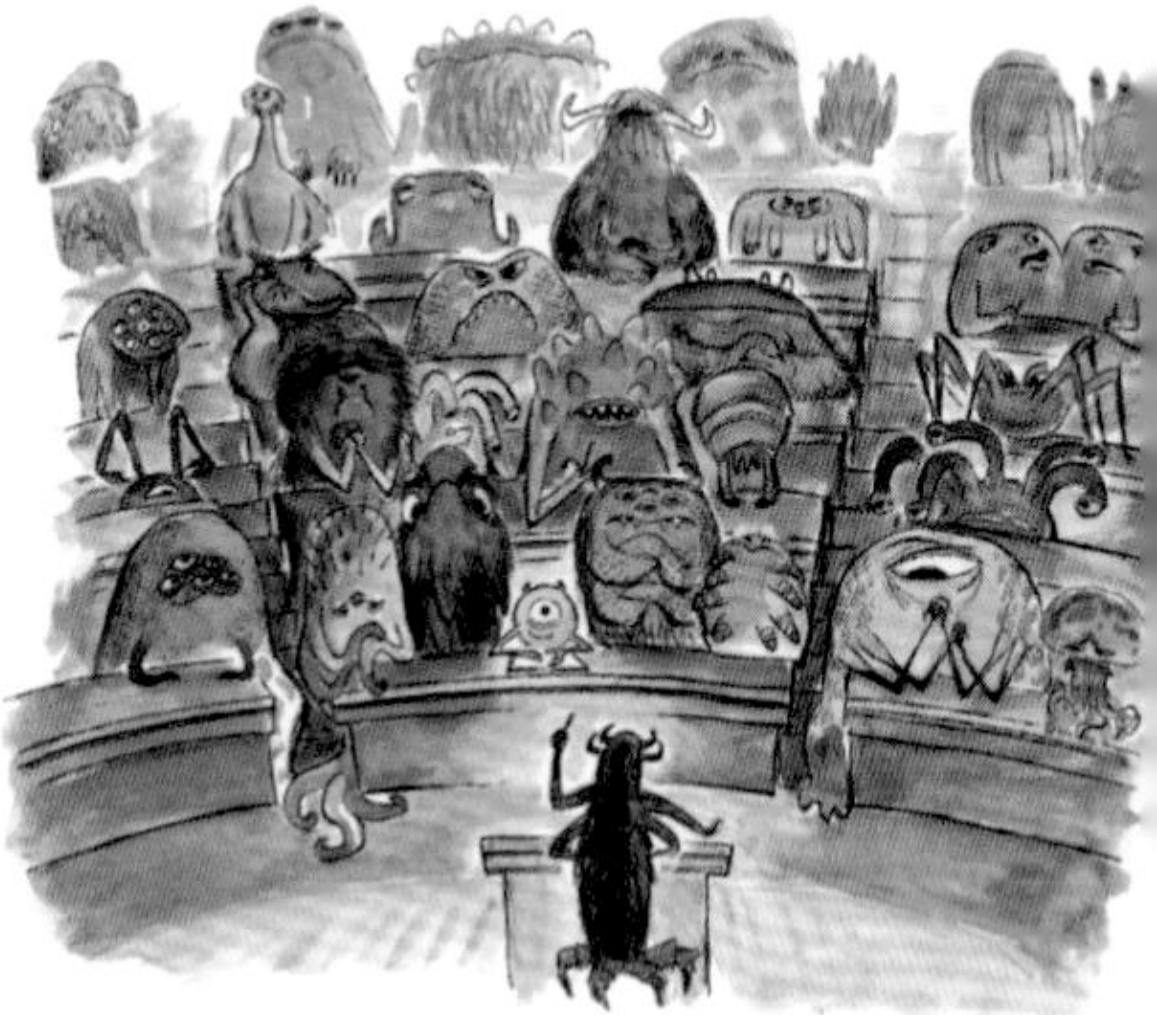

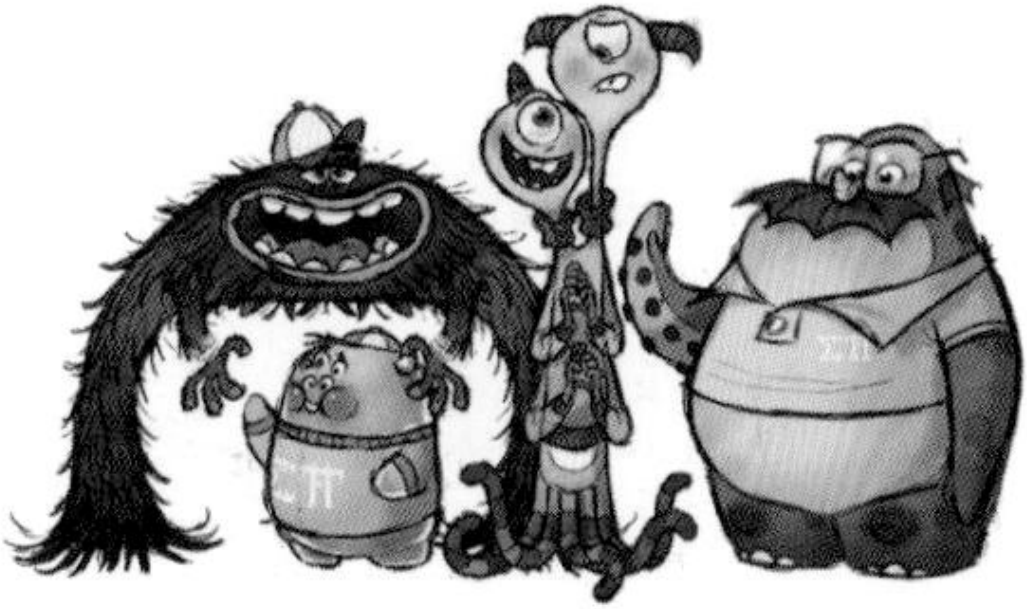

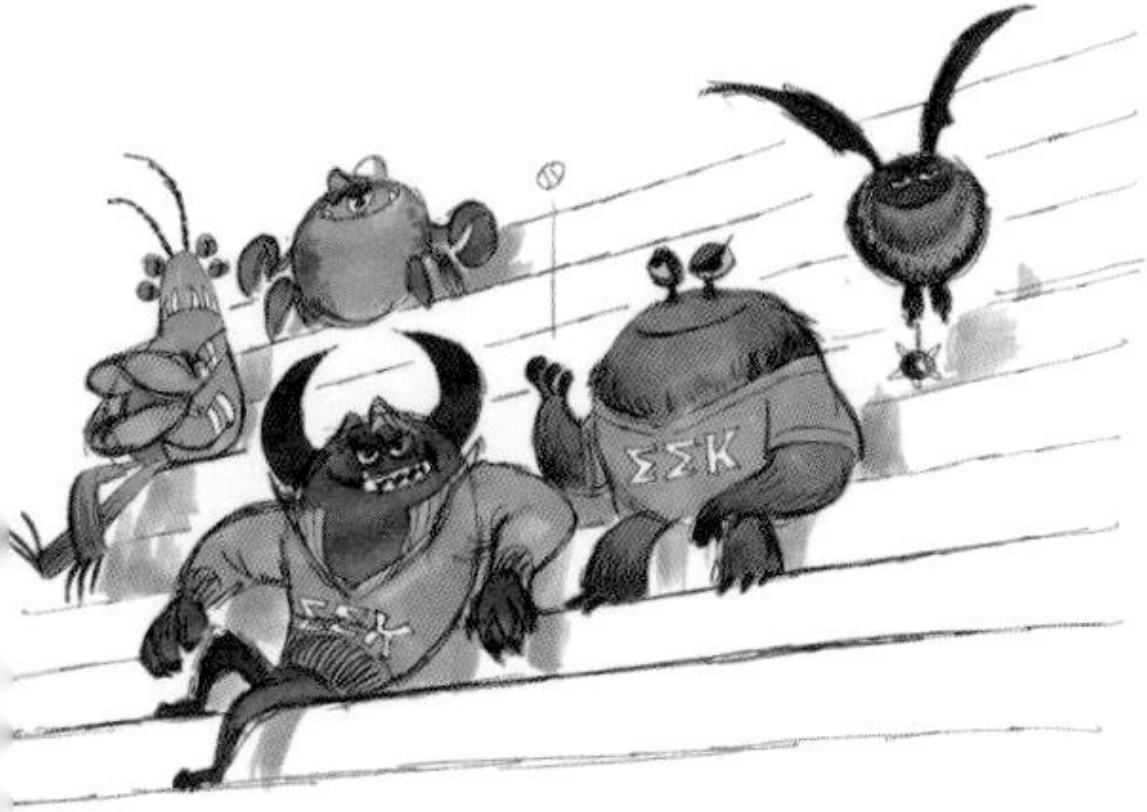
ΣΣΚ

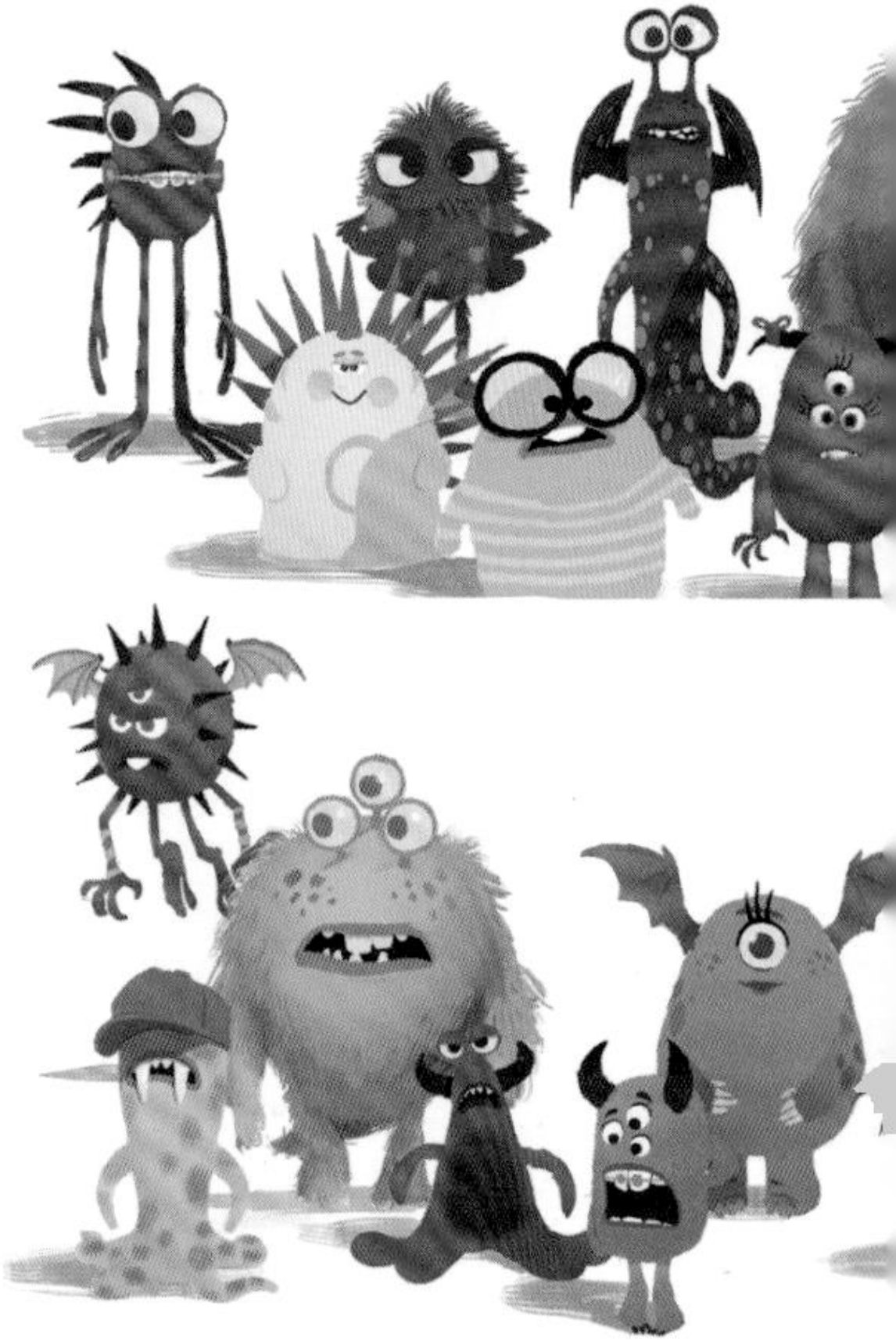

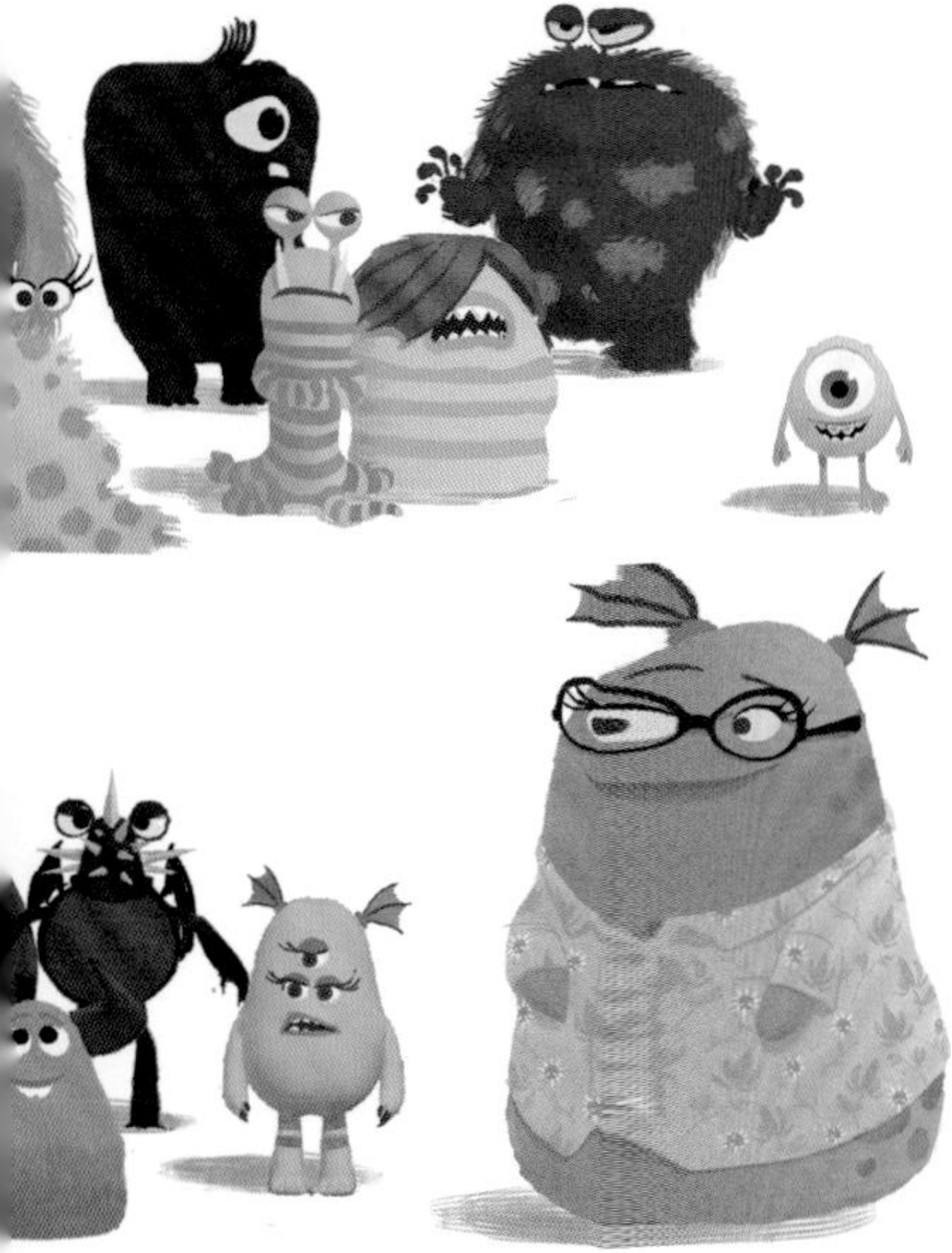

SHORT
LAVA
2014

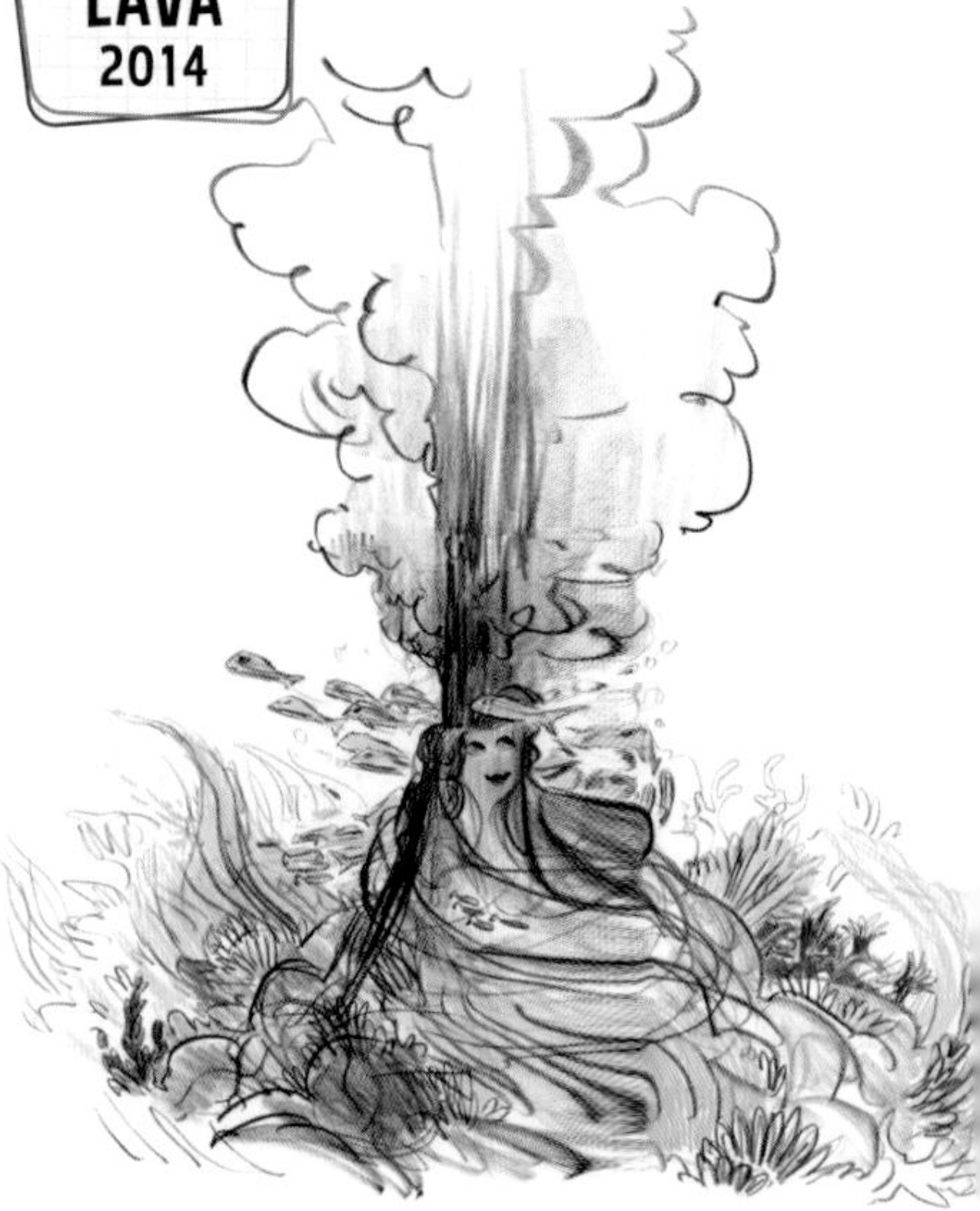

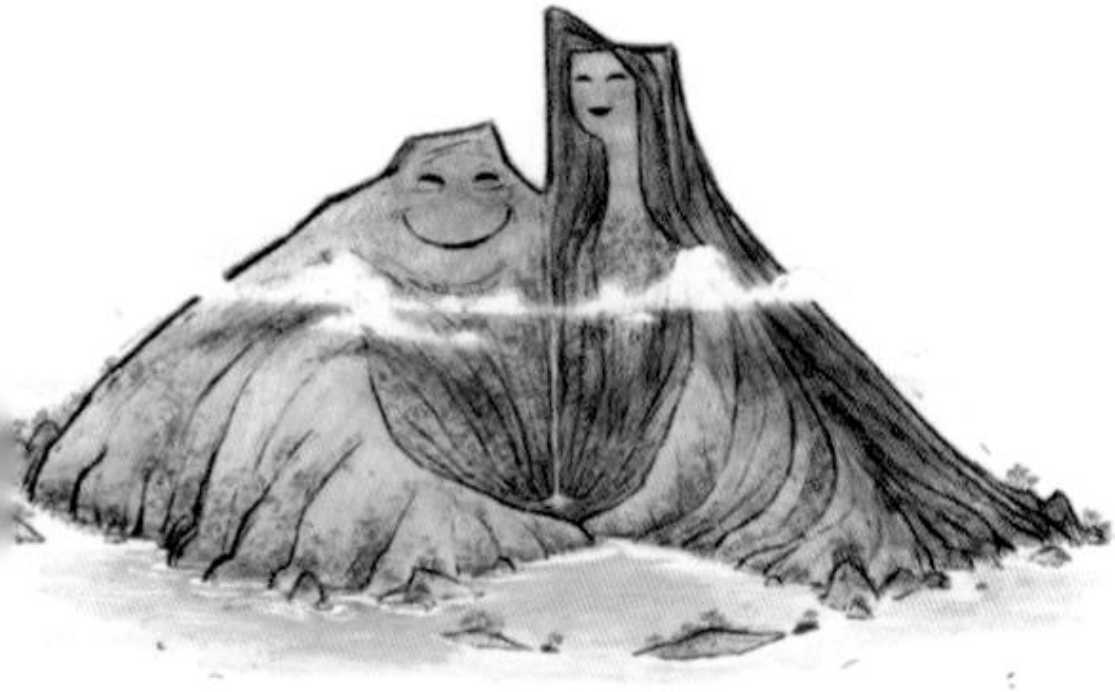

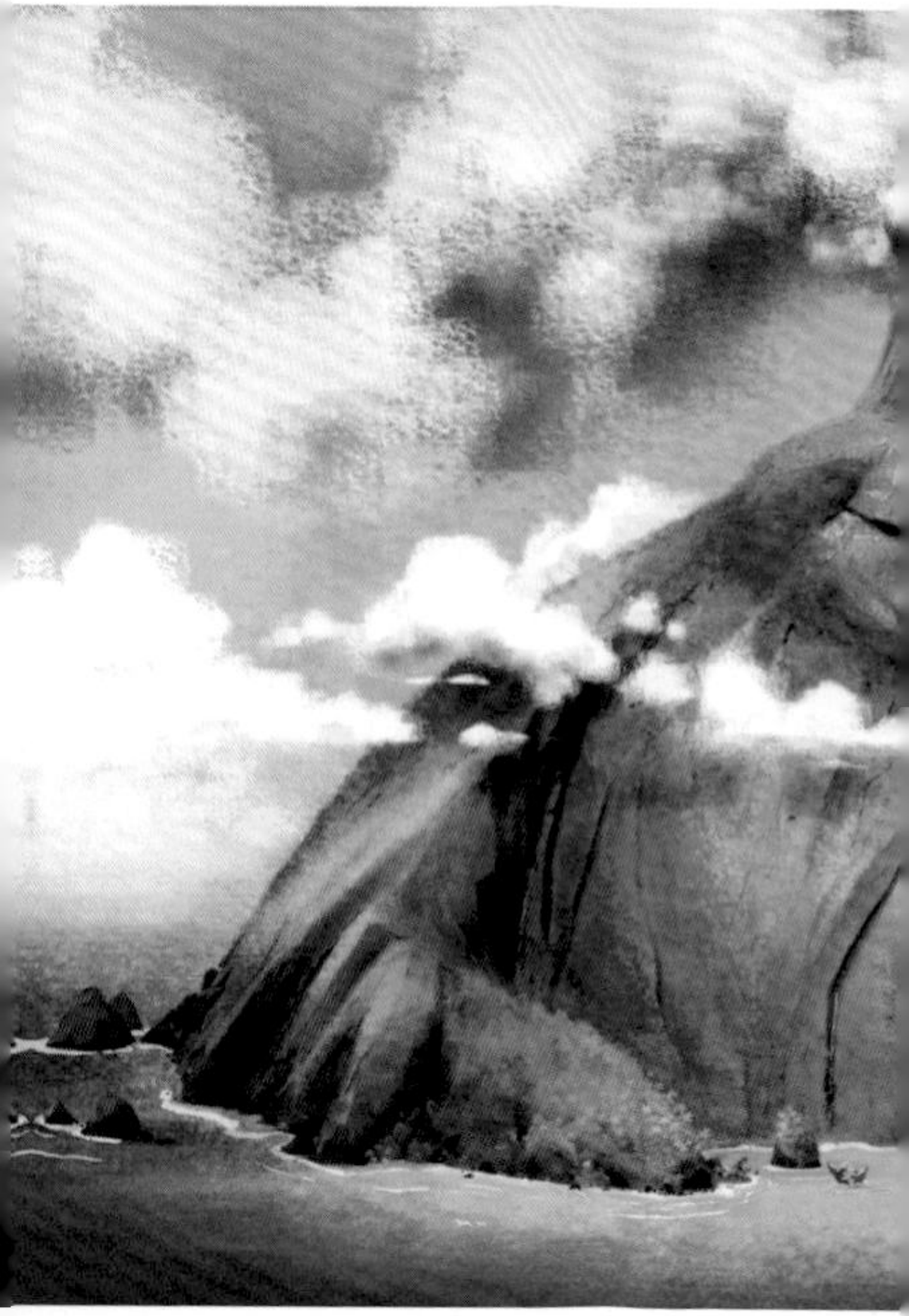

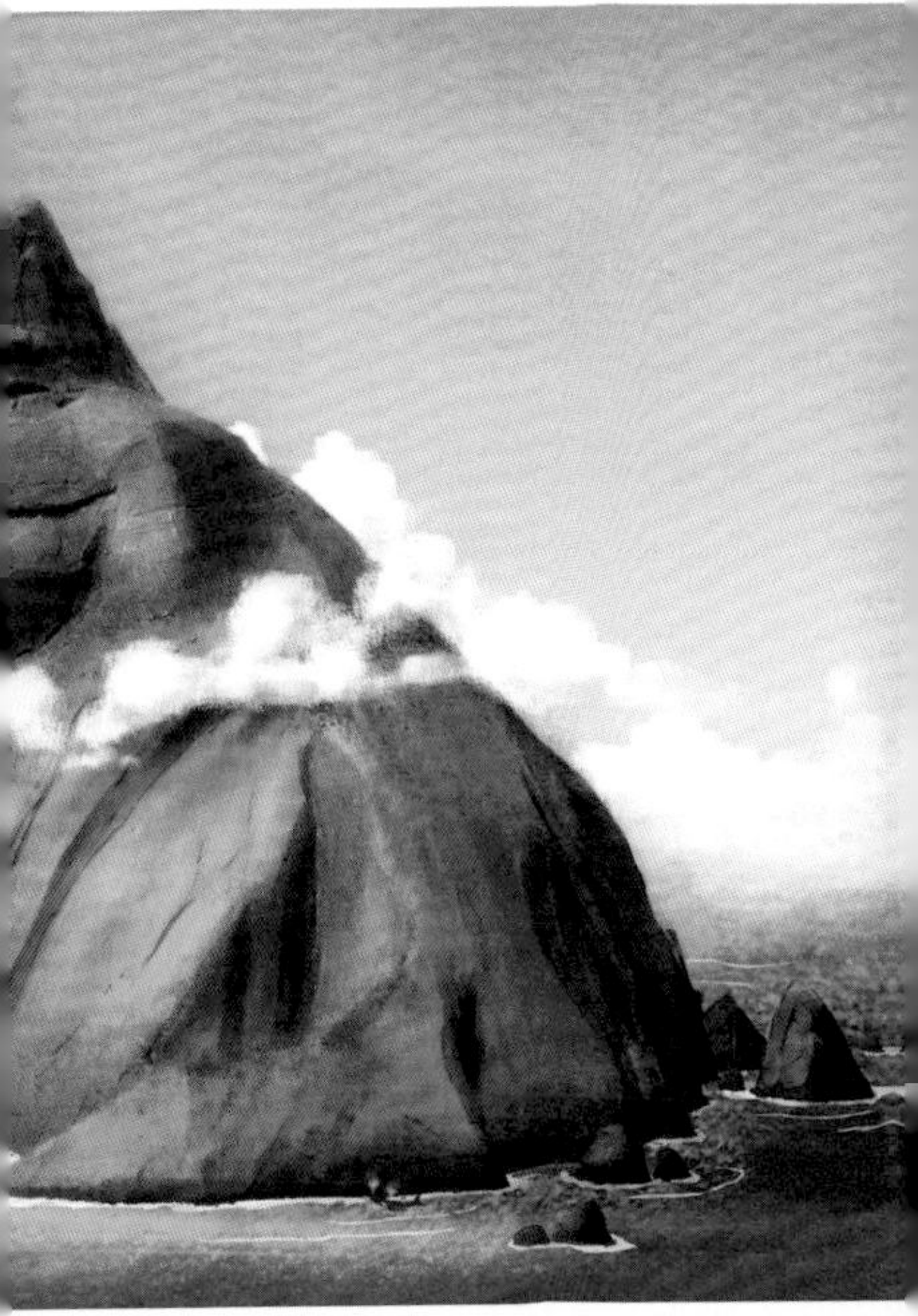

INSIDE OUT
2015

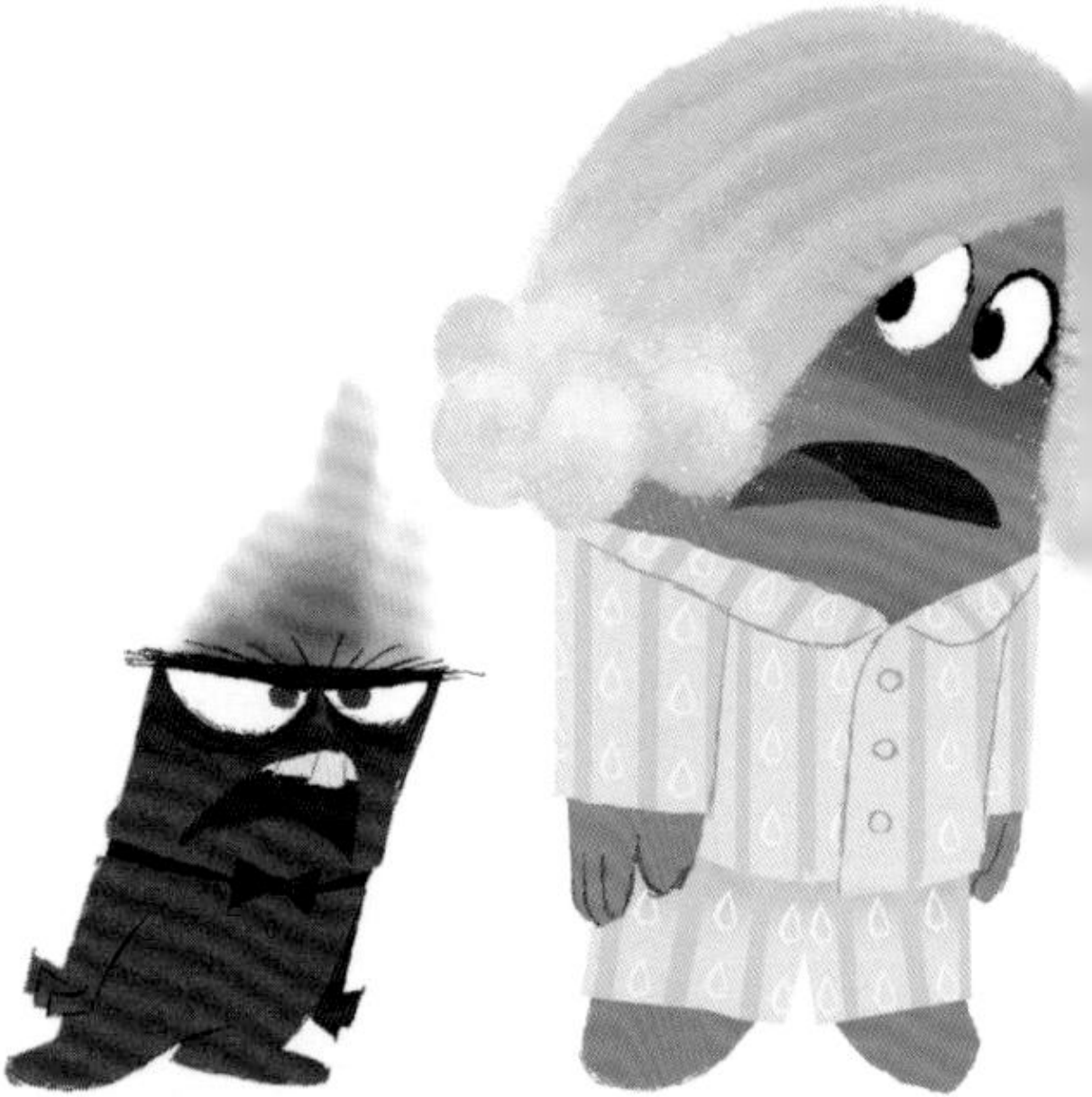

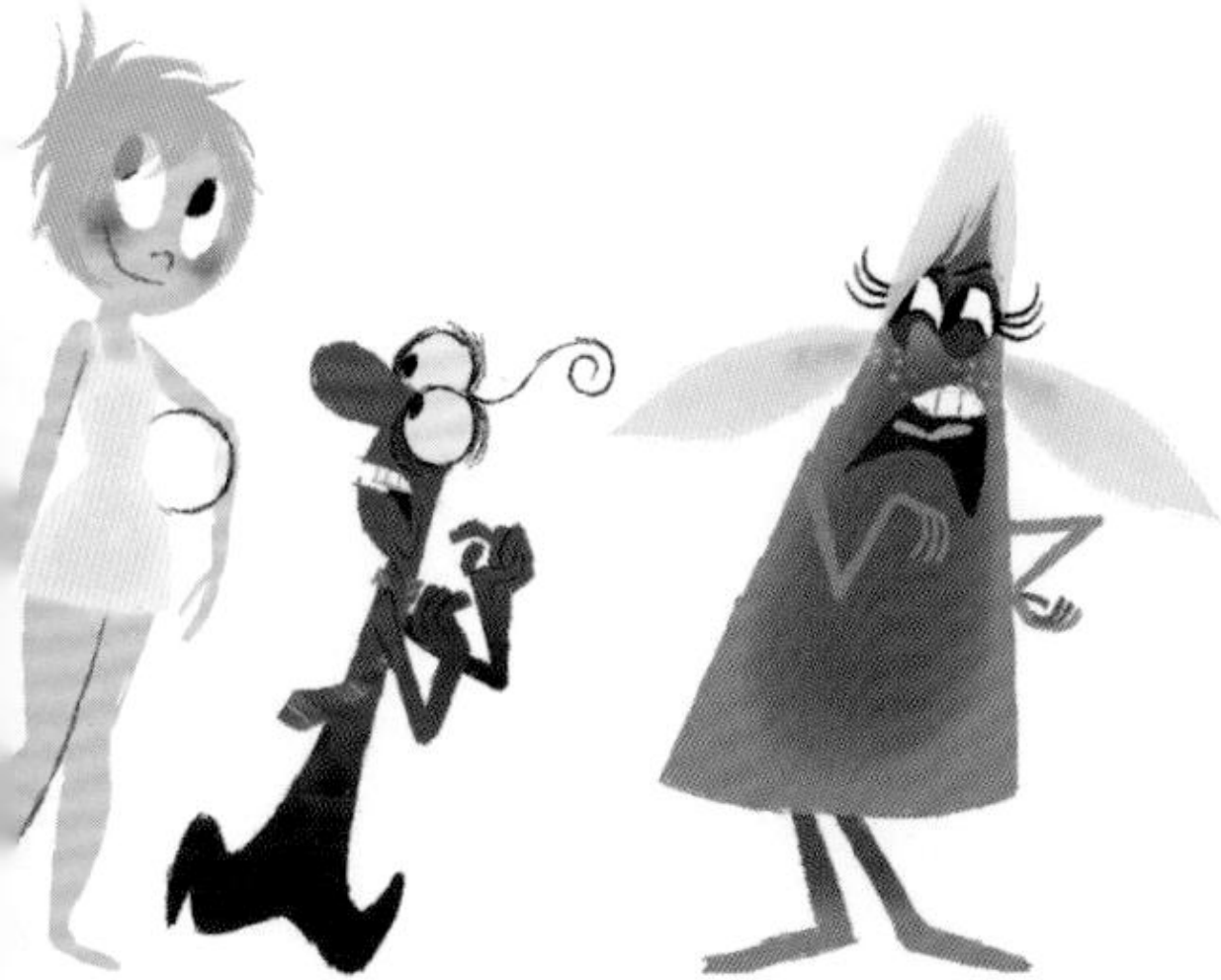

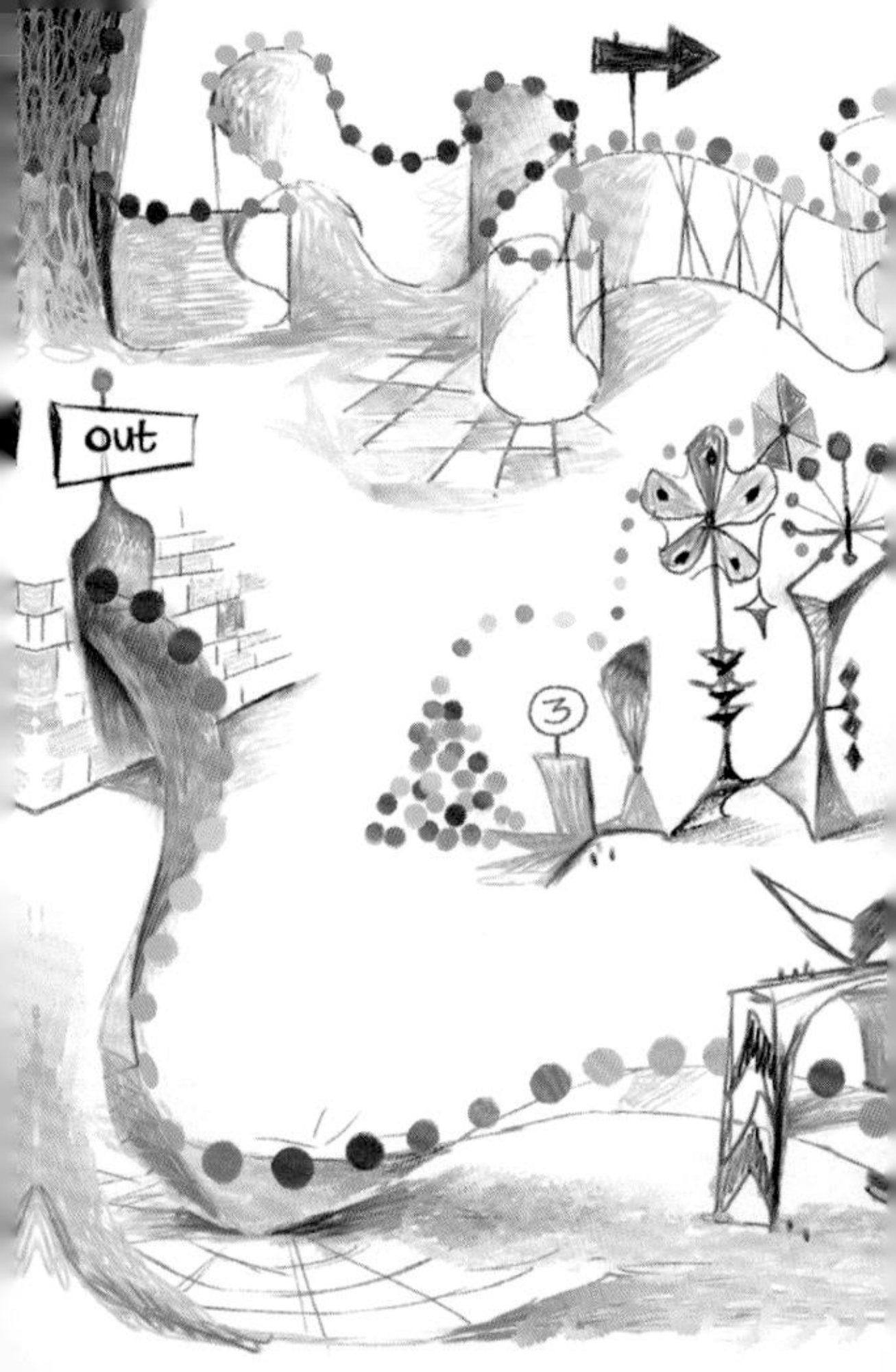
out
3

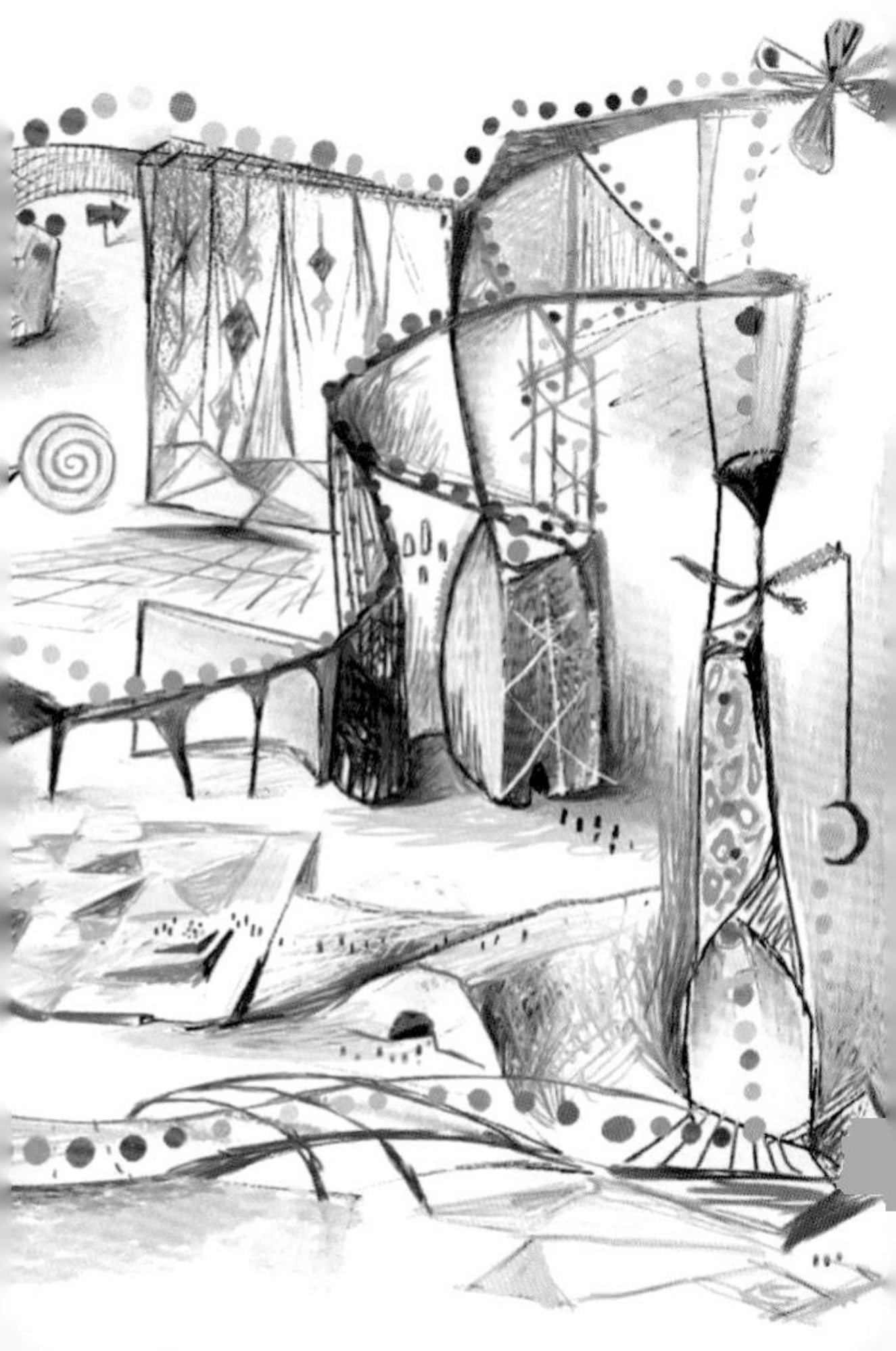

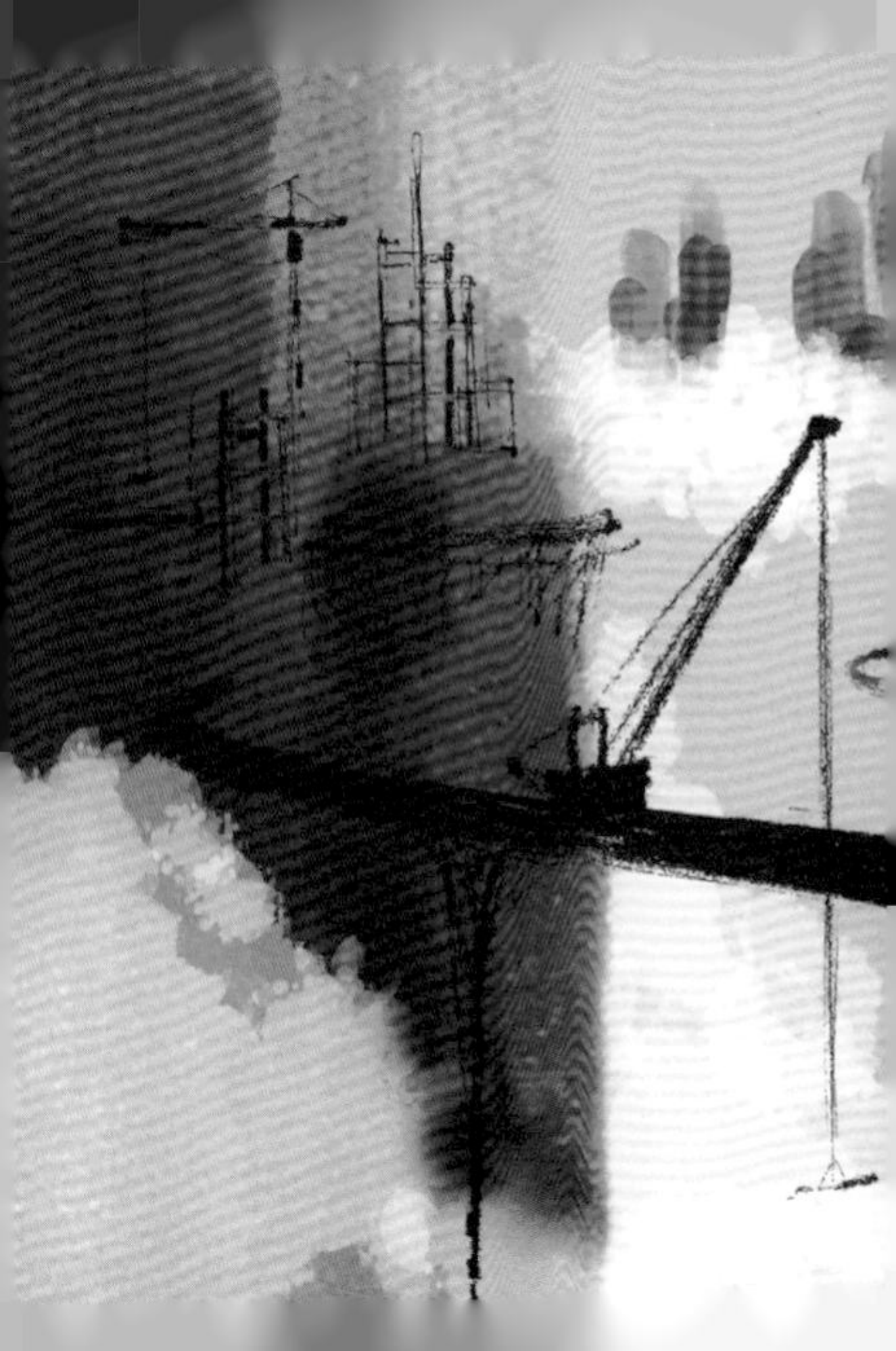

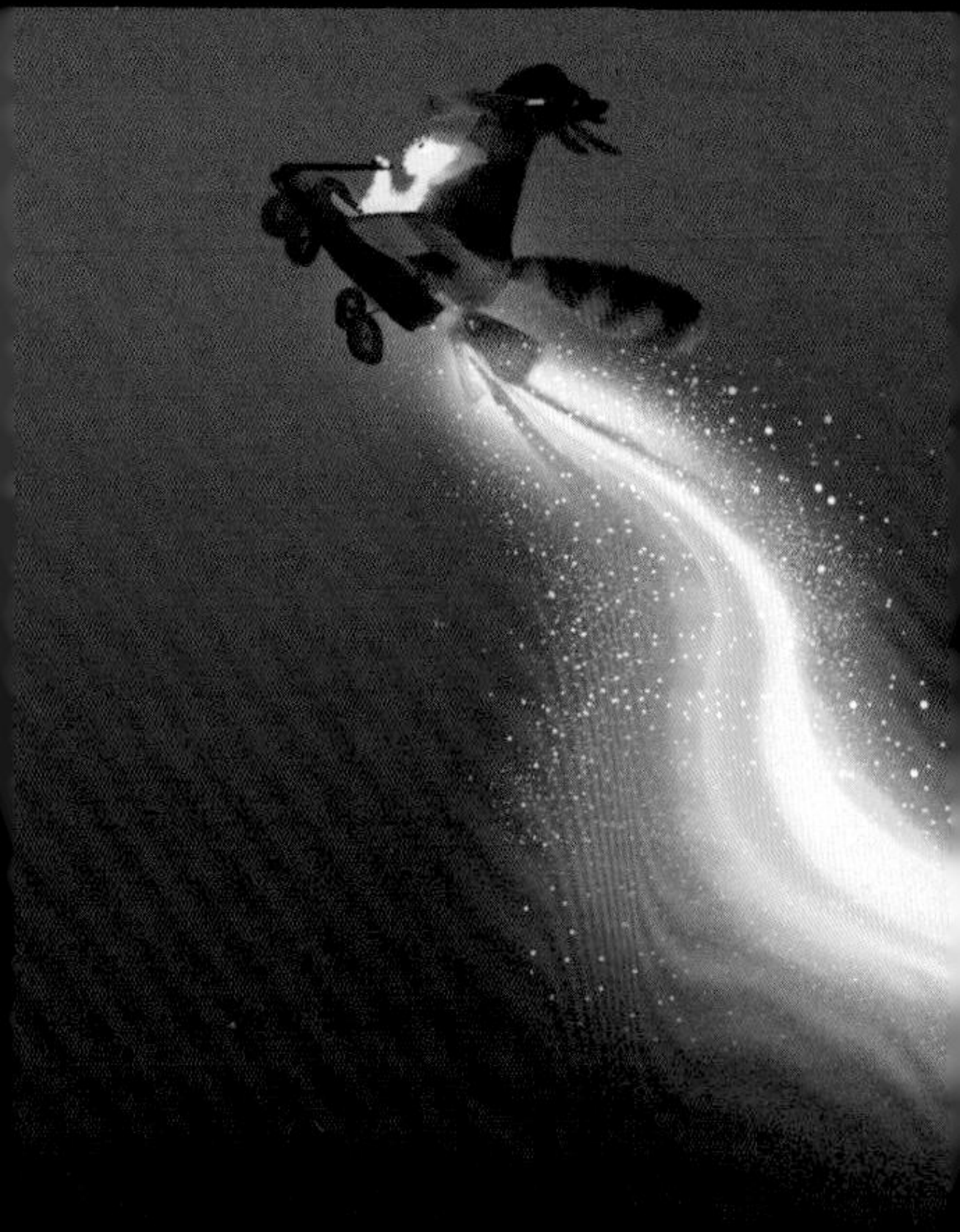

SHORT

SANJAY'S SUPER TEAM

2015

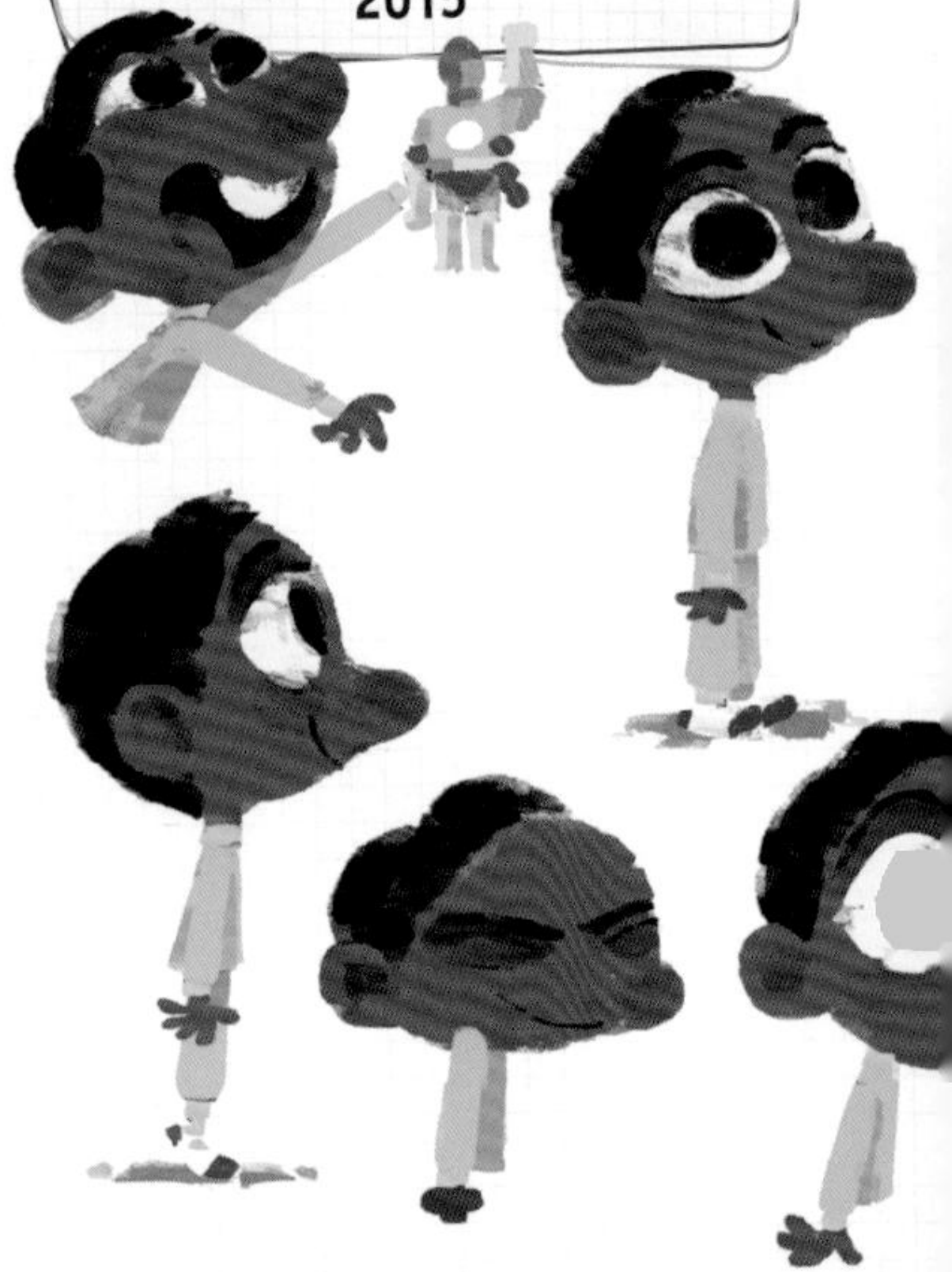

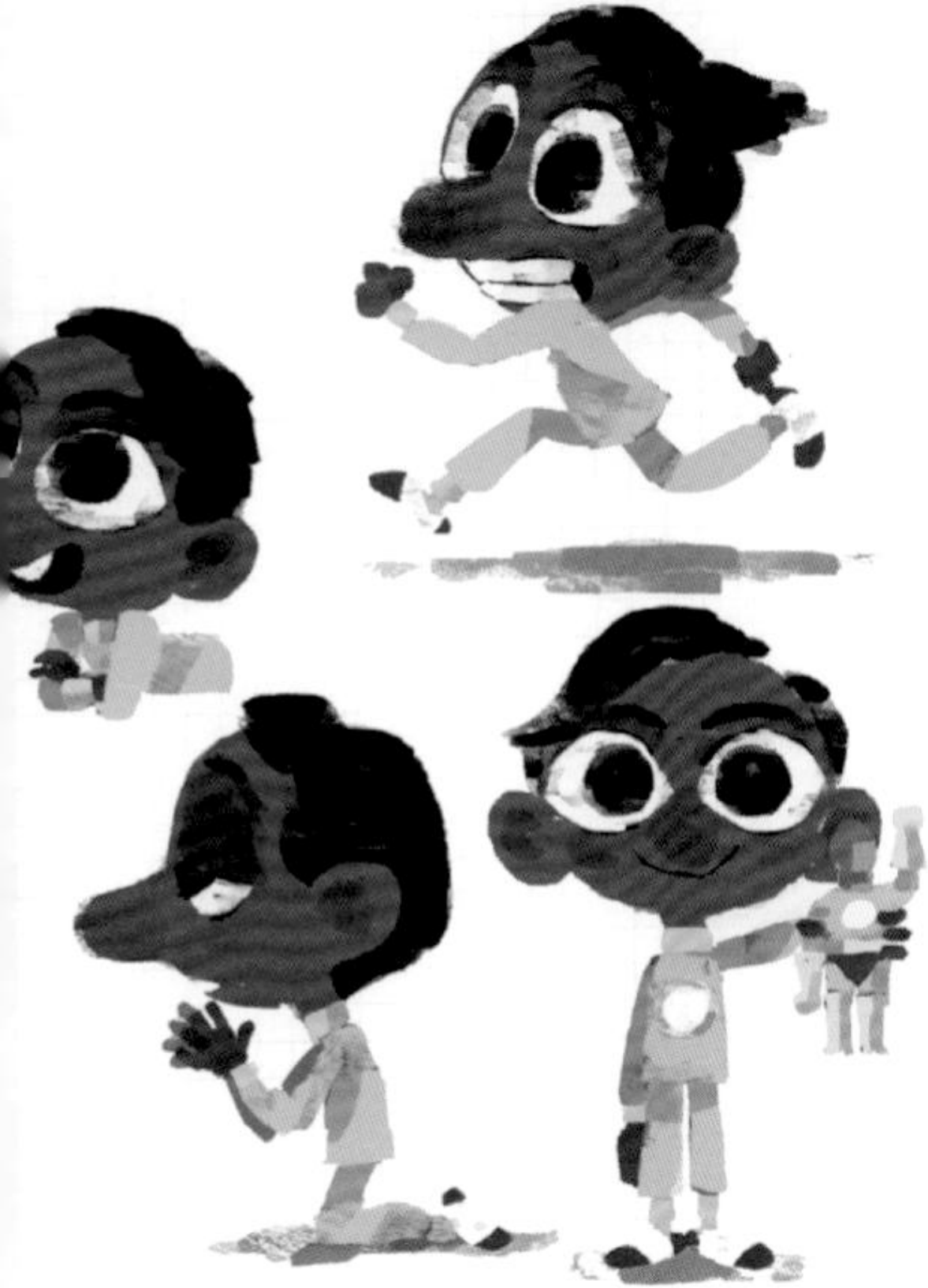

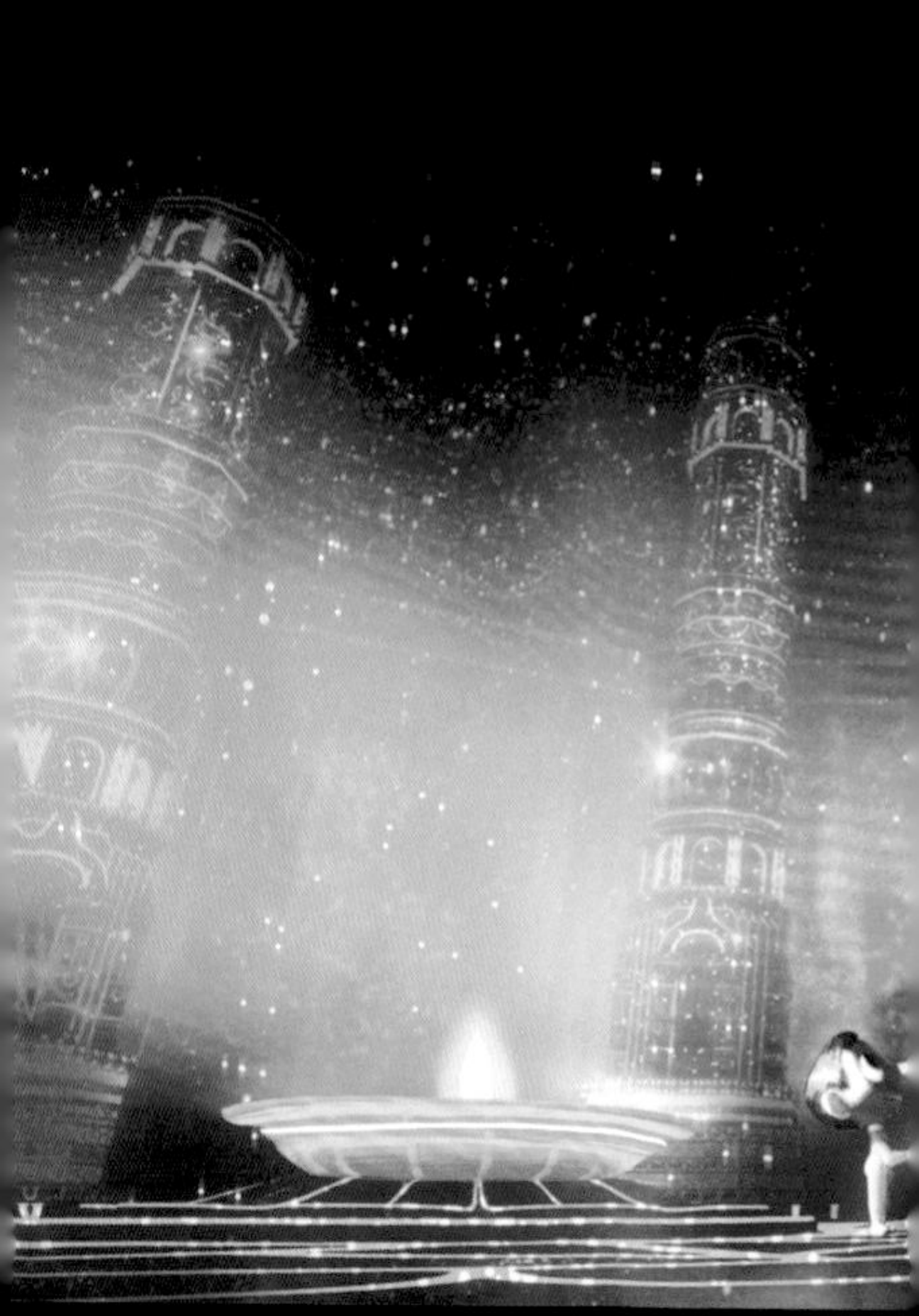

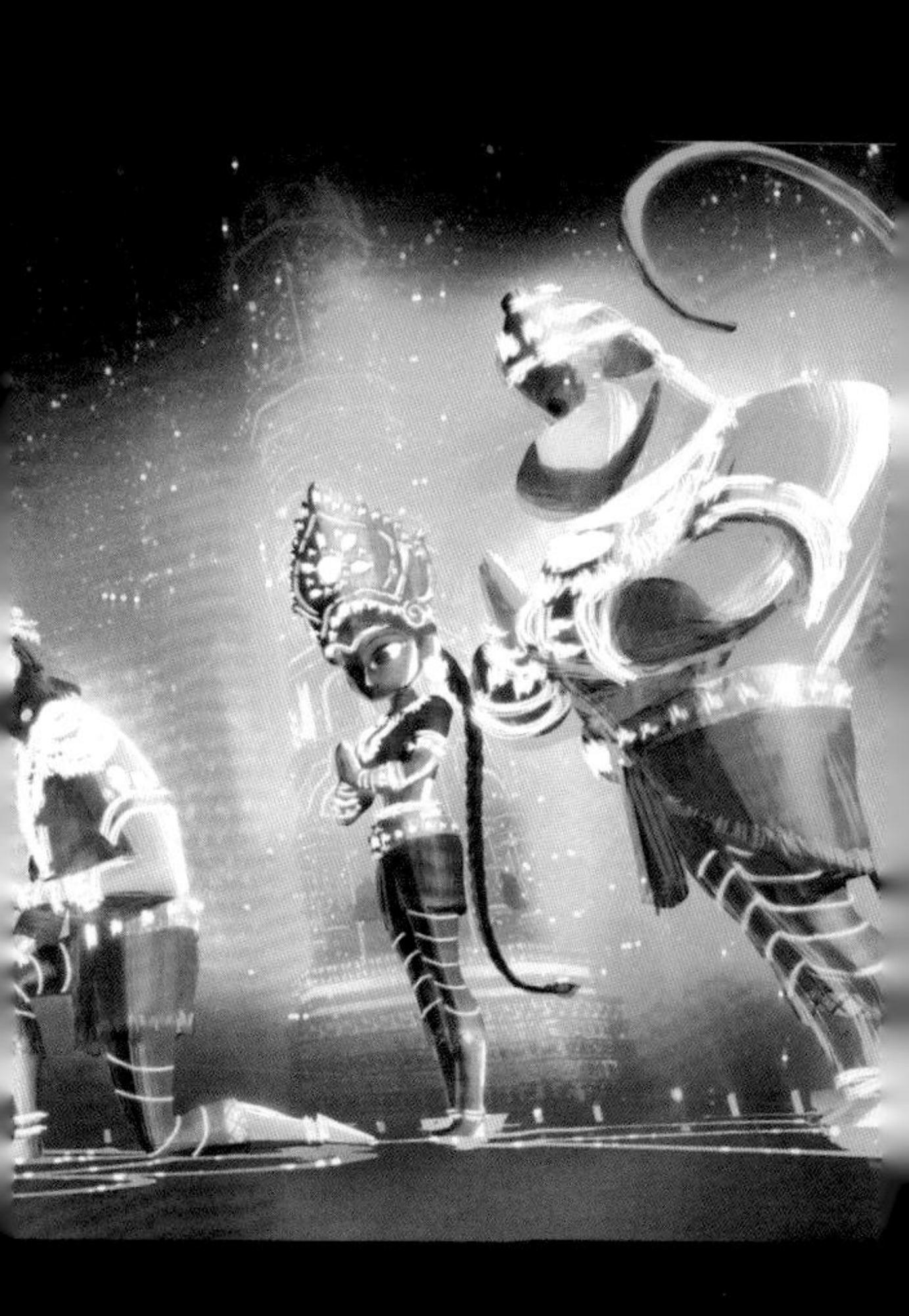

THE GOOD DINOSAUR
2015

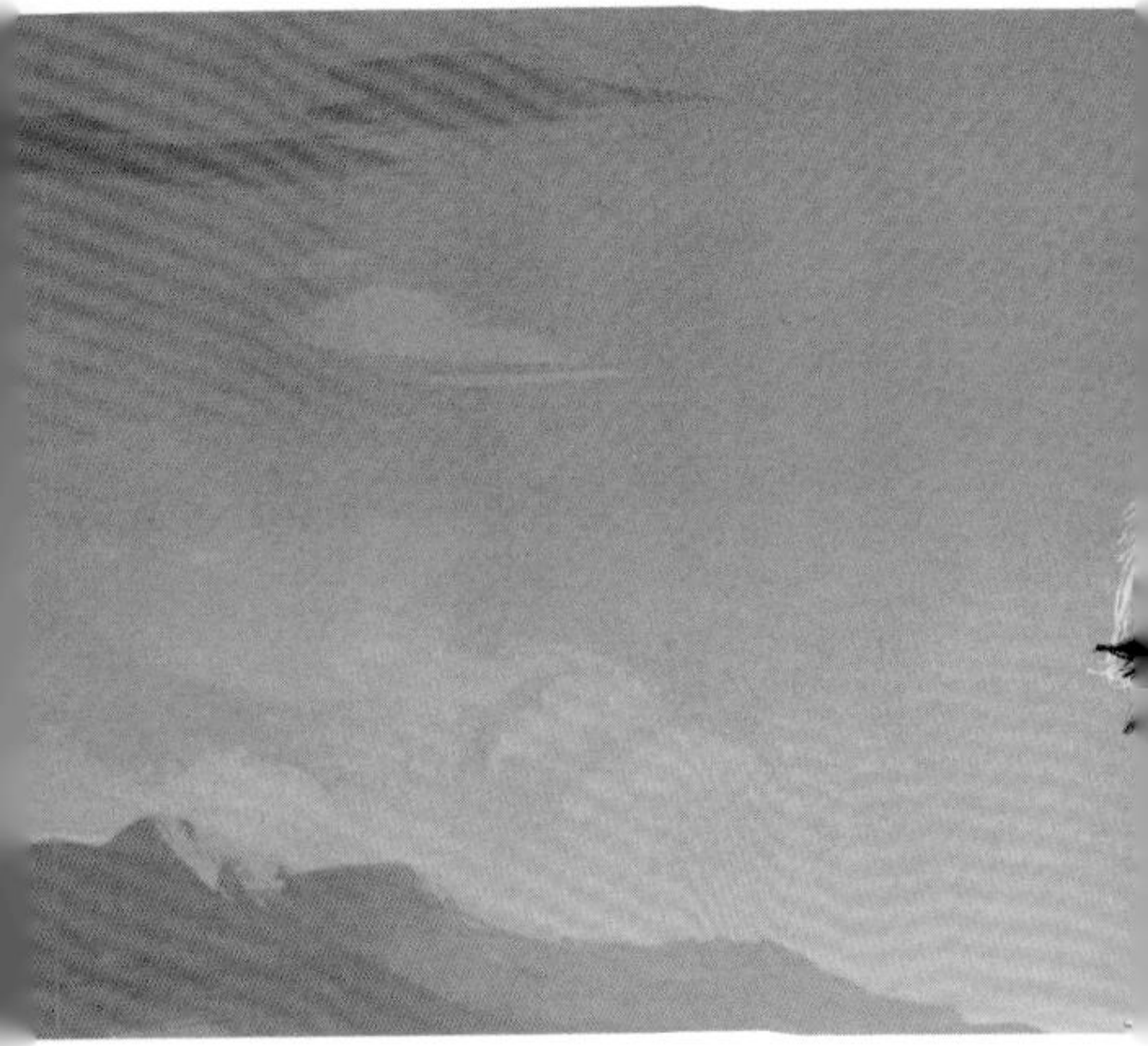

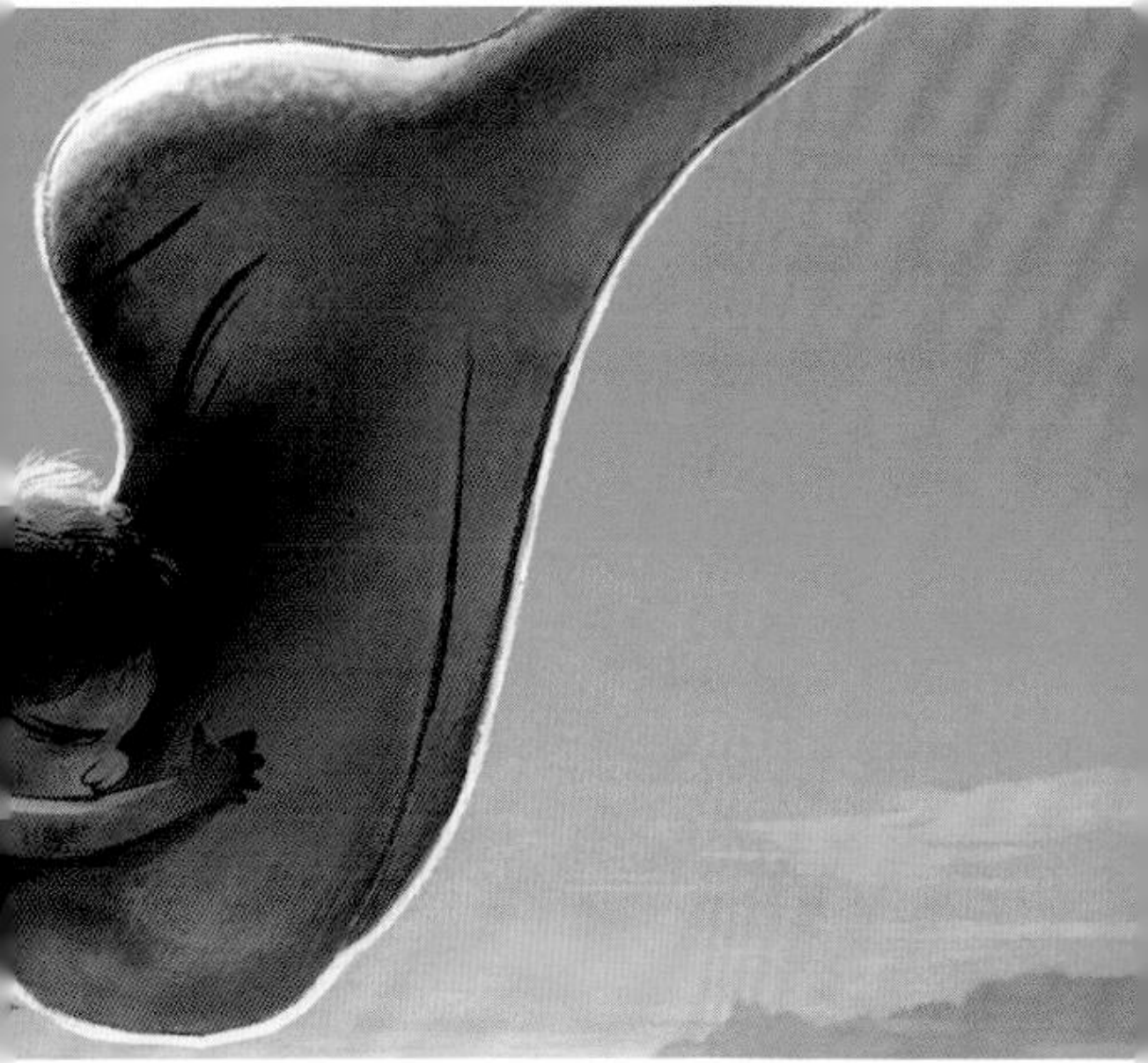

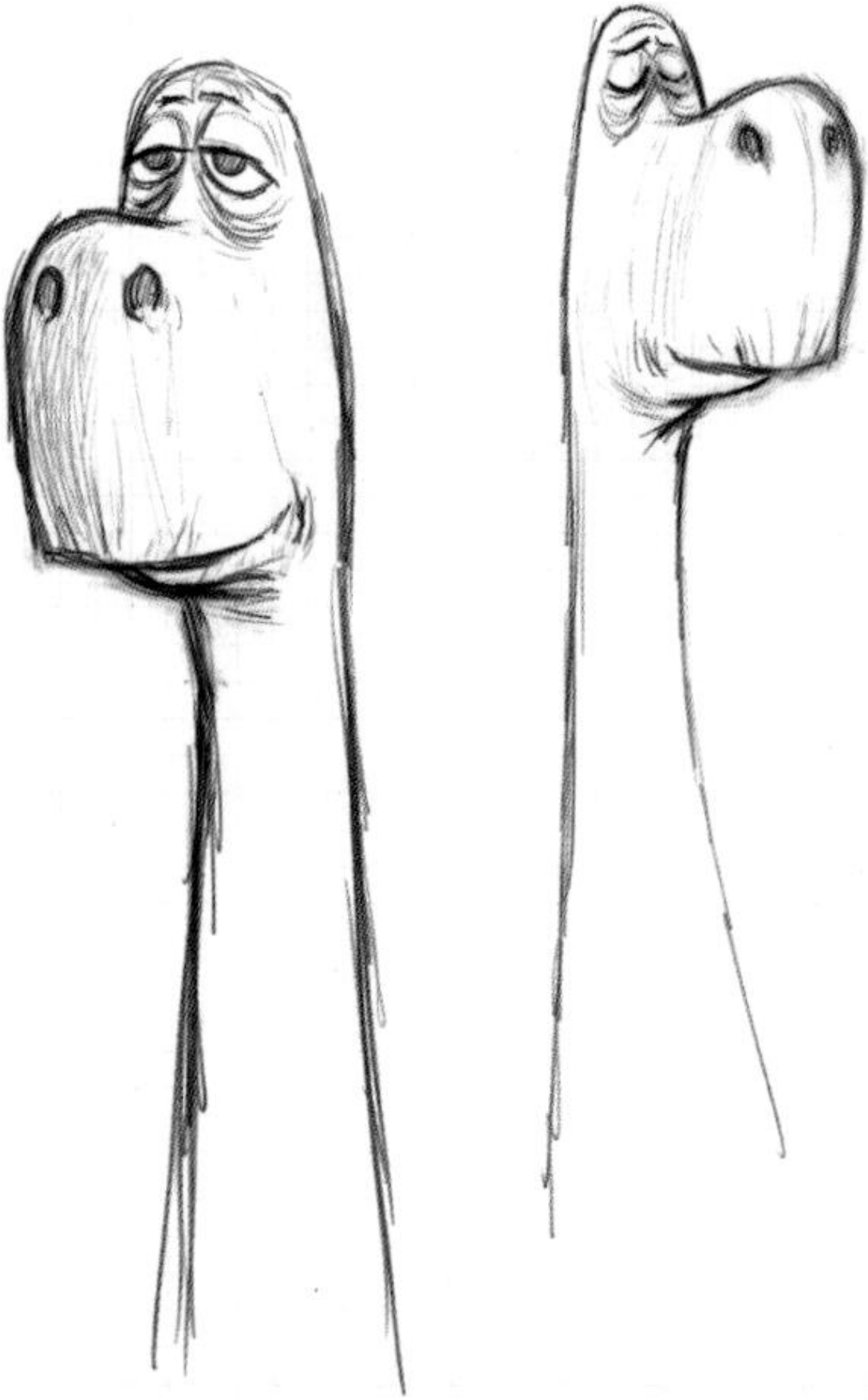

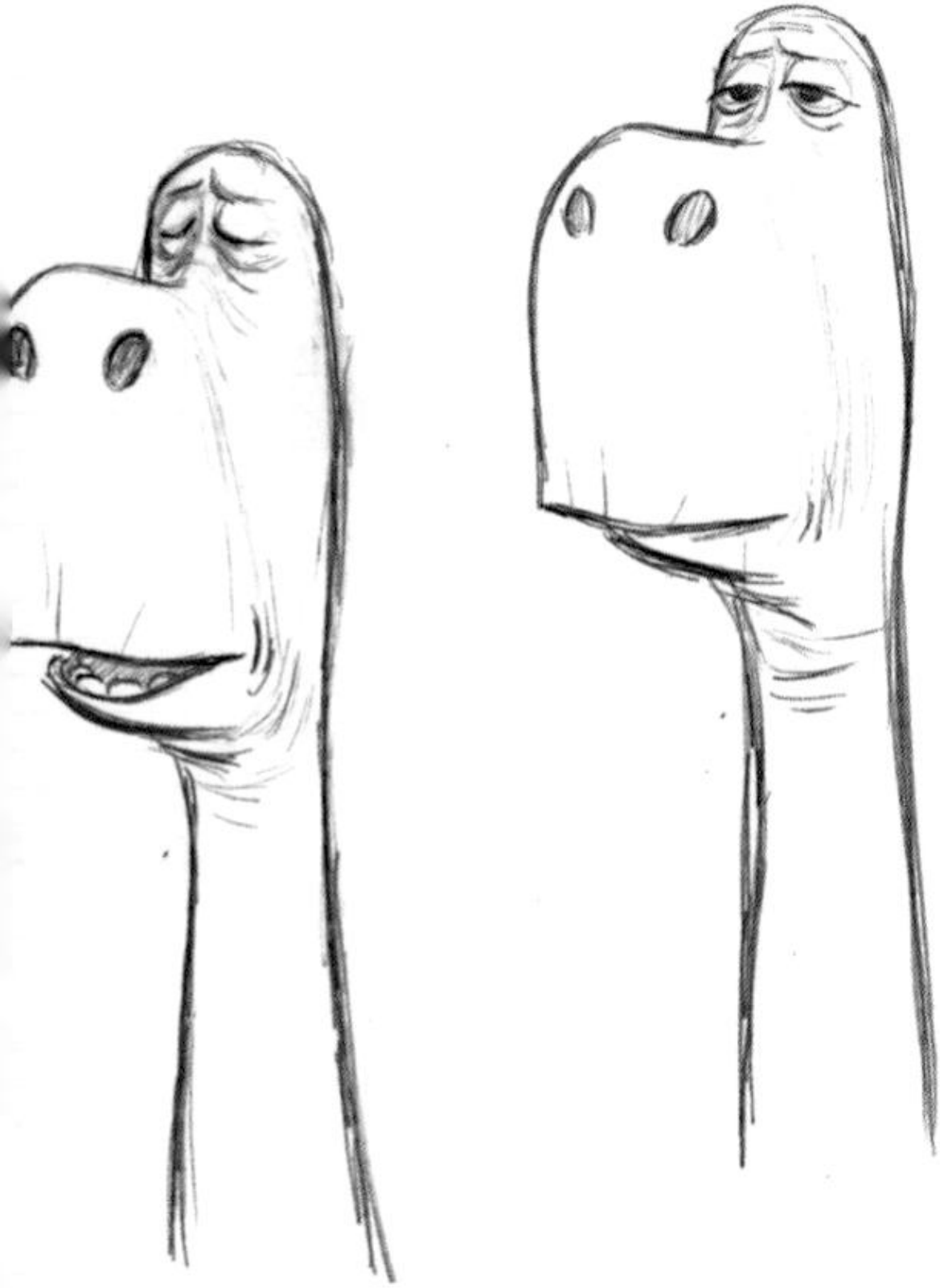

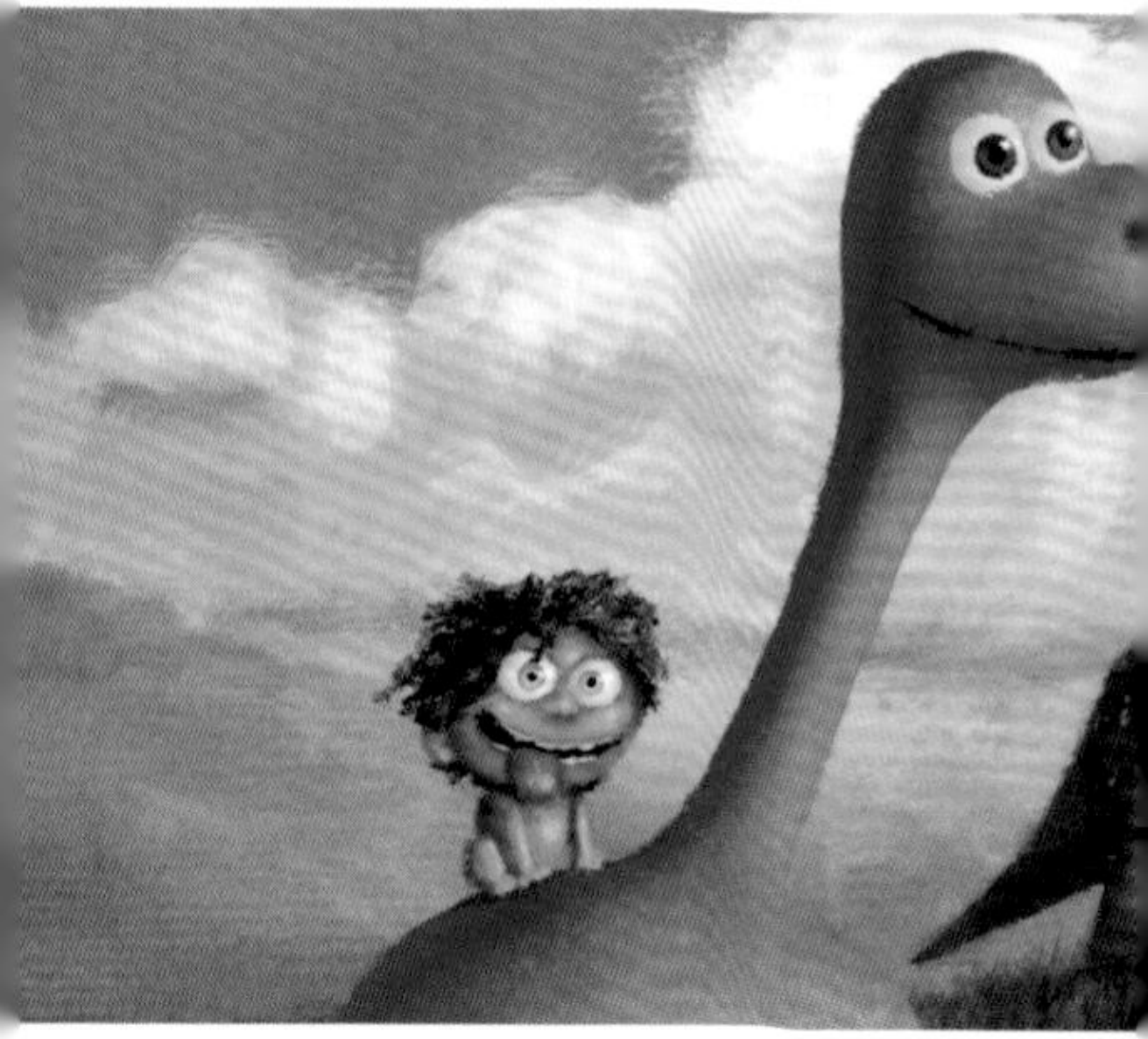

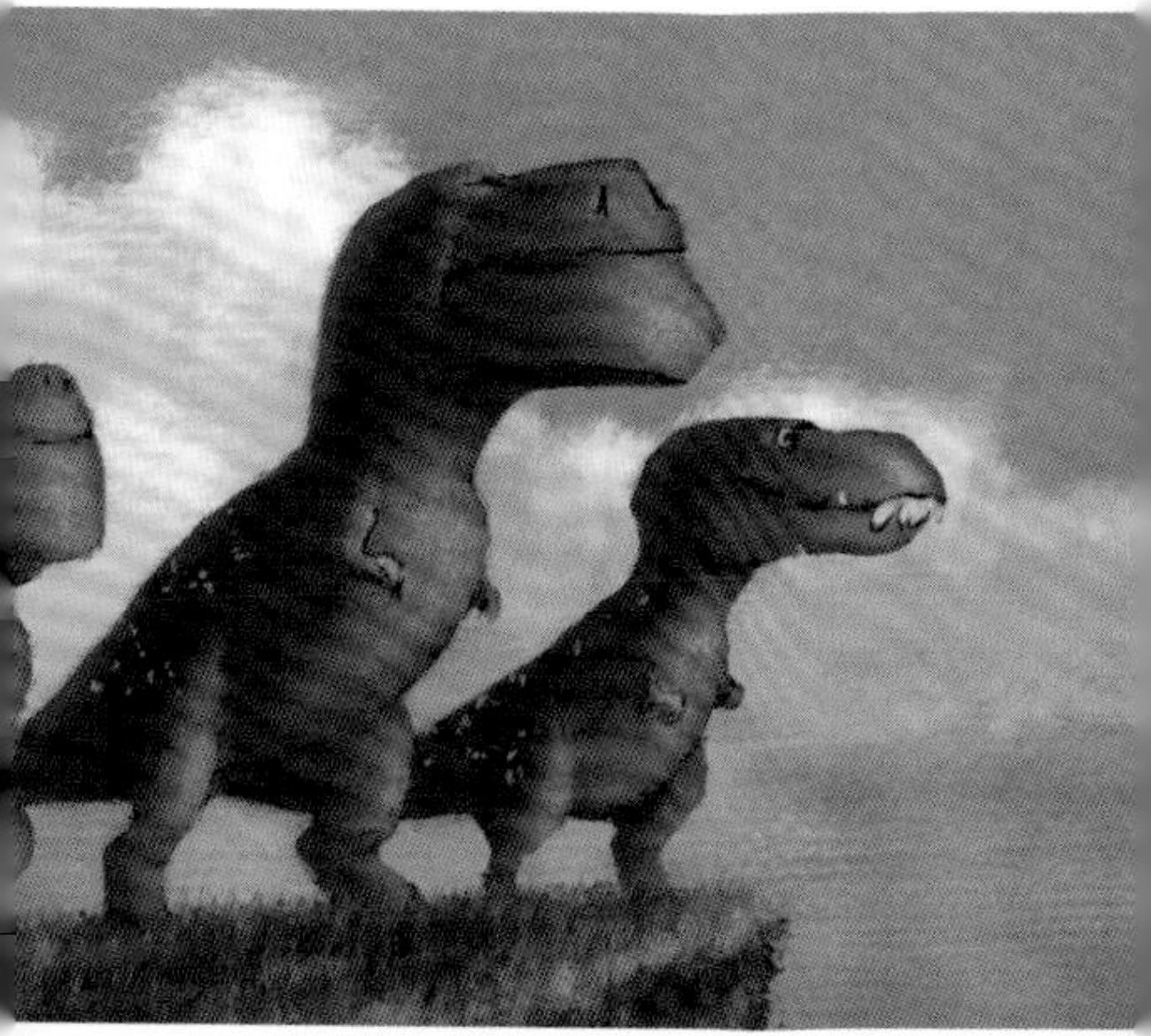

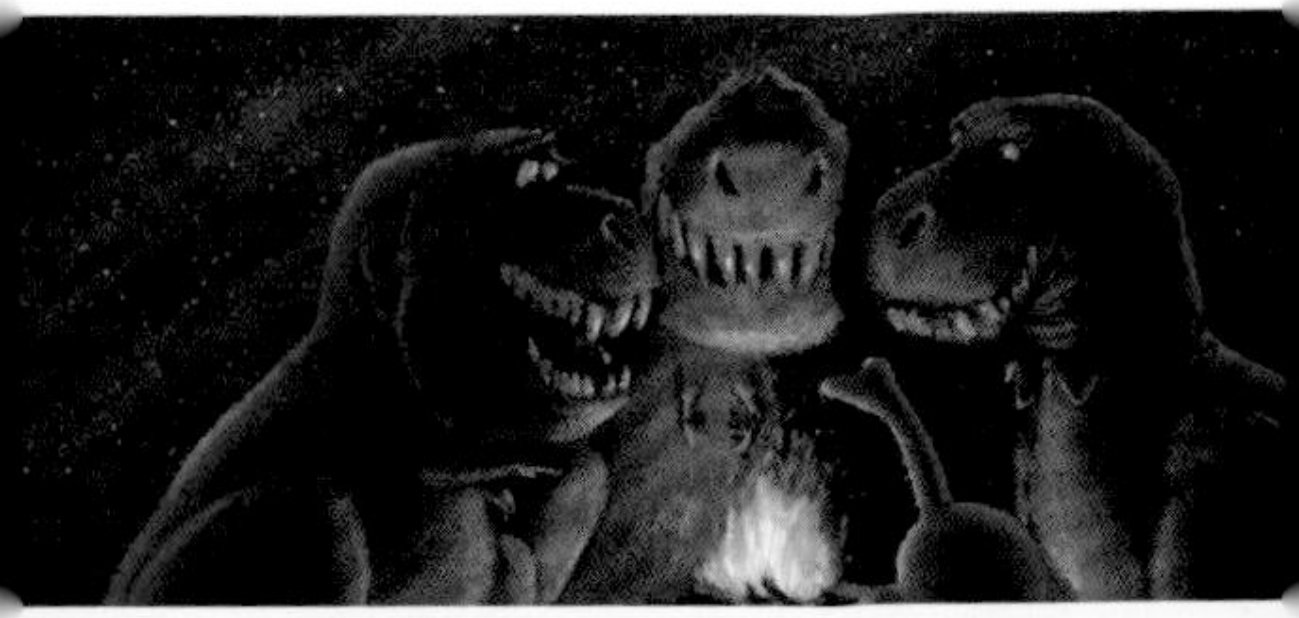

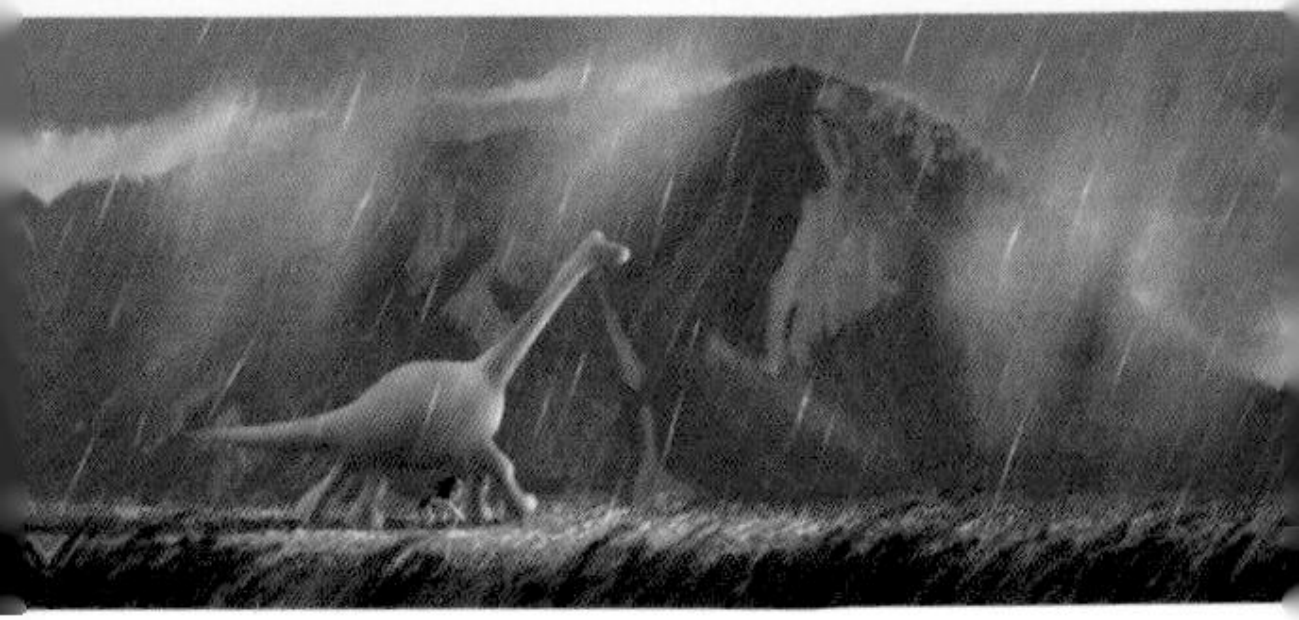

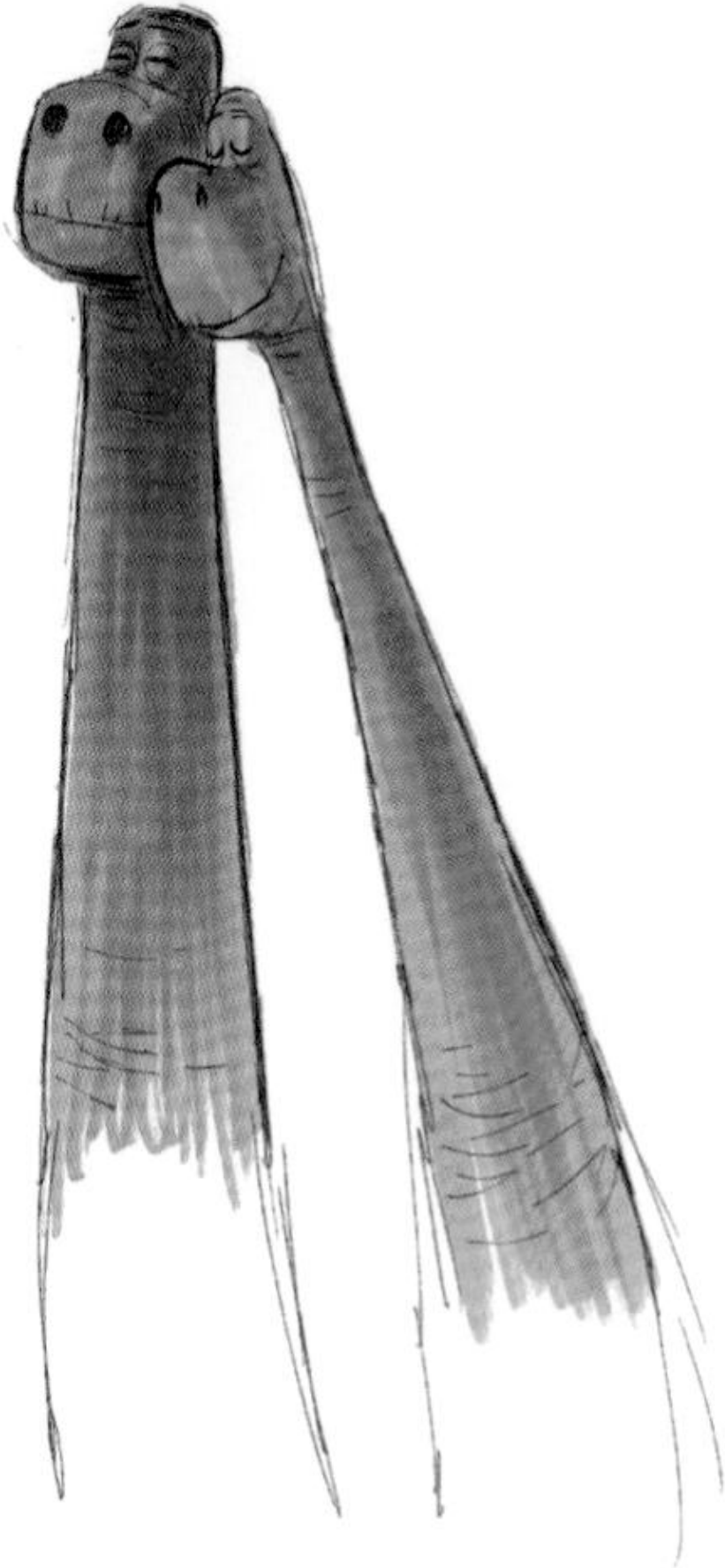

SHORT

PIPER

2016

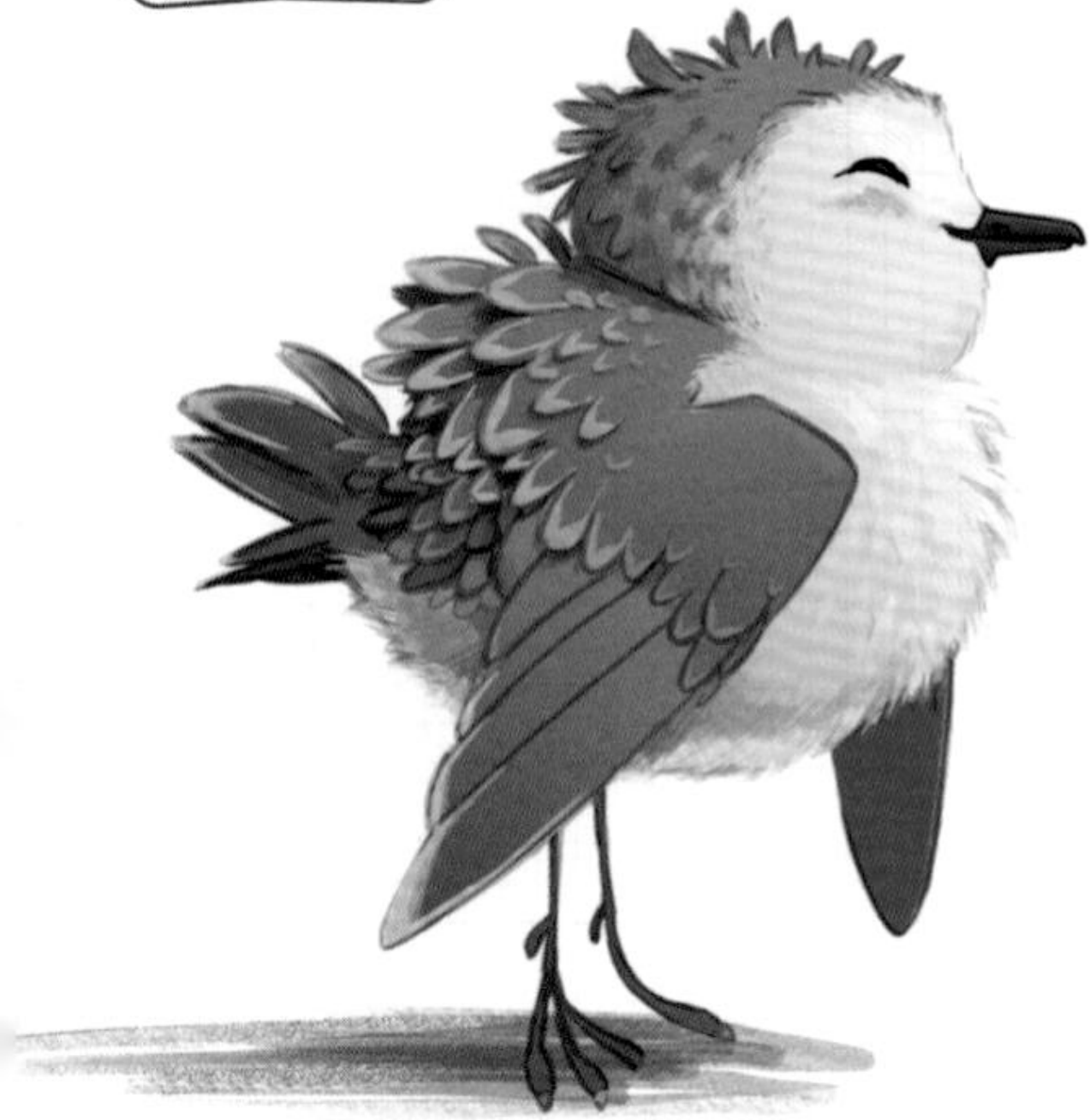

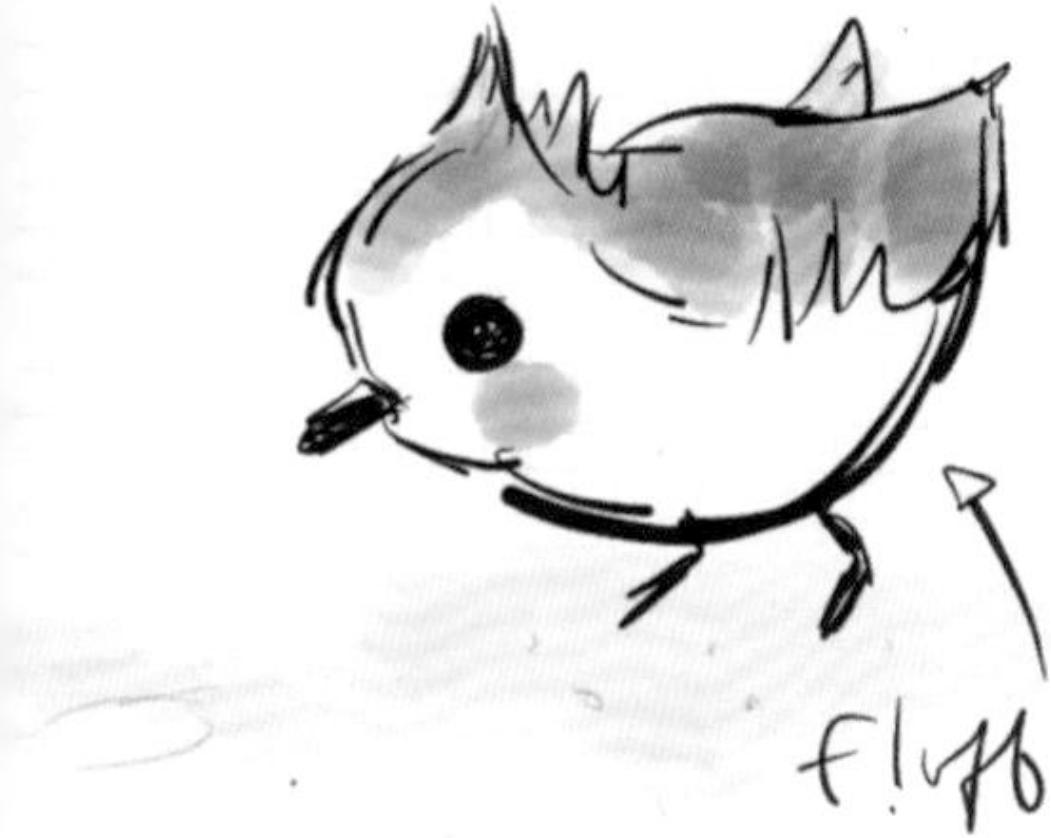
Flufi

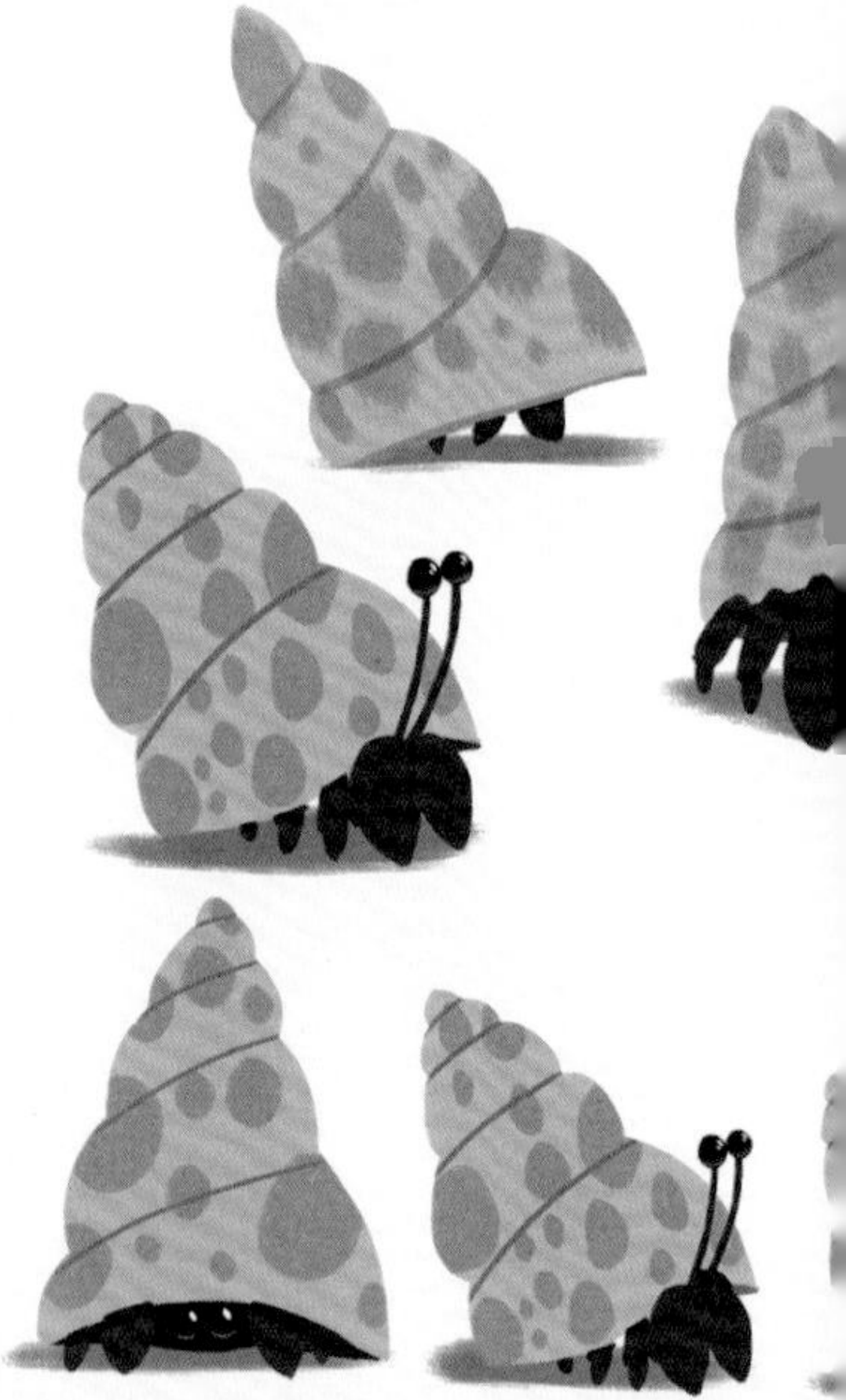

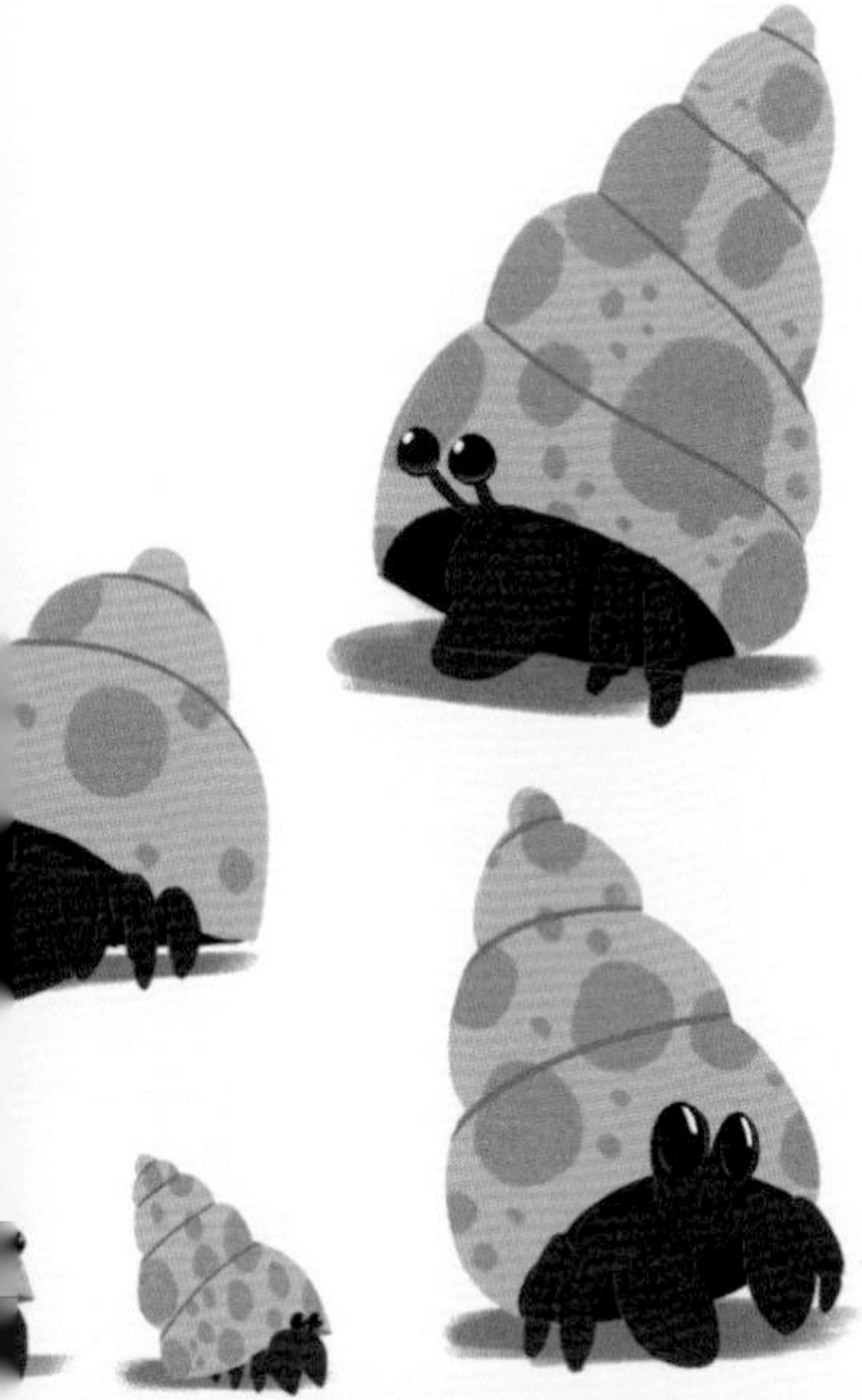

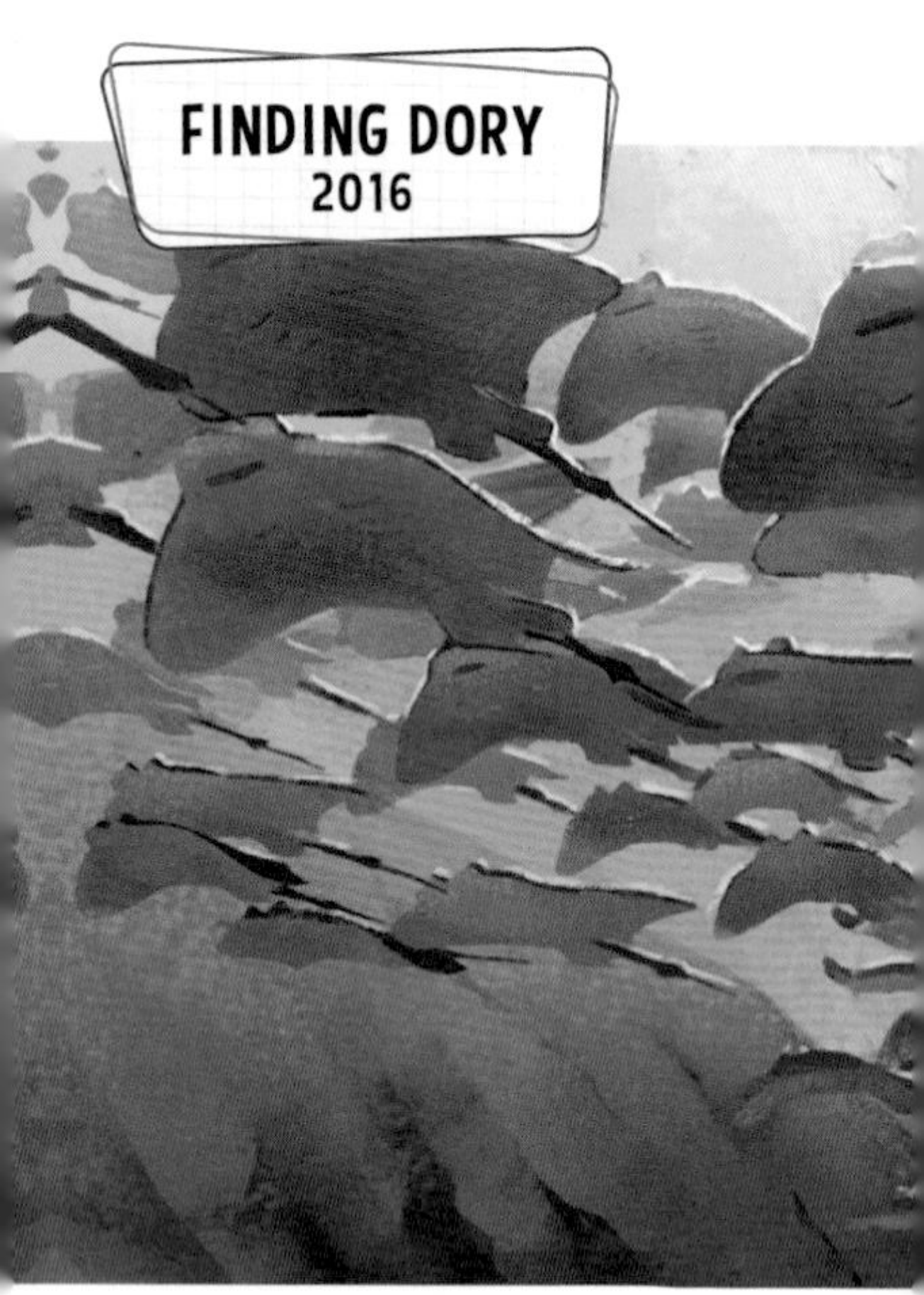
FINDING DORY
2016

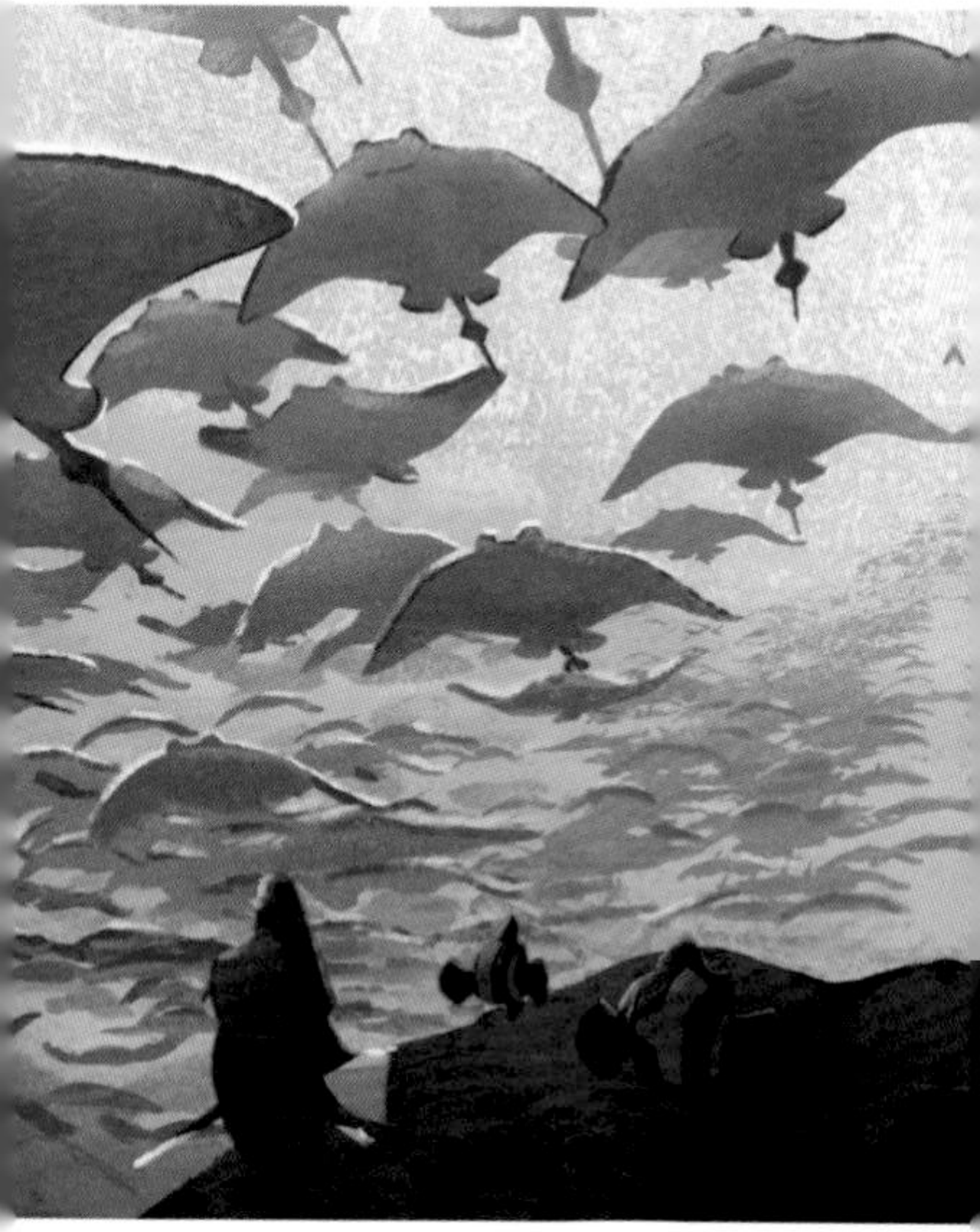

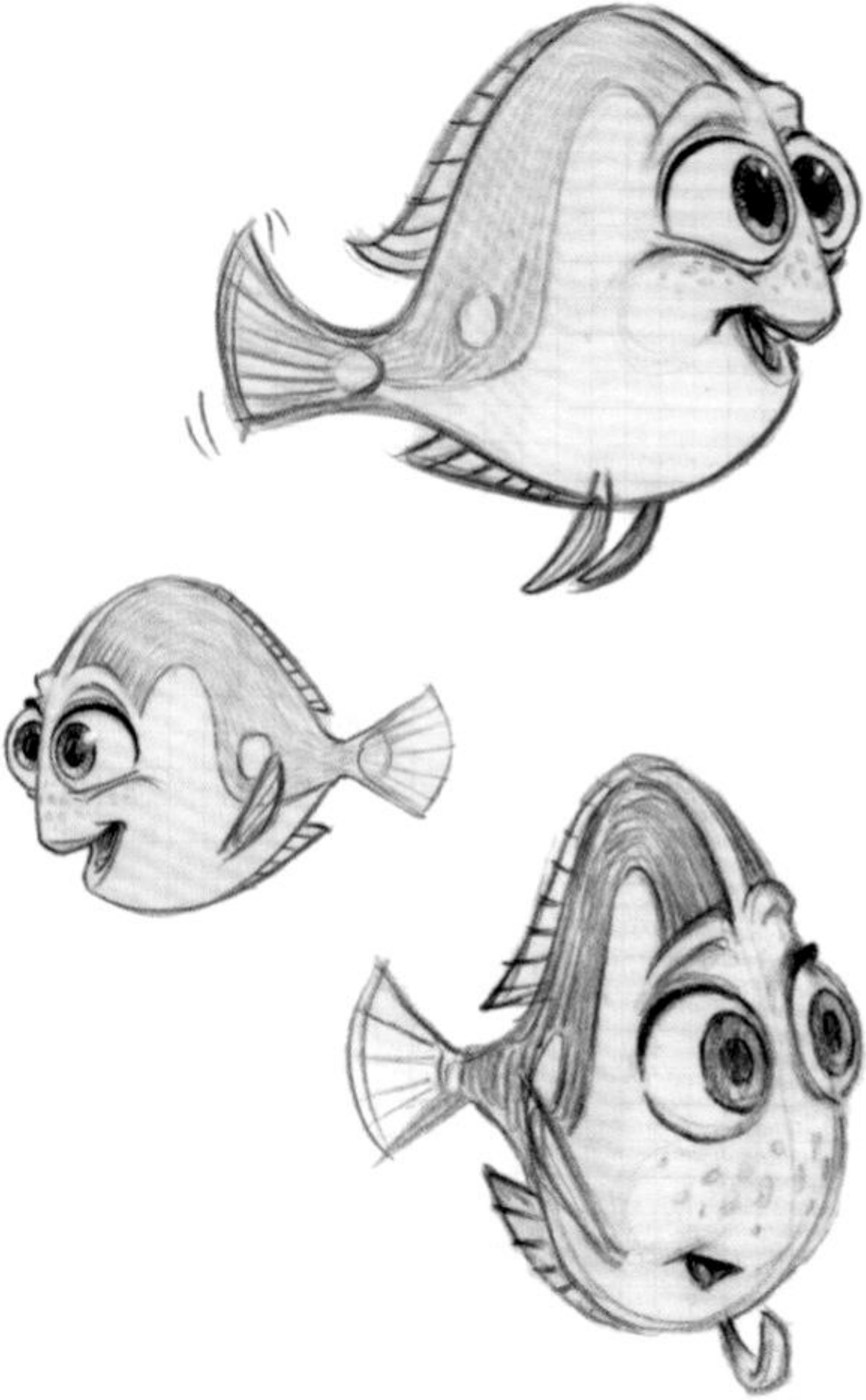

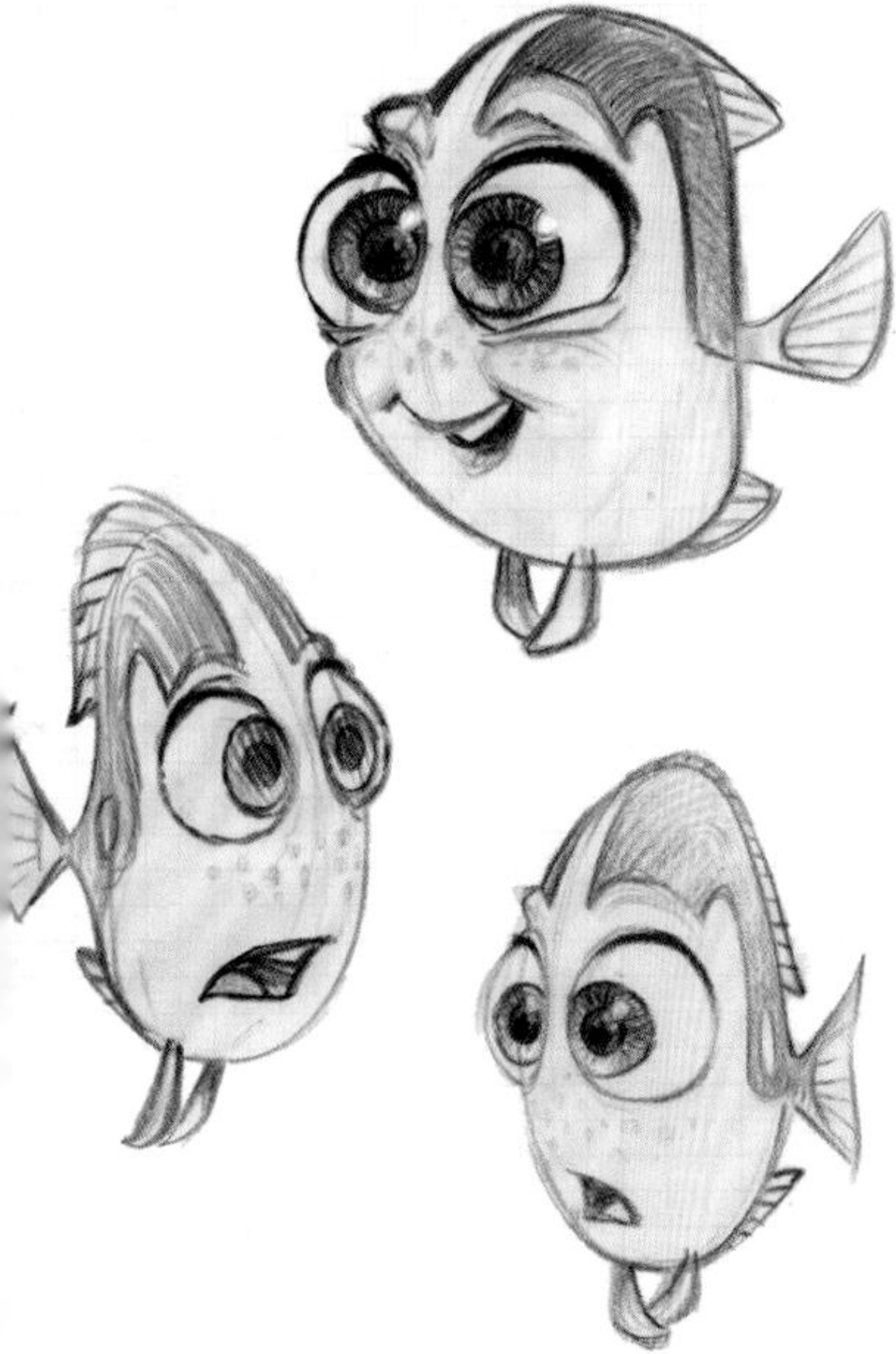

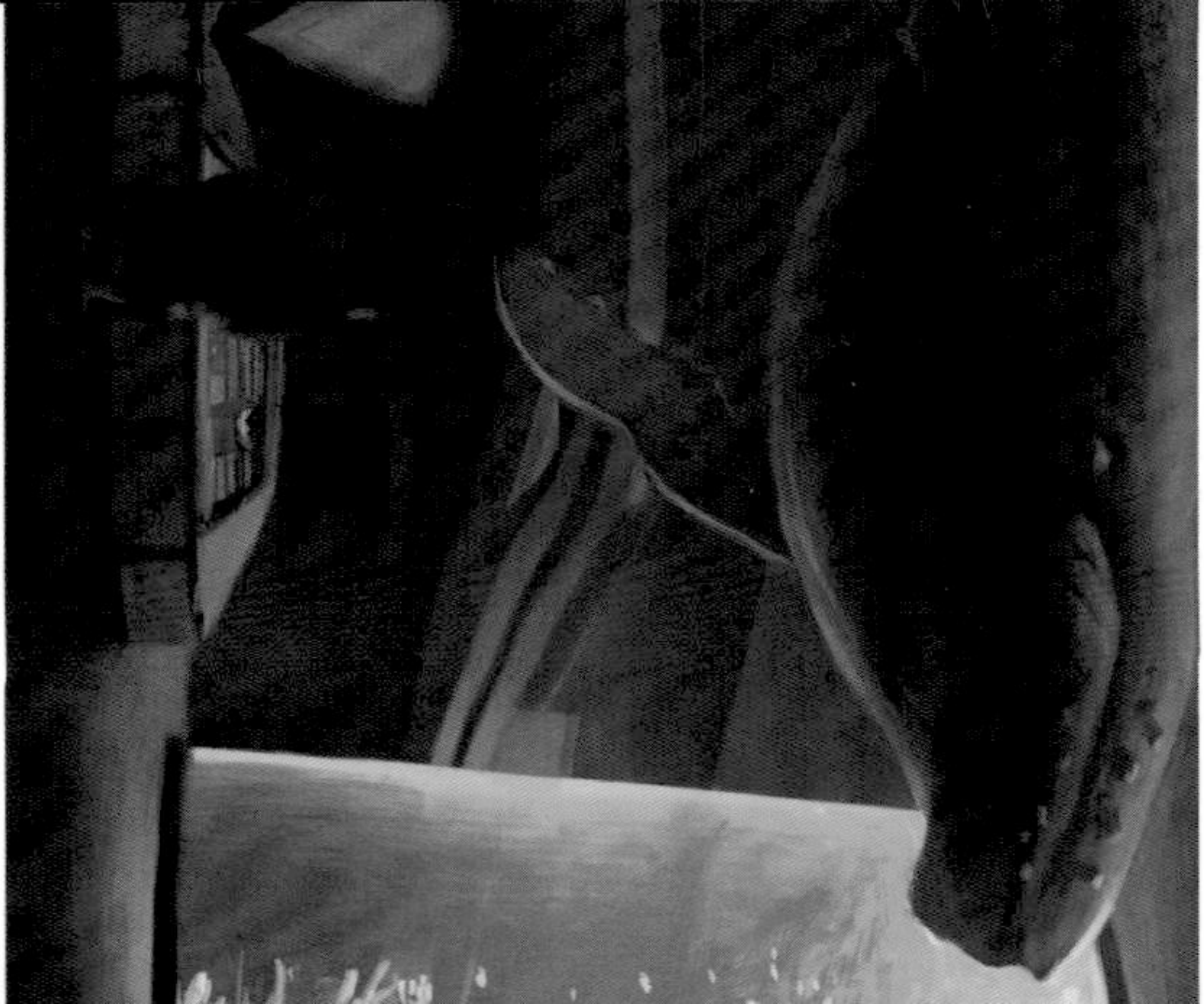

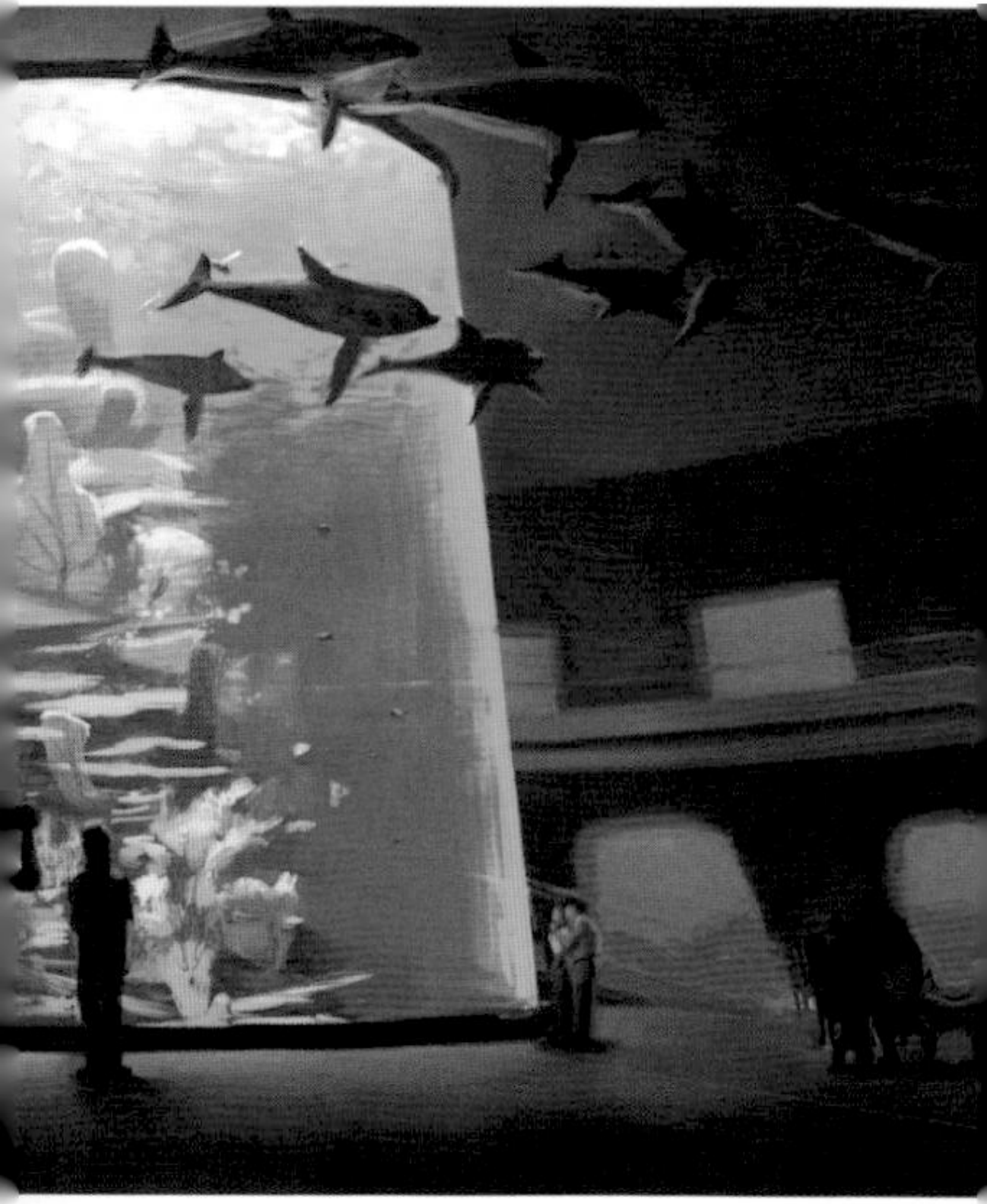

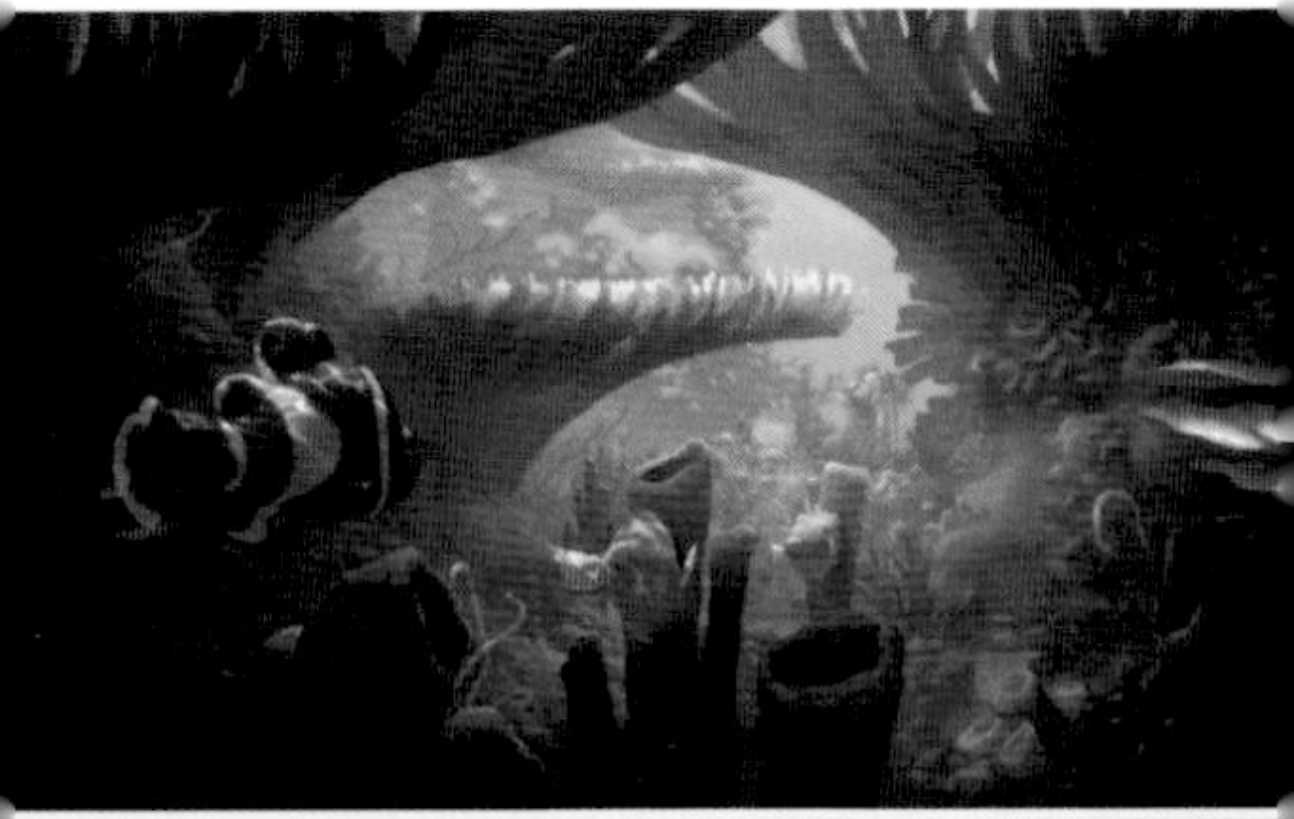

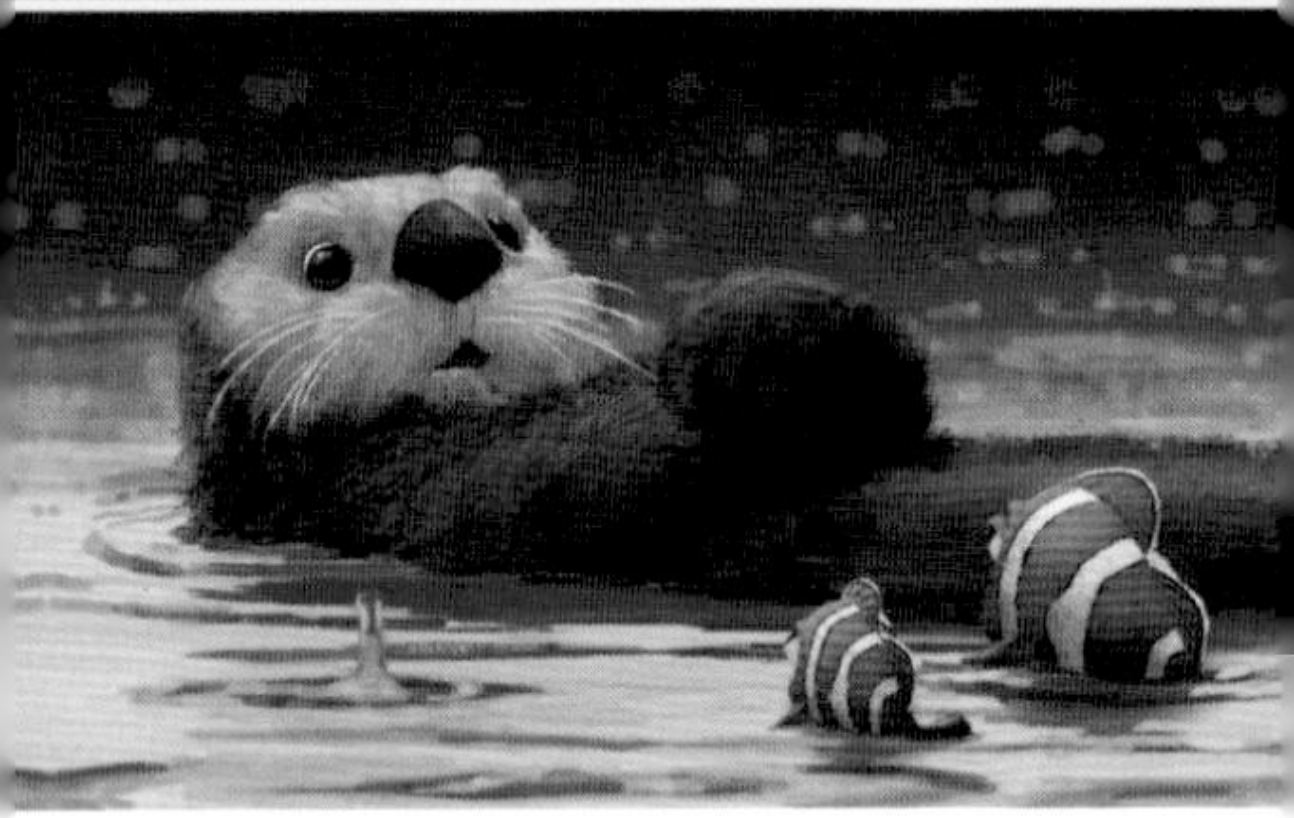

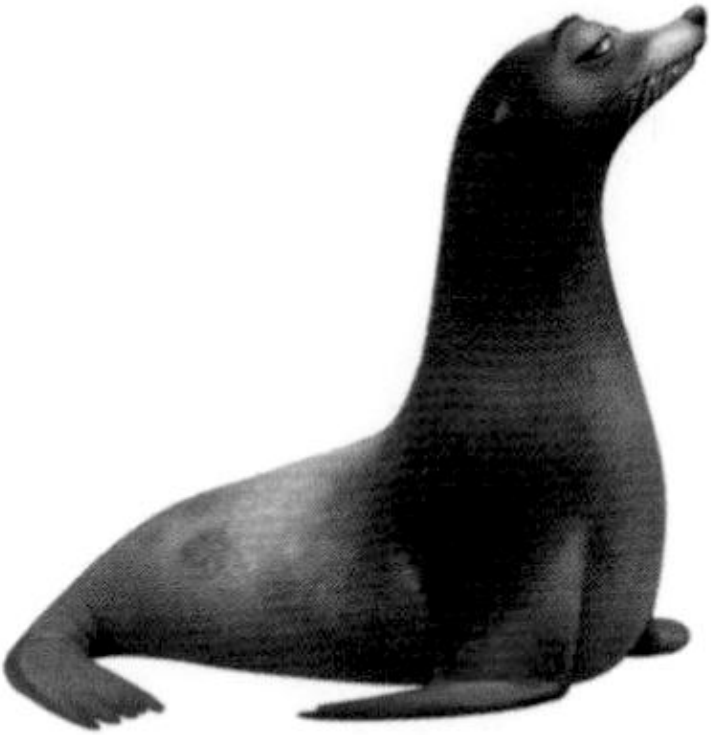

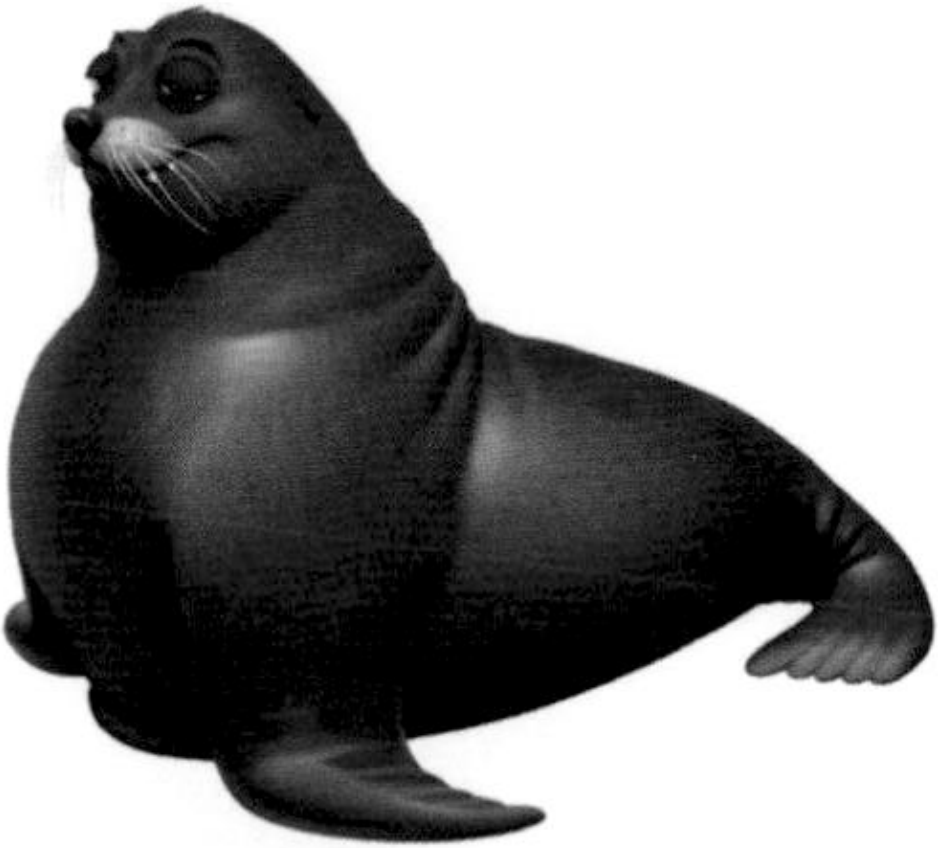

SHORT
LOU
2017

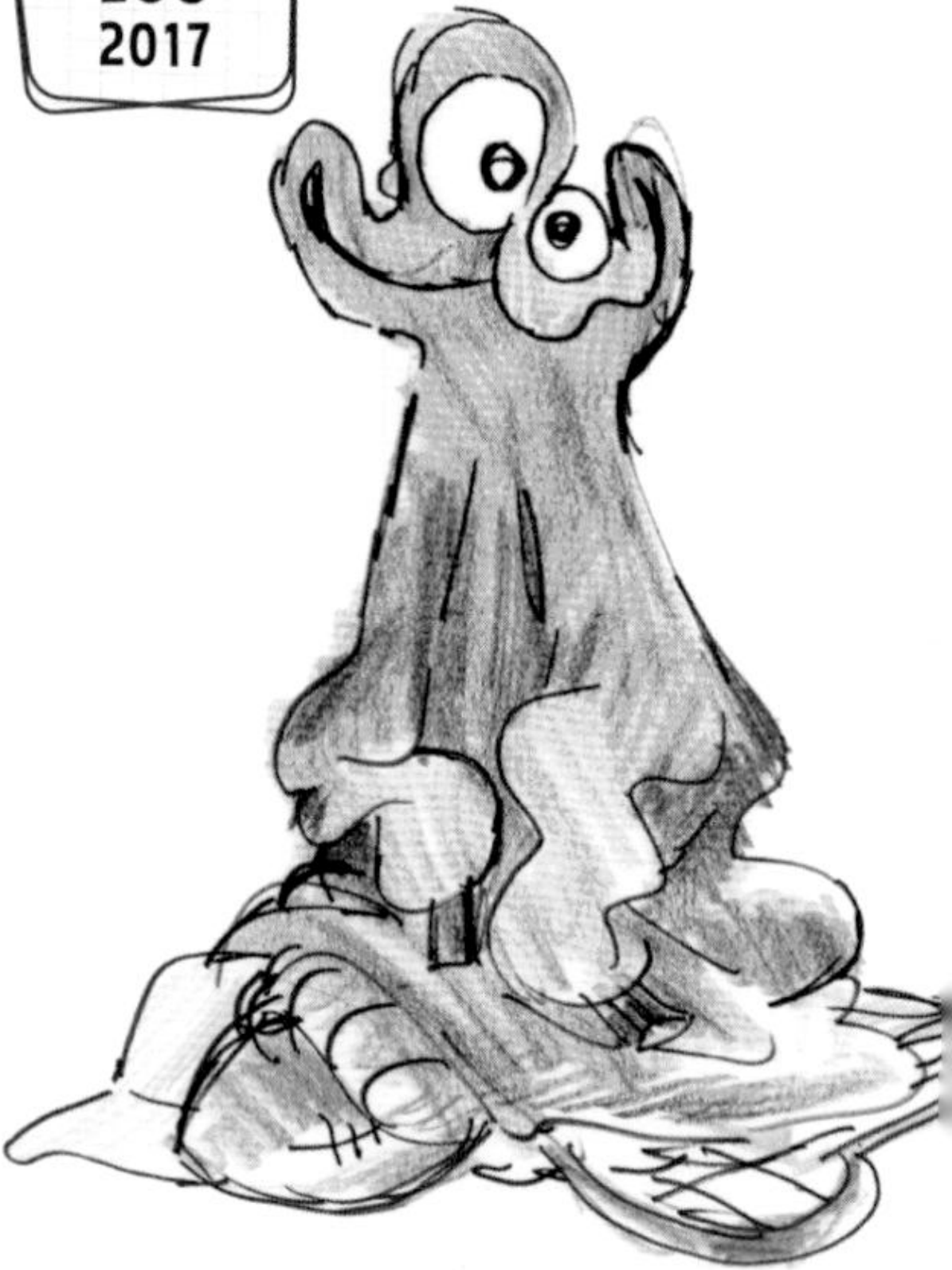

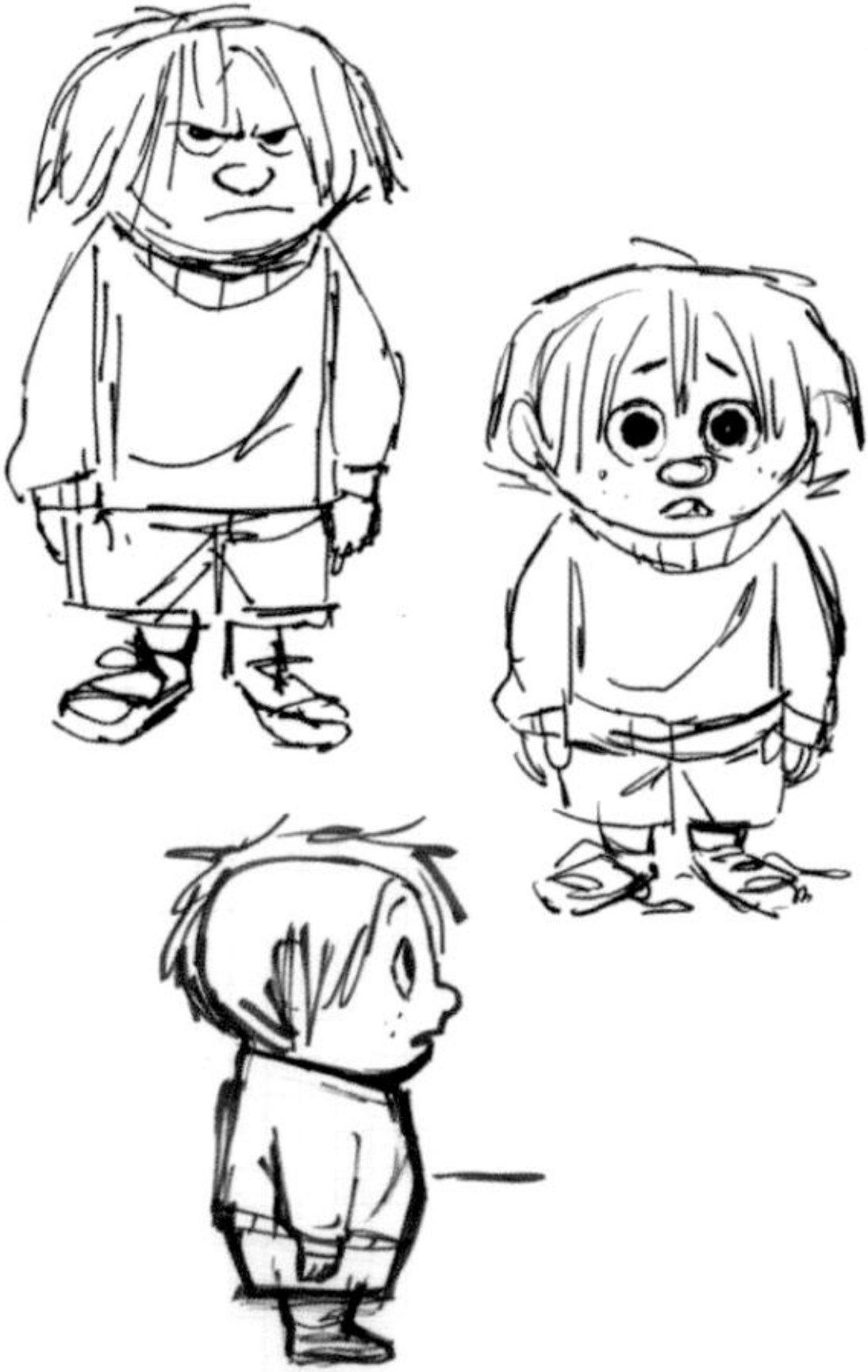

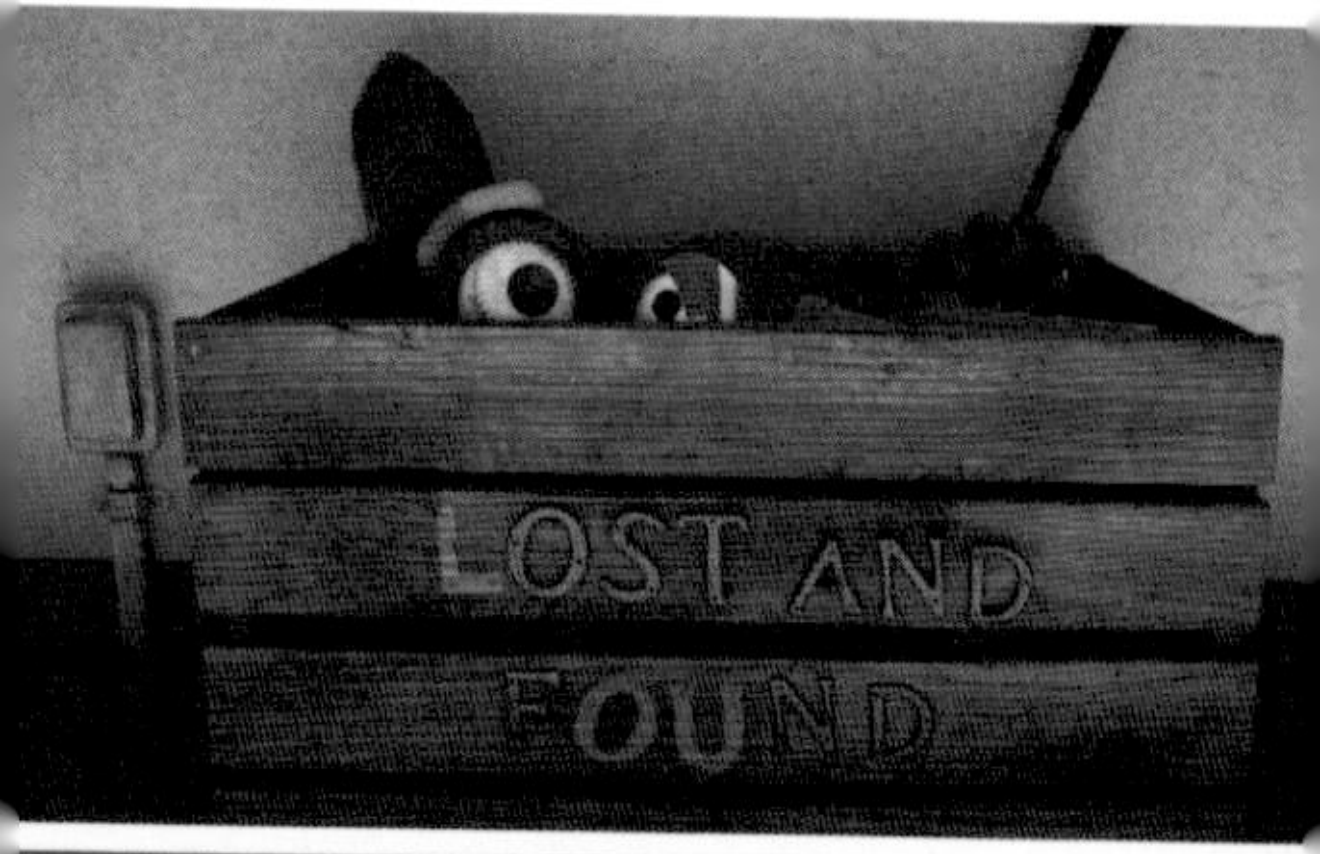
LOST AND
FOUND

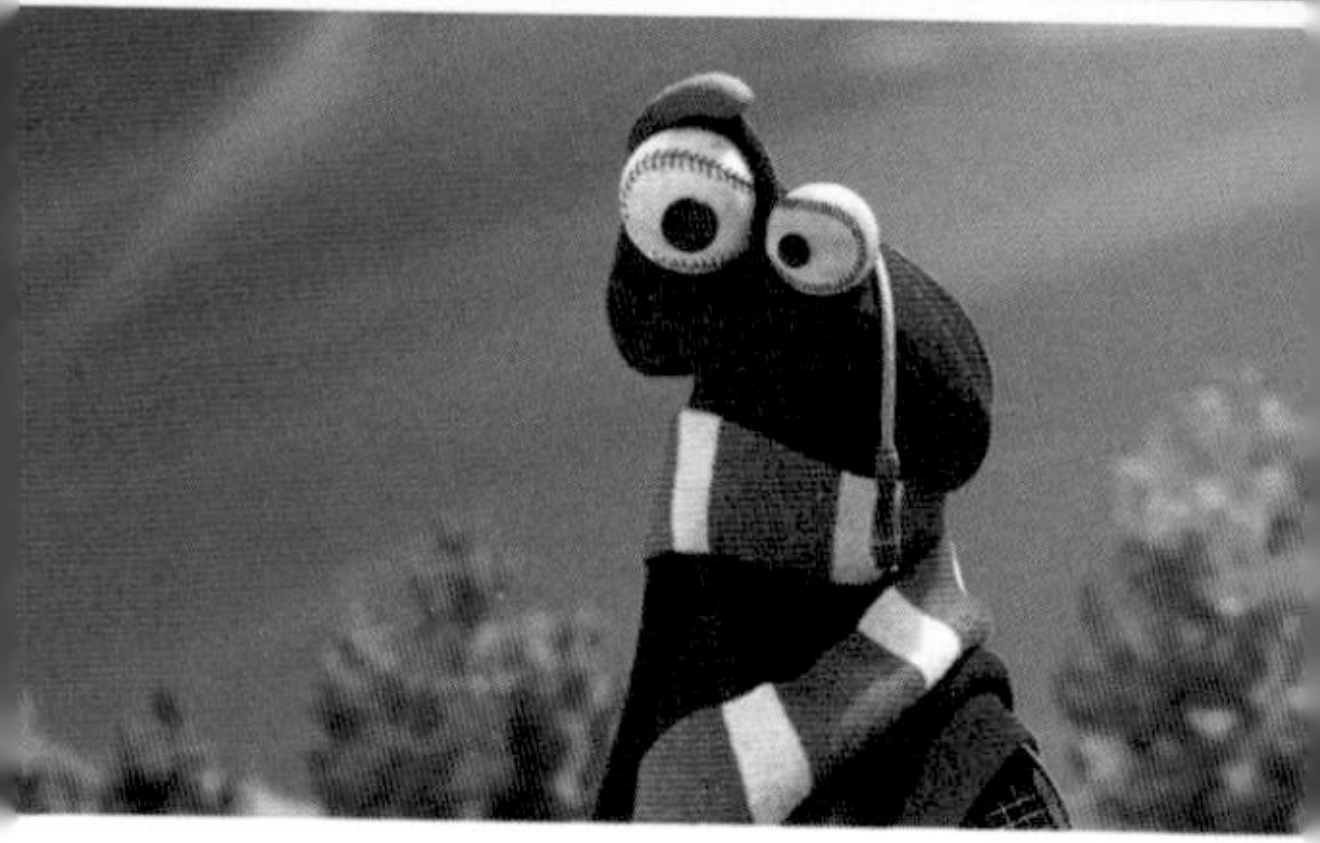

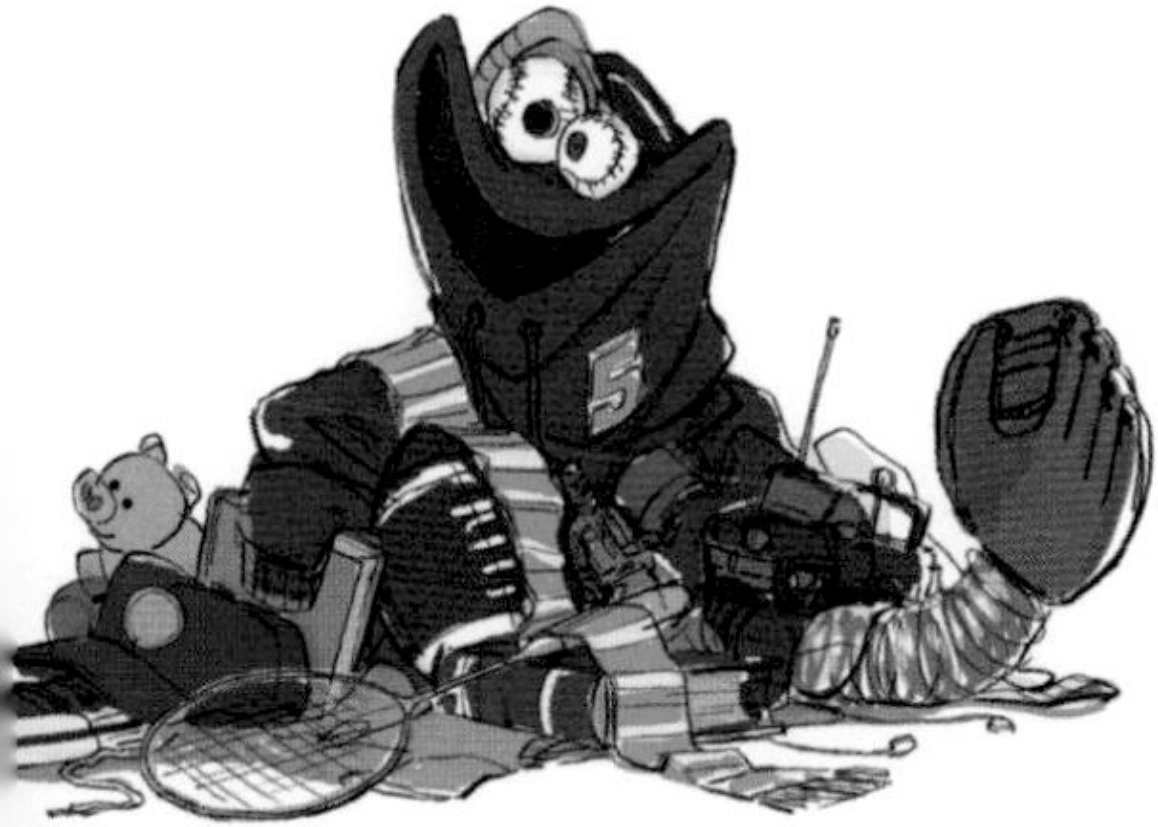
5

CARS 3
2017

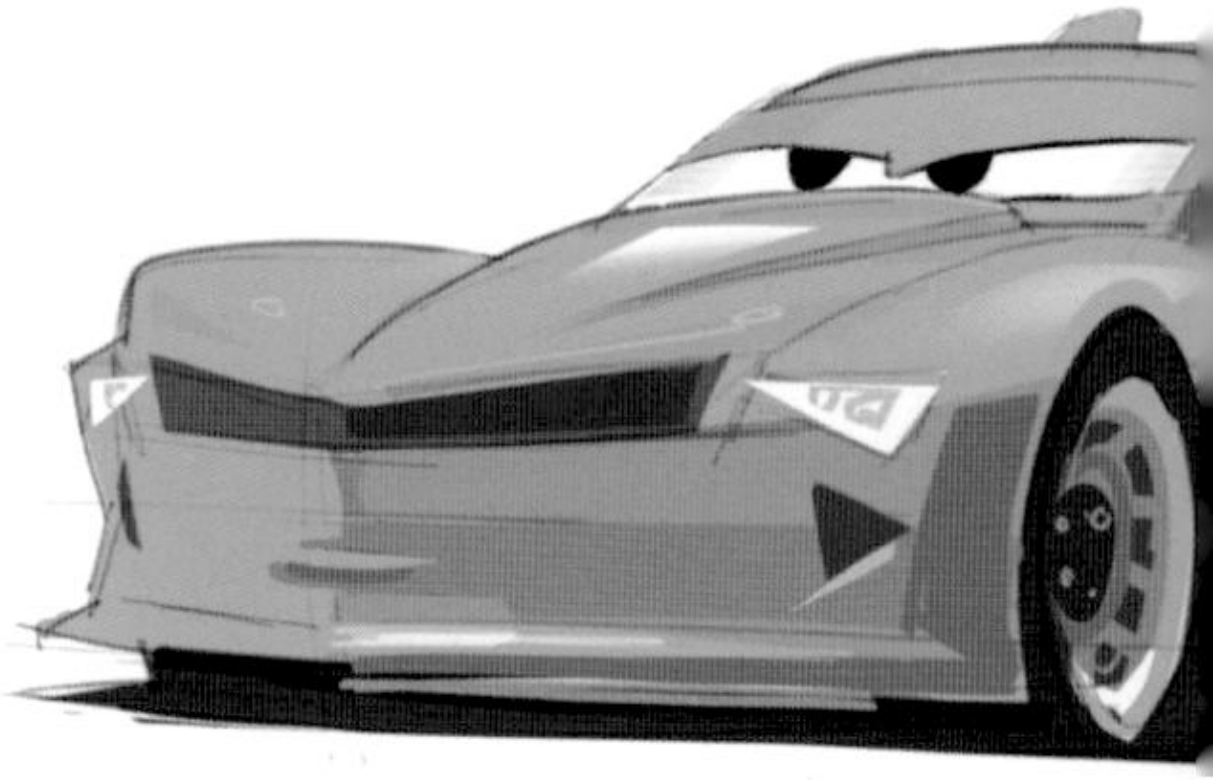

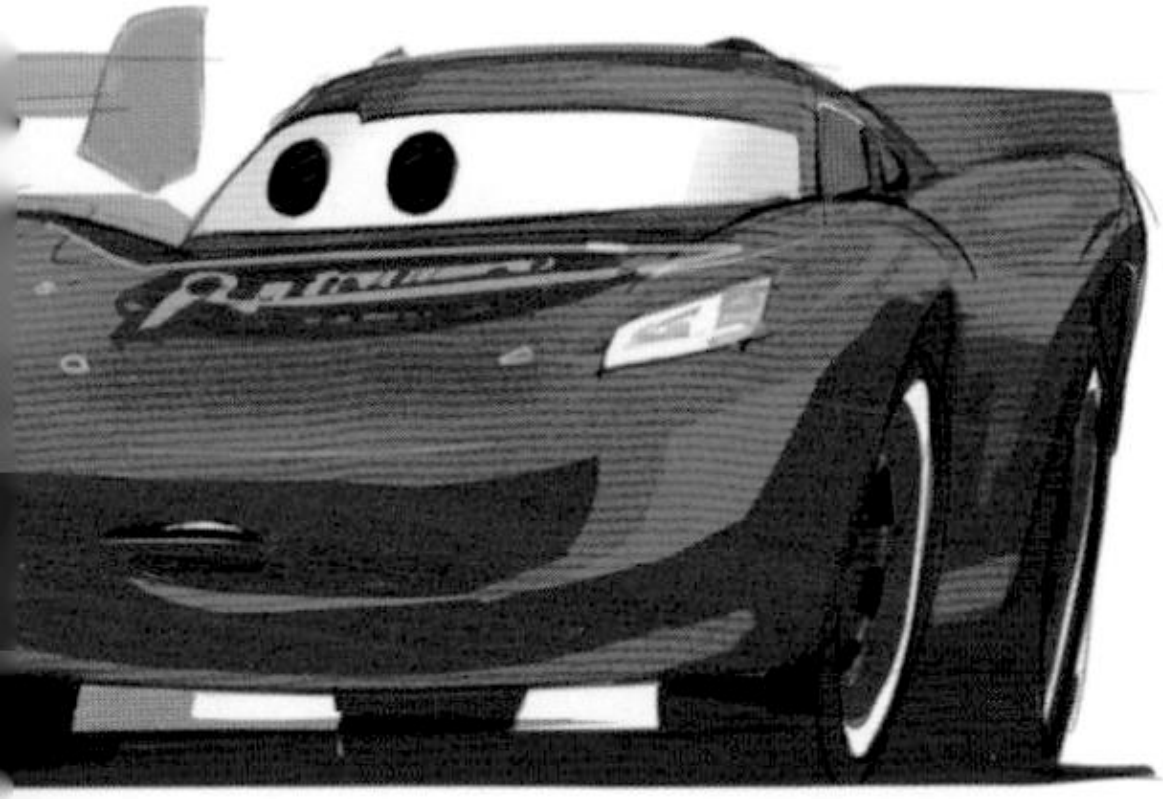

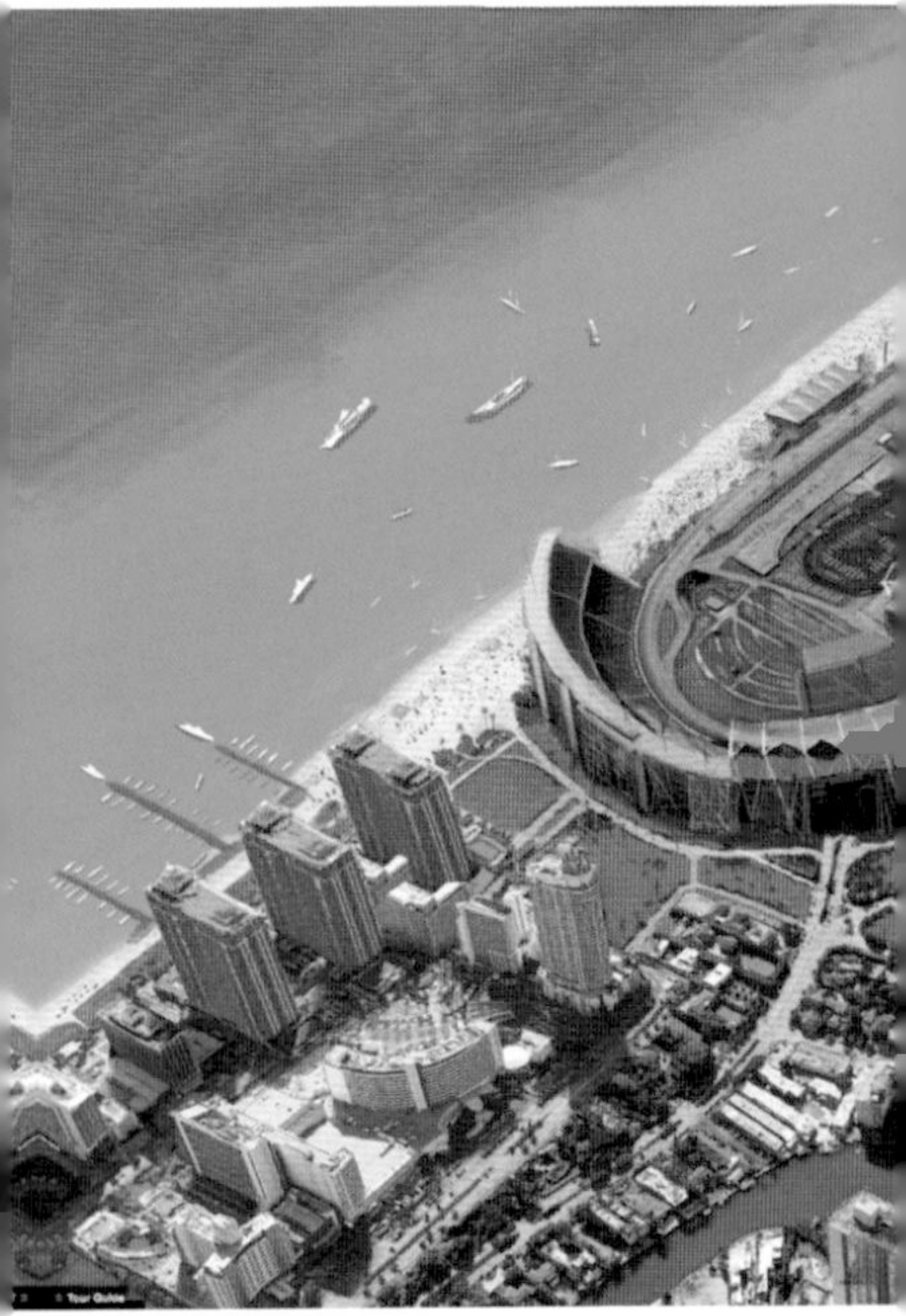

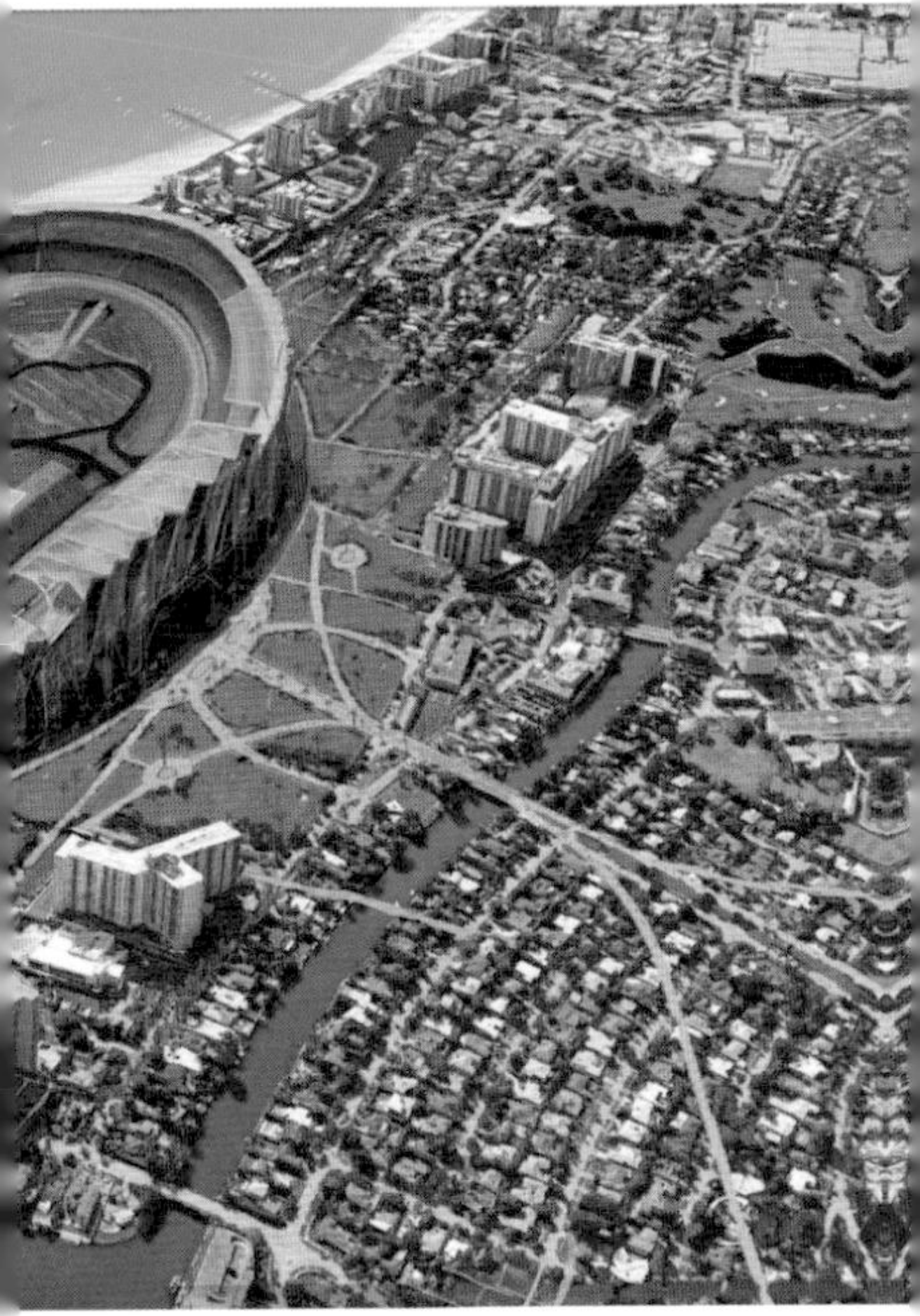

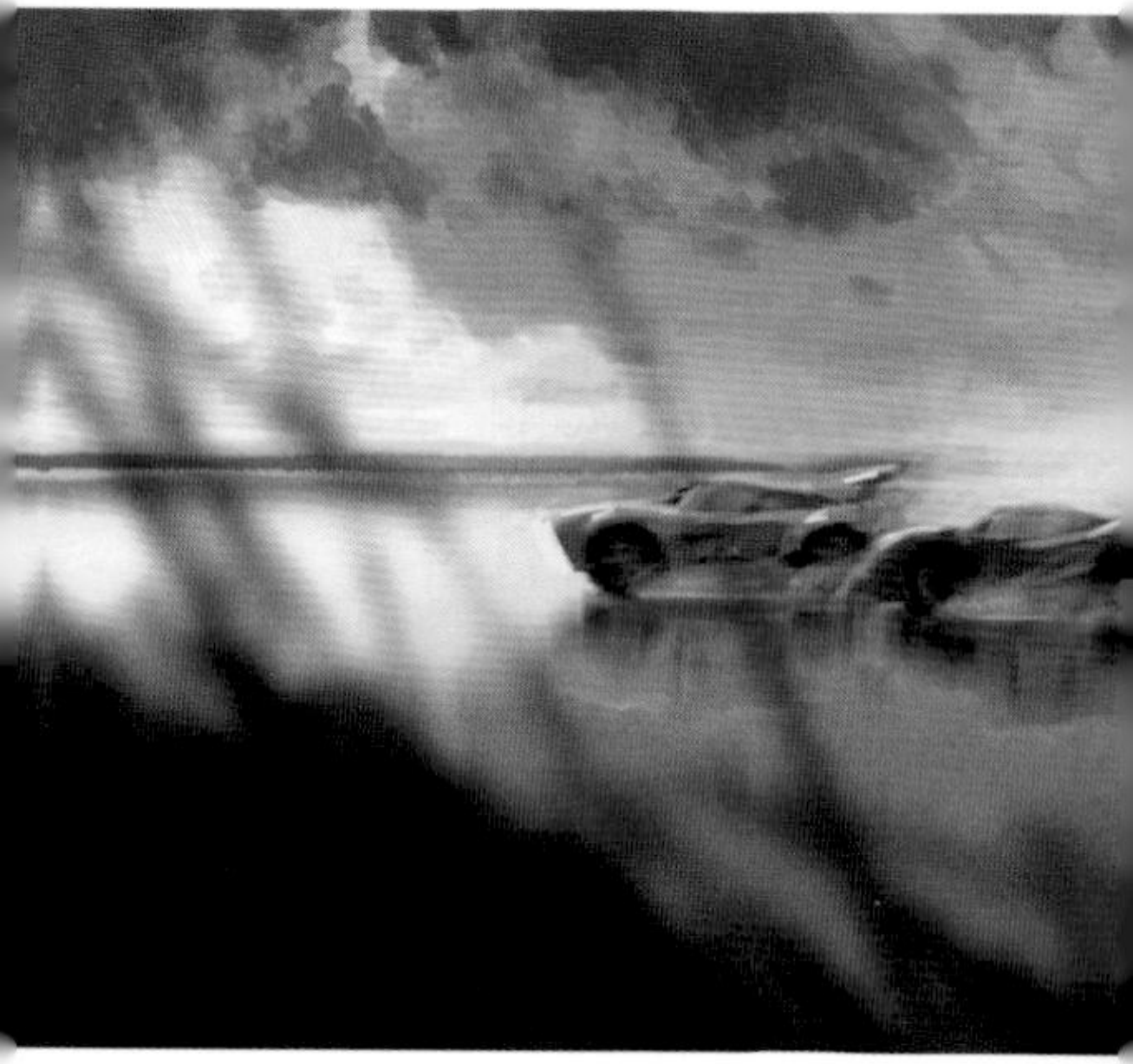

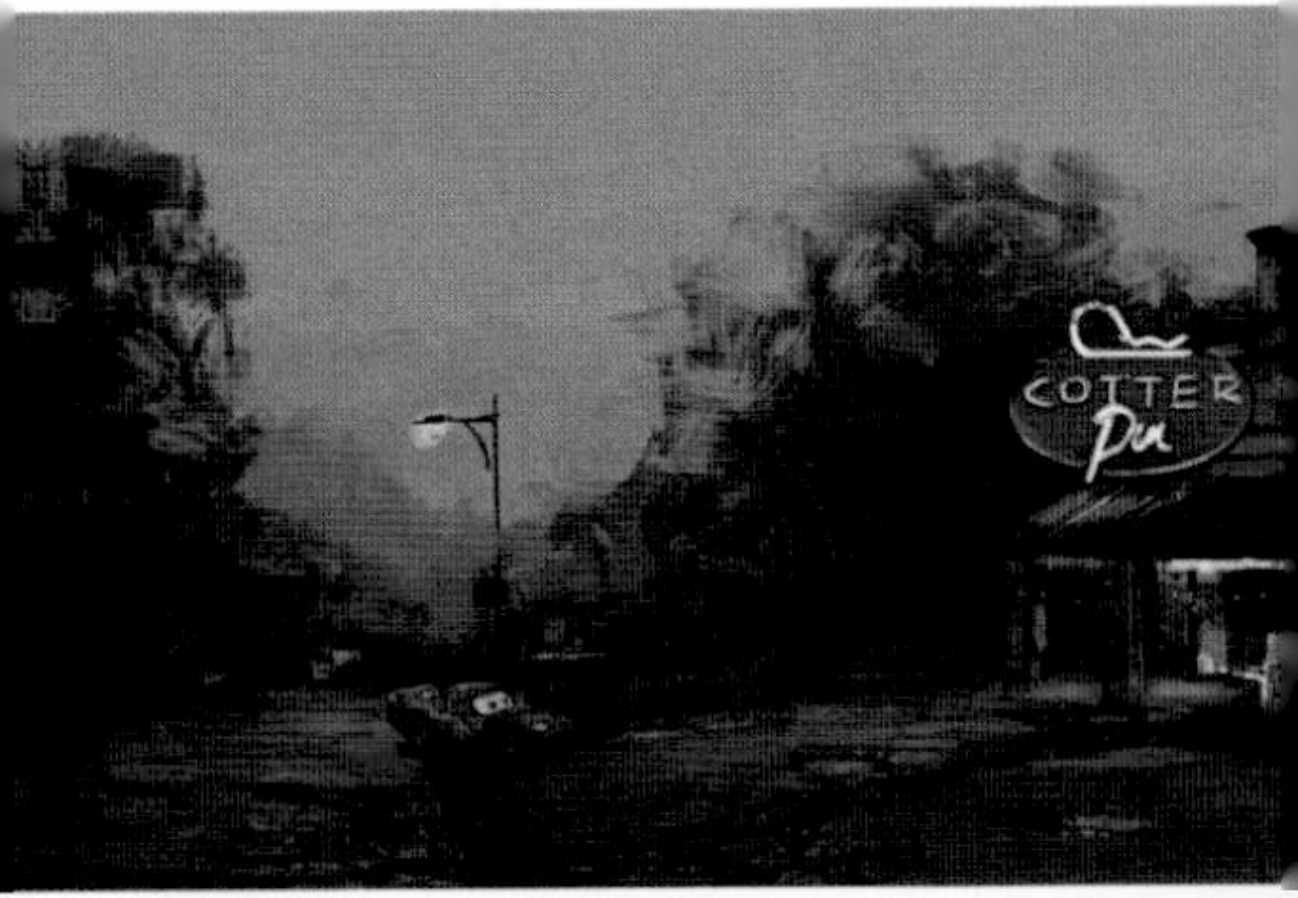
COTTER
Pin

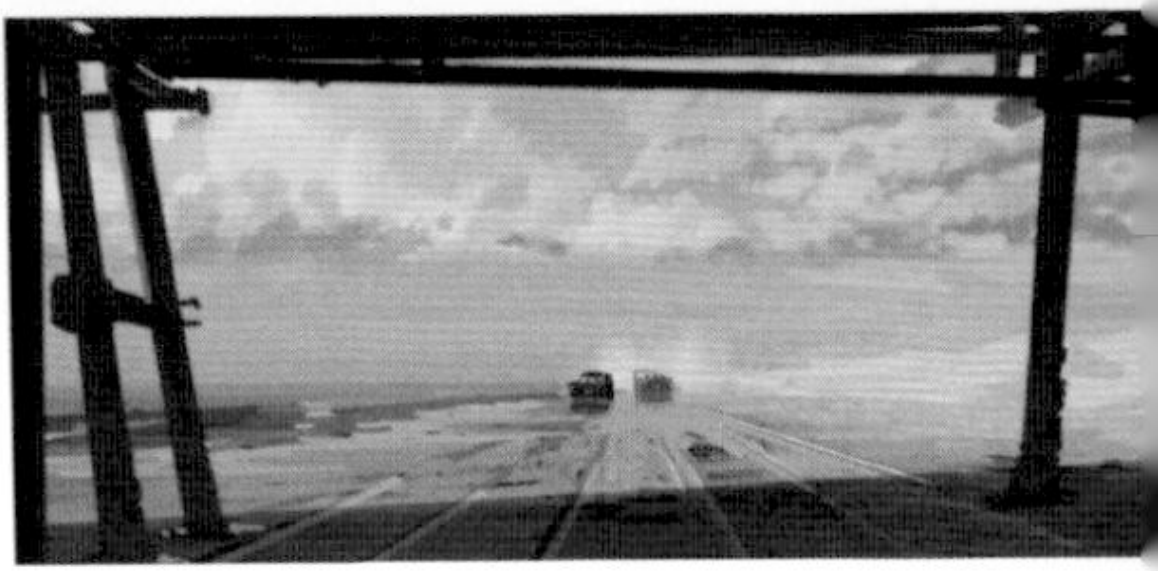

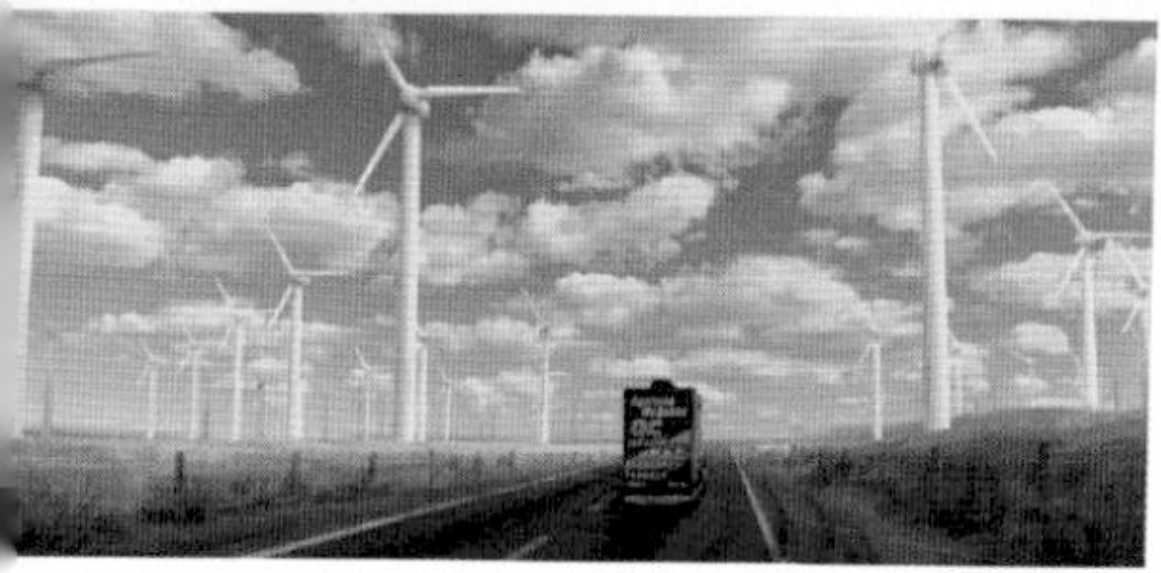

COCO
2017

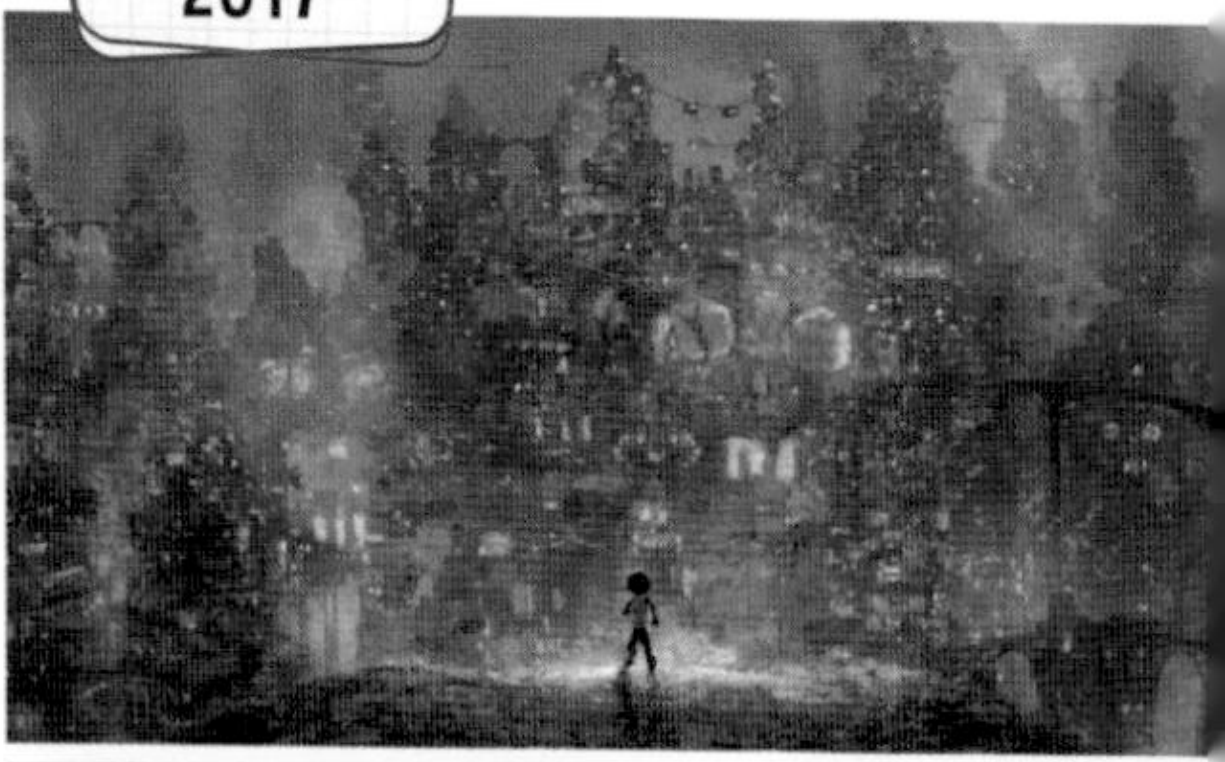

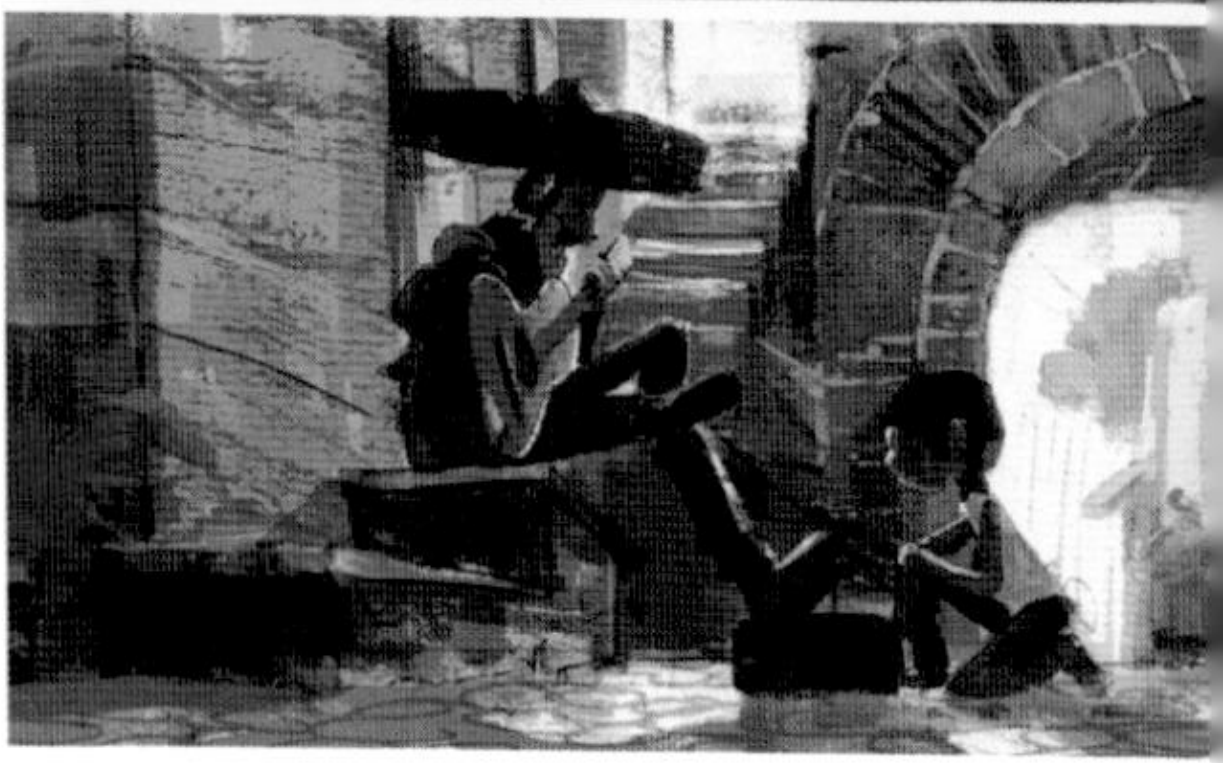

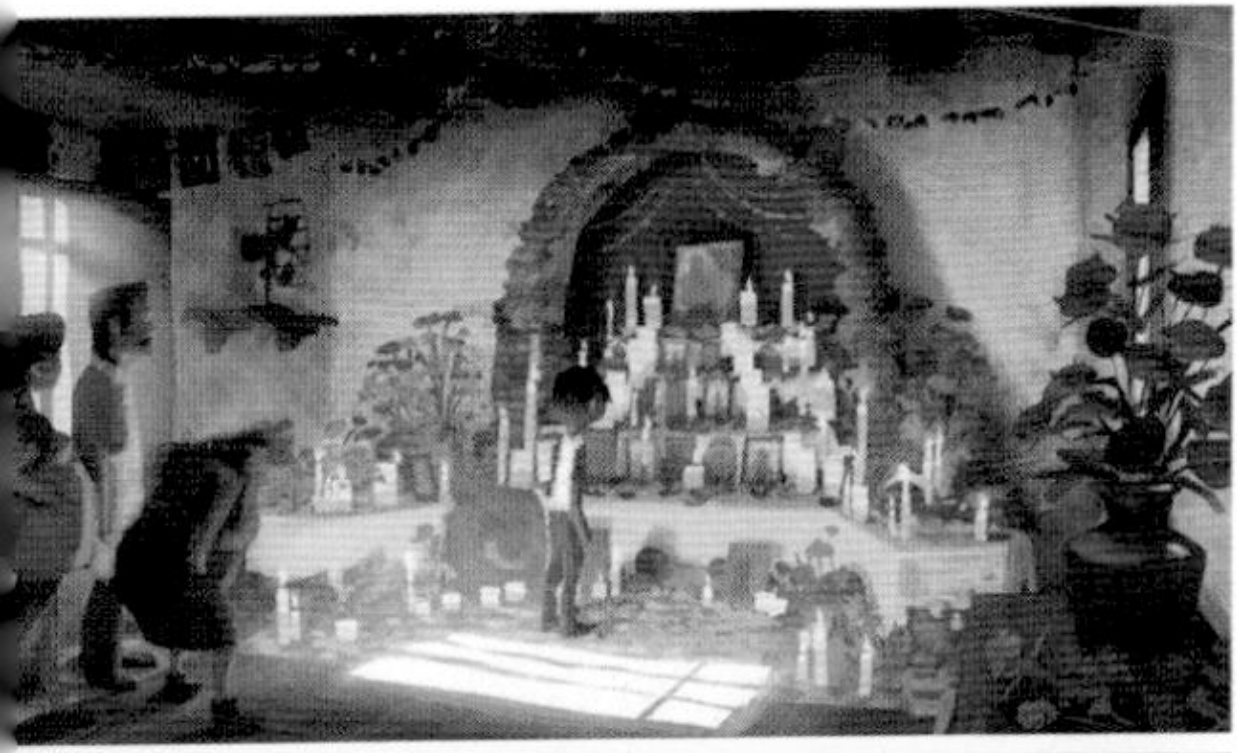

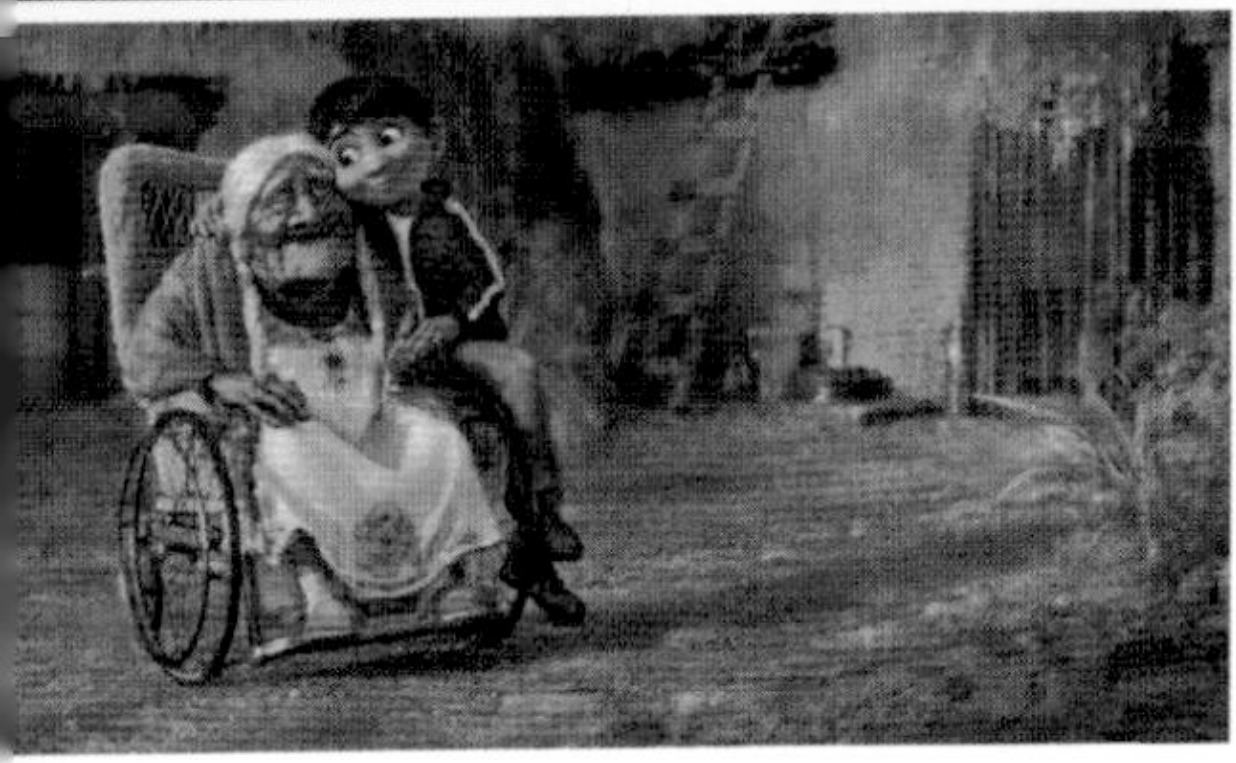

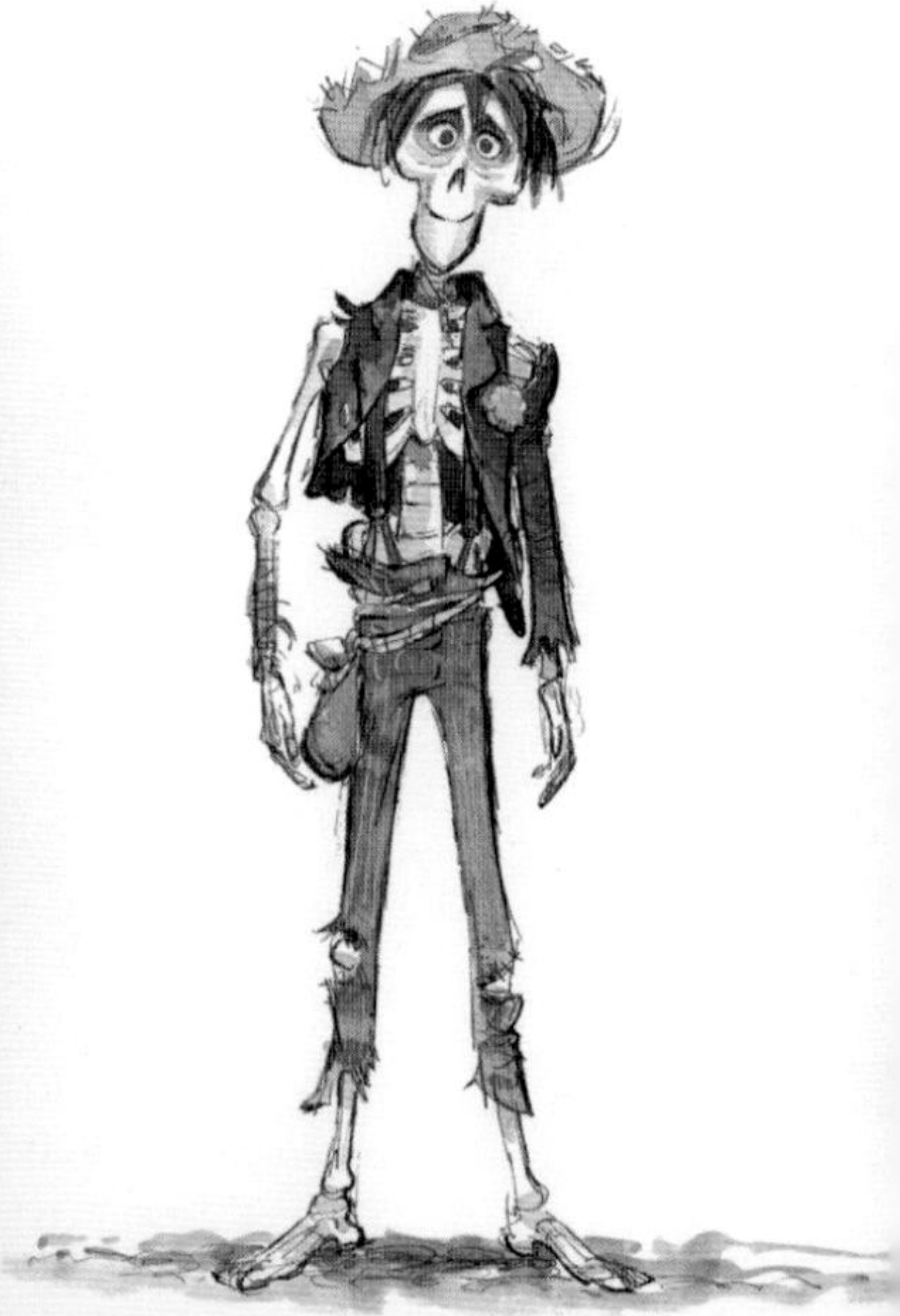

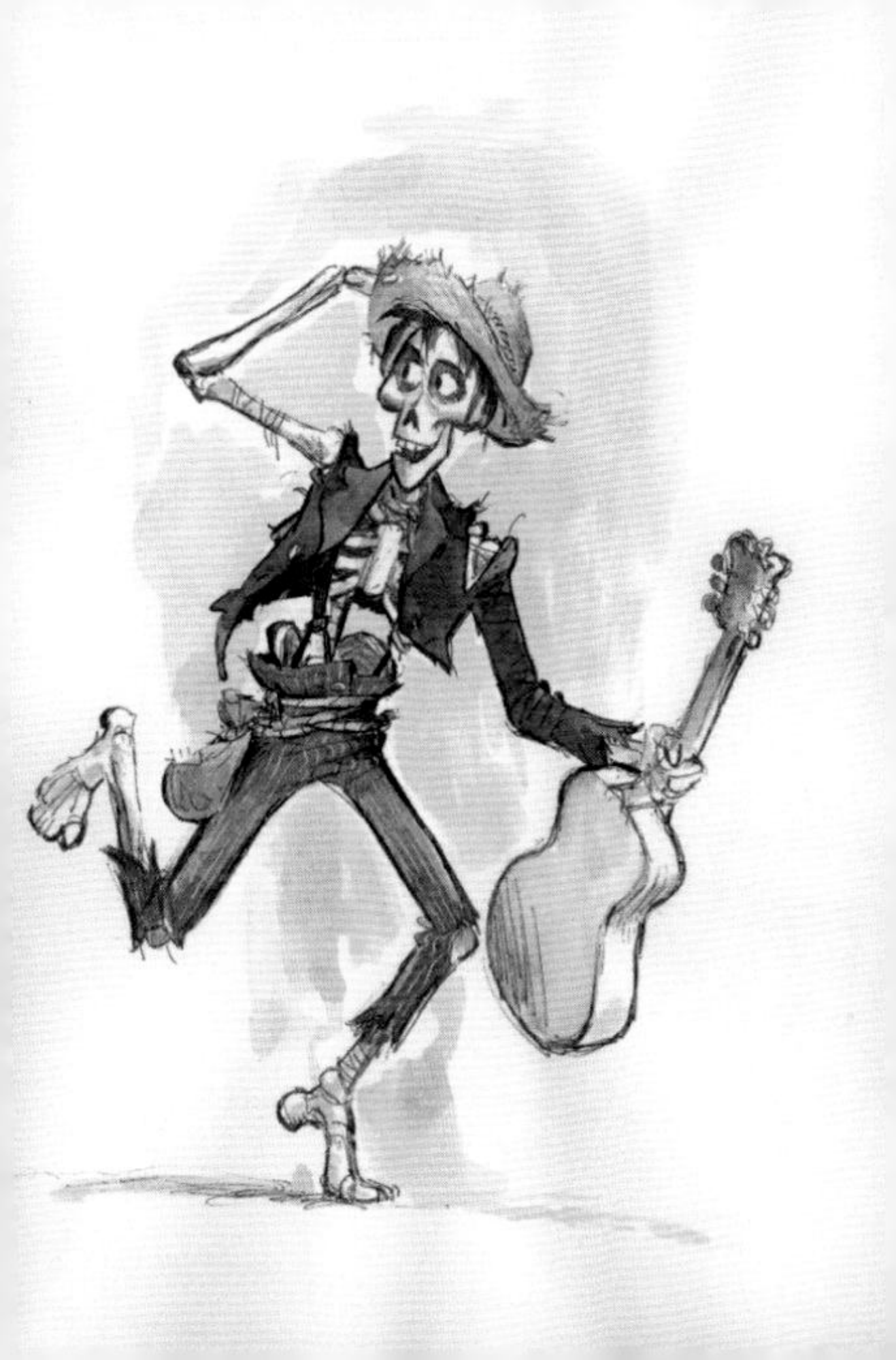

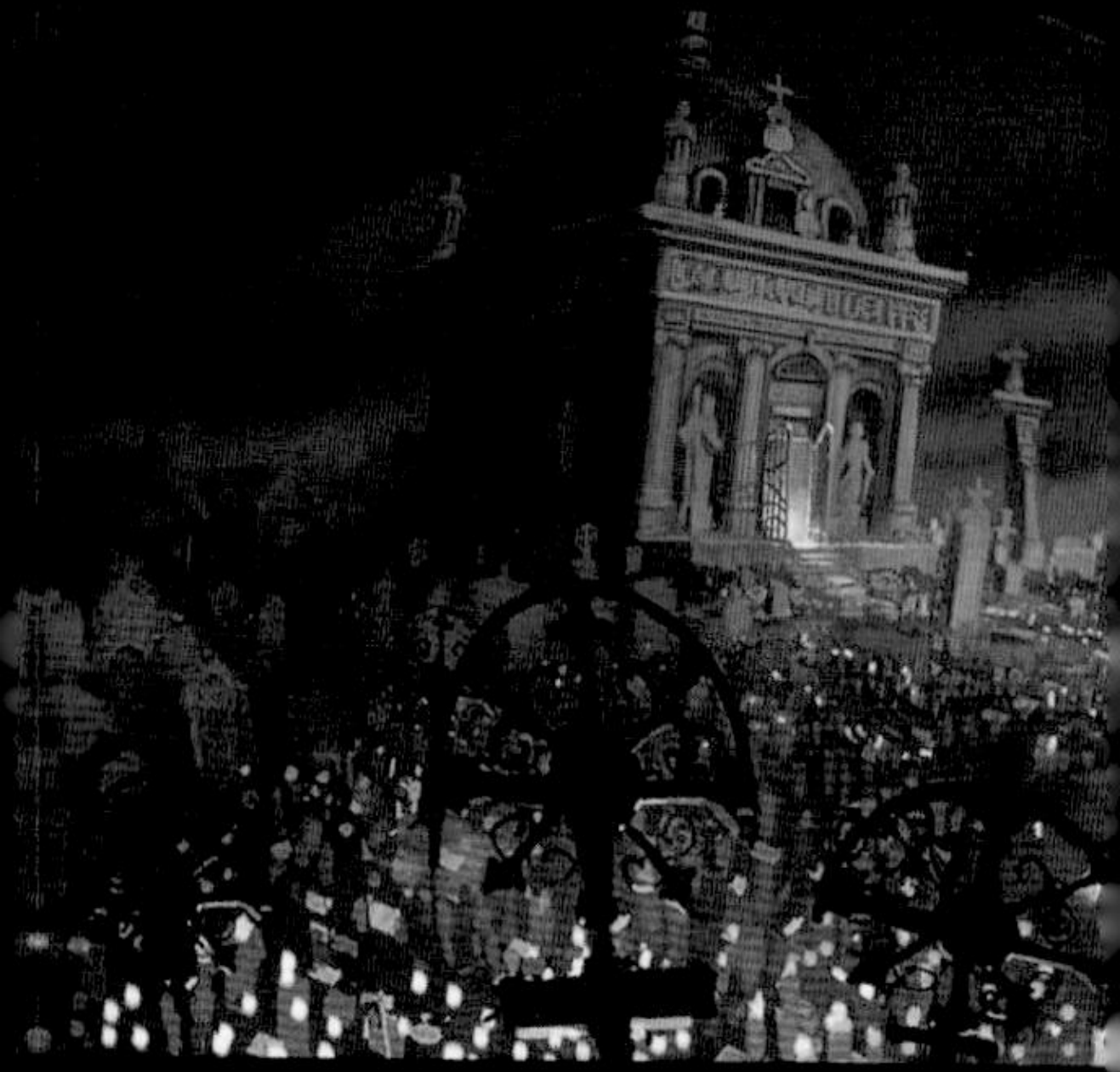

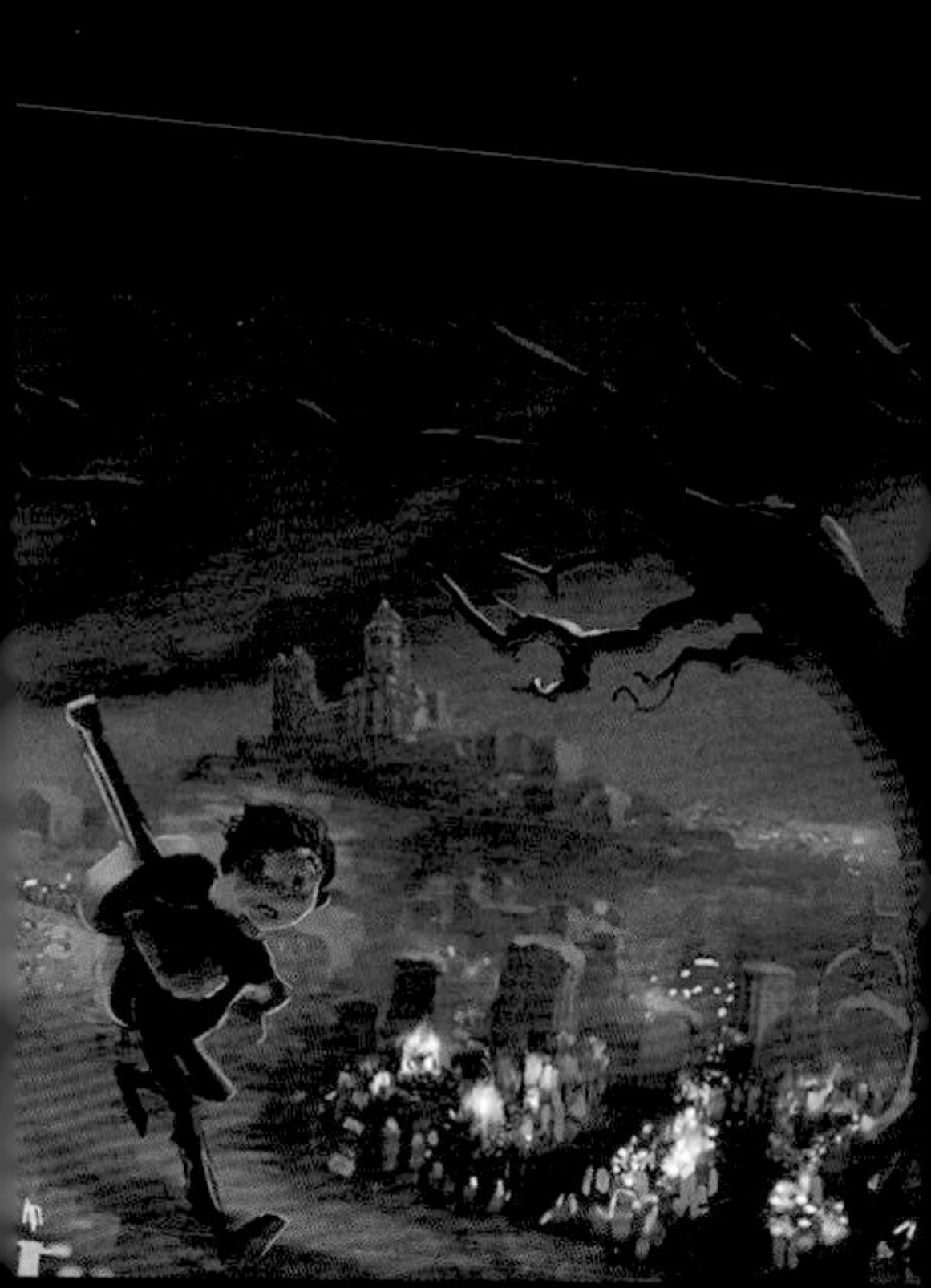

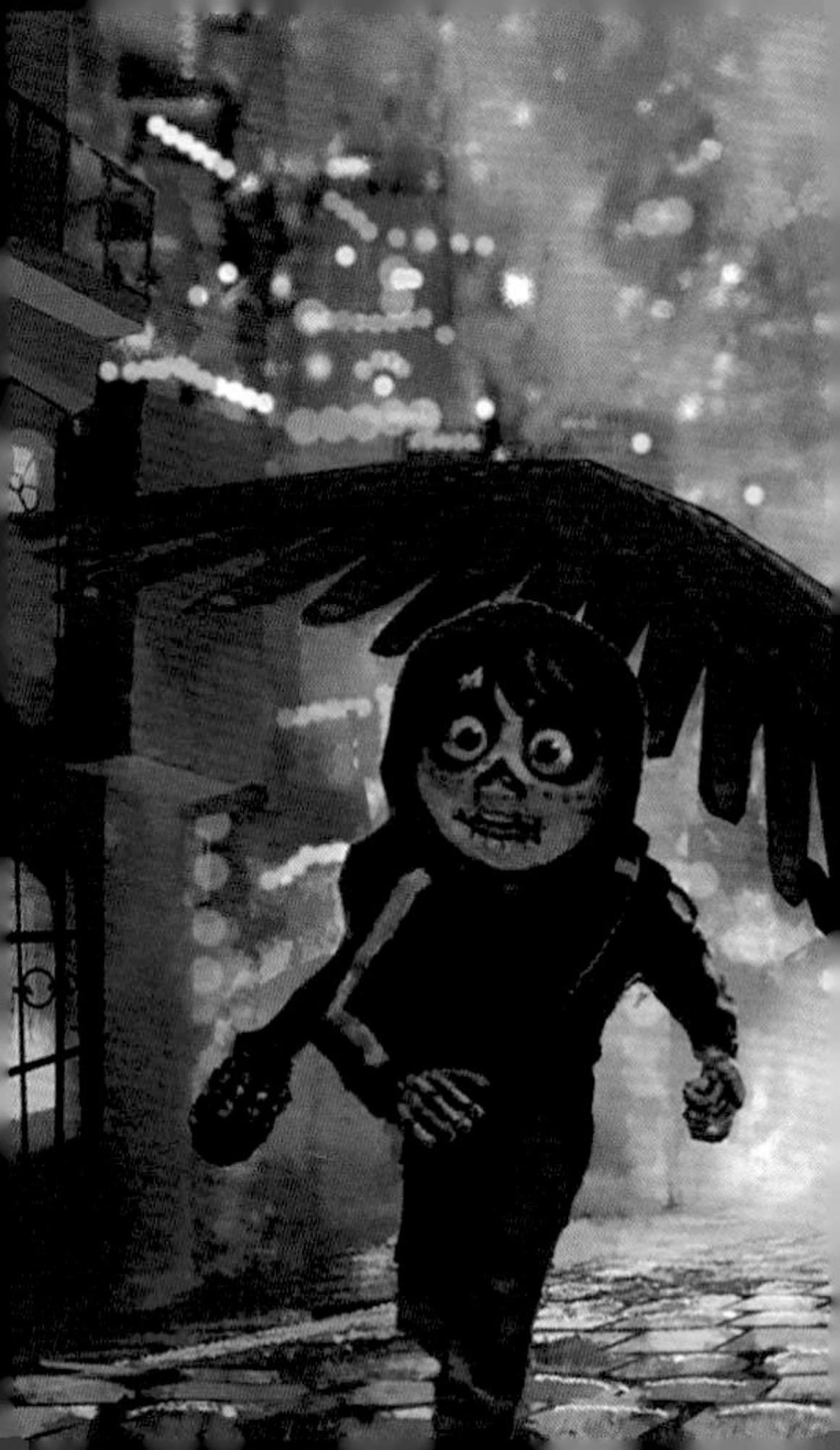

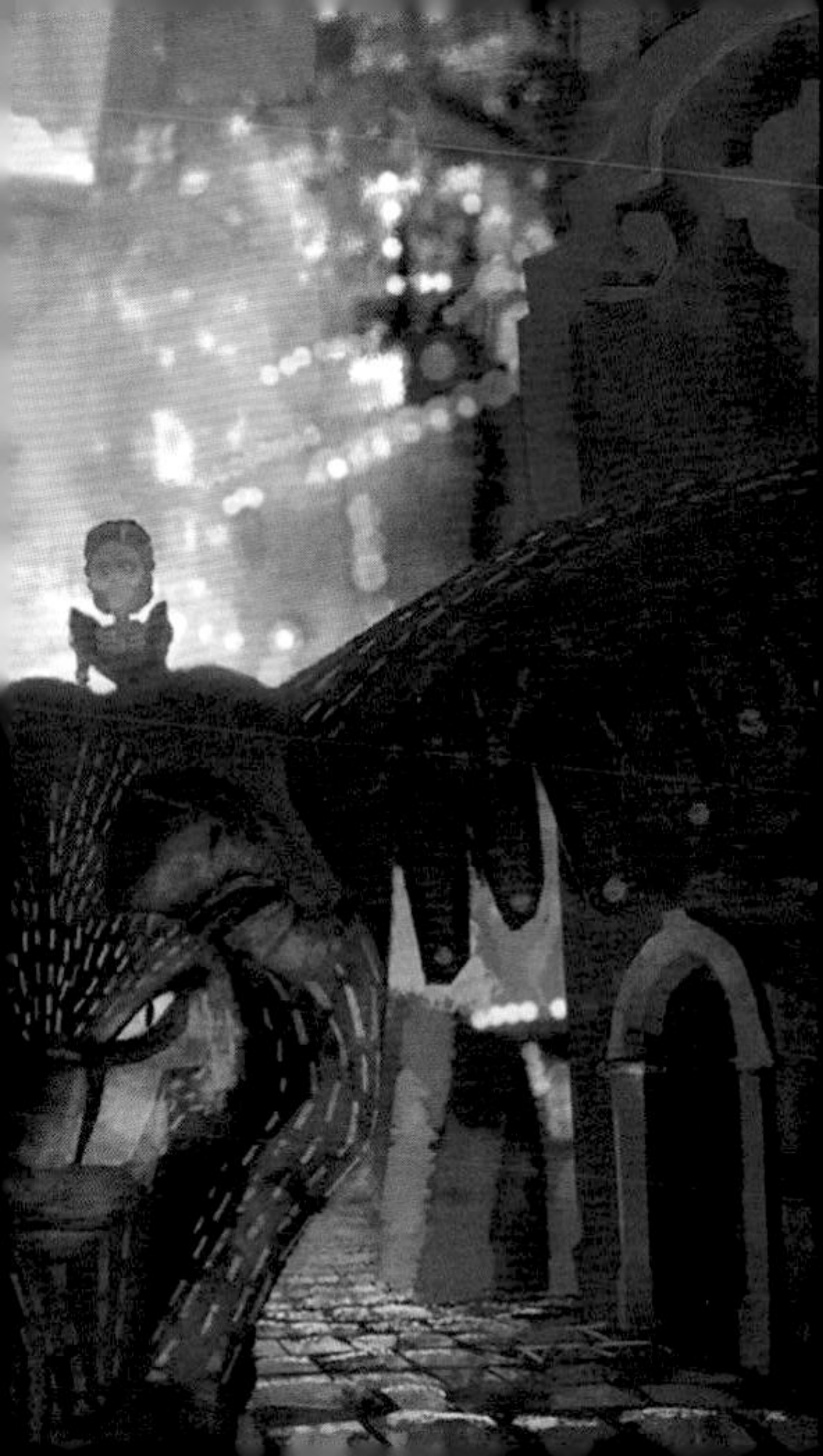

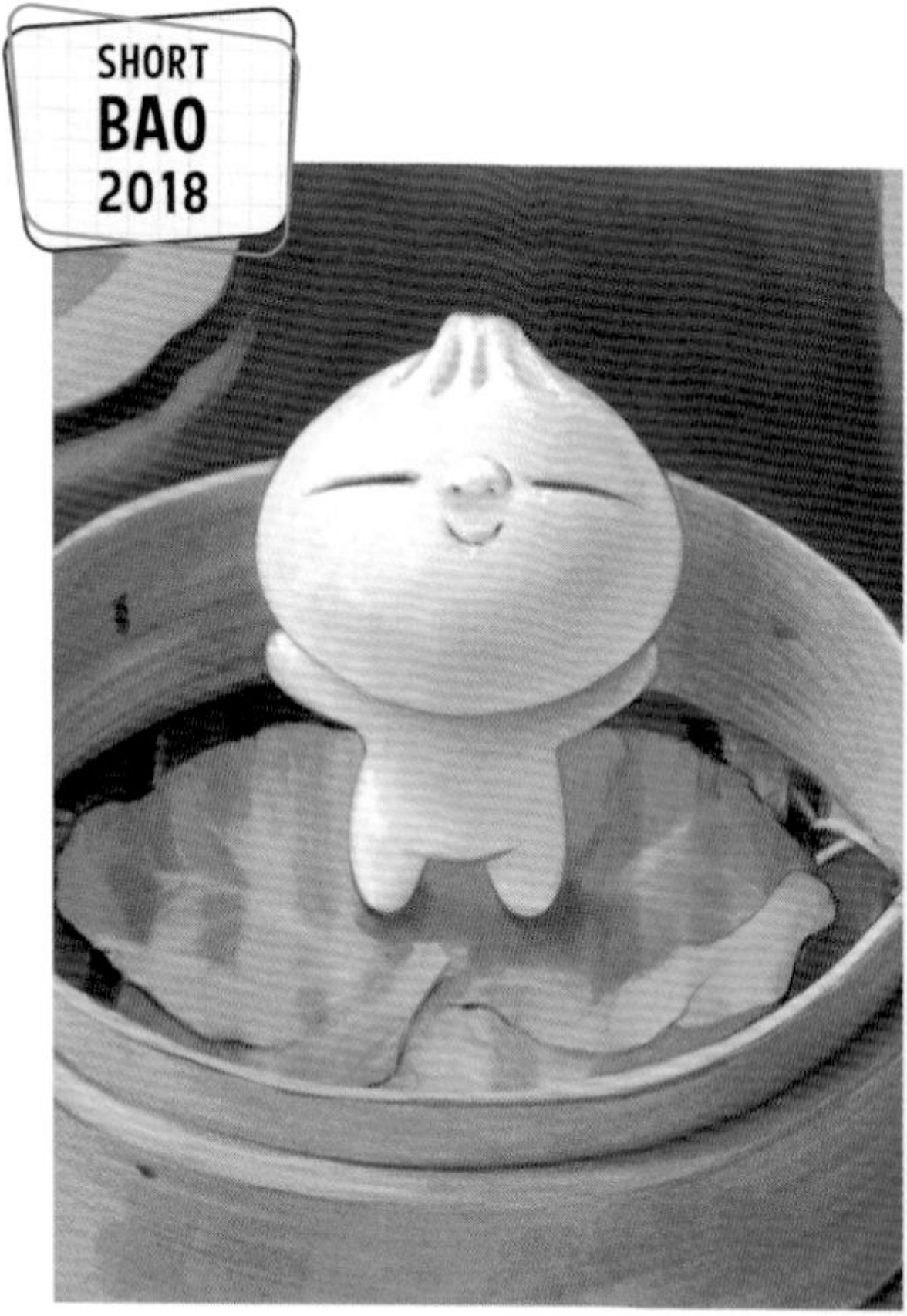
SHORT
BAO
2018

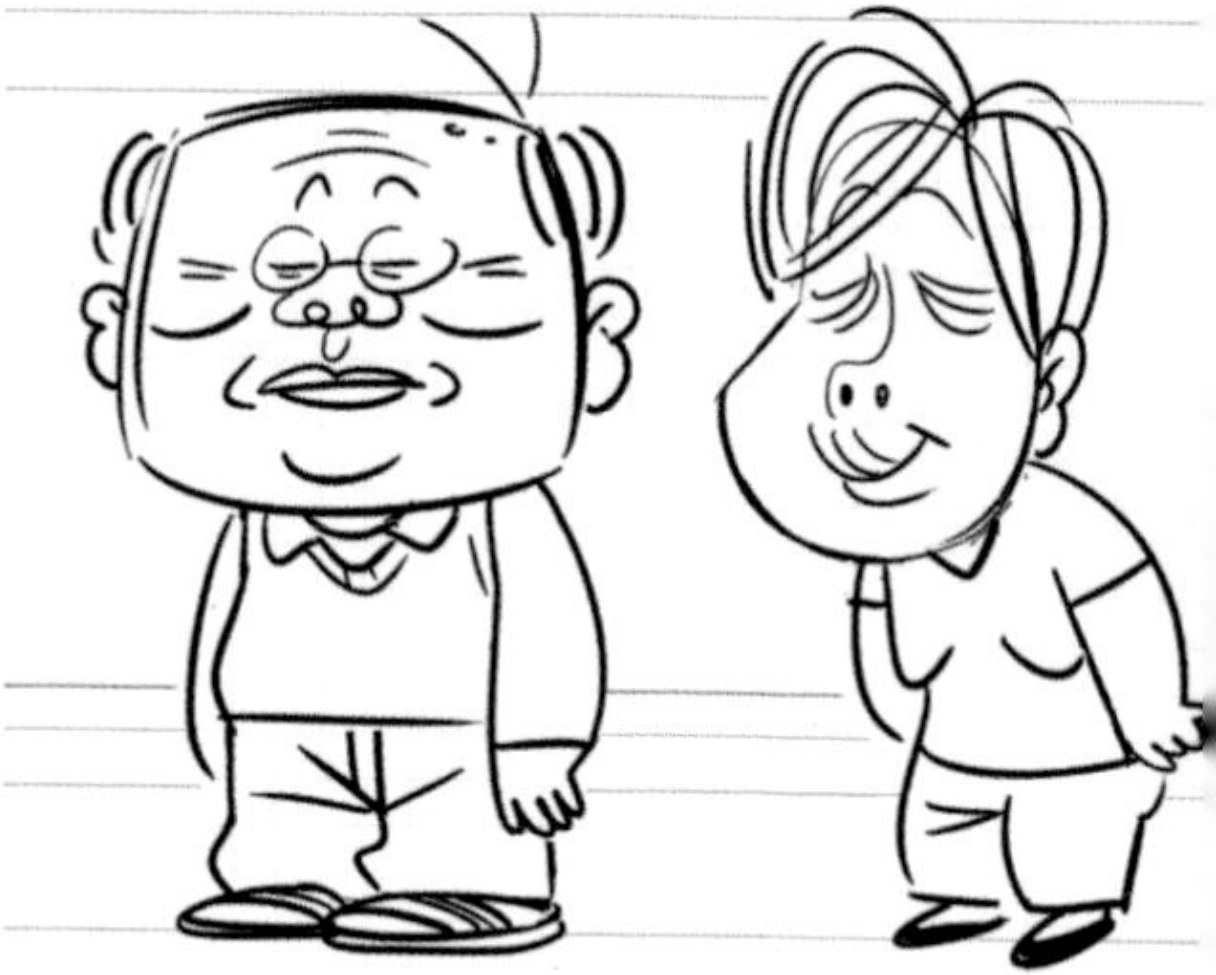

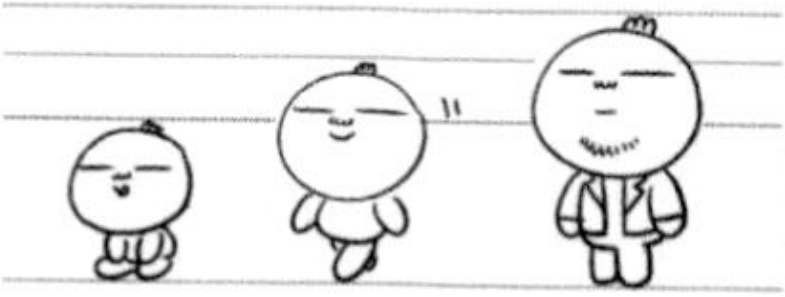

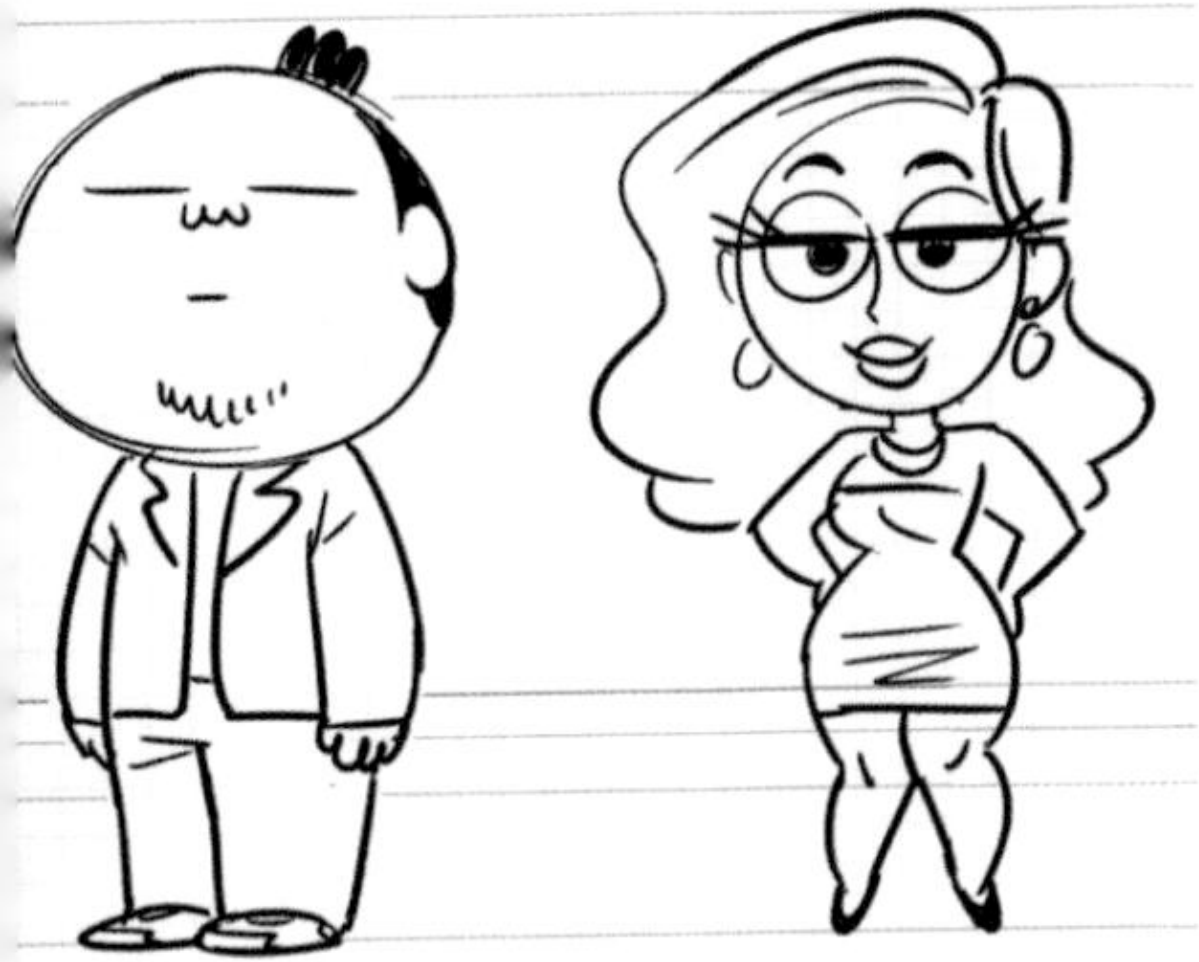

THE INCREDIBLES 2
2018

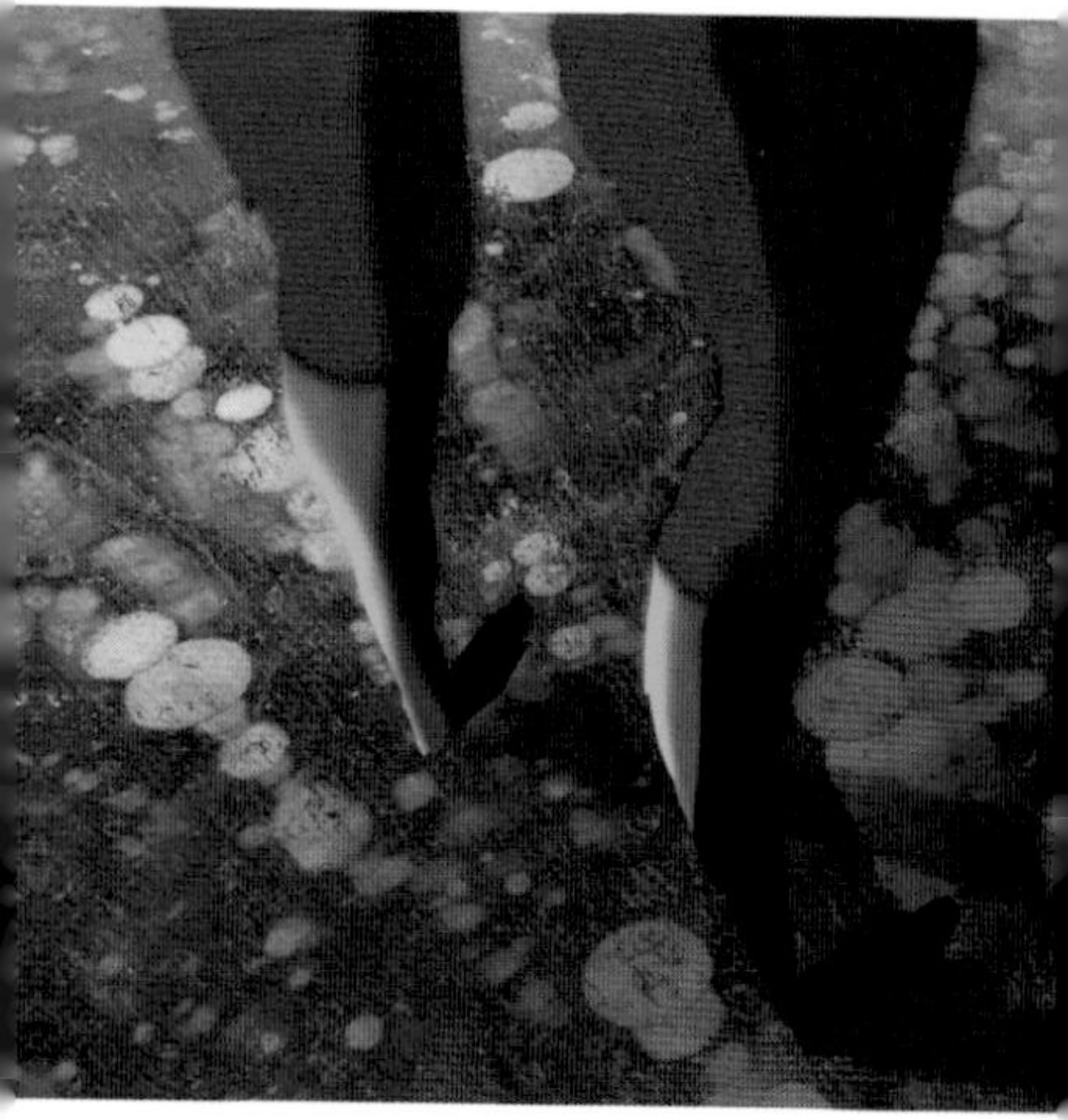

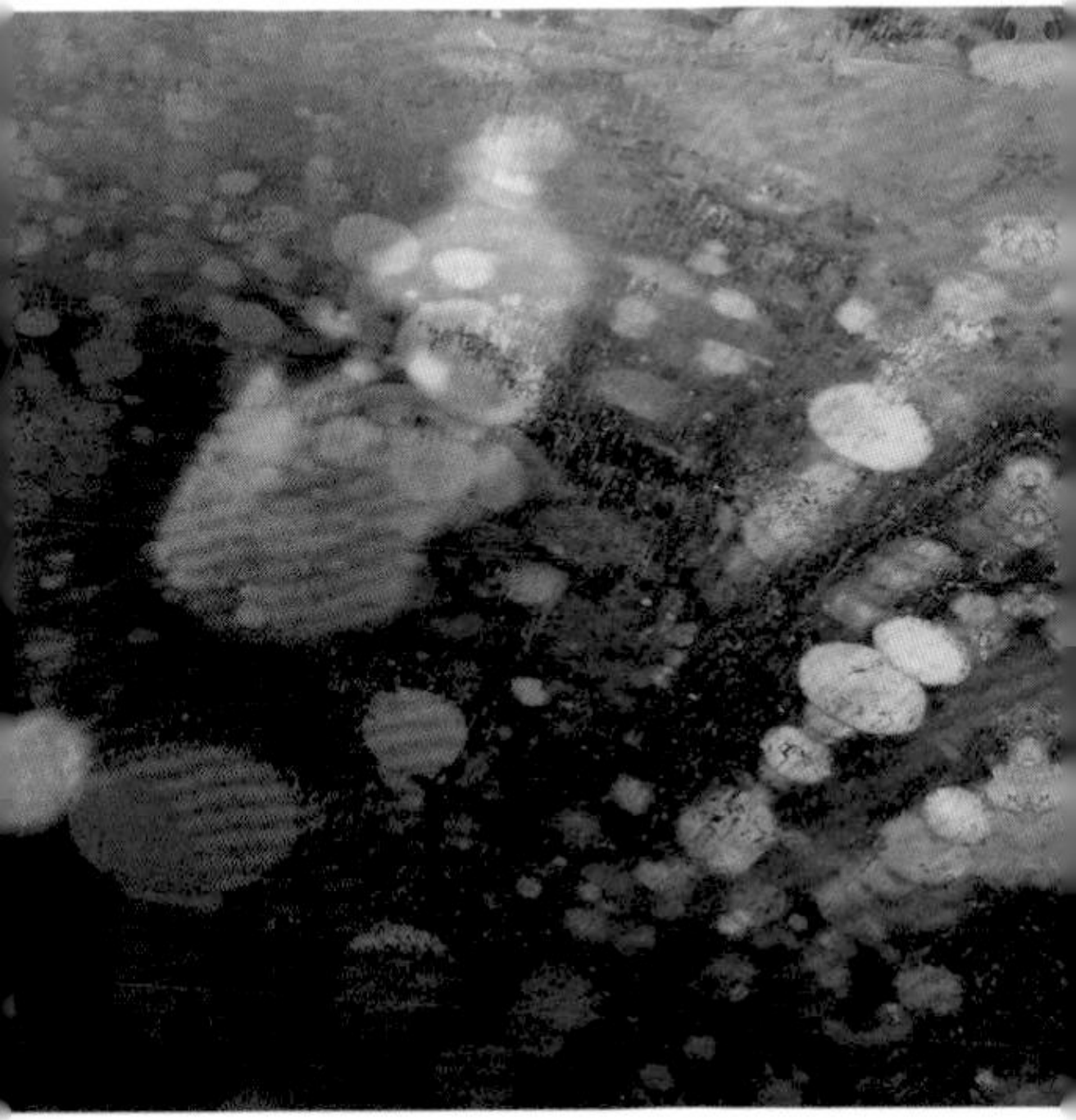

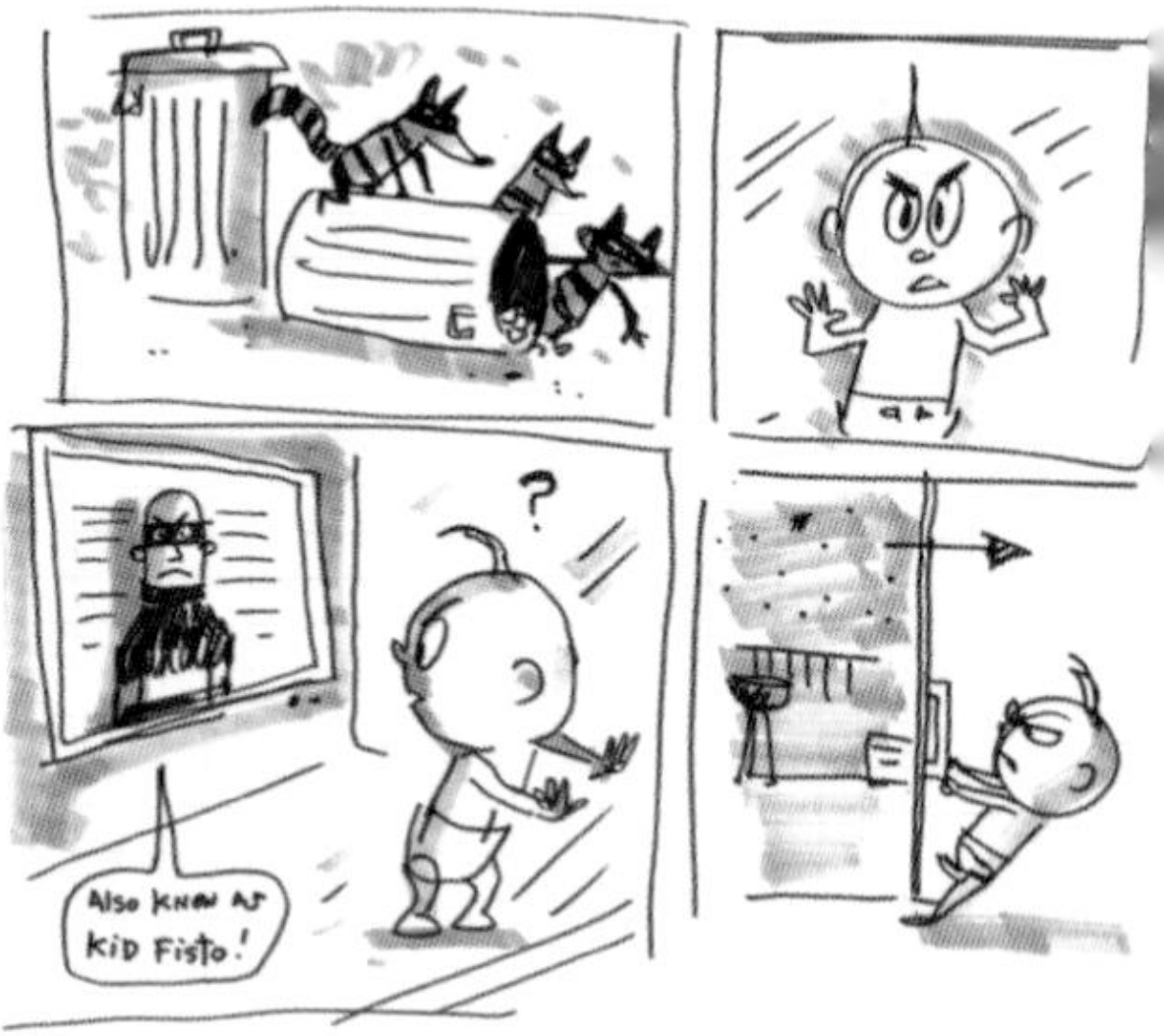
?
Also know as Kid Fisto!

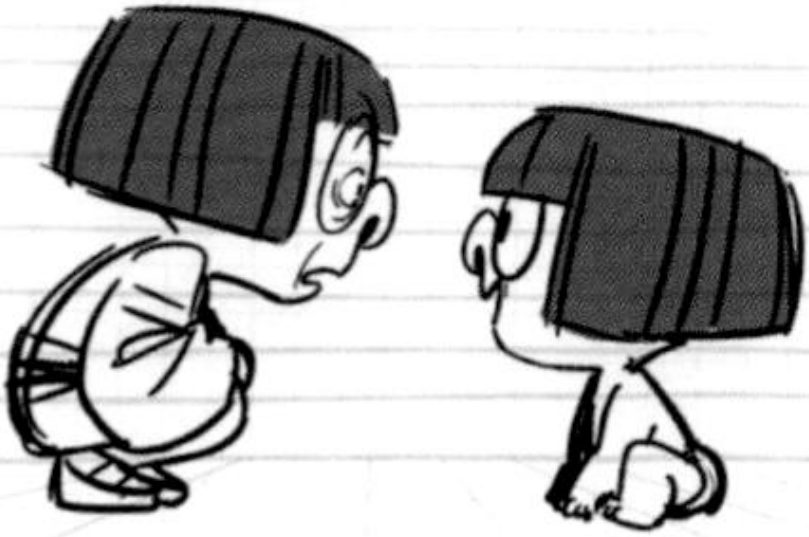

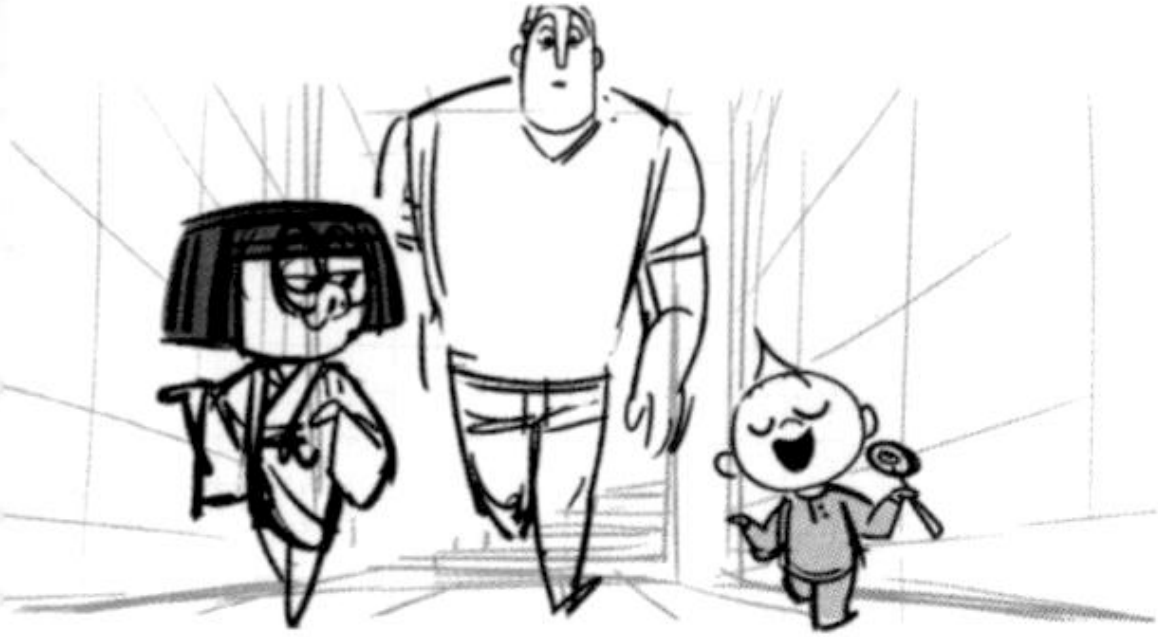

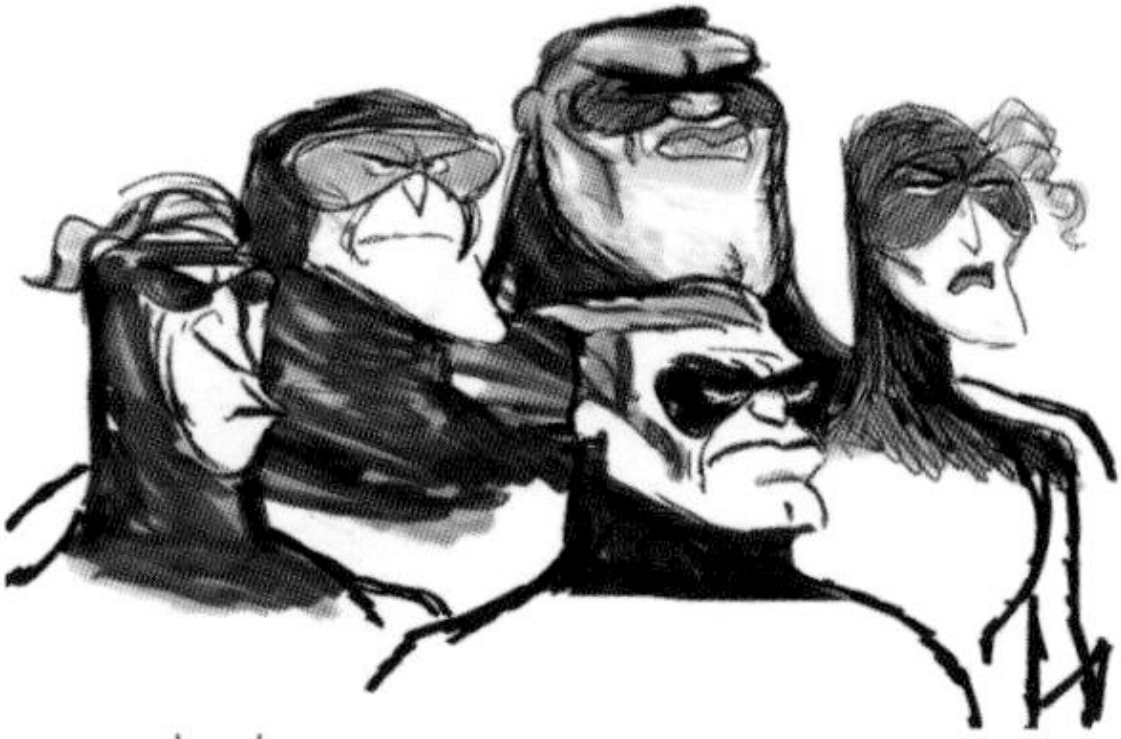

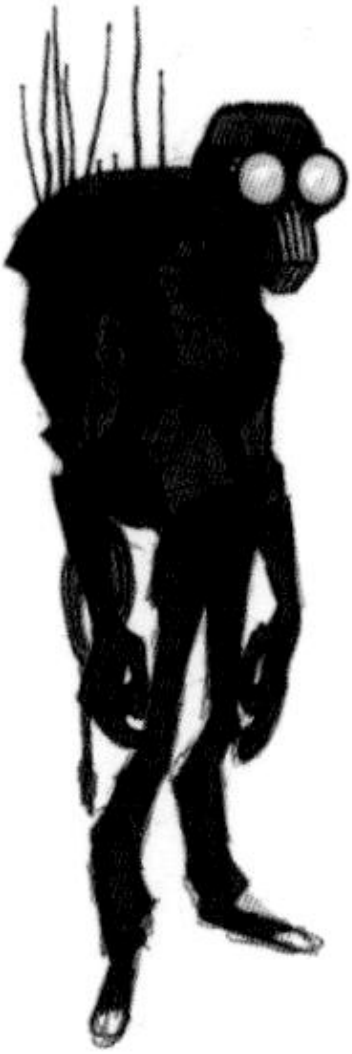

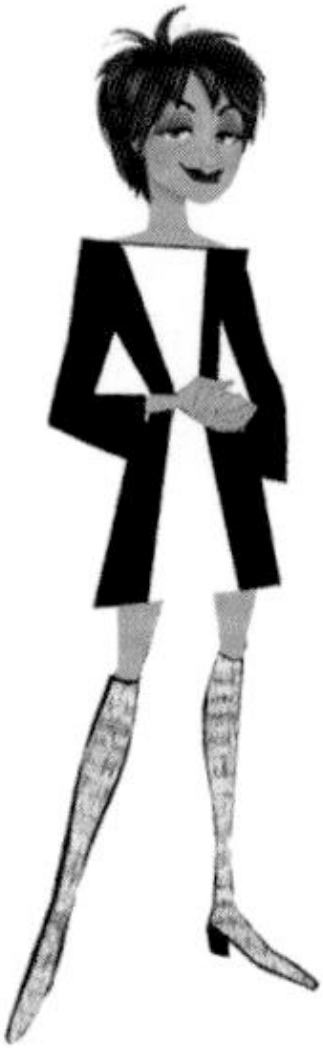

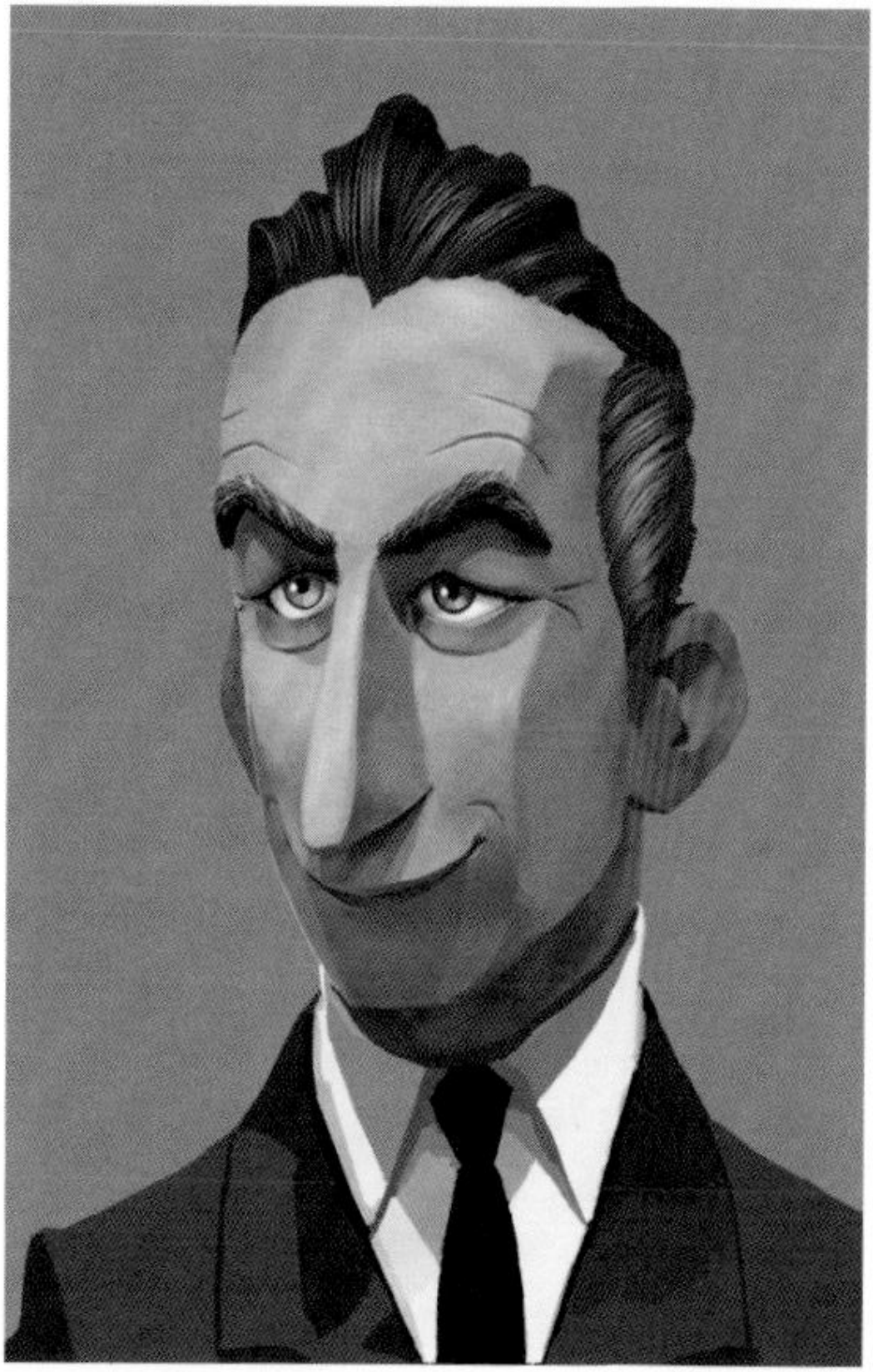

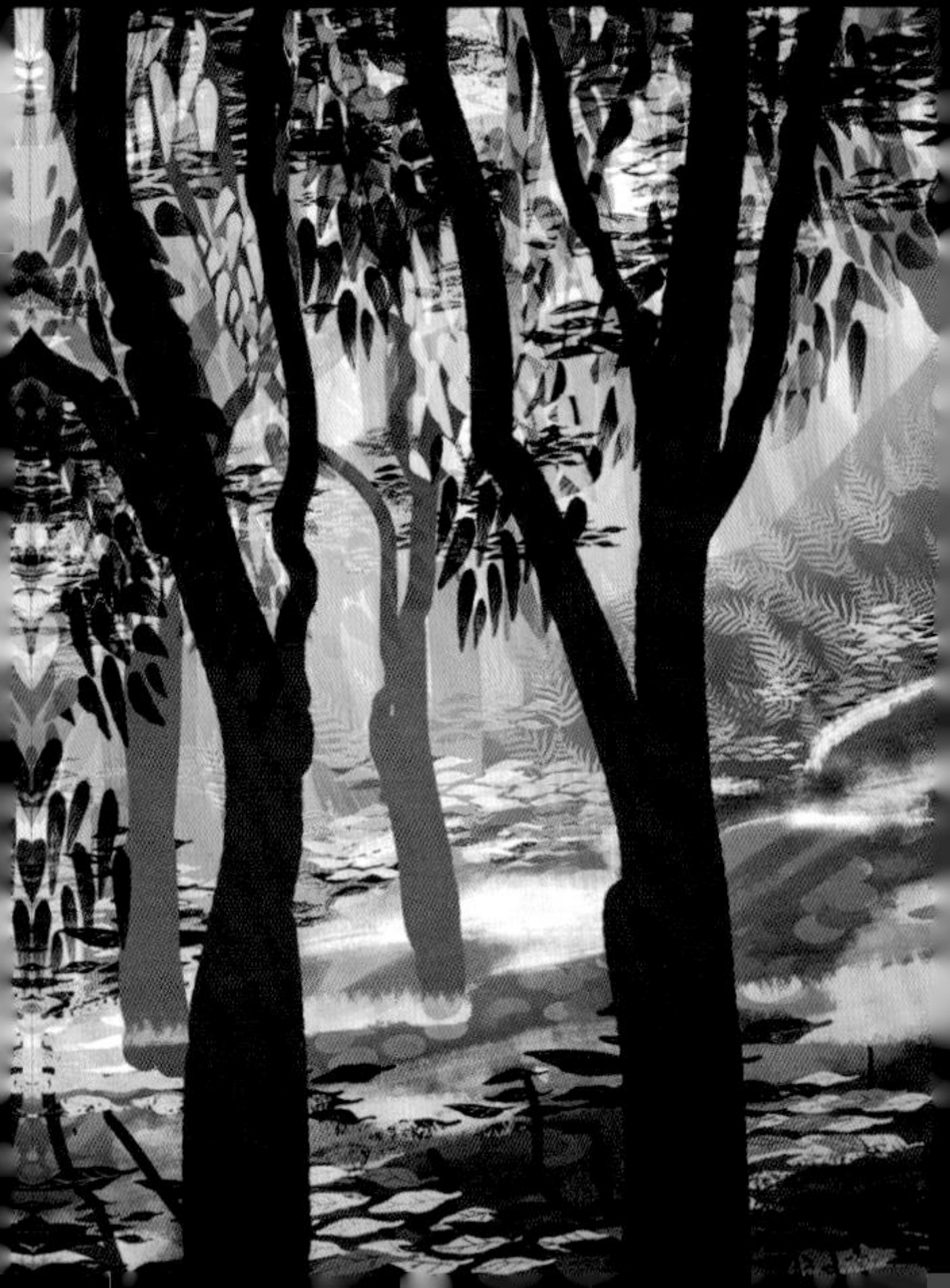

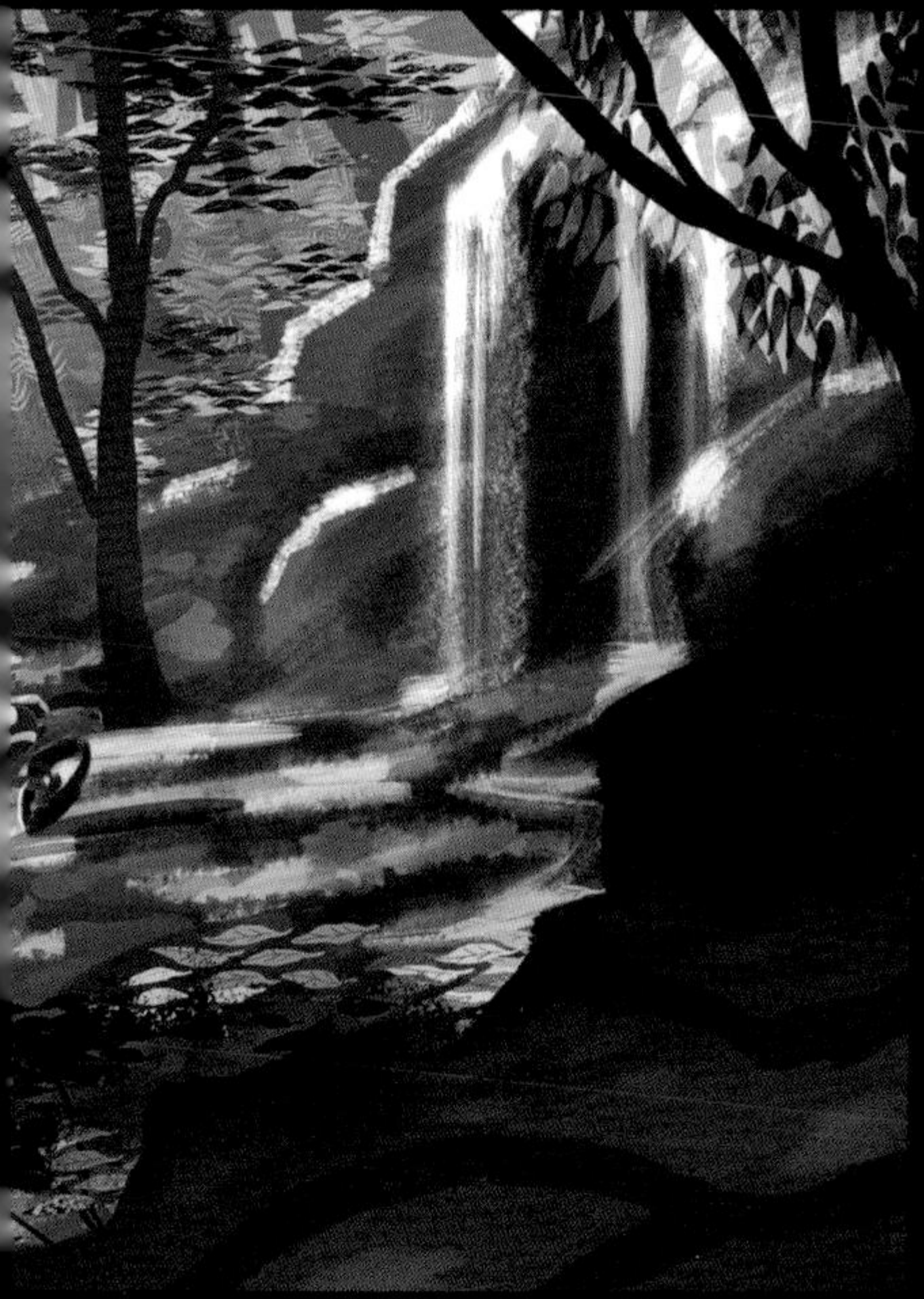

TOY STORY 4
2019

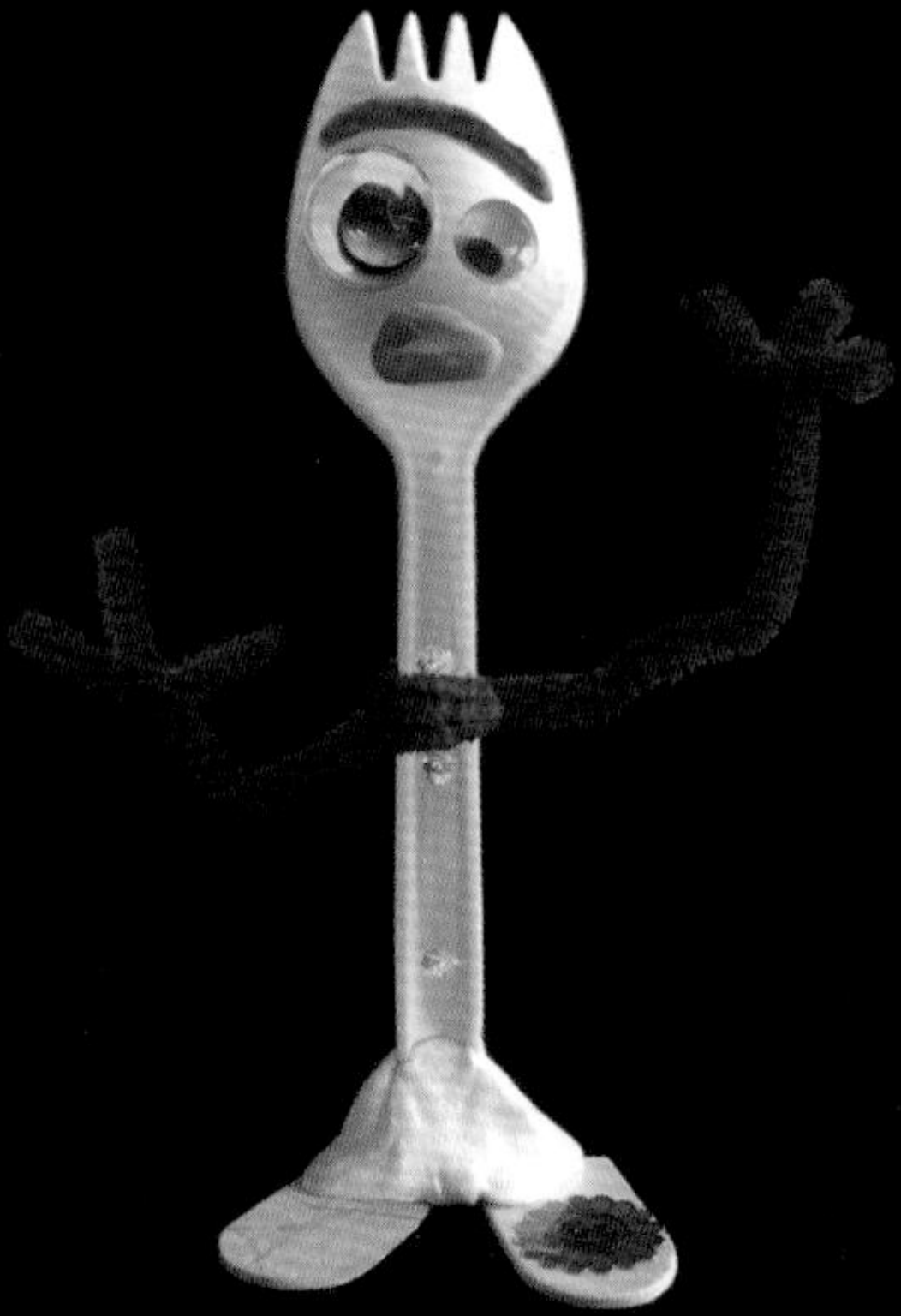

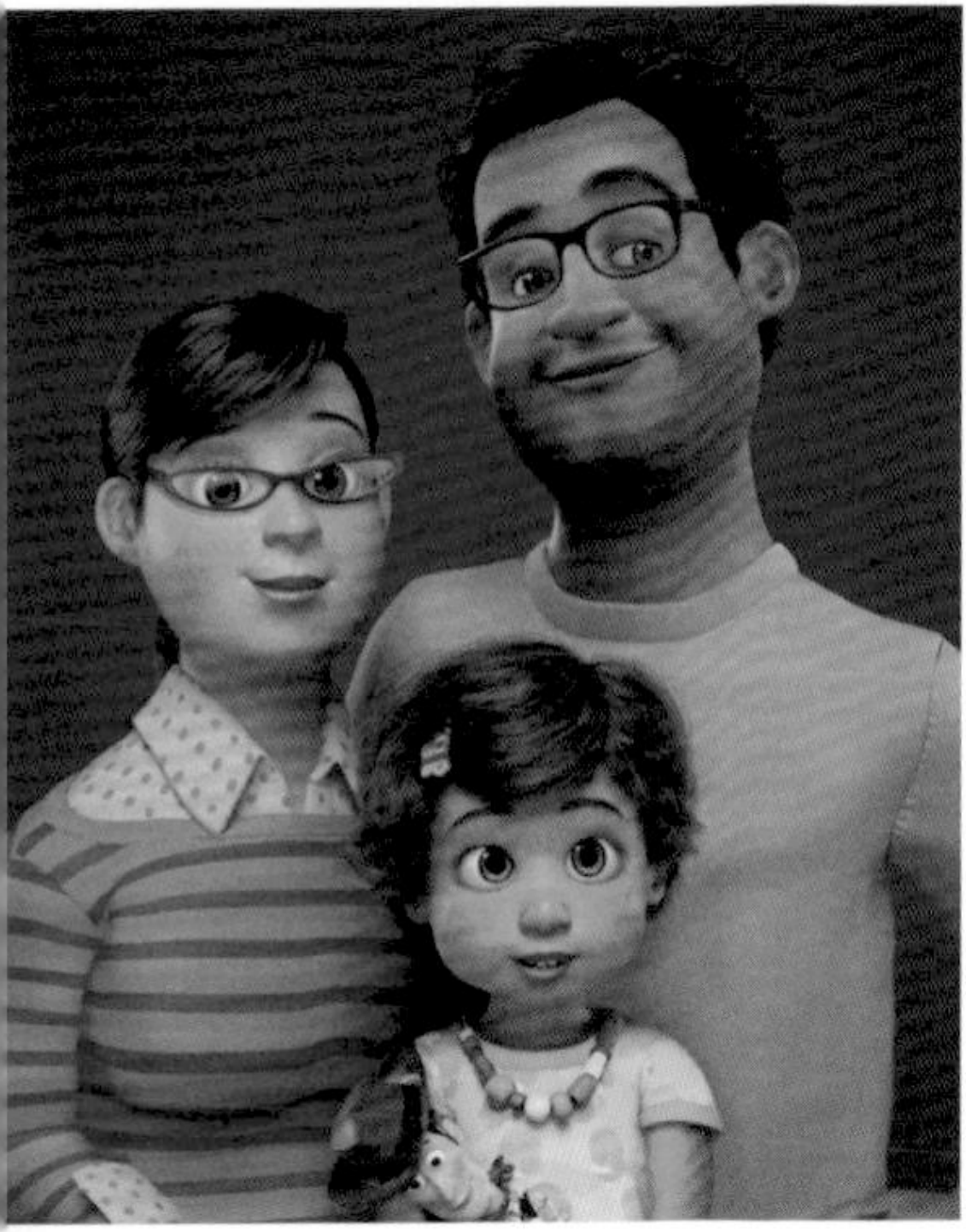

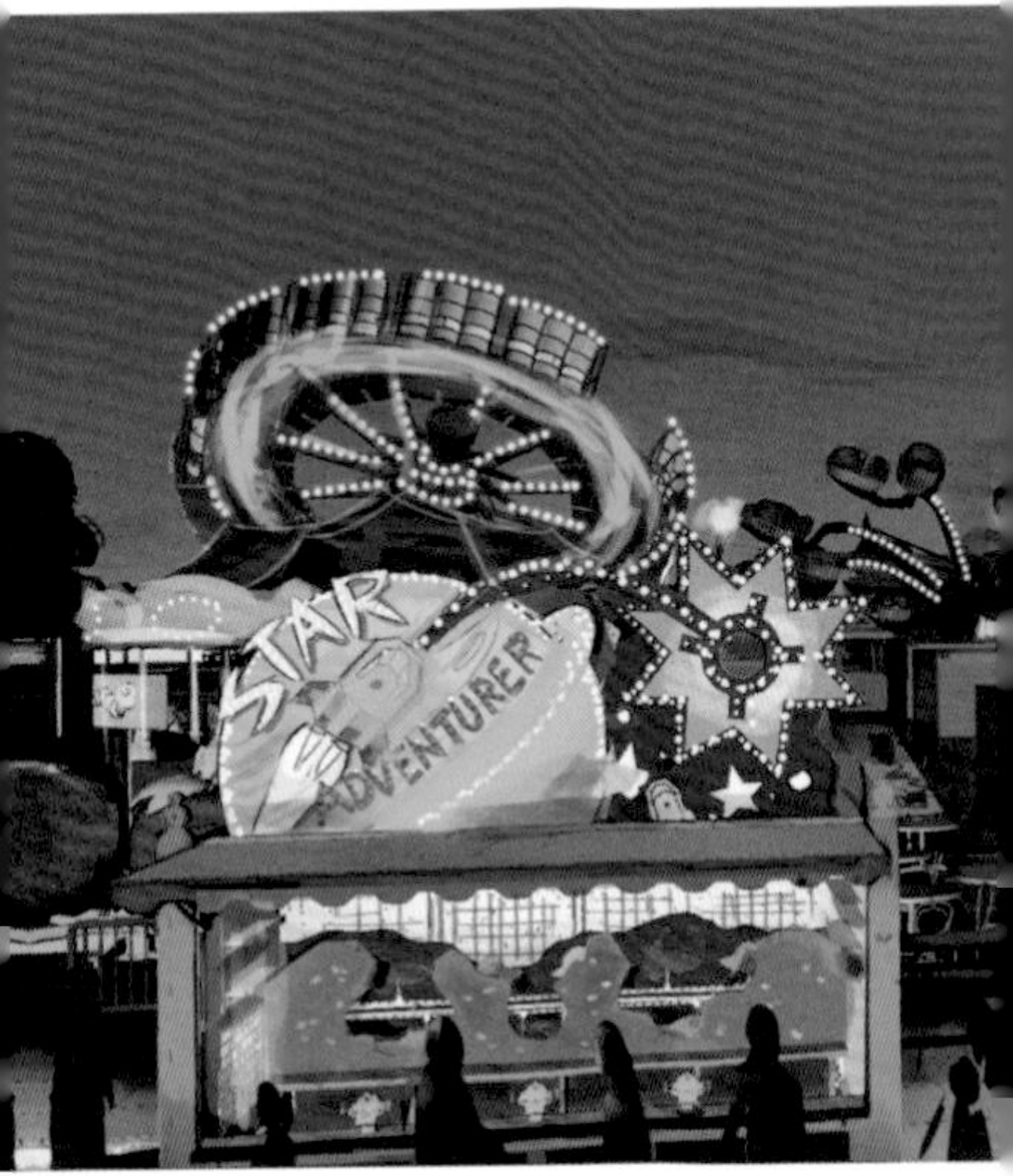
STAR
ADVENTURER

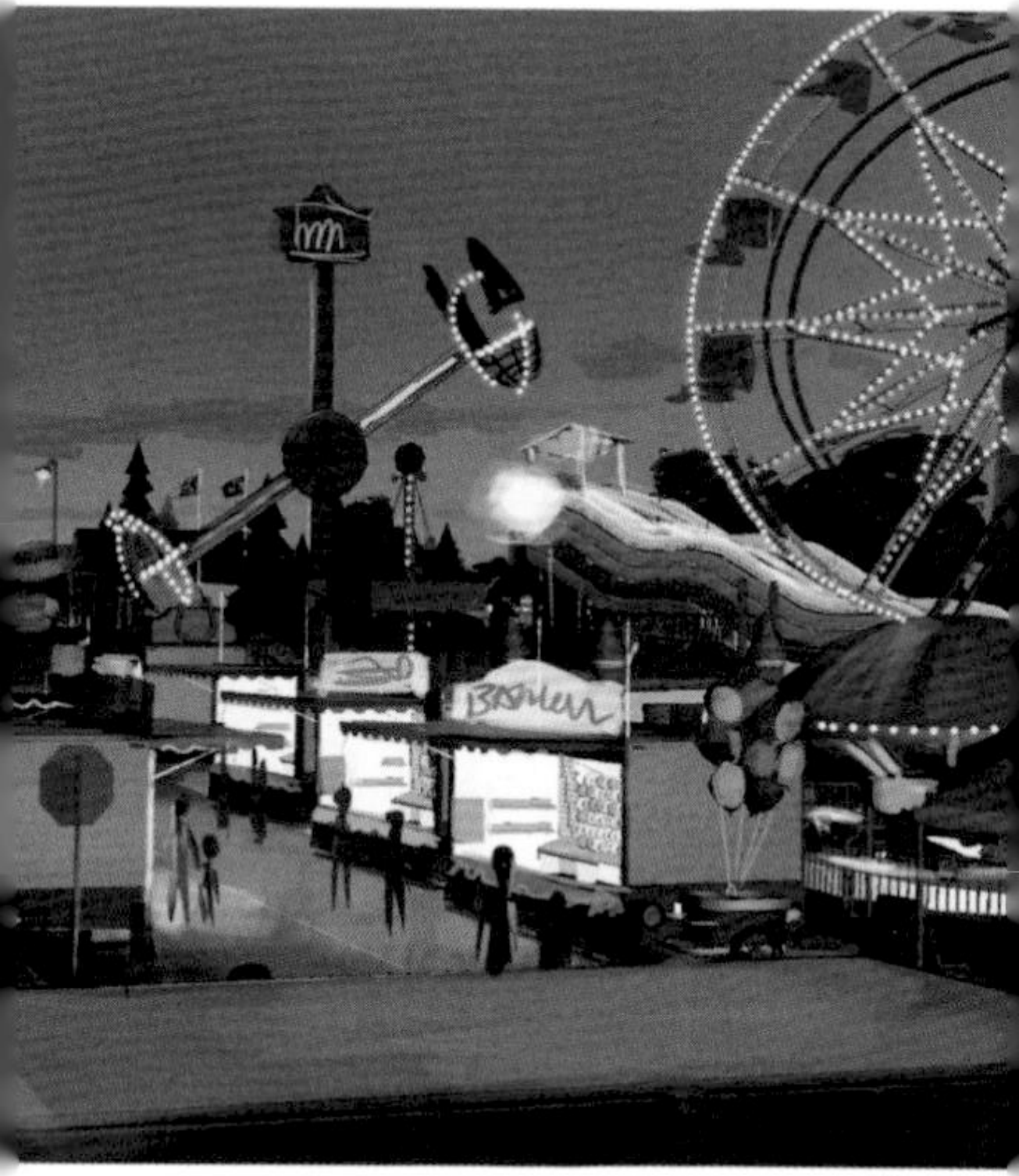

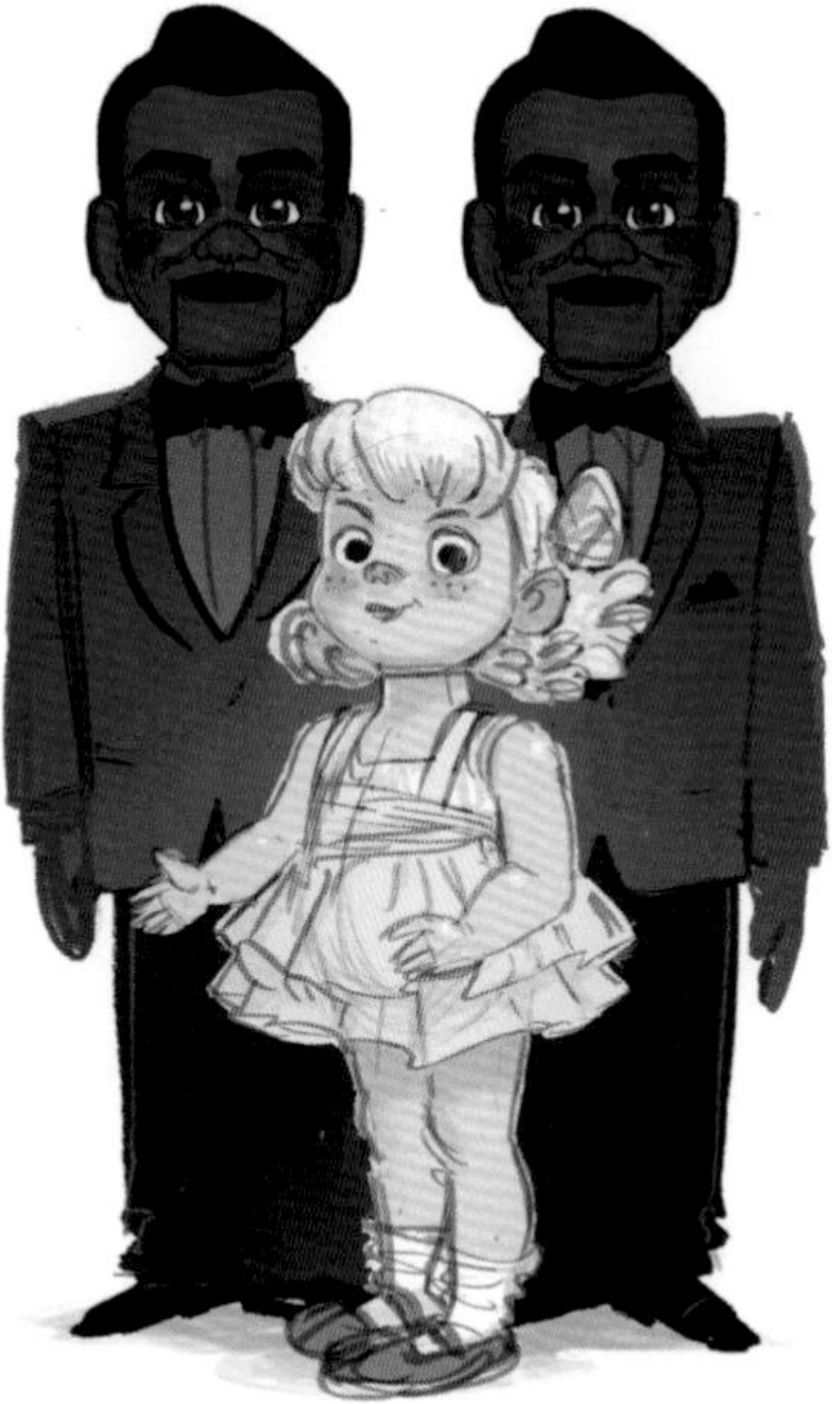

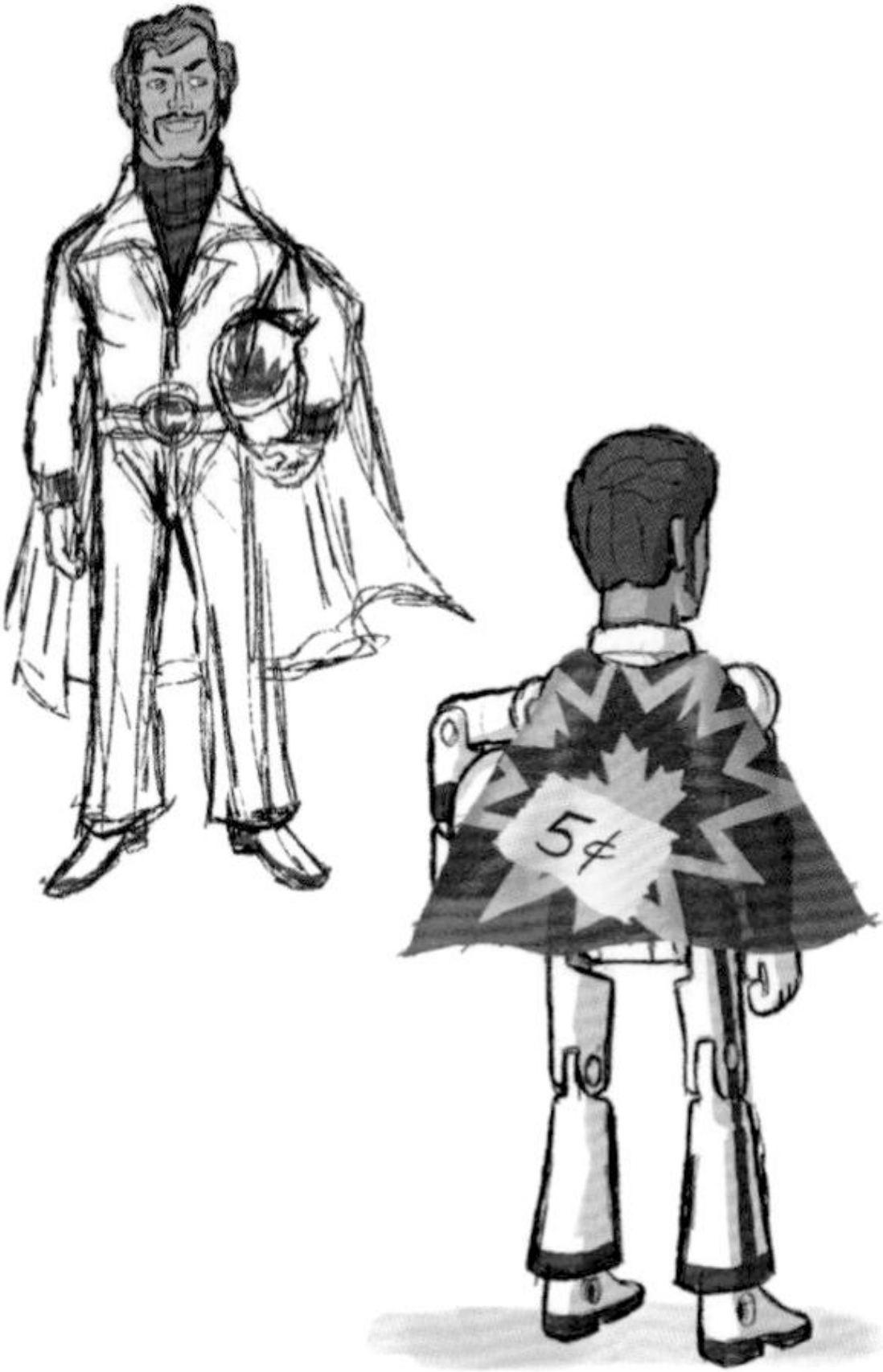
5¢

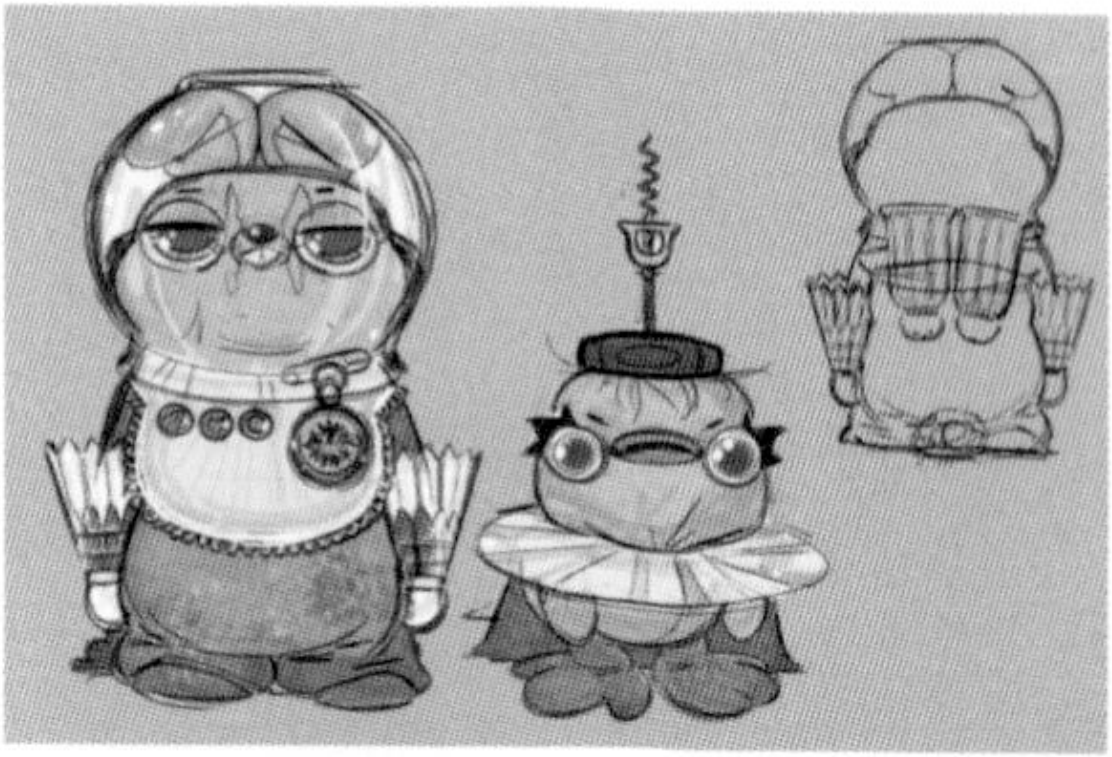

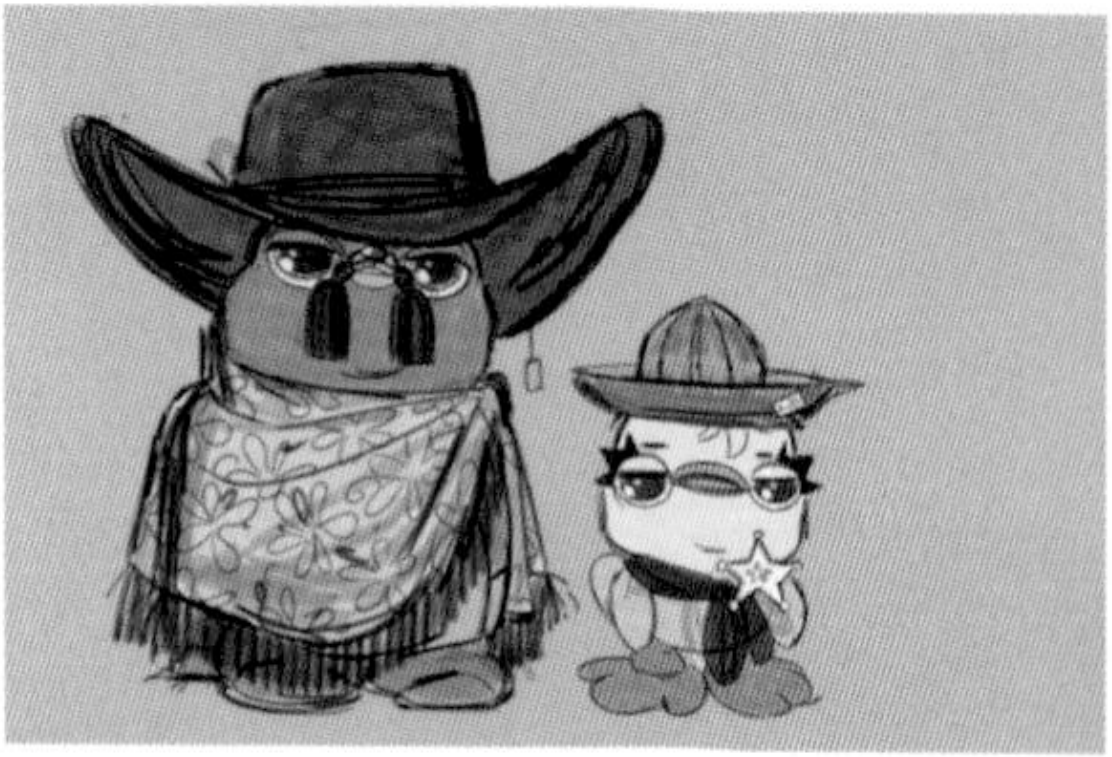

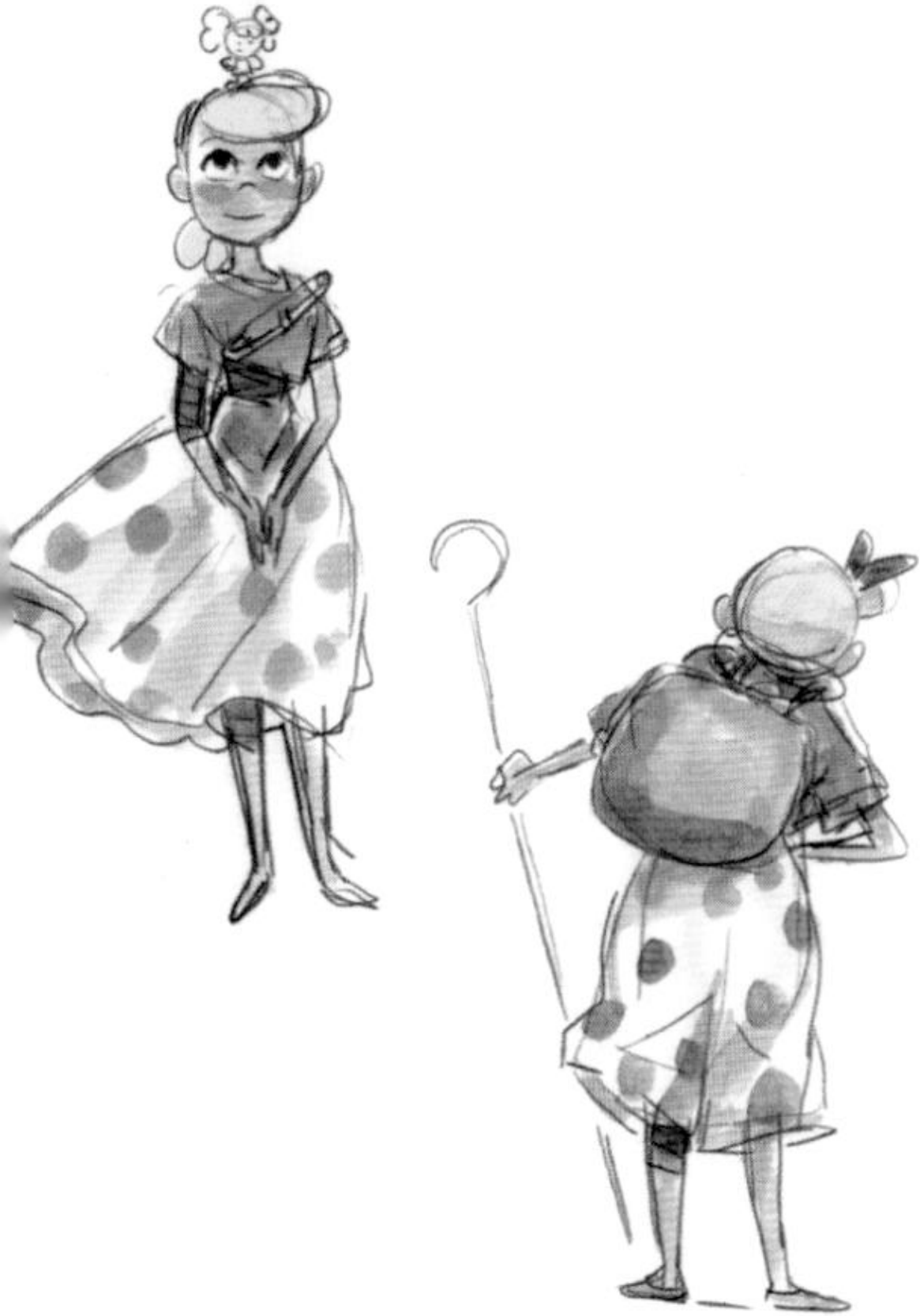

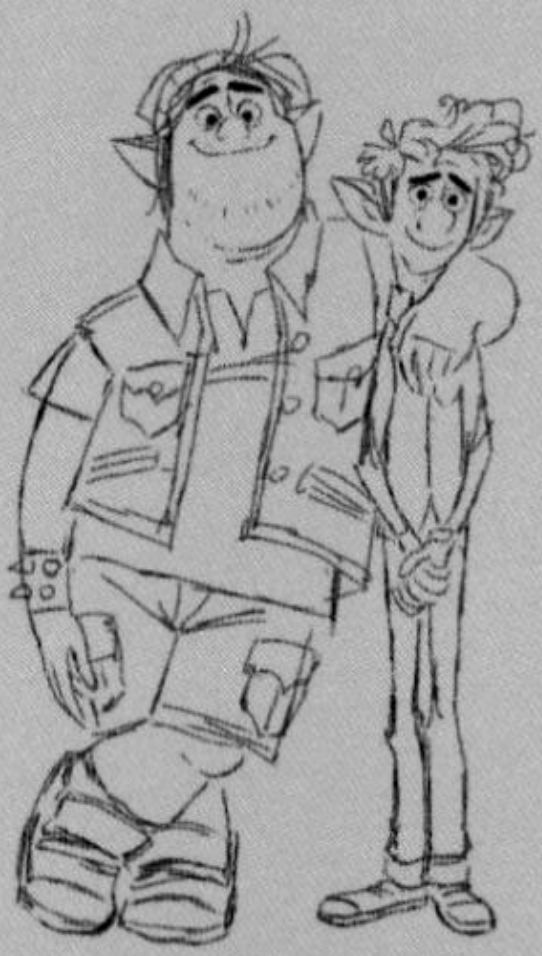

2020s

As the studio moves toward the future, there is little doubt that it will continue to push the envelope on the ways in which technology and art coexist. With every film the studio creates, Pixar demonstrates an enduring commitment to the creation of compelling, inventive, and ultimately transformative visual storytelling.

ONWARD
2020

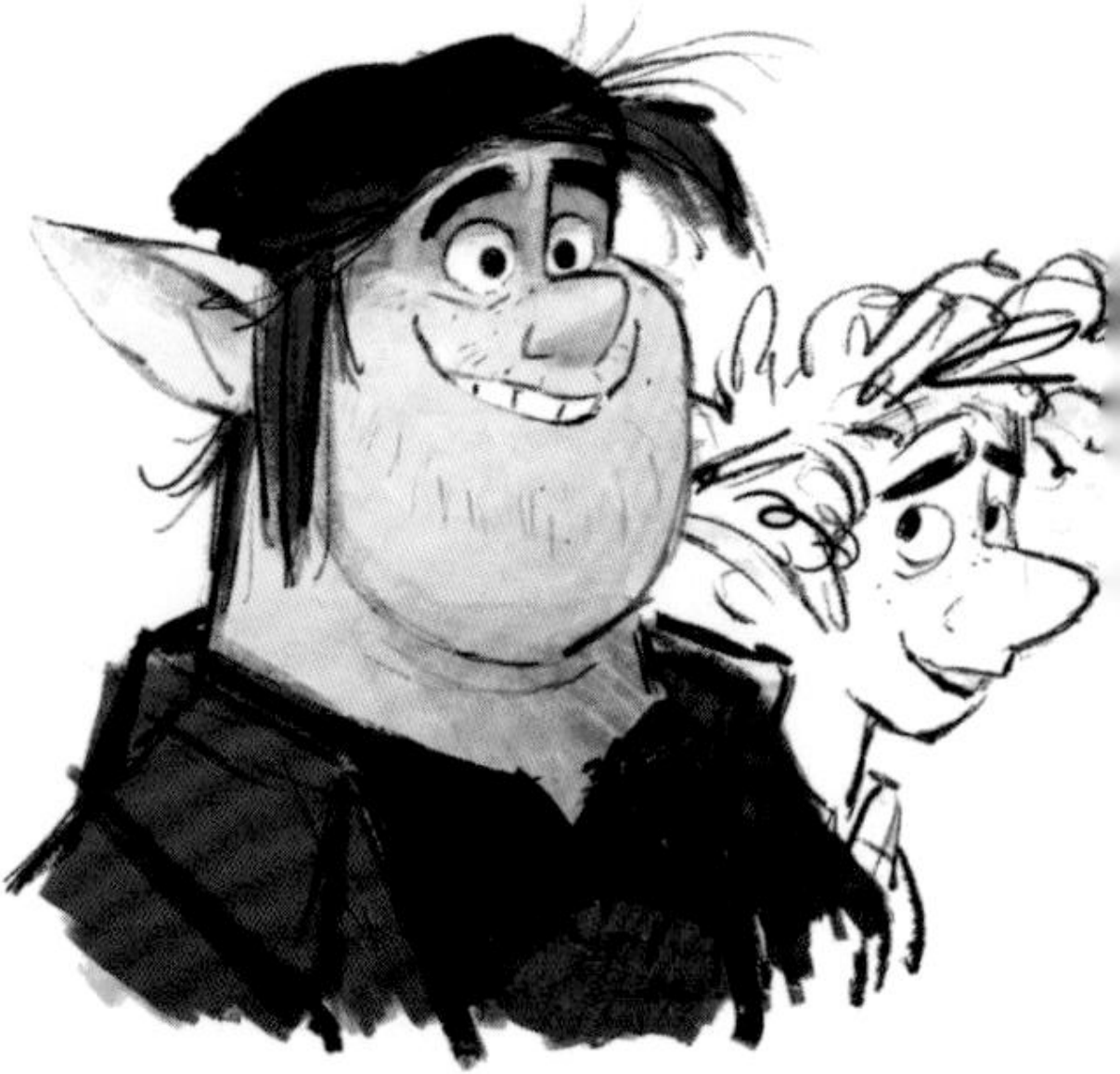

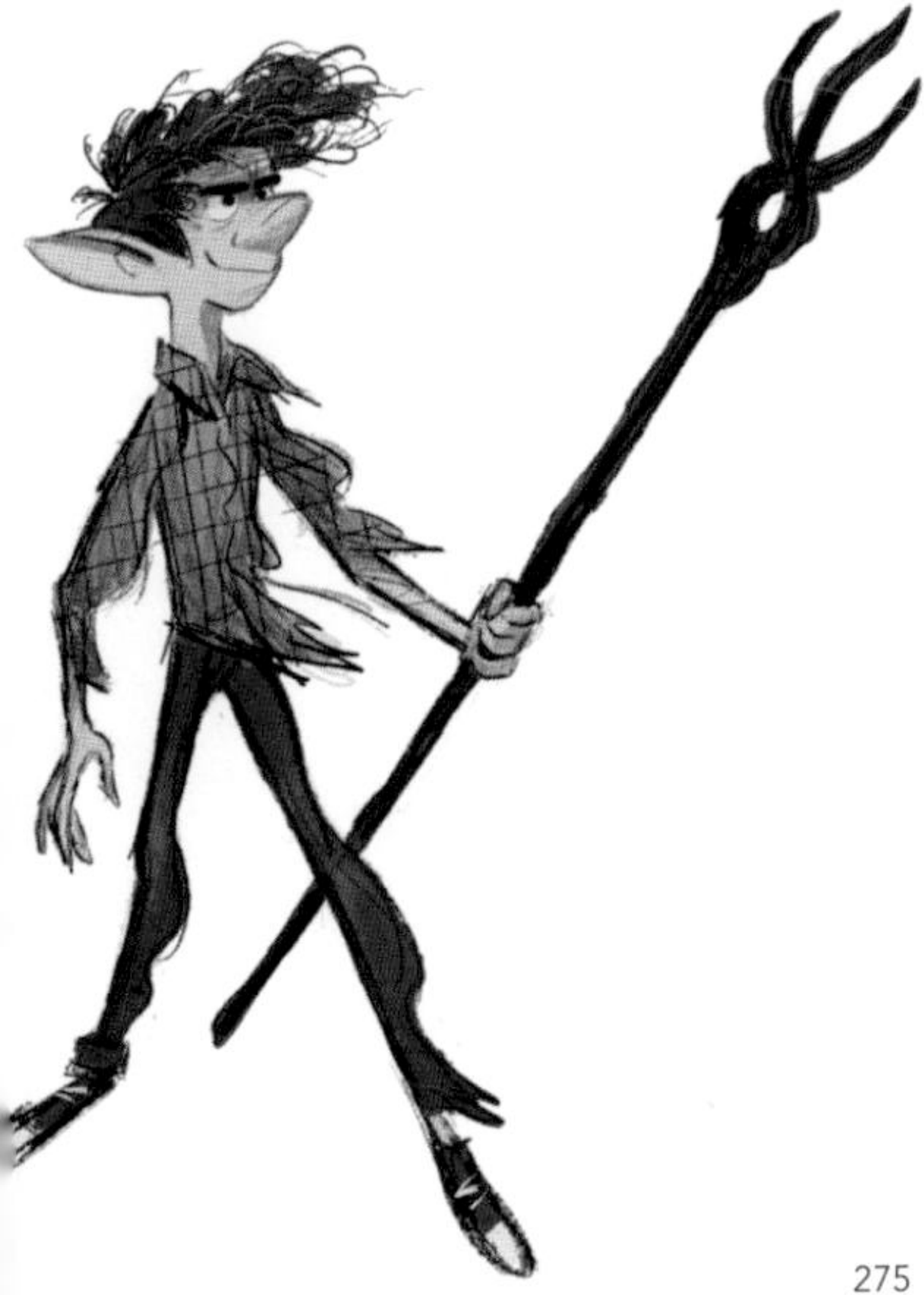

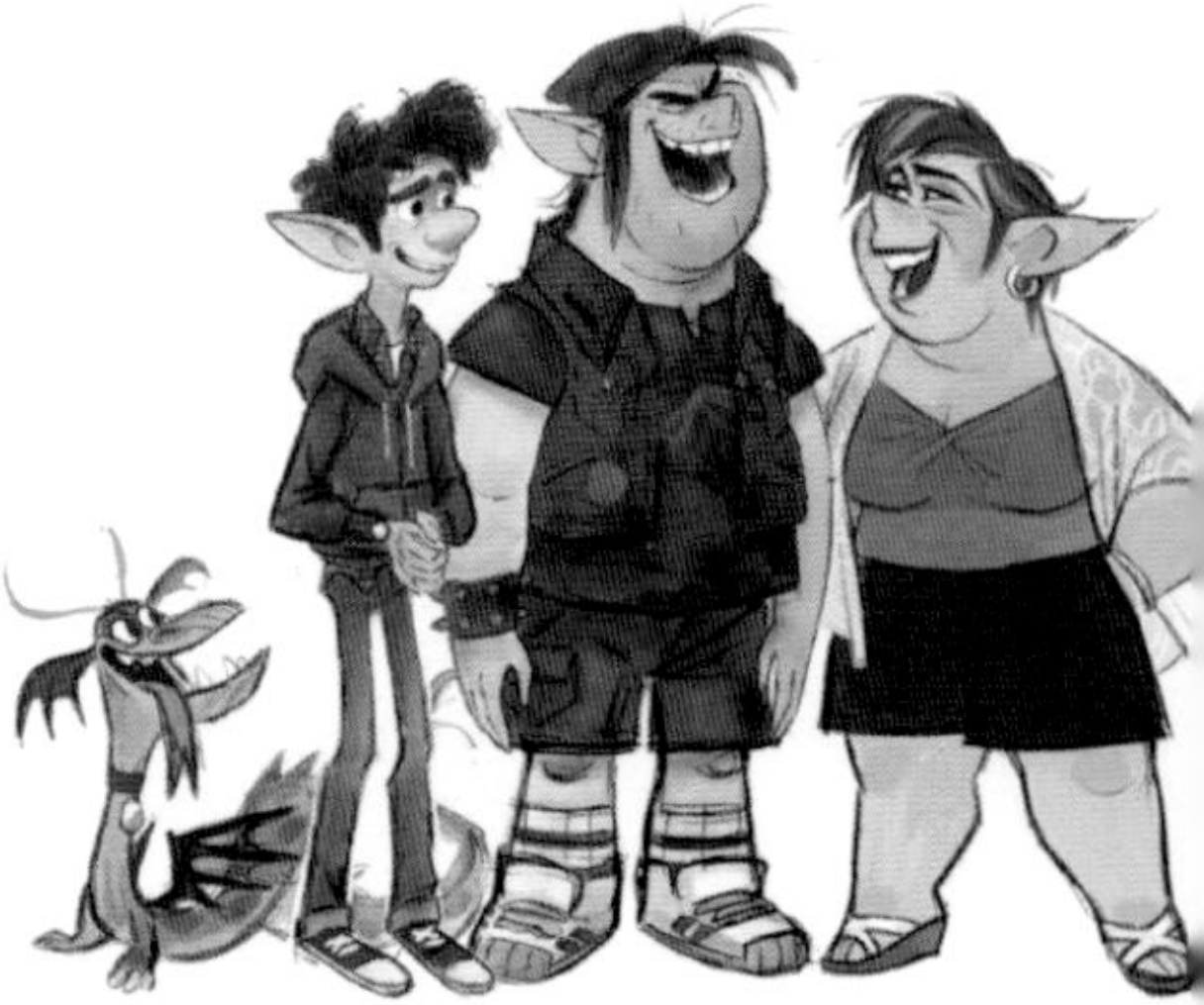

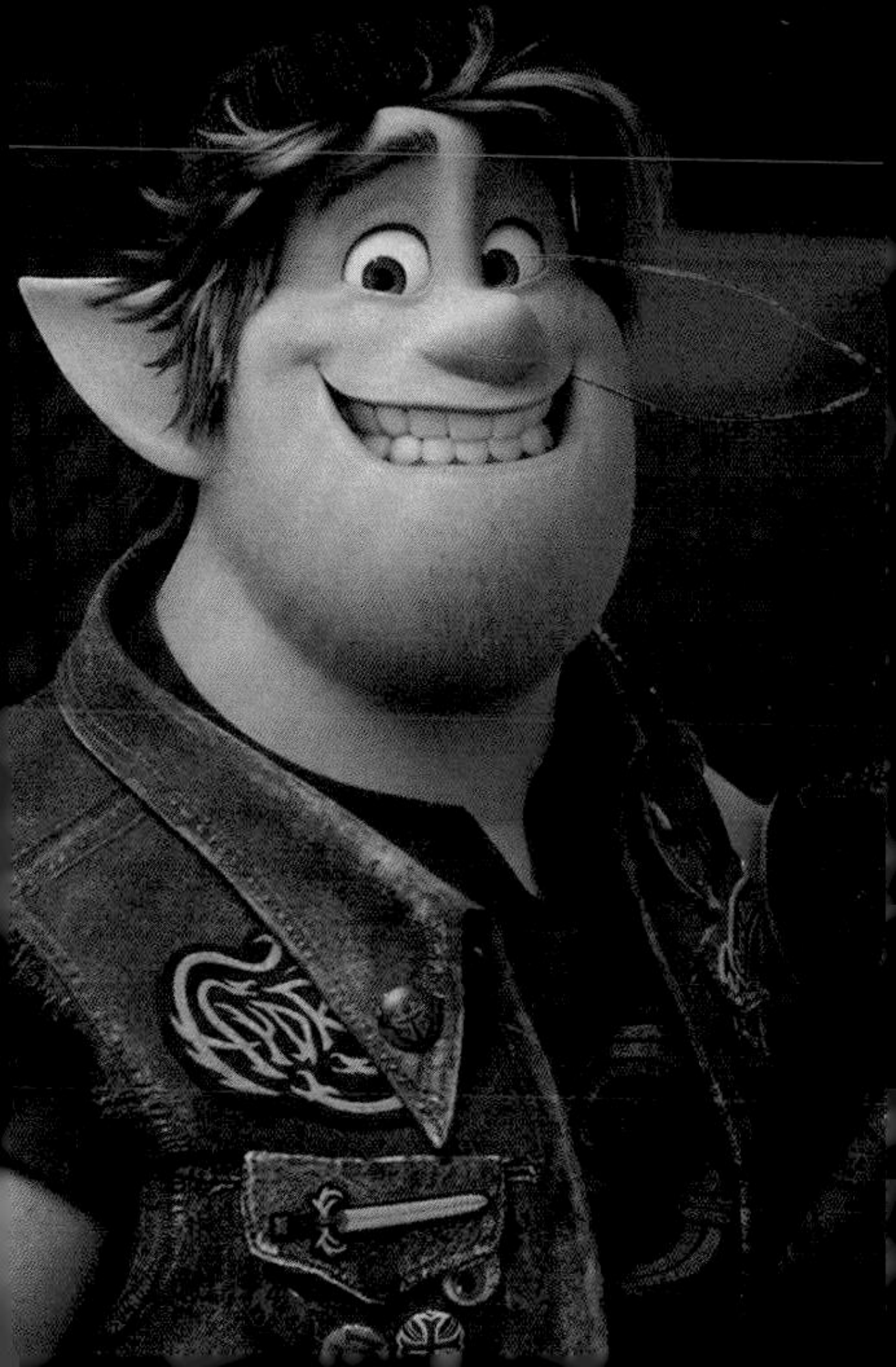

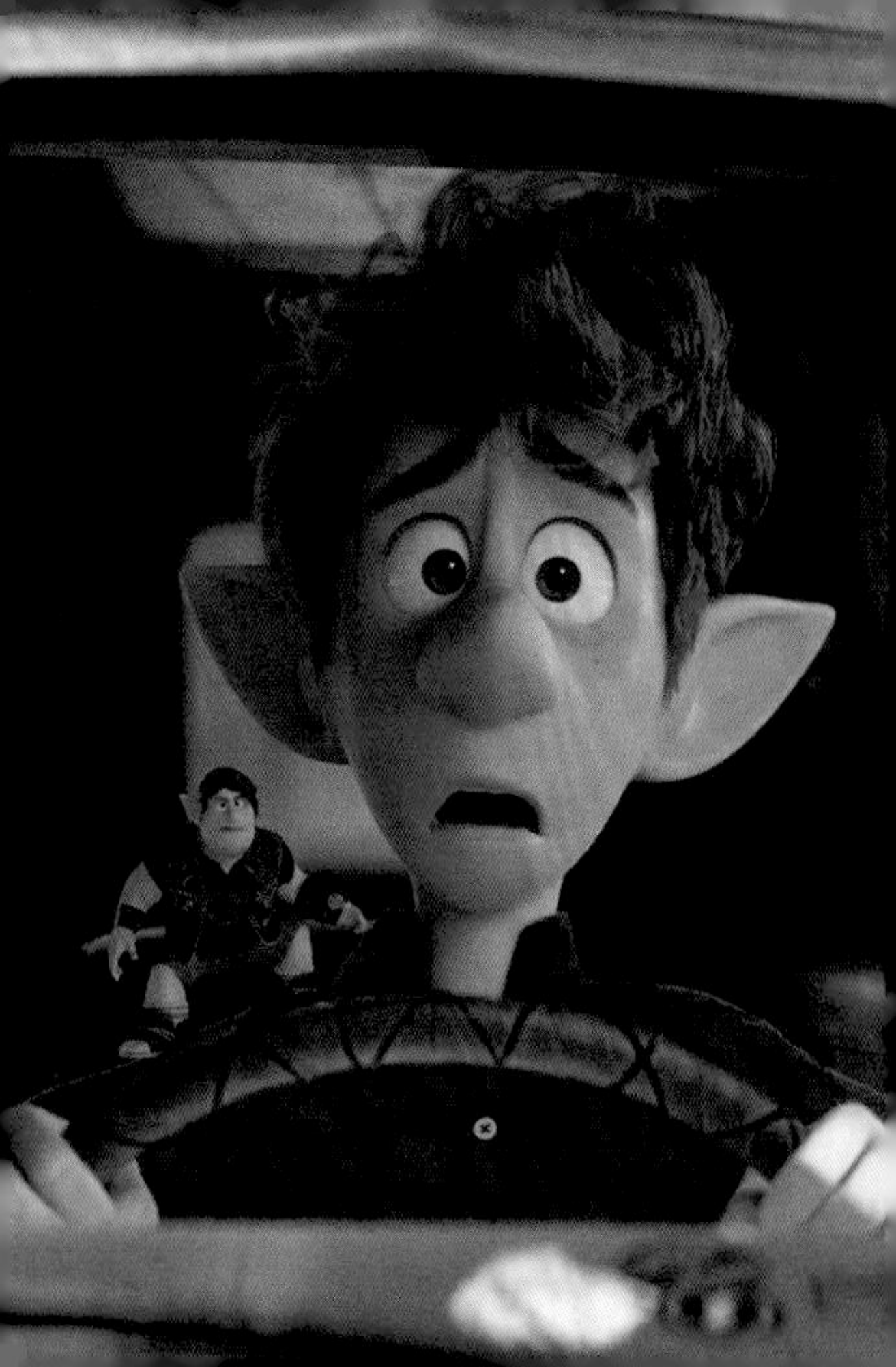

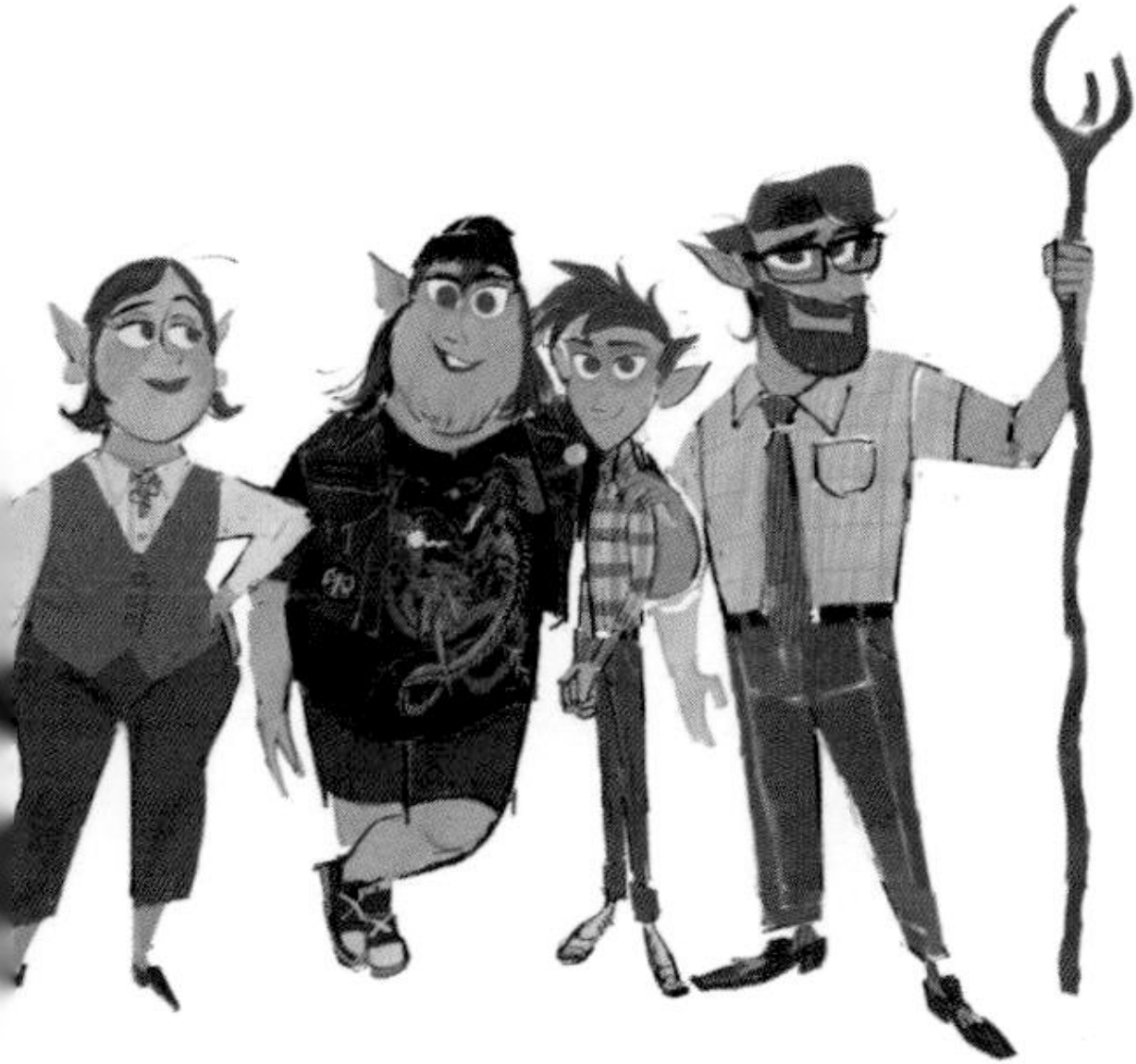

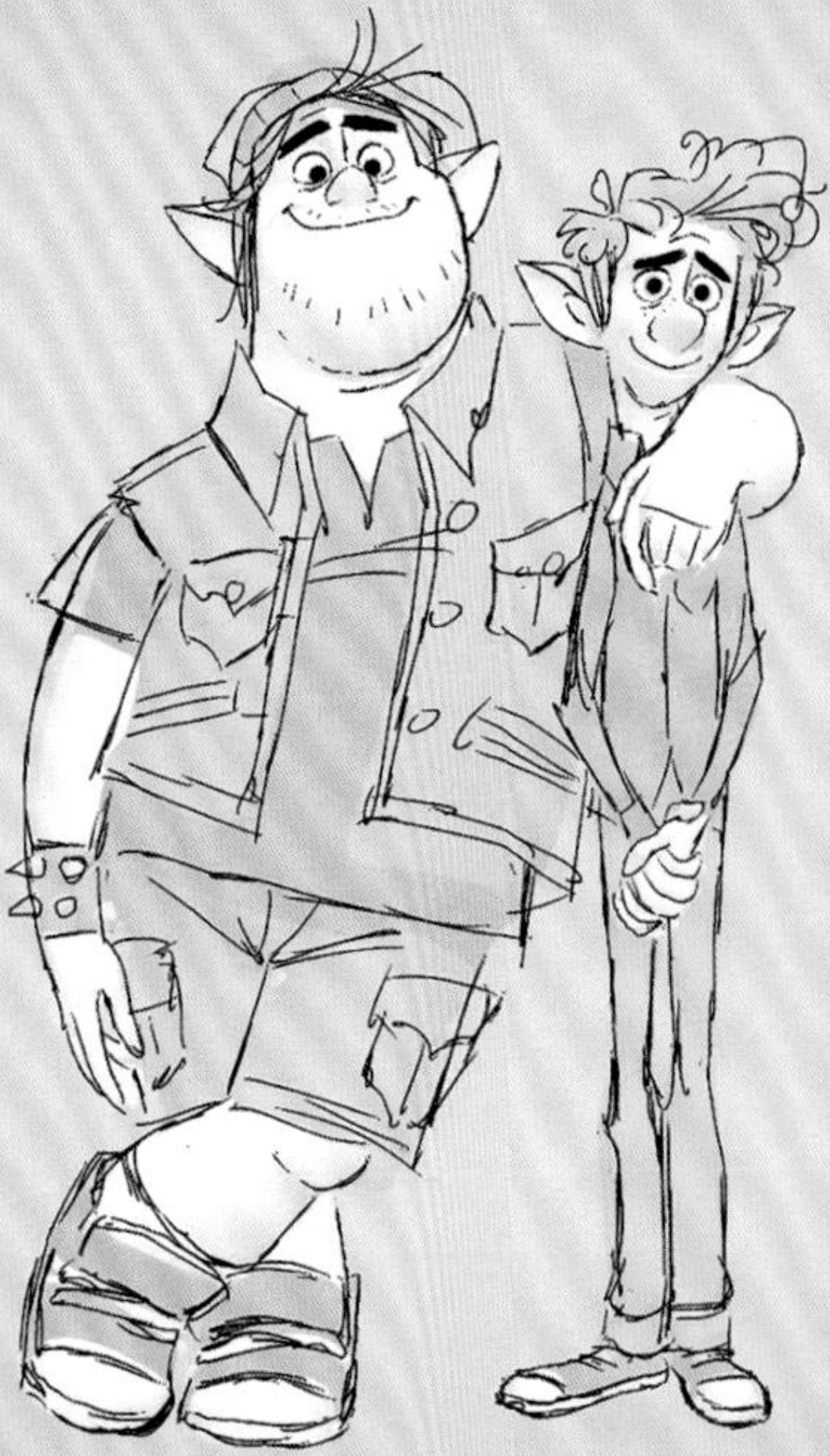

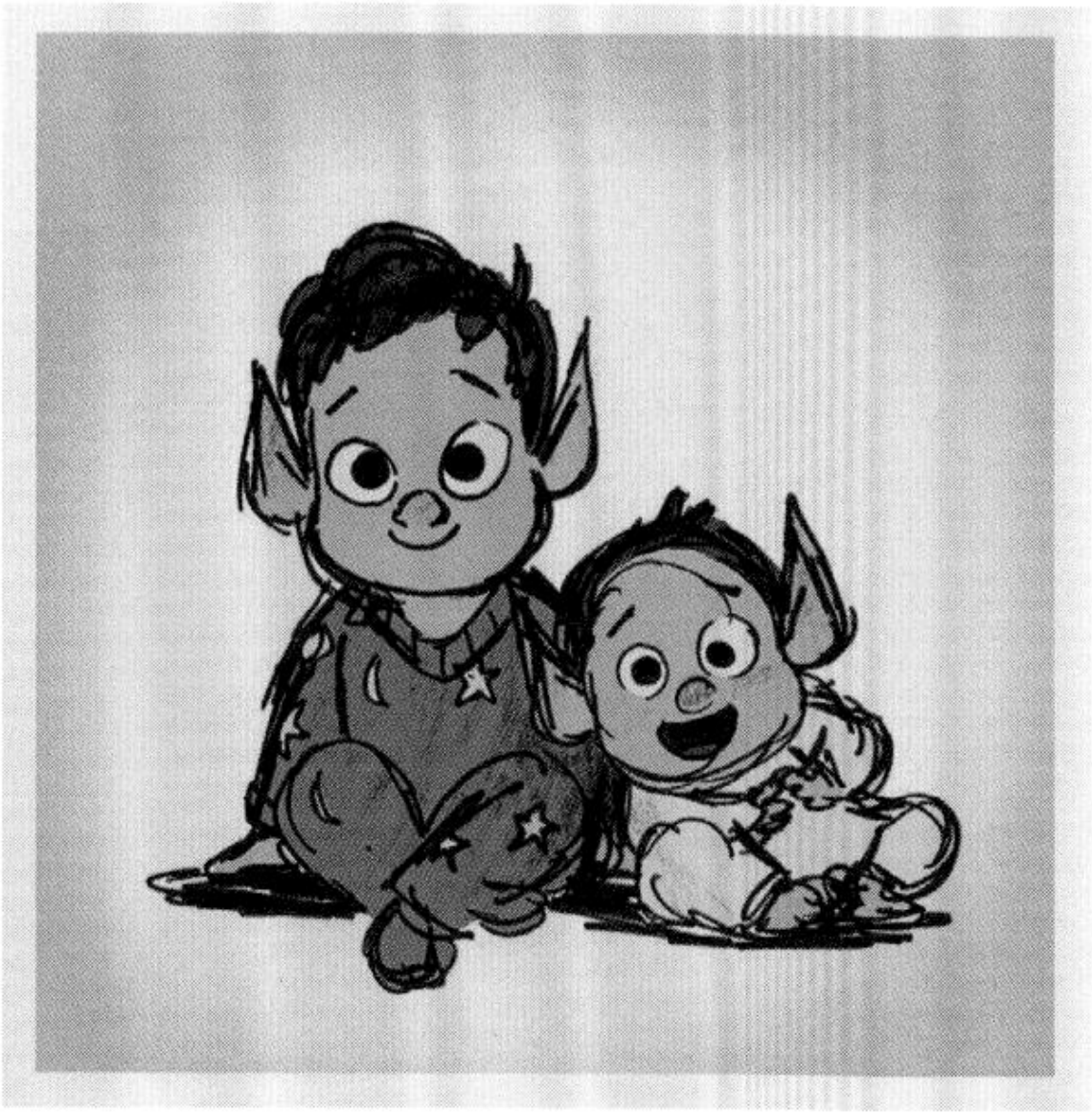

SOUL
2020

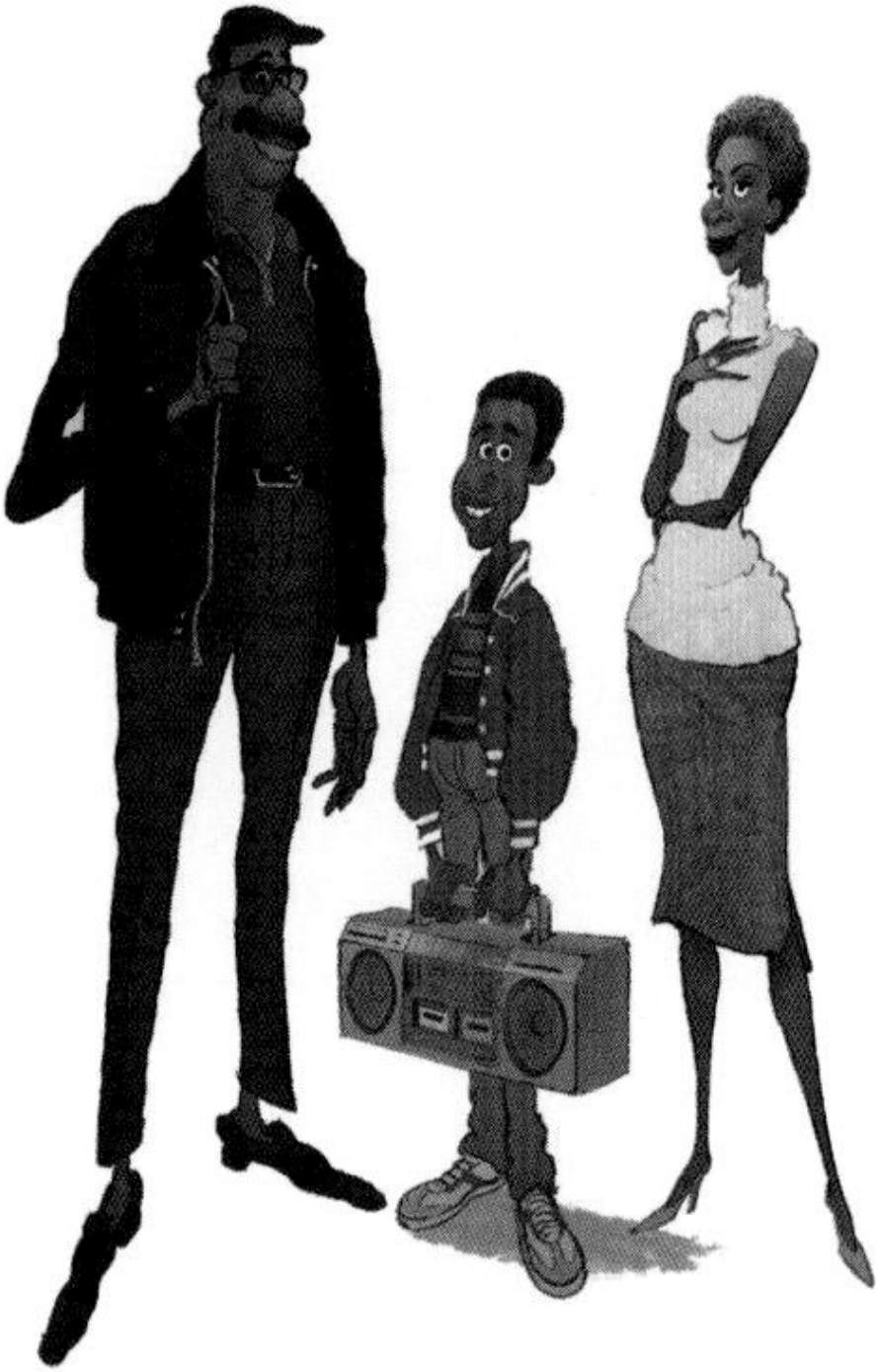

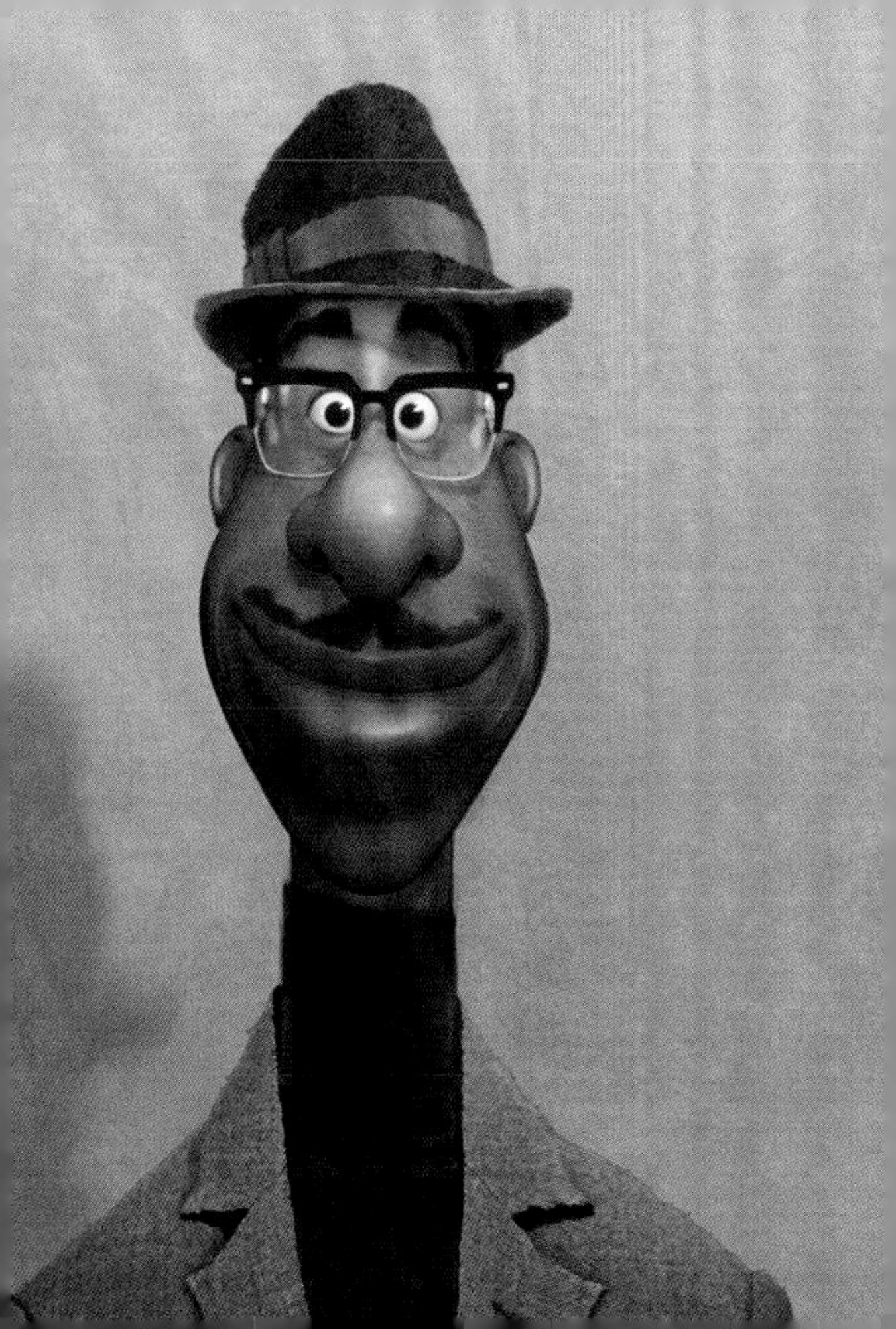

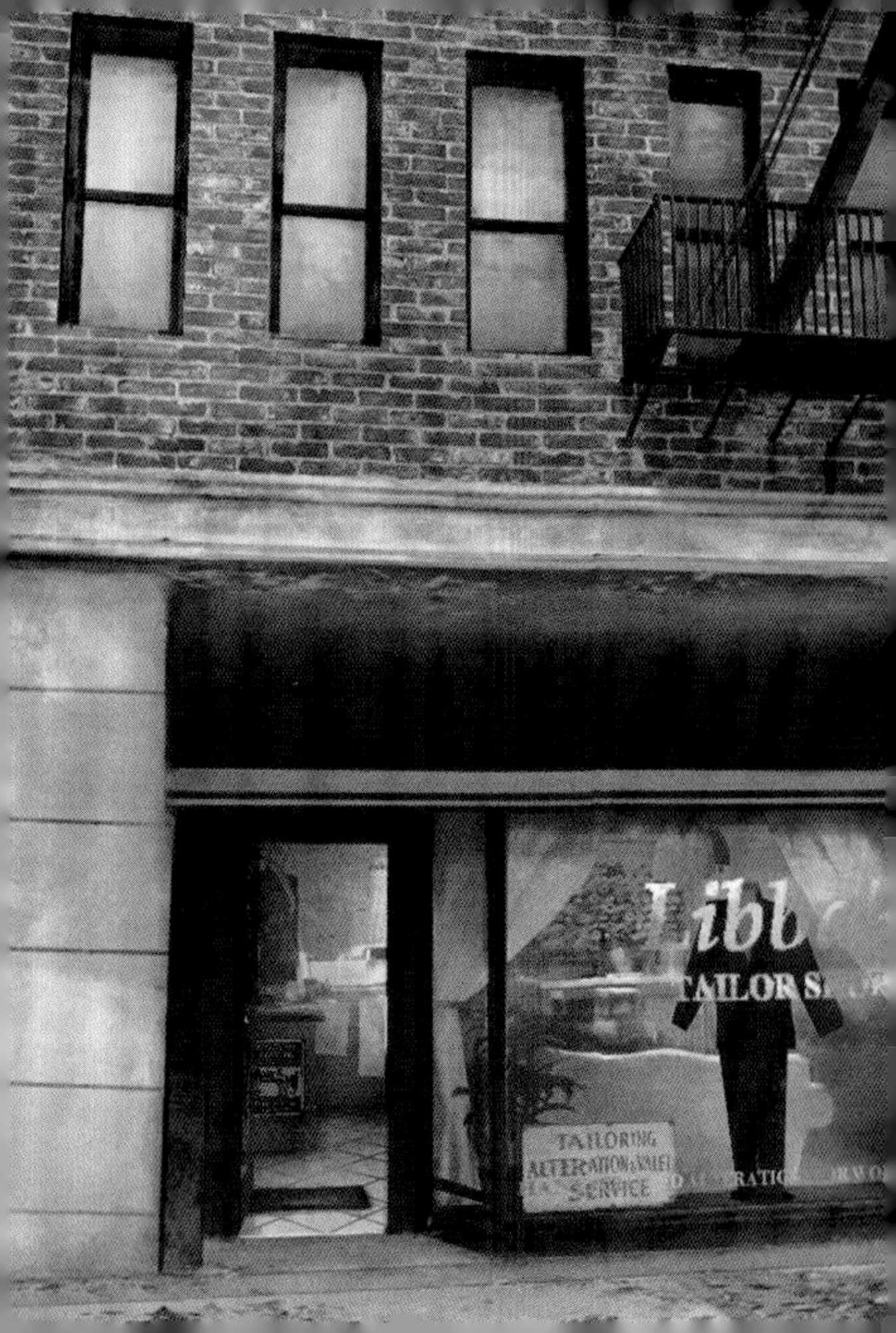
TAILORING
SERVICE

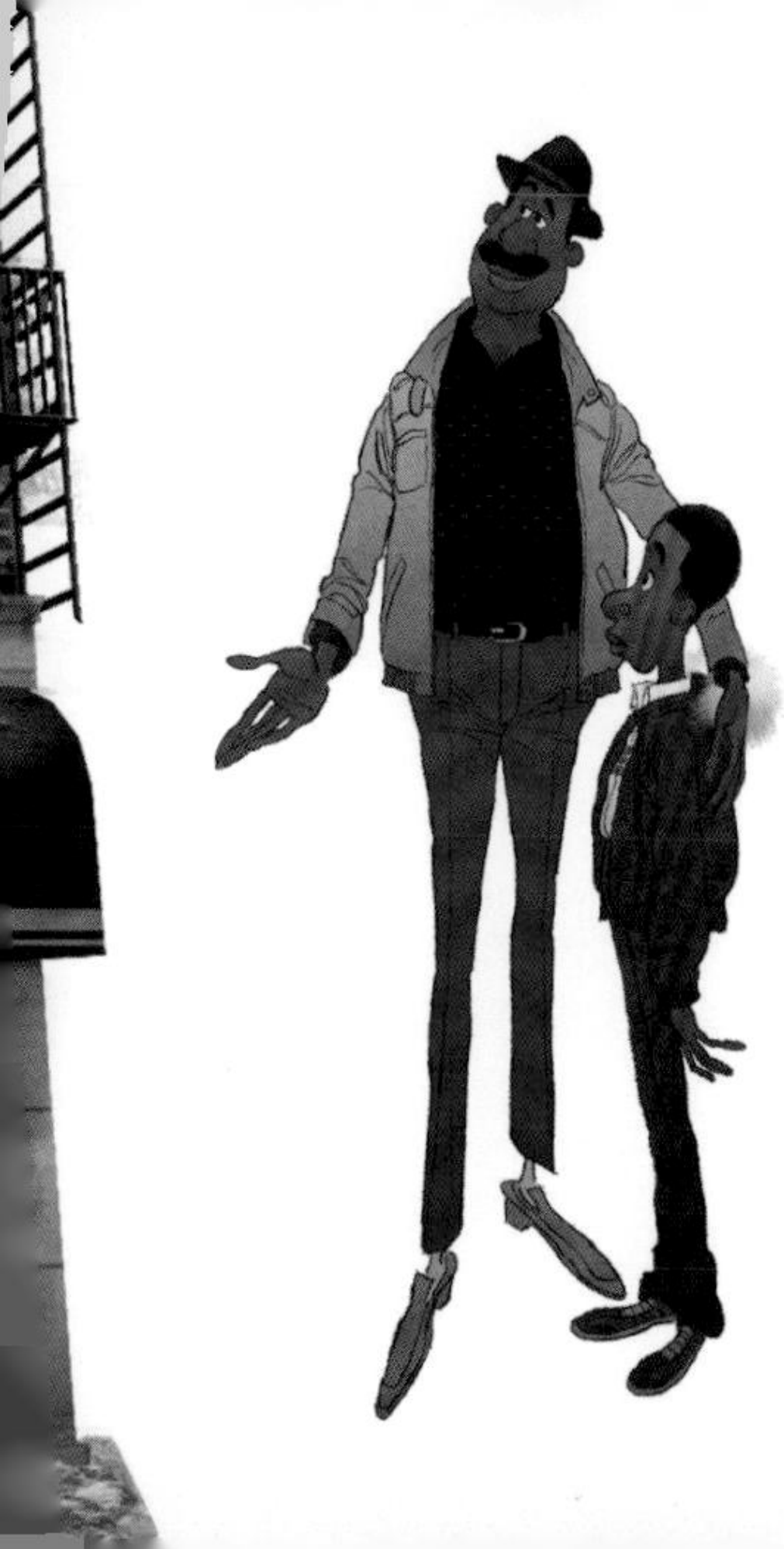

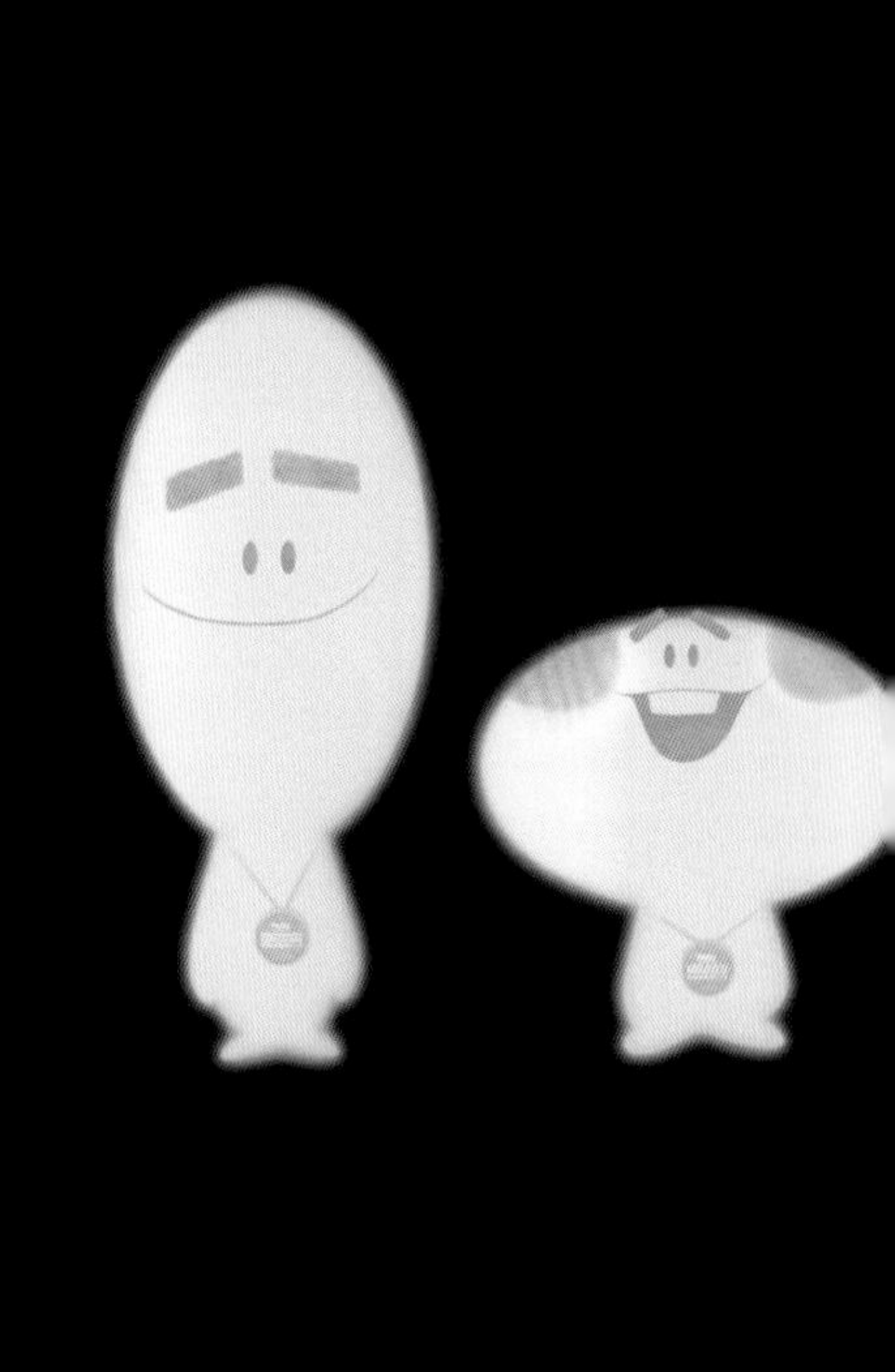

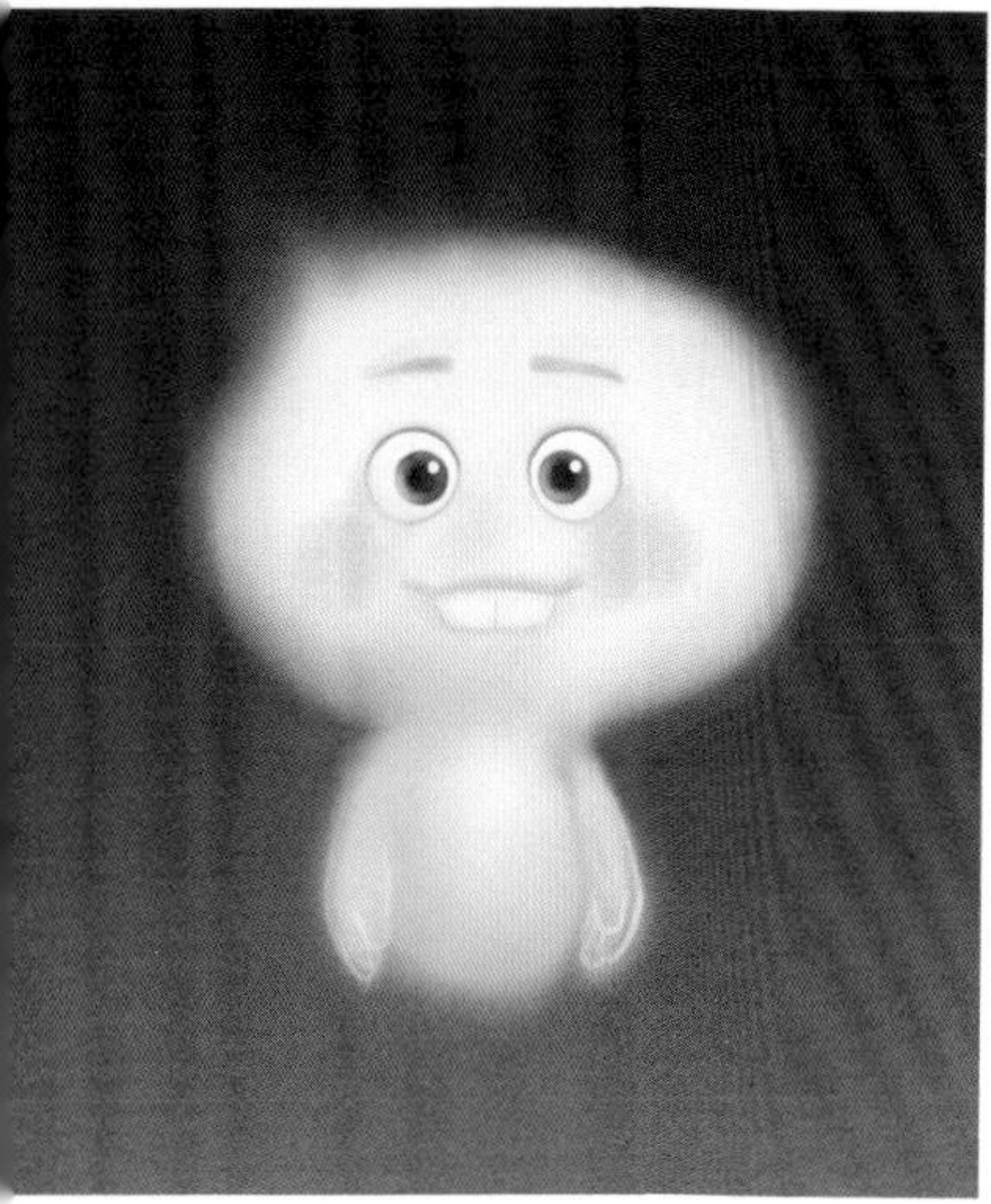

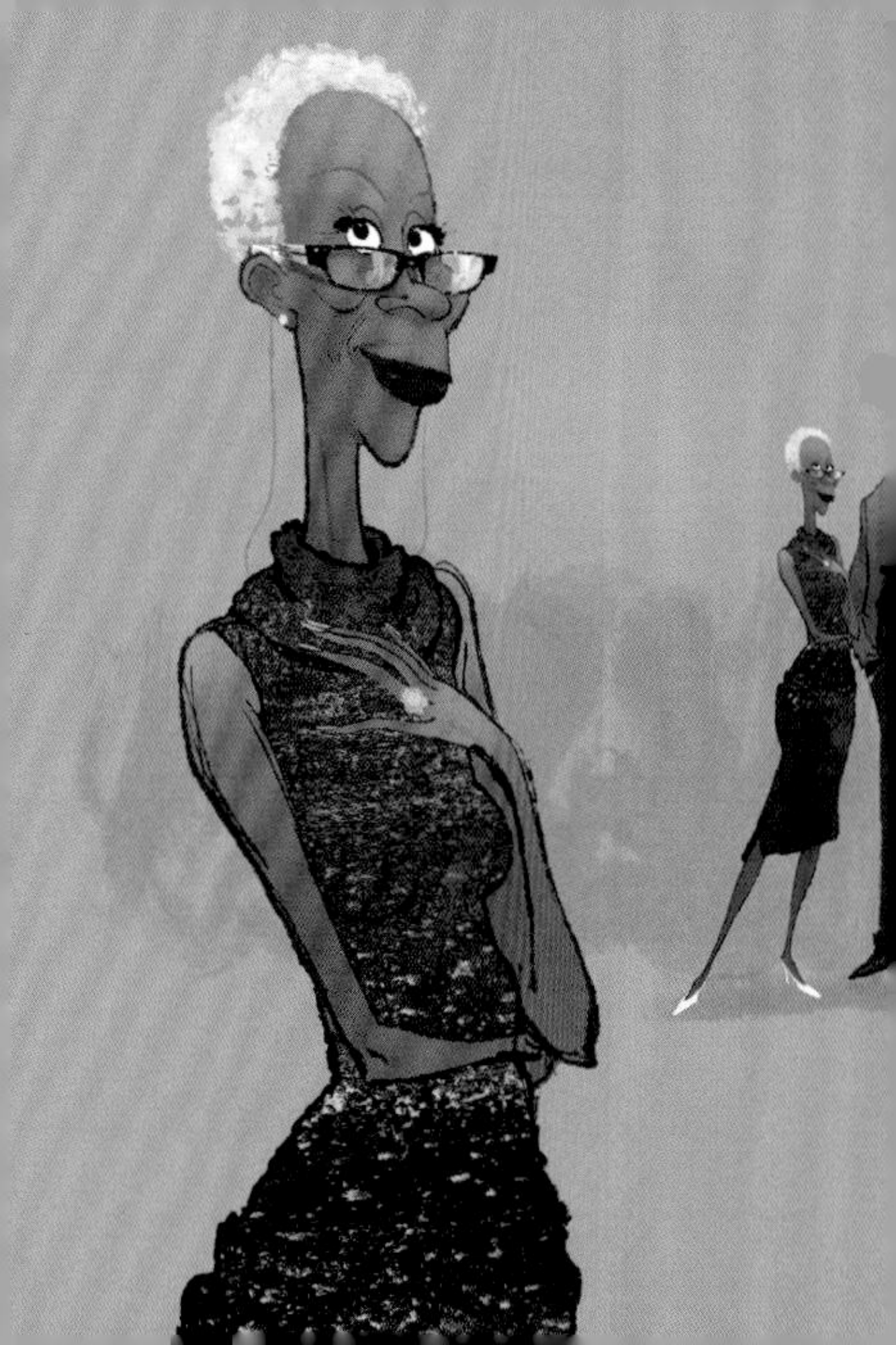

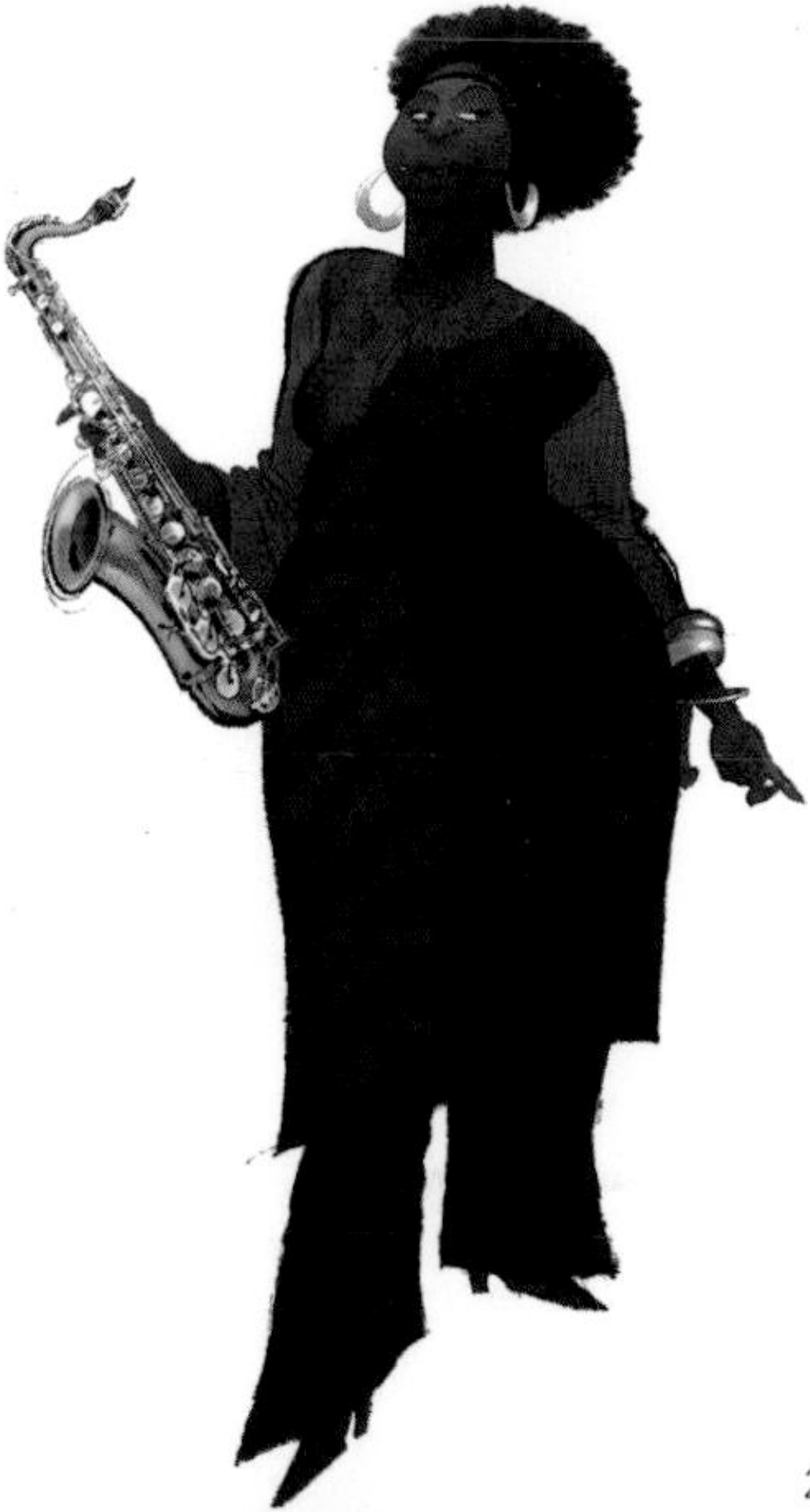

CREDITS

Page 1: Carrie Hobson, digital
Page 2: Daniel Arriaga, digital
Pages 4–5: Tia Kratter, layout by Bob Pauley, acrylic
Pages 6, 264: Albert Lozano, photo collage and digital
Pages 8–9: Ralph Eggleston, digital painting
Pages 10, 123: Harley Jessup, digital and pencil
Page 12: Jason Deamer, pencil
Pages 14–15: Ralph Eggleston, pastel
Page 17: Jan Pinkava, pencil
Page 18: John Lasseter, pencil
Page 19: John Lasseter, pastel
Page 20: John Lasseter, pencil
Page 21: John Lasseter, pastel
Page 26: John Lasseter, pencil
Page 27: John Lasseter, pencil
Page 29: John Lasseter, marker
Pages 30–31: John Lasseter, pencil
Pages 34–35: John Lasseter, pencil; Yael Milo, Tony Apodaca, Eben Ostby, Flip Phillips, and Craig Good, pencil

Page 48: Jan Pinkava, pencil; Jan Pinkava, crayon
Page 49: Bob Peterson, pen
Page 50: Jan Pinkava, pencil
Page 51: Jan Pinkava, pencil
Page 68: Dan Lee, pencil
Page 70: Ralph Eggleston, crayon
Page 71: Ralph Eggleston, marker
Pages 72–73: Ralph Eggleston, pastel
Page 74: Ricky Nierva, gouache
Page 75: Ricky Nierva, gouache
Page 76: Pete Doctor, marker; Dan Lee, pencil
Page 77: Dominique Louis, layout by Geefwee Boedoe, pastel
Pages 78–79: Dominique Louis, layout by Harley Jessup, pastel
Pages 80–81: Dominique Louis, pastel
Page 82: Dan Lee, pencil
Page 83: Ralph Eggleston, pastel; August Hall, acrylic
Page 84: Ralph Eggleston, pastel and marker
Page 85: Brett Coderre, color pencil
Page 86: James S. Baker, color pencil and wash; Jason Deamer, pencil, color pencil, and marker
Page 87: Randy Berrett, digital

Page 88: Dominique Louis, layout by Nelson Bohol, pastel

Page 89: Ralph Eggleston, pastel

Pages 90–91: Bud Luckey, pencil

Pages 92–93: Bud Luckey, pencil

Page 94: Lou Romano, pencil and marker

Page 95: Lou Romano, gouache

Page 96: Mark Andrews, digital

Page 97: Lou Romano, gouache; Teddy Newton, collage

Pages 98–99: Lou Romano, gouache

Page 100: John Lee, layout by Scott Caple, acrylic

Page 101: Glen Kim, digital

Page 102: Ronnie del Carmen, pencil

Page 103: Mark Andrews, marker

Page 104: Ronnie del Carmen, pencil; Ronnie del Carmen, pencil and Photoshop

Page 106: Bob Pauley, mixed media; Bob Pauley, pencil

Pages 108–109: Jay Shuster, pencil and marker

Page 110: Bud Luckey, pencil; Steve Purcell, ink and pencil

Page 111: Bob Pauley, pencil and marker; Bud Luckey, pencil

Pages 112–113: Tia Kratter, acrylic
Page 118: Dan Lee, pencil; Peter DeSeve, pencil; Jason Deamer, pencil
Page 119: Dominique Louis, shading study
Page 120: Jason Deamer, pencil and marker
Page 121: Robert Kondo, digital paint over sculpt by Greg Dykstra
Page 122: Harley Jessup, pencil and marker
Page 124: Dominique Louis, layout by Harley Jessup, pastel; Dominique Louis, layout by Harley Jessup, digital
Page 125: Belinda Van Valkenburg and Robert Kondo, digital paint over sculpt by Greg Dykstra
Page 130: Ralph Eggleston, digital
Page 131: Nelson Bohol, pen and marker
Pages 132–133: John Lee, layout by Jay Shuster, digital
Page 134: John Lee, digital
Page 135: John Lee, digital
Pages 136–137: John Lee, digital
Page 142: Tony Fucile, digital
Page 143: Daniel López Muñoz
Page 144: Albert Lozano, pencil/digital paint

Page 145: Don Shank, digital

Pages 146–147: Albert Lozano, digital

Pages 148–149: Ricky Nierva, gouache

Pages 156–157: Robert Kondo, layout by Bob Pauley, digital

Page 158: Tom Gately, pencil

Page 159: Tom Gately, pencil

Page 160: Dice Tsutsumi, digital

Page 161: Daniel Arriaga, digital

Pages 162–163: Robert Kondo, digital

Pages 164–165: Harley Jessup, digital

Page 166: Sharon Calahan, digital paint over set render

Page 167: Jay Shuster, color by Jack Chang, digital; Sharon Calahan, digital paint over set render

Pages 168–169: Harley Jessup, digital

Page 176: Matt Nolte, pencil

Page 177: Steve Pilcher, pencil

Pages 178–179: Louis Gonzales, pencil

Pages 180–181: Matt Nolte, pencil

Pages 182–183: Huy Nguyen, digital

Page 188: Jason Deamer, digital

Page 189: Ricky Nierva, digital; Shelly Wan, digital

Pages 190–191: Shelly Wan, digital
Page 192: Daniela Strijleva, pen and watercolor
Page 193: Daniela Strijleva, marker; Chris Sasaki, pencil
Pages 194–195: Jason Deamer, digital
Pages 200–201: Chris Sasaki, digital painting
Pages 202–203: Don Shank, colored pencil
Pages 204–205: Dan Holland, watercolor and digital painting
Pages 206–207: Chris Sasaki, digital painting
Pages 212–213: Kyle Macnaughton
Pages 214–215: Daniela Strijleva
Pages 216–217: Sharon Calahan
Page 218: Sharon Calahan, layout by Ricky Nierva; Eric Benson
Page 219: Daniela Strijleva
Pages 224–225: Rona Liu, digital painting
Pages 226–227: Jason Deamer, pencil
Pages 228–229: John Lee, layout by Tim Evatt, digital painting
Page 230: Shelly Wan, digital painting; Rona Liu and Sharon Calahan, digital painting
Page 231: Steve Pilcher, digital painting

Pages 236–237: Jay Shuster, digital

Pages 238–239: Kristian Norielus, digital

Pages 240–241: Noah Klocek, digital

Pages 242–243: Drew Hartel, digital; Bill Cone, digital; Paul Abadilla, digital

Page 244: Huy Nguyen, layout by Xavier Riffault and Dean Kelly, digital

Page 245: Shelly Wan, layout by Manny Hernandez, digital; Sharon Calahan, digital

Pages 246–247: Daniela Strijleva, pen and gouache

Pages 248–249: Armand Baltazar and John Nevarez, digital

Pages 250–251: Harley Jessup, digital

Pages 256–257: Ralph Eggleston, digital

Page 258: Teddy Newton, pencil

Page 259: Domee Shi, digital

Page 260: Matt Nolte, marker; Matt Nolte, pencil and digital; Bryn Imagire, digital

Page 261: Bryn Imagire, clay sculpt by Greg Dykstra, digital painting

Pages 262–263: Ralph Eggleston, digital

Page 265: Laura Phillips, digital painting

Pages 266–267: Nathaniel McLaughlin, digital

Page 268: Jason Deamer, digital

Page 269: Albert Lozano, digital
Page 270: Deanna Marsigliese, digital
Page 271: Michael Yates, pencil and watercolor
Page 282: Grant Alexander and Daniel López Muñoz, digital
Page 283: Daniel López Muñoz, digital
Page 284: Ernesto Nemesio, digital
Page 285: Grant Alexander, digital
Page 286: Ricky Nierva and Steve Pilcher, digital
Page 287: Bryn Imagire, digital
Page 288: Daniel López Muñoz, digital
Page 289: Daniel López Muñoz, digital
Pages 300–301: Jason Deamer, digital painting
Pages 302–303: Zaruhi Galystan, digital
Page 304: Tony Fucile and Teddy Newton, pencil and marker
All other pages: Courtesy Disney/Pixar

Etch A Sketch © The Ohio Art Company. Slinky® Dog is a registered trademark of © Just Play, LLC. Mr. and Mrs. Potato Head® and Playskool Portable Baby Monitor® are registered trademarks of Hasbro, Inc. All rights reserved. Mattel and Fisher-Price toys used with permission. © Mattel, Inc. All rights reserved.

Materials and characters from the movies Cars, Cars 2, and Cars 3. Copyright © 2020 Disney/Pixar, not including underlying vehicles owned by third parties; and, if applicable: Dodge, Hudson Hornet, Plymouth Superbird, Pacer, Gremlin are trademarks of Chrysler LLC; Jeep® and the Jeep® grille design are registered trademarks of Chrysler LLC; Petty marks used by permission of Petty Marketing LLC; Mack is a registered trademark of Mack Trucks, Inc.; Maserati logos and model designations are trademarks of Maserati S.p.A. and are used under license; Fairlane, Mercury, and Model T are registered trademarks of Ford Motor Company; Darrell Waltrip marks used by permission of Darrell Waltrip Motor Sports; Porsche is a trademark of Porsche; Sarge's rank insignia design used with the approval of the U.S. Army; Volkswagon trademarks, design patents, and copyrights are used with the approval of the owner, Volkswagen AG; Audi a trademark of Audi AG; Bentley is a trademark of Bentley Motors Limited; BMW is a trademark of BMW AG; Mustang is a trademark of Ford Motor

Company; Citroën is a trademark of Automobiles Citroën; Datsun is a trademark of Nissan Morot Co., Ltd.; FIAT, Alfa Romeo, and Topolino are trademarks of FIAT S.p.A.; Honda is a trademark of Honda Motor Co., Ltd.; Cadillac Coupe DeVille, H-1 Hummer, Pontiac GTO, Monte Carlo, Corvette, El Dorado, and Chevrolet Impala are trademarks of General Motors; Mini Cooper is a trademark of BMW AG; Nissan is a trademark of Nissan Motor Co., Ltd.; the trademarks OPEL, VAUXHALL, ASTRA, CORSA, MERIVA, and ZAFIRA are registered trademarks of Opel Eisenach GmbH/GM UK Ltd.; Peugeot is a trademark of Automobiles Peugeot; Piaggio is a trademark of Piaggio & C. S.p.A.; is a registered trademark of General Motors; Renault. Ferrari Elements produced under the license of Ferrari S.p.A. FERRARI, the PRANCING HORSE device, all associated logos and distinctive designs are property of Ferrari S.p.A. The body designs of the Ferrari cars are protected as Ferrari property design, trademark and trade dress regulations. PETERBILT and PACCAR trademarks licensed by PACCAR INC, Bellevue, Washington, U.S.A.; KENWORTH and PACCAR trademarks licensed by PACCAR INC, Bellevue, Washington, U.S.A.; Mazda Miata is a registered trademark of Mazda Motor Corporation; background inspired by the Cadillac Ranch by Ant Farm (Lord, Michels and Marquez) © 1974. The term OMNIDROID used by permission of Lucasfilm Ltd.

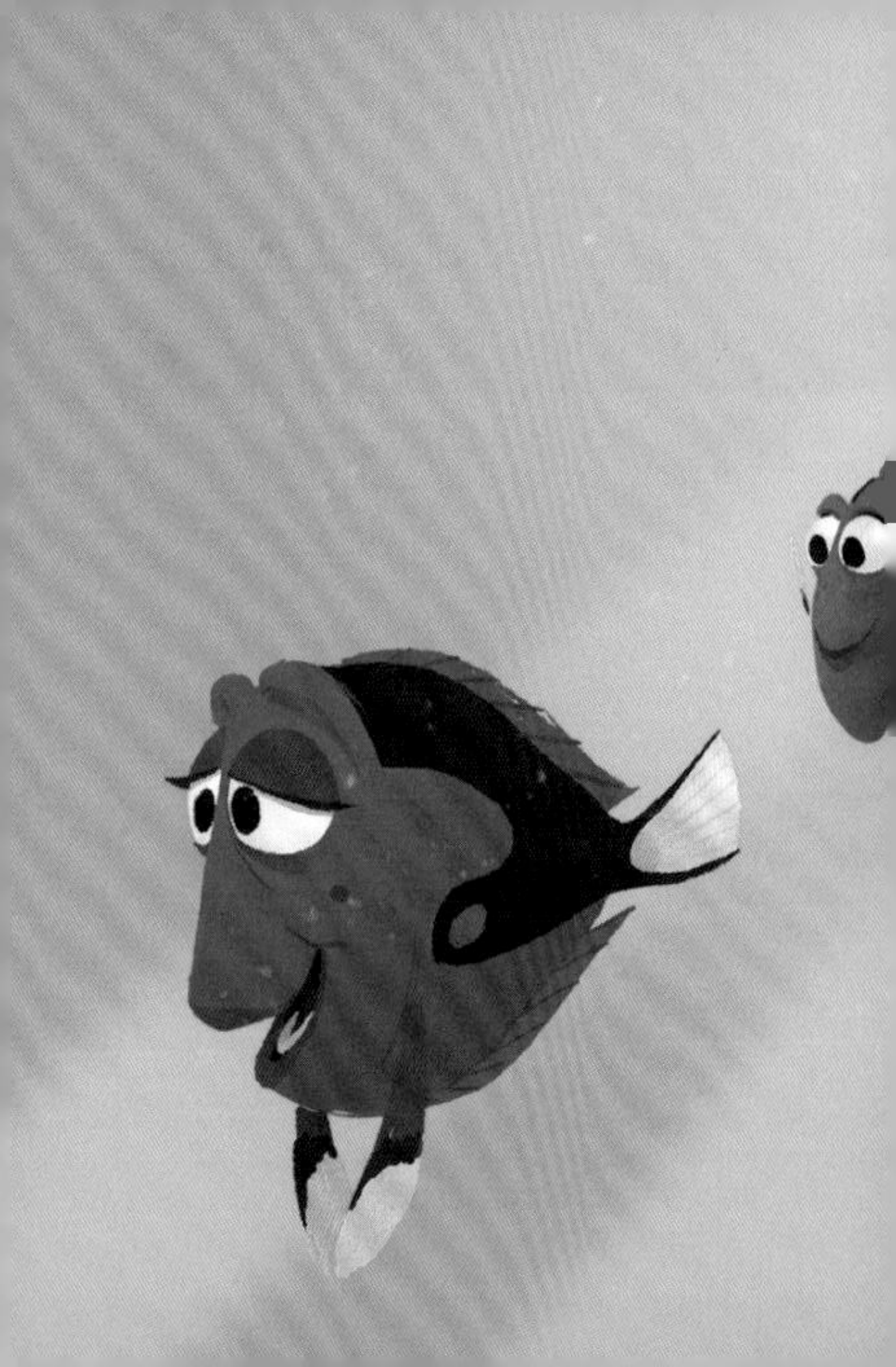

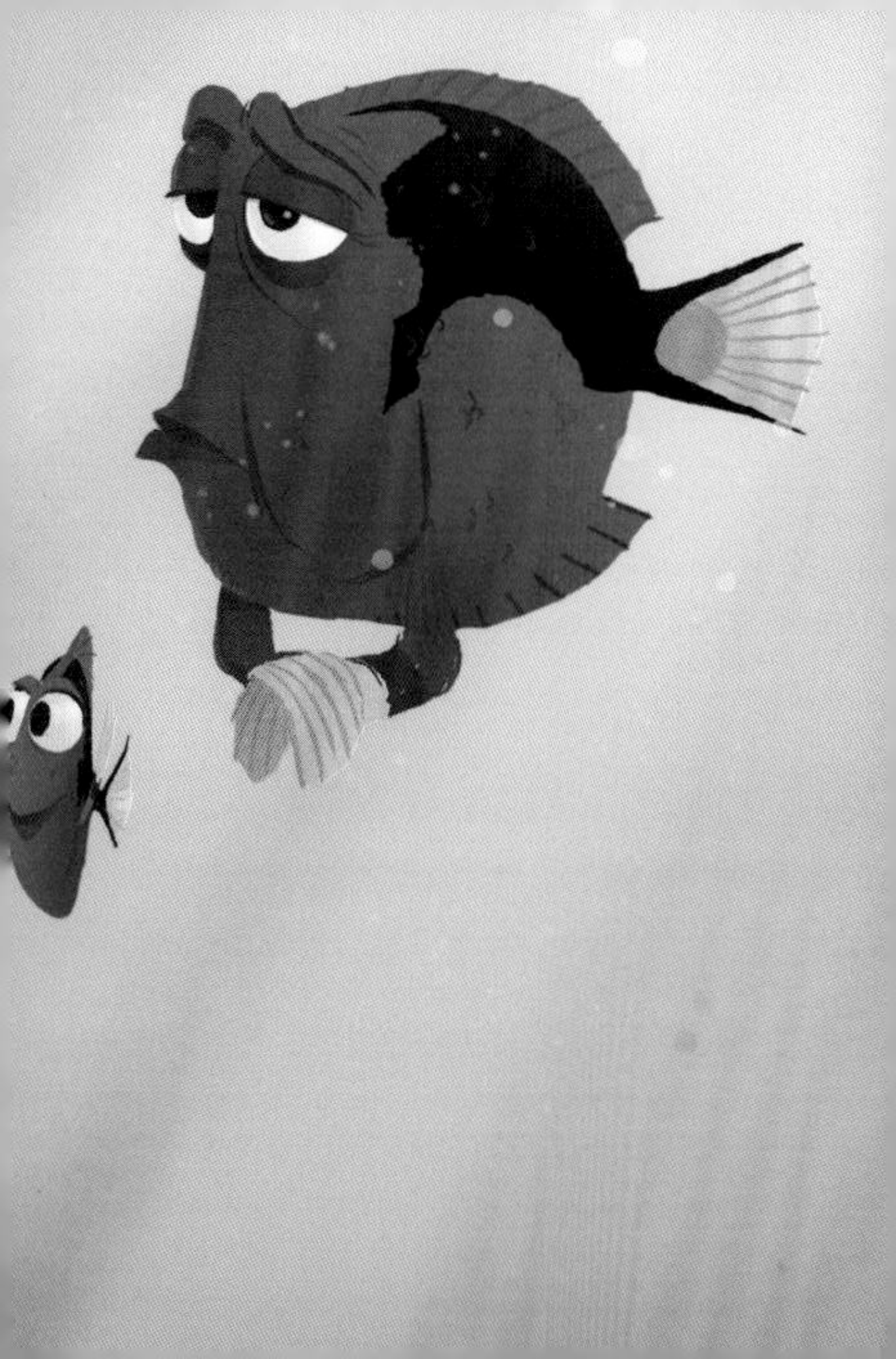

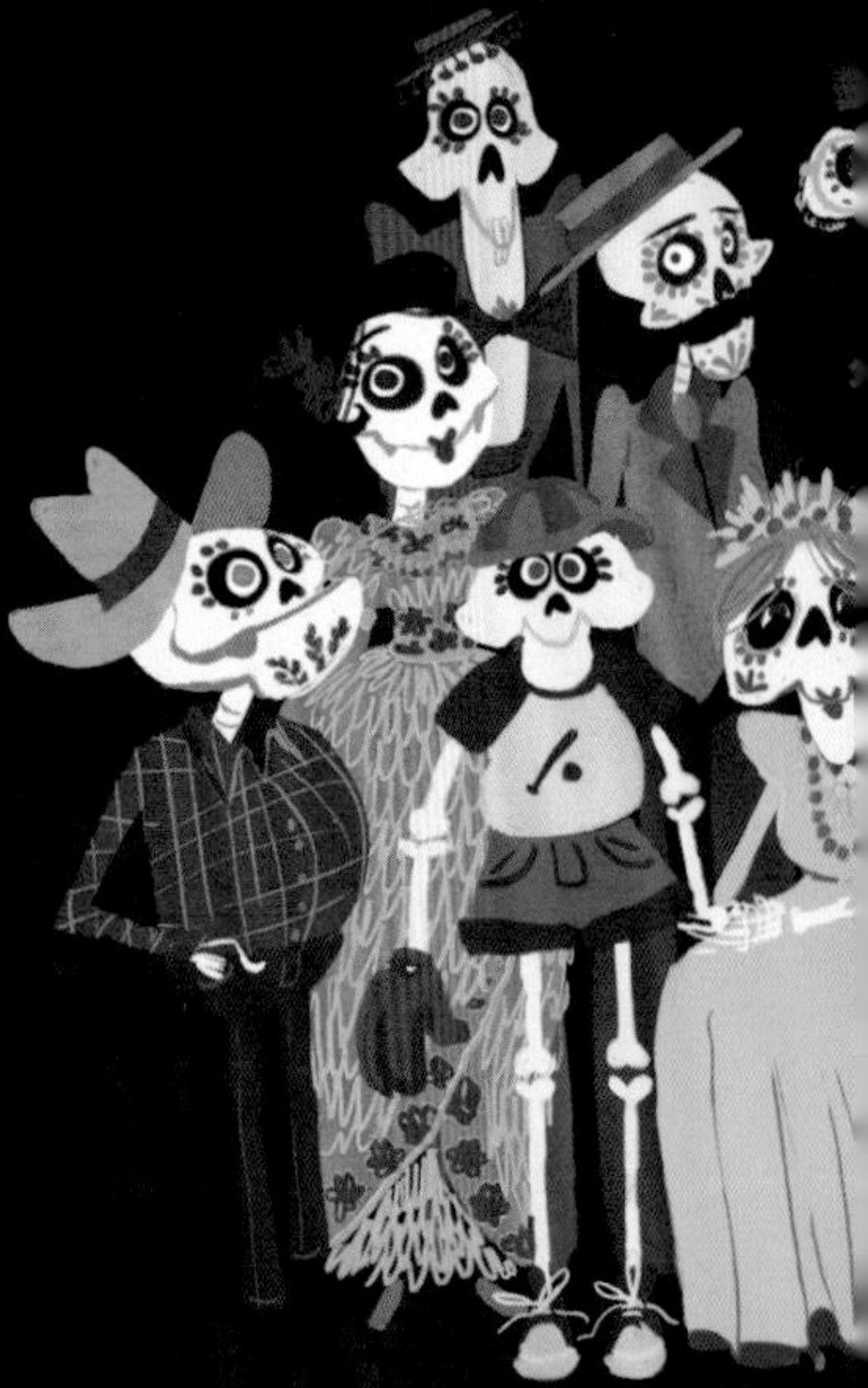

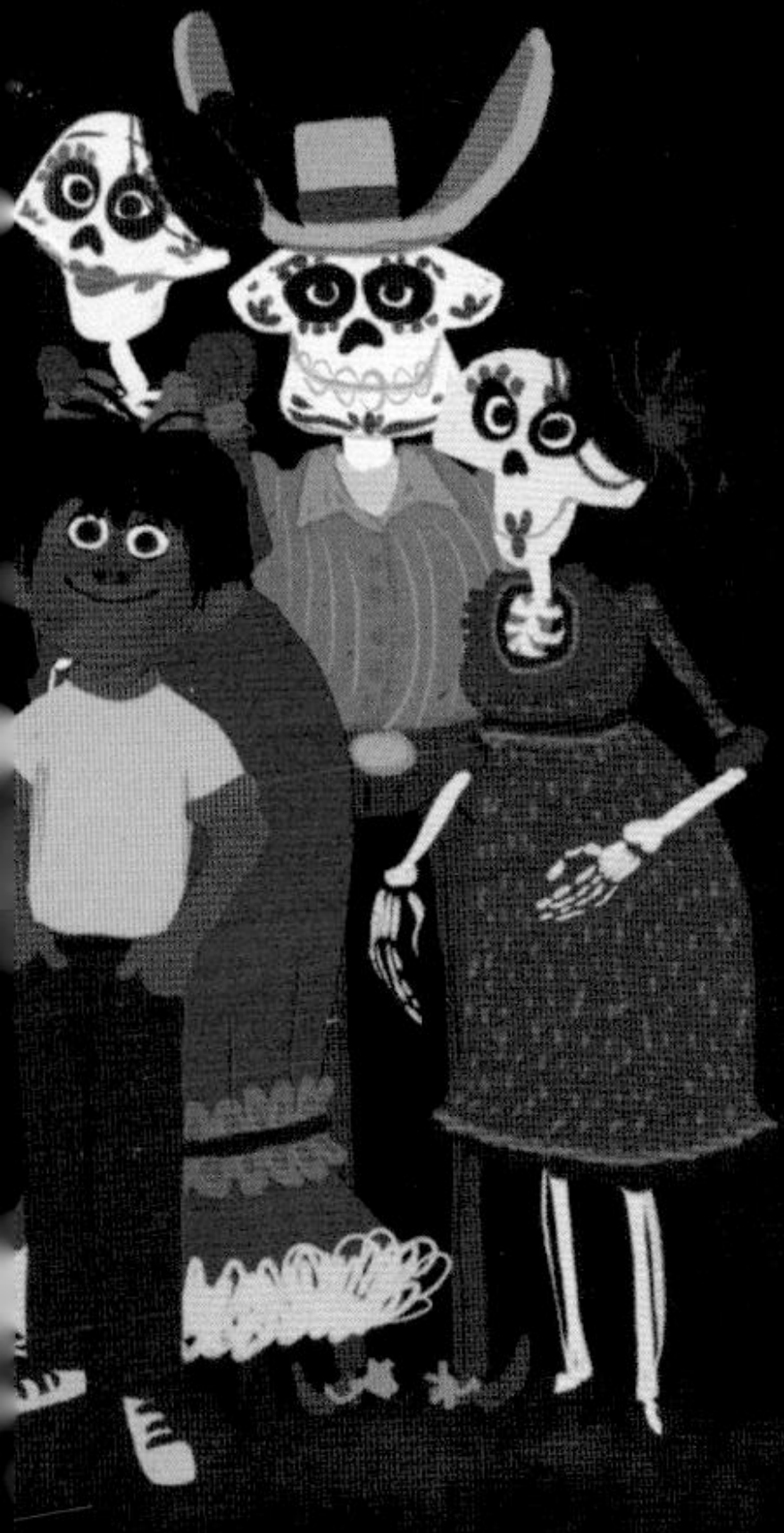

INSIGHT
EDITIONS

PO Box 3088
San Rafael, CA 94912
www.insighteditions.com

Find us on Facebook:
www.facebook.com/InsightEditions

Follow us on Twitter: @insighteditions

Design by Leah Lauer

Copyright © 2021 by
Disney Enterprises, Inc./Pixar
Text by Brooke Vitale

All rights reserved. Published by Insight Editions, San Rafael, California, in 2021. No part of this book may be reproduced in any form without written permission from the publisher.

ISBN: 978-1-68383-866-1

Manufactured in China by Insight Editions

10 9 8 7 6 5 4 3 2

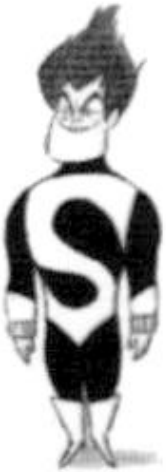